CHEMISTRY FOR TODAY

3rd Edition

RANDAL L. HENLY

FOLENS PUBLISHERS
International

Artwork: Michael Phillips.
Page Make-up and Design: European Text Resources Ltd.
Typeset: European Text Resources Ltd. Bookman 10, Helvetica 10.
Output: on Linotronic 300 at the Type Bureau.
ISBN 0 86121 171 5
Printed at the press of the Publisher.

Table of Contents

INTRODUCTION FOR TEACHERS

Chemistry For Today is a text written specifically for the Leaving Certificate chemistry syllabus of the Department of Education, and it covers the complete course up to higher level in a very comprehensive manner. As well as providing all the necessary academic material, the content of the book shows many instances of chemistry and its applications in pupils' everyday lives and surroundings. The text is written in an easy-to-read style, and emphasis is placed on the explaining of principles rather than on just given facts.

The main changes in this third edition are as follows:

(a) The integration of experimental details into the appropriate parts of the text.

(b) The addition of some extra experiments which time has shown to be of examination importance, and the deletion of some experiments of lesser importance.

(c) The expansion of the section on partial pressures and the addition of extra problems relevant to that topic.

(d) The inclusion of more structured questions and more short-answer questions of the type which are a feature of current examination papers.

(e) A complete rewrite of the section on pH calculations, making it appropriate to the fact that all such calculations are now done using electronic calculators in the solving of quadratic equations.

(f) The addition of a 'Review' at the end of each chapter, listing what should be known when the chapter has been covered.

(g) An increased number of Worked Examples of the various types of calculation described.

The text is fully up to date and contains the modern units, symbols and IUPAC nomenclature as recommended by the Association for Science Education. An appendix equates modern names with the older and still often used ones. Two points might be mentioned regarding units: the terms 'molar' (meaning a concentration of 1.0 mole per litre) and 'molarity' (meaning the concentration in moles per litre), although not strictly the recommended terms are retained - mainly for the want of equally explanatory terms to replace them; secondly, the litre is used throughout rather than the decimetre cubed. The former is now a familiar everyday unit and is much simpler to read and write than the dm^3. As well, the recent decision to accept L as its symbol rather than I is particularly constructive. All teachers will be aware of pupils' errors caused by their confusing the letter I with the figure 1. Consequently, L is used throughout the text as the symbol for the litre.

Material which is only necessary for those doing the higher course is marked by a vertical line in the margin beside the text. For the benefit of pupils who have done little or no chemistry at the start of their Leaving Certificate course, some basic chemistry is included in the text - most of it occurring in the first two chapters.

The text is well illustrated with line drawings and photographs, and these, along with some background reading, show the importance of chemistry in industry and its applications in everyday life. In some sections, the treatment of a topic has been covered in somewhat greater detail than is required - in order to make it more understanding and meaningful. For example, for the manufacture of sulphuric acid, the syllabus states that only the principles of the contact process are required. However, an account giving only the principles would be very incomplete, particularly when the process illustrates other features of chemical interest, such as catalysis, equilibrium, energy conservation and anti-pollution measures. The importance of organic chemistry is emphasised by referring to such products as plastics, detergents, dyes, antiseptics, oils, etc. To help the learning of factual material summarising charts are given at the end of many of the organic chapters.

In order to stress the fact that today's knowledge did not just happen and that it is due to the work and efforts of various people from the past, pictures and short biographies of a number of scientists are given. Knowing something about the lives of such people is part of any good education.

A plentiful supply of questions is provided, both at the ends of the chapters and also within many of the chapters - to provide exercises for the topic in hand. Chapter 30 of the text is essentially a revision chapter and contains a wide selection of questions and problems. Altogether there are more than 600 questions and problems in the book.

The order in which the syllabus is laid out is not, nor is it meant to be, the recommended teaching order. No two teachers are likely to agree on the most suitable sequence of the various topics, and so it would have been futile to arrange the chapters in a teaching order. They are therefore set in a logical order, viz. basic chemistry first; then the physical; followed by the inorganic chemistry of the appropriate elements in order of their Periodic Groups; and finally organic chemistry. Teachers should strive, as far as possible, to take the chapters in an order in which the work of one does not depend on another which has yet to be done. More recommendations about a teaching order appear in the Teachers' Guide.

Finally, I would like to acknowledge the help, interest and cooperation which I have had from many people and organizations listed below, during the time in which both this edition and the two previous editions were in preparation.

TEACHERS' GUIDE AND RESOURCE BOOK

This book, published separately, contains the following:

(i) Guidelines and practical suggestions about laboratory organisations, with lists of the apparatus and the chemicals which are needed for the course;

(ii) Details of how to prepare all of the reagents needed;

(iii) Lists of the apparatus and chemicals needed for each of the experiments, additional and helpful hints for many of them, and typical results for most of the quantitative ones;

(iv) Suggestions about a sensible and logical teaching order for the various topics of the syllabus

(v) The worked solutions to all of the numerical problems in the text;

(vi) Experimental instruction sheets for 30 recommended experiments; each of these lists the requirements for the experiment, gives detailed practical instructions, includes spaces for the results and calculations, and summaries what should be included in the experimental report. These are supplied as copyright-free master sheets, so that teachers can make photocopies in bulk as required.

ACKNOWLEDGEMENTS

I am indebted to many individuals and organisations for help and suggestions in the preparation of both this new edition and the previous editions. These include: Drs.Adrian Somerfield and Roy Brown, Messrs. Declan Kennedy, Oliver Harrington, Hugh Dobbs and Graham Hewston, I.C.I.Ltd., B.P. Chemicals, National Coal Board, British Steel Corporation, the Controller of the Stationery Office, Dublin.

I thank the following for supplying photographs and/or diagrams, for permission to reproduce copyright diagrams or for allowing photographs to be taken on their premises: BBC Hulton Picture Library, British Oxygen Corporation, British Steel Corporation, Cavendish Laboratory, Central Fisheries Board, Colibri Components, Dublin County Council, Esso Petroleum Co., An Forus Taluntais, Gouldings Chemicals Ltd., and Dallas Camier, Hugh Grant, I.C.I. Agricultural Division, I.C.I. Fibres, Irish Times, Lever Bros.Ltd., M & B Ltd., Manchester Corporation, N.B.S.T., National Coal Board, National Museum of Ireland, Nitrigin Eireann Teo., Permutit Co., Royal Institution, Science Museum London, Shell, Karl Winkelmann.
Biophoto Associates, ZEFA Picture Library, Merseyside Photographic Services, James Davis Photography.
Cover Slide: Tony Stone Photo Library.

I must also record my thanks to pupils, many of whom were often constructively critical and could always suggest better ways of expressing things. Finally I thank the staff of Folens and Co. who, as always, have been helpful, cooperative and easy to work with.

Randal L. Henly.
Mount Temple School,
Malahide Road,
Dublin 3.

INTRODUCTION TO PRACTICAL CHEMISTRY

Chemistry is a practical science and the carrying out of experimental work is essential to a full understanding of the subject. The description of each experiment consists essentially of practical instructions, and apart from a brief introduction to the topic, the theory is not explained. However, it must be emphasised that while doing an experiment, it is essential to know the theory behind the work being done, and the appropriate section of the book should be consulted if necessary. Carrying out an experiment by just following instructions and neither knowing why you are doing what you are doing, nor understanding the chemistry involved, is largely a complete waste of time. Before starting an experiment, make sure you are aware of the aim, and as you come to each stage, the reason for the procedure involved.

Experimental reports   Every chemist has to be able to write concise reports of the work and experiments which he does, and learning how to do this correctly is part of the practical chemistry course. A course report should be written up under the following headings:

Title, or aim of experiment

Date — optional

Diagram of apparatus, if appropriate.
There is no need to draw diagrams for experiments which only involve standard pieces of equipment, such as

burettes and pipettes, evaporating basins and tripods, etc. In diagrams, stands and clamps are not usually drawn.

Procedure
The account of the procedure should be comprehensive but concise - important information should be given but irrelevant details omitted. For instance, it is irrelevant to know whether a flask being heated was held in a clamp or placed on a tripod, or whether a beaker was 250 or 400 cm^3 in size. The account should be written in the past tense and passive voice, *i.e.,it should read "The apparatus was set up as shown. Some water was allowed to run into the flask and the gas which was produced was collected."* and not *"We set up the apparatus as shown. We allowed some water to run into the flask and we collected the gas which was produced"*.

Readings, Measurements, etc., if any
In quantitative experiments *i.e.*,those which involve measurement), all measurements taken should be recorded, in the form of a table and along with their units. *e.g.*,

Mass of beaker ....72.38 g
Mass of beaker and compound ....87.61 g
Mass of compound ....15.23 g
Volume of solution ....75 cm^3
Temperature of solution ....21°C

Calculations, (graph), etc. if any
Sufficient calculations should be shown, so that a reader of the report can follow the reasoning, from the measurements taken to the final conclusions. Do not clutter the report with subtractions, multiplications, logs and so on; do these on scrap paper or use a calculator.

Conclusion
This should be a clear statement confirming the objective of the experiment or giving a numerical value if the aim was to measure something, *e.g.*, *"Molecular mass of compound = 74"*. Do not give a result as *"x = 74"*.
As far as possible, put diagrams, tables of results, etc. on squared paper and reserve the lined paper for writing.

Safety, prevention of accidents and laboratory common sense
A chemistry laboratory, even a school one, can be a potentially dangerous place, but if common sense is exercised by all and the instructions for the experiment are carried out exactly as described, there is little or no danger of anything going wrong. Remember that many chemicals are poisonous, irritating to the eyes, lungs and/or throat or are highly inflammable and care is required at all times. Where such a chemical is in use in an experiment, attention is drawn to its nature in a footnote. Broken glass is probably the most common cause of school laboratory accidents. Glassware with sharp or jagged edges is dangerous and such pieces should be brought to the teacher. Be sure to read and heed safety rule number 7.

Safety rules

1. Follow experimental instructions exactly and do not try variations of the experiments, without your teachers permission.

2. Never taste laboratory chemicals; poisonous substances are not always labelled as such. If you get something into your mouth, spit it out at once, wash your mouth with lots of water and report the matter to your teacher.

3. Smell substances carefully, by gently wafting the smell towards your nose to start with, and do not inhale smells, as large quantities may be dangerous.

4. Use concentrated acids with great care and only when specifically instructed to do so. Acids and other corrosive liquids, if spilt, should be washed away immediately with large quantities of water.

5. When heating vessels, heat gently at first, until the vessel becomes hot. Do not heat thick glass containers such as graduated cylinders or reagent bottles. When heating test tubes, use a test tube holder and make sure that the tube is not pointing at yourself or anyone else, in case the contents are suddenly ejected.

6. Long hair must be tied back, and ties, cardigans, etc. should not be allowed to hang freely.

7. When inserting glass tubing (or a thermometer) into a stopper, hold the tube in a protective cloth, wet the tube to lubricate it and then ease it into the stopper with a screwing motion. Do not push it (with force) straight in.

8. Do not place apparatus, especially tall pieces like graduated cylinders, near the edge of a bench or shelf.

9. Never rush, run or throw things about in the laboratory — it can be dangerous.

10. All accidents and breakages, however slight, must be reported to your teacher.

Know the hazard symbols

The symbols used for the labelling of hazardous materials are shown below, together with their meanings.

OXIDISING AGENT

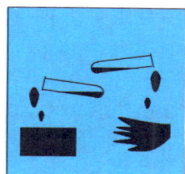
CORROSIVE

HARMFUL OR IRRITANT

FLAMMABLE

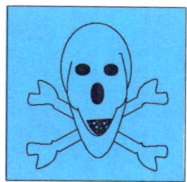
TOXIC

EXPLOSIVE

Fluted filter paper

When filter paper is folded by the conventional method there are three thicknesses of paper on one side of the filter and this slows the filtration process. A fluted paper is one folded in such a way that there is only one thickness of paper all around; filtration is therefore faster when a paper folded in such a way is used. Filter paper is fluted as follows:

Place the filter paper on the bench, fold it exactly in half and make a definite crease. Open it out (but do not turn it over), and fold it in half again - at exactly right angles to the previous fold, crease it, and open it out. Without turning the paper over, make two more folds, at 45° to those already there. The paper should then appear as in Fig. 1.

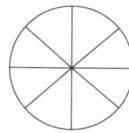
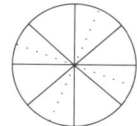
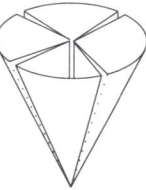

Turn the paper over, and make two more creases - at right angles to each and exactly half way between two of the pairs of creases that are already there. Because the paper has been turned over, these new folds are in the opposite direction to those already there (Fig. 2).

The paper is now ready, and provided the folding has been done accurately, it will fit snugly into a filter funnel (Fig. 3). Once it is wet, it will remain in the funnel and will not tend to pop up.

Thermometers
Thermometers are expensive and if treated roughly are easily broken. If the thermometer for an experiment is not in use, it should be kept in its case and preferably put near the back of the bench where it will not roll off. A hot thermometer should never be cooled in cold water before being put away; if left for a few minutes, it will cool itself.

Cleaning Glassware
As far as possible, glassware should be cleaned immediately after use. Most of the substances encountered in this chemistry course are water soluble so that brushing with cold water will clean most vessels. If not, hot water with detergent will be more effective, but if this is used, a rinse in plain water should follow. There is usually no need to dry glassware - if it is left upside down to drain,(though this is not recommended for flasks) it will normally be dry when next required.

Tidying Up
When the experiment has been finished, all apparatus should be returned to its correct place and the bench should be wiped up, if necessary, with a damp cloth. Used filter paper and other solid waste should be put in the waste bins, not thrown into the sink or onto the floor.

LIST OF EXPERIMENTS

1.1 To measure melting point
1.2 Recrystallisation of an impure compound
1.3 Paper chromatography
1.4 To measure the length of a molecule
3.1 Flame tests for metals
4.1 Properties of covalent and ionic compounds
6.1 To determine the relative molecular mass of a volatile liquid
6.2 To measure the relative molecular mass of a volatile liquid
7.1 To determine water of crystallisation in a hydrated salt
7.2 To determine the empirical formula of copper iodide
7.3 To find the percentage of carbon dioxide evolved when sodium hydrogen carbonate is decomposed
7.4 To find the formula of black copper oxide
7.5 To find the formula of copper carbonate by its thermal decomposition
8.1 Preparation of copper(II) sulphate
8.2 Preparation of magnesium sulphate
8.3 Tests for anions (acid radicals)
9.1 To prepare 0.5 M sodium carbonate solution
9.2 To standardise sodium hydroxide solution
9.4 To determine the percentage of water of crystallisation in 'washing soda'
9.5 To find the percentage of ethanoic acid in vinegar
9.6 To determine the percentage of water of crystallisation in ethanedioic acid crystals
9.7 To determine the relative molecular mass of citric acid
9.8 To determine the amount of magnesium hydroxide in a 'Milk of Magnesia tablet'
9.9 To determine the mass of acetylsalicylic acid in an 'Aspirin' tablet
11.1 To prepare 0.1 M ammonium iron(II) sulphate solution

Symbol	Quantity or Unit
A_r	relative atomic mass
M_r	relative molecular mass
L	Avogadro Constant
N	number of molecules
n	amount of substance (*i.e.* number of moles)
M	molarity (*i.e.* number of moles per litree)
F	faraday
g	gram
kg	kilogram
mg	milligram
mol	mole
kJ	kilojoule
cm^3	{ centimetre cubed } { cubic centimetre }
dm^3	{ decimetre cubed } { cubic decimetre } (L)
L	litre (= dm^3)
Pa	pascals pressure (= N/m^2)
mmHg	millimetres of mercury pressure
tm	atmospheres pressure
C	coulomb
A	ampere

ABBREVIATIONS USED IN THIS BOOK

conc.	concentrated
b.p.	boiling point
dil.	dilute
e^-	electron
f.p.	freezing point
LCH	Leaving Certificate, higher level
LCO	Leaving Certificate, ordinary level
m.p.	melting point
p.p.m.	parts per million
ppt.	precipitate
s.t.p.	standard pressure and temperature
$\equiv$	reacts exactly with
(^{1})	see footnote

Relative Atomic Masses (for calculations)

Aluminium	27
Barium	137
Bismuth	209
Bromine	80
Calcium	40
Carbon	12
Chlorine	35.5
Chromium	52
Cobalt	59
Copper	64
Fluorine	19
Hydrogen	1
Iodine	127
Iron	56
Lead	207
Lithium	7
Magnesium	24
Manganese	55
Mercury	201
Nickel	59
Nitrogen	14
Oxygen	16
Phosphorus	31
Potassium	39
Silicon	28
Silver	108
Sodium	23
Sulphur	32
Tin	119
Titanium	48
Zinc	65

Matter

Chemistry is the study of what substances or materials are made of, what effects they have on one another and what changes they undergo. Matter, the scientific name for materials or substances, can be described as that which occupies space or which has mass.

There are three different states in which matter can exist — **solid, liquid** and **gas** (or **vapour**). A solid has both fixed shape and fixed volume, a liquid has no fixed shape but its volume is fixed, *i.e.* it cannot be compressed, whereas a gas has neither fixed shape nor fixed volume.

Changes of State

Although every substance is most familiar in one state, most substances can also exist in both of the other two states. Heating or cooling changes the state of most substances. The changing of a solid into a liquid is called **melting**, and the reverse change (liquid to solid) is known as **freezing**. Both **boiling** and **evaporation** refer to the changing of a liquid to a gas (or vapour). In boiling, the change occurs at a fixed temperature and throughout the liquid, but in evaporation, the change occurs at lower temperatures and only from the surface of the liquid. When a gas becomes a liquid, the change is known as **condensing**. Some solids do not melt when heated, but change directly to a gas or vapour; this is called **sublimation**. Iodine, solid carbon dioxide and ammonium chloride are some of the few substances which sublime.

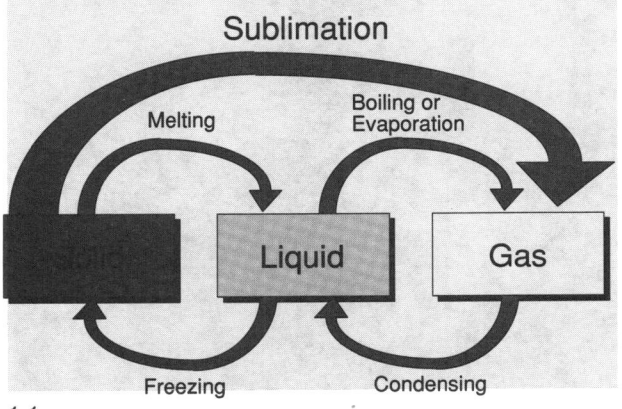

1.1

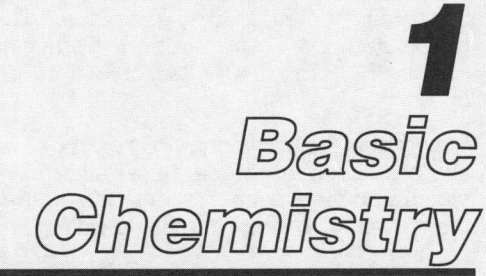

1
Basic Chemistry

The temperature at which a solid melts is known as its **melting point** and the temperature at which a liquid boils is called its **boiling point**.

Experiment 1.1
To measure melting point

Measurement of the melting point of a substance is one of the standard tests used for identification and also as a test of the purity of the substance. The simplest method of measuring a melting point is as follows.

Introduce a small portion of the substance, which must be finely powdered and quite dry, into a dry capillary tube. (One end of the capillary tube must be closed, and if this is not so, seal one end by rotating the tube slowly with the end just protruding into a blue bunsen flame, until the end closes.) Attach the tube to a suitable thermometer — surface tension may hold it, but if not, a convenient method is by using a band cut from some rubber tubing — and support the arrangement in a beaker or large test tube of water or other liquid containing a stirrer.

Slowly heat the container, while gently and continuously stirring to keep the temperature uniform. Watch the solid closely, and when it melts, note the temperature on the thermometer. This is the melting point.

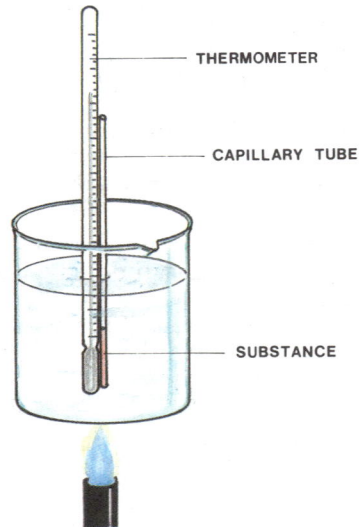

THERMOMETER

CAPILLARY TUBE

SUBSTANCE

1.2

1.3 — Part of a modern chemical works — the ammonia plant at N.E.T., Marino Point, Cork. The efficient operation of such a process depends on the specialised knowledge and skills of many groups of people, such as chemists, physicists, engineers and electricians. A large chemical works contains many steel towers and tanks, of all shapes and sizes, linked together by many miles of roads, pipelines and wires.

Atoms

All matter is made up of particles called atoms. Atoms are very, very small, so small in fact that inside an empty matchbox there are about one thousand million, million, million atoms of oxygen and nitrogen. There are different kinds of atoms — just over one hundred altogether. Ninety two of these are naturally occurring. *i.e.* they are found on the earth, and the remainder have been artificially made in nuclear reactors.

Molecules

As a general rule, atoms do not exist singly. They occur in groups called molecules. A molecule can be described as a group or cluster of atoms — either the same or different — joined together chemically.

Elements

If the atoms in a molecule of a substance are all alike, the substance is called an element. Because there are about one hundred different kinds of atom, there are about one hundred different elements. **An element can be defined as a substance which cannot be broken down into simpler substances by chemical means**. All elements are different and each has its own characteristic properties. See the appendices on Page 379 for a full list of the elements.

Every element has its own symbol, which represents one atom (or sometimes one mole) of that element. Many of the symbols are the initial letters of the elements; others have a second letter where there is more than one starting with the same letter (in these, the capital initial is followed by a **SMALL** second letter). Some of the symbols are derived from the latin names for the elements (**ferrum** = iron; **stannum** = tin), since a number of the elements were known in Roman times.

It is important to realise and remember that the chemical symbol of an element represents one atom of that element. **"H"** stands for **one** atom of hydrogen[i] and not just "hydrogen". Likewise the chemical formula of a substance stands for **one molecule** of that substance. H_2O stands for **one** molecule. The difference between "**2H**" and "**H_2**" must also be understood.

"**2H**" represents **two separate atoms** of hydrogen, while

"**H_2**" means **one molecule** of hydrogen— in which two atoms are combined together.

Some elements can exist in different physical forms (differing in colour, hardness, melting point, etc). These different forms are called **allotropes**. Allotrophy is described more fully in chapters 5 and 18.

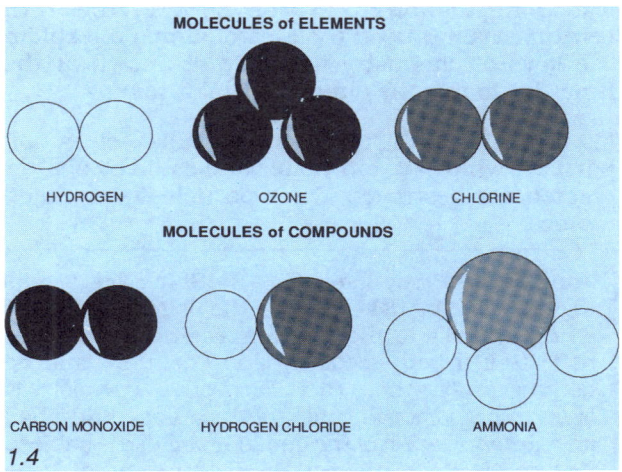

MOLECULES of ELEMENTS

HYDROGEN   OZONE   CHLORINE

MOLECULES of COMPOUNDS

CARBON MONOXIDE   HYDROGEN CHLORIDE   AMMONIA

1.4

Compounds

If the molecules of a substance consist of two or more different kinds of atom, the substance is known as a **compound**.

A compound can be defined as a substance which is formed by the chemical combination of two or more elements. There are millions of different chemical compounds. Just as every element has its own symbol, every compound has its own formula. The formula shows which elements are present in the compound and how many atoms of each kind are in a molecule of the compound.

(i)   It can also mean one mole of hydrogen atoms (Chapter 6).

When elements combine to form compounds, the reaction is called **synthesis**. Synthesis is the building up of a compound by combining simpler substances together. Unlike elements, compounds **can** be split up into simpler substances. The splitting up of compounds into simpler substances is called **decomposition**. The commonest ways of decomposing compounds are by heating and by passing electricity through them (electrolysis).

John Dalton

The first man to realise the importance of atoms was John Dalton, who was born in the 18th century. Dalton used the idea of atoms to explain the laws of chemistry which were known at the time. To do this, he stated the following:

(i)   All matter is made up of extremely small particles which are indivisible and could be neither created nor destroyed; these particles were called atoms.

(ii)   Atoms of one element were all exactly alike and had the same "weight", but they differed from, and had a different "weight" than atoms of any other element.

(iii)   When elements react to form compounds, their atoms combine in simple numerical ratios such as 1:1, 1:2, 1:3, etc.

Dalton's ideas were remarkably true for a scientist of his time but in the light of present day knowledge, they are not absolutely accurate. Since the discovery of isotopes (see page 32) it is known that the atoms of any given element are not all alike; secondly, atoms are nowadays created, destroyed and changed into one another — in nuclear reactions.

Dalton invented a system of chemical symbols for atoms and using these, explained how atoms unite in simple proportions to form "compound atoms" (*i.e.* molecules).

Jons Jacob Berzelius (1779-1848) of Sweden was the one who, in 1811, devised the present system of giving symbols to the chemical elements. Berzelius had studied both medicine and chemistry and he became a professor in each. His work in chemistry is outstanding for its originality and accuracy, and it had an enormous effect of the development of the subject. He was the first to make a detailed study of catalysis — the property which some substances have of being able to speed up chemical reactions without themselves being used up. Catalysts are highly important in modern chemical processes. He investigated the electrolysis of salts and was the first to put forward the idea that when two elements combine together, the forces which hold them are partly electrical (long before electrons had been discovered), he thus had the idea of ionic bonds). He discovered several new elements (cerium, selenium, silicon, thorium); he introduced the blowpipe in chemical analysis and wrote a book on the subject; he showed that hydrogen was contained in all acids and not oxygen as had previously been thought; he introduced the terms **allotropes, isomerism** and **catalysis**.
He measured the "atomic weight" of most of the chemical elements which were known at the time, and in 1828 he published the first accurate table of atomic weights, listing those of 54 elements.

1.5

Except in three cases, his values were in good agreement with modern figures. His work in analysis enabled him to give an accurate chemical formula to a great number of substances. It is a sad omission that no element has ever been named "berzelium", for if ever a chemist deserved to be remembered in this way, it is surely Berzelius.

However, these symbols were too inconvenient to use and J.J. Berzelius replaced them by the symbols which are used today — and which are given in the list at the end of the book.

1.6 — *Dalton's interest in gases led him to his ideas about atoms and molecules. In this picture, he is collecting marsh gas. Dalton is stirring up the mud at the bottom of the stagnent pond while his assistant catches the bubbles in a wide mouthed bottle.*

Mixtures and Compounds

Both elements and compounds are pure substances — because each consists of molecules which are all alike. There is however, another type of substance — made up of different kinds of molecules — and this is called a **mixture**. A mixture consists of two or more different substances, not chemically joined together, but just mingled with each other or all "jumbled up together". Mixtures occur everywhere — the air is a mixture, so also is practically all food, the soil in the ground, oil and petrol and many other everyday substances. An **alloy** is a very important kind of mixture in modern life. It consists of two or more different metals mixed uniformly together, and is made by mixing the metals when they are molten. Some common alloys (and what they consist of) are brass (copper and zinc), "silver" coinage metal (copper and nickel), stainless steel (iron, chromium and nickel), solder (lead and tin) and bell metal (copper and tin).

Solution and Crystallisation

A solution can be described as a uniform or homeogeneous mixture of a substance (usually a solid) and a liquid in a solution, the molecules of the substance are distributed evenly amongst the molecules of the liquid.

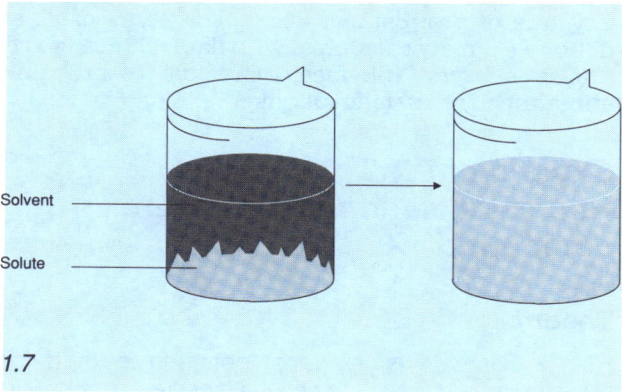

Solvent

Solute

1.7

When a substance dissolves in a liquid, the substance is said to be **soluble**, and if a substance does not dissolve, it is **insoluble**. In a solution, the solid substance which dissolves is called the **solute**, and the liquid which dissolves it is known as the **solvent**. When salt is dissolved in water, the salt is the solute and water the solvent. A **saturated solution** is one which contains as much solute as the solvent can hold, at a particular temperature (an **unsaturated solution** can

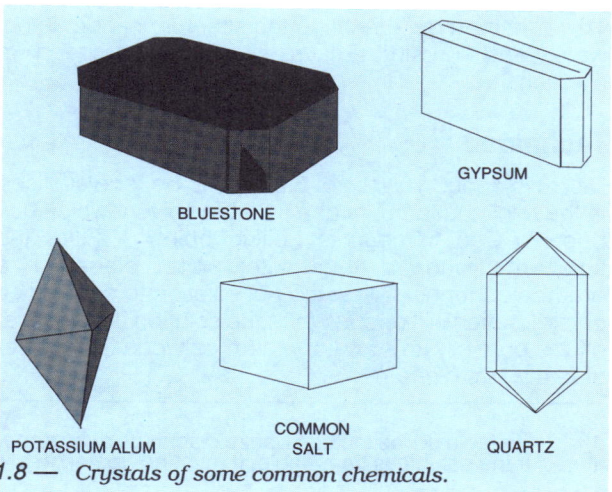

BLUESTONE

GYPSUM

POTASSIUM ALUM

COMMON SALT

QUARTZ

1.8 — *Crystals of some common chemicals.*

dissolve more solute). As a general rule, hot solvents can dissolve more solute than the same quantity of the cold solvent. When a hot saturated solution is cooled, the solvent is unable to hold all of the solute, and some of it appears in the form of crystals. This process is called **crystallisation**. Crystals of a substance are solid pieces of it, of definite geometrical shape, with flat faces and fixed angles between the faces. Crystals of any one substance are usually all alike.

Experiment 1.2
Recrystallisation of an impure compound

Theory

Recrystallisation is the most common method for purifying a solid. It is based on the fact that the solubility of a solute in a particular solvent increases with temperature, i.e. the solvent when hot can dissolve more solute that it can when cold. Thus, when a hot saturated solution of the solute is allowed to cool, the solute comes out of the solution and is deposited as crystals. Insoluble impurities are filtered off before cooling and a solvent is chosen so that soluble impurities remain in solution. Commonly used solvents include water, ethanol or methylated spirits, glacial ethanoic acid and propanone (acetone). The solution must not be allowed to cool unduly as it is being filtered so that crystallisation does not commence prematurely. This is helped by (i) heating the filter funnel (e.g. in hot water) and (ii) using a fluted filter paper to speed up filtration.

Technique [i]

Dissolve about 1 — 2 g of the solid to be recrystallised in the minimum amount of a suitable solvent which has been heated to near its boiling point [ii]. Filter the solution through a fluted filter paper placed in a pre-heated funnel. Allow the hot solution to cool, when crystallisation will occur. When the solution is cold, filter off the pure crystals and dry them between filter paper or in a warm place.

Separating mixtures

There are many different methods for separating mixtures, the method used being dependent on the

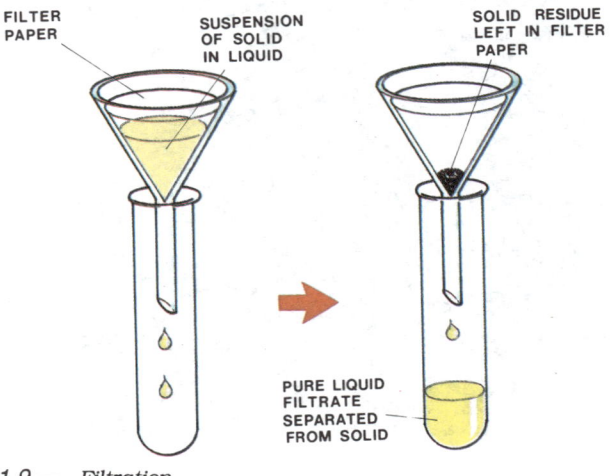

1.9 — Filtration

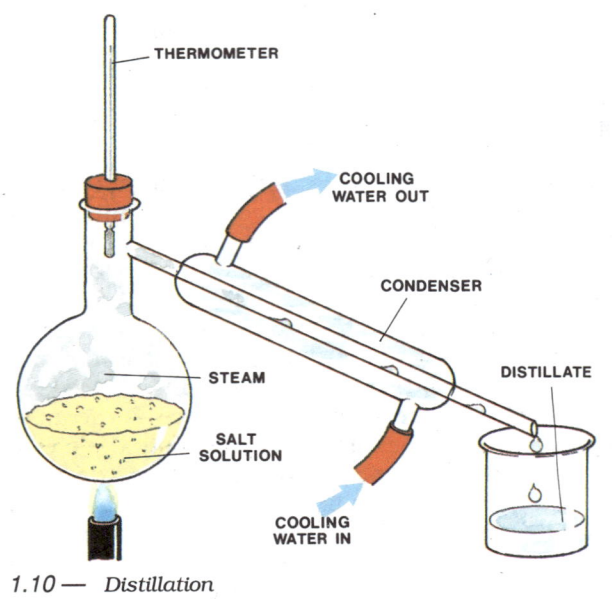

1.10 — Distillation

(i)   Suitable solids include benzoic acid (using water as a solvent), and naphthalene (using ethanol).
(ii) If the soluble is flammable, it must be heated in a water bath.

type of mixture. Some of the more common methods are filtration, distillation, evaporation, use of separating funnel, and chromatography, and these methods are illustrated.

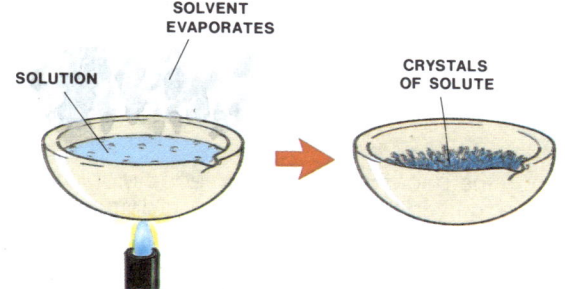

1.11 — *Evaporation*

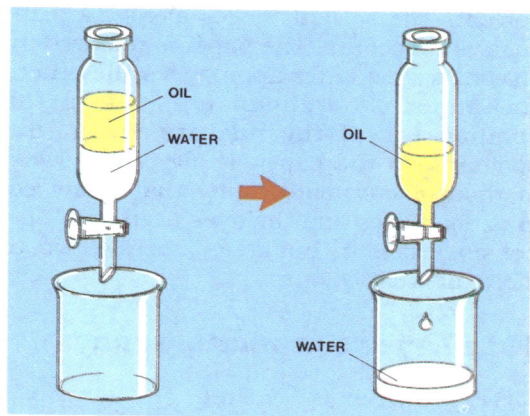

1.12 — *Using a separating funnel to separate oil and water.*

Chromatography

Chromatography is a method of separating chemical substances from each other and is one of the most versatile and important techniques of modern chemical analysis. It can be used to separate substances which are physically and chemically very similar to each other and which would be difficult and time consuming to separate by other methods. It can be used for most complex mixtures, and for extremely small quantities of substances — as small as microgram (10^{-6}g) samples.

The name chromatography literally means "colour writing", since the technique was originally used to separate mixtures of coloured substances. It is no longer restricted to such, however, and colourless substances can be separated from each other just as easily as those which have colour.

Separation by chromatography makes use of **adsorption**. This is the name given to the way in which atoms, molecules or ions become attached to the surfaces of solids. There are various types of chromatography — paper, thin layer, column and gas chromatography, but the basic principle of each method is the same. The mixture to be separated is dissolved in a suitable solvent and then the solution is allowed to flow through an adsorbing medium, which can be a strip of suitable paper or an inert chemical such as silica gel or alumina. As the solvent moves, the mixture moves with it, but because the different substances in it will have different affinities for the solvent and for the adsorbing medium, they travel at different rates and so become separated from each other.

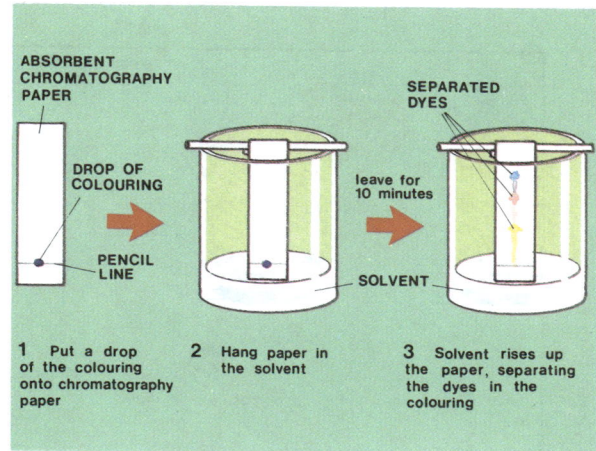

1.13

Paper chromatography is a simple and fast method of separation and is very useful for coloured substances. The adsorbing medium is specially prepared paper rather like filter paper (although filter paper is quite satisfactory) and a variety of solvents can be used, *e.g.* water, ethanol, or mixtures of these with each other and with other solvents. A spot of the mixture to be separated is placed near one end of a strip of the paper, which is then arranged with this end dipping into the solvent. The solvent moves along the paper and separation occurs. The paper is removed from the solvent as the latter approaches the other end of the paper, whereupon it is found that the components of the mixture are at different positions on the paper. It may be shown by the method of chromatography that many coloured inks, food dyes and the dyes used in felt pens are not single colours but are mixtures of two, three or more different colours.

Thin Layer Chromatography

This method is rather similar to paper chromatography but differs in the adsorbing substance. Instead of the solvent travelling along a paper strip, it travels along a thin layer of an adsorbent substance supported by, and adhering to, a glass plate. For small scale experiments, a microscope slide makes a suitable glass plate. The technique is similar to that used for paper chromatography.

Experiment 1.3.
Paper Chromatography

Take a piece of chromatography paper and on it rule a straight pencil line 2 to 3 cm from the bottom edge. On this line place a spot of each of the colours, to be separated into its components. The spots should be about 3 mm in diameter and at least 3 cm apart.

Arrange the paper with its bottom edge dipping into a suitable solvent (two methods for doing this are illustrated), and then leave the arrangement where it will not be disturbed. When the solvent approaches the top of the paper — this will take 15 to 30 minutes — carefully remove the paper from the liquid and leave it to dry. The chromatogram can then be safely examined. Suitable substances to separate are the colours in felt pens or markers, coloured inks and food dyes. It is an interesting exercise to separate the colours from a complete set of markers and find out how many basic dyes are present in the set. Water is a suitable solvent for most of the cheap sets of markers which are available.

1.14 — *Nine colours from a set of felt pens are shown in this chromatogram to be made up of seven dyes. Only the yellow and blue markers consist of single dyes. Note: In order to show the original colours, a second set of spots was put on to the paper after the chromatogram had been run and allowed to dry out.*

Nomenclature of Compounds

The modern method of naming chemical compounds is due to an organisation called the International Union of Pure and Applied Chemistry ('IUPAC'). Using this method, names of compounds give much information about their composition, and once the system is understood, a knowledge of the formula of a compound usually enables it to be named. Some general rules of the method are as follows:

1.   Compounds containing two elements have names ending in **-ide** and the names of the two elements form the name of the compound. For example, sodium chloride is composed of sodium and chlorine (and nothing else), calcium hydride is made up of calcium and hydrogen, and silver oxide consists of silver and oxygen.

The two main exceptions to this rule are those of hydroxides and ammonium salts. Hydroxides contain hydrogen and oxygen in addition to the metal. "Ammonium" (which consists of nitrogen and hydrogen) takes the place of the metal in many compounds, so that the compound ammonium chloride, even though its name ends in **-ide**, contains three elements, nitrogen, hydrogen and chlorine.

2.   The name of a compound ends in **-ate** when it contains oxygen as well as the elements mentioned in its name. Thus, sodium carbonate contains sodium, carbon and oxygen, and zinc sulphate consists of zinc, sulphur and oxygen.

3.   Where an element has more than one valency (explained on page 60), the valency in use is shown in Roman numerals in brackets, immediately after the name of the element. Thus in "copper(I) oxide", the valency of copper is one, and in "copper(II) oxide", it is two. This method replaces an older method in which the suffixes **-ous** and **-ic** denoted the lower and higher valencies respectively.

Atomicity

This means the number of atoms in each molecule of a substance. A few substances are made up of single atoms, and such substances are described as being **monatomic**; helium, neon and the other noble gases are examples.

Substances which are **diatomic** contain two atoms per molecule. All the common gases which are elements (hydrogen, oxygen, nitrogen, chlorine,

fluorine) are diatomic. Examples of diatomic compounds are hydrogen chloride (HCl) and carbon monoxide (CO).

Triatomic means that there are three atoms in each molecule of the substance. Examples of triatomic substances are carbon dioxide (CO_2), water (H_2O) and ozone (O_3).

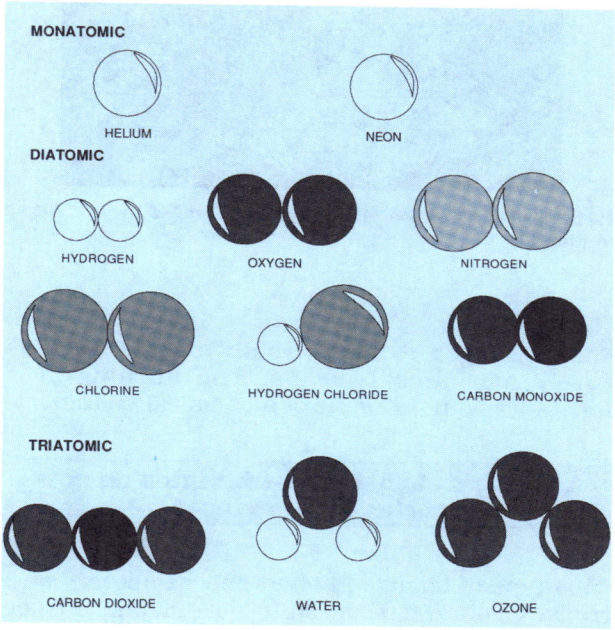

1.15

Chemical and Physical Changes

Substances undergo two types of change — chemical and physical.

> **A chemical change is one in which a new substance is produced**

The new substance has properties which are usually very different from those of the original substance. A chemical change involves the breaking up of molecules and the rearrangement of their atoms into new molecules.

1.16 — *Both physical and chemical changes occur when a candle burns.*

Such changes cannot usually be reversed by purely mechanical means. The burning of a substance is an example of a chemical change.

A physical change is one in which no new substance is produced.

This type of change is often only temporary and involves a change in the state (solid, liquid, gas) or in the appearance of the substance. The melting of a substance is an example of a physical change.

Water of Crystallisation

Water of crystallisation is water which is chemically combined in many substances and which is responsible for the colour and crystalline shape of those substances. "Bluestone" or crystalline copper(II) sulphate is a example of such a substance; the compound is both blue and crystalline because of the water of crystallisation in it. On being heated, the water is driven off from the crystals and their colour and crystalline shape are lost. The white powder which is produced is "anhydrous copper(II) sulphate" (**anhydrous means "without water"**). A substance which contains water of crystallisation is said to be **hydrated**.

Law of Conservation of Matter

There are many different laws of chemistry — statements summarising important facts and relationships — which have been either verified experimentally or deduced theoretically, or often both. One very basic and important law which is assumed throughout the chemistry course is the **Law of Conservation of Matter** (or mass). This law states:

In a chemical change, matter is neither created nor destroyed.

Or expressed another way, it states: **In a chemical change, the total mass of the reactants is the same as the total mass of the products** (the reactants are the substances which react and the products are those which are produced).

A simple experiment such as that illustrated below can be used to verify this law.

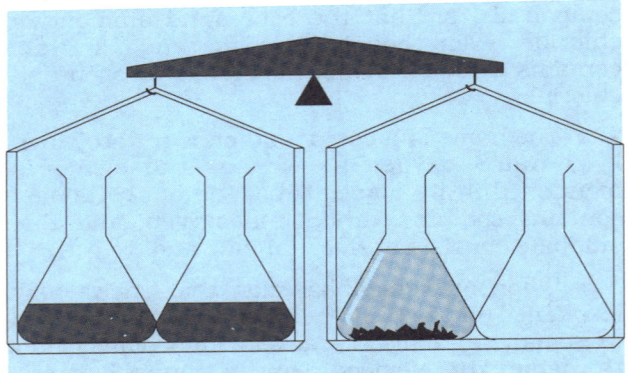

1.17 — *On the left hand pan of the balance are two substances which can react together (e.g. solutions of lead nitrate and potassium iodide); on the right hand pan the substances have been mixed and reaction has taken place. There is no change in mass.*

Another important basic law is the **Law of Constant Composition**, which states:

A given compound always contains the same elements, united together in the same fixed proportions by mass.

Diffusion and Kinetic Theory

Molecules in both liquids and gases can be shown by several simple experiments to be constantly in motion. As a consequence of this, gases and liquids spread themselves throughout any space into which they are put — a process called **diffusion.**In gases and liquids, the molecules are not joined together — so making diffusion possible; but in solids, molecules are held together.

In a solid, the molecules are packed very closely together and are arranged in a regular manner. They are not free to move about, due to the forces of attraction between them, but they can vibrate about their mean positions. This structure explains the fact that solids have both fixed shape and fixed volume.

In a liquid, the molecules are also close together, but they are not arranged in any pattern. They are continuously moving about because the force of attraction between them is small. A liquid therefore flows, and it takes the shape of its container. Because the molecules are close together, a liquid cannot be compressed.

In a gas, there is little force of attraction between the molecules and they have complete freedom from each other. They are widely separated and are moving about in all directions at high speeds. For these reasons, a gas fills any space into which it is put, and it can easily be compressed into a smaller space.

Copper sulphate crystals in a measuring cylinder

Water is gently added

After several days the blue colour has spread through the water

1.18 — *Diffusion of copper sulphate in water.*

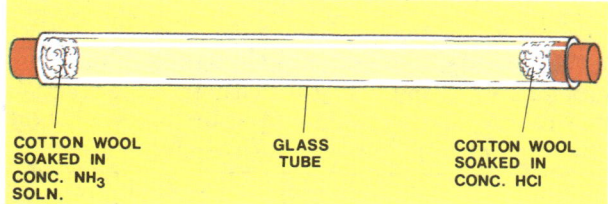

COTTON WOOL SOAKED IN CONC. NH₃ SOLN.

GLASS TUBE

COTTON WOOL SOAKED IN CONC. HCl

1.19 — *Gaseous diffusion is illustrated in this experiment. The two gases, ammonia (NH₃) and hydrogen chloride (HCl) diffuse towards each other, and after a few minutes, meet and react together, forming a white deposit of ammonium chloride on the sides of the tube.*

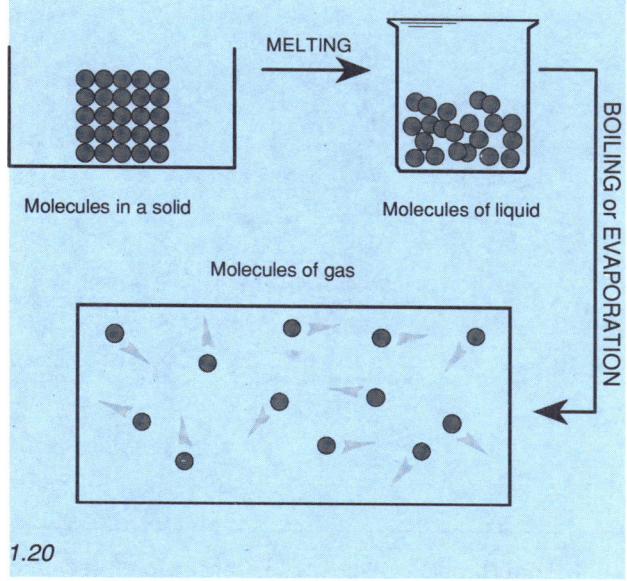

Molecules in a solid

MELTING

Molecules of liquid

BOILING or EVAPORATION

Molecules of gas

1.20

Molecular Size

Individual molecules are so small that they cannot be seen, even under the highest powered microscope. However, molecular sizes can be determined by several methods, one of which is now described.

Oil Film Experiment

A rough value of the size of certain molecules can be obtained by a method which originally devised by the English scientist Lord Rayleigh[i], in 1899.

From chemical studies, it is known that molecules of certain oils and fatty acids are longer than they are wide, and that one end has an affinity for water. When a drop of such a substances is placed on a water surface, it spreads out to form an approximately circular film, with the molecules standing upright like the pile of a carpet. When the spreading out stops, it is reasonable to assume that the oil film is one molecule thick, and also that the molecules are in contact with each other, since latent heat is required to separate them from each other. The thickness of the oil layer is thus approximately equal to the length of a molecule of a substance used. The oil is added as a very dilute solution in ether, alcohol or another volatile solvent. When a drop of the solution is placed onto the water surface it spreads out rapidly, the solvent evaporates and a monomolecular layer (*i.e.* one molecule thick) of the oil remains. If talc or lycopodium powder has been lightly shaken onto the water surface, it is pushed aside by the spreading drop and the area covered by the oil made clearly visible.

Worked Example

In such an experiment, one drop of a 0.01% solution of a suitable oil dissolved in ether was placed on a water surface which had been lightly covered with talc. When the solvent had evaporated, a circular oil film, about 6 cm in diameter, was formed.

Hence:

$$\text{Area of Film } (\pi r^2) = 3.14 \times (3)^2 = 28 \text{ cm}^2$$

$$\text{Volume of Film} = 28t \text{ cm}^3$$
(where t = thickness of film)

The volume of a drop was found by letting 50 drops run out of a burette and noting the change in the butette's scale reading. On doing this, it was discovered that the volume of 50 drops was 2.5 cm^3. Therefore:

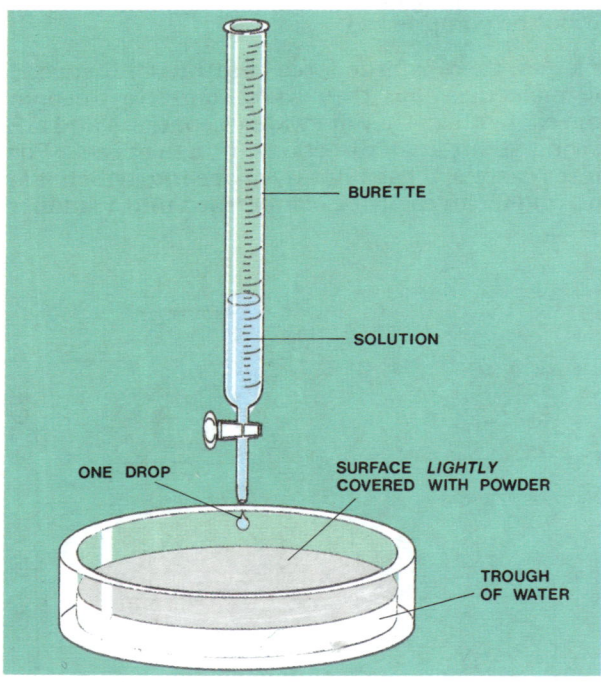

BURETTE

SOLUTION

ONE DROP

SURFACE *LIGHTLY* COVERED WITH POWDER

TROUGH OF WATER

1.21

(i) Lord Rayleigh (1842 - 1919) became professor of experimental physics at Cambridge University in 1879. For his many discoveries in physics he received a Nobel prize in 1904. He is probably best remembered for his discovery, along with Sir William Ramsey, of argon, in 1894. This resulted from his determining the density of atmospheric nitrogen very accurately, and finding that it was very slightly greater than the density of pure nitrogen. He concluded that atmospheric nitrogen must have a very small amount of a denser gas with it. His colleague, Ramsey, subsequently discovered helium, krypton, neon and xenon.

$$\text{Volume of Drop} = \frac{2.5}{50} = 0.05 \text{ cm}^3$$

$$\text{Volume of Oil in Drop} = 0.01\% \text{ of } 0.05 \text{ cm}^3$$

$$= 0.000005 \text{ cm}^3$$

$$= 5 \times 10^{-6} \text{ cm}^3$$

$$\text{So } 28t = 5 \times 10^{-6}$$

$$t = \frac{5 \times 10^{-6}}{28}$$

$$2 \times 10^{-7} \text{ cm}$$

So the length of the oil molecules is about 2×10^{-7} (or 0.0000002) cm. This value must only be regarded as an order of magnitude, because a number of assumptions made in the experiment are not fully valid. However, the experiment does indicate just how very small the oil molecules are. It might be pointed out too, that these oil molecules are very much larger than molecules of common substances like water, carbon dioxide or methane.

Experiment 1.4
To estimate the length of a molecule

Procedure

Fill a burette with 0.01% solution of a suitable oil (*e.g.* oleic acid). Measure the volume of one drop by either counting the drops to form 1 cm^3 or by measuring the volume of, say, 50 drops.

Fill a clean tray or trough to a depth of a few cm with water. When it becomes quite still, lightly cover its surface with talc or lycopodium powder (a pepper pot makes a suitable shaker). Then place one drop of the oil solution from the burette in the centre on the tray. The solvent quickly evaporates and the oil spreads out to form an approximately circular patch on the water. Measure, as best you can, the diameter of this circle.

Repeat the experiment once or twice, and obtain an average value for the diameter of the oil film. Wash the tray and clean it with a sponge soaked in a little ethanol each time before refilling it with fresh water.

Results

Record your measurements in table form as follows:
No. of drops of solution counted . . . . . . =
Volume of solution . . . . =
Volume of one drop of solution . . . . =
Concentration of solution . . . . = 0.01%
Volume of oil in one drop . . . . =
Diameter of oil circle (1) . . . . =
Diameter of oil circle (2) . . . . =
Diameter of oil circle (3) . . . . =
Average diameter . . . . =
Radius of oil film . . . . =
Thickness of oil film . . . . =

From the volume of one drop and the concentration of the oil solution, (0.01% = 1 part in 10,000) calculate the volume of the oil present in each drop. The value of the oil circle is given by $\pi r^2 h$, where r is the radius of the circle and h its thickness. Hence, h can be calculated (a worked example is given).

Brownian Movement

Although molecules in gases and liquids are constantly moving, the movement cannot be seen — because of the minute size of molecules. However, it is possible to see the **effect** of molecular movement — in an experiment such as is illustrated below.

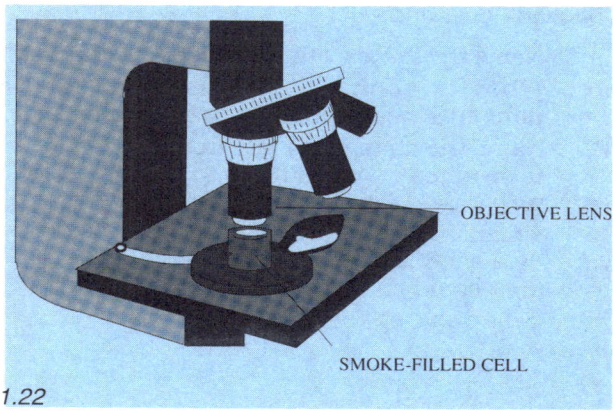

OBJECTIVE LENS

SMOKE-FILLED CELL

1.22

A small transparent cell is filled with smoke and placed under a microscope. A lens is arranged to focus light from a bulb onto the cell, making the smoke visible. When viewed through the microscope, the movement of the smoke particles is continuous and erratic — as shown overleaf.

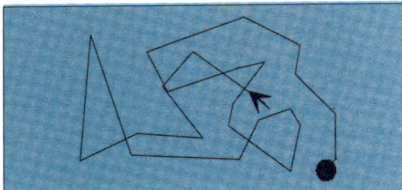

1.23 — The type of erratic pattern traced out by particles using Brownian motion.

The effect is called **Brownian Movement**, after Robert Brown, a Scottish botanist who first noticed it in 1827. Brown was observing pollen grains under a microscope and he noticed this constant erratic movement. (Pollen is a substance produced by the stamens of plants. If a buttercup, for example, is rubbed between the fingers, the yellow dust which rubs off is pollen). Brown was not able to explain the motion of the particles; it just did not occur to him that molecules had anything to do with it. The explanation is that the very small particles are made to move about by being continuously but irregularly bombarded by molecules of the gas or liquid. Brownian movement is experimental evidence which supports the kinetic theory of both liquids and gases, as described previously.

Questions

Q.1.1 Give short answers to each of the following questions;

(a) Name the three states in which matter exists.

(b) What is common to, and what is the difference between, boiling and evaporation?

(c) Name the change of state from
(i) solid to gas, and (ii) gas to liquid.

(d) What name denotes the temperature at which
 (i) a solid changes to a liquid, and
(ii) a liquid changes to a gas?

(e) Distinguish between an element and a compound.

(f) How did John Dalton envisage atoms?

(g) What is each of: mixture, alloy, solution?

(h) What is a saturated solution? What happens when such a solution is cooled?

(i) What is meant by solubility? How does solubility vary with temperature?

(j) By what method could you separate;
(i) a liquid and an insoluble solid?
(ii) a liquid containing a dissolved solid,
(iii) the dyes in a coloured ink?

Q.1.2

(a) Name the elements which are contained in
 (i) copper sulphide,
(ii) copper sulphate,
(iii) aluminium phosphate,
(iv) ammonium phosphate.

(b) Name
(i) a diatomic gaseous element,
(ii) a triatomic gaseous compound.

(c) Define a chemical change, and give an example of such.

(d) What is meant by hydrated? What word has the opposite meaning?

(e) State the Law of Conservation of Matter.

(f) What is the difference between the arrangement of the molecules in a liquid and a gas?

(g) Give an example of a substance diffusing.

(h) How can a very thin oil film on a water surface be made visible?

(i) What is Brownian movement, and what does it prove?

(j) What is meant by each of
(i) atomicity, (ii) monomolecular?

All matter is composed of elements, and all elements are composed of atoms. Until about the beginning of the twentieth century, it was believed that atoms were the fundamental particles, that is, there were no smaller particles than atoms — there was no evidence to suggest otherwise.

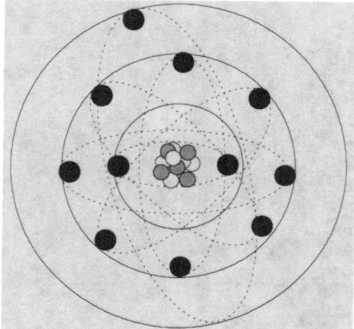

2.1 — *If an atom of sodium were magnified about 300 million times, it might look this size, but it would not look solid, as John Dalton at the beginning of the 19th century had thought; it might look something like the above.*

One of the important inventions of the nineteenth century, that of the induction coil — by Nicholas Callan at Maynooth, Co. Kildare — made possible the investigation of the passage of electricity through gases. It was from such an investigation that a famous scientist J. J. Thomson, at Cambridge University, discovered, in 1895, that there were particles of negative electricity in all atoms and that the mass of these particles was about 2000 times less than that of hydrogen atoms — the lightest atoms known. These particles he called **electrons**, a name which had already been proposed by Professor Johnstone Stoney of Galway for the fundamental charge of electricity in electrolysis.

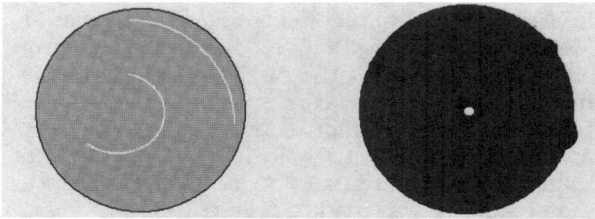

2.2 — *Dalton's atom of 1800 was a tiny, solid, indivisible and indestructible particle. Thomson's atom of 1900 was a sphere of positive charge with negative electrons embedded in it.*

2
Atomic Structure 2

This changed the whole idea of the concept of the atom. Thomson now visualised an atom as a "plum pudding" in which the electrons (the plums) were embedded in a "pudding" of positive charge. However, in 1911, another famous scientist, Ernest Rutherford, upset this idea when he discovered a most amazing fact — that atoms consist mainly of space! and that in the middle of each atom is a small hard dense core (now called the **"nucleus"**) which contains practically all the mass of the atom. This nucleus contains particles of positive electricity which he named **protons**.

Rutherford was professor of physics at Manchester University when, along with two of his assistants, Geiger and Marsden, he carried out the classic experiment in which the atomic nucleus was identified. A narrow beam of alpha particles from a radioactive substance was directed at thin gold foil, with a detector for alpha particles on the far side of the foil. The detector was arranged so that it could rotate in a horizontal plane, and the whole apparatus was enclosed in an evacuated chamber.

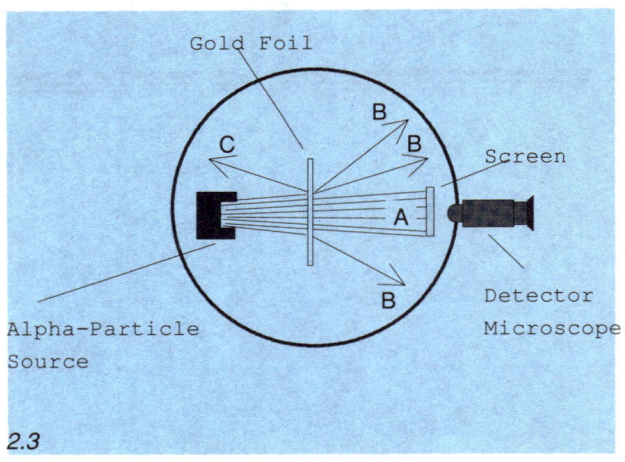

2.3

Alpha particles from the source struck the foil, and in the experiment Rutherford investigated where they then went. This was done by rotating the eyepiece and counting the number of particles which were coming from the foil at different angles. The results showed that most of the particles passed straight through the foil (A), but without making holes in it, and this indicated to Rutherford

2.4 —

J.J.Thomson (1856-1940) who was from Manchester, is famous for two great achievements. He was responsible for building up the Cavendish laboratory in Cambridge into one of the greatest centres of research in the world, especially for atomic physics. He was professor of physics there for 34 years and it was during this time that he discovered the electron — while carrying out research on the conductivity of electricity through gases. Thomson, who received the Nobel prize for physics in 1906 and was knighted in 1912, was succeeded as Cavendish professor by Rutherford.
Ernest Rutherford (1871-1937) was a New Zealander who came to England in 1895, to do research at Cambridge, working under Thomson. At the age of 27, he was made professor of physics at Magill University in Canada, but he returned to England in 1907 to become professor of physics at Manchester. It was in 1911 that his investigations of alpha particles led to the discovery of the atomic nucleus and the atom consisting mainly of space. He received the Nobel prize for chemistry in 1908, and was knighted in 1914. In 1919, he returned to Cambridge and here many more great discoveries were made. He was made a peer in 1931.
This photograph, taken in 1933, is characteristic of the two great men. Thomson invariably wore his bowler hat when he went outdoors, and Rutherford would often use his hands as he explained things.

that the particles had passed right through the atoms of gold, which therefore must consist mainly of empty space. But more surprising to him was the fact that a few of the particles were deflected through large angles (B) and some, about one in every 8,000 were even turned back again in the direction of the source (C). In this modern age, when most school pupils know about atomic structure and accept it, it is difficult to appreciate the significance of these results. Here was a piece of solid metal which would allow tiny "bullets" to pass through (but without making holes in it) and yet every so often one bounced right back. Rutherford's words expressed his amazement "*It was about as credible*", he wrote, "*as if you had fired a 15 inch shell at a piece of tissue paper and it came back and hit you*".

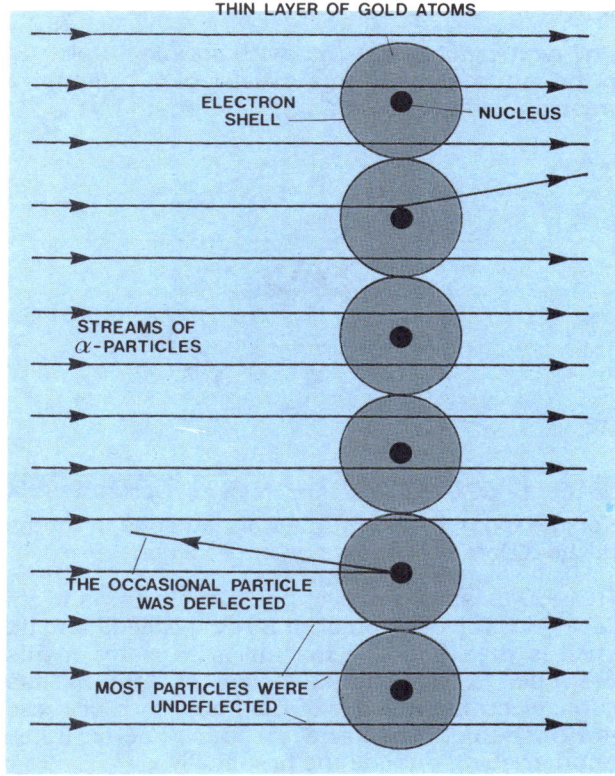

2.5

His explanation was that all the positive charge and mass must be concentrated in a very tiny volume or nucleus at the centre of the atom, and he calculated that the diameter of the nucleus was at least 10,000 times smaller than that of the atom.

Finally, in 1932, another scientist, **James Chadwick**, discovered a second kind of particle in the nucleus; this time, with no electrical charge. These particles were called **neutrons.**

Many scientists have been involved in unravelling the structure of the atom, and if you are specifically interested, you should read about the work of the following in science books and/or encyclopedias: Crooks; Thomson; Millikan; Becquerel; the Curies; Rutherford; Chadwick; Mosely; Aston; Geiger; Soddy; Bohr.

The effect of streams of electrons can be seen in an apparatus called a **cathode ray tube**. There are many types of cathode ray tube; that shown is the maltese cross tube.

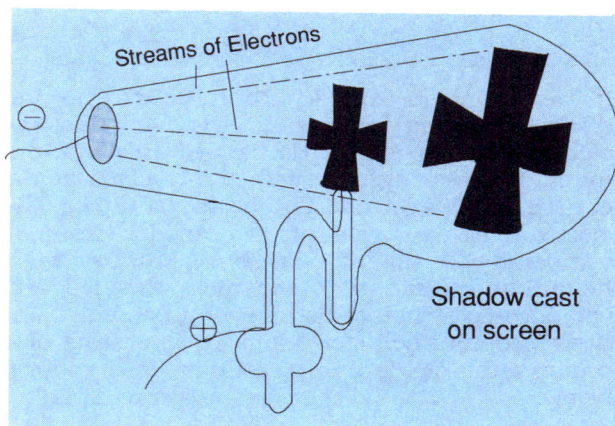

2.6 — *The Maltese Cross tube*

When the tube is connected to a suitable source of electricity, cathode rays which are streams of electrons, travel outwards, from the cathode, towards the maltese cross and the end of the tube. They cause a glow, or "fluorescence", when they strike the glass at the end of the tube, and a shadow is cast by the cross where it is in the way of the electron beam. Streams of electrons are like light in this respect.

If a magnet is now brought near the tube, the shadow is deflected, because a magnet exerts a force on an electron beam. In this way, streams of electrons are **not** like light.

So, atoms are made up of three different types of particle — which differ in their electric charge, where they are found, and also in their mass. Masses of atoms are so small that if they were expressed in grams, there would be about 23 zeros after the decimal point before the first digit of the number! **Atomic mass units** are used; these are a scale of masses on which the mass of the lightest atom (an atom of hydrogen) is about 1. On this scale, both the proton and neutron have a mass of 1, and the mass of an electron, which is very much smaller, is about $1/1,840$. The following summarises these facts:

Particle	Mass (a.m.u)	Charge	Location
Proton	1	+1	in the nucleus
Neutron	1	0	in the nucleus
Electron	$1/1,840$	-1	orbiting the nucleus in a series of "shells"

It was a Danish scientist, **Niels Bohr**, who first discovered something about the way that the electrons are arranged. He likened an atom to a miniature solar system, with the nucleus at the centre, and around which are rotating the electrons in various orbits. His model is simple compared with that of today, but a study of it is a helpful introduction to the more detailed and complicated structure as known at present. Bohr described the hydrogen atom as consisting of a proton with a single electron orbiting it — as shown below.

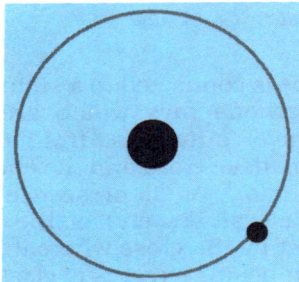

2.7

In reality, the electron orbit is not circular, as the diagram suggests, but is spherical — so that an atom occupies some particular volume. As well, it must be realised that diagrams such as are shown

here are completely out of scale. In reality, about 99.9999% of an atom consists of space! If a hydrogen atom were magnified until it were about 10 metres across, then the electron would be like a ball bearing revolving around the nucleus — which would be like another ball bearing at the centre.

> **The atomic number of an element is the number of protons in an atom of that element.**

It is also equal to the number of electrons. This means that an atom is electrically neutral, since there are equal numbers of positive and negative charges. Further, the chemical properties of an element are determined by the number and arrangement of the electrons in its atoms, and so atoms of different atomic number are atoms of different elements.

The next element (*i.e.* that with atomic number 2) is helium and its atoms consist of 2 protons, 2 neutrons and 2 electrons.

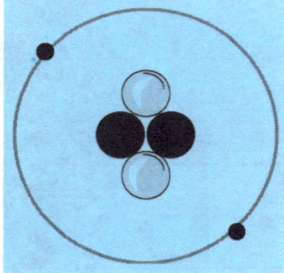

2.8

Electron Arrangement

For the moment the number of neutrons in atoms of the different elements will not be considered.

Helium, as shown above, has two electrons in its "shell" (as the electron orbit is often called), and its shell is then full. The maximum capacity of this first shell is two. The third element, lithium, has three electrons in each of its atoms; two of these are in the first shell and the extra one occupies another shell, outside the first shell.

The capacity of this second electron shell is eight, so that in lithium and the following seven elements, there are different numbers of electrons in this shell.

Oxygen is one of the elements in this set; its atomic number is 8 and so its atom can be represented as shown below.

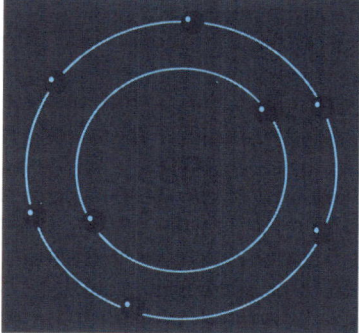

2.9

In element no. 10, the second electron shell is then full and for element no. 11 (sodium) the extra electron enters a new shell, *i.e.* the third shell. Thus, in sodium, the electron arrangement is 2,8,1.

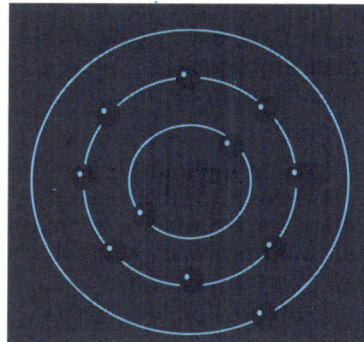

2.10

The capacity of this third electron shell is 18, **but**, once there are 8 electrons in it, the extra electron in the next element potassium, enters the fourth shell. This is because the arrangement 2,8,8,1 is more stable than a 2,8,9 arrangement. The reason for this will be understood after Chapter 3 has been studied. The electron structure in the atoms of the first 20 elements is given in the table below.

Element	Atomic number	Number of electrons in different shells			
		1st	2nd	3rd	4th
Hydrogen	1	1			
Helium	2	2			
Lithium	3	2	1		
Beryllium	4	2	2		
Boron	5	2	3		
Carbon	6	2	4		
Nitrogen	7	2	5		
Oxygen	8	2	6		
Fluorine	9	2	7		
Neon	10	2	8		
Sodium	11	2	8	1	
Magnesium	12	2	8	2	
Aluminium	13	2	8	3	
Silicon	14	2	8	4	
Phosporus	15	2	8	5	
Sulphur	16	2	8	6	
Chlorine	17	2	8	7	
Argon	18	2	8	8	
Potassium	19	2	8	8	1
Calcium	20	2	8	8	2

The Noble Gases

Eight electrons in the outer shell of an element is a very important and very stable electron arrangement; in fact it is the most stable structure of all and the elements which have this structure are called the **noble gases**. These gases are very inert or unreactive, and most of them form no compounds. Helium, which has 2 electrons in its outer (and only) shell, is also included in this group, because its shell is full and it is inert like the others.

Gas	Electron structure				
Helium	2				
Neon	2	8			
Argon	2	8	8		
Krypton	2	8	18	8	
Xenon	2	8	18	18	8

The Transition Elements

After a noble gas, the next element always has its extra electron in a new shell— even though the previous shell may not be completely full. The structure of potassium is 2,8,8,1 and that of calcium is 2,8,8,2, although the capacity of the third shell is 18. However, in the elements following calcium, the extra electrons again start entering the third shell and they continue doing so until it is complete *i.e.* until it contains 18 electrons.

Element	Atomic number	Number of electrons in shells			
		1st	2nd	3rd	4th
Scandium	21	2	8	9	2
Titanium	22	2	8	10	2
Vanadium	23	2	8	11	2
Chromium	24	2	8	13	1
Manganese	25	2	8	13	2
Iron	26	2	8	14	2
Cobalt	27	2	8	15	2
Nickel	28	2	8	16	2
Copper	29	2	8	18	1
Zinc	30	2	8	18	2
Gallium	31	2	8	18	3

These elements in which the difference in electron structure between successive members occurs in the penultimate shell (*i.e.* the last but one) are the **transition elments**. The electron structure of the first series of transition elements is shown above. More about the transition elements will be found in Chapters 3 and 17.

Neutrons and Isotopes

Practically all of the mass of an atom is due to its protons and neutrons (both of which have a mass of 1), and so is concentrated at the centre of the atom.

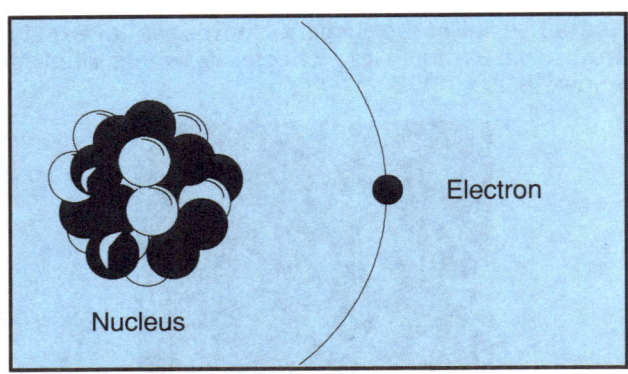

2.11 — *The nucleus contains the protons and neutrons.*

> **The mass number of an element is the number of protons and neutrons in an atom of that element.**

The mass of an atom has the same value as the mass number of that atom. In, for example, the neon atom illustrated above, there are 10 protons and 10 neutrons, and so its mass number is 20. Also, its mass is 20 units (the mass of the 10 electrons is so tiny ($^{10}/_{1,840}$) that it can be ignored).

Remembering that the atomic number of an element is the number of protons (and is usually the same as the number of electrons) and the mass number is equal to the number of protons and neutrons together, a knowledge of these 2 numbers enables you to tell how many of each of the 3 kinds of particle are present in an atom.

Atoms of the same element always contain the same number of electrons, but not always the same number of neutrons. Look at the two atoms represented below.

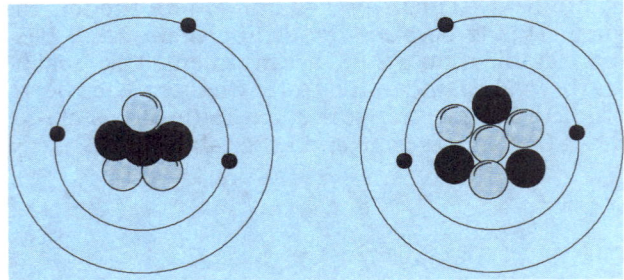

2.12 — *Isotopes of lithium (the red particles represent protons and the green represent neutrons).*

Each has 3 protons *i.e.* each has an atomic number of 3, so therefore each is an atom of lithium. But (a) has 3 neutrons, making its mass 6, whereas (b) has 4 neutrons and so its mass is 7. These different forms of lithium are known as isotopes.

> **Isotopes are atoms of the same element (*i.e.* same atomic number) but which have different masses due to different numbers of neutrons in the nuclei.**

Isotopes exist for most elements; hydrogen has only one isotope of importance whereas tin has about 10. An atom of "ordinary" hydrogen consists of one proton and one electron, but there is also an isotope of hydrogen, called deuterium, which consists of a proton, and an electron, as in ordinary hydrogen, but with a neutron in the nucleus.

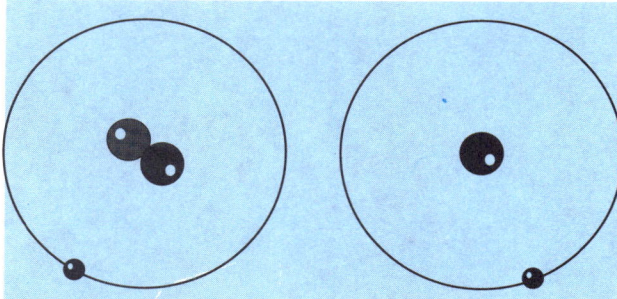

2.13 —   *Isotopes of hydrogen*

The chemical properties of an element depend on the arrangement of the electrons in the atom, and so the different isotopes of any element have the same properties.

The different isotopes of an element are not usually given special names, but symbols, showing both the atomic numbers and the mass *e.g.*

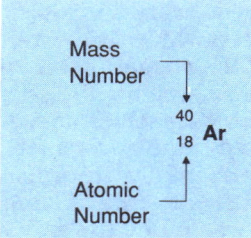

Mass Number

$^{40}_{18}$ **Ar**

Atomic Number

This symbol, which is for the element argon, shows that its atomic number is 18 and the mass of that

particular isotope is 40. There are thus 18 protons, 18 electrons and 22 neutrons in each of its atoms.

The Periodic Table

Wherever there exists a large number of similar objects, it is usually helpful and logical to arrange them in some sort of order. In your school library for instance, the books are likely to be arranged according to their subjects, and if you collect stamps or coins, they ar probably classified according to countries — Irish, British, French, Dutch and so on. Likewise it is necessary to arrange the 100 elements which are known today.

History

No single person just decided to write out the first Periodic Table. Rather, it evolved over a period of fifty years or so, in the 19th century. By about 1817, there were 49 known elements. Dalton's atomic theory of nine years back was gaining acceptance and "atomic weights" (these are known nowadays as "relative atomic masses") were being measured, although with no great accuracy.

Dobereiner's Triads

In that year, J.W. Dobereiner (1780-1849), who was a professor at the University of Jena in Germany, noticed that three recently discovered elements — calcium, strontium and barium — had similar properties, and that the atomic weight of strontium (88) was about midway between those of the other two (40 and137). He called this group of elements a "triad".

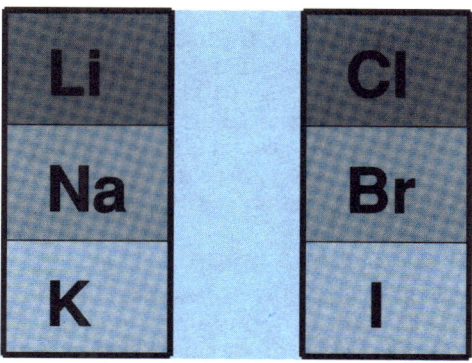

2.14 —   *Two of Dobereiner's Triads*

Later, he picked out other triads from the known elements; chlorine/bromine/ iodine and lithium /sodium/potassium and in each case the same relationship applied. He thought he had discovered the key to the pattern of the elements — they fitted together in threes. However, this kind of grouping was found to apply to only a limited number of elements, and Dobereiner's triads received only scant attention.

Newlands' "Octaves"

By 1863, about 60 elements had been discovered and more accurate ways of measuring atomic weights had been devised. John Newlands, an English chemist, listed all the known elements in order of increasing atomic weight, and noticed a regular repeating pattern. He found that each eighth element, starting from a given one, is similar in its chemical properties to the first one, like the eighth note in an octave of music. So he called his discovery the **Law of Octaves**

H	Li	Be	B	C	N	O
F	Na	Mg	Al	Si	P	S
Cl	K	Ca	Cr	Ti	Mn	Fe

2.15

But his pattern really only worked for the first 16 or so elements. In the above list, while lithium, sodium and potassium obviously belong to each other, iron, for example, is clearly out of place — it just is not chemically similar to oxygen and sulphur. At a meeting of scientists at which Newlands presented his findings, he was ridiculed and asked sarcastically if he had ever examined the elements according to their initial letters! However, Newlands was basically correct in his idea and in time this was realised. Twenty years later, the Royal Society presented him with the Davy Medal in recognition of his work.

Lothar Meyer's Curves

The next year a German professor, Lothar Meyer (1830-1895) published some results which supported the idea of periodic recurrence of properties as put forward by Newlands. Meyer had worked out the "atomic volume" of each of the known elements. This value was obtained by dividing the atomic weight of the element by its relative density (in the solid state), and it represented the volume occupied by an atom of the relevant element. Meyer's findings took the form of a graph of atomic volume plotted against atomic weight, and this graph (Fig.2.16) showed definite patterns, the most obvious being that the elements which have the largest atomic volumes are the alkali metals, *viz.* lithium, sodium, potassium and so on. Graphs of other physical properties (density, m.p., b.p.) plotted against atomic weight show similar characteristics and these provide confirmation that many properties of the elements are 'periodic' *i.e.* they recur at regular intervals.

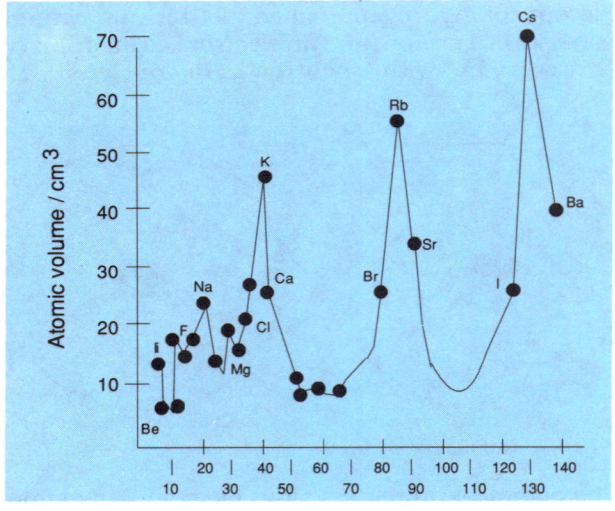

2.16 — Lothar Meyer's curves

Dimitri Mendeleeff

The most satisfactory method for classifying the elements was put forward in 1869 by a Russian chemist, Dimitri Mendeleeff. Mendeleeff discovered that if the elements were listed in order of increasing atomic weight, the properties of the elements repeated themselves at regular intervals and he constructed a table in which the elements were arranged horizontally, in order of increasing atomic weight, with elements of similar properties in columns. This was much the same as Newlands had done, but Mendeleeff made some significant changes.

2.17 — *Dimitri Ivanovitch Mendeleeff was Russian and lived from 1834 to 1907. He was professor of chemistry at St. Petersburg (now Leningrad) for 25 years and it was during this time that he put forward his famous Periodic law, in 1869.*

In order that the elements would fall into the correct groups as indicated by their chemical properties, he found it necessary to leave blank spaces occasionally. He predicted that these spaces would be filled by the discovery of new elements, and he even went so far as to predict, from a knowledge of the properties of the elements above and below the spaces, what these undiscovered elements would be like. For example, the element germanium (no. 32) was one of the undiscovered ones at the time. Mendeleeff reasoned from the atomic weights of silicon and tin, that there must be an element in between them. He referred to this missing element as "eka-silicon", and he predicted a number of properties about it (see accompanying table). When germanium was discovered 17 years later and it was found that his predictions were remarkably accurate, there was little doubt that Mendeleeff's ideas of classification were correct. Other predictions about missing elements (gallium, discovered 1875, and scandium, discovered 1879) were similarly successful. So not only did Mendeleeff's table account for known facts, but could also be used to predict unknown ones.

Property	Mendeleeff's predictions about "eka-silicon"	Observed properties of germanium.
Atomic mass	72	72.6
Appearance	Light grey metal	Dark grey metal
Melting point	$\approx 800°C$	950°C
Density	5.5 g/cm^3	5.4 g/cm^3
Oxide	EsO_2	GeO_2
b.p. of oxide	high	1,116°C
Density of oxide	4.7 g/cm^3	4.7 g/cm^3
Chloride	$EsCl_4$	$GeCl_4$
b.p. of chloride	less than 100°C	86°C
Density of chloride	about 1.9 g/cm^3	1.887 g/cm^3

Mendeleeff also found that he had to reverse the order of several pairs of elements to make them fall into groups which contained elements of similar properties. Elements numbers 52 and 53 are an example of this; tellurium (no.52) has an atomic weight greater than that of iodine (no. 53) but must be placed before iodine so that both elements will fall into their correct groups (other pairs of elements for which this is necessary are numbers 27 and 28, and numbers 18 and 19). Mendeleeff presumed that the atomic weights known at the time were incorrect and that more accurate values would be determined in time, which would reverse the order of such elements. However, he was wrong in this presumption, and it was not until the 20th century that the correct explanation was discovered.

Lord Rayleigh (1842 - 1919) is probably best known for his work which led to the discovery of the noble gases. In 1893, he determined the density of atmospheric nitrogen very accurately, and showed that it was slightly greater than the density of nitrogen which had been prepared from a nitrogen compound. He concluded that atmospheric nitrogen contained a small quantity of a more dense gas as an impurity. The following year, along with Sir William Ramsey, he isolated argon from the air and showed, by means of its spectrum, that it was a hitherto unknown element. Ramsey subsequently, along with others, discovered helium, neon, krypton and xenon.

	I		II		III		IV		V		VI		VII		VIII
Group															
Sub-Group	A	B	A	B	A	B	A	B	A	B	A	B	A	B	
1st Period														H	
2nd Period	Li		Be			B		C		N		O		F	
3rd Period	Na		Mg			Al		Si		P		S		Cl	
4th Period	K		Ca				Ti		V	As	Cr	Se	Mn		Fe Co Ni
		Cu		Zn										Br	
5th Period	Rb		Sr		Y		Zr		Nb	Sb	Mo				Ru Rh Pd
		Ag		Cd		In		Sn				Te		I	
6th Period	Cs		Ba		La+ rare earths				Ta		W				Os Ir Pt
		Au		Hg		Ti		Pb		Bi					

2.18 — *Mendeleeff's Periodic Table.*
The modern layout of the table (see back cover) differs in several ways. It has —

(i)   the addition of the noble gases (Group 0), which were undiscovered in Mendeleeff's time,

(ii)   the inclusion of atomic numbers, which, again, were undiscovered in Mendeleeff's time,

(iii)   no spaces; the gaps left for Mendeleeff for undiscovered elements (e.g. Sc, Ga, Ge) have now been filled,

(iv)   the transition elements listed in a separate block; Mendeleeff included these in Groups 1 - 8, under sub group headings

Moseley and Atomic Numbers

In 1911, Ernest Rutherford had discovered that the atom consists of a positively charged nucleus with the electrons revolving around it. Two years later, a young research student of Rutherford's called Henry Moseley, found that the positive charge in a atomic nucleus was of a definite amount, and it was different for atoms of each element — in much the same way as the atomic weight was different for each element. Hydrogen's atoms had one unit of charge, helium's had two, lithium's three and so on. The number of units of charge in the nucleus came to be called the **atomic number** of that element. Moseley found that if the elements were arranged in order of increasing atomic number, they fell into the same periodic pattern as devised by Mendeleeff, but whereas Mendeleeff had to reverse the order of some elements to make them fit the pattern, Moseley did not — the elements fell neatly into place, each in its correct group. So it came to be realised that atomic numbers are more fundamental than atomic weights, and that the properties of the elements are more closely related to atomic numbers than to atomic weights.

Today, there are no gaps in the Periodic Table; all the elements which occur in nature have been discovered. In this nuclear age, many elements which do not occur in nature have been man-made, or synthesised in nuclear explosions, nuclear reactors or "atom-smashers". The element of highest atomic number which occurs naturally is uranium, number 92. The first of the artificial elements neptunium, number 93, was identified in 1940 amongst the products of an experiment in which uranium had been bombarded with neutrons, and since that time, the number of new elements has steadily increased. In most cases, only minimal quantities of these elements have been produced and they are mainly of theoretical interest.

Structure of the Periodic Table

In the modern periodic table, the elements are listed in order of increasing atomic numbers and arranged according to the number of electrons in the outer shells of their atoms. Those elements whose atoms have the same numbers of outer electrons are placed in columns called **Groups**. Because all the elements in any one group have the same number of outer electrons, they have similar properties.

> **The group number of an element is equal to the number of electrons in the outer shell of an atom of that element.**

Several of the groups have special names: the **Group 1** elements are called the **alkali metals** (which thus contain one electron in the outer shells of their atoms); **Group 7** are known as the **halogens**; and the **noble gases** make up **Group 0**, at the extreme right-hand side of the table.

Periods \ Groups	I	II	III	etc.
1	H			
2	Li	Be	B	
3	Na	Mg	Al	
etc.				

The horizontal rows of elements are called **Periods**. All the elements in any given period have the same number of electron shells.

> **The period number of an element is equal to the number of electron shells in an atom of that element.**

A new period starts when a new outer electron shell begins to fill. The first 3 periods are known as short periods; the periods thereafter are called long periods, since each of these contains a series of transition elements, *i.e.* those in which the differences in electron structure between successive members occurs in the penultimate shell. Period 4 thus contains those elements in which the electron differences occur in the third shell (elements numbers 21 to 30).

The properties of the transition elements are fairly similar to each other (because they have the same outer shell electron structure) and resemble those of their horizontal neighbours (non-transition).

Characteristic properties of these elements are:

(i)   variable valency or oxidation state,

(ii) formation of coloured compounds (*i.e.* their ions are coloured),

(iii) action as catalysts in chemical reactions.

Hydrogen is difficult to classify fully satisfactorily; some of its properties resemble those of the alkali metals while others are like those of the halogens. Some periodic tables place hydrogen in both groups.

Metals and Non-metals

Although the Periodic Table does not classify the elements into metals and non-metals, there is a reasonably clear division between the two. This is shown by the heavy line like a "steps of stairs" on the Table (printed on the back cover), non-metals being in the top right hand corner.

Metalloids

Iron, copper and zinc are clearly metals, while carbon, sulphur and nitrogen are clearly non-metals. However, some elements have properties which are intermediate between the two and are called "metalloids". Silicon and germanium are examples, and since they are neither very good nor very poor conductors of electricity, they are known as **semi-conductors**. These elements are used to make devices like diodes, transistors and ICs (integrated circuits) which are small, robust and relatively cheap, and have made possible modern electronic equipment, like small portable radios and recorders, calculators, video games and computers.

Questions

Q.2.1   Give short answers to each of the following questions.

(a)   Who discovered
(i) that an atom is mainly space but with a dense nucleus in the centre, and
(ii) that electrons are negatively charged?

(b)   What are the relative charges on the proton and the electron?

(c)   What does the cathode ray tube experiment show?

(d)   Which element has
(i) the smallest number,
(ii) the largest number, of electrons?

(e)   What is the electron structure of an atom of
(i) sodium, (ii) sulphur?

(f)   What is the electron capacity of each of the first, second and third electron "shells"?

(g)   What is common to the structure of the noble gases and what is the effect of this structure on their properties?

(h)   What is a transition element ? Name one.

(i)   Name two characteristic properties of the transition element.

Q.2.2
(a)   Define
(i) atomic number, and (ii) mass number.

(b)   Give the definition of isotopes.

(c)   How do atoms of $^{23}_{11}$ Na and $^{24}_{11}$ Na
(ii) differ from each other, and
(ii) resemble each other?

(d)   How many
(i) electrons, (ii) neutrons,
are in an atom of $^{59}_{27}$Co?

(e)   Give the exact symbols for the isotopes which contain
(i) 17 protons and 18 neutrons, and
(ii) 17 protons and 20 neutrons.

(f)   How many protons and neutrons are in an atom of $^{45}_{21}$Sc, and what is the arrangement of its electrons?

Q.2.3
(a)   How did
(i) Dobereiner, and (ii) Newlands,
classify the elements which were known when they lived?

(b)   State two ways in which Mendeleeff's Periodic Table differs from the modern form.

(c)   **What is the electron structure of each of boron and aluminium? Why are these elements in the same Periodic Group?**

(d)   Give the name of the Periodic Group which contains neon.

(e)   What is the group number of
(i) the alkali metals, (ii) the halogens?

(f)   What is common to all the elements in any given period of elements?

(g)   What are the mass number and atomic number of the element which is in Group 3 and Period 3 of the Periodic Table?

(h)   How many
(i) shells of electrons, and
(ii) outer shell electrons, in an atom of element no. 84?

(i)   Why is hydrogen difficult to classify on the Periodic Table?

Q.2.4   Draw diagrams showing the numbers of protons, neutrons and electrons in atoms of boron, magnesium, phosphorus and potassium. Show the electron arrangements also.

Q.2.5   What was Thomson's model of the atom and why was it discarded? Describe Rutherford's gold foil experiment and explain what is shown about the nature of the atom, and how it did this.

Q.2.6   Use the data in the Data Section at the end of the book to plot (on the same graph) melting and boiling points of elements numbers 1 to 20 against atomic number. What can be deduced from these graphs?

(a)   What elements occur at or near the peaks on the boiling point curves?

(b)   Which elements occur in the troughs on the melting point curves?

(c)   Which elements are liquid over very large temperature ranges?

9.2.7 A section of the Periodic Table is shown. Some of the elements are represented by letters (but these letters are **not** the symbols for the elements).

(a) What letter represents the element which
(i) is a noble gas,
(ii) is a halogen,
(iii) belongs to Group 3,
(iv) has 4 outer shell electrons.

(b) What is the name of the group to which A and L belong? Why are these elements in the same group.

(c) Name the group to which Q belongs. List two characteristic properties of the elements in the same group?

(d) What are the electron structures of M,Q and T?

(e) What two elements do Z and E represent? Name and give the formula of the compound formed by these two elements.

(f) Which two elements belong to Period 3. Give the electron structure of each of these.

(g) What actual elements do A,D,J,L and Q represent? What actual element occurs in the Periodic Table between
(i) D and E, and (ii) A and L?

Review When you know Chapter 2 you should be able to:

(a) Name the three fundamental sub-atomic particles, and state the mass, charge and location of each.

(b) Give definitions of: atomic number, mass number, isotopes, periodic group, group number, period, period number.

(c) Describe the arrangement of the electrons (according to Bohr) for the 36 elements.

(d) Describe the similarities and differences between any pair of named isotopes.

(e) Explain in terms of electron structure each of: noble gas, transition element, halogen, alkali metal.

(f) Describe the distinctive features of the transition metals.

(g) Describe Rutherford's experiment in which the atomic nucleus was discovered.

(h) State the contribution of each of: Dobereiner, Newlands, Lothar Meyer, Mendeleeff, to the evolution of the modern periodic table.

(i) State how the modern periodic table differs from Mendeleeff's table.

3
Atomic Structure 2

Experiment 3.1
Flame Tests for Metals

Most elements can be made to give out light, and when they do so, the light is of a colour which is characteristic of that particular element. The colour of the light emitted by an element is often used as a means of identification of that element. One of the simplest ways of making metal atoms emit light is to heat a salt of the metal in a flame. Salts of many metals require to be heated to very high temperatures, but those listed below can emit light when heated with a good bunsen burner. Metal chlorides are particularly suitable for this purpose because they are usually more volative than other salts of metals.

Salts (preferably the chlorides) of the following metals are suitable: lithium, sodium, potassium, calcium, nickel, copper, strontium, barium.

Procedure

1.   Clean a platinum or nichrome wire by dipping it into concentrated hydrochloric acid (contained in a small test tube or on a watch glass) and then heating it red or white hot in a non-luminous bunsen flame. Do NOT use the bottle of acid for this purpose as the acid would become contaminated. Repeat the procedure until the wire gives no colour to the flame.

2.   Dip the wire into concentrated hydrochloric acid and then into a small sample of the salt of the metal to be investigated. Heat the wire in the bunsen flame and observe the flame colour.

3.   Investigate as many metal salts as are available. Leave the sodium salt until last as its flame colour is very persistent and can remain long after the salt has been removed from the flame.

4.   Prepare a chart of the results, listing the metal, and the colour of the flame which was observed.

Atomic Emission Spectra

When atoms are "excited" (given energy) either by heating them or subjecting them to an electric discharge, they usually emit coloured light — or some other form of electromagnetic radiation. The light emitted by such sources (*e.g.* street lights, neon signs, coloured flames) generally consist of a mixture of a small number of individual colours or wavelengths. If this light is passed through a spectroscope (spectrometer), the spectrum which is produced is generally very different from the continuous spectrum obtained from an

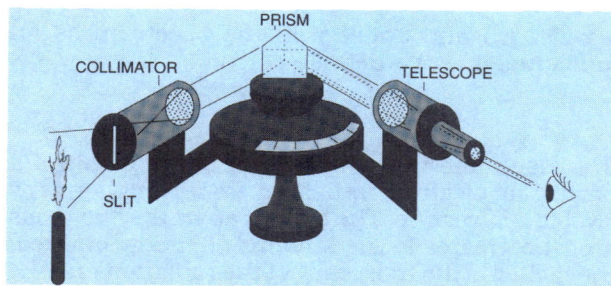

3.1 — A spectroscope. Light from the source passes through the slit and is converted by the collimator into a parallel beam. This is then dispersed by the prism into various colours, which are focussed by the telescope, forming a spectrum.

incandescent source such as an ordinary electric bulb. The latter produces a continuous spectrum — from red, through various colours, to violet — but the spectra from excited atoms are not continuous; they consist of a number of distinct lines, each coresppnding to a definite wavelength of light. The visible spectrum of hydrogen, shown below, consists of four distinct lines.

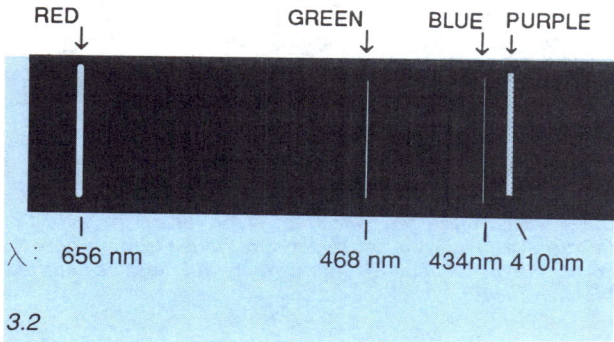

3.2

Bohr's Theory

Niels Bohr discovered that the electrons in atoms are arranged around the nucleus in a series of "shells" or energy levels. He obtained his clues about this from a study of the hydrogen spectrum. The fact that the spectrum consists of lines indicated to him that only certain energy emissions are possible, and this is accounted for as follows:

1. In an atom, electrons revolve around the nucleus in certain allowed "orbits" or "shells". While in a particular "shell" an electron has a definite amount of energy.

2. An **energy level** is one of the discrete amounts of energy which an electron can have when it is in an atom. It is dependent on the distance of the electron from the nucleus.

3. The energy levels are numbered, that of lowest energy being denoted by $n = 1$, that of next greatest energy has $n = 2$, and so on. The main energy level number (the "shell" number) is known as the **principal quantum number**. The maximum electron capacity of each main energy level has been found to be $2n^2$. When $n = 1$, the electron capacity is 2, when $n = 2$, the capacity is 8, for $n = 3$, the capacity is 18 and for $n = 4$, it is 32.

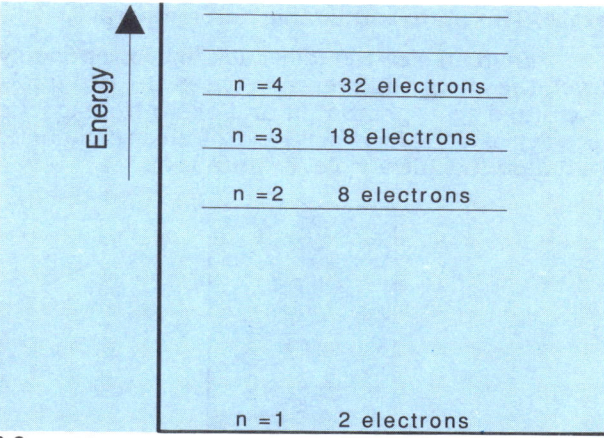

3.3 — The energy levels of the various shells.

4. Electrons normally occupy the lowest available energy levels. The **ground state** of the atom refers to the state of the atom when all of its electrons are in their lowest available energy levels.

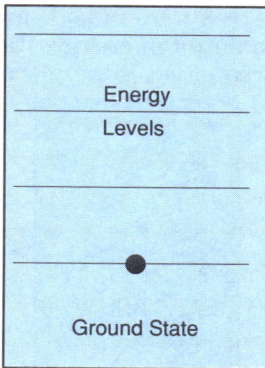

3.4

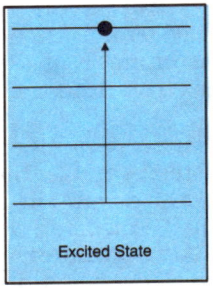

3.5

5.   When energy is given to an atom, one or more of the electrons are promoted to higher energy levels. The atom is then said to be in the **excited state**. This state is unstable and temporary.

6.   When an electron falls back to a lower energy level, the energy difference between the two levels is emitted as a "photon" (a unit of electromagnetic energy) of light or other kind of electromagnetic radiation (*i.e.* ultra violet or infra red).

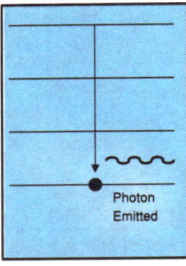

3.6

7.   The energy and frequency of the radiation are related by $E = hf$, where E is the energy, f the frequency and h is a constant known as Planck's constant (value 6.6×10^{-34} Js). Since the photon has a definite amount of energy, the emitted light has a definite frequency. It therefore has a definite

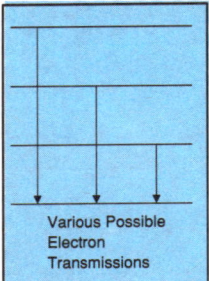

3.7

wavelength and appears in the spectrum as an individual line of a definite colour.

$$E_1 - E_2 = hf$$

8.   Each line in the spectrum is the result of a particular electron transition from a high energy level to a lower one. The further apart the two levels are, the greater is the amount of energy emitted, the higher is the frequency of the radiation and the shorter the wavelength of the light.

The Hydrogen Spectrum

Each element has its own characteristic emission spectrum. That of hydrogen, being the element with the simplest atomic structure, is most easily explained. The complete hydrogen spectrum is made up of several series of lines; in addition to the lines in the visible region of the spectrum, there are others in both the ultra-violet and the infra-red.

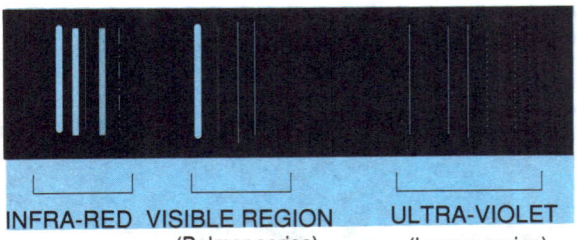

INFRA-RED   VISIBLE REGION   ULTRA-VIOLET
                (Balmer series)   (Lyman series)

3.8 — The hydrogen spectrum. (The lines in both the infra-red and ultra-violet regions, although shown here in colour, are invisible to the human eye, and must be detected by other means.

The existence of several series of lines can be explained in terms of electron transitions to each different level from all the levels above it. The lines in the ultra-violet (called the Lyman series) are caused by electrons falling to the $n = 1$ level (the lowest possible level) from all higher levels. These electron transitions release most energy, so that the lines have the shortest wavelengths.

The lines in the visible spectrum (of slightly longer wavelength and therefore caused by electron transitions of somewhat less energy) result from electrons falling to the $n = 2$ level, from all levels above it. Likewise, the lines in the infra-red are caused by electrons falling to the $n = 3$ level (less energy emitted and therefore longer wavelengths).

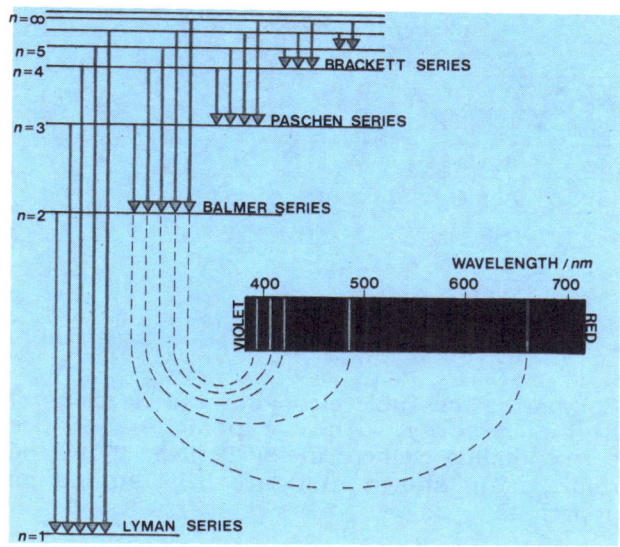

3.9 *The origin of the visible lines in the hydrogen spectrum.*

Energy Levels and Sublevels

Bohr's theory explains the wavelengths of the various lines in the hydrogen spectrum with remarkable accuracy, but when applied to other elements, it needs much modification. A close study of the spectra of many elements shows that each main energy level or "principal shell" must be divided into one or more sublevels or "subshells". The number of sublevels in each main level is equal to its principal quantum number. Thus, the first level has only one sublevel, the second has two, and so on. The sublevels are designated by the letters, s, p, d and f[(i)], and the electron content of each — irrespective of its principal quantum number — is fixed; each **s** subshell holds two electrons, each **p** holds six, each **d** ten and each **f** fourteen. The energy level of an electron indicates the quantity of energy which it has in an atom.

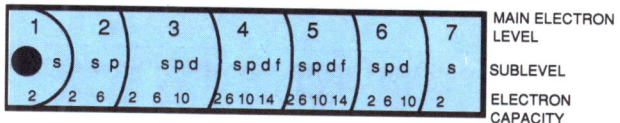

3.10

In any given level, the energy of the electron in the sublevels increases in the order s < p < d < f, but in some cases, the d (and f where it exists) sublevel of a lower main level or shell, overlaps the s (and sometimes p) sublevel of the next higher main level or shell. For example, the 4s level is of lower energy than the 3d level.

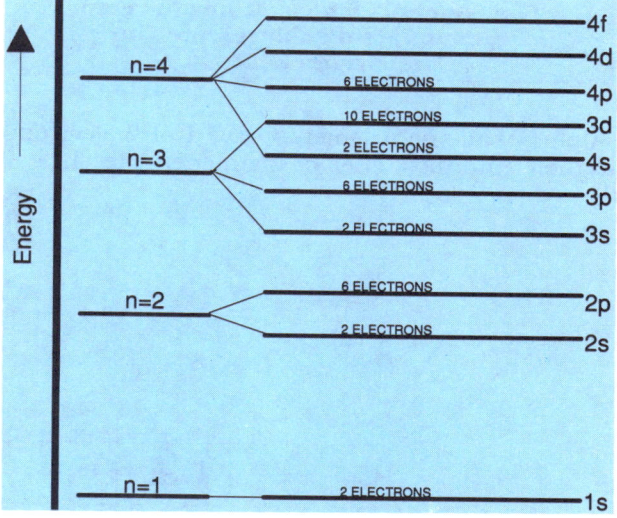

3.11 — *Energy level diagram.*

(i)   The letters are derived from 'sharp', 'principal', 'diffuse' and 'fundamental', terms which are used in spectroscopy

The **Aufbau Principle**, one of the rules which governs electron arrangement in atoms, states that

> **electrons occupy the lowest available energy level.**

This means that as atoms are being built up, the 1s sublevel is the first to fill, then the 2s, the 2p, 3s and so on, in the order shown in Figure 3.11.

Electrons in normal atoms only enter higher energy levels after the lower energy levels have been filled to capacity. Since the 3d level is of higher energy than the 4s, it means that when electrons are filling this level (the 3d), there are already electrons in the next higher main level (the 4s).

> **The elements whose atoms have an incomplete d sublevel, are the transition elements.**

Atoms of all such elements have 1 or 2 electrons in their outermost shell or main energy level.

Highest energy levels of the electrons in atoms of element numbers 1 to 38	
5s	Rb, Sr
4p	Ga, Ge, As, Se, Br, Kr
3d	Sc to Zn
4s	K, Ca
3p	Al, Si, P, S, Cl, Ar
3s	Na, Mg.
2p	B, C, N, O, F, Ne.
2s	Li, Be
1s	H, He

Comparing the sublevel holding the electrons of highest energy with the positions of the corresponding element in the Periodic table, the relationship shown in figure 3.12 should be apparent.

Knowing the above pattern, the order in which the sublevels are filled can be read off from the Periodic Table. The transition elements are sometimes referred to as the "d-block" elements because they have their highest energy electrons in d sublevels. More about the transition elements will be found in Chapter 17.

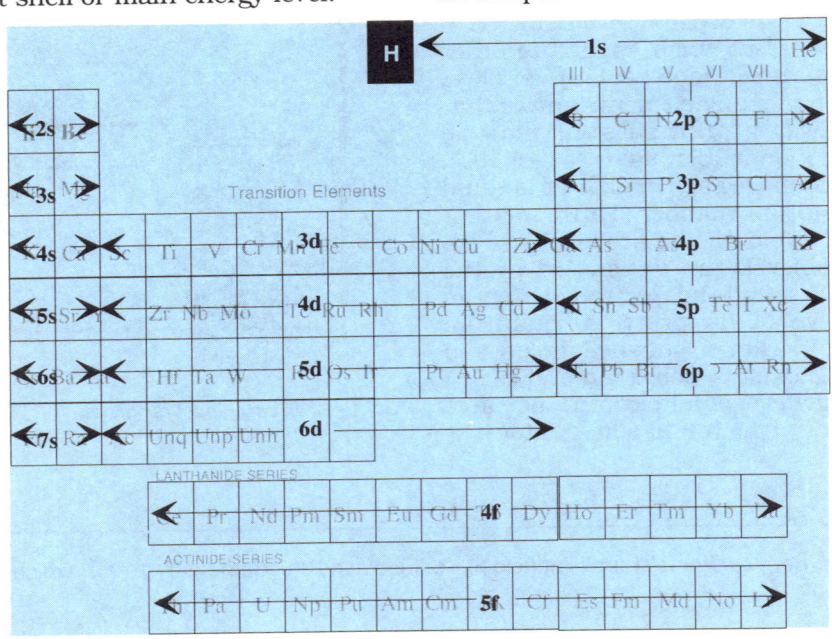

3.12 —

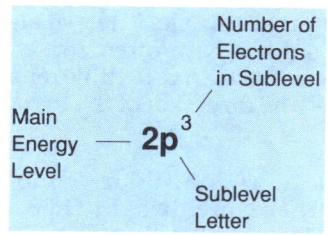

The electron configuration of an element shows the numbers of electrons in each of the various sublevels in an atom. Chlorine, for example, is given by $Cl = 1s^2, 2s^2, 2p^6, 3s^2, 3p^5$. This means that there are two electrons in the 1s sublevel, two in the 2s, six in the 2p and so on.

Questions

9.3.1 Write out the electronic configuration in atoms of:
(a) the elements Be, Ne, Si, Sc, Se;
(b) elements of atomic number 7, 13, 19, 29, 38.

9.3.2. What elements are represented by
(a) $1s^2, 2s^2, 2p^6, 3s^1$,
(b) $1s^2, 2s^2, 2p^6$,
(c) $1s^2, 2s^2, 2p^6, 3s^2, 2p^6, 4s^2, 3d^{10}$
(d) $1s^2, 2s^2, 2p^6, 3s^2, 3p^6, 4s^2, 3d^2$.

Atomic Orbitals

Bohr's simple theory, in which he envisaged the electrons revolving around the nucleus in various circular "orbits" was soon superseded after the discovery, by the French physicist de Broglie, that electrons have wave characteristics. The study of electron sutruture which involves their wave characteristics is known as **wave mechanics** and was developed mainly during the 1920s by the German physicist Heisenberg, and the Austrian physicist Schrodinger. The electrons moving about a nucleus are described in wave mechanics by complex mathematical functions, known as the Schrodinger wave equations. These equations are very complicated, even for the simple hydrogen atom. Solutions have been found for some of them and, when plotted on polar diagrams, they indicate that electrons in atoms occupy regions of space — now called orbitals, to distinguish them from Bohr's orbits.

> **Atomic orbitals can be defined as regions in space around the nucleus of an atom in which the electrons are most likely to be found.**

Atomic orbitals may be regarded as the modern equivalent of Bohr's orbits. There are four types of orbital — **s**, **p**, **d**, and **f,** one characteristic of each energy sublevel. They are of different shapes and the number of orbitals in each main energy level depends on its principal quantum number. An orbital can hold two electrons.

The simplest type of orbital is an **s** orbital and it is spherical in shape. Each **s** sublevel is made up of one **s** orbital.

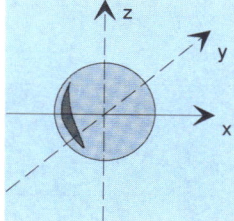

3.13 — *An s orbital*

A **p** orbital is sort of dumb-bell shaped and is usually represented by two spheres. Each **p** sublevel is made up of three **p** orbitals — all mutually at right angles to each other and designated by p_x, p_y and p_z. Since each can hold two electrons, the total electron capacity of a **p** sublevel is six (see Fig 3.14(b)).

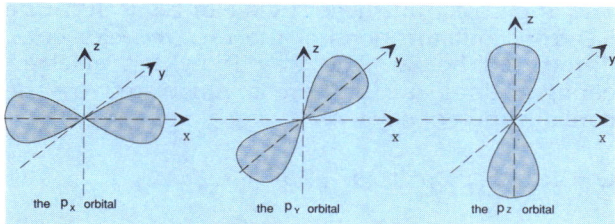

3.14 (a) — *The p orbitals*

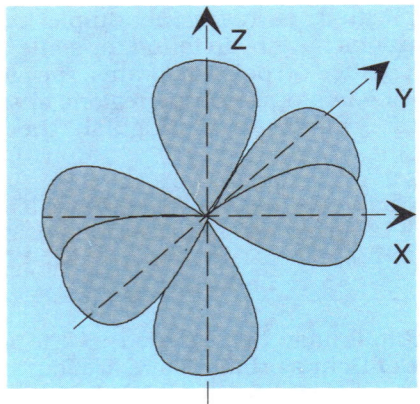

3.14 (b) — *The arrangement of the three p orbitals*

The shapes of **d** and **f** orbitals are complex and cannot easily be represented in two dimensions. Each **d** sublevel consists of five **d** orbitals and each **f** sublevel of seven **f** orbitals.

Orbitals and Electrons in each main energy level.

Main Energy Level or "Shell"	Sub level	Number of Orbitals	Electron Capacity	Total Electron Capacity
$n=1$	s	1	2	2
$n=2$	s	1	2	8
	p	3	6	
$n=3$	s	1	2	18
	p	3	6	
	d	5	10	
$n=4$	s	1	2	
	p	3	6	
	d	5	10	32
	f	7	14	

Electron Distribution in Orbitals

An orbital can hold two electrons. It has been shown, however, that when two electrons occupy the same orbital, they differ in one respect — they have opposite spin. Evidence for this comes from experiments on the magnetic properties of different elements. In any given orbital, a pair of electrons

of opposite spin are stable. The two electrons in an **s** orbital or sublevel are often represented as ↑↓ and the six electrons in a **p** sublevel are indicated by ↑↓ ↑↓ ↑↓ — the direction of the arrows signifying the spin.

In addition to the Aufbau Principle, stated previously, there are two further rules which summarise electron distribution in atoms. These are **Hund's Rule of Maximum Multiplicity,** which states:

> **When two or more orbitals of equal energy are available to electrons, the electrons occupy them singly before filling them in pairs**

and the **Pauli Exclusion Principle,** which asserts that;

> **No more than two electrons can occupy an orbital, and this they can only do if they have opposite spin.**

To summarise the rules about the way the electrons are distributed in atoms:

1. An orbital can hold a maximum of two electrons.

2. When an electron is added to an atom, it goes into the orbital of lowest energy level.

3. If two orbitals of equal energy are available, the electron goes into an orbital which is not already occupied by another electron.

4. A pair of electrons in the same orbital have opposite spin.

5. Unpaired electrons in different orbitals have the same spin.

The application of these rules can be seen in the electron configurations of the first ten elements, illustrated below. The way in which electron configurations are written is illustrated by the configuration of oxygen:

$O = 1s^2, 2s^2, 2p_x^2, 2p_y^1, 2p_z^1$

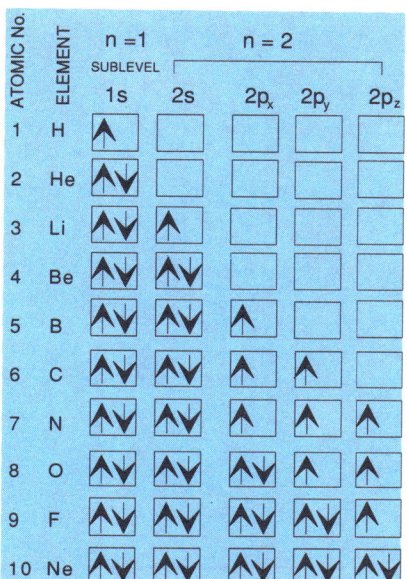

3.15 — *The electron configuration of the first 10 elements.*

Questions

Q.3.3 Write the full electronic configuration (s, p_x, p_y, p_z,) for atoms of lithium, aluminium, calcium, arsenic.

Q.3.4 What is the full electron configuration in atoms of elements numbers 4, 10, 14, 21 and 34?

Atomic Radii

Radii of atoms cannot be determined directly, since an isolated atom has no well-defined boundary. Values of atomic radii are usually found from the inter-atomic spacings of atoms in solids or when they are combined together. Half of the distance between the centres of adjacent atoms is taken to be the atomic radius. The distance between two chlorine atoms bonded together has been found to be 0.198 nm, and so the atomic radius is taken to be 0.099 nm.

Examination of the values shows definite trends. In general, as one moves from left to right across any given period, the values decrease. Despite the

fact that succeeding elements have a greater number of electrons, the larger the nuclear charge, the greater is the force of attraction between the nucleus and the outer electrons, and so the smaller is the radius. The transition elements show little variation in atomic size, since the difference in electron structure is in the penultimate[i] shell.

Moving down any given group, the values of the radii increase — due to the extra "shell" of electrons in succeeding elements. Ionisation energies and electronegativities are closely related to atomic radii.

Atomic Radii							
I	II	III	IV	V	VI	VII	VIII
H 37							He 54
Li 123	Be 106	B 88	C 77	N 74	O 66	F 64	Ne 112
Na 157	Mg 140	Al 126	Si 117	P 110	S 104	Cl 99	A 154
K 203	Ca 174	*Ga 126	Ge 122	As 118	Se 117	Br 111	Kn 169
Rb 216	Sr 191	*In 150	Sn 141	Sb 136	Te 132	I 128	Xe 190
Cs 235	Ba 198	*Th 155	Pb 154	Bi 152	Po 153	At	Rn 220

units = pm (picometres= 10^{-12}m)
*Transition elements omitted.

Ionisation Energy

When an electron is removed from an atom, the resulting particle is a positively charged ion. The process, called **ionisation**, can be represented as $Na - e^- \rightarrow Na^+$, and the energy required to cause it is ionisation energy.

> **The first ionisation energy of an element is the minimum energy required to completely remove the most loosely bound electron from an isolated atom of the element.**

An isolated atom means that the element must be in the gaseous state. Values of ionisation energies are usually expressed in kilojoules per mole.

(i)   second last

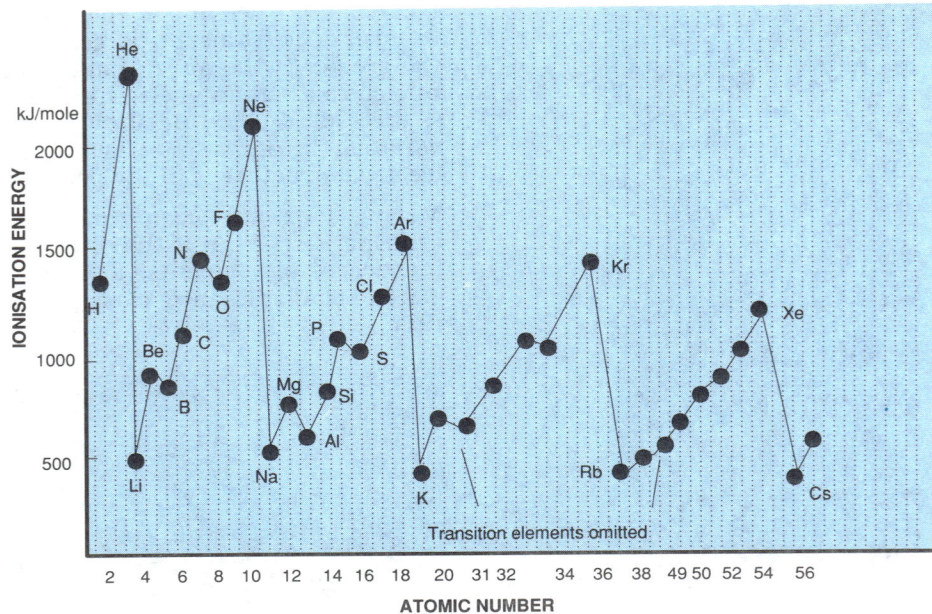

3.16

Ionisation energies vary considerably from element to element, as can be seen in the accompanying graph.

The following points should be noted:

1.   The peak values are for the noble gases — because these elements are the most stable and require the most energy to remove electrons from their atoms.

2.   The troughs are the values for alkali metals (Group 1 elements), showing that these elements can have electrons removed most easily.

3.   In general, ionisation energies gradually increase in moving across any given period, from an alkali metal to the next noble gas (*e.g.* Li to Ne).

Moving across the period, the nuclear charge (atomic number) increases and the atomic radius decreases. The change in both of these factors causes the outer electrons to be held more firmly, and so the ionisation energy values increase.

There are two exceptions to this generalisation — beryllium and nitrogen, whose values are abnormally high. Ionisation of beryllium involves the removal of an electron from a complete **s** orbital, whereas when boron is ionised, the electron removed is the single electron from the **p** orbital. A full orbital is relatively stable and so beryllium has a higher value than boron.

Nitrogen has the electron configuration $1s^2$, $2s^2$, $2p_x{}^1$, $2p_y{}^1$, $2p_z{}^1$. A half filled orbital is the next most

Trends in Values in Period 2							
Element	Li	Be	B	C	N	O	F	Ne
Atomic number	3	4	5	6	7	8	9	10
Atomic radius (nm)	0.123	0.106	0.08	0.077	0.074	0.066	0.064	0.112
Ionisation energy (kJ /mol)	520	900	800	1090	1400	1310	1680	2080

stable state after a full orbital and this is why nitrogen has a higher value than oxygen.

4. Ionisation energies gradually decrease in moving down any given group — the values for the noble gases (the peak values) for example, decrease as atomic number increases. The same trend may be seen by looking at the values for the elements of any other group (see table)

Trends in Values in a Given Group, e.g. Group 1.

Element	Atomic number	Atomic radius (nm)	Ionisation energy (kJ /mol)
Li	3	0.12	520
Na	11	0.16	500
K	19	0.20	420
Rb	37	0.22	400
Cs	55	0.24	380

Moving down the group, the values decrease (despite the increasing nuclear charge) because of (a) the increasing distance of the outer electrons from the nucleus and (b) the "screening" effect of the completed inner shells.

Second and Successive Ionisation Energies

The second ionisation energy of an element is the energy required to remove the second most loosely bound electron from an atom. The second ionisation energy does not include the energy for the first ionisation. It is the extra energy required for the change $X^+ - e^- \rightarrow X^{2+}$. Third, fourth etc. ionisation energies can be defined in a similar manner.

The second ionisation energy is necessarily greater than the value for the first ionisation because of the attraction of the electron for the positive ion formed in the first ionisation. The third ionisation energy must be higher still. A comparison of the successive ionisation energies of any one element gives considerable information about its electron structure. For sodium, magnesium and aluminium, the first four ionisation energies are given in the chart below.

The values for sodium show that only one electron is relatively easily removed. The great increase in the value of the second I.E. means that the second available electron is from a full shell. For magnesium, the great increase occurs at the third

I.E., indicating that two electrons are relatively easily lost, but that the third electron is from a full shell.

Element	1st I.E	2nd I.E.	3rd I.E.	4th I.E.	5th I.E.
Na	0.49	4.55	6.95	9.50	13.4
Mg	0.74	1.45	7.72	10.52	13.36
Al	0.58	1.81	2.73	11.30	14.8
Si	0.79	1.58	3.2	4.4	16.1

Questions

Q.3.5 Values for successive ionisation energies of an element are shown in Fig.3.17.

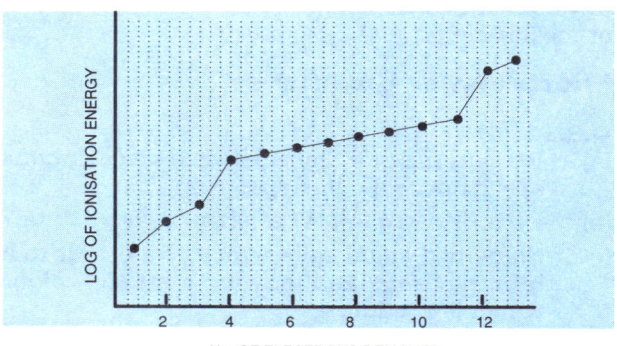

3.17

Explain why:

(a) there is a sharp increase for the 4th value:

(b) why the values for electrons 4 to 11 show a fairly linear increase;

(c) why there is again a sharp increase in the value for the 12th electron;

(d) why there are only thirteen values given.

Q.3.6 The first four ionisation energies of an element are: 800, 2420, 3650, 24960 kJ/mol. Why is the last so great? What can you tell about the electron structure of the element which has these values?

Q.3.7 The first ionisation energies of eight successive elements in the Periodic Table are (in kJ/mol): 580, 780, 970, 940, 1140, 1350, 400 and 540. From this information, place each element in its correct group.

Q.3.8 Make out a chart showing the electronic configurations of elements numbers 11 to 18, in the same style as that shown in Fig. 3.12.

Q.3.9 Write out the electronic configuration of
(i) the Fe^{2+} ion,
(ii) the Fe^{3+} ion.

Which structure do you think is more stable, and why?

Q.3.10 Write an essay on how the concept of the atom has changed in the last hundred years. The work of the following should be mentioned: Thomson; the Curies; Rutherford; Bohr; Chadwick; Aston; Heisenberg; Schrodinger. It will be necessary to consult other chemistry and/or physics textbooks or encyclopaedias in your school or local library.

Short Answer Questions

Q.3.11
(a) Explain the difference between a continuous spectrum and a line spectrum.

(b) Define an orbital. What shape is a **p** orbital?

(c) Name two metal salts which give colour to a bunsen flame, and for each state the colour which is produced.

(d) For what purpose is a spectroscope used in chemistry?

(e) Identify the species represented by
(i) $1s^2, 2s^2, 2p^6, 3s^2, 3p^6, 4s^2, 3d^2$,
(ii) $[1s^2, 2s^2, 2p^6, 3s^2, 3p^6]^{2-}$.

(f) Explain why the atomic radius of potassium is greater than that of
(i) sodium, (ii) calcium.

(g) Write an equation for the 3rd ionisation energy of aluminium.

(h) Explain why nitrogen has a higher ionisation energy than that of
(i) carbon, (ii) oxygen.

(i) Which of the following, Mg^{2+}, Ne, O^{2-}, Al^{3+}, F^-, all of which have the same electron structure, has
(i) the smallest radius
(ii) the largest radius?

(j) Explain each of
(i) photon,   (ii) energy level,
(iii) ground state (iv) excited state.

(k) Write out the full electron configurations of phosphorus and manganese atoms.

(l) How do ionisation energies vary
(i) across a period of elements
(ii) down a group of elements?

(m) How many orbitals are present in the 2nd main energy level? What symbol denotes each of these orbitals?

(n) Explain what each of the symbols in the equation $E_1 - E_2 = hf$ signifies. What does the equation tell?

(o) What names are normally given to the changes represented by
(i) $X - e^- \rightarrow X^+$, (ii) $X^+ - e^- \rightarrow X^{2+}$?

(p) What is the electron configuration of
(i) Na, (ii) F, (iii) Na^+, (iv) F^- .

(q) State
(i) Hund's Rule of Multiplicity,
(ii) Pauli's Exclusion Principle.

(r) What were the contributions of each of
(i) Bohr (ii) de Broglie,
to the structure of the atom?

Exam Questions

Q.3.12.
(a) What are
(i) neutrons; (ii) isotopes?
Show the atomic structure of the isotopes of carbon or of chlorine.

(b) What is meant by
(i) energy levels (ii) atomic orbitals?
In what respect does a 2s orbital differ from a 1s orbital?

(c) Write down the elctronic configuration (s,p) of lithium, neon, sodium. Suggest a reason why
(i) sodium is more reactive than lithium
(ii) neon in unreactive.

Q.3.13.
(a) Describe how the emission spectrum of hydrogen could be observed. What evidence about atoms did Bohr deduce from a study of such a spectrum. Briefly explain Bohr's reasoning.

(b) What is an atomic orbital? Draw diagrams of an s orbital or a p orbital. What is the electron capacity of each?

(c) Write down the electron configurations of atoms of elements numbers 16 and 21.

Q.3.14.

(a) Explain each of the following terms: line spectrum, ground state of an atom, excited state of an atom, energy level.

(b) Describe using diagrams, how the visible lines in the hydrogen spectrum are caused. Who first explained this and what was its historical importance?

(c) State the number of electrons present in each of the following particles, and write out the electron configuration of each; Na, Na^+, Cl^-, Fe^{2+}, Fe^{3+}. Which of the latter two would you expect to be more stable and why?

(d) State Hund's Rule and Pauli's Exclusion Principle.

Q.3.15

(a) Define first ionisation energy.

(b) Describe the atomic spectrum of hydrogen and indicate how the ionisation energy of hydrogen is related to the energy content of the various energy levels in the hydrogen atom.

(c) State and explain the variation in first ionisation energies down Group 1 of the Periodic Table.

(d) Explain how the variation in first ionisation energies along Period 2 provides evidence for electron sub-levels.

(e) Write equations for
(i) the first ionisation,
(ii) the second ionisation, of an element X. Which of these two values is greater, and why?

(f) Sketch a rough graph to show to show how the successive ionisation energies of carbon vary with the number of electrons removed, and explain the shape of the graph.

Review   When you know Chapter 3 you should be able to:

(a) describe an experiment in which the flame colour produced by a given metal salt is observed.

(b) explain why excited atoms emit light.

(c) describe Bohr's explation of the hydrogen spectrum, and say what electron transitions cause the lines in the visible region of the spectrum.

(d) explain each of: emission spectrum, continuous spectrum, line spectrum, energy level, ground state, excited state, photon, transition element, the formula $E_1 - E_2 = hf$.

(e) state the Aufbau Principle, Hund's Rule, Pauli's Exclusion Principle.

(f) define principal quantum number, ionisation energy.

(g) list the atom's main and sub energy levels in increasing order of energy.

(h) describe an orbital and draw diagrams showing the shapes of s and p orbitals.

(i) state the order in which the electrons fill the various orbitals.

(j) write the electron configuration for any given element (up to No. 38).

(k) state and explain the trends in ionisation energy values.

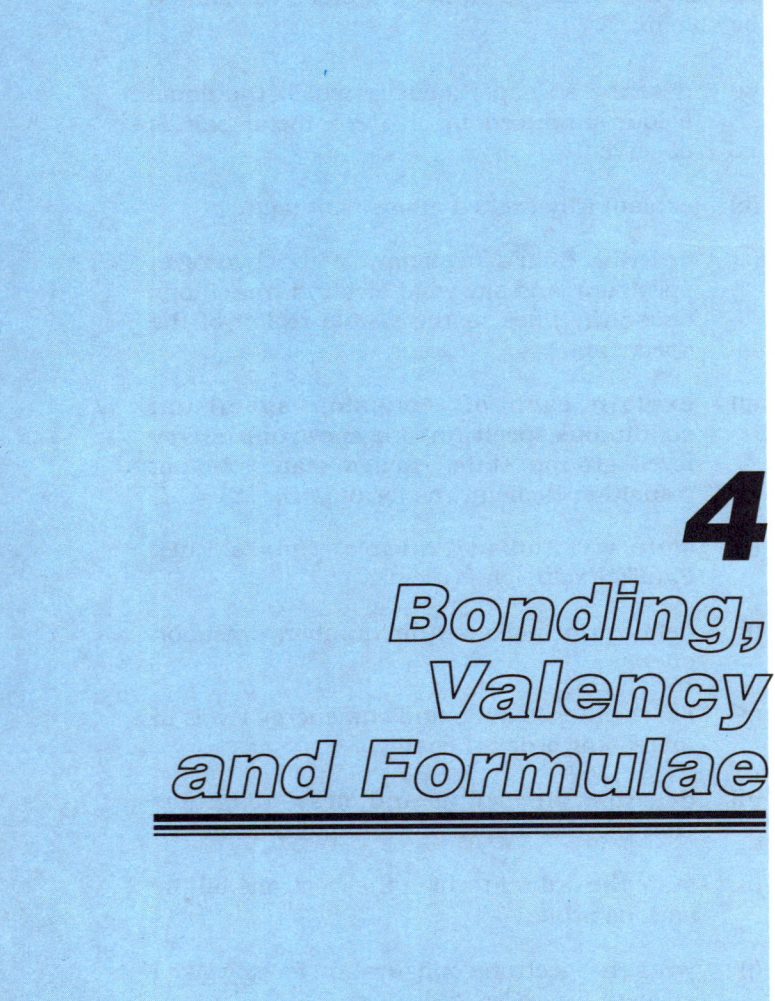

4

Bonding, Valency and Formulae

Atoms join together to form compounds and they do this in several different ways. The forces of attraction which holds atoms together are called **bonds**; bonding between atoms essentially involves electrons, particularly those in the outer shells of the atoms. The **"octet rule"** is a guide to understanding bonding. The most stable electron structure in atoms is that of noble gas, *i.e.* an outer shell containing 8 electrons. **In bonding, atoms try to attain this stable structure and they do so by gaining, losing or sharing electrons.** It must be stressed however that the octet rule[i] is only a useful guide; it is **not** a rigid chemical law never disobeyed.

There are 2 main types of bonding; that in which electrons are **lost and gained** is called **ionic** (or **electrovalent**) **bonding**, and that in which electrons are **shared** by atoms is known as **covalent bonding.**

Ionic Bonding

In this type of bonding, which occurs between metals and non-metals, one or two electrons are completely transferred from one atom to another, so that each atom contains its octet. Sodium chloride is a typical compound in which an ionic bond is present.

A sodium atom has the electron structure 2,8,1, and in a chlorine atom it is 2,8,7. Sodium attains its octet by losing its single outer electron while chlorine does so by gaining an extra electron, and this is what happens when sodium and chlorine combine together. The outer electron of the sodium atom is transferred to the chlorine atom as shown opposite.

The chlorine is then no longer a neutral atom; since it has gained an extra electron, it carries an overall negative charge. Likewise, the sodium is no longer a neutral atom; it has lost an electron and so has a positive charge.

(i)   The main exceptions to the "octet rule" in ionic bonding are:
1. Lithium, whose electron structure is 2.1. The nearest noble gas structure to lithium is that of helium, which has 2 electrons in its outer (and only) shell. A Li$^+$ ion has thus the helium structure.
2. The transition metal ions, which can have up to 18 electrons in their outer shells. However, considering bonding in terms of octets is a simplified explanation, and other and better theories exist.

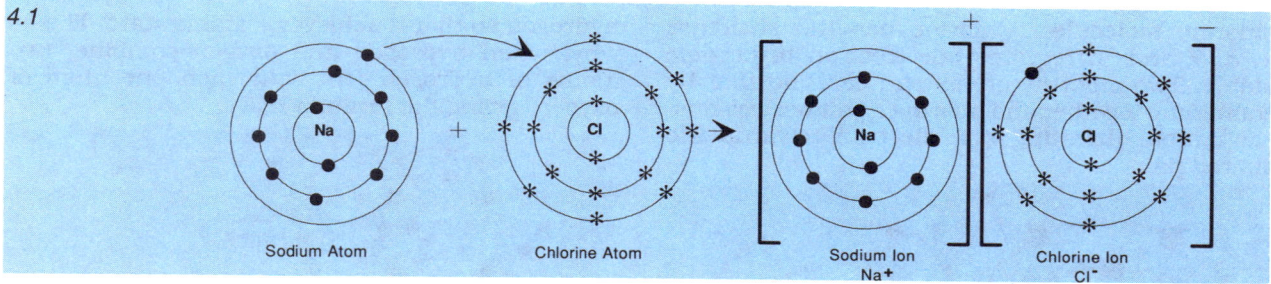

4.1

Sodium Atom   Chlorine Atom   Sodium Ion Na+   Chlorine Ion Cl⁻

Atoms (or groups of atoms) which have either lost or gained electrons, and so have become either positively or negatively charged, are known as ions.

In the example, the sodium atom is converted to a sodium ion (represented as Na^+) and the chlorine atom has become a chloride ion (written as Cl^-). Because the ions are oppositely charged, they attract each other and hold together.

An ionic bond can be defined as the force of attraction between the oppositely charged ions which are produced when electrons are transferred from one atom to another.

This force of attraction occurs in all directions around an ion, so that a compound such as sodium chloride consists of, not just a pair of ions held together, but a huge number of ions of each kind held together in a 3-dimensional regular and repeating pattern. Compounds containing ionic bonds are therefore normally crystalline.

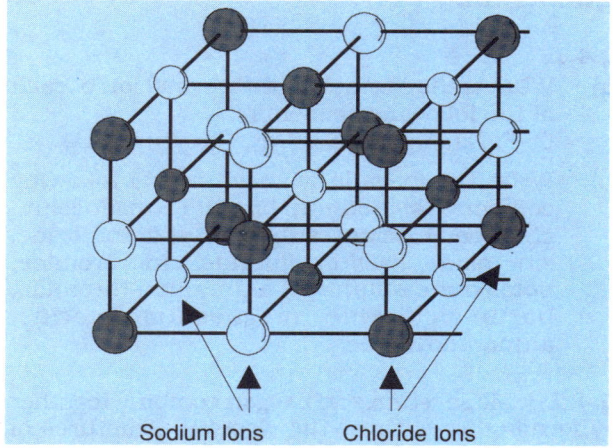

Sodium Ions   Chloride Ions

4.2 — The crystal lattice of sodium chloride.

That the ions are much more stable than the atoms of the elements is evident from the properties of each. Both sodium and chlorine are very reactive elements and readily undergo many chemical reactions, but the compound sodium chloride, common salt, is a rather unreactive sort of substance and to change it back into its elements, a large amount of energy is required.

Magnesium combines with chlorine in a similar manner, but since magnesium is in Group 2, it must lose 2 electrons to become stable *i.e.* to attain the structure of neon. Chlorine has 7 electrons and only requires one more. When these two elements combine, a magnesium atom loses its 2 electrons to 2 chlorine atoms, one electron to each, and in this way, all 3 atoms acquire their octets.

Magnesium has lost 2 negative charges and therefore becomes an ion with a charge of +2 and is written as Mg^{2+}. The chlorine atoms, as before, become Cl^- ions, only this time 2 of them are necessary to balance the +2 charge on each magnesium ion. The formula of the compound is thus $MgCl_2$.

Covalent Bonding

In this type of bonding, molecules are formed by the combination of atoms which share their electrons with each other — to give each atom the stable structure of a noble gas.

A covalent bond consists of one or more shared pairs of electrons, each of the bonded atoms contributing one electron towards the shared pair.

The electron pair may be shared either equally or unequally, forming pure covalent, or polar covalent bonds, respectively.

It is a fact that chlorine atoms do not exist on their own; they combine together in pairs, forming chlorine molecules. Chlorine has the structure 2, 8, 7 and so requires one electron to become stable. Two chlorine atoms can each do that by combining together and sharing a pair of electrons, each atom donating one electron towards the shared pair.

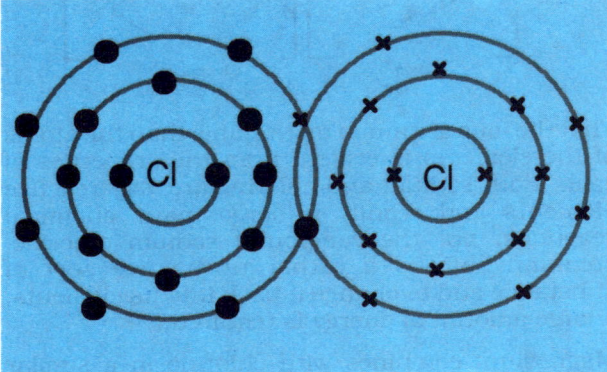

4.3 — *Chlorine molecule*

In the chlorine molecule, each of the atoms has 8 electrons in its outer shell. The 2 shared electrons which hold the atoms together constitute a covalent bond. It is a very strong bond and much energy is normally required to break it. Diagrammatically, a covalent bond is often represented by a dash:

$$Cl^{\bullet} + Cl^{\bullet} \rightarrow Cl - Cl$$

Molecules formed by covalent bonding usually contain a small number of atoms, joined specifically to each other. No electrons are either lost or gained and so there are no ions. There is little force of attraction between molecules, so that they do not form a lattice structure, as ionic compounds do. Covalent compounds usually exist as small separate individual molecules and are therefore either gases or liquids (unlike ionic compounds, which are mainly solids).

In many hydrogen compounds, covalent bonds are present. When hydrogen combines by sharing, it attains the stable structure of helium *i.e.* it acquires an extra electron so that it has 2 electrons in its outer (and only) shell. Some compounds of hydrogen in which covalent bonds are present are shown in the chart opposite.

Since oxygen has 2 electron spaces in its outer shell, it must share electrons with 2 atoms of

hydrogen so that it achieves a stable state. This is why, when hydrogen and oxygen combine, two atoms of hydrogen join with each one atom of oxygen, giving the formula H_2O.

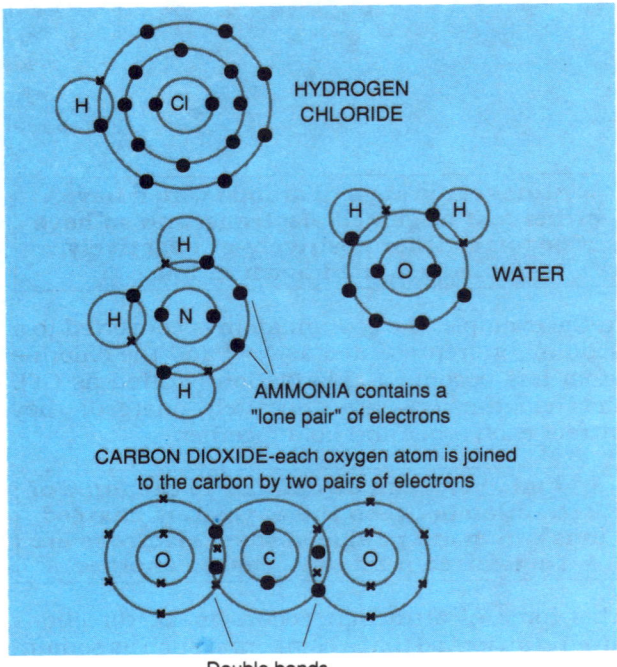

4.4 — *In carbon dioxide each oxygen atom is joined to the carbon by two pairs of electrons, i.e. by a "double bond".*

Questions

Q.4.1.

(a) What is the symbol for the normal ion of each of the following elements?
O, F, Na, Mg, Al, S, Cl, K, Ca, Zn, Br, Ba.

(b) Write the formula for each of the following compounds: Sodium bromide, magnesium chloride, calcium sulphide, sodium oxide, zinc oxide, calcium fluoride, zinc bromide, potassium sulphide, aluminium bromide, barium chloride, magnesium fluoride, aluminium oxide.

Q.4.2 Magnesium and oxygen combine together by forming ions. Draw the electron structures of the ions formed from each atom and give their symbols also.

Q.4.3. With the aid of a periodic table, work out what ions are formed, and the formulae of the compounds produced, when the following pairs of elements combine together:

(a) potassium and oxygen;
(b) magnesium and bromine;
(c) lithium and chlorine;
(d) aluminium and fluorine.

Q.4.4. Draw diagrams showing the structure (protons, neutrons and electrons) of

(a) a chlorine atom
(b) a chloride ion
(c) a chlorine molecule.

Q.4.5 The compounds listed below contain covalent bonds. For each of these draw the electron structures of the atoms of the 2 elements; decide in what ratio the atoms must unite to form a molecule so that each atom attains a noble gas structure, then draw a diagram of the molecule showing how the electrons are arranged:

(a) methane (carbon and hydrogen);
(b) hydrogen sulphide (hydrogen and sulphur);
(c) tetrachloromethane (carbon and chlorine);
(d) phosphine (phosphorus and hydrogen);
(e) nitrogen fluoride (nitrogen and fluorine).

Q.4.6 What type of bonding occurs in each of the following compounds? Draw a diagram showing the structure of each: KF, PH_3, Cl_2O, K_2O, MgF_2, OF_2, $HOCl$, K_2S.

Electrochemistry

By means of a simple electrical circuit, such as illustrated, it can easily be shown that some liquids conduct electricity while others do not.

When an ionic compound,[i] either in the molten state or dissolved in water, is placed in the beaker, the bulb lights, showing that the substance is conducting electricity; a covalent compound used instead does not conduct. Ionic compounds, when either molten or dissolved in water, conduct

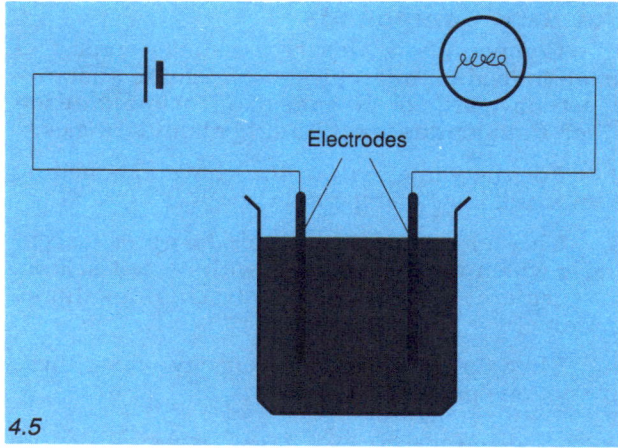

Electrodes

4.5

electricity because, in both of these states, the ionic lattice has broken down, leaving the ions free to move. The breaking apart of the ions from an ionic lattice is called ionisation. A more detailed account of electrochemistry is given in Chapter 16.

Properties of Compounds

Ionic Compounds

1. Compounds are composed, not of separate molecules, but of two types of ion, which form a rigid crystalline "close-packed" structure or lattice.

2. Because of the attraction between the ions in the crystalline lattice, a large amount of energy is required to separate them from each other. Ionic compounds have therefore high melting points and high boiling points.

3. They are usually soluble in water (the reason for this is explained on page 57)

4. When either molten or dissolved in water, ionic compounds conduct electricity — because in these states the ions are not attached to each other and are free to move.

(i) Compounds which contain ionic bonds are called **ionic** compounds, whereas **covalent** compounds are those containing covalent bonds **only.**

Covalent Compounds

1.   Compounds of this type usually consist of small individual molecules — of definite shape — which have little or no force of attraction for each other. Compounds are thus either liquids or gases.

2.   For the same reason, they have low melting points and low boiling points.

3.   They are usually insoluble in water (except those which react chemically with it), but soluble in covalent solvents (*e.g.* tetrachloromethane, benzene).

4.   They do not conduct electricity, since there are no ions present.

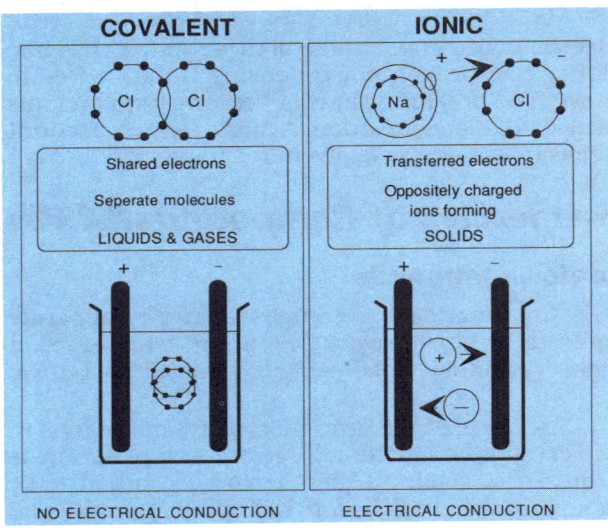

4.6

Experiment 4.1
Properties of covalent and ionic Compounds

In this experiment some of the characteristic properties of both ionic and covalent compounds are illustrated. Then, using a knowledge of these properties, various compounds are tested in order to find out whether they are ionic or covalent.

1. As a general rule, ionic compounds are soluble in water and covalent compounds are not; the latter are usually soluble in covalent solvents, *i.e.* solvents in which the atoms in each molecule are held together covalently.

Take a small crystal of iodine and add it to about 10 cm^3 of water in a test tube. Cover the top of the tube and shake.

Does the crystal dissolve?

What does this suggest about the type of bond in iodine?

Now add some 1,1,1-trichloroethane to the mixture and shake. What happens?

What does this suggest about the bonding in trichloroethane?

Why do the two liquids not mix?

2. Another difference between ionic and covalent compounds is that ionic compounds, when either molten or dissolved in water, conduct electricity whereas covalent compounds do not.

Arrange a circuit as shown above. Check that the circuit is working by placing a piece of metal across the electrodes — the bulb should light. If it does not, find the fault and rectify it.

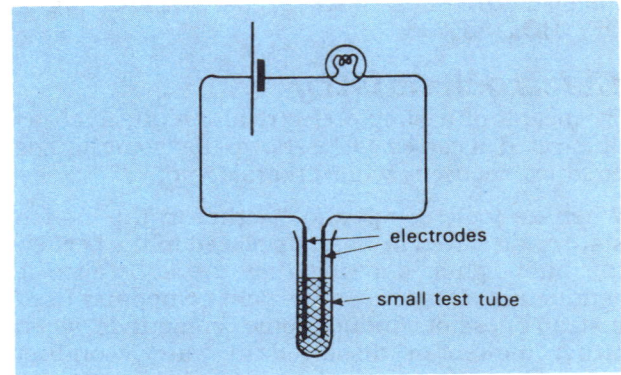

4.7

Place some water in the test tube. Does the bulb light?

Why/ why not?

What type of bonding is present in water?

Now add some sodium chloride and shake the tube to dissolve it? Does the bulb light?

What type of bond does sodium chloride contain?

3. Use the same apparatus to find out which of various compounds are ionic and which are covalent. Test as many of those listed as are available and classify them into two groups, ionic and covalent. If the substance is solid, dissolve it in water before testing it, and after testing each, rinse the test tube and the electrodes with water before testing the next.

Compounds : water; paraffin oil; copper sulphate; sugar; urea; borax; lead bromide; dilute sulphuric acid; potassium iodide; methylated spirits; sodium hydroxide; dilute nitric acid; dilute hydrochloric acid; trichloroethane.

4. Place some solid lead bromide in the test tube and insert the electrodes.

Does it conduct electricity?

Why/ why not?

Now heat the tube gently at first and then more strongly, until the solid melts.

Does it conduct?

Explain why it conducts in one case and not in the other.

Electronegativity

Dividing chemical compounds into two groups, ionic and covalent, is simplifying the subject of bonding to a considerable extent. A great many compounds have bonding which is neither fully one nor the other; their properties indicate that they are partially ionic and partially covalent.

Electronegativity is a property which can be used to predict the type of bond formed when two elements combine.

> **The electronegativity of an element is a measure of the power of attraction of an atom of that element for the shared pair of electrons in a covalent bond.**

Atoms of high electronegativity (*i.e.* non-metals in general) readily gain electrons (from metals) forming negative ions. They also share electrons

H 2.1							He ----
Li 1.0	Be 1.5	B 2.0	C 2.5	N 3.0	O 3.5	F 4.0	Ne ----
Na 0.9	Mg 1.2	Al 1.5	Si 1.8	P 2.1	S 2.5	Cl 3.0	Ar ----
K 0.8	Ca 1.0	Ga 1.6	Ge 1.8	As 2.0	Se 2.4	Br 2.8	Kr ----

Some electronegativity values. There are no units; the scale is an arbitrary one, indicating values which are relative to one another. The commonly used electronegativity values were determined by Professor Linus Pauling, an American chemist. The full table of electronegativities is given at the end of the book.

with each other and form molecules. They have small atomic radii and the number of electrons in their outer shells approaches eight.

Atoms of low electronegativity (*i.e.* metals in general) are known as **electropositive** because they easily lose electrons (to non-metals) to form positive ions. They have large atomic radii and only a small number of electrons in their outer shells.

A covalent bond consists of a shared pair of electrons, but unless the two joined atoms have the same attraction for the electron pair, the latter will not be shared equally.

In a chlorine molecule, two identical atoms are joined together and so the shared pair of electrons forming the bond is equally divided between the atoms *i.e.* Cl **:** Cl

In a hydrogen chloride molecule however, in which the two atoms have different powers of attraction for the electrons, the shared pair is not equally divided. Since the electronegativity of chlorine (3.0) is higher than that of hydrogen (2.1), the chlorine atom has a greater share of the electron pair, *i.e.* H $\overset{..}{}$Cl This causes a slight negative charge on the chlorine atom and a slight positive charge on the hydrogen. This separation of charge in the molecule is denoted as:

$$\overset{\delta^+}{H} \overset{\delta^-}{——— Cl}$$

(where δ indicates a partial charge). The bond is described as being polar (covalent) and the molecule is said to possess a dipole moment.

> **A polar (or polar covalent) bond is a covalent bond in which the shared pair of electrons is attracted more to one of the joined atoms than to the other.**

The **difference** in the electronegativity values of two joined atoms can be used to tell whether the bond between them is ionic or covalent, and if covalent, how polar that bond is.

If there is no difference between the electronegativities of the two joined atoms, the bond is a pure covalent one. For example:

$$Br ——— Br$$
$$2.8 \qquad 2.8$$
no difference,
no polarity
∴ pure covalent

If there is a difference, but it is less than about 1.7, the bond is polar covalent *e.g.*

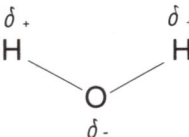

There are two separate but identical bonds here, so the same reasoning applies to both. For each bond, the difference in the electronegativities of the two joined atoms is 1.4 and so each bond is polar, the shared pair of electrons being attracted more by oxygen than by the hydrogen atom. Thus, the oxygen becomes slightly negative and each of the hydrogens slightly positively charged.

If the difference between the electronegativities of two atoms is more than 1.7, the bond will be ionic — since one of the atoms pulls electrons completely away from the other:

$$Na \qquad Br$$
$$0.8 \qquad 2.8$$
$$Diff. = \qquad 2.0,$$
Therefore, Na^+ and Br^-

Polar covalent bonds are essentially intermediate between pure covalent bonds and ionic bonds, and have therefore a certain amount of ionic character. When the amount of ionic character is more than 50%, the bond is regarded as being essentially ionic. The accompanying table relates the percentage ionic character of a bond with the difference in the electronegativities of the two joined atoms.

Percentage ionic character of a single bond.

Difference in electronegativity	% ionic character
0	0
0.2	1
0.4	4
0.6	9
0.8	15
1.0	22
1.2	30
1.4	39
1.6	47
1.7	51
1.8	55
2.0	63
2.2	70
2.4	76
2.6	82
2.8	86
3.0	89
3.2	92

Hydrogen Bonding

Water — an unusual substance

Water is a covalent compound and its molecule, with only 3 atoms, is very small ($M_r = 18$) so that it might be expected to be a gas. When frozen, it forms a crystalline structure of the type formed by ionic compounds and this crystalline structure requires an unusually high amount of energy to melt it, *i.e.* to separate the molecules from each other. It also has an abnormally high boiling point and specific latent heat of vaporisation. These abnormal properties of water are illustrated in the following table and graph.

Specific Latent Heats of Fusion of some Liquids	
Water	334 kJ/kg
Benzene	126 kJ/kg
Ethanol	100 kJ/kg
Phenylamine	88 kJ/kg
Trichloromethane	78 kJ/kg
Carbon disulphide	58 kJ/kg
Tetrachloromethane	16 kJ/kg

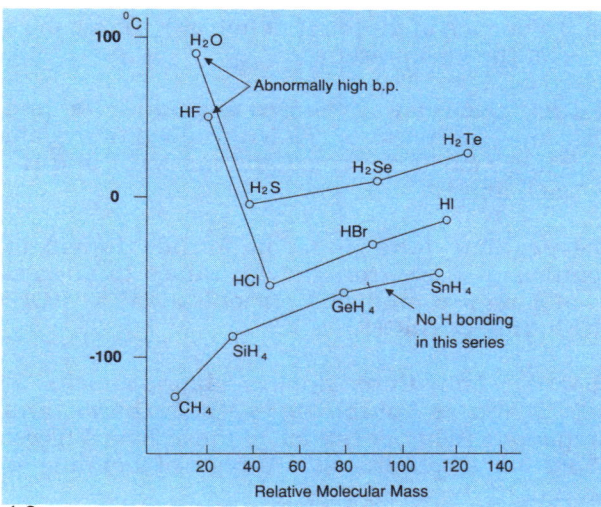

4.8

The properties of water indicate that there is some force holding molecules of water together. This force is due to the considerably polar nature of the water molecule — the difference between the electronegativities of the 2 elements is 1.4, which makes water about 39% ionic in character.

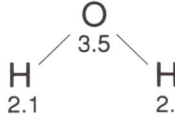

The polarity of the molecule and the small size of the hydrogen atom causes adjacent molecules to associate into groups or chains — the molecules

held together by the force of electrical attraction between the slightly positive hydrogen atoms and the slightly negative oxygen atoms. The links are called **hydrogen bonds**.

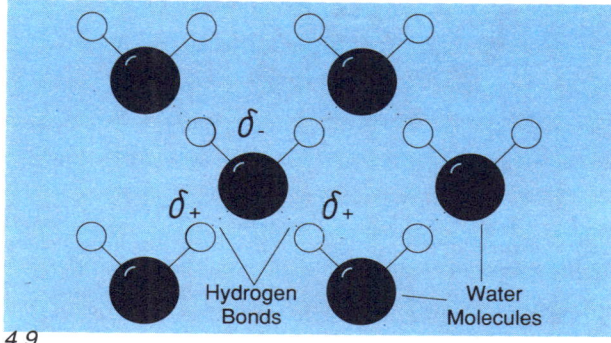

4.9

These associated molecules behave as a much larger molecule and explain the abnormal properties of water *i.e.* its high melting point and boiling point; its high specific latent heats; the crystalline structure of ice; the expansion of water on freezing (the ice lattice occupies more space than the liquid water molecules).

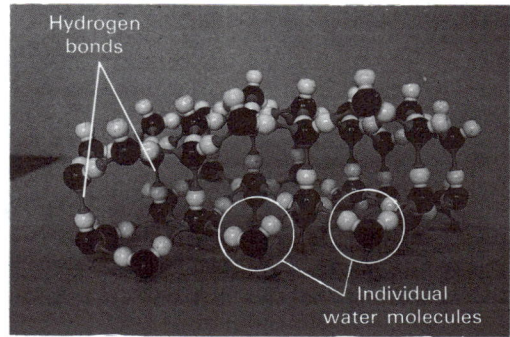

4.10 — *A model showing the structure of ice.*

The extent of hydrogen bonding in water decreases as the water is heated and at 100°C all of the hydrogen bonds finally break, as the liquid is changed to a vapour.

Because water molecules are polar, water is a good solvent for ionic compounds. The slightly positive hydrogen atoms in the water molecule attract the negative ions of the ionic compound, and the slightly negative oxygen atoms attract the positive ions.

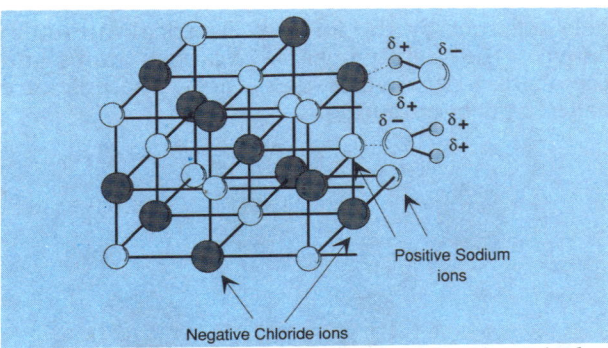

4.11 — *The crystal lattice of sodium chloride being broken apart because of the attraction of the polar water molecules for the ions in the lattice.*

Since a covalent compound contains no ions, water does not normally either dissolve or mix with covalent compounds.

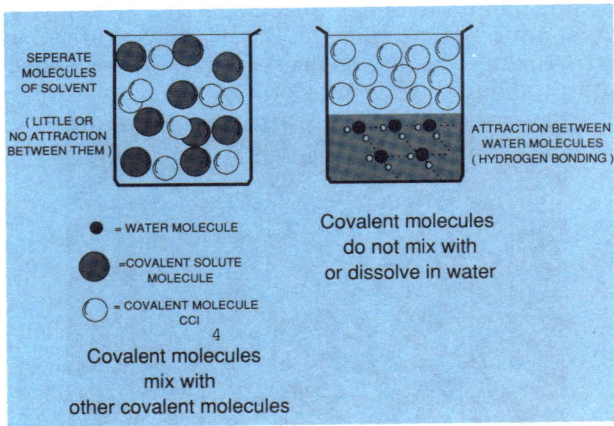

4.12

Hydrogen bonding also occurs in other compounds in which a hydrogen atom is joined to a very electronegative element, particularly in HF and (to a lesser extent) in NH_3. The properties of these compounds indicate that their molecular masses are greater than their molecular formulae suggests — again due to association of molecules.

Questions

Q.4.7

(a) Divide the following list of substances into 3 groups, *viz.* those which contain
(i) pure covalent bonds;
(ii) polar covalent bonds
(iii) ionic bonds
Br_2, KCl, H_2O, CaF_2, AlF_3, CS_2, ICl, K_2O.

(b) For each of those in list (i) draw the structure of the molecule showing how the electrons are arranged.

(c) For each of those in list (ii), show where the polarity arises in the molecule (in the manner of the diagram of the water molecule which is shown on page 58)

(d) For each of those in list (iii), give the symbols of the ions present.

Q.4.8 NaOH always ionises to produce Na^+ and OH^- ions. Use electronegativity values to explain why these ions are formed and not NaO^+ and H^-, or NaO^- and H^+.

Q.4.9. The following compounds ionise in solution. Use electronegativity values to suggest what ions are produced on ionisation: — KOH, HOCl, HONO, NaONO, KSCl.

Q.4.10 Anhydrous iron(III) chloride melts at 282°C and is soluble in water, ethanol and propanone. What does each of these facts suggest about its structure? What type of bonding is present in the molecule?

Q.4.11 When a charged rod is held close to a stream of water from a tap, the water is deflected. This does not happen with a stream of tetrachloromethane.

(a) Explain both of these facts.

(b) Name two other liquids which would be deflected and two which would not.

Valency

Atoms combine together in different ratios — depending on what atoms they are. Sodium chloride is NaCl but calcium chloride is $CaCl_2$. Valency is a means of expressing the "combining power" of atoms of an element.

> **The valency of an element is defined as the number of electrons which an atom of that element must either lose or gain to achieve a noble gas structure.**

Valency is thus equal to either the periodic group number or 8 minus the group number; the normal valency is usually the smaller of the 2 possible numbers.

Oxygen is in group 6 and so it needs to lose 6 electrons or to gain 2; invariably it gains 2, *i.e.* its normal valency is 2.

When the valencies of two elements which combine together are known, the formula for the compound which they produce is easily worked out. Calcium atoms for example have two electrons in their outer shells (*i.e.* their valency is 2) and chlorine atoms have 7 — or space for one more (*i.e.* their valency is 1). To take the electrons from each calcium atom, 2 chlorine atoms are necessary; they combine in the ratio of 1:2 and the formula for the compound is $CaCl_2$. When calcium and oxygen combine together, the ratio is 1:1 (since each element has a valency of 2) and the formula for the compound formed in this case is CaO.

Many elements have several different valencies and where such an element occurs in a compound, the name of the compound shows which valency is utilised; the valency is denoted by a Roman numeral in brackets after the name of the element[i]. Lead, for example, has valencies of 2 and 4 and so it forms two different oxides, *viz.* lead(II) oxide (in which the valency of the lead is 2) and lead(IV) oxide (in which it is 4).

Questions

Q.4.12   In the form of a table, list the common elements under its correct valency. Include elements numbers, 1, 6 - 9, 11 - 17, 19, 20, 26, 29, 30, 35, 50, 53, and 82

Q.4.13   Give formulae for the compounds produced when the following pairs of elements combine together:

(a)   calcium and bromine;
(b)   silicon and fluorine;
(c)   calcium and hydrogen;
(d)   silicon and hydrogen;
(e)   lead and chlorine;
(f)   sodium and hydrogen;
(g)   silicon and oxygen;
(h)   phosphorus and bromine;
(i)   aluminium and chlorine;
(j)   aluminium and oxygen.

Q.4.14   Titanium (Ti) has valencies of 2, 3 and 4. Write the formulae for

(a)   the 3 chlorides of titanium;
(b)   the 3 oxides.

Q.4.15
(a)   What is the formula for each of the following ionic compounds?
magnesium chloride, sodium oxide, zinc sulphide, calcium iodide, lead(II) oxide, lead(IV) oxide, tin bromide, tin oxide, sodium nitride, aluminium fluoride.
(b)   For each of those compounds, give the symbols for the ions of which it is composed.

Q.4.16   Write the formula for each of the following: phosphorus(III) chloride, phosphorus(V) chloride, mercury(I) sulphide, mercury(II) sulphide, tin(II) chloride, tin(IV) chloride, iron(II) oxide, iron(III) oxide, manganese dioxide, sulphur trioxide.

Q.4.17   Ions are particles which can have an independent existence, and they also have their own characteristic colours. From the colours of the listed salts, work out the colour of following ions: Fe^{3+}, Fe^{2+}, Ni^{2+}, CrO_4^{2-}, Cu^{2+}, Na^+, SO_4^{2-}, Cl^-, OH^-.

NaCl white, KCl white, $FeCl_2$ green, $FeCl_3$ brown, $FeSO_4$ green, $CuCl_2$ blue, $NiCl_2$ green.

Na_2SO_4 white, K_2SO_4 white, $CuSO_4$ blue, $NiSO_4$ green.

(i)   This is a slight simplification; the Roman numeral really shows the oxidation number, but it is sufficient for the present to regard it as valency.

Na_2CrO_4 yellow, K_2CrO_4 yellow, $CuCrO_4$ green.

NaOH white, KOH white, $Fe(OH)_2$ green, $Fe(OH)_3$ brown, $Cu(OH)_2$ blue.

Chemical Equations

A chemical equation is a convenient way of representing a chemical change; it shows what substances react together and what is produced. A correctly written equation also shows the numbers of atoms or molecules of each of the substances involved in the reaction.

In order to write an equation, it is necessary to know what substances react and what is produced. An equation does not tell whether a reaction will take place or what is produced in one which does. It is possible to write many "equations" for reactions that do not occur, e.g.

$$MgO + H_2O \longrightarrow MgH_2 + O_2$$

is a correctly balanced equation, but no such reaction has ever been observed. An equation merely summarises a known fact.

To show how an equation is constructed the equation for the reaction of magnesium with oxygen, in which the compound magnesium oxide is produced, is explained.

1. The equation is written in words:

magnesium + oxygen $\longrightarrow$ magnesium oxide

2. The correct formula for each substance is written in place of its name:
$$Mg + O_2 \longrightarrow MgO$$
(Remember that the common element gases are diatomic).

3. The equation is balanced, so that there are the same number of each kind of atom on each side (in accordance with the law of conservation of matter). In this reaction it is necessary to put a "2" before the Mg (denoting 2 atoms of it) and a "2" before the MgO (denoting 2 molecules of it).

$$2Mg + O_2 \longrightarrow 2MgO$$

The correct formula of a substance must never be altered in order to balance an equation.

Further information from equations

An equation can be modified to give further information by adding "state symbols" in brackets after the formula of each substance:-(s) indicates a solid, (l) a liquid, (g) a gas and (aq) a solution of the substance in water. Also, an arrow pointing upwards means that the substance is a gas which is given off and an arrow pointing downwards means that the substance is insoluble and is precipitated. The equation

$$Zn(s) + 2HCl(aq) \longrightarrow ZnCl_2(aq) + H_2(g)\uparrow$$

tells that solid zinc reacts with a solution of hydrogen chloride in water and produces zinc chloride (also dissolved in water) and gaseous hydrogen.

Information about the masses of the substance involved in the reaction is also obtainable from its equation; how this is done is explained in Chapter 7.

Information not given by equations

An equation tells nothing about the conditions necessary for the reaction — whether heat or light are necessary; whether the reaction, once started, will continue of its own accord; how fast it will proceed; or what will be observed. It tells nothing about the mechanism of the reaction and whether there are any intermediate substances formed in the process.

Questions

Q.4.18 Write equations for the following reactions:

(a) zinc + oxygen → zinc oxide
(b) sodium + chlorine → sodium chloride;
(c) sodium + oxygen → sodium oxide;
(d) hydrogen + chlorine → hydrogen chloride;
(e) calcium + chlorine → calcium chloride;
(f) phosphorus + chlorine →
     phosphorus(V) chloride;
(g) phosphorus + oxygen →
     phosphorus(V) oxide;
(h) zine + bromine → zinc bromide;
(i) sodium + hydrogen → sodium hydride;
(j) hydrogen + oxygen → water.

Q.4.19 Write and balance equations for the following:

(a)   calcium + oxygen →

(b)   zinc + chlorine →

(c)   nitrogen + hydrogen →

(d)   potassium + hydrogen →

(e)   hydrogen + sulphur →

(f)   potassium + bromine →

Q.4.20 Balance the following equations:

(a) $Fe_2O_3 + CO \rightarrow FeO + CO_2$;

(b) $PCl_5 + H_2O \rightarrow H_3PO_4 + HCl$;

(c) $NiS + O_2 \rightarrow NiO + SO_2$;

(d) $SiH_4 + O_2 \rightarrow SiO_2 + H_2O$;

(e) $HNO_2 \rightarrow NO + NO_2 + H_2O$;

(f) $CuO + NH_3 \rightarrow Cu + H_2O + N_2$;

Q.4.21 Balance each of the following equations:

(a) $CO + O_2 \rightarrow CO_2$;

(b) $Fe + O_2 \rightarrow Fe_2O_3$;

(c) $CH_4 + O_2 \rightarrow CO_2 + H_2O$;

(d) $H_2SO_4 + NaCN \rightarrow Na_2SO_4 + HCN$;

(e) $N_2 + O_2 \rightarrow NO$;

(f) $SO_2 + O_2 \rightarrow SO_3$;

(g) $Fe + HCl \rightarrow FeCl_2 + H_2$;

(h) $N_2 + H_2 \rightarrow NH_3$;

(i) $CaCl_2 + Na_3PO_4 \rightarrow NaCl + Ca_3(PO_4)_2$;

(j) $C_3H_8 + O_2 \rightarrow CO_2 + H_2O$;

(k) $P_2O_5 + H_2O \rightarrow H_3PO_4$.

Q.4.22 Write a balanced equation for each of the following changes;

(a)   Ammonium chloride (NH_4Cl) is heated to form hydrogen chloride and ammonia.

(b)   Nitrogen is reacted with chlorine to form nitrogen chloride.

(c)   Methane is burned in oxygen, forming carbon dioxide and water vapour.

(d)   Zinc reacts with fluorine to form zinc fluoride.

(e)   Hydrogen peroxide (H_2O_2) is decomposed to produce oxygen and water.

(f)   Calcium hydroxide, $Ca(OH)_2$, is neutralised with HCl to produce calcium chloride and water.

(g)   Iron(III) hydroxide is heated, forming iron(III) oxide and water vapour.

(h)   Boron oxide is reacted with magnesium, producing boron and magnesium oxide.

Q.4.23 Give short answers to each of the following questions.

(a)   Define an ionic bond.

(b)   Name three properties characteristic of covalent compounds.

(c)   What is a lone pair? Name a molecule containing such.

(d)   How does a double bond differ from a single bond?

(e)   Classify each of oxygen, ammonia, salt, as (i) ionic, (ii) pure covalent, (iii) polar covalent.

(f)   What are the normal ions of Zn, I, Al?

(g)   Which two of the first 36 elements would form a compound with the greatest ionic character?

(h)   How many (i) electrons, (ii) neutrons, are in the ion $_{25}^{55}Mn^{3+}$

(i)   Which element has the highest electronegativity? Why?

(j)   Why is $MgCl_2$ a solid but SCl_2 a liquid?

(k)   Give the definition of electronegativity.

(l)   How do electronegativity values vary (i) across a Period, (ii) down a Group?

(m)   Complete and balance the equation: $P + Cl_2 \rightarrow ?$

(n)   Which is larger and why, a bromine atom or a bromide ion?

(o)   What binding force holds the particles together in (i) calcium oxide, (ii) ice?

(p)   Name an electropositive element. Why is it electropositive?

(q)   What is the valency of each of: magnesium, nitrogen, iodine?

(r)   What is the formula of (i) magnesium iodide, (ii) nitrogen chloride?

(s)   What are the symbols for the copper(I) ion and the copper(II) ion?

(t)   Name two ways of making sodium chloride conduct electricity.

Q.4.24 List 3 characteristic properties of covalent compounds and 3 characteristic properties of ionic compounds. From the following list of elements:-, H, C, O, Na, Mg, S, Cl, choose:

(a)   Any 2 elements (except H) and give the formula of a chloride of each of them, indicating whether the bonding is ionic or covalent in each case.

(b)   Any 2 elements and give the name and formula of a covalent compound of each with hydrogen.

Q.4.25   Distinguish between a covalent bond and an ionic bond, using as examples, elements selected from K, Mg, O, Br. Describe a simple electrical experiment which could be performed to decide if a given substance were covalent or ionic.

Q.4.26   Draw the electron structures of each of the following molecules and ions: ClF, OH^-, SiH_4, BH_4^-, $SnCl_2$, H^-, SiO_2.

Q.4.27   List all the information that you can derive from this equation:

$$MgCO_3(s) + 2HCl\ (aq) \rightarrow$$
$$MgCl_2(aq) + CO_2(g) + H_2O(l).$$

Q.4.28   Classify the following compounds as ionic or covalent. For those that are covalent, state whether they are polar or non-polar:—
KF, NO, Br_2, IBr, CaO, F_2, MgS, $NaBr$, HCl.

Q.4.29   Give the reason for each of the following statements:

(a)   Helium forms no compounds.

(b)   Aluminium has a valency of 3.

(c)   Solid lithium bromide does not conduct electricity but a solution of it in water does.

(d)   Potassium bromide is a solid but hydrogen bromide is a gas.

(e)   A rubbed polythene rod deflects a stream of water from a tap.

(f)   Silver conducts electricity but sulphur does not.

(g)   A sodium ion is Na^+ but a magnesium ion is Mg^{2+}.

(h)   Iodine crystals dissolve in tetrachloromethane but not in water.

(i)   The electronegativity of chlorine is much greater than that of sodium.

(j)   There is a compound PCl_5 but not NCl_5.

Review   When you know chapter 4, you should be able to:

(a)   Define an ionic bond, an ion, a covalent bond, electronegativity, valency.

(b)   Explain what is meant by:— a lone pair, a double bond, a polar compound, ionisation.

(c)   Name four ionic compounds, write the symbols for, and draw the electron structures of the ions present.

(d)   Name four covalent compounds and draw the electron structures of their molecules.

(e)   List four characteristics of
(i) ionic compounds, and
(ii) covalent compounds.

(f)   Explain how the properties mentioned result from the structures of the substances.

(g)   Describe an experiment to distinguish between ionic and covalent compounds.

(h)   State how electronegativity values vary
(i) across a period, and
(ii) down a group, of the Periodic Table.

(i)   Say in which part of the Table
(i) the most electronegative elements and
(ii) the most electropositive elements,
occur.

(j)   Say what is the difference in electronegativity values of two elements which combine to form a compound which is 50% covalent and 50% ionic.

(k)   State what type of bonding occurs in any given compound given the electronegativities of the component elements.

(l)   Indicate the polarity in any named polar covalent compound.

(m)   Explain what a hydrogen bond, and how it accounts for some of the abnormal properties of water.

(n)   State the normal valency of any given element, with the aid of a Periodic table.

(o)   Write out the formula for any simple compound.

(p)   Write and balance the equation for any simple reaction.

(q)   Give the meaning of the various state symbols which are used in equations.

Crystal Structure

Crystals have a definite geometrical shape due to the fact that they have regular and orderly internal structure, a fact for which there is much experimental evidence. A crystal is made up of a repeating structure of close-packed units (atoms, ions or molecules) arranged in a regular pattern — known as a **lattice**. There are three types of crystal lattice, on which the units or 'building blocks' are, respectively, atoms, ions and molecules.

Ionic Crystals

These consist of positively and negatively charged ions arranged in a lattice. The best known example is that of sodium chloride. Crystals of this, which are cubic in shape, consist of positive sodium ions (Na^+) and negative chloride ions (Cl^-) held together by electrostatic forces of attraction, in a simple cubic lattice.

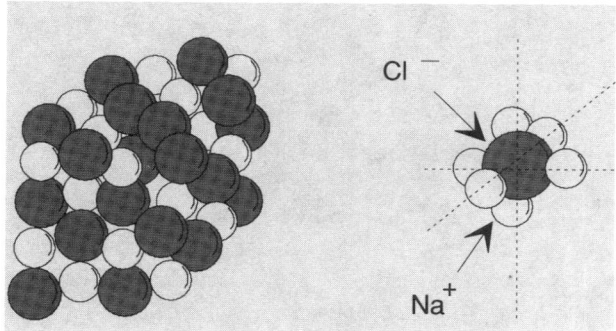

5.1

The ions are independent units and occupy alternate positions on the lattice; molecules of sodium chloride do not exist. Each sodium ion is surrounded by six chloride ions and each chloride by six sodiums.

When such a crystal is placed in water, there are forces of attraction between the ions and the water molecules (due to the polarity of the latter.) If these forces are greater than the forces between the ions in the crystal, the ionic lattice generally breaks down, *i.e.* the crystal dissolves. Ionic substances do not dissolve in non-polar solvents like tetrachloromethane, because molecules of such compounds have little or no attraction for ions.

5

Crystals and Molecules

Atomic Crystals or Covalent Crystals

These consist of atoms, arranged in a regular pattern, joined by covalent bonds. The two most common examples of this type of crystal are diamond and graphite, which are allotropes of carbon.

1. Diamond

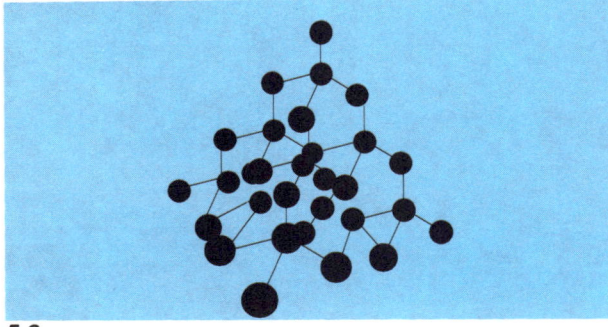

5.2

In this structure, each carbon atom is strongly bonded to four neighbouring atoms — arranged tetrahedrally. The covalent bonds bind all the atoms in the diamond crystal together, into a single giant molecule, and the very compact and firmly bound structure which results is responsible for the extreme hardness of diamond and its lack of chemical reactivity.

2. Graphite

This allotrope consists of layers of carbon atoms arranged in hexagonal rings.

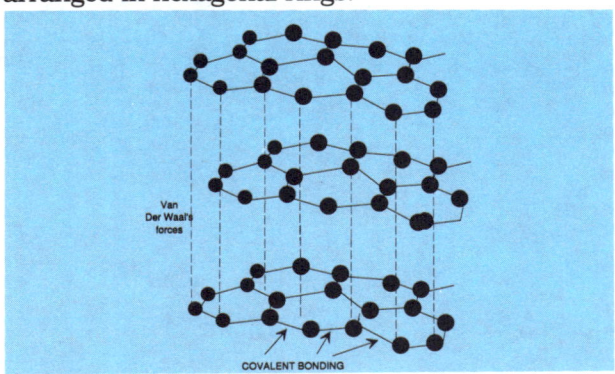

Van Der Waal's forces

COVALENT BONDING

5.3

The atoms in each layer are covalently bonded to three neighbouring atoms at an angle of 120° to each other. Adjacent layers are held together by weak forces known as **van der Waals forces**. These forces are very weak and so adjacent layers can slide over one another — resulting in the soft flaky nature of graphite and its use as a lubricant.

Molecular Crystals

The structural units in these types of crystals are molecules, and examples are ice (H_2O), iodine (I_2), sulphur (S_8), and solid carbon dioxide (or 'dry ice') CO_2.

Ice consists of water molecules held together in a rigid lattice by hydrogen bonds (as described in the previous chapter). In iodine crystals and solid CO_2, the molecules are held together by the weak van de Waals forces.

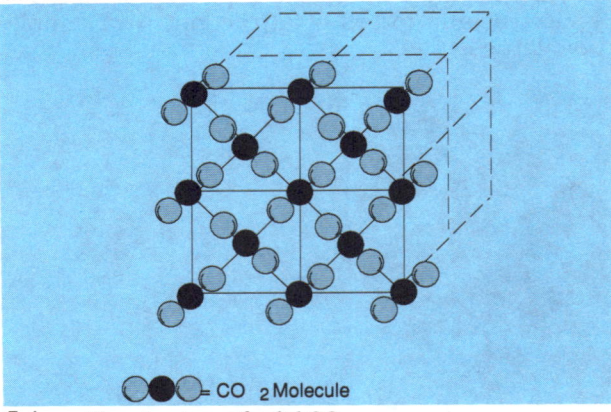

= CO_2 Molecule

5.4 — *The structure of solid CO_2*

Such crystals are characterised by low melting and boiling points, because the bonding forces between the individual molecules are weak. It is important to realise that on melting and boiling, the covalent bonds within the molecules are unaffected and the molecules remain intact.

Summary of Crystal Structure.

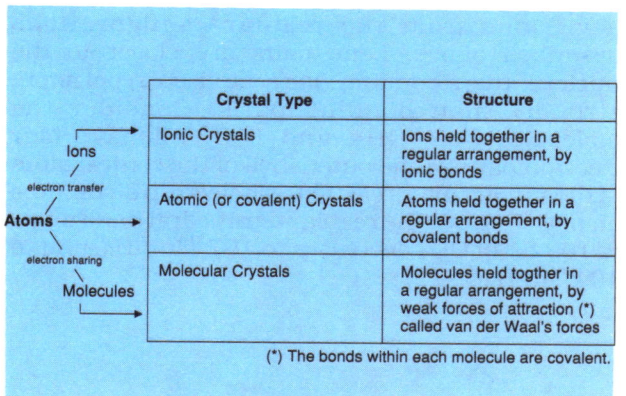

Crystal Type	Structure
Ionic Crystals	Ions held together in a regular arrangement, by ionic bonds
Atomic (or covalent) Crystals	Atoms held together in a regular arrangement, by covalent bonds
Molecular Crystals	Molecules held togther in a regular arrangement, by weak forces of attraction (*) called van der Waal's forces

(*) The bonds within each molecule are covalent.

(*) The bonds within each molecule are covalent

Shapes of Molecules

Electron Pair Repulsion Theory

One important difference between covalent and ionic compounds is that covalent compounds consist of separate molecules, whereas ionic compounds do not; the latter are composed of positive and negative ions built up into a giant structure or crystalline lattice. The electron pair repulsion theory, put forward in the 1930s, enables the shape of a molecule to be predicted from its structure. The main features are as follows:

1.   **Covalent molecules generally have a definite shape.** Covalent bonds consist of shared pairs of electrons, and where one atom is joined to several others by such bonds, the resulting molecule has a definite shape due to the repulsive forces between the electron pairs in that atom.

2.   **In molecules, covalent bonds generally arrange themselves surrounding a central atom.** In most small molecules which consist of several atoms, there is one central atom to which the others are attached. For example, in a molecule of the type XY_3 (see Fig 5.5, below), the arrangement is invariably (a) and never (b) or (c) or any other variation.

3.   **The shape of the molecule is determined by the total number of electron pairs in the central atom.** The shape of the molecule is essentially due to the arrangement in space of the covalent bonds, and it has been discovered that this depends on the **total** number of electron pairs in the central atom. Total number means the number of bonding pairs (*i.e.* covalent bonds) and lone pairs.

4.   **Electron pairs repel one another and arrange themselves in space so as to be as far apart from each other as possible**. This happens because of the mutual repulsion between pairs of electrons. Thus, 2 electron pairs will adopt a **linear** arrangement, 3 pairs will form a **triangular** shape, and 4 pairs will arrange themselves **tetrahedrally**.

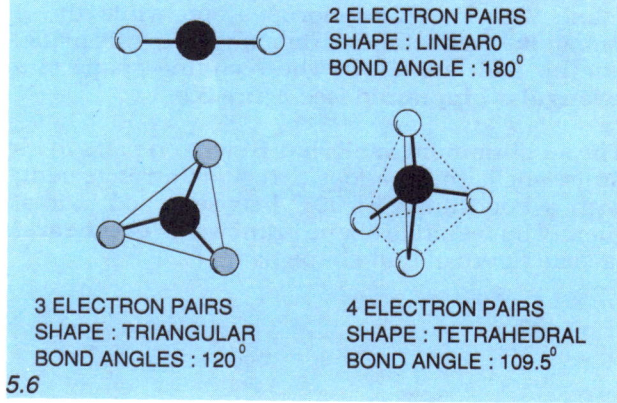

2 ELECTRON PAIRS
SHAPE : LINEAR0
BOND ANGLE : 180°

3 ELECTRON PAIRS
SHAPE : TRIANGULAR
BOND ANGLES : 120°

4 ELECTRON PAIRS
SHAPE : TETRAHEDRAL
BOND ANGLE : 109.5°

5.6

5.5

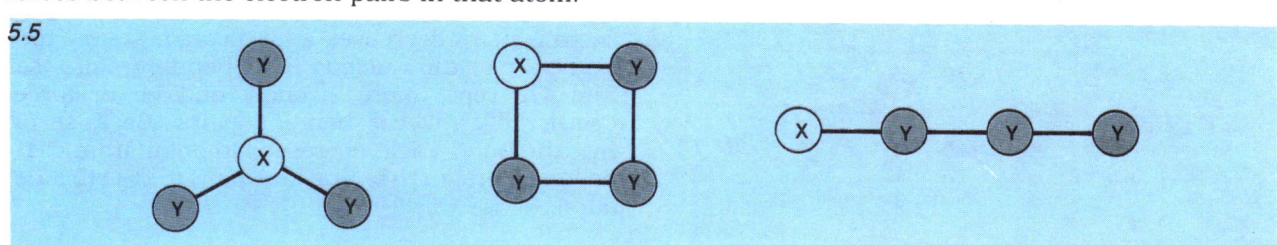

Before considering further shapes, it should be stressed that the 'octet rule' is not a rigid chemical law and while it is a useful guide in many cases, it does not always hold; molecules of BeH_2, BF_3, PCl_5, and SF_6 (shown in figure 5.7) have 4, 6, 10 and 12 electrons respectively in the outer shell of the central atom.

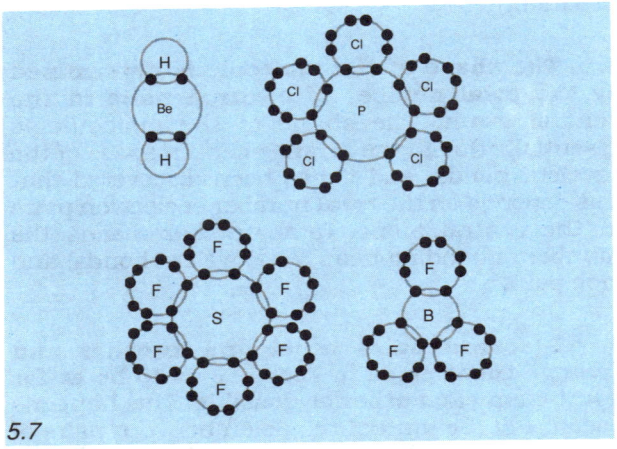

5.7

In the PCl_5 molecule, the phosphorus atom has 5 electron pairs in its outer shell; 3 of these form a triangular shape (with a bond angle of 120 $^\circ$) on a plane with the phosphorus atom, while the 2 remaining pairs stand at right angles to this plane, one up and one down. The resulting shape is a **triangular bipyramid** (see figure 5.8).

The sulphur atom in SF_6 has 6 electron pairs in its outer shell; these adopt a regular arrangement, with a bond angle of 90 $^\circ$ between each pair of them. The resulting shape is known as **octahedral** (a solid figure of that shape has 8 faces).

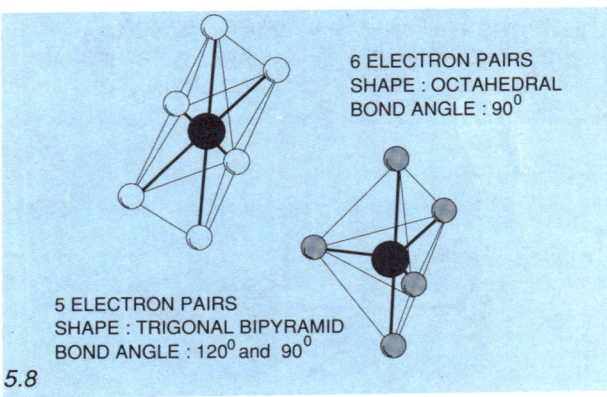

6 ELECTRON PAIRS
SHAPE : OCTAHEDRAL
BOND ANGLE : 90^0

5 ELECTRON PAIRS
SHAPE : TRIGONAL BIPYRAMID
BOND ANGLE : 120^0 and 90^0

5.8

5. Deviations from regular configurations occur when lone pairs of electrons are present.
When there are lone pairs of electrons present in the central atom of the molecule, there are slight deviations from the regular configurations described above. Lone pairs are closer to the nucleus than bonding pairs, and so repel more strongly than bonding pairs. Consider the molecules CH_4, NH_3, and H_2O. All have four electron pairs in the outer shell of the central atom of their molecules (refer to their electron structures on page 54), but the regular tetrahedral bond angle of 109.5 $^\circ$ of CH_4 decreases to 107 $^\circ$ in NH_3, and to 104 $^\circ$ in H_2O.

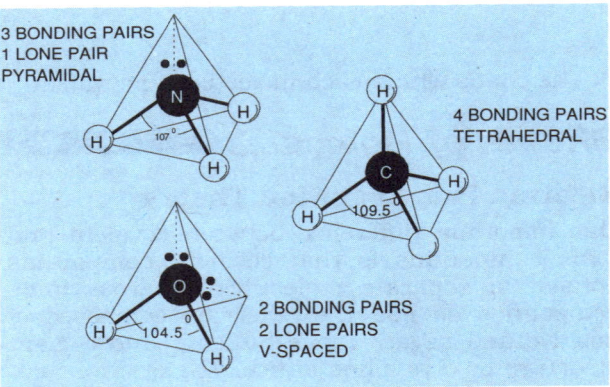

3 BONDING PAIRS
1 LONE PAIR
PYRAMIDAL

4 BONDING PAIRS
TETRAHEDRAL

2 BONDING PAIRS
2 LONE PAIRS
V-SPACED

5.9 — Molecules based on the tetrahedral structure. (The electron structures of these molecules are shown on page 54).

6. Repulsion between electron pairs decreases in the order:
l.p/l.p > l.p/b.p > b.p/b.p.
The decreasing angles referred to above have been explained by assuming that the repulsion between electron pairs decreases as indicated. Lone pairs are closer to the nucleus than bonding pairs, so they will repel more strongly and hence force together slightly the bonding pairs. Because of this, the bond angle decreases in going from CH_4 (no lone pairs) to NH_3 (one lone pair) to H_2O (2 lone pairs).

5.10

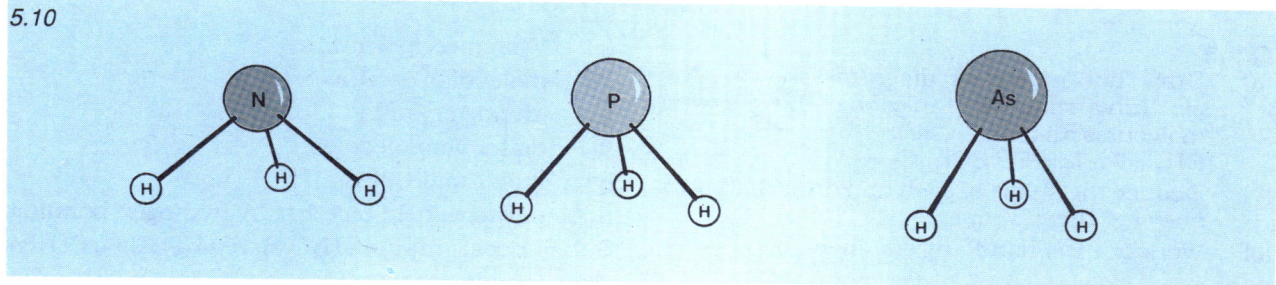

The bond angle also depends on what the central atom is. Consider the three molecules: NH_3, PH_3, and AsH_3. All have similar electron structures, but the bond angle decreases from 107° in NH_3 to 94° in PH_3 to 92° in AsH_3. This is due to the increasing atomic radius and the decreasing electronegativity of the central atom.

As the atomic radius increases and the electronegativity decreases, the shared pairs of electrons are further away from the central atom and therefore from each other; so there is a smaller force of repulsion between them and the bonds can become closer and make a smaller angle with each other.

Summary of Molecular Shapes

Table 1 : Molecules with NO Lone Pairs			
Number	Shape of molecules	Bond angle(s)	Examples
2	Linear	180°	BeH_2
3	Triangular Planar	120°	BF_3
4	Tetrahedral	$109\frac{1}{2}^\circ$	CH_4
5	Trigonal Bipyramid	120° and 90°	PCl_5
6	Octahedral	90°	SF_6

Table 2 : Molecules WITH Lone Pairs			
Electron pairs	Shape of molecule	Approx. bond angle(*)	Examples
4 b.p.	Tetrahedral	$109\frac{1}{2}^\circ$	CH_4 (included for comparison)
3 b.p 1 l.p.	Pyramidal	107°	NH_3
2 b.p. 2 l.p.	V - shaped	$104\frac{1}{2}^\circ$	H_2O(*)
1 b.p. 3 l.p.	Linear	180°	HCl (**)

(*)Bond angle also depends on electronegativity of central atom.

(**)Any molecule containing 2 atoms **must** be linear.

Questions

Q.5.1.

(a) Draw 'dot and cross' diagrams showing the electron arrangements in molecules of: SiH_4, $AlBr_3$, PBr_3, $BeCl_2$, OCl_2, H_2S

(b) Deduce the shape of each, and draw diagrams showing these shapes.

(c) Label each of the bond angles as best you can.

Q.5.2

(a) Draw 'dot and cross' diagrams showing the electron arrangement in each of the following molecules and ions: $SnCl_2$, NH_4^+, $FeCl_2$, NF_3, $SiCl_4$, PCl_3, $SnCl_4$, AlH_3, SCl_2, HBr.

(b) Deduce the shape of each, and draw diagrams to illustrate.

(c) Label the bond angle(s) in each molecule or ion.

Q.5.3

(a) Draw 'dot and cross' diagrams showing the electron arrangement in each of the following molecules and ions: $GeCl_4$, SbH_3, BBr_3, OF_2, BH_4^-, $TeCl_4$, PF_5, CCl_4, CO_2, NH_2^-

(b) Deduce the shape of each and draw diagrams showing these shapes.

(c) Work out the bond angle(s) in each.

Q.5.4 What type of bond occurs in each of the following substances: $LiCl$, $BeCl_2$, $CaCl_2$, BCl_3, CF_4, NCl_3, ICl_3, H_3O^+ ?

For each of the covalent substances, draw a diagram showing the electron structure of that substance and describe its shape.

Q.5.5 Name the particles present in the crystal lattices of (i) potassium chloride; (ii) diamond (iii) carbon dioxide.

Explain the following in terms of structures of the substances involved; (i) solid potassium chloride does not conduct electricity, but the molten salt does; (ii) potassium chloride has a high melting point, whereas carbon dioxide is a gas at room temperature; (iii) potassium chloride will dissolve in water but diamond will not; (iv) diamond is extremely hard but solid carbon dioxide is soft.

Q.5.6 Explain (i) why both H_2O and H_2S have V-shaped molecules, and (ii) why H_2O has a bond angle of about $104°$ but the angle in H_2S is about $92°$.

Q.5.7 From the given list of substances, select one which is composed of;

(a) covalent crystals

(b) ionic crystals

(c) V-shaped molecules

(d) molecular crystals

(e) atomic crystals

(f) diatomic molecules

(g) linear molecules

(h) particles held together by hydrogen bonding.

Substances: graphite, $H_2O(s)$, H_2O (l), $KI(s)$, $CO_2(g)$, H_2, CH_4, Zn.

Q.5.8 What binding force holds together the

(a) carbon atoms in diamond,

(b) atoms in a molecule of water

(c) H_2O molecules in ice,

(d) particles in potassium iodide

(e) molecules in iodine crystals

(f) atoms in an atomic crystal

Review When you know Chapter 5, you should be able to:

(a) State the three different types of crystal lattice, know what particles occupy the lattice points, and what type of force holds them together.

(b) Give examples of each of the above types.

(c) Classify a crystalline substance into its correct category.

(d) State the main features of the electron pair repulsion theory.

(e) Predict the shape of a molecule, given its formula.

(f) Draw diagrams illustrating linear, triangular planar, tetrahedral, pyramidal and V-shaped molecules.

The Gas Laws

Gases do not have a fixed volume; they fill any space into which they are put. The volume of a gas can easily be changed — in two different ways. If the temperature of a gas is increased, the gas expands and occupies a greater volume; whereas if the pressure on a gas is increased, the gas becomes compressed and occupies a smaller volume. Two scientists carried out investigations, one to find out how the volume of a gas changes with temperature, and the other to find out how it changes with pressure. Professor Charles investigated the effect of changing temperature and Robert Boyle the effect of changing pressure.

Boyle's Law

6.1 —   Robert Boyle (1624 - 1691)

When a fixed mass of gas is kept at constant temperature, the graph showing how its pressure and volume are related looks like that shown overleaf.

This graph shows that as the pressure is increased, the volume is decreased, i.e. the two quantities are inversely proportional to each other. If several different values of the pressure are selected and the corresponding volumes at each of those pressures read from the graph, it can be shown that the product of the pressure and the volume is constant.

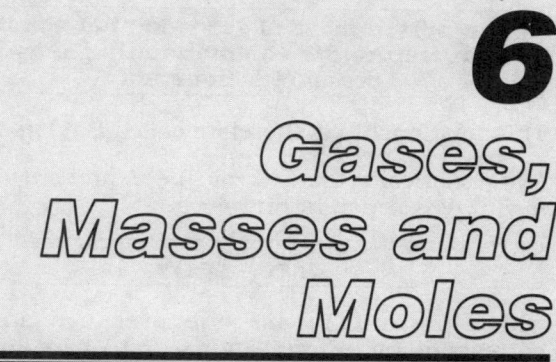

6

Gases, Masses and Moles

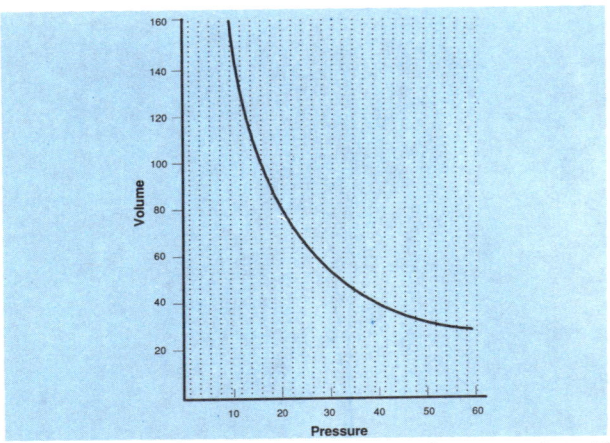

6.2 — *Graph showing how the volume of a gas varies with pressure.*

What Boyle discovered in the 17th century is that,

> **when a fixed mass of gas is kept at constant temperature, its volume multiplied by its pressure is constant.**

This relationship is therefore called **Boyle's Law.**

Mathematically the law can be expressed in the form: *pV* is constant or:

$$p_1 V_1 = p_2 V_2$$

where p_1 and V_1 are one pressure and its corresponding volume, and p_2 and V_2 are another pressure and volume.

Another way of expressing **Boyle's Law** is that:

> **At constant temperature, the volume of a fixed mass of gas is inversely proportional to its pressure,** *i.e.*
> $$p \propto \frac{1}{V}$$

Knowing the relationship between the two quantities, it is possible to calculate the volume of gas at one pressure when its volume at another pressure is known.

Units of Pressure

In the laboratory, one is usually dealing with pressures in the region of atmospheric pressure, and the most convenient way of expressing such is in **millimetres of mercury**, which have the symbol **mmHg**. Standard atmospheric pressure is 760 mmHg.

In industry, where very high pressures are common, it is more convenient and meaningful to express pressure in **atmospheres** *i.e.* the number of times the pressure is greater than standard atmospheric pressure:

$$1 \text{ atm} = 760 \text{ mmHg}$$

From a theoretical point of view, since pressure is force per unit area, the correct SI unit is the **newton per square metre** (N/m^2), also known as the **pascal** (Pa). Many data books express pressure in pascals:

$$1 \text{ atm} = 1.013 \times 10^5 \text{ Pa} = 101.3 \times 10^3 \text{ Pa}$$
$$= 101.3 \text{ kPa}$$

Boyle's Law holds for all units of pressure (and volume), provided that the same units are used on both sides of the equation.

Charles' Law

When a certain mass of gas is kept at constant pressure, the graph showing how its volume depends on the temperature is as follows:

The graph of volume and temperature being a straight line means that the two quantities are directly proportional to each other. Charles' law states this relationship as follows;

> **The volume of a fixed mass of gas, kept at constant pressure, is directly proportional to the absolute temperature.**[i]

(i)   Note that the temperature is expressed on the Kelvin or Absolute scale. This is the scale of the temperature which has zero at the lowest temperature possible, absolute zero, which is the same as - 273 $^{\circ}$C on the Celsius scale. Temperatures on the Kelvin scale are easily found — by adding 273 to the Celsius temperature. K = $^{\circ}$C + 273

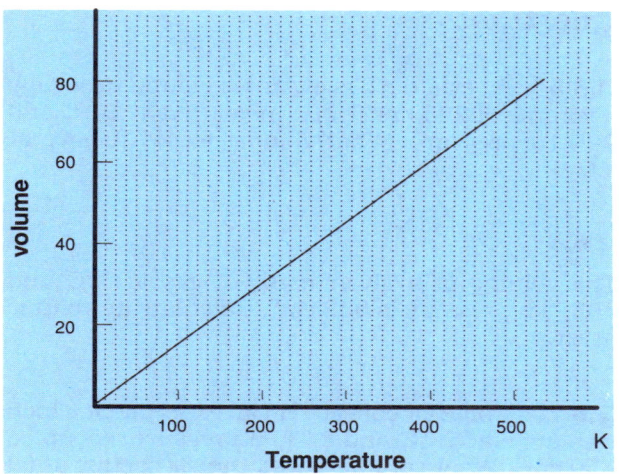

6.3 — Graph showing how the volume of a gas varies with temperature.

Mathematically, this law can be expressed in the form;

$$V \propto T$$

or as:

$$\frac{V}{T} \text{ is constant.}$$

Using this relationship, the volume of a gas at any given temperature can be calculated, provided that its volume at some other temperature is known. It must be remembered that in such calculations, the temperature must be expressed on the Kelvin scale.

Questions

Q.6.1   In an experiment, 85 cm^3 of hydrogen were collected when the pressure was 93 kPa. What would have been its volume if the pressure were 101 kPa

Q.6.2   A gas occupies 2 litres when the pressure is 95 kPa. What volume will it occupy at 100 kPa pressure.

Q.6.3   The volume of a fixed mass of gas is 546 cm^3 at 0°C. What will be its volume when it is heated to (a) 10°C, (b) 100°C.

Q.6.4   In a chemical experiment, 580 cm^3 of hydrogen were collected at the laboratory temperature of 17°C. What volume would this hydrogen occupy at 0°C?

Standard Temperature and Pressure

In laboratory experiments which involve the measuring of volumes of gases, it is often necessary to calculate what volume the gas would occupy at a standard temperature and pressure. 0°C (273 K) and 1.01325 × 10^5 Pa (= 101.3 kPa) are the values of universally accepted standard temperature and pressure. These standard conditions are necessary for several reasons.

6.4 —

Wiliam Thomson, who became Lord Kelvin, was Scottish — although he was born in Belfast. He entered Glasgow University at the remarkably early age of 11, and at the age of 22 he became Professor of Natural Philosophy, a position which he held for 53 years. He became one of the greatest scientists of Victorian times. He was very interested in heat and is best remembered for the scale of temperature which starts at absolute zero or -273°C, i.e. the Kelvin or absolute scale. Other achievements included perfecting the mariners' compass and the insulation of undersea cables; and the invention of hte mirror galvanometer and electric lamp wire or 'flex'. He was knighted in 1866 and made a baron in 1892, when he took the title Lord Kelvin. He is buried in Westminster Abbey, next to Newton.

Volumes of gases, being so easily changed, cannot be compared, unless temperature and pressure are specified, and a table of values of densities of gases must be at a particular temperature and pressure to be of any use. However, an accuracy of five decimal places is seldom required in expressing standard pressure, and 1.01×10^5 Pa is usually quite adequate (more conveniently, this value is 101 kPa).

Standard temperature and pressure (usually abbreviated to s.t.p.) can therefore be taken as 101 kPa and 0°C or 273 K.

The General Gas Law

The results of Boyle's and Charles' laws can be combined into a single expression which takes the form;

$$\frac{pV}{T} \text{ is constant, or } \frac{p_1 V_1}{T_1} = \frac{p_2 V_2}{T_2}$$

Using this equation, the volume of a gas at any temperature and pressure can be calculated, provided that its volume at some other given temperature and pressure is known. The following example shows the method involved in the calculation.

Worked Example 1

A certain mass of gas was found to occupy a volume of 269 cm^3 when the temperature was 17 °C and the pressure 99.7 kPa. What volume would the gas occupy at s.t.p.?

p_1 = 99.7 kPa p_2 = 101 kPa

V_1 = 269 cm^3 V_2 = ?

T_1 = 17°C = 290 K T_2 = 0°C = 273 K

$$\frac{p_1 V_1}{T_1} = \frac{p_2 V_2}{T_2}$$

$$\frac{99.7 \times 269}{290} = \frac{101 \times V_2}{273}$$

$$290 \times 101 \times V_2 = 99.7 \times 269 \times 273$$

$$V_2 = \frac{99.7 \times 269 \times 273}{290 \times 101}$$

$$= 250 \text{ cm}^3$$

Questions

Q.6.5 A certain mass of gas was found to occupy a volume of 225 cm^3 when measured at 20°C and 96 kPa pressure. What volume would it have at s.t.p.?

Q.6.6

The volume of a given mass of gas at 7°C and 105 kPa pressure is 532 cm^3. Calculate its volume at s.t.p.

Q.6.7 Some air collected in an experiment which was done at 27°C and 94 kPa pressure, occupied 250 cm^3. What volume would the air occupy at (a) s.t.p. (b) 77°C and 98 kPa pressure?

Q.6.8 In a high pressure experiment, 100cm^3 of a gas were collected at 100°C and 500 kPa pressure. What volume would the gas have at s.t.p.?

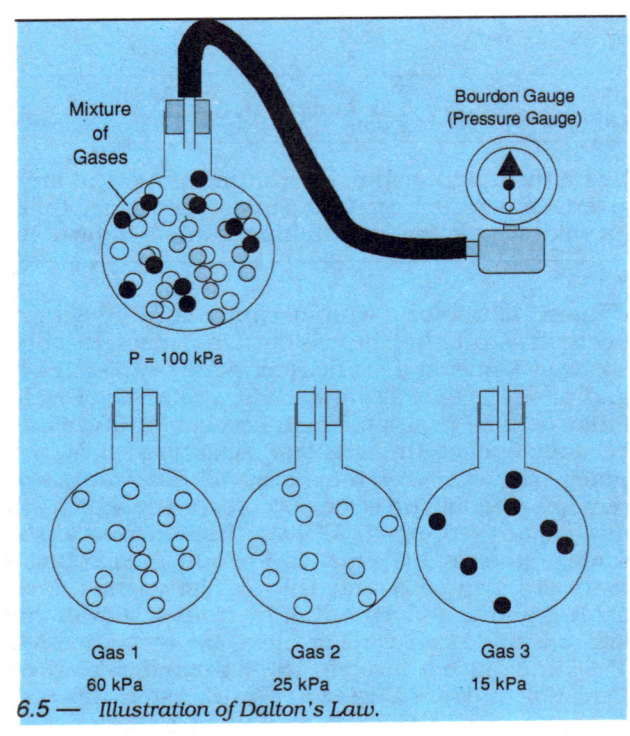

6.5 — *Illustration of Dalton's Law.*

Dalton's Law of Partial Pressures.

This law states

> **The pressure exerted by a mixture of gases is equal to the sum of the pressures which each gas would exert if it alone occupied the container — assuming that the gases do not react chemically.**

The pressure exerted by any one gas in a mixture is known as the **partial pressure** of that gas.

The partial pressure of a gas in a mixture is proportional to the amount of that gas present. If, for example, a mixture of 1 part nitrogen and 3 parts of hydrogen exert a pressure of 400 kPa, then the partial pressures of the nitrogen and hydrgoen are 100 and 300 kPa respectively.

Questions

Q.6.9 Assuming that the air consists of one fifth oxygen and four fifths nitrogen, and exerts a pressure of 100 kPa, what are the partial pressures of the oxygen and the nitrogen?

Q.6.10 75 cm^3 of hydrogen, 15 cm^3 of nitrogen, and 90 cm^3 of carbon dioxide (all at the same temperature and pressure) were put into a flask; the total pressure was then 2.4 atmospheres. Calculate the partial pressure of each gas.

Q.6.11 A flask contains oxygen at a pressure of 0.3 atm. Hydrogen is admitted until the total pressure is 0.8 atm., and then nitrogen is put in until the total pressure reaches 0.9 atm. What is then the partial pressure of each gas?

Masses of Atoms and Molecules

Atoms and molecules are much too small for their masses to be expressed in grams; the mass of one of the largest atoms, that of uranium for example, is only 0.00000000000000000000395 g.

A scale of relative atomic masses is therefore used. This scale was originally defined in terms of the hydrogen atom — whose mass was taken to be exactly one unit, but the present standard for the scale is the carbon 12 isotope — whose mass is defined as exactly 12.0 units.

> **The relative atomic mass of an element is the mass of an atom of that element compared with one-twelfth of the mass of the carbon-12 isotope.**

The symbol for relative atomic mass is A_r. On this scale, a hydrogen atom has a mass of 1.008 units. The atomic mass of an element does not refer to any particular isotope; it is the mass of an average atom of the naturally occurring element. It will be noticed when looking at a list of relative atomic masses that most of them are almost, but not quite, whole numbers (*e.g.* neon = 20.18), this is because practically every element has isotopes, and these cause the mass of an "average" atom to be slightly more or slightly less than a whole number. Neon, for example, is a mixture of two isotopes, *viz* $^{20}_{10}$Ne and $^{22}_{10}$Ne. 91% of the atoms are of the former type (of mass 20) and 9% of the latter (of mass 22). Averaging these values gives the atomic mass of 20.18.

91 atoms of mass =	1820
9 atoms of mass =	198
Total mass of 100 atoms =	2018
Average mass of each atom =	20.18

To help in understanding relative atomic mass, it can be thought of as being the mass of an atom compared with the mass of a hydrogen atom. Remember that the atomic number is, and must be, a whole number. The same applies to the mass number. The relative atomic mass can be, and usually is, fractional, since it is an average value. Masses of molecules are expressed on the same scale.

> **The relative molecular mass (symbol M_r) of an element or compound is the mass of one molecule of that element or compound compared with one-twelfth of the mass of the carbon-12 isotope.**

If the formula of a compound is known, its molecular mass can be calculated by adding together the masses of all the atoms in the molecule.

For example, the molecular mass of nitric acid (HNO_3) is 63

(H=1, N=14, O=16) $1 + 14 + (3 \times 16) = 63$.

Avogadro's Law

Amadeo Avogadro was a Professor of Physics in Italy in the 19th century and he put forward a most useful hypothesis relating molecules and volumes. This states that:

> **Equal volumes of all gases, measured at the same temperature and pressure, contain equal numbers of molecules.**

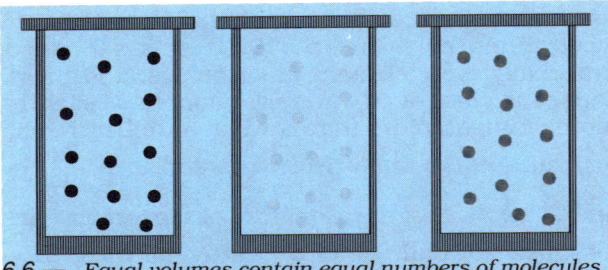

6.6 — *Equal volumes contain equal numbers of molecules.*

Although there is no direct proof of this statement there is little doubt about its truth since there is much indirect evidence which supports it. It is now regarded as a law.

Some important deductions from **Avogadro's Law** follow:

1. The hydrogen molecule must be diatomic.

It is an experimental fact that equal volumes of hydrogen and chlorine combine together and produce twice the volume of hydrogen chloride, *i.e.*

1 volume of hydrogen
+ = 2 volumes of hydrogen chloride
1 volume of chlorine

Applying **Avogadro's Law** this becomes:

n molecules of hydrogen
+ = 2*n* molecules of hydrogen chloride
n molecules of chlorine

Therefore,

1 molecule of hydrogen
+ = 2 molecules of hydrogen chloride
1 molecule of chlorine

Since each of the hydrogen chloride molecules formed must contain both hydrogen and chlorine,

the molecules of those substances must contain 2 atoms:

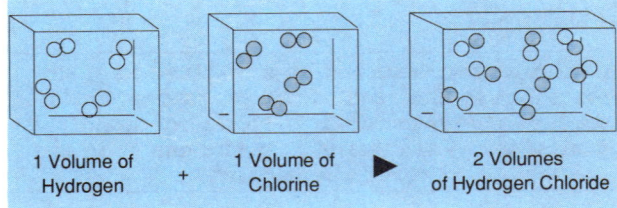

1 Volume of Hydrogen + 1 Volume of Chlorine ▶ 2 Volumes of Hydrogen Chloride

6.7

It can, in a similar manner, be shown that molecules of oxygen, nitrogen and fluorine are also diatomic.

2. Volumes and molecules are interchangeable in reactions involving gases.

The equation for the reaction, between hydrogen and oxygen for example, is:

$$2H_2 \ + \ O_2 \longrightarrow 2H_2O$$

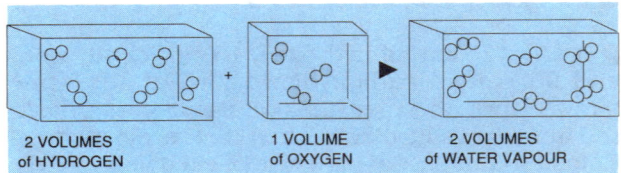

2 VOLUMES of HYDROGEN + 1 VOLUME of OXYGEN ▶ 2 VOLUMES of WATER VAPOUR

6.8

In addition to this equation showing the ratio in which molecules react, it also shows that two volumes of hydrogen (*e.g.* 2 litres) react exactly with 1 volume of oxygen (*i.e.* 1 litre), to produce water.

Counting Atoms — Moles

Atoms are far too small to be counted in the usual way. Instead, they are "counted" by weighing them, just as in banks, for instance, coinage is often "counted" by weighing it.

Because atoms are so very tiny, they have to be weighed out in enormous numbers. The standard enormous number which is used in chemistry is called the Avogadro Constant.

> **The Avogadro Constant is the number of carbon atoms in exactly 12 grams of the carbon-12 isotope.**

Obviously this is a gigantic number. Its value is 6.02×10^{23} and it is denoted by the symbol L. Some concept of the size of this number may be obtained from the following:

1. A large test tube half full of water contains about 6×10^{23} molecules. If they evaporate at the rate of one million molecules per second, it would take 19 billion years for all of the water to evaporate !

2. 6×10^{23} "Smarties" spread over the area of Ireland would form a "pillar" about 7,583 km high!

This number has been determined by several different methods, all of which very closely agree in the result that they give for it. Methods used in its determination involve the study of crystals by X-ray diffraction; counting radioactive disintegrations in an element of known half life, *e.g.* radium; and making use of the charge on the electron as measured by Millikan's experiment.

It should readily be seen that 24 g of magnesium, for example, must contain the same number of atoms as 12 g of carbon; a magnesium atom has a mass of twice that of the carbon atom so that in twice the amount of it (*i.e.* 24 g) there will also be the Avogadro Constant number of atoms.

Likewise, the atomic mass of any other element, expressed in grams, will also contain the same number of atoms.

The Avogadro Constant number of particles is used in defining the standard amount of a substance used in Chemistry, an amount known as a **mole**.

> **A mole of any substance is that amount of it which contains the Avogadro Constant number of particles.**

A mole of any substance is equal to its molecular mass, formula mass[i] or atomic mass expressed in grams. Remember that the mole is not just a number; it is an **amount** of a substance, the

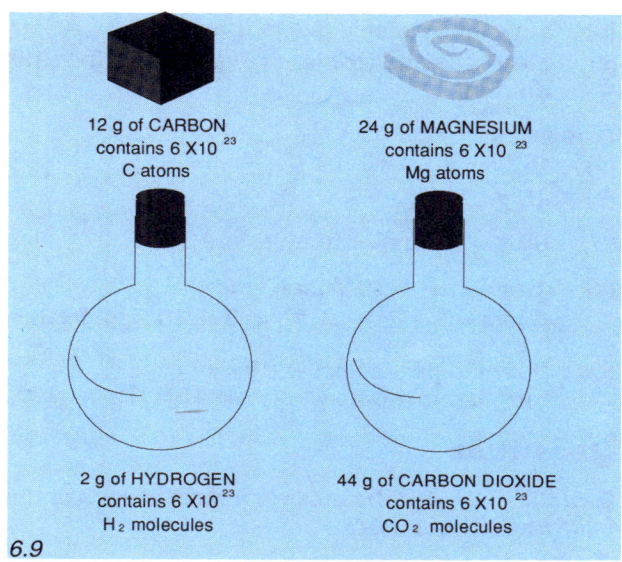

12 g of CARBON contains 6×10^{23} C atoms

24 g of MAGNESIUM contains 6×10^{23} Mg atoms

2 g of HYDROGEN contains 6×10^{23} H_2 molecules

44 g of CARBON DIOXIDE contains 6×10^{23} CO_2 molecules

6.9

amount which contains that enormous number of particles, whether they be atoms, molecules, ions, electrons or any other kind. The usefulness of the mole as a unit will become apparent with further work.

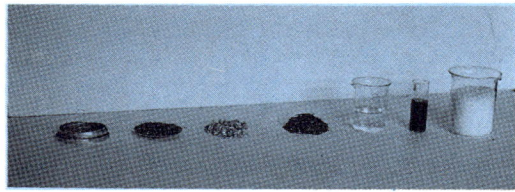

6.10 — Moles of various substances: (left to right) magnesium; graphite; zinc; copper; sulphuric acid; water; magnesium sulphate.

Worked Example 1

(a) What is the molecular mass of water?

(b) What is the mass of a mole of water?

(c) How many moles of water are contained in 90 g of water.

(i) It is strictly incorrect to refer to the " molecular mass " of a compound which exists in the form of a crystalline lattice, such as sodium chloride (made up of Na^+ and Cl^- ions), since there are no actual molecules present. The term "formula" mass is more correct for such substances.

(d)   How many molecules is that?

(e)   How many **atoms** are present in that amount.

Answers

(a) H_2O = 2 + 16 = 18

(b)   18 g

(c) $90 g = \dfrac{90}{18}$ mol = 5 moles of H_2O

(d)   1 mol = 6 × 10^{23} molecules,
       5 mol = 5 × 6 × 10^{23} = 3 × 10^{24} molecules

(e)   3 atoms per molecule, therefore
       number of atoms = 3 × 3 × 10^{24} = 9 × 10^{24}

Questions

Q.6.12   What is the mass of a mole of each of the following substances?

(a)   helium atoms
(b)   hydrogen molecules
(c)   magnesium atoms
(d)   nitrogen molecules
(e)   chlorine molecules
(f)   water molecules

Q.6.13   How many moles of particles (*i.e.* atoms or molecules) are there in

(a)   1 g of helium atoms
(b)   1 g of hydrogen molecules
(c)   2.4 g of magnesium atoms
(d)   7 g of nitrogen molecules
(e)   7.1 g of chlorine molecules
(f)   9 g of water molecules.

Q.6.14
(a)   What is the mass of a mole of each of
       (i) helium,
       (ii) calcium,
       (iii) carbon,
       (iv) oxygen?

(b)   How many moles of atoms are contained in each of:
       (i) 10 g helium,
       (ii) 10 g calcium,
       (iii) 48 g carbon,
       (iv) 48 g oxygen?

(c)   What is the actual number of atoms present in each of the above quantities (see part (b))?

Q.6.15
(a)   What is the mass of a mole of each of
       (i) nitrogen,
       (ii) carbon dioxide,
       (iii) ammonia,
       (iv) methane?

(b)   How many moles of molecules are present in 10 g of each of
       (i) nitrogen
       (ii) carbon dioxide
       (iii) ammonia
       (iv) methane?

(c)   How many molecules are present in each of those quantities?

(d)   How many atoms are present in each of those quantities?

Q.6.16   How many
(a)   moles of molecules,
(b)   molecules,
(c)   atoms, are present in each of :
       (i) 10 g hydrogen
       (ii) 8 g oxygen
       (iii) 7 g carbon monoxide?

Q.6.17   How many
(a)   molecules,
(b)   atoms, are contained in each of :
       (i)   1.8 g water
       (ii   640 g of sulphur dioxide,
       (iii) 4.9 g sulphuric acid
       (iv) 34 g ammonia
       (v) 0.63 g nitric acid?

Q.6.18
(a)   How many iron atoms are there in a typical 5 cm nail, which has a mass of 5.6 g?

(b)   How many water molecules are contained in a glass of water, of volume 200 cm^3 (density of water = 1 g/cm^3)?

Q.6.19   The mass of one molecule of a compound is 7.33 × 10^{-23} g. Calculate its relative molecular mass. Which of the following could it be: H_2O_2, CO_2, NO_2, N_2O, HCl?

Molar Volume

According to Avogadro's Law, equal volumes of gases contain equal numbers of molecules; conversely, equal numbers of molecules of gases, for example 6 × 10^{23} must occupy equal volumes.

This means that one mole of every gas (at the same temperature and pressure) has the same volume.

The volume occupied by one mole of a gas is easily calculated. One mole of hydrogen (H_2) has a mass of 2 g, and the density of hydrogen is 0.0893 grams per litre at s.t.p..

$$\text{Density} = \frac{\text{mass}}{\text{volume}},$$

therefore, $\text{volume} = \frac{\text{mass}}{\text{density}}$.

therefore, the volume of one mole of hydrogen (at s.t.p.) is $\frac{2}{0.0893}$ L = 22.4 litres.

This volume is known as the **molar volume** (at s.t.p.).

> **The molar volume of any gas is the volume occupied by 1 mole of that gas, and is 22.4 litres at s.t.p.**

At room temperature (20°C), the volume is slightly greater and is usually taken to be 24 litres. The value of the molar volume is used in calculations involving the density of a gas, and in questions in which mass, volume and/or number of moles have to be related. Some examples follow.

Worked Example 2

Calculate the density of nitrogen (*i.e.* the mass of unit volume of it) at s.t.p.

N_2 = 28

22.4 litres have a mass of 28 g.

1 litre has a mass of $\frac{28}{22.4}$ g = 1.25 g

Therefore: Density of nitrogen = 1.25 g/litre

Worked Example 3

Calculate the volume occupied by 4 g of CO_2 (at s.t.p.)

$$CO_2 = 44$$

44 g have a volume of 22.4 litres.

Therefore:

4 g have a volume of $\frac{22.4}{11}$ litres = 2.04 litres.

Questions

Q.6.20   Calculate, at s.t.p.:

(a)   the density of chlorine;
(b)   the mass of 50 litres of methane;
(c)   the volume occupied by 85 g of ammonia;
(d)   the density of carbon monoxide
(e)   the volume occupied by 8 g of oxygen;
(g)   the mass of 1 litre of sulphur dioxide.

Q.6.21   Calculate the density of each of the following gases, using the value of the molar volume (22.4 L, at s.t.p.); nitrogen; carbon dioxide; oxygen; phosphine (PH_3); methane; ethene.

Q.6.22   Calculate the volume occupied by;

(a)   14 g of nitrogen;
(b)   4.4 g of carbon dioxide
(c)   8 g of oxygen
(d)   68 g of phosphine
(e)   1 g of methane
(f)   1 g of ethene.

Q.6.23   Calculate the mass of :

(a)   1 litre of nitrogen
(b)   2 litres of carbon dioxide
(c)   3 litres of oxygen
(d)   4 litres of phosphine
(e)   5 litres of methane;
(f)   6 litres of ethene.

Q.6.24
(a)   One litre of a gas at s.t.p. has a mass of 0.718 g. Calculate its molecular mass. Which of the following gases could it be; CO_2, CO, O_2, CH_4?
(b)   What is the molecular mass of a gas 250 cm^3 of which, at s.t.p. weighs 1.116 g?
(c)   350 cm^3 of a gas (at s.t.p.) weighs 1.00 g. Calculate its relative molecular mass. Given that it is an oxide of sulphur, what is its formula?

The Ideal Gas Equation

Very accurate measurements of the effects of temperature and pressure on gases show that they do not obey Boyle's and Charles' laws absolutely, particularly at high pressures and low temperatures, when the molecules are pushed closer together. A gas which **does** obey the gas laws at all temperatures and pressures is called an **ideal gas**. In reality, no such gas exists, but it is a useful concept. However, at ordinary temperatures and pressures, most permanent gases behave like an ideal gas would, and for these a useful equation relating a number of variables for gases, can be deduced.

It has been shown that $\frac{pV}{T}$ for a gas is constant; the constant is usually denoted by R but no mention has been made so far of its value. A little thought should show that the value, must depend on the amount of gas involved, and also on what units are used in expressing both the temperature and the pressure. Using the SI units of these — Kelvins and N/m^2 (or pascals) — its value is calculated, below, for one mole of a gas. At s.t.p. one mole of an ideal gas occupies 22.4 litres, which is 0.0224 m^3, So:

$$R = \frac{pV}{T} = \frac{101325 \times 0.0224}{273}$$

$$= 8.31 \; ^{Nm}/_{K} \; mol$$

or 8.31 J/K mol, $(JK^{-1} \, mol^{-1})$

The equation

$$\frac{pV}{T} = R$$

can be rearranged as $pV = RT$ where R is the gas constant just calculated and p, V and T are expressed in SI units. For n moles of the gas, the equation becomes;

$$pV = nRT$$

and this equation is known as the **ideal gas equation,** or the **equation of state for an ideal gas.**

Determination of Relative Molecular Mass

There are several experimental methods for the determination of the molecular masses of substances. One well known method, which is used for volatile liquids, was devised by Victor Meyer, a German chemist of the last century. The principle of his method is that a known mass of the liquid is taken and vaporised, and then the volume occupied by the vapour is measured, along with the temperature and pressure. Calculation, using either the molar volume (22.4 L) or the ideal gas equation (**pV=nRT**) leads to the molecular mass of the liquid. The experiment described below is a modern version of Victor Meyer's method.

Experiment 6.1
To Determine the Relative Molecular Mass of a Volatile Liquid

The apparatus consists of a graduated gas syringe enclosed in a container which can be heated by passing steam through it. The syringe is closed by a self-sealing cap, through which the liquid can be injected.

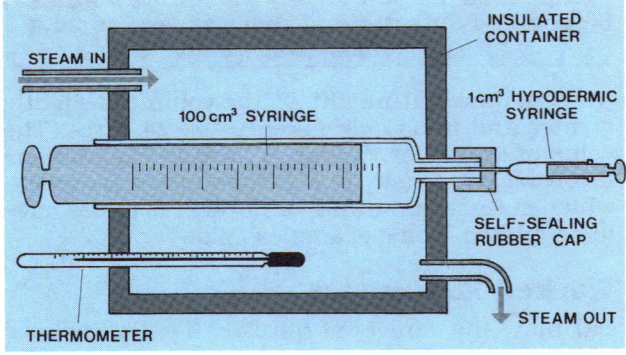

6.11 — *Apparatus to determine relative molecular mass.*

A few cm^3 of air are drawn into the syringe and the rubber cap fitted over the nozzle. Steam is passed through the container, until the thermometer reading and the volume of air in the syringe become steady. The temperature and the volume of air are recorded.

Some of the liquid whose molecular mass is required is taken into the hypodermic syringe, and the latter is then weighed. A small volume (about 0.2 cm^3) of this liquid is then injected into the gas syringe, through the self-sealing cap. The hypodermic syringe is removed and reweighed. By subtraction, the mass of liquid injected into the gas syringe is found. The liquid in the heated gas syringe vaporises and the plunger is pushed out. The volume is recorded once it has become steady. Finally, the atmospheric pressure is noted.

Specimen Results

Initial volume of air in gas syringe . . . . 10 cm^3

Final volume of air + vapour in syringe . . 75 cm^3

Volume of vapour . . . . 65 cm^3

Temperature at which vapour is collected
. . . . 99° C (= 372 K)

Initial mass of hypodermic syringe . . . . . .32.48 g

Final mass of hypodermic syringe . . . . . .32.30 g

Mass of liquid injected and vaporised . . .0.18 g

Atmospheric pressure . . . . .99.9 kPa.

Volume of vapour . . . . .65 cm^3

$$= 65 \times 10^{-6} \text{ m}^3$$

Pressure . . . . 99.9 kPa = 99.9 × 10^3 Pa

Temperature . . . . .372 K

Gas Constant . . . . .8.31 J/K mol

$$pV = nRT$$

$$n = \frac{pV}{RT} = \frac{99.9 \times 10^3 \times 65 \times 10^{-6}}{8.31 \times 372}$$

$$= 0.0021 \text{ moles}$$

0.0021 moles have a mass of 0.18 g

Therefore, 1 mole has a mass of $\dfrac{0.18}{0.0021}$ g = 86 g

i.e. relative molecular mass = 86

Experiment 6.2.
To measure the Relative Molecular Mass of a Volatile Liquid.

The principle of this experiment, which is based on Dumas' method for measuring molecular mass, is to find the mass of vapour which occupies a given volume at a known temperature and pressure. By calculation, the number of moles of vapour in the flask is then found and hence the molar mass.

Take a clean dry conical flask (about a 250 cm^3 size), a circle of aluminium foil about twice the diameter of the mouth of the flask and a rubber band. Weigh these together. Pour about 8 cm^3 of the given liquid into the flask. Make the aluminium foil into a cap for the flask by

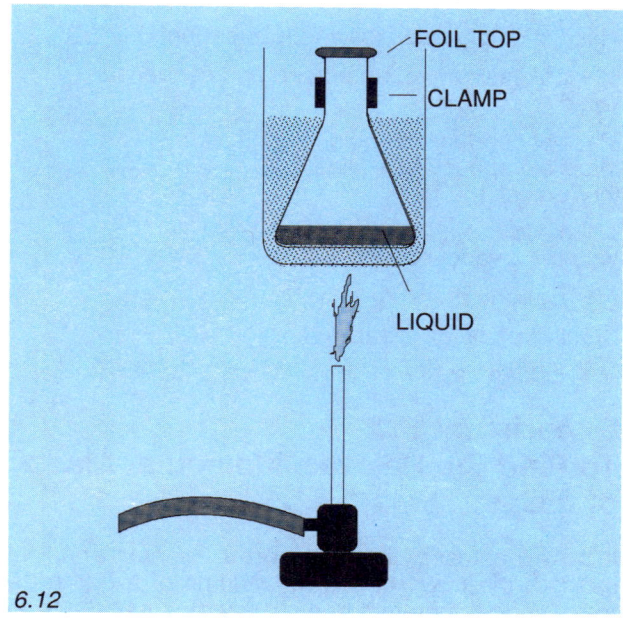

6.12

placing it on top and pressing it down over the sides. Stretch the rubber band around it (several times if necessary) to hold it tight. Make a **very small** hole in the cap using the point of a pin. Clamp the flask in a suitable container of boiling water as shown — as much as possible of the flask should be covered by the water. The liquid boils and expels the air from the flask. When all the liquid has vaporised (none left on the bottom of the flask or condensed around the top — this will take about five minutes), the flask is then full of the vapour of the liquid, at 100° C and at the day's atmospheric pressure. Remove the flask from the boiling water and **on no account put it back again**.

Allow the flask to **cool to room temperature**, dry the outside of it (and the foil top if necessary). Reweigh, to find the mass of the vapour — which has now condensed to a liquid. Find the volume of the flask by filling it with water (to the level of the foil) and pouring the water into a graduated cylinder.

Results — Record these as follows and then use the ideal gas equation to calculate the number of moles of vapour, and hence find its molecular mass. A worked examples of this type of calculation is given above.

Determination of Relative Molecular Mass

Mass of empty flask, foil and rubber band . =

Mass of flask, foil, rubber band and condensed liquid . . . . =

Mass of condensed liquid
Mass of vapour which filled) . . . . =
the flask at 100 °C

Volume of flask
Volume of vapour at 100°C) . . . . =

Atmospheric pressure . . . . =

Number of moles of vapour . . . . =

Molecular mass . . . . =

Experiment 6.3
To Find the Relative Molecular Mass of a Gas.

In this experiment, which is based on Regnault's original method, the mass of a given volume of a gas (at a measured temperature and pressure) is found. Using the ideal gas equation, the number of moles of it is calculated, and this leads to its relative molecular mass. Ideally a gas syringe should be used, but a large plastic syringe, if it is air tight, will suffice.

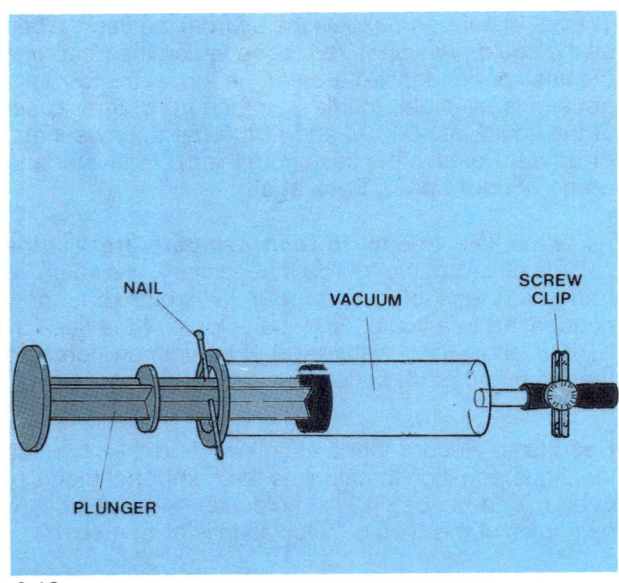

6.13

"Empty" the syringe of air. This is done by pressing the plunger in fully, closing the screw clip, pulling the syringe open so that there is a vacuum within, and then putting the nail in position to hold the plunger out. Now weigh it, preferably to 3 decimal places.

Next fill it with the gas whose molecular mass is to be determined. This can be done by connecting the rubber tube to a cylinder of the gas and opening the screw clip. It is advisable to flush it out once or twice with the gas before putting back the nail and returning the plunger to its marked position. Disconnect the gas supply and close the screw clip. Reweigh the syringe (including the nail and clip). Note the volume of gas in the syringe, and record the values of the temperature and the atmospheric pressure.

Calculate the number of moles of gas contained in the syringe, and then, using the mass of gas which it contained, work out its relative molecular mass.

Problems

Q.6.25 Calculate the relative molecular mass of a volatile liquid from the following results of a gas syringe experiment:

Initial mass of small syringe + liquid = 30.490 g
Mass of syringe + liquid after injection = 30.244 g
Initial volume of air in gas syringe = 8 cm³
Final volume of air + vapour in gas syringe = 48 cm³
Temperature of vapour = 100°C
Atmospheric pressure = 100 kPa

Q.6.26 0.5 g of a volatile liquid element was vaporised in a heated gas syringe and was found to occupy a volume of 97 cm³ at 100 ° C and 98.8 kPa pressure. Calculate the relative molecular mass of the element, and with the aid of a Periodic Table, identify it.

Q.6.27 0.18 g of an organic liquid, when vaporised, occupied 92 cm³ at 101°C and 104.9 kPa pressure. Calculate the relative molecular mass of the liquid.

Q.6.28 0.25 cm³ of a liquid of density 0.91 g/cm³ was injected into a gas syringe at a temperature of 160° C. The liquid vaporised completely and occupied 81cm³ at 102 kPa pressure. Calculate the molecular mass of the liquid.

Q.6.29 In an experiment to measure the relative molecular mass of a volatile liquid, a flask whose capacity was 410 cm^3, contained 3.0 g of the vapour of a volatile liquid at a temperature of 100°C and 101.4 kPa pressure. Calculate
(i) the number of moles of vapour in the flask, and
(ii) its relative molecular mass.

Q.6.30 The density of a gas is 3.17 g/L at 20°C and 2.35 atm. pressure. Calculate the relative molecular mass of that gas.

Q.6.31. The following measurements refer to a small cylinder of gas:

Mass of empty cylinder	= 80.00 g
Mass of cylinder full of gas	= 80.50 g
Capacity of cylinder	= 100 cm^3
Temperature	= 0 °C

Pressure of gas inside cylinder = 4.0 atmospheres
Calculate the molecular mass of the gas in the cylinder.

Q.6.32. An evacuated gas syringe has a mass of 123.45 g. When 87 cm^3 of a gas at 102 kPa and 22°C were drawn into it, its mass increased to 123.66 g. Calculate the molecular mass of the gas.

Diffusion

Diffusion is the way in which gaseous molecules spread themselves and fill any space into which they are put. Some simple experiments on diffusion are described in Chapter 1.
Different gases diffuse at different rates. Graham, in the 19th century, investigated this and discovered that the less dense a gas is, the more rapidly it diffuses.

Graham's law of Diffusion

This law states that:

> **Gases diffuse at rates which are inversely proportional to the square roots of their densities (temperature being constant),** *i.e.*

$$r \propto \sqrt{\frac{1}{d}}$$

or, in the case of 2 gases

$$\frac{r_1}{r_2} = \sqrt{\frac{d_2}{d_1}}$$

Since the density of a gas is proportional to its molecular mass (Avogadro: equal volumes contain

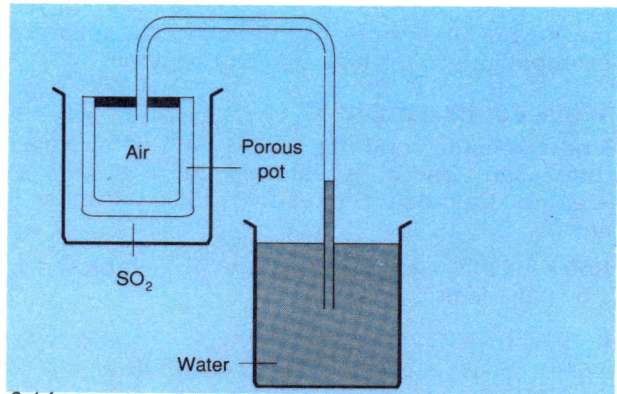

6.14 — *When the beaker of SO$_2$ is placed outside the porous pot, the gases (the air and the SO$_2$) start to diffuse into each other. The air, being the less dense, diffuses out faster than the SO$_2$ diffuses in; the pressure inside the pot is thus reduced and this is shown by the water rising up the tube.*

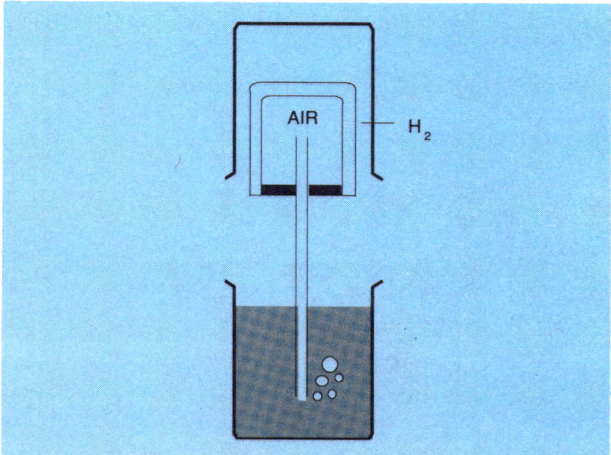

6.15 — *When hydrogen is placed outside the porous pot, it, being less dense than air, diffuses in faster than the air diffuses out; the pressure is thus increased and bubbles of gas are driven out through the water.*

equal numbers of molecules), the ratio of the densities of two gases is the same as the ratio of their molecular masses. **Graham's Law** can therefore be given as:

$$\frac{r_1}{r_2} = \sqrt{\frac{m_{r_2}}{m_{r_1}}}$$

This is a more useful form of the law, since it enable the molecular masses of gases to be compared by measuring their rates of diffusion. The following example illustrates how this can be done.

Worked Example 4

Under similar conditions, 300 cm^3 of hydrogen diffuses in 12 seconds, and 250 cm^3 of gas X in 47 seconds. Calculate the relative molecular mass of gas X.

Rates of diffusion are conveniently expressed in cm^3 per second. So:

For the hydrogen,

$$r_1 = 300 \text{ cm}^3 \text{ in 12 seconds}$$

$$= \frac{300}{12} \text{ cm}^3 \text{ per second}$$

$$M_r = 2$$

For gas X,

$$r_2 = \frac{250}{47} \text{ cm}^3 \text{ per second}$$

$$M_r = x$$

$$\frac{300/12}{250/47} = \sqrt{\frac{x}{2}}$$

$$\sqrt{x} = \sqrt{2} \times \frac{300}{12} \times \frac{47}{50} = 6.64$$

$$x = (6.64)^2 = 44$$

Questions

Q.6.33 Hydrogen diffused through a porous pot at the rate of 16 cm^3/sec. Another gas diffused at the rate of 4 cm^3/sec. Calculate the molecular mass of the other gas. Given that it is a gaseous element, identify it.

Q.6.34 30 cm^3 of oxygen diffused in 10 s, and the same volume of another gas, under the same conditions, diffused in 15 s. Calculate the relative molecular mass of the other gas.

Q.6.35 A fixed volume of oxygen diffused through a porous pot in 84.8 sec; an equal volume of gas Y took 120 sec to diffuse. Calculate the molecular mass of Y.

Q.6.36 A certain volume of oxygen diffused in 100 s. An equal volume of Z took 141.4 s. What is the molecular mass of Z?

Q.6.37 20 cm^3 of hydrogen diffused through a porous material in 16 seconds. How long would an equal volume of methane take?

Q.6.38 In 3 minutes, 7.5 cm^3 of carbon dioxide diffused. What volume of helium would diffuse in the same time, under the same conditions?

Measuring Relative Atomic Masses

In the mid 19th century when the idea of atoms and molecules had become well established, chemists devised several methods for measuring the masses of atoms of the different elements. Some of these gave quite accurate results but they are now only of historical interest.

The Mass Spectrograph

Atomic masses are now determined by means of the **mass spectrograph**. This apparatus, which was devised by F.W. Aston at Cambridge in the early 1920s, basically "sorts out" atoms into groups, each group containing atoms of the same mass. It can thus separate the different isotopes of an element and it enables the relative masses of these isotopes to be determined.

The element whose atomic mass is to be determined is placed in a discharge tube at low pressure and a high potential difference applied across it.

Due to collisions with high energy electrons in the tube, gaseous atoms of the elements have electrons knocked out of their shells and so are converted to positive ions. These positive ions travel towards the cathode (*i.e.* the negative electrode), in which there is a slit, so that a beam of positive ions emerges from this slit. The beam then passes through an electrostatic field which allows only ions of the same speed to enter the part of the spectrograph which actually separates the isotopes.

In this part, the beam of ions passes through a strong magnetic field which causes it to be deflected, after which it falls on a photographic plate. The ions of smallest mass are deflected most and those of greatest mass, least. After the plate has been developed, lines are produced where it

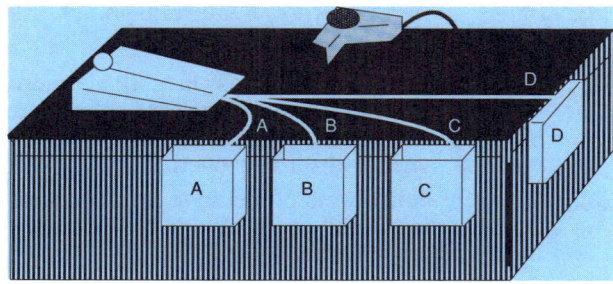

6.16 — *The principle on which the mass spectrograph is based is illustrated in this experiment. When the blower is switched off, spheres roll down the slope, travelling along path d. When the blower is switched on, a force acts on the spheres and they are deflected; those of smallest mass (e.g. table tennis balls) are deflected most — along path a —, while those of greatest mass (e.g. golf balls) are deflected least — along path c.*

has been struck by the ions and from the positions of these lines, the relative masses of the ions can be calculated.

Nowadays, the ions are detected electronically rather than by a photographic plate. The intensity of the ion beam is measured at different positions and the results are automatically recorded as a graph, by a chart recorder. Below, is shown the mass spectrum of a sample of mercury.

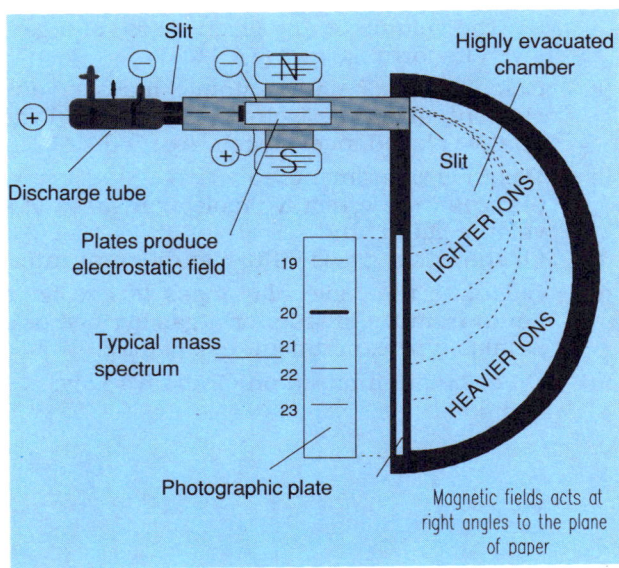

6.17

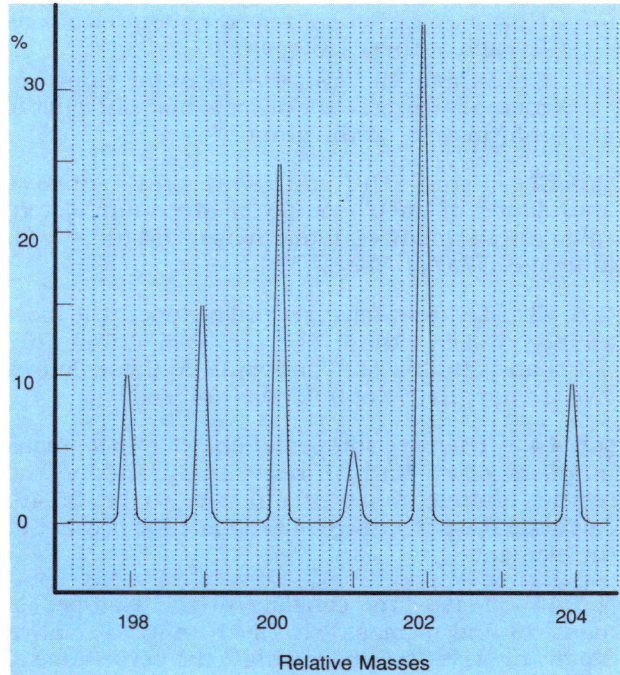

6.18 — *The mass spectrum of germanium, showing the isotopes present and their relative abundance.*

6.19

The invention of the mass spectroscope made possible great advances in chemistry, particularly by enabling isotopes of elements to be separated; several distinct lines were produced from one element, each line corresponding to a particular mass. From the intensity of the lines, the relative abundance of each isotope was estimated. There is a worked example of a calculation on page 75.

Questions

Q.6.39   An element consists of two isotopes of masses 35 and 37 respectively. Three-quarters of the atoms are of the former type and the remainder of the latter. What value do these figures give for the relative atomic mass of the element.

Q.6.40   Naturally occurring boron consists of two isotopes, of mass numbers 10 and 11, present in the ratio of 18.8 to 81.2 respectively. Calculate the relative atomic mass of boron.

Q.6.41   Refer to the mass spectrum of mercury shown in Fig.6.19.

(a)   What are the mass numbers of the two most abundant isotopes?

(b)   How many protons, neutrons and electrons in each of these isotopes?

(c)   Calculate the relative atomic mass of mercury (correct to 2 decimal places) from the information on the graph.

Q.6.42   From the masses and relative abundance of each isotope of strontium listed, calculate its relative atomic mass:- 84 (0.5%); 86 (9.9%); 87 (7.0%); 88 (82.6%).

Q.6.43   Lead contains several isotopes, the most abundant being those of mass 206 (25%), 207 (23%) and 208 (52%). What value do these figures give for the relative atomic mass of lead?

Q.6.44   The two isotopes of chlorine have mass numbers of 35 and 37 respectively. Taking the relative atomic mass of chlorine to be 35.46, calculate the percentage of each isotope present in the element.

Q.6.45   Potassium consists of the isotopes of mass 39 and of mass 41. Given that its relative atomic mass is 39.096, calculate the percentage of each isotope present.

Review   When you know Chapter 6 you should be able to:

(a)   State Boyle's law, Charles' law, the general gas law, Dalton's law, Avogadro's law, the ideal gas equation (and know what the various symbols in it represent).

(b)   Give the definitions of: relative atomic mass, relative molecular mass, Avogadro constant, mole, molar volume.

(c)   Say what the following symbols and abbreviations represent:
p, V, T, n, A_r, M_r, s.t.p., mol

(d)   Convert $^\circ$C to K, and cm^3 to m^3.

(e)   Convert volumes to s.t.p., and to room temperature and pressure.

(f)   Explain isotopes, diffusion, the principle of the mass spectrometer (spectrograph).

(g)   State the values of standard temperature, standard pressure, molar volume.

(h)   Calculate the mass of a mole of any substance, given its formula.

(i)   Calculate the number of moles and the number of molecules in a stated mass of any given substance, e.g. Q.6.16.

(j)   Calculate
(i) the density,
(ii) the mass of any given volume,
(iii) the volume of any given mass, of a gas, given its formula, e.g. Q 16.20.

(k)   Calculate the relative atomic mass of any element, given the isotopes present and the relative abundance of each, e.g. Q.6.42.

(l)   Describe experiments to
(i) measure the relative molecular mass of a volatile liquid, and
(ii) show that gases diffuse at different rates.

(m)   Calculate the molecular mass of a volatile liquid from the results or a gas syringe or a Dumas type experiment, e.g. Q.6.26.

(n)   Do calculation based on Graham's Law, e.g. Q.6.33.

Stoichiometry means the determination of the combining quantities of elements and the mass relationships in chemical substances and reactions. Much quantitative information can be gained from chemical formulae and equations and this chapter explains the most important information which is so obtainable.

Calculation of the relative molecular mass of a compound from its formula.

This is found by adding together the relative atomic masses of each of the atoms present in a molecule of the compound *e.g.*

NaOH $= 23 + 16 + 1 = 40$

$H_2SO_4 = (2 \times 1) + 32 + (4 \times 16) = 98$

Calculation of the percentage of each element present in a compound, from the formula of the latter.

This is calculated from the relative atomic masses of the atoms present in a molecule of the compound. The following examples illustrate the method.

Worked Examples 1 and 2

(a)   Calculate the % of carbon in carbon dioxide.

$$CO_2, \quad M_r = 44$$

Relative mass of molecule = 44

Relative mass of carbon present = 12

% of carbon present $= \dfrac{12}{44} \times 100 = 27.3\%$

(b)   Calculate the % of oxygen in sulphur acid

$$H_2SO_4, \quad M_r = 98$$

Relative mass of molecule = 98

Relative mass of oxygen present = $4 \times 16 = 64$

% of oxygen present $= \dfrac{64}{98} \times 100 = 65.3\%$

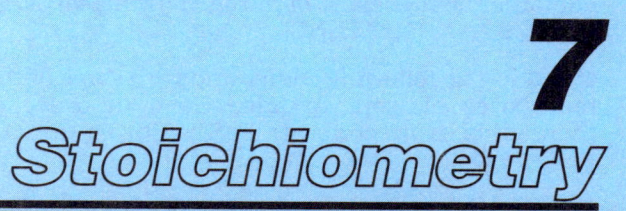

7

Stoichiometry

Questions

9.7.1 Penecillin has the formula

$$C_{14}H_{20}O_4N_2S$$

How many atoms are in a molecule of this, and what is its relative molecular mass?

9.7.2 Calculate the relative molecular mass of each of the following compounds: sulphuric acid; carbon dioxide; magnesium chloride; sodium oxide; water; nitric acid; potassium nitrate; magnesium nitrate; calcium carbonate.

9.7.3 What is the % of nitrogen in each of NO_2, HNO_3, $Cu(NO_3)_2$, NH_3, Mg_3N_2?

9.7.4 Which of the following compounds contains the highest % of nitrogen (by mass): NH_3; $(NH_4)_2SO_4$; N_2H_4; NH_4NO_3 ?

9.7.5 The following compounds are some of the main ores of iron. Arrange them in order of increasing iron content: FeS_2; Fe_2O_3; Fe_3O_4; $Fe_2O_3H_2O$.

9.7.6 Calculate the % of water of crystallisation in "bluestone" ($CuSO_45H_2O$).

9.7.7 Find the % of each of the elements present in ammonium chloride NH_4Cl.

9.7.8 What is the % of oxygen in each of the following compounds; MgO; P_2O_5; H_2SO_4; $Cu(NO_3)_2$; Al_2O_3.

9.7.9 Calculate the percentage of both carbon and hydrogen in

(a) ethene (C_2H_4) and
(b) propene (C_3H_6).

Calculation of the empirical formula of a compound from its percentage composition.

> **The empirical formula of a compound is a simple formula showing only the ratio in which the different atoms are present in a molecule of the compound**

This may or may not be the same as the molecular formula of the compound — which shows the actual number of each type of atom present. A molecule of glucose, for example, consists of carbon, hydrogen and oxygen atoms, present in the ratio of 1 : 2 : 1 respectively; the empirical formula is thus CH_2O. The actual numbers of each kind of atom present are 6 carbons, 12 hydrogens and 6 oxygens; the molecular formula is therefore $C_6H_{12}O_6$.

To determine the empirical formula of a compound, the % of each element present in the compound is divided by the relative atomic mass of that element. The empirical formula is the simplest whole number ratio between the figures so obtained. Two examples showing this technique follow.

Worked Example 3

A compound contains 40% sulphur and 60% oxygen. What is its empirical formula?

Element	%	$\dfrac{\%}{A_r}$	Simplest ratio	Formula
Sulphur	40	$\dfrac{40}{32} = 1.25$	1	
Oxygen	60	$\dfrac{60}{16} = 3.75$	3	SO_3

Worked Example 4

What is the simplest formula of a compound which contains 54.5% carbon, 9.1% hydrogen and 36.4% oxygen.

Element	%	$\dfrac{\%}{A_r}$	Simplest ratio	Formula
Carbon	54.5	$\dfrac{54.5}{12} = 4.54$	2	
Hydrogen	9.1	$\dfrac{9.1}{1} = 9.1$	4	C_2H_4O
Oxygen	36.4	$\dfrac{36.4}{16} = 2.27$	1	

Calculation of molecular formula, from empirical formula and relative molecular mass.

The relative molecular mass of a compound provides the information that decides whether the molecular formula is the same as the empirical formula or, if not, how many empirical formula "units" are contained in the molecular formula.

In the previous worked example, an empirical formula was shown to be C_2H_4O. If the relative molecular mass of the same compound was found to be 88, then the molecular formula of the compound must be $C_4H_8O_2$, since the relative mass of "C_2H_4O" is only 44, but that of $C_4H_8O_2$ is 88.

Q.7.10 What is the empirical formula of each of the following compounds:—propene C_3H_6; ethanoic acid $C_2H_4O_2$; ethyl ethanoate $C_4H_8O_2$; benzene C_6H_6; dichloroethane $C_2H_4Cl_2$; tetrachlorobutane $C_4H_6Cl_4$?

Q.7.11 Find the empirical formula of each of the following compounds, from its percentage composition:

(a)   zinc 80.3%, oxygen 19.7%

(b)   tin 62.6%, chlorine 37.4%

(c)   iron 70%, oxygen 30%

(d)   sulphur 21.9%, fluorine 78.1%.

Q.7.12 Calculate the empirical formulae of the compounds which contain the following:

(a)   sulphur 23.7%, oxygen 23.7%, chlorine 52.6%

(b)   sodium 32.2%, zinc 45.4%, oxygen 22.4%

(c)   magnesium 12.0%, chlorine 34.9%, water 53.1%.

(d)   magnesium 9.8%, sulphur 13.0%, oxygen 26.0%, water 51.2%

Q.7.13 Find the simplest formula of the compounds which contain the following;

(a)   sodium 29.1%, sulphur 40.5%, oxygen 30.4%

(b)   barium 56.15%, chlorine 29.10%, water 14.75%

Q.7.14 A compound contains 26.6% of potassium, 35.5% of chromium, and the rest is oxygen. Calculate its empirical formula.

Q.7.15 An organic compound contains 40% carbon, 6.7% hydrogen and 53.3% oxygen. Find its empirical formula. Find also its molecular formula if its molecular mass is

(a)   60; (b)   90.

Q.7.16 A compound of relative molecular mass 34 contains 5.88% hydrogen and 94.12% oxygen. What is the compound?

Gravimetric Analysis

The principle of gravimetric analysis (analysis based on the weighing of substances) is that the substance being determined is either (a) converted to a compound of known composition, or (b) extracted from the compound containing it. The substance formed is then isolated, purified and weighed. The result(s) obtained can then be used to calculate a percentage composition or an empirical formula.

The success of a gravimetric analysis depends on (i) accuracy in weighing, (ii) cleanliness of apparatus, and (iii) ensuring the NONE of the required substance(s) is lost at any stage in the analysis. The following illustrate some of the standard gravimetric procedures.

Experiment 7.1.
To determine water of crystallisation in hydrated salt.

Water of crystallisation in a compound can usually be driven off by heating the compound. It is thus easily determined — the compound is weighed, heated sufficiently, cooled and reweighed.

Weigh a clean dry crucible and lid and then accurately weigh into it about 3 g of crystals of the given salt. Place the crucible on a pipeclay triangle on a tripod and heat gently for a few minutes with the lid a little to one side. Then increase the temperature and heat to dull redness for five minutes. Allow to cool for ten minutes and reweigh. Calculate the percentage of water in the salt.

Results

Mass of crucible and lid . . . .

Mass of crucible, lid and crystals . . . .

Mass of crystals . . . .

Mass of crucible, lid and anhydrous salt . . . .

Mass of water driven off (*i.e.* loss in mass) . . . . . .

Percentage of water of crystallisation in the salt . .

Calculation of Formulae from Experimental Results

Worked Example 5

In an experiment 2.6 g of chromium were heated in an excess of chlorine and it was found that 7.93 g of a chloride of chromium was formed. Calculate the empirical formula of the chromium chloride. If its molecular mass was found to be 158, what is the molecular formula for the compound?

Mass of chromium chloride = 7.93 g

Mass of chromium = 2.6 g

$\therefore$ Mass of chlorine = 5.33 g

If the mass of each element in the compound is known, there is no need to calculate the percentage of each present, because the ratio in grams will be the same as the percentage ratio. Hence:

Element	Mass Present	Mass $\overline{A_r}$	Ratio
Chromium	2.6 g	$\frac{2.6}{52} = 0.05$	1
Chlorine	5.33 g	$\frac{5.33}{35.5} = 0.15$	3
$\therefore$ Empirical Formula = CrCl$_3$			

Since $M_r = 158$, and

$$CrCl_3 = 52 + 3(35.5) = 158.5$$

the molecular formula is the same as the empirical formula.

$$\text{Formula} = CrCl_3$$

Experiment 7.2
To determine the Empirical Formula of Copper Iodide.

Copper iodide on being strongly heated, decomposes into its elements. In this experiment, a weighed sample of it is decomposed, the iodine is released as iodine vapour, and the copper which remains is then weighed. Calculation leads to the mass of iodine released, and to the empirical formula for the compound.

Weigh, as accurately as possible, a clean dry test tube. Add 2 to 3 g of copper iodide and reweigh. In the fume cupboard, heat the test tube, gently at first and then

more strongly, until no more purple vapour of iodine is evolved. Allow the tube to cool and reweigh.

Calculate
(i) the mass of copper iodide taken,

(ii) the mass of copper remaining,

(iii) the mass of iodine evolved,

(iv) the number of moles of copper,

(v) the number of moles of iodine atoms,

(vi) the empirical formula for the copper iodide.

Experiment 7.3
To find Percentage of Gas Evolved when Sodium Hydrogencarbonate is decomposed.

All metal hydrogencarbonates decompose on being heated, releasing carbon dioxide and water vapour, and forming the corresponding carbonate. In this experiment, the compound being investigated is sodium hydrogencarbonate, and so sodium carbonate is formed.

Weigh, as accurately as possible, a clean dry evaporating basin, along with a glass stirring rod. Add about 5 g of sodium hydrogencarbonate and reweigh. Place the basin on a tripod and gauze, and heat, gently at first and then more strongly, until all of the carbon dioxide has been evolved (it should be obvious when this stage has been reached). Stirring the solid with the glass rod during the heating will help the process. Allow to cool, and reweigh.

Calculate the mass of the hydrogencarbonate taken originally, the mass of the carbonate remaining, and hence the mass of gas evolved. Express this as a percentage of the original mass.

List the results as follows:

Mass of empty basin . . . . =

Mass of basin + hydrogencarbonate . . . =

Mass of hydrogencarbonate taken . . . . . =

Mass of basin + residual carbonate . . . . =

Mass of carbonate formed . . . . =

Mass of CO_2 and H_2O released . . . . ⎞ =
Loss of Mass . . . . ⎠

Percentage loss of mass . . . . =

Further work:

Make dilute solutions of
(i) the original sodium hydrogencarbonate, and
(ii) the final sodium carbonate.

To each add some magnesium sulphate solution. Observe and explain what happens.

Experiment 7.4
To find the Formula of "Black Copper Oxide"

Copper is a transition metal and has therefore variable valency. It has two oxides, one black and the other reddish-brown. In this experiment, the black oxide is prepared from copper metal, and its formula determined.

Copper is not easily oxidised to copper oxide because it is low in the electrochemical series. However, on reaction with nitric acid (which is a good oxidising agent), it is oxidised to copper nitrate — and the nitric acid reduced to nitrogen dioxide in the process. Copper salts are easily decomposed (for the same reason as copper is not easily oxidised), and copper nitrate on being heated yields copper oxide — nitrogen dioxide again being formed, along with another gas. By finding the mass of the initial copper and the mass of the final copper oxide, the formula for the compound can be calculated.

Procedure

Weigh an empty boiling tube, add about 1 g of copper pieces and reweigh. Very carefully, add about 6 cm^3 of concentrated nitric acid from a burette or small graduated cylinder and place the boiling tube in the fume cupboard for the reaction to occur. When all the copper has reacted, heat gently and evaporate to dryness — still working in the fume cupboard. Then continue heating until all the copper nitrate (which is green) has been converted to black copper oxide. Allow the tube to cool, and reweigh.

Record your results in table form, as shown below. From the mass of copper and its relative atomic mass (63.5) calculate the number of moles of it present. Likewise, calculate the number of moles of oxygen atoms present. The simplest whole number ratio between the amounts of copper and oxygen is the empirical formula for the copper oxide.

Results

Mass of empty boiling tube . . . . =
Mass of boiling tube + copper . . . . =
Mass of copper . . . . =
Mass of boiling tube + copper oxide . . . =
Mass of copper oxide . . . . =
Mass of oxygen in the copper oxide . . . . =
Number of moles of copper present . . . . =
Number of moles of oxygen atoms present=

Empirical formula for the copper oxide . . =

Experiment 7.5
To find the Formula of "Copper Carbonate" by its Thermal Decomposition

Many metal carbonates decompose on being heated, releasing carbon dioxide and forming an oxide of the metal e.g.,

$$copper\ carbonate \rightarrow CuO + CO_2$$

Since copper is a transition metal, "copper carbonate" could refer to copper(I) carbonate or to copper(II) carbonate. By finding the ratio of CuO to CO_2 in the carbonate, its formula may be deduced.

Weigh a clean dry crucible and lid. Place in it about 5 g of copper carbonate and reweigh. Place the crucible and lid on a pipeclay triangle over a tripod. Heat it, gently at first and then more strongly, for about 10 minutes. Allow to cool and reweigh.

Calculate the mass of the copper carbonate taken, the mass of the copper oxide remaining and hence the mass of the carbon dioxide released. By using the relative molecular masses of copper oxide (79.5) and of carbon dioxide (44), find the number of moles of (i) copper oxide, and (ii) carbon dioxide. The mole ratio of CuO to CO_2 is the same as the mole ratio of Cu to CO_3. Hence find out if the given compound was copper(I) carbonate (Cu_2CO_3) or copper(II) carbonate ($CuCO_3$).

Specimen results:

Mass of crucible + lid . . . . = 18.24 g

Mass of crucible, lid + carbonate. = 23.70 g

Mass of crucible + lid + oxide .. = 21.76 g

Worked Example 6

In an experiment, 15 g of sodium sulphate crystals on being heated left a residue of 7.95 g of the anhydrous salt. Calculate (a) the percentage of water of crystallisation in the crystals, and (b) the value of "x" in the formula $Na_2SO_4xH_2O$.

(a)   Mass of crystals ....15.00 g
        Mass of anhydrous salt................... 7.95 g
  ∴ Mass of water of crystallisation ... 7.05 g

$$\text{Percentage water} = \frac{7.05 \times 100}{15.00} = 47\%$$

(b)   Mass of anhydrous salt...............7.95 g $\Big)$ *
        Mass of water.............................7.05 g

        Molecular mass of Na_2SO_4 ....142 $\Big)$ *
        Molecular mass of xH_2O ....$18x$

(* these pairs of values must be in the same ratio.)

$$\therefore \frac{7.95}{7.05} = \frac{142}{18x}, \quad \text{Solve for } x; \; x = 7$$

$$x = 7, \therefore Na_2SO_4 \, 7H_2O$$

Q.7.17   A stream of chlorine was passed over 1.12 g of heated iron fillings. The mass of the product was found to be 3.25 g.

(a)   How many moles of iron reacted?
(b)   What mass of chlorine was present in the compound?
(c)   How many moles of chlorine **atoms** are present?
(d)   In what ratio did the atoms combine?
(e)   What was the formula for the product?
(f)   What is its correct name?

Q.7.18   Sketch a suitable apparatus in which a stream of dry hydrogen could be passed over heated copper oxide. In such an experiment, 4.3 g of the oxide was reduced to 3.8 g of copper. Calculate the formula for the copper oxide and write an equation for the reaction which occurred.

Q.7.19   Lead iodide on being strongly heated, decomposes into its elements. In an experiment, the following measurements were obtained:

Mass of test tube .... 30.11 g
Mass of test tube + lead iodide   .... 33.56 g
Mass of test tube + lead .... 31.66 g

Calculate the number of moles of
(i) lead atoms, and
(ii) iodine atoms, and hence find the formula of the lead iodide.

Q.7.20   Copper on being reacted with sulphur, forms a copper sulphide. In an experiment 1.00 g of copper formed 1.25 g of the sulphide. Calculate its formula.

Q.7.21   In an experiment, a sample of copper weighing 1.23 g was converted to copper iodide. This compound, when purified, was found to weigh 3.69 g. Calculate
(i) the percentage of iodine in the copper iodide, and
(ii) the empirical formula for the compound.

Q.7.22   In an experiment to find the formula of zinc carbonate, a 2.50 g sample of it was heated until all of the carbon dioxide which it contained was evolved. The residue of zinc oxide (ZnO) was found to weigh 1.62 g. Calculate
(i) the percentage of carbon dioxide in the carbonate, and
(ii) the formula for the zinc carbonate.

Q.7.23   A hydrated aluminium sulphate $Al_2(SO_4)_3 \, x \, H_2O$, contains 8.1% of aluminium by mass. Find the value of x.

Q.7.24   Many substances crystallise in a hydrated form. Chlorine gas, when cooled sufficiently, crystallises as a hydrate Cl_2xH_2O. When 21.5 g of chlorine hydrate are decomposed, 14.4 g of water are obtained. Determine the value of x.

Q.7.25   In an experiment, 4.9 g of a metal X formed 8.1 g of its oxide, XO. Calculate the relative atomic mass of the metal.

Q.7.26   The oxide of a trivalent metal contains 31.6% of oxygen. Calculate the relative atomic mass of X.

Q.7.27   An oxide of the type XO_2 contains 36.8% of oxygen. Calculate the relative atomic mass of X.

Calculation of the Reacting Masses of Substances.

A balanced chemical equation, as well as showing what substances react and what substances are produced, shows also the quantities of each of those substances. Consider the equation:

$$C + O_2 \rightarrow CO_2$$

The information given here is that 1 atom of carbon combines with 1 molecule of oxygen to produce 1 molecule of carbon dioxide.

It also means that 1 mole of carbon atoms (*i.e.* 6×10^{23}) combines with 1 mole of oxygen molecules to produce 1 mole of CO_2 molecules. The mass of 1 mole of carbon atoms is 12 g. 1 mole of oxygen molecules is 32 g (*i.e.* O_2) and that of 1 mole of CO_2 molecules is 44 g, so therefore the equation also tells that 12 g of carbon combine with 32 g of oxygen to produce 44 g of carbon dioxide.

C	+	O_2	$\rightarrow$	CO_2
1 atom	+	1 molecule	$\rightarrow$	1 molecule
1 mole	+	1 mole	$\rightarrow$	1 mole
12 g	+	32 g	$\rightarrow$	44 g

The volume of a gas which is produced (or which reacts) in a chemical change may also be determined from the chemical equation, by making use of the fact that 1 mole of very gas occupies 22.4 litres (at s.t.p.) or 24 litres (at room temperature).

Worked Example 7

A problem such as "What mass of zinc sulphate, and what volume of hydrogen (at s.t.p.) are produced when 6.5 g of zinc react with excess dilute sulphuric acid" is solved as follows:

Zn	+	H_2SO_4	$\rightarrow$	$ZnSO_4$	+	H_2
1 atom	+	1 molecule	$\rightarrow$	1 molecule	+	1 molecule

Since the acid is in excess, the quantities of the products depend only on the mass of zinc used. No information is required about the amount of the acid used, and so in this problem, there is no need to include it in the calculations. From the information given by the equation, 1 mole of zinc atoms (= 65 g) produces 1 mole of zinc sulphate (= 161 g) and 1 mole of hydrogen (= 2 g); the latter occupies 22.4 litres (at s.t.p).

Zn + H_2SO_4	$\longrightarrow$	$ZnSO_4$	+ H_2		
1 mole	$\longrightarrow$	1 mole	+ 1 mole		
65 g	$\longrightarrow$	161 g	+ 2 g	=	22.4 L
6.5 g	$\longrightarrow$	16.1 g	+ 0.2 g	=	2.24 L

The answer therefore to the problem is that 6.5 g of zinc reacts with excess acid to produce 16.1 g of zinc sulphate and 2.24 litres of hydrogen (at s.t.p.).

The final example is of a problem involving calculation of moles mass, and volume, in the same chemical reaction.

Worked Example 8

Copper reacts with concentrated sulphuric acid according to the equation:

$$Cu + 2H_2SO_4 \rightarrow CuSO_4 + SO_2 + 2H_2O$$

If, in such a reaction, 12.7 g of copper were used, calculate the following;

(a)   the number of moles of copper used;

(b)   the number of moles of sulphuric acid required;

(c)   the mass of copper sulphate produced;

(d)   the volume (at room temperature) of sulphur dioxide formed;

(e)   the number of molecules of sulphur dioxide.

Solution

(a)   63.5 g Cu = 1 mol.

$\therefore$ 12.7 g $= \dfrac{12.7}{63.5}$ mol $= 0.2$ mol

(b)   Refer to balanced equation:

Cu	+	$2H_2SO_4$	$\longrightarrow$	....
1 mol	+	2 mol		
$\therefore$ 0.2 mol	+	0.4 mol		

(c)

Cu + $2H_2SO_4$	$\longrightarrow$	$CuSO_4$ + ...
1 mol	$\longrightarrow$	1 mol
$\therefore$ 0.2 mol	$\longrightarrow$	0.2 mol

1 mol $CuSO_4$ = 159.5 g

$\therefore$ 0.2 mol = (0.2 $\times$ 159.5) g = 31.9 g

(d)   Again, from equation,

0.2 mol Cu $\longrightarrow$ 0.2 mol SO_2

Amount of SO_2 = 0.2 mol

= 0.2 $\times$ 24 litres (at room temp.)

= 4.8 litres

(e)   Moles of SO_2 = 0.2

Number of molecules = (0.2 $\times$ 6 $\times$ 10^{23})

= 1.2 $\times$ 10^{23}

Questions

Q.7.28   What (i) mass and (ii) volume of chlorine (at room temperature and pressure), combines with 4.6 g of sodium?

Q.7.29 Iron burns in chlorine to form iron(III) chloride. Write a balanced equation for the reaction. Calculate the mass of iron(III) chloride formed from 14 g of iron.

Q.7.30 What is the mass and the volume (at room temperature and pressure) of oxygen which combines exactly with 4.8 g of magnesium?

Q.7.31 Work out the values which are missing from the following statement.

One mole of Ca (....g) and half a mole of oxygen gas (...g) combine to form ... mol of calcium oxide (...g). 4.0 g of calcium and ...g of oxygen combine to form ....g of calcium oxide. When 0.4 g of calcium reacts with oxygen, the increase in mass is ....g. If 6 moles of calcium oxide were decomposed to calcium and oxygen, ... moles of Ca and ... moles of oxygen gas would be obtained. The percentage of calcium in calcium oxide is ...%

Q.7.32 What mass of each of the following elements combines with exactly 22.4 litres of oxygen:
(a) magnesium; (b) hydrogen: (c) carbon; (d) potassium?

Q.7.33 Nitrogen can be made to combine directly with hydrogen to produce ammonia, NH_3. Calculate the volume (at s.t.p.) of nitrogen which combines with exactly (a) 6 litres of hydrogen; (b) 6 g of hydrogen.

Q.7.34 Joseph Priestly discovered oxygen in 1774 by using a burning glass to focus the heat of the sun on "red calx of mercury" (now called mercury(II) oxide). On doing this, the compound decomposed. Write an equation for the reaction. Calculate (a) the mass and (b) the volume of oxygen (at room temperature and pressure) which would be produced by decomposing 10.8 g of mercury(II) oxide.

Q.7.35 Nitrous oxide, N_2O (often known as "laughing gas') can be made by heating ammonium nitrate, NH_4NO_3. The one other product is an everyday substance. Write an equation for the reaction. Calculate the mass and volume (at s.t.p) of nitrous oxide formed by heating 40 g of ammonium nitrate.

Q.7.36 From the time of their discovery up to the mid 'sixties, it was thought that the noble gases could not form compounds and they were usually called the "inert" gases. A number of their compounds are now known, however, and have been prepared. Xenon hexafluoride (hex = 6) is prepared by the direct combination of the elements. Write an equation for its preparation. Calculate the mass of fluorine needed to prepare 22.8 g of xenon hexafluoride.

Q.7.37 "Washing soda" has the formula $Na_2CO_31OH_2O$.

(a) Calculate the % of water of crystallisation in washing soda crystals

(b) Calculate
(i) the mass and
(ii) the volume of carbon dioxide (at s.t.p) evolved, when 28.6 g of washing soda crystals are reacted with excess dilute acid.

Q.7.38. Methane burns in air to form carbon dioxide and water (vapour). Write a balanced equation for the reaction. Assuming that 16 g of methane are burned, calculate the following.

(a) the volume of that methane;

(b) the volume of oxygen required for combustion.

(c) the volume of CO_2 formed

(d) the mass of water formed.

Q.7.39 Sodium hydrogencarbonate on being heated, decomposes and is changed to sodium carbonate, carbon dioxide and water vapour.

(a) Write a balanced equation for the reaction.

(b) Calculate the mass of sodium carbonate obtained when 16.8 g of sodium hydrogen-carbonate is completely decomposed.

(c) What volume of CO_2 (at s.t.p) is liberated in the same reaction?

Q.7.40 In a reaction, 4.35 g of manganese dioxide reacted completely with concentrated hydrochloric acid according to:

$$MnO_2 + 4HCl \rightarrow MnCl_2 + Cl_2 + 2H_2O$$

(a)   How many moles of MnO_2 is 4.35 g?
(b)   How many moles of HCl were needed?
(c)   What mass of $MnCl_2$ was produced?
(d)   What volume of Cl_2 at s.t.p. was produced?
(e)   What was the number of chlorine molecules?

Q.7.41 Nitrogen dioxide is produced in the reaction between copper and concentrated nitric acid according to the equation:

$$Cu + 4HNO_3 \rightarrow Cu(NO_3)_2 + 2NO_2 + 2H_2O.$$

In a reaction, 25.4 g of copper was reacted with sufficient concentrated nitric acid to complete the reaction:

(a)   How many moles of nitric acid were required?
(b)   What mass of nitric acid was required?
(c)   If "concentrated nitric acid" has a density of 1.5 g/cm^3, what volume of the concentrated acid was required?

(d)   What mass of $Cu(NO_3)_2$ was produced?
(e)   How many moles of NO_2 were formed?
(f)   What was the volume, at s.t.p., of the NO_2?
(g)   How many molecules of water were produced in the reaction?

Review   When you know Chapter 7 you should be able to:

(a)   Calculate the relative mass of a compound from its formula.

(b)   Calculate the percentage of any element in a compound, given its formula.

(c)   Calculate the empirical formula of a compound, given its composition.

(d)   Describe experiments in which
(i) the amount of water of crystallisation in a compound is found,
(ii) the empirical formula of a compound is determined.

(e)   Calculate the amounts, masses and volumes of reacting substances, from given chemical equations.

8

Acids, Bases & Salts

For many hundreds of years acids have been recognised as a group of compounds which have a number of properties in common: sour taste; ability to change the colour of certain dyes, *e.g.* litmus; corrosive action on common metals; reaction with metal carbonates to produce carbon dioxide; ability to neutralise bases.

There have been various definitions of just what an acid is; in the eighteenth century it was described as a compound containing hydrogen which can be replaced by a metal, to form another compound called a salt.

Towards the end of the last century, Arrhenius proposed the more precise definition:

> **an acid is a substance which produces H^+ ions in solution, and a base is a substance which produces OH^- ions in solution.**

Neutralisation was then the reaction in which H^+ and OH^- ions combined to form water, *i.e.*

$$H^+ + OH^- \rightarrow H_2O$$

While these definitions were satisfactory for many purposes, they have been found to be generally inadequate in several ways:

(i) H^+ ions are no longer accepted as having an independent existence in solution; they are known to become hydrated — forming H_3O^+ ions, called hydronium ions.

(ii) The nature of the solvent often determines whether a substance is acidic or not. Hydrogen chloride (HCl) for example acts as an acid when dissolved in water, but when dissolved in methylbezene (toluene), it shows no acidic properties whatever — the solution does not affect litmus, react with carbonates or conduct electricity.

(iii) NH_3, which neutralises acids and forms salts similar to those formed by NaOH, is not regarded as a base by the Arrhenius definition.

(iv) There are many reactions in which neither H^+ nor OH^- ions are involved but which are essentially the same as those in which H^+ and OH^- ions do take part. The Arrhenius definitions would not class such reactions as neutralisations.

Brønsted-Lowry Definitions

In 1923, much more general definitions of acids and bases were put forward, independently, by two chemists, J.N. Brønsted, who was Danish, and T.M. Lowry, of England. These Brønsted-Lowry definitions (as they are known) are:

> **An acid is a substance (molecule or ion) which can donate protons, and a base is a substance which can accept protons.**

Remembering that a proton is a hydrogen ion (H^+) the Brønsted-Lowry definition is not completely different from the earlier definition.

$$HCl \longrightarrow H^+ + Cl^- \qquad (1)$$
$$\text{acid} \qquad \text{proton}$$

$$HNO_3 \longrightarrow H^+ + NO_3^- \qquad (2)$$
$$\text{acid} \qquad \text{proton}$$

$$OH^- + H^+ \longrightarrow H_2O \qquad (3)$$
$$\text{base} \quad \text{proton}$$

$$NH_3 + H^+ \longrightarrow NH_4^+ \qquad (4)$$
$$\text{base} \quad \text{proton}$$

In order for a proton to be donated by one substance, another substance must be present to accept it, *i.e.* a base. An acid can only act in the presence of a base, and an acid-base reaction is one in which a proton is transferred from one substance to another.

In aqueous solution, HCl acts as an acid; the proton which it donates (equation (1) above) is accepted by a water molecule forming an hydronium[i] ion :

$$H^+ + H_2O \longrightarrow H_3O^+$$

Water thus acts as the Brønsted base. The net change is that a proton is transferred from the HCl molecule to a water molecule; see Fig.8.1:

$$HCl + H_2O \longrightarrow H_3O^+ + Cl^- (5)$$

When dissolved in methylbezene, HCl is unable to act as an acid because methylbezene molecules ($CH_3C_6H_5$) being non-polar, are unable to accept protons. A HCl molecule is an acid in the presence of ammonia (NH_3), because the latter can accept protons (equation (4) above). The net change here is the transference of a proton from each HCl molecule (the Brønsted acid) to each ammonia (the Brønsted base):

$$HCl + NH_3 \longrightarrow NH_4^+ + Cl^-$$

Two water molecules can react with each other, one acting as an acid and the other as a base, see Fig. 8.2:

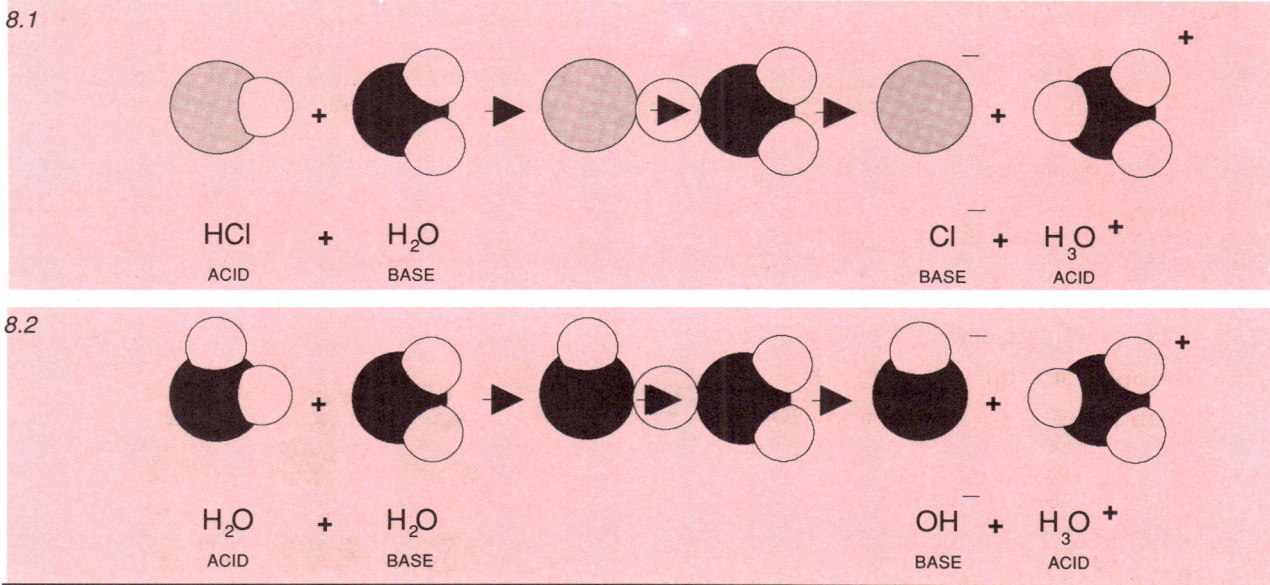

8.1

$$HCl \quad + \quad H_2O \qquad\qquad\qquad Cl^- \quad + \quad H_3O^+$$
ACID   BASE   BASE   ACID

8.2

$$H_2O \quad + \quad H_2O \qquad\qquad\qquad OH^- \quad + \quad H_3O^+$$
ACID   BASE   BASE   ACID

(i)   also known as the oxonium ion.

$$H_2O + H_2O \rightarrow H_3O^+ + OH^-$$

This is what happens when water ionises — which it does to a very small extent.

> **A substance which can act both as an acid and as a base is described as amphoteric.**

In a way, the terms **acid** and **base** can be thought of, not so much as labels for substances, but as an indication of the way in which a substance reacts. However, most substances which are classified as acids only react as acids and most which are classified as bases only react as bases. It is only a few substances which can react in both ways. Water, as explained is one. Hydrogen fluoride, HF, is another, for a molecule of it can both donate and accept a proton:

as an acid: $HF \rightarrow H^+ + F^-$

as a base : $HF + H^+ \rightarrow H_2F^+$

Conjugate Pairs

> **Two substances which differ by a proton are called a conjugate pair.**

When a Brønsted acid donates a proton, it is converted to its conjugate base:

$$\underset{\substack{\text{Brønsted} \\ \text{acid}}}{HCl} \rightarrow H^+ + \underset{\substack{\text{conjugate} \\ \text{base}}}{Cl^-}$$

Cl^- is the conjugate base of the acid HCl.

Conversely, when a Brønsted base accepts a proton, it becomes its conjugate acid:

$$NH_3 + H^+ \rightarrow NH_4^+$$

NH_4^+ is the conjugate acid of the base NH_3.

Other examples of conjugate pairs are:

$$\underset{\text{acid}}{H_2O} \text{ and } \underset{\text{base}}{OH^-} \; ; \quad \underset{\text{acid}}{HNO_3} \text{ and } \underset{\text{base}}{NO_3^-} \; ;$$

$$\underset{\text{acid}}{H_3O^+} \text{ and } \underset{\text{base}}{H_2O} \; .$$

Q.8.1. From each of the following equations name the Brønsted acid and the Brønsted base and list the two conjugate pairs present: (cont..)

(a) $HNO_3 + H_2O \rightarrow H_3O^+ + NO_3^-$
(b) $H_2O + H_2S \rightarrow H_3O^+ + HS^-$
(c) $H_2CO_3 + OH^- \rightarrow HCO_3^- + H_2O$
(d) $NH_2^- + H_2O \rightarrow NH_3 + OH^-$
(e) $NH_3 + H_2SO_4 \rightarrow HSO_4^- + NH_4^+$

Q.8.2   What are the conjugate bases of each of the following Brønsted acids: HCN; $HClO_3$; NH_4^+; H_2S; HF; H_2O; H_2SO_4?

Q. 8.3   What are the conjugate acids of each of the following Brønsted bases: HCO_3^-; NH_2^-; H_2O; Cl^-; SO_4^{2-}; HF; NH_3?

Q.8.4
(a)   What is the conjugate base of each of the following acids; H_2CO_3; HSO_4^-; C_6H_5OH; NH_3; HCO_3^-; H_2?

(b)   What is the conjugate acid of each of the following bases: ClO_4^-; HSO_4^-; HF; H^-; H_2O; CO_3^{2-}?

Properties of Acids

Regardless of how acids are defined, they all have many similar properties. The three common laboratory acids or "mineral" acids are **hydrochloric, nitric** and **sulphuric** acids. Of these, the latter two are dangerous corrosive liquids and this is probably responsible for the general ideal that all acids are highly dangerous liquids with mysterious powers of eating through metals, clothes and flesh. This is very much a false idea; many acids are solids and many occur in everyday substances, including foods.

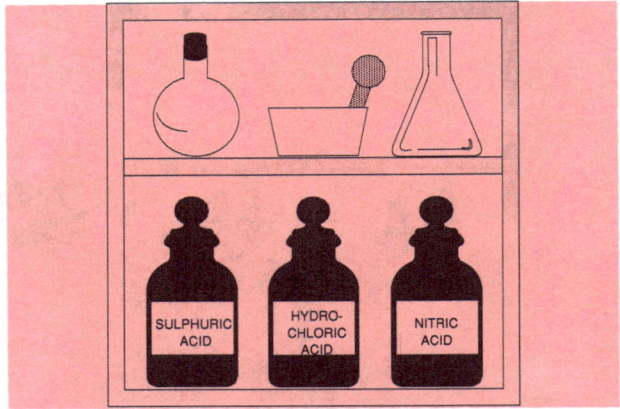

8.3 — The three common laboratory acids, H_2SO_4 HCl, HNO_3.

1.   An important property of acids is that they **form salts when they react.** Sulphuric acid, for example, reacts with zinc to produce zinc sulphate and hydrogen:

$$Zn + H_2SO_4 \rightarrow ZnSO_4 + H_2$$

Zinc sulphate is the salt formed in this reaction. All the salts formed from sulphuric acid are called sulphates; likewise, hydrochloric acid forms salts called chlorides and nitric acid forms nitrates.

2.   Acids **liberate carbon dioxide from metal carbonates** and hydrogencarbonates, in addition to forming salts and water:

$$Na_2CO_3 + H_2SO_4 \rightarrow Na_2SO_4 + H_2O + CO_2$$

$$ZnCO_3 + 2HCl \rightarrow ZnCl_2 + H_2O + CO_2$$

$$NaHCO + HNO_3 \rightarrow NaNO_3 + H_2O + CO_2$$

This latter reaction is often used as a test for acids or acidic substances. Hydrogencarbonates are very easily decomposed, even by very weak acids, so if carbon dioxide is liberated when a substance is added to it, that substance is acidic.

3.   Acids have a **sour taste**; the taste of sour milk, for example, is due to lactic acid and that of lemon juice is due to citric acid.

4.   Acids **change the colour of various vegetable dyes** and other chemical compounds — such substances are described as indicators. Litmus, which is the best known indicator, is red in acidic solution and blue in alkaline solution.

5.   Acids **ionise in aqueous solution** and hence conduct electricity. This is discussed more fully on page 197.

Basicity of Acids

This is the number of available protons or replaceable hydrogen atoms per molecule of acid. Simple acids like hydrochloric (HCl) and nitric (HNO_3) acids contain only one available proton and such acids are known as **monobasic** or monoprotic. Sulphuric acid is an example of a **dibasic** acid since it has two available protons per molecule:

$$H_2SO_4 \rightarrow 2H^+ + SO_4^{2-}$$

Phosphoric(V) acid is the only common example of a **tribasic** acid. It has the formula H_3PO_4 and three protons are obtainable from each molecule of it.

Bases

In practical terms, the most important property of a base is that when it reacts with an acid, it produces a salt (and water). In such a reaction — which is called a **neutralisation** — both the acid and the base lose their characteristic properties. Most of the bases found in the laboratory are either metal oxides, metal hydroxides, or ammonia.

ACID   ALKALI

8.4 — *Neutralisation*

Some reactions of acids with bases are illustrated

Acid	+	Base	→	Salt	+	Water
H_2SO_4 Sulphuric acid	+	CuO Copper(II) oxide	→	CuSO4 Copper(II) sulphate	+	H_2O
$2HNO_3$ Nitric acid	+	PbO Lead(II) oxide	→	Pb(NO3)2 Lead(II) nitrate	+	H_2O
HCl Hydrochloric acid	+	NaOH Sodium hydroxide	→	NaCl Sodium chloride	+	H_2O
H_2SO_4 Sulphuric acid	+	Mg(OH)2 Magnesium hydroxide	→	MgSO4 Magnesium sulphate	+	$2H_2O$

Alkalis

An alkali is a base which is soluble in water.

All alkalis form OH^- ions in solution and the most important of them are sodium hydroxide (NaOH), potassium hydroxide (KOH), calcium hydroxide [Ca(OH)$_2$] and ammonia (NH$_3$). The latter requires some explanation.

Ammonia is a gas and has the formula NH_3. When it reacts with water, it accepts a proton and forms the ammonium ion NH_4^+:

$$NH_3 + H_2O \rightarrow NH_4^+ + OH^-$$

Because of the OH^- ions which are also formed, the solution is alkaline.

When ammonia reacts with an acid, it forms an **ammonium** salt, since it contains the ammonium ion:

$$NH_3 + HCl \rightarrow NH_4Cl \ (NH_4^+ \text{ and } Cl^-)$$
ammonium chloride

$$NH_3 + HNO_3 \rightarrow NH_4NO_3 \ (NH_4^+ + NO_3^-)$$
ammonium nitrate

Ammonium salts are very similar to sodium and potassium salts.

Remember,

NH_3 = ammon**IA** (the compound)

NH_4 ....= ammon**IUM**........

Properties of Alkalis

1. The strong alkalis (NaOH and KOH) are good solvents for oil and grease and hence are corrosive to handle; their solutions have a slippery, soapy feel because they react with the skin. They are commonly called caustic soda and caustic potash (caustic = "burning").
2. Solutions of alkalis affect indicators — reversing the colour change caused by acids.
3. Like all bases, alkalis neutralise acids, producing salts and water.
4. Alkalis ionise in aqueous solution and hence conduct electricity:

$$NaOH \rightarrow Na^+ + OH^-$$

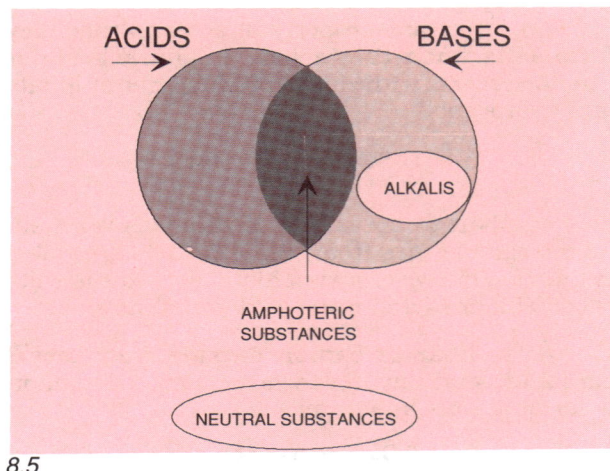

8.5

Salts

An acid and a base react together to produce a salt and water. A salt is the compound produced when the hydrogen of the acid is replaced by a metal — or by the ammonium radical (NH_4^+).

The name of the salt is derived from both the metal and the acid. The group of atoms which makes up the non-metal part of the salt — and behaves in many ways like a single atom — is known as a **radical**. Sulphuric acid (H_2SO_4) for example, can be converted to zinc sulphate ($ZnSO_4$) or to sodium sulphate (Na_2SO_4). The group of atoms consisting of one sulphur and four oxygen atoms is the sulphate radical.

A radical cannot exist on its own; it must be combined with either hydrogen or a metal (or both in some cases) — which means that each radical has a definite valency. This is due to the fact that such a group of atoms exist as a negative ion in solution, carrying one or more extra electrons. Such negative ions are known as **anions**. The common radicals and anions are listed opposite.

Radical	Formula	Valency	Ion
Nitrate	NO_3	1	NO_3^-
Hydroxide	OH	1	OH^-
Hydrogen-carbonate	HCO_3	1	$HCO3^-$
Sulphate	SO_4	2	$SO4^{2-}$
Sulphite	SO_3	2	$SO3^{2-}$
Carbonate	CO_3	2	$CO3^{2-}$
Phosphate	PO_4	3	$PO4^{3-}$
Ammonium	*NH_4*	*1*	*NH_4^+*

The ammonium radical is somewhat different to the others; it behaves as a metal atom because it exists as a positive ion in solution (just like Na^+ or K^+). Ammonium chloride for example consists of NH_4^+ and Cl^- ions.

When a compound contains a radical, the valency of the radical must be satisfied — just as valencies of elements must be satisfied in compounds. Zinc sulphate is $ZnSO_4$, but zinc nitrate is $Zn(NO_3)_2$; this is because the sulphate and nitrate radicals have different valencies. When the same radical occurs twice in a formula, it is written in brackets, with a small "2" following it — as in the formula for zinc nitrate above.

The name of a salt consists of the names of both the metal and the acid radical. When lead reacts with nitric acid, the salt formed is thus lead nitrate.

The formation of a salt from its corresponding acid can be carried out in several ways, *viz*, by reacting the acid with the metal, with the metal oxide or hydroxide (*i.e.* with a base) or with the metal carbonate. The following equations show examples of these reactions:

$$\underset{\text{metal}}{Mg} + \underset{\text{acid}}{2HCl} \longrightarrow MgCl_2 + H_2$$

$$\underset{\substack{\text{metal}\\\text{oxide}}}{CuO} + \underset{\text{acid}}{H_2SO_4} \longrightarrow CuSO_4 + H_2O$$

$$\underset{\text{alkali}}{KOH} + \underset{\text{acid}}{HNO_3} \longrightarrow KNO_3 + H_2O$$

$$\underset{\substack{\text{metal}\\\text{carbonate}}}{CaCO_3} + \underset{\text{acid}}{2HCl} \longrightarrow CaCl_2 + H_2O + CO_2$$

Insoluble salts can be formed by a reaction known as "ion exchange". Such a reaction can be represented in general by:

$$AX + BY \longrightarrow AY + BX$$

where A and B are metal atoms and X and Y are acid radicals. For the reaction to occur, both AX and BY must be soluble salts and either AY or BX must be insoluble. On mixing the reactants, the insoluble product is precipitated.

For example, when solutions of barium chloride and sodium sulphate are mixed, insoluble barium sulphate is precipitated:

$$BaCl_2 + Na_2SO_4 \rightarrow BaSO_4 (\downarrow) + 2NaCl.$$

Solubilities of salts in water

The following generalisations apply to the salts of the common metals:

1. **Salts which are soluble**: all sodium, potassium and ammonium salts; all nitrates and hydrogencarbonates, all chlorides except those of silver, lead and mercury(I); all sulphates except those of barium, lead and calcium.

2. **Salts which are insoluble**: all carbonates except those of sodium, potassium and ammonium; all hydroxides [i] except those of sodium, potassium, ammonium, calcium (slightly soluble) and barium (slightly soluble).

Questions

Q.8.5 Give the names of the salts produced in each of the following reactions:-

(a) magnesium + sulphuric acid;
(b) magnesium + nitric acid
(c) magnesium + hydrochloric acid;
(d) silver + nitric acid;

(i) Hydroxides are bases rather than salts; but are included here for convenience.

(e)   silver + sulphuric acid
(f)   lithium + hydrochloric acid;
(g)   calcium + nitric acid;
(h)   lithium + sulphuric acid;
(i)   aluminium + nitric acid
(j)   zinc + hydrochloric acid;
(k)   nickel + sulphuric acid;
(l)   barium + nitric acid.

Q.8.6   Give the name of each of the following compounds and state whether it is an acid, a base or a salt;

HCl;	$MgSO_4$;	$FeCl_3$;	$Cu(OH)_2$
NaOH;	$CaCl_2$;	Na_2CO_3;	KNO_3;
NaCl;	HNO_2;	CuO;	H_2CO_3.
MgO;	Fe_2O_3;	$CuSO_4$;	

Q.8.7   Using the valencies of both elements and radicals, write the formula of each of the following compounds:—

magnesium sulphate;   potassium hydroxide;
magnesium chloride;   zinc sulphate;
magnesium hydroxide;   zinc hydroxide;
magnesium carbonate;   zinc bromide;
magnesium nitrate

Q.8.8   Write down the formula for each of the following compounds:

zinc nitrate;   iron(II) sulphate;
copper(I) chloride;   iron(III) sulphate;
copper(II) chloride;   aluminium sulphate;
copper(I) sulphate;   aluminium carbonate;
copper(II) sulphate;   lead(II) nitrate;
tin(II) nitrate;
tin(IV) nitrate;

Q.8.9   Write and balance the equations for each of the following reactions:

(a)   magnesium + sulphuric acid→
                magnesium sulphate + hydrogen
(b)   zinc + hydrochloric acid→
                zinc chloride + hydrogen
(c)   zinc oxide + hydrochloric acid →
                zinc chloride + water
(d)   zinc oxide + nitric acid → zinc nitrate + water
(e)   sodium hydroxide + sulphuric acid →
                sodium sulphate + water
(f)   zinc hydroxide + sulphuric acid →
                zinc sulphate + water

(g)   potassium hydroxide + nitric acid →
                potassium nitrate + water
(h)   copper(II) oxide + nitric acid →
                copper(II) nitrate + water
(i)   magnesium carbonate + sulphuric acid →
      magnesium sulphate + carbon dioxide + water
(j)   magnesium carbonate +   nitric acid →
      magnesium nitrate + carbon dioxide + water.

Q.8.10   Write and balance equations for each of the following reactions:

(a)   iron + sulphuric acid →
(b)   iron(II) oxide + sulphuric acid→
(c)   iron(II) oxide + hydrochloric acid →
(d)   iron(III) oxide + hydrochloric acid →
(e)   iron(III) oxide + nitric acid →
(f)   magnesium hydroxide + hydrochloric acid→
(g)   magnesium hydroxide + sulphuric acid→
(h)   **magnesium hydroxide + nitric acid** →
(i)   calcium carbonate + hydrochloric acid→
(j)   sodium carbonate + nitric acid→
(k)   aluminium oxide + sulphuric acid →
(l)   ammonia + sulphuric acid→

Experiment 8.1
Preparation of copper(II) sulphate (from copper(II) oxide and sulphuric acid)

Take about 50 cm^3 of dilute sulphuric acid and heat it to near boiling (until bubbles begin to appear). Remove the heat source. Add copper(II) oxide, in small portions at a time, until no more will react, *i.e.* until there is excess on the bottom of the beaker (about 7 g will be required). Filter the solution into an evaporating basin and set it aside to crystallise. When this has happened, remove the crystals and dry them on absorbent paper. If desired, the rest of the solution may be further crystallised by evaporating it to about half its volume and again setting it aside to cool and crystallise.

Further work

Lead(II) nitrate may be prepared in an identical manner. Use about 50 cm^3 of dilute nitric acid and 10 g of lead(II) oxide. Evaporate the solution slightly before leaving it to crystallise.

Experiment 8.2
Preparation of magnesium sulphate (from magnesium carbonate and sulphuric acid).

Measure about 50 cm^3 of dilute sulphuric acid into a beaker. Add magnesium carbonate, in small portions at a time, until no more will react, *i.e.* until a portion of it when added and stirred, causes no further effervescence and some unreacted solid remains in the beaker. Heat the solution to boiling and then filter it into an evaporating basin. Evaporate the filtrate until the solid begins to separate and then set the basin aside to cool. When it is cold, decant off the remaining solution and dry the crystals on absorbent paper.

Further work

Barium chloride may be prepared in an identical manner. Take about 25 cm^3 of dilute hydrochloric acid and add barium carbonate in the manner described above.

Experiment 8.3
Tests for Acid Radicals or Anions

The chemical tests used to confirm the presence of the common radicals or anions are described in their appropriate chapters. These can be found as follows:

Chlorides, bromides, iodides, page 295
Sulphates, sulphites, thiosulphates, page 282, 283
Nitrates, page 242
Carbonates, hydrogencarbonates, pages 230-232

Carbonates and Hydrogencarbonates

To about 1 g of the solid carbonate or hydrogencarbonate in a test tube, add about 5 cm^3 of dilute hydrochloric acid. Insert a stopper fitted with a bent glass tube, such as that shown. Pass the gas which is formed through limewater. The formation of a milky precipitate means that the gas is carbon dioxide and the original compound is a carbonate or hydrogencarbonate.

Now prepare dilute solutions of both the carbonate and hydrogencarbonate by dissolving about 0.1 g of each (as much as will fit on the tip of a spatula) in about 5 cm^3 of water. To distinguish between them, add about the same volume of magnesium sulphate solution to each. The formation of a precipitate confirms the presence of

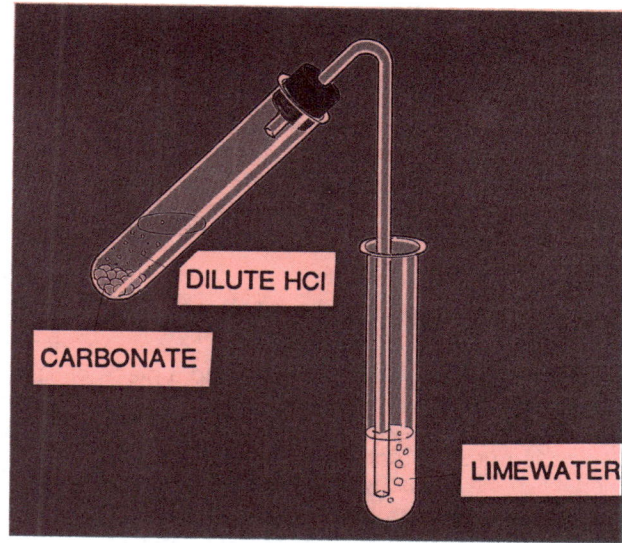

8.6

a carbonate, whereas the absence of a precipitate means that the substance is a hydrogencarbonate.

Sulphates and Sulphites

Prepare dilute solutions of these by dissolving about 0.1 g of each in about 5 cm^3 portions of water. To each add 1 or 2 cm^3 of barium chloride solution. Note that each forms a white precipitate.

To both tubes add about the same volume of dilute hydrochloric acid. The sulphite precipitate dissolves whereas the sulphate precipitate remains.

Thiosulphates

To a small quantity of thiosulphate crystals, add a few cm^3 of dilute hydrochloric acid. Note the formation of a yellow precipitate of sulphur and the characteristic smell of sulphur dioxide gas.

Halides (chlorides, bromides and iodides)

Prepare dilute solutions of these by dissolving about 0.1 g of each in about 5 cm^3 of water. To each add a few drops of silver nitrate solution. Note that the chloride forms a white precipitate, the bromide gives a yellowish precipitate and the iodide produces a distinctly yellow one.

To each tube then add about the same volume of ammonia solution and invert to mix. The chloride precipitate fully dissolves, the bromide partially dissolves and the iodide precipitate remains.

Nitrates

To a solution of a nitrate in water, add about an equal volume of freshly-prepared iron(II) sulphate solution. Mix the solutions by inverting the tube several times. Hold the tube in a sloping position and **slowly and carefully** pour some concentrated sulphuric acid down the inside of the tube. The formation of a brown ring at the junction of the two liquids confirms the presence of the nitrate ion.

Testing for Sulphur dioxide

This gas can be identified either by its characteristic smell of burning sulphur, or by holding a piece of filter paper which has been dipped in acidified potassium permanganate solution in the gas. If the permanganate (which is purple in colour) is decolorised by the gas, then it is most probably sulphur dioxide.

How Acidic is an Acid?— pH

So far, substances have been classified as either acidic or alkaline — which is all litmus indicator can tell about them. But there are degrees of acidity and alkalinity and these are measured on a scale of numbers called the pH scale — which goes from 0 to 14.

A substance which is neutral has a pH of 7; a pH of less than 7 means that the substance is acidic and a pH of more than 7 indicates an alkaline substance. The further away from 7 that the pH of a substance is, the stronger it is. Thus, strong acids have very low pH values and strong alkalis have very high values. pH is explained fully in Chapter 14.

Strong and Weak Acids

"Strong" and "weak" are terms which are applied to acids (and bases) according to the extent of how much they dissociate into ions (i.e. ionise) in solution — or to how readily they donate protons.

A strong acid is one which is largely dissociated in solution; it **donates protons readily** and therefore exists in solution mainly as ions. In dilute hydrochloric acid, for example, there are few undissociated molecules — practically all have ionised:

$$HCl \rightleftharpoons H^+ + Cl^-, \text{ or more fully,}$$

$$HCl + H_2O \rightleftharpoons H_3O^+ + Cl^-$$

The other strong acids of importance are sulphuric (H_2SO_4) and nitric (HNO_3). Solutions of such acids have low pH values and have high electrical conductivities because they are present mainly as ions.

A weak acid is one which is only slightly dissociated in solution; it **is a poor donor of protons** and exists in solution mainly as undissociated molecules. Ethanoic (acetic) acid is a common example of a weak acid; in dilute solution (1.0 M) only four molecules in each thousand are dissociated:

$$CH_3COOH \rightleftharpoons H^+ + CH_3COO$$

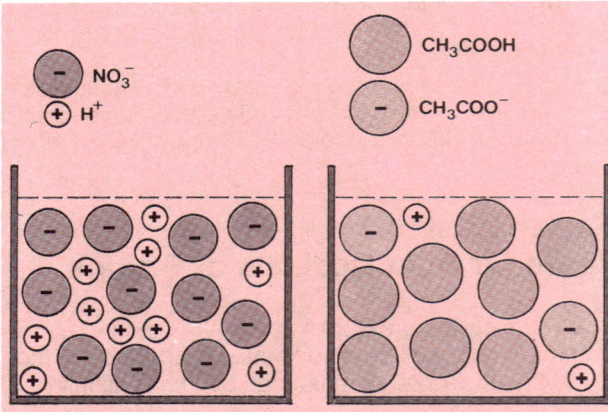

8.7

Other weak acids are carbonic (H_2CO_3), phosphoric (H_3PO_4) and most of the organic acids. Such acids have pH values in the region of 4 to 5 and are weak electrolytes, i.e. they have poor electrical conductivity in solution.

It follows from the above that since HCl readily donates protons, then the Cl^- ion (its conjugate base) has little tendency to combine with or accept a proton, i.e. Cl^- is a weak base:

$$\underset{\substack{\text{strong} \\ \text{acid}}}{HCl} + H_2O \rightleftharpoons H_3O^+ + \underset{\substack{\text{weak} \\ \text{base}}}{Cl^-}$$

Conversely, since CH_3COOH is a poor proton donor (it is more stable as undissociated molecules), then the CH_3COO^- ion (its conjugate base) is a good proton acceptor, i.e. it is a strong base.

$$CH_3COOH + H_2O \xleftarrow{\quad} H_3O^+ + CH_3COO^-$$
weak
acid
strong
base

A strong acid has therefore a weak conjugate base and a weak acid has a strong conjugate base. The weaker the acid, the stronger the conjugate base.

Note "strong" and "weak" as applied to acids must not be confused with "concentrated" and "dilute"; the latter terms refer to the amount of acid (which can be either strong or weak) per unit volume — this is usually expressed in either grams per litre or moles per litre. "Bench Sulphuric Acid" is a dilute solution of a strong acid (it usually contains about 1.5 moles of H_2SO_4 per litre) but it is almost completely dissociated. "Glacial Acetic Acid" is concentrated (there are about 18 moles per litre) but is weak, since little, if any, is dissociated into ions.

Strong and Weak Bases

Similar definitions apply to bases. **A strong base is a good acceptor of protons and a weak base is a poor acceptor.** The OH^- ion is a strong base since it readily combines with any available proton (to become H_2O) but NH_3 accepts protons much less readily and is therefore a weak base:

$$OH^- + H^+ \xleftarrow{\quad} H_2O$$
strong
base
weak acid

$$NH_3 + H^+ \xleftarrow{\quad} NH_4^+$$
weak
base
strong
acid

A strong base has a weak conjugate acid and a weak base has a strong conjugate acid.

Relative Strengths of Conjugate Acid and Base Pairs.

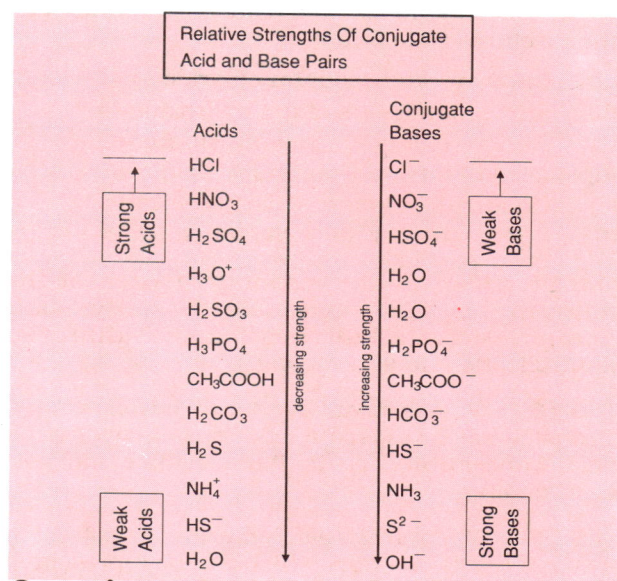

Questions

Q.8.11. Write out each of the following equations and mark (a) the acids, (b) the bases and (c) the two conjugate pairs present.

(i) $$H_2S + H_2O \xleftarrow{\quad} H_3O^+ + HS^-$$

(iii) $$CH_3COO^- + H_2O \xleftarrow{\quad} OH^- + CH_3COOH$$

(iii) $$H_3O^+ + NH_3 \xleftarrow{\quad} NH_4^+ + H_2O$$

(iv) $$H_2O + H_2SO_4 \xleftarrow{\quad} H_3O^+ + HSO_4^-$$

(v) $$HNO_3 + H_2F_2 \xleftarrow{\quad} H_2NO_3^+ + HF_2$$

(vi) $$O^{2-} + H_2O \xleftarrow{\quad} OH^- + OH^-$$

(vii) $$NaNH_2 + H_2O \xleftarrow{\quad} NH_3 + NaOH$$

Q.8.12 What is the name of each of the following compounds: $AgNO_3$; $FeCl_2$; $FeCl_3$; K_2SO_4; $KHSO_4$; $CuSO_4$; Cu_2SO_4; Na_2CO_3; $NaHCO_3$; NH_4Cl; $(NH)_2SO_4$; PbO; PbO_2; Na_3PO_4; Na_2SO_4; Na_2SO_3; $MnSO_4$; $Mn_2(SO_4)_3$; $(NH_4)_2CO_3$.

Q.8.13 The following are ion exchange reactions in which an insoluble compound is produced. Write the equation for each reaction and underline the insoluble compound:

(a) Silver nitrate + sodium chloride →
(b) Zinc sulphate + sodium hydroxide →
(c) Barium chloride + sodium sulphate →
(d) Lead(II) nitrate + sulphuric acid →
(e) Copper(II) sulphate + barium nitrate →
(f) Sodium carbonate + calcium nitrate →

Q.8.14 Explain the meaning of each of the following terms:— diatomic; basicity; salt; amphoteric; alkali; dibasic; diprotic; neutralisation; ionise; radical.

Q.8.15 What is meant by each of the following:— Brønsted acid; conjugate acid; strong acid; weak acid; concentrated acid; dilute acid; monobasic acid; organic acid?

Q.8.16 When hydrogen chloride dissolves in water, a reaction occurs which can be represented by: $HCl + H_2O \rightarrow H_3O^+ + Cl^-$

Which compound in this reaction is the acid, and which is the base? When the solution of hydrogen chloride is mixed with sodium hydroxide solution, another reaction occurs. What name is given to this type of reaction. Write an equation to represent it.

Q.8.17 Distinguish between each of the following pairs of terms; (a) Brønsted acid and Brønsted base; (b) strong acid and weak acid; (c) strong acid and concentrated acid; (d) base and alkali; (e) sulphurous acid and sulphuric acid.

Q.8.18 From the list of compounds given below select:

(a) a compound that is not a salt;
(b) two insoluble salts
(c) a coloured salt;
(d) table salt;
(e) a compound which reacts with sulphuric acid to give a white precipitate;
(f) two compounds which would react together to form a precipitate;
(g) the precipitate which would be formed (in the reaction mentioned in (f)).

NH_4Cl; $CuSO_4$; $NaCl$; $NaOH$; $BaCl_2$; $AgCl$; $MgCl_2$; $BaSO_4$

Q.8.19 Rewrite the following paragraph, selecting the correct word from each of the pairs enclosed by brackets.
Acids are compounds, most of which dissolve in water to produce (hydrogen/hydroxide) ions. Sulphuric acid is one example. It is (strong/weak) acid, which can be neutralised by (acids/alkalis) to form salts called (nitrates/sulphates). Many (metals/non-metals) react with acids to give a gas called (hydrogen/carbon dioxide). Solutions of acids are (good/poor) conductors of electricity. They often affect indicators. For example, phenolphthalein turns (pink/colourless) in acids, while litmus turns (red/blue). The strength of an acid is shown by its (concentration/pH) value. The (higher/lower) the number, the stronger the acid.

Q.8.20 Four colourless solutions P, Q, R and S are:
dilute HCl; $BaCl_2$; Na_2SO_4 and Na_2CO_3 (but not in that order). The table shows the effect of mixing each pair of substances. Identify each of the lettered compounds.

	P	Q	R
Q	White ppt.	—	—
R	White ppt.	—	—
S	—	gas evolved	—

Review When you know Chapter 8, you should be able to:

(a) define: Brønsted acid, Brønsted base, conjugate acid, conjugate base, conjugate pair, and give an example of each.
(b) select each of the above substances from any acid-base equation, *e.g.*
$HSO_4^- + NH_3 \rightarrow NH_4^+ + SO_4^{2-}$
(c) give the names and formula for the common laboratory acids and alkalis,
(d) list the characteristic properties of the above,
(e) write the correct formula for any named salt,
(f) write the balanced equation for any acid-base or for any acid-carbonate reaction,
(g) explain what an ion exchange reaction is,
(h) explain the differences between strong and weak acids, and give examples of each,
(i) explain; amphoteric, monobasic, dibasic, radical, base, alkali.

Volumetric analysis is a system of chemical analysis which is based on the measurement of volumes of solutions which react together — as distinct from gravimetric analysis, which is based on weighings only. In general, a volumetric analysis is carried out by finding the volume of one solution (whose concentration is known) which reacts exactly with a given volume of another solution — in a known chemical reaction, *e.g.* an acid reacting with an alkali.

Concentration

There are several ways of expressing the concentration of a solution:

1. The most useful method in chemistry is in terms of the number of moles of the substance per litre of solution (mol/L) (N.B. A litre is the same as a decimetre cubed, dm^3).

2. Mass (sometimes incorrectly called "weight") per unit volume, abbreviated w/v. The most usual units are grams per litre (g/L).

3. Mass per unit mass (w/w), *e.g.* the number of grams of the substance per 100 g of the solvent, and this is usually referred to simply as a percentage.

4. Parts per million (p.p.m.). This is mainly used for very dilute solutions (or suspensions) and is the number of parts of the substance per million parts of the liquid. Milligrams per litre (mg/L) are the same as p.p.m., since a litre of water has a mass of a million milligrams.

Concentrations in volumetric analysis are mainly expressed in moles per litre.

Definitions and relationships

A solution which contains one mole of a substance per litre of solution is known as a **molar solution** of that substance. For example, a molar solution of sulphuric acid contains 98 g (H_2SO_4 = 98) of the acid per litre of solution. The concentration of a solution expressed in moles of the substance per litre of solution is known as the **molarity** of the solution. For example, a solution of sulphuric acid containing 49 g (= 0.5 mol) of sulphuric acid per litre of solution is 0.5 molar (0.5 M).

A **standard solution** of a substance is one whose concentration is known, *e.g.* 0.2 molar, 10 grams per litre (which may be written as 10 g/L).

9

Volumetric Analysis I

The concentration of a solution in grams per litre is equal to its molarity multiplied by the molecular mass of the solute *e.g.* 0.5 M sulphuric acid contains 49 g of H_2SO_4 (= 0.5 mol = 0.5 × 98 g) per litre of solution.

Concentration (in g/L) =
                          Molarity × **Molar mass**

No. of moles = Volume (in L) × **Molarity**

No. of grams = No. of moles × **Molar Mass**

Questions

Q.9.1   What is the concentration (in g/L) of each of the following solutions

(a)   1.0 M HCl,
(b)   0.2 M NaOH,
(c)   0.1 M H_2SO_4,
(d)   5 M HNO_3,
(e)   0.2 M KOH,
(f)   0.05 M $Mg(OH)_2$

Q.9.2   How many moles of HNO_3 are in each of the following solutions?

(a)   1 litre of 2 M HNO_3,
(b)   100 cm^3 of 2 M HNO_3,
(c)   100 cm^3 of 0.5 M HNO_3,
(d)   100 cm^3 of 10 M HNO_3,
(e)   100 cm^3 of x M HNO_3,

Q.9.3   How many grams of NaOH are in each of the following solutions?

(a)   1 litre of 2 M NaOH,
(b)   1 litre of 0.2 M NaOH,
(c)   0.5 litre of 0.2 M NaOH,
(d)   2 litres of 0.5 M NaOH.

Q.9.4   What is the molarity of each of the following solutions?

(a)   20 g of NaOH per litre,
(b)   5.85 g of NaCl in 500 cm^3,
(c)   4.9 g of H_2SO_4 in 200 cm^3,
(d)   5.4 g of $KHCO_3$ in 500 cm^3

(e)   6.3 g of HNO_3 in 250 cm^3,
(f)   3 g of $H_2C_2O_4$ in 10 cm^3.

Q.9.5   How many grams of each of the various solutes are required to prepare:

(a)   1 litre of 1.0 M H_2SO_4,
(b)   2 litres of 1.0 M NaCl,
(c)   500 cm^3 of 0.1 M HNO_3,
(d)   250 cm^3 of 0.5 M NaOH,
(e)   100 cm^3 of 0.2 M KOH,
(f)   250 cm^3 of 0.5 M Na_2CO_3.

Standard Solutions

In the determination of the concentration of an acid, a standard solution of an alkali is used, and conversely, to determine the concentration of an alkali, a standard acid is required. However, before any determinations at all can be made, a starting, accurately standardised solution is required — from which to standardise (*i.e.* find the exact concentration of) other solutions.

Standard solutions of the common laboratory acids and alkalis cannot be prepared directly, for various reasons; hydrochloric acid is a solution of a gas in water, so that it is not easy to obtain 36.5 g (1 mole) of "HCl"; sulphuric acid is supplied at approximately 98% purity (the rest being water), so that 98 g of the acid is not 98 g (1 mole) of H_2SO_4; nitric acid is volatile so that an exact quantity of that it cannot be weighed out. Sodium and potassium hydroxides cannot be weighed out accurately, since both of these substances are deliquescent and by the time that a certain quantity might be weighed out, some moisture would be present in that quantity.

Anhydrous sodium carbonate is obtainable in a very pure state and it is easy to dry, weigh out, and dissolve in water. Such a substance is called a **primary standard**. A molar solution of this substance contains 106 g (Na_2CO_3 = 106) of it in 1 litre of solution. However, for the standardisation of approimately molar hydrochloric acid, half molar (0.5 M) sodium carbonate is more useful. 0.5 M sodium carbonate thus contains 53 g (0.5 × 106) of Na_2CO_3 per litre.

Experiment 9.1
To Prepare 0.5 M Sodium Carbonate Solution

0.5 M sodium carbonate contains 53 g of the solute per litre of solution. However, a litre of solution will not be required, and 250 cm³ is quite sufficient. This volume contains 13.25 g (53/4) of the sodium carbonate.

Weight out accurately 13.25 g of pure dry anhydrous sodium carbonate. Take about 100 cm³ of water in a beaker and, **WHILE STIRRING CONTINUOUSLY,** slowly add the sodium carbonate. Failure to do this will result in the formation of a hard dense lump of the solid, which will not dissolve easily. Keep stirring until all of the solid has dissolved.

Pour the solution into a 250 cm³ volumetric flask, rinse the beaker with water and pour this rinse water into the flask also. Repeat this once more, and then add water to bring the solution up to the mark on the neck of the flask (a wash bottle is very helpful for this). Stopper the flask and mix well by inverting the flask several times. This solution should now be exactly 0.5 M.

When an acid and an alkali neutralise each other, the ratio of the number of moles of acid to the number of moles of alkali depends on which acid and which alkali are reacting. For example, when hydrochloric acid neutralises sodium hydroxide, the ratio is 1:1, but when sulphuric acid neutralises sodium hydroxide, the ratio is 1:2, since each mole of acid reacts with 2 moles of alkali.

$$HCl + NaOH \rightarrow NaCl + H_2O$$

$$H_2SO_4 + 2NaOH \rightarrow Na_2SO_4 + 2H_2O$$

Q.9.6 Complete and balance the following equations, and hence find the number of moles of acid and alkali which neutralise each other.

(a) $HCl + KOH \rightarrow$

(b) $H_2SO_4 + KOH \rightarrow$

(c) $HNO_3 + KOH \rightarrow$

(d) $HCl + Ca(OH)_2 \rightarrow$

(e) $HNO_3 + Mg(OH)_2 \rightarrow$

(f) $HNO_3 + NaOH \rightarrow$

(g) $HCl + Mg(OH)_2 \rightarrow$

If 25 cm³ of 1.0 M HCl neutralises 50 cm³ of NaOH solution, then it should be seen that since the volume of alkali is twice the volume of acid, the concentration of the alkali must be half that of the acid, *i.e.* 0.5 M. It is not so obvious though, that if, for example, 25 cm³ of 1.2 M HCl neutralises 30 cm³ of NaOH, the latter must be 1.0 M. However, it is possible to derive a formula which relates all the different variables in such a problem. This important formula is:

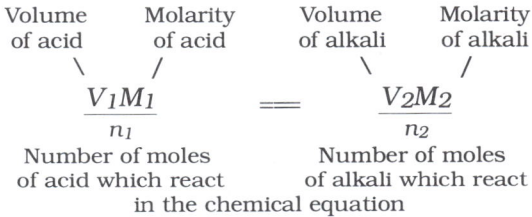

Note : This same relationship applies to reactions between oxidising agents and reducing agents.

Titrations

The standard solution of sodium carbonate just prepared can be used to find out the concentration of (*i.e.* to **standardise**) a solution of hydrochloric acid.

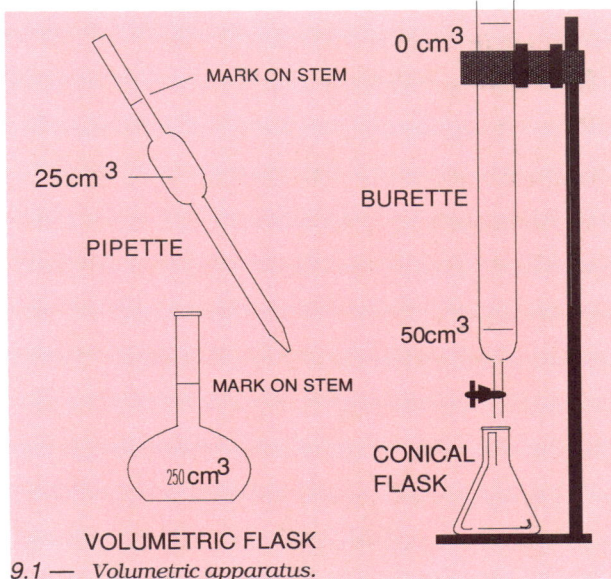

9.1 — *Volumetric apparatus.*

This is done by finding out what volume of acid is required to neutralise a given volume (usually 25 cm^3) of the 0.5 M sodium carbonate solution. The latter solution is accurately measured out (by pipette) into a conical flask, and the quantity of acid needed to neutralise it is found by running the acid from a burette into the flask until a suitable indicator, also in the flask, changes colour. This process is called a **titration** and the amount of solution added from the burette is known as the **titre**. Methyl orange is a suitable indicator to show the "end point" of this reaction as it changes colour at the correct pH value. A titration is usually done several times, and the average titre used in the calculations.

Worked Example 1

A solution of hydrochloric acid was standardised by titrating it against 0.5 M sodium carbonate, using methyl orange indicator. The results of titrating the acid against 25 cm^3 portions of the sodium carbonate were as follows:

Burette Readings	Trial 1	Trial 2	Trial 3	Trial 4
1st reading	0.0	23.2	0.0	22.6
2nd reading	23.2	45.9	22.6	45.4
Titres	23.2	22.7	22.6	22.8

Calculate the concentration of the acid in (i) moles per litre and (ii) grams per litre.

Solution

Ignoring the first titre (which is inconsistent with the others), the average works out to be 22.7 cm^3

Titration conclusion:

$$25 \text{ cm}^3 \ 0.5 \text{ M Na}_2\text{CO}_3 \equiv 22.7 \text{ cm}^3 \text{ HCl}$$

Balanced equation

$$\text{Na}_2\text{CO}_3 + 2\text{HCl} \rightarrow 2\text{NaCl} + \text{H}_2\text{O} + \text{CO}_2$$

$$\frac{V_1 M_1}{n_1} = \frac{V_2 M_2}{n_2}$$

$$\frac{25 \times 0.5}{1} = \frac{22.7 \times x}{2}$$

$$x = \frac{25 \times 0.5 \times 2}{22.7 \times 1} = 1.1 \text{ M}$$

Result: the acid is 1.1 molar, or its concentration is 1.1 moles per litre. Since 1 mol of HCl is 36.5 g, then its concentration in grams per litre is $1.1 \times 36.5 = 40.15$ g/L.

Experiment 9.2
To Standardise a Solution of Hydrochloric Acid

Fill the burette (see note 1) with the acid to be standardised. Pipette 25 cm^3 (see note 2) of 0.5 M sodium carbonate solution into a conical flask and add a few drops of methyl orange indicator. Note the reading on the burette. While continuously shaking or swirling the flask, run in the acid from the burette until the indicator changes colour. If a white tile is placed underneath the flask, the colour change is much easier to see and hence the "end point" will be more accurately found. Note the final reading on the burette and hence find the volume of acid needed to neutralise the carbonate solution. Record your results in table form, as in the worked example.

Wash out the conical flask and repeat the titration at least twice. These latter titrations should be done more accurately, and if their results are not consistent, a further titration should be carried out.

mean titre	——— cm^3
conclusion	——— cm^3 of 0.5 M NaCO$_3$
neutralises =	——— cm^3 of x HCl

Using the relationship

$$\frac{V_1 M_1}{n_1} = \frac{V_2 M_2}{n_2}$$

and the information given in the titration conclusion and in the balanced equation, calculate the concentration of the hydrochloric acid in (i) moles per litre and (ii) grams per litre.

Notes

1. A burette should be either clean and dry before being filled, or should be washed with the solution which it is going to contain. To do this, pour about 10 cm^3 of the solution into the burette

(use a funnel, and make sure that the burette tap is closed), then tilt and rotate it so that the inside surfaces are rinsed with the solution. Empty this solution into the sink. Fill the burette with the solution (again using the funnel) Open the top momentarily so that the glass jet below it becomes filled with the solution. Remove the funnel from the top of the burette and it is then ready for use.

2. A pipette should either be clean and dry before use, or should be washed with what it is going to contain. Do this by sucking up into it a small amount of the solution, swirling it around inside, and then emptying this solution into the sink. When emptying a pipette, let it drain by itself and do not blow out the last drop: a pipette is designed to deliver the stated volume without blowing.

Once a supply of both acid and alkali have been standardised, analysis of the most acidic and basic substances can be carried out. The following worked examples illustrated what sort of analyses can be done, and how the calculations are worked out in such experiments.

Worked Example 2

10.0 g of impure sodium hydroxide were weighed out, dissolved in water and solution made up to 250 cm^3 in a volumetric flask. 25 cm^3 of this solution, on being titrated with 1.1 M HCl, required 21.8 cm^3 of the acid for neutralisation. Calculate the % purity of the original sodium hydroxide.

Titration conclusion:

$$25 cm^3 \; x \; NaOH \equiv 21.8 \; cm^3 \; 1.1 \; M \; HCl$$

Balanced equation:

$$NaOH + HCl \rightarrow NaCl + H_2O$$

$$\frac{V_1 M_1}{n_1} = \frac{V_2 M_2}{n_2}$$

$$\frac{25 \times x}{1} = \frac{21.8 \times 1.1}{1}$$

$$x = \frac{21.8 \times 1.1}{25}$$

$$= 0.96 \; M$$

The concentration of sodium hydroxide was 0.96 moles of NaOH per litre; the actual volume of the solution was 250 cm^3 (i.e. one quarter litre) so

the number of moles of NaOH present was $\frac{0.96}{4}$, which is 0.24.

1 mole of NaOH has a mass of 40 g; 0.24 mole is therefore 0.24 × 40 g i.e. 9.6 g. The actual mass of NaOH present in the 10 g of impure sodium was thus 9.6 g.

The % purity is therefore, $\frac{9.6 \times 100}{10}$ = 96%

Worked Example 3

In an experiment to find the amount of water of crystallisation in "Washing Soda" (hydrated sodium carbonate), 7.15 g of the crystals were dissolved in water and made up to a volume of 250 cm^3 of solution. 25 cm^3 portions of this solution were titrated with 0.25 M hydrochloric acid and the average titre was found to be 20.0 cm^3. Calculate (i) the percentage of water in the crystals, and (ii) y in the formula $Na_2CO_3 \; yH_2O$.

Let the molarity of the sodium carbonate solution be x.

Titration conclusion :

$$25 \; cm^3 \; x \; Na_2CO_3 \equiv 20 \; cm^3 \; 0.25 \; M \; HCl$$

Balanced equation:

$$Na_2CO_3 + 2HCl \rightarrow 2NaCl + CO_2 + H_2O$$

$$\frac{V_1 M_1}{n_1} = \frac{V_2 M_2}{n_2}$$

$$\therefore \frac{25 \times x}{1} = \frac{20 \times 0.25}{2}$$

Solve for x; x = 0.1 mol/L = 0.025 mol /250 cm^3

Amount of Na_2CO_3 present =

$$0.025 \; mol = 0.025 \times 106 \; g = 2.65 \; g$$

Mass of Na_2CO_3 crystals (i.e. $Na_2CO_3 yH_2O$) = 7.15 g

Therefore mass of water of crystallisation =

$$7.15 - 2.56 = 4.50 \; g$$

$$\%H_2O = \frac{4.5 \times 100}{7.15} = 62.9 \, \%$$

	£
Calcium chloride hexahydrate	500 g **2.04**
"AnalaR"	3 kg **7.54**
$CaCl_2.6H_2O$ M. W. 219.08	50 kg **POA**
Description: Colourless deliquescent	
crystals	
Minimum assay 98.0%	
Maximum Limits of Impurities	
Insoluble matter 0.003%	
Free Acid (HCL) 0.0007%	
Free alkali 0.02ml N%	
Nitrate (NO_3) 0.001%	
Phosphate (PO_4) 0.001%	
Silicate (SiO_4) 0.005%	
Ammonium (NH_4) 0.0025%	
Aresenic (As) 0.0001%	
Barium and strontium (Ba + Sr) 0.01%	
Iron (Fe) 0.0002%	
Heavy metals (Pb) 0.0005%	
Magnesium (Mg) 0.01%	
Potassium (K) 0.005%	
Sodium (Na) 0.05%	

Sulphuric Acid	2.5 1 **1.51**
H_2SO_4 M. W. 98.08	
Assay (acidimetric) 97 - 99%	
Wt. per ml at 20^0 C About 1.835 g	
Maximum Limits of Impurities	
Non-volatile matter 0.01%	
Hydrochloric acid (HCl) 0.01%	
Nitric acid (HNO_3) 0.001%	
Aresenic (As) 0.0002%	
Iron (Fe) 0.002%	
Lead (Pb) 0.002%	
Reducing substances 0.02 ml N%	

Zinc oxide "AnalaR"	500 g **1.70**
ZnO M. W. 81.38	1 kg **3.29**
Description: A white amorphous powder	2 kg **6.10**
Minimum assay (after ignition) 99.7%	30 kg **POA**
Maximum Limits of Impurities	
Acid-insoluble matter 0.01%	
Loss at 600^0 C 0.5%	
Carbonate (CO_3) 0.25%	
Chloride (Cl) 0.002%	
Sulphur Compounds (SO_4) 0.01%	
Aresenic (As) 0.0001%	
Cadmium (Cd) 0.002%	
Iron (Fe) 0.0003%	
Lead (Pb) 0.02%	
Manganese (Mn) 0.001%	
Metallic zinc (Zn) 0.002%	
Reducing substances (O) 0.0016%	

9.2 — *Chemicals of 100% purity are virtually non-existant; even analytical grade ('Analar') chemicals contain impurities. Chemical catalogues give details of the impurities in each of the substances listed. These three extracts are taken from the catalogue of a major chemical supplier.*

Mass of Na_2CO_3 = 2.65 g

Mass of water of crystallisation = 4.50 g

Molecular mass of Na_2CO_3 = 106

Molecular mass of yH_2O = 18y

Therefore, $\dfrac{2.65}{4.50} = \dfrac{106}{18y}$

Solve for y; $y = 10$

Formula for compound = $Na_2CO_3 10H_2O$

Experiment 9.3
To Standardise Sodium Hydroxide Solution

Use the same acid in the burette as in the previous experiment. Pipette 25 cm^3 of the sodium hydroxide solution into a conical flask and add a few drops of indicator (any indicator is suitable). Titrate with the acid in the manner already described. Carry out three titrations, record the results in table form, and calculate the average titre.

Write out the titration conclusion and the balanced equation for the reaction. As before, calculate the concentration of the alkali. Express the result in (i) moles per litre and, (ii) grams per litre.

Experiment 9.4
To Determine the Percentage of Water of Crystallisation in "Washing Soda" (hydrated sodium carbonate).

Weigh out accurately about 10 g of washing soda crystals. Dissolve these in about 100 cm^3 of water in a beaker, and pour the solution into a 250 cm^3 volumetric flask. Rinse the beaker twice and pour the rinse water into the flask each time. Make the solution up to the 250 cm^3 mark with water. Stopper the flask and mix well.

Pipette 25 cm^3 of the solution into a conical flask, add a few drops of methyl orange indicator and titrate with 0.5 M hydrochloric acid until the indicator changes colour. Carry out three titrations, record the results in table form and calculate the average titre.

Write the titration conclusion and the balanced equation for the reaction. Calculate the concentration of the carbonate solution, expressing the results in (i) moles per litre (ii) grams per litre, and (iii) grams per 250 cm^3.

Hence the mass of actual (*i.e.* anhydrous) Na_2CO_3 is found. Subtract this from the mass of Na_2CO_3 crystals in order to find the mass of the water of crystallisation.

Calculate the percentage of water of crystallisation in the crystals.

Finally, calculate the formula for the crystals (*i.e.* "*y*" in the formula $Na_2CO_3yH_2O$) by using the relationship:

$$\frac{\text{Mass of anhydrous } Na_2CO_3}{\text{Mass of water of crystallisation}} =$$

$$\frac{\text{Relative molecular mass of } Na_2CO_3}{\text{Relative molecular mass of } y\,H_2O}$$

(A worked example of this calculation is given on page 92)

Experiment 9.5
To find the Percentage of Ethanoic Acid in Vinegar

This determination is done by titrating a solution of vinegar against standard alkali. The reaction between ethanoic acid and sodium hydroxide is given by:

$$CH_3COOH + NaOH \rightarrow CH_3COONa + H_2O$$

Measure out 25 cm^3 of vinegar and dilute this to exactly 100 cm^3 with water. This is most conveniently done in a 100 cm^3 volumetric flask, but if such is not available, mix the 25 cm^3 of vinegar with 75 cm^3 of water, measured out by using the pipette three times. Mix the solution well.

Pour the diluted vinegar into a burette and titrate against 25 cm^3 portions of sodium hydroxide, using phenolphthalein indicator. Carry out three titrations and record the results in the usual manner.

Write out the titration conclusion and the balanced equation for the reaction. Calculate the concentration of ethanoic acid in the diluted vinegar. Knowing that the original vinegar was diluted four times (25 cm^3 made up to 100 cm^3) calculate the concentration of the acid in the original vinegar. Express this in (i) moles per litre, (ii) grams per litre, and (iii) grams per 100 cm^3, *i.e.* as a percentage.

Experiment 9.6
To Determine the Percentage of Water of Crystallisation in Ethanedioic Acid Crystals ($H_2C_2O_4,yH_2O$)

Weight out accurately about 10 g of the acid, dissolve it in water in a beaker, rinse the beaker and add the rinse water to the flask and then make the solution up to the 250 cm^3 in the usual manner. Fill the burette with this solution.

Titrate against 25 cm^3 portions of 0.5 M sodium hydroxide solution, using phenolphthalein indicator. Carry out three titrations and record the results in the usual manner.

Calculate the concentration of the acid in (i) moles per litre (ii) grams per litre and (iii) grams per 250 cm^3. Hence find the mass of $H_2C_2O_4$. Subtract from the mass of the crystalline acid in order to find the mass of water of crystallisation. Express as a percentage and also calculate "*y*" in the formula for the crystalline acid.

Experiment 9.7
To Determine the Molecular Mass of Citric Acid

Citric acid is a tribasic, water soluble, crystalline organic acid which occurs in appreciable amounts in citrus fruits such as lemons and grapefruit. In this experiment its molecular mass is found as follows. A solution containing a known number of grams per litre is prepared. The molarity of this solution is found by titrating it against standard alkali. Calculation leads to the concentration in moles per litre, and since the mass present is known, the molecular mass can be calculated.

Weigh out accurately about 10 g of the acid, dissolve it in water in a beaker and make the solution up to a volume of 250 cm^3 in the usual manner. Fill the burette with this solution. Titrate against 25 cm^3 portions of 0.5 M sodium hydroxide solution using phenolphthalein indicator. Record the results in the usual manner.

Write out the titration conclusion and the balanced equation for the reaction (write the formula for the acid as H_3C, where C represents "citrate"). Calculate the concentration of the acid in (i) moles per litre, and (ii) grams per 250 cm^3. Since the mass of this number of moles is known, the molecular mass can be calculated.

Back Titrations

Substances which are insoluble in water (such as most metal carbonates) cannot be determined by direct titration, and a method known as back titration is used for these. The principle of this method is that a known quantity of the substance being determined is dissolved in an excess (but known) amount of acid, then the amount of excess is found by titration against standard alkali. Knowing the amount of acid taken initially, and the amount remaining (the excess), the amount used to react with the insoluble substance can be calculated. The method can be compared to the paying of 50 p in a shop and receiving back 20 p change. The amount used was therefore 30 p.

The method of calculation is illustrated in the following worked example.

Worked Example 4

2g of a sample of limestone were dissolved in 50 cm^3 of 1.0 M HCl. The resulting solution was made up to 250 cm^3 with water. 25 cm^3 of this solution required 11.6 cm^3 of 0.1 M NaOH for neutralisation. Assuming that the only basic material in limestone is $CaCO_3$, calculate the % of it present.

Titration conclusion:

$$25 \text{ cm}^3 \ x \text{ HCl} \ \equiv \ 11.6 \text{ cm}^3 \ 0.1 \text{ M NaOH}$$

Balanced equation:

$$HCl \ + \ NaOH \ \rightarrow \ NaCl \ + \ H_2O$$

$$\frac{V_1 M_1}{n_1} = \frac{V_2 M_2}{n_2}$$

$$\frac{25 \times x}{1} = \frac{11.6 \times 0.1}{1}$$

$$x = \frac{11.6 \times 0.1}{25} = 0.0464$$

i.e. the concentration of the excess acid is 0.0464 moles per litre; this is the same as

$$\frac{0.0464}{4} \text{ moles per 250 cm}^3$$

which is 0.0116 moles.

The amount of excess acid is thus 0.0116 moles.

Acid taken initially	= 50 cm^3 of 1.0 M HCl
Number of moles present	= $\frac{50}{100} \times 1.0 = 0.05$

Acid taken initially	= 0.05 moles
Acid excess	= 0.0116 moles
Therefore, acid used	= 0.0384 moles

$$2HCl \ + \ CaCO_3 = CaCl_2 + \ H_2O \ + \ CO_2$$

2 moles HCl react with 1 mole $CaCO_3$

therefore, 0.0384 moles HCl react with ½ of 0.0384 moles $CaCO_3$

$$= 0.0192 \text{ moles CaCO}_3$$

$$= 1.92 \text{ g of CaCO}_3 \ (CaCO_3 = 100)$$

Mass of $CaCO_3$ = 1.92 g

Mass of limestone sample = 2 g

Therefore % of $CaCO_3$ in limestone sample

$$= \frac{1.92}{2} \times 100 = 96\%$$

Experiment 9.8
To Determine the Amount of Mg(OH)₂ in "Milk of Magnesia" Tablets.

Pipette two 25 cm^3 portions of 1.0 M hydrochloric acid into a 250 cm^3 volumetric flask and add a "Milk of Magnesia" tablet. When the tablet has dissolved, make the solution up to the mark on the neck of the flask with water. Stopper the flask and mix the solution well.

Fill the burette with this solution. Pipette 25 cm^3 of 0.1 M sodium hydroxide solution into a conical flask, add a few drops of indicator (any indicator is suitable), and titrate with the acid solution until the indicator changes colour. Carry out several more titrations and record the results in the usual manner.

Calculate the concentration of the acid solution in moles per litre and hence find the number of moles of acid in the 250 cm^3 of solution. Calculate the total amount (i.e. number of moles) of acid taken initially, and subtract to find the amount used to react with the Mg(OH)₂.

Write out the balanced equation for the reaction between the $Mg(OH)_2$ and the hydrochloric acid, and hence find the number of moles of $Mg(OH)_2$ which were present in the tablet. Finally, calculate the mass of that number of moles of $Mg(OH)_2$. This is the required figure — mass of $Mg(OH)_2$ per tablet.

Experiment 9.9
To Determine the Mass of Acetylsalicylic Acid in an "Aspirin" Tablet.

Aspirin is a drug which both relieves pain and lowers body temperature. Its chemical name is acetylsalicylic acid and it is effectively a compound of two acids, acetic (ethanoic) acid and salicylic acid. When heated with sodium hydroxide solution, it is hydrolysed (split up) into the two acids, each of which is then neutralised. The reaction is given by:

$$CH_3COOC_6H_4COOH + 2NaOH \rightarrow$$

$$CH_3COONa + HOC_6H_4COONa + H_2O$$

The experiment is done by reacting a weighed quantity of aspirin tablets with an excess of standard alkali. The amount of excess alkali is determined by titration with standard acid. So the amount of alkali used is found, and hence the amount of acetylsalicylic acid in the tablets.

Weigh out accurately about 1.5 g of Aspirin tablets (about 5) into a conical flask. Add 25 cm^3 of 1.0 M sodium hydroxide solution and about the same volume of water. Simmer the mixture gently (**DO NOT BOIL**) for 10 minutes to hydrolyse the aspirin.

Cool the mixture and transfer it with washings to a 250 cm^3 volumetric flask. Make the solution up to the mark in the usual way. Mix well. Titrate 25 cm^3 portions of the solution with 0.1 M hydrochloric acid using phenolphthalein indicator. Carry out three titrations and record the results as usual.

Calculate the concentration of the excess sodium hydroxide solution, and then the amount of it present in the 250 cm^3 of solution. Subtract from the amount of alkali taken initially in order to find the amount which reacted with the acetylsalicylic acid. Hence, and with the aid of the equation given above, find the amount of acetylsalicylic acid present. Express this (i) in grams and (ii) as a percentage of the total mass of tablets which were used.

Questions
Standardisations

9.9.7 How many moles of NaOH would neutralise each of the following:

(a)   1 mole HCl
(b)   1 mole H_2SO_4
(c)   0.1 mole HNO_3
(d)   2.5 moles H_2SO_4
(e)   3.65 g HCl
(f)   9.8 g H_2SO_4

9.9.8 How many cm^3 of molar (1.0 M) hydrochloric acid would neutralise each of:

(a)   1 litre of 1.0 M NaOH
(b)   1 litre of 1.0 M $Ca(OH)_2$
(c)   100 cm^3 of 1.0 M KOH
(d)   100 cm^3 of 0.1 M KOH
(e)   100 cm^3 of 0.1 M $Mg(OH)_2$
(f)   4 g of NaOH
(g)   74 g of $Ca(OH)_2$

9.9.9 In an experiment, 20 cm^3 of sodium hydroxide solution were neutralised by 25 cm^3 of 1.0 M hydrochloric acid. Calculate the concentration of the sodium hydroxide in (a) moles per litre and (b) grams per litre.

9.9.10 If 23 cm^3 of 1.0 M sodium hydroxide neutralised 20 cm^3 of a given sulphuric acid solution, what was the concentration of the latter in terms of (a) moles per litre and (b) grams per litre.

9.9.11 20 cm^3 of 0.1 M sulphuric acid were required to neutralise 25 cm^3 of a solution of potassium hydroxide. What was the concentration of the latter in (a) moles per litre and (b) grams per litre?

9.9.12 Some sodium hydroxide was weighed out, dissolved in water and made up to 200 cm^3 of solution. 25 cm^3 of that solution neutralised 30 cm^3 of 1.0 M HCl. What was the mass of the sodium hydroxide taken?

9.9.13 Hydrochloric acid was standardised against 0.5 M Na_2CO_3 solution. 25 cm^3 of the latter required 24 cm^3 of the acid for neutralisation.

Calculate the concentration of the acid in (a) moles of HCl per litre and (b) grams of HCl per litre.

Q.9.14 25 cm^3 of 0.2 M Na$_2$CO$_3$ required 20 cm^3 of nitric acid for neutralisation. Calculate the concentration of the latter in terms of (a) moles per litre, and (b) grams per litre.

Q.9.15 10 cm^3 of concentrated hydrochloric acid were diluted to 1 litre with water. 27 cm^3 of this diluted acid were required to neutralise 25 cm^3 of 0.05 M sodium carbonate solution. Calculate the concentration of the original acid in (a) moles per litre, and (b) grams per litre.

Q.9.16 100 cm^3 of *Milk of Magnesia* (which is a suspension of Mg(OH)$_2$ in water) were diluted to 1 litre with water. 25 cm^3 portions of this solution were then titrated against 0.5 M HCl and it was found that 14.7 cm^3 of the acid were required for neutralisation. Calculate the concentration of the original Milk of Magnesia in terms of grams of Mg(OH)$_2$ per litre.

Q.9.17 3.65 g of HCl were dissolved in water and the solution made up to a volume of 500 cm^3. By titration, it was found that 30 cm^3 of the solution neutralised 25 cm^3 of a solution of sodium carbonate.

(a) Calculate the molarity of the hydrochloric acid solution.

(b) Work out the concentration of the sodium carbonate (i) in mol/L, and (ii) in g/L.

Q.9.18 2.5 g of anhydrous sodium carbonate are made up to 500 cm^3 of solution. What volume of 0.1 M hydrochloric acid will be neccessary to neutralise 25 cm^3 of this solution ?

Water of Crystallisation.

Q.9.19 Washing soda is crystalline sodium carbonate. Calculate (a) the % of water of crystallisation in the crystals and (b) 'x' in the formula Na$_2$CO$_3$xH$_2$O from the following experimental results:

4.3 g of washing soda crystals were dissolved in water and the solution made up to 250 cm^3 of solution. 25 cm^3 of this solution required 15 cm^3 of 0.2 M HCl for neutralisation, using methyl orange indicator.

Q.9.20 5 g of a sample of "washing soda" (hydrated sodium carbonate) which had partially effloresced were dissolved in water and made up to 250 cm^3 of solution. When 25 cm^3 portions of this solution were titrated against 0.2 M hydrochloric acid, using methyl orange indicator, the average titre was 18.6 cm^3. Calculate the % of water of crystallisation in the original crystals and also the average number of water molecules attached to each sodium carbonate molecule.

Q.9.21 Oxalic acid is a dibasic organic acid which reacts with sodium hydroxide as follows:

$$H_2C_2O_4 + 2NaOH \rightarrow Na_2C_2O_4 + 2H_2O$$

The crystalline acid contains water of crystallisation. Calculate the number of moles of water of crystallisation per mole of acid from the following experimental results.

3.15 g of the crystalline acid were made up to 250 cm^3 of solution. 25 cm^3 of this solution neutralised 20 cm^3 of 0.25 M NaOH solution.

Q.9.22 3.1 g of hydrated sodium carbonate were dissolved in water and made up to 500 cm^3 with water. When 25 cm^3 of this solution were titrated with 0.085 M hydrochloric acid, 29.4 cm^3 of the acid were required for neutralisation. Calculate the percentage of water in the hydrated salt, and the value of x in the formula Na$_2$CO$_3$xH$_2$O

Q.9.23 25 cm^3 of a solution containing 8.18 g/L of oxalic acid, H$_2$C$_2$O$_4$xH$_2$O were just neutralised by 26.0 cm^3 of 0.125 M sodium hydroxide solution. Calculate the value of x.

Q.9.24 Sodium "sesquicarbonate" reacts with hydrochloric acid according to:

$$Na_2CO_3NaHCO_3 + 3HCl \rightarrow 3NaCl + 2H_2O + 2CO_2$$

A solution containing 11.3 g of Na$_2$CO$_3$NaHCO$_3$xH$_2$O per litre was titrated with 0.3 M hydrochloric acid and it was found that 25 cm^3 of the solution reacted with 12.5 cm^3 of the acid. Calculate the value of x.

Molecular Mass Determination

Q.9.25 7.3 g of a dibasic organic acid were made up to 250 cm^3 of solution with water. 25 cm^3 of this solution neutralised 22.5 cm^3 of 0.5 M sodium hydroxide solution. Calculate the relative molecular mass of the acid.

Q.9.26   4 g of a dibasic organic were dissolved in water and made up to 250 cm^3 of solution. 8.1 cm^3 of this solution neutralised 25 cm^3 of 0.1 M NaOH. Calculate the relative molecular mass of the acid.

Q.9.27   Citric acid is a tribasic, water soluble, crystalline organic acid which occurs in appreciable quantities in citrus fruits. Calculate its relative molecular mass from the following experimental results:

10 g of the acid were dissolved in water and made up to 200 cm^3 in a volumetric flask. This solution was titrated against 0.5 M NaOH; 25 cm^3 of the alkali required 17.5 cm^3 of the acid for neutralisation.

Q.9.28   A solution contained 10 g per litre of a Group 1 metal hydroxide. 25 cm^3 of this solution were neutralised by 22.3 cm^3 of 0.1 M sulphuric acid. Calculate the molecular mass of the metal hydroxide, identify the metal and name the compound.

Back Titrations and Others.

Q.9.29   7 g of an indigestion mixture were added to 50 cm^3 of 1.0 M hydrochloric acid and the solution then diluted to 250 cm^3. 25 cm^3 of this diluted solution required 24 cm^3 of 0.1 M sodium hydroxide to neutralise the excess acid present. If all the basic material in the mixture is Mg(OH)$_2$ calculate the % of it present.

Q.9.30   7.2 g of the oxide of a divalent metal were dissolved in 500 cm^3 of 0.5 M hydrochloric acid. The resulting solution was diluted to 1 litre, and 20 cm^3 of this solution just neutralised 10 cm^3 of 0.1 M sodium hydroxide solution. Calculate the molecular mass of the metal oxide and hence the atomic mass of the metal.

Q.9.31   Calculate the relative molecular mass of the carbonate of a divalent metal X from the following data: 1.0 g of the anhydrous metal carbonate was added to 50 cm^3 of 1.0 M hydrochloric acid. The excess of acid required 30 cm^3 of 1.0 M sodium hydroxide for neutralisation. Calculate also, the relative atomic mass of X.

Q.9.32   4.77 g of a divalent metal oxide were dissolved in 150 cm^3 of 0.5 M sulphuric acid. The excess of acid from this reaction was just neutralised by 30 cm^3 of 1.0 M sodium hydroxide. Calculate the relative molecular mass of the oxide.

Q.9.33   1.0 g of an ore containing zinc oxide was dissolved in 25 cm^3 of 0.5 M sulphuric acid, and the solution was made up to a volume of 100 cm^3 with water. By titration, it was found that 20 cm^3 of this solution neutralised 16 cm^3 of 0.1 M sodium hydroxide. Calculate the percentage of zinc oxide in the ore.

Q.9.34   2.05 g of impure sodium hydroxide are dissolved in water and diluted to 500 cm^3 of solution. 25 cm^3 of this solution are just neutralised by 24.7 cm^3 of a solution of hydrochloric acid containing 3.65 g of HCl per litre. Calculate the percentage purity of the alkali.

Q.9.35   An excess of calcium hydroxide was shaken with water until no more would dissolve. 25 cm^3 of the resulting solution required 12 cm^3 of 0.1 M hydrochloric acid to neutralise it. Calculate the solubility of calcium hydroxide in water.

Q.9.36   50 cm^3 of vinegar were diluted to 250 cm^3 with water. 25 cm^3 of this solution required 21 cm^3 of 0.2 M sodium hydroxide for neutralisation. Calculate the percentage of ethanoic acid in the vinegar (Ethanoic acid is a monobasic acid of formula CH$_3$COOH; only the latter hydrogen atom is acidic);

Practical Questions

Q.9.37   A wet burette is to be filled with 0.5 M hydrochloric acid. Describe all that should be done so that it is ready for a titration to be carried out.

Q.9.38   The following questions refer to the titration of sodium carbonate solution with hydrochloric acid.

(a)   Which solution is put into the burette ? Why?

(b)   Why is a conical flask used in preference to (i) a beaker, (ii) a round bottomed flask.

(c)   What is **observed** in the flask during the titration.

(d)   What indicator is used ? What is the colour change at end point?

(e)   Why is the first titre often ignored ?

Q.9.39 Distinguish between essentials and precautions in carrying out a titration. Which of the following are essentials and which are precautions? Explain your answers.

(a) titrating into a **conical flask**,
(b) using an indicator
(c) using a pipette,
(d) using a burette,
(e) swirling the flask,
(f) reading the **bottom** of the liquid meniscus,
(g) titrating slowly,
(h) using a white tile.

Review   When you know chapter 9 you should be able to:

(a) give the definitions of: standard solution, molar solution, molarity, primary standard,

(b) state the relationship between concentration, molarity, molecular mass, number of moles, volume, mass,

(c) describe how to prepare a standard solution,

(d) describe the correct way of filling and using burettes and pipettes,

(e) describe how to carry out a titration, and know the precautions should be observed in order to obtain an accurate result,

(f) state the colours of litmus, methyl orange and phenolphthalein indicators in both acidic and alkaline solutions,

(g) balance the equation for any acid/alkali reaction,

(h) say when a back titration method is necessary,

(i) write the formula used in volumetric calculations, and know what each symbol in it represents,

(j) calculate the result of any titration experiment or problem.

The term "oxidation" originally meant the combining of oxygen with an element or compound; magnesium, for example, on combustion, is oxidised to magnesium oxide, and carbon monoxide to carbon dioxide.

$$Mg + O \quad \rightarrow \quad MgO^{(i)}$$

$$CO + O \quad \rightarrow \quad CO_2$$

Many other reactions, of apparently different nature, are also described as oxidations; hydrochloric acid is said to be oxidised to chlorine: $HCl \rightarrow Cl$, and iron(II) chloride is oxidised to iron(III) chloride: $FeCl_2 \rightarrow FeCl_3$.

Reduction, conversely, was originally applied to reactions in which oxygen was removed from compounds. Iron oxide, for example, is reduced to iron: $FeO \rightarrow Fe^{\ (ii)}$

Other reactions which are described as reduction reactions are:
chlorine $\rightarrow$ hydrogen chloride
iron(III)chloride $\rightarrow$ iron(II)chloride.

What is common to all of these oxidation and reduction reactions is that electrons are transferred from one substance to another.

Oxidation and Electrons

> **Oxidation can be defined as a process in which there is a loss of electrons from an atom or ion.**

This change occurs in such reactions as:

1. addition of oxygen (or other electronegative element), *e.g.* $Mg \rightarrow MgO$
2. removal of hydrogen, *e.g.* $HCl \rightarrow Cl$,
3. increase in valency, *e.g.* $FeCl_2 \rightarrow FeCl_3$.

1. Magnesium is oxidised to magnesium oxide — which is composed of magnesium ions (Mg^{2+}) and of oxide ions (O^{2-}); the fundamental change is

10
Oxidation-Reduction

(i)   Strictly, the above reactions should be written as $2Mg + O_2 \rightarrow 2MgO$ and $2CO + O_2 \rightarrow 2CO_2$; however, for the sake of simplicity, single atoms of oxygen are shown.
(ii) To keep the concept simple for the moment, how these changes are carried out in practice, is not mentioned above. They are:(i) $4HCl + MnO_2 \rightarrow Cl_2 + MnCl_2 + 2H_2O$ (ii) $2FeCl_2 + Cl_2 \rightarrow FeCl_3$
(iii) $FeO + H_2 \rightarrow Fe + H_2O$

that each magnesium atom loses its 2 outer electrons to become a magnesium ion:

$$Mg - 2e^- \rightarrow Mg^{2+}$$

2. In a simple way, this change can be regarded as the conversion of H^+Cl^- to Cl, *i.e.* each chloride ion, Cl^-, loses its extra electron to become a neutral chlorine atom.

However, HCl is not a completely ionic compound; the differences between the electronegativities of the two elements is 1.4; this means that while the bond is more covalent than ionic, it is very polar and is best denoted as

$$\overset{\delta^+}{H} \text{---} \overset{\delta^-}{Cl}$$

The chlorine atom has a greater share of the electron pair than the hydrogen atom. So, when the hydrogen is removed, the chlorine atom loses its extra share of electrons and is therefore oxidised according to the definition of oxidation.

3. $FeCl_2$ is composed of iron(II) ions (Fe^{2+}) and chloride ions, and $FeCl_3$ consists of iron(III) ions (Fe^{3+}) and chloride ions. The change from Fe^{2+} to Fe^{3+} is brought about by the loss of an electron from each Fe^{2+}; the Fe^{2+} is therefore oxidised to Fe^{3+};

$$Fe^{2+} - e^- \rightarrow Fe^{3+}$$

Reduction and Electrons

Reduction is a process in which an atom or ion gains electrons.

This occurs in:

1. removal of oxygen, *e.g.* $MgO \rightarrow Mg$;
2. addition of hydrogen, *e.g.* $Cl \rightarrow HCl$ and,
3. decrease in valency, *e.g.* $FeCl_3 \rightarrow FeCl_2$.

The changes in terms of electrons are:

1. $Mg^{2+} + 2e^- \rightarrow Mg$
2. $Cl + e^- \rightarrow Cl^-$
3. $Fe^{3+} + e^- \rightarrow Fe^{2+}$.

Questions

Q.10.1 Classify each of the following changes as an oxidation or a reduction. (N.B. equations are unbalanced).

(a) $S \rightarrow SO_2$
(b) $NH_3 \rightarrow N_2$
(c) $PCl_3 \rightarrow PCl_5$
(d) $CO_2 \rightarrow CO$
(e) $C_2H_4 \rightarrow C_2H_6$
(f) $C_2H_4O \rightarrow C_2H_4O_2$
(g) $HgCl \rightarrow HgCl_2$
(h) $SiO_2 \rightarrow Si$
(i) $S \rightarrow H_2S$
(j) $NO \rightarrow NO_2$
(k) $As_2O_3 \rightarrow As$
(l) $Na_2SO_3 \rightarrow Na_2SO_4$

Q.10.2 State about each of the following reactions, whether it is an oxidation or a reduction (N.B. equations are unbalanced)

(a) $Ca \rightarrow CaO$
(b) $HBr \rightarrow Br_2$
(c) $SnCl_2 \rightarrow SnCl_4$
(d) $CuO \rightarrow Cu$
(e) $FeCl_3 \rightarrow FeCl_2$
(f) $Cu_2O \rightarrow CuO$
(g) $FeO \rightarrow Fe_2O_3$
(h) $Br \rightarrow Br^-$
(i) $Na \rightarrow NaCl$
(j) $Cu \rightarrow CuS$
(k) $CuCl_2 \rightarrow CuCl$
(i) $ZnO \rightarrow Zn$

Q.10.3 For each of the above reactions, explain in terms of electron loss or gain, why it is an oxidation or a reduction.

Simultaneous Oxidation and Reduction.

The two processes are complementary and must occur together, since, in order for one substance to gain electrons, another substance must lose them

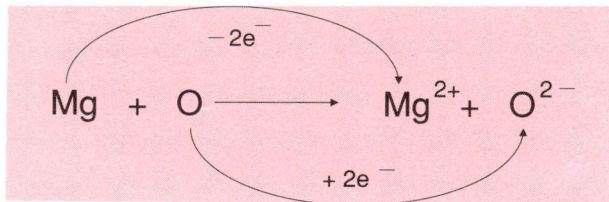

In the above, magnesium is oxidised to Mg^{2+} ions, by the oxygen — which is reduced to oxide, O^{2-}, at the same time.

The substance which does the oxidising (*i.e.* that which removes the electrons) **is known as the oxidising agent**, and it is itself reduced in the process, since it gains electrons.

Conversely, **the substance which does the reducing** (*i.e.* that which provides the electrons) **is called the reducing agent**, and it is oxidised in the change, since it loses electrons.

One perhaps unexpected feature of oxidation-reduction reactions is that neither oxygen nor hydrogen need take part in the reaction at all. In the reaction in which sodium combines with chlorine to form sodium chloride (NaCl, *i.e.* Na^+ and Cl^-); sodium is oxidised and chlorine is reduced:

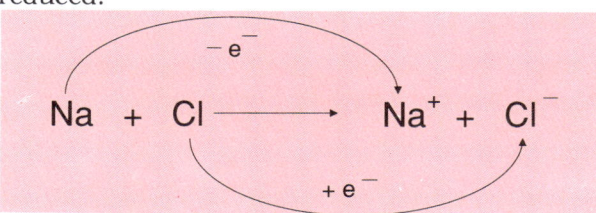

The chlorine has oxidised the Na to Na^+, while at the same time, the sodium has reduced the Cl to Cl^-. Chlorine is thus the oxidising agent and sodium the reducing agent.

Q.10.4 For each of the following reactions, list (i) the substance which is oxidised, (ii) the substance which is reduced, (iii) the oxidising agent, and (vi) the reducing agent. (N.B. equations are unbalanced).

(a) $CuO + H_2 \rightarrow Cu + H_2O$
(b) $H_2 + O_2 \rightarrow H_2O$
(c) $Zn + Cl_2 \rightarrow ZnCl_2$
(d) $CO_2 + Mg \rightarrow C + MgO$
(e) $H_2O_2 + HBr \rightarrow Br_2 + H_2O$
(f) $Cu + S \rightarrow Cu_2S$

Q.10.5 For each of the following equations, list (i) the substance which is oxidised, (ii) substance which is reduced, (iii) oxidising agent (iv) reducing agent. (N.B. equations are unbalanced).

(a) $FeCl_2 + Cl_2 \rightarrow FeCl_3$
(b) $Br_2 + I^- \rightarrow Br^- + I_2$
(c) $N_2 + I_2 \rightarrow NI_3$
(d) $N_2 + Mg \rightarrow Mg_3N_2$
(e) $Zn + Cu^{2+} \rightarrow Zn^{2+} + Cu$
(f) $Mg + HCl \rightarrow MgCl_2 + H_2$

Q.10.6 Balance each of the above equations.

Oxidation Numbers or Oxidation State.

In order to keep a check on electron movement in chemical compounds and reactions, a scheme of numbers, called oxidation numbers, is used.

> **The oxidation number of an element is the charge which an atom of that element has, or appears to have, in a compound.**

"Appears to have" is an important term in the definition, because for oxidation number purposes, when 2 atoms are joined by a polar covalent bond, the shared electrons are assigned completely to the more electronegative of the 2 atoms. HCl is polar and, as already mentioned, the molecule is best represented as

$$\overset{\delta^+}{H} \text{——} \overset{\delta^-}{Cl}$$

For oxidation number purposes, it is regarded as H^+ and Cl^-, *i.e.* the oxidation number of hydrogen is +1 and of chlorine -1.

In ammonia, NH_3, which has the structure:

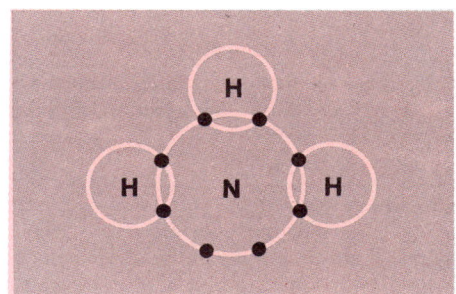

10.1

the shared electrons are counted with the more electronegative nitrogen atom, so that the compound is regarded as N^{3-} and $3H^+$, *i.e.* nitrogen has an oxidation number of -3, and each of the hydrogen atoms, +1. Ammonia is not, of course, ionic, and oxidation number is therefore only a convention, but a most useful one, as will be seen.

The oxidation number of each of the elements in a compound is easily calculated, provided some simple rules are observed.

Rules for Oxidation Numbers

1. In free elements, each atom has an oxidation number of zero.
2. In simple ions (ions consisting of a single atom) the oxidation number is equal to the charge on the ion. (Group I elements always form compounds by losing their single outer electron and forming +1 ions; so their oxidation number in compounds is always +1. Similarly, the oxidation number in Group II elements in compounds is always +2.)
3. In simple compounds (those containing two elements), the halogens (Group VII) have an oxidation number of -1.
4. In most compounds, oxygen has an oxidation number of -2. There are 2 exceptions: in peroxides it is -1, and in the compound OF_2 it is +2 (see following note)
5. In most compounds, hydrogen has an oxidation number of +1, the exception being in metal hydrides, in which it is -1 (see notes below).
6. In neutral molecules, the oxidation numbers of all the atoms present add up to zero. In complex ions (those containing more than one atom, *e.g.* NO_3^-) the oxidation numbers of all the atoms present add up to the charge on the ion.

Notes

Rule 4: Peroxides are compounds which contain -O-O-, and in the oxygen-oxygen bond, the electron pair is shared equally between the two like atoms. The apparent charge on each oxygen is thus -1.

In OF_2, in which oxygen is combined with the more electronegative fluorine (the only element which is more electronegative than oxygen itself) the shared electrons are counted with the fluorine atoms, and so oxygen has the apparent charge of +2.

Rule 5: In metal hydrides, e.g. NaH, hydrogen is joined to a less electronegative element and the electron pair is therefore counted with the hydrogen, i.e. it appears to be $\underset{-}{H}$.

Rule 6: As an example of applying the rules here, the oxidation number of sulphur in (i) H_2SO_4 and (ii) SO_3^{2-} is calculated

(i) There are 2 hydrogen atoms, each of which has an oxidation number of +1, making +2; there are 4 oxygen atoms, each of which has oxidation number of -2, making -8. The sum of the oxidation numbers of the hydrogen and oxygen atoms is thus -6. For the total sum of oxidation numbers to be zero, sulphur must have a value of +6.

$$\underset{2(+1)}{H_2} \quad \underset{?}{S} \quad \underset{4(-2)}{O_4}$$
$$\therefore S = +6$$

(ii) 3 oxygen atoms, each of which has a value of -2 add up to -6; the total sum is -2, therefore sulphur must have a value of +4.

$$\underset{?}{S} \quad \underset{3(-2)}{O_3^{2-}}$$
$$\therefore S = +4$$

Questions

Q.10.7   What is the oxidation number of each of the atoms in the following compounds?
NaBr; HBr; CO_2; LiH; NaOH; Na_2O_2; Mg_3N_2; Na_2CO_3.

Q.10.8   Calculate the oxidation number of sulphur in each of the following substances:

SO_2; Na_2S; SF_6; $Na_2S_2O_3$; SO_4^{2-}; H_2S; $MgSO_4$; S_8; $S_2O_7^{2-}$; $H_2S_2O_4$.

Q.10.9   What is the oxidation number of nitrogen in each of the following?

NO; NH_3; NO_2; NO_3^-; N_2; NH_2OH; KNO_3; NH_4^+; NO_2^-; NH_4Cl.

Q.10.10   For each of the equations listed in Q.10.4, write the oxidation number of each element underneath its symbol. It will be observed that when a substance is oxidised, its oxidation number is increased, and when a substance is reduced, the oxidation number is decreased. The first two of those equations, with this done, are shown:

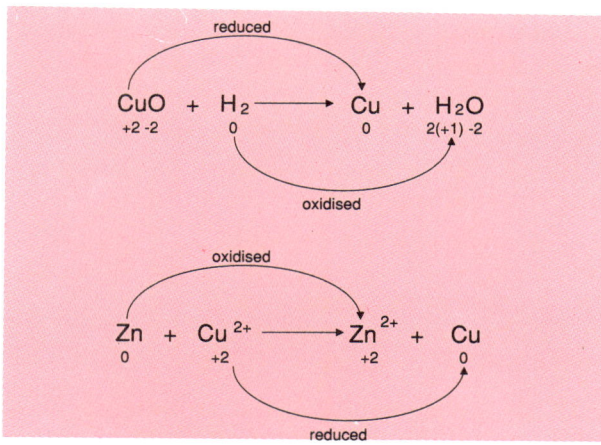

Increase in oxidation number means oxidation; decrease in oxidation number means reduction.

Balancing Redox Equations.

One of the most useful applications of the concept of oxidation numbers is that it provides a means of balancing equations of redox (i.e. oxidation-reduction) reactions; of the 3 main types of chemical reaction, ones in which electron transfer occurs are the most common.

The total increase in oxidation number in whatever is being oxidised must equal the total decrease in whatever is being reduced. This is really another way of stating that the total number of electrons gained by one substance must equal the total number lost by another substance.

The following equation is that of the reaction between hydrochloric acid and manganese dioxide; in this reaction, HCl is oxidised to chlorine — by the MnO_2, which is reduced to Mn^{2+}. Hydrogen ions, H^+, are necessary for the change, and water is a by-product of the reaction:

$$HCl + MnO_2 + H^+ \rightarrow Mn^{2+} + Cl_2 + H_2O$$

In order to balance the equation, the oxidation number of each element present is written underneath its symbol; the equation then appears as:

$$\underset{+1\,-1}{HCl} + \underset{+4\,-2}{MnO_2} + \underset{+1}{H^+} \rightarrow \underset{+2}{Mn^{2+}} + \underset{0}{Cl_2} + \underset{+1\,-2}{H_2O}$$

It is then seen that the oxidation number of chlorine is increased by 1 (i.e. from -1 to zero), while the

oxidation number of the Mn is decreased by 2 (i.e. from +4 to +2). This means, effectively, that each chlorine atom loses one electron, while each manganese atom gains 2. To provide 2 electrons for each of the Mn atoms, 2 chlorine atoms must react. The ratio in which the substances react is therefore two HCl molecules to each one MnO_2 molecule:

$$2HCl + MnO_2 + H^+ \rightarrow Mn^{2+} + Cl_2 + H_2O$$

Completing the numbers of each of the other molecules follows: $2H_2O$ molecules must be produced since there are 2 oxygen atoms in the MnO_2, hence 4 hydrogen atoms are necessary; 2 of these are provided by the 2 HCl, so that 2 H^+ are required to provide the remaining 2. The final balanced equation is thus:

$$2HCl + MnO_2 + 2H^+ \rightarrow Mn^{2+} + Cl_2 + 2H_2O$$

Balancing such an equation is relatively simple and could be done by inspection, but in the case of the following equation, and of many others, balancing it systematically using oxidation numbers, considerably reduces the time and effort necessary.

Summary of Method

$$P + HNO_3 \rightarrow H_3PO_4 + H_2O + NO_2$$

1. Write in the oxidation number of each element.

2. Observe what is oxidised and by how much its oxidation number increases (in the case of the above equation, the oxidation number of phosphorus increases from zero to +5).

3. Observe what is reduced and by how much its oxidation number decreases (in the above, the oxidation number of nitrogen decreases from +5 to +4).

4. From the information gained in 2 and 3, fill in the ratio in which the substance being oxidised must react with the substance being reduced, so that the total increase in oxidation number equals the total decrease (in the above, since P increases by 5, and N decreases by 1, five HNO_3 molecules must react with each one P atom).

5. Complete the number of each of the other substances to make the equation balance:

$$P + 5HNO_3 \rightarrow H_3PO_4 + H_2O + 5NO_2$$

(since all the N atoms in the HNO_3 are converted to NO_2 and there are five N atoms altogether, five NO_2 molecules must be formed).

Questions

Q.10.11. Make a list of the words which are needed to complete the following paragraph.

.... can be regarded in several ways: (i) as the .... of a substance with .... or some other non-metal, (ii) as the loss of ...., and (iii) as the .... of electrons. Reduction occurs when (i) the substance combines with ...., (ii) when there is a loss of .... from the substance, and (iii) when electrons are .... by it. As .... and .... must occur simultaneously, such reactions are described as .... reactions. .... agents cause .... and are themselves .... in the process. Similarly, ... agents are oxidised as they cause .... to occur.

Q.10.12 Work out the oxidation number of the stated element in each of the following substances:

(a) Cl in $NaCl$, ClO_2, ClO^-, $KClO_3$, $AlCl_3$,

(b) Mn in MnO_2, $KMnO_4$, $MnCl_2$, Mn_2O_7, MnO_4^-, $MnF3$.

(c) Sn in SnO_2, SnO_3^{2-}, $Sn(OH)_2$, $Sn(SO_4)_2$, $SnCl_4$, SnO_2^{2-}

(d) Fe in $FeSO_4$, $Fe(OH)_3$, Fe_2O_3, FeO_4^{2-}, K_2FeO_4, Fe_3O_4.

Q.10.13 What is meant by (a) an oxidising agent; (b) a reducing agent. Explain each in terms of electrons, using the reaction between calcium and sulphur as an example.

Q.10.14 For each of the following reactions, work out (a) what ions the product consists of; (b) which element in the reaction is oxidised and which is reduced; (c) which is the oxidising agent and which is the reducing agent.

(i) $K + F_2 \rightarrow KF$

(ii) $Na + O_2 \rightarrow Na_2O$

(iii) $Al + Cl_2 \rightarrow AlCl_3$

(iv) $Mg + F_2 \rightarrow MgF_2$

(v) $K + S \rightarrow K_2S$

(vi) $Ba + Cl_2 \rightarrow BaCl_2$

(N.B. Equations are unbalanced.)

Q.10.15 Define oxidation and reduction in terms of electron transfer. State, with reasons, which (if any) of the following reactions are oxidation-reduction (redox) reactions:

(i) $2Na + Cl \rightarrow 2NaCl$

(ii) $AgNO_3 + NaCl \rightarrow AgCl + NaNO_3$

(iii) $Mg + S \rightarrow MgS$

(N.B. equations are unbalanced)

Q.10.16 What are the rules about oxidation numbers that apply to:

(a) an atom of a free element;

(b) a simple ion,

(c) oxygen in its compounds,

(d) hydrogen in its compounds;

(e) a neutral molecule.

Q.10.17 Which of the following are oxidation-reduction reactions, and why?

(a) $Mg + Br_2 \rightarrow MgBr_2$

(b) $MgO + H_2O \rightarrow Mg(OH)_2$

(c) $Mg + N_2 \rightarrow Mg_3N_2$

(d) $MgCO_3 \rightarrow MgO + CO_2$

(e) $Mg + H_2O \rightarrow MgO + H_2$

(f) $MgCl_2 \rightarrow Mg + Cl_2$

(g) $MgBr_2 + Cl_2 \rightarrow MgCl_2 + Br_2$

(h) $Mg_3N_2 + H_2O \rightarrow Mg(OH)_2 + NH_3$

(i) $Mg + H_2SO_4 \rightarrow MgSO_4 + H_2$

(j) $Mg + S \rightarrow MgS$

Q.10.18. Define oxidation in terms of (i) electron transfer, (ii) change in oxidation number. Use oxidation numbers to determine whether or not each of the following is an oxidation-reduction reaction and if so state which species is being oxidised and which is being reduced:

$$H_2SO_3^- + OH^- \rightarrow HSO_3^- + H_2O$$
$$Cu_2O + 2H^+ \rightarrow Cu + Cu^{2+} + H_2O$$
$$Ag + H^+ + NO_3^- \rightarrow Ag^+ + NO + H_2O$$
$$K_2Cr_2O_7 + HCl \rightarrow KCl + CrCl_3 + H_2O + Cl_2$$
$$Cl_2 + OH^- \rightarrow Cl^- + ClO_3^- + H_2O$$
$$AgNO_3 + HCl \rightarrow AgCl + HNO_3$$

For those which are redox reactions, use oxidation numbers to balance their equations.

Q.10.19 Write equations for the reactions between (a) lead(II) oxide and hydrogen; (b) copper(II) oxide and carbon; (c) magnesium and hydrochloric acid; (d) aluminium and iron(III) oxide. Show where electrons are lost and gained in each reaction, and also name the oxidising agent.

Q.10.20 Is hydrogen an oxidising or a reducing agent? In the reactions of hydrogen with each of the following substances, show what loses and what gains electrons; (a) Cl_2 ; (b) CuO; (c) Na. What is the oxidising agent in each reaction?

Q.10.21 Titanium forms three oxides, in which it has valencies of 2, 3, and 4 respectively. Write the formula for each of the three oxides. Write equations for (a) the reduction of titanium(IV) chloride by sodium — to form titanium; (b) the reduction of titanium(IV) oxide by aluminium — again to form titanium.

Q.10.22 Define oxidation in terms of (a) electron transfer; (b) change in oxidation number. In the following examples indicate clearly, by showing electron loss or gain, which species is being oxidised and which is being reduced:

(c) $2Al + 3Cl_2 \rightarrow AlCl_3$

(d) $MnO_4^- + 5Fe^{2+} + 8H^+ \rightarrow Mn^{2+} + Fe^{3+} + 4H_2O$

(e) $F_2 + \frac{1}{2}O_2 \rightarrow OF_2$

(f) $SO_2 + H_2O + NaClO \rightarrow NaCl + H_2SO_4$

(g) $2K + 2H_2O \rightarrow 2KOH + H_2$

(h) $2FeCl_2 + Cl_2 \rightarrow 2FeCl_3$

(k) $Cl_2 + H_2S \rightarrow 2HCl + S$

Q.10.23 Balance each of the following equations using oxidation numbers:

(a) $Fe^{2+} + Cl_2 \rightarrow Fe^{3+} + Cl^-$

(b) $Cu + HNO_3 + H^+ \rightarrow Cu^{2+} + NO_2 + H_2O$

(c) $HI + O_2 \rightarrow H_2O + I_2$

(d) $NH_3 + O_2 \rightarrow H_2O + N_2$

(e) $Cl_2 + SO_3^{2-} + H_2O \rightarrow Cl^- + SO_4^{2-} + H^+$

(f) $MnO_4^- + I^- + H^+ \rightarrow Mn^{2+} + I_2 + H_2O$

(h) $Cu + HNO_3 + H^+ \rightarrow Cu^{2+} + NO + H_2O$

10.24 Which of the following equations are oxidation-reduction reactions? Balance those which are of this type and label both the oxidising agent and the reducing agent:

(i) $ZnO + HCl \rightarrow ZnCl_2 + H_2O$

(ii) $Zn + HCl \rightarrow ZnCl_2 + H_2$

(iii) $Cu + H_2SO_4 \rightarrow CuSO_4 + SO_2 + H_2O$

(iv) $Mg(OH)_2 + H_2SO_4 \rightarrow MgSO_4 + H_2O$

(v) $CaC_2 + H_2O \rightarrow Ca(OH)_2 + C_2H_2$

(vi) $Na_2S_2O_3 + I_2 \rightarrow NaI + Na_2S_4O_6$

(vii) $Na + O_2 \rightarrow Na_2O$ (cont..)

(viii) $F_2 + O_2 \rightarrow OF_2$

Q.10.25 Using oxidation numbers balance each of the following equations:

(a) $H_2O_2 + I^- + H^+ \rightarrow I_2 + H_2O$

(b) $HNO_3 + Fe^{2+} + H^+ \rightarrow NO_2 + Fe^{3+} + H_2O$

(c) $KIO_3 + KI + HCl \rightarrow I_2 + H_2O + KCl$

(d) $ClO^- + Sn^{2+} + H^+ \rightarrow Cl^- + Sn^{4+} + H_2O$

(e) $MnO_4^- + C_2O_4^{2-} + H^+ \rightarrow Mn^{2+} + CO_2 + H_2O$

(f) $H_2O_2 + Fe^{2+} + H^+ \rightarrow Fe^{3+} + H_2O$

(g) $MnO_4^- + Fe^{2+} + H^+ \rightarrow Mn^{2+} + Fe^{3+} + H_2O$

(h) $IO_3^- + I^- + H^+ \rightarrow I_2 + H_2O$

Q.10.26 Write equations for each of the following reactions. Name the substance oxidised and the substance reduced:

(a) the addition of sodium to water

(b) the reaction of hydrogen sulphide with moist sulphur dioxide.

(c) the reaction of hydrogen peroxide with acidified potassium iodide:

(d) the conversion of lead(II) oxide to lead, using hydrogen;

(e) the reaction of tin(II) chloride and mercury(II) chloride;

(f) the action of steam on magnesium;

(g) the reaction of hydrochloric acid and manganese dioxide;

(h) the passage of hydrogen over heated sodium;

(i) the burning of sodium in chlorine.

Review When you know Chapter 10 you should be able to:

(a) Define oxidation and reduction in terms of loss or gain of electrons.

(b) State the three different forms of reaction in which oxidation and reduction occur.

(c) Explain what is meant by an oxidising agent and a reducing agent.

(d) Select from any redox equation what is oxidised, what is reduced, the oxidising agent and the reducing agent.

(e) Define oxidation number and state the rules for calculating such numbers.

(f) Calculate the oxidation number of an element in a compound of a given formula.

(g) Balance any redox equation using oxidation numbers.

11

Volumetric Analysis II

Potassium Permanganate or Potassium Manganate(VII)[i]

Potassium permanganate, $KMnO_4$, is a powerful oxidising agent, and so reacts with, and can be used for the estimation of reducing agents, *e.g.*, iron(II) ions (Fe^{2+}), ethanedioic acid ($H_2C_2O_4$) and sulphite ions (SO_3^{2-}). There are two ways of regarding how permanganate oxidises: (a) in terms of oxygen and (b) in terms of electrons. The net result is, of course, the same in each case.

(a)   In acidic solution, the permanganate ion oxidises and is, therefore, itself reduced, to Mn^{2+}, as follows:

$$2MnO_4^- + 6H^+ \rightarrow Mn^{2+} + 3H_2O + 5[O]$$

↑
not released as oxygen gas, but taken by the substance being oxidised

Thus **two** permanganate ions provide **five** oxygen atoms available for oxidation. Note that the manganese is reduced from +7 oxidation state (in MnO_4^-) to the +2 state (in Mn^{2+}). This reaction only happens when there is a substance present which can react with the available oxygen atoms (*i.e.* a reducing agent).

(b)   In terms of electrons, the permanganate ion oxidises according to:

$$MnO_4^- + 8H^+ + 5e^- \rightarrow Mn^{2+} + 4H_2O$$

Thus, each permanganate ion can accept five electrons. As before, the reaction can only happen when there is a supplier of electrons (*i.e.* a reducing agent) present.

When potassium permanganate is acidified, there is no change until a reducing agent is added. This can easily be shown by a simple experiment, done as follows:

Take a dilute solution of potassium permanganate and acidify it by adding some dilute sulphuric acid; there is no change. Add a suitable reducing agent. A few crystals of sodium sulphite (Na_2SO_3) are convenient and react quickly. In aqueous solution, this substance is easily oxidised to sodium

(i)   The MnO_4^- ion is known both by its traditional name permanganate, and by the IUPAC name manganate(VII)

sulphate (Na_2SO_4), and so it is a reducing agent. Stir the mixture and observe the disappearance of the purple colour of the permanganate ions. The Mn^{2+} ions which are produced are virtually colourless and so the solution becomes decolorised as the permanganate is reduced.

In titrating permanganate solution against a reducing agent, decolorisation occurs as long as there is reducing agent present. Once all the reducing agent has been used up, decolorisation no longer takes place, and the purple colour of the permanganate remains. No indicator is thus necessary in titrating permanganate; it acts as its own indicator.

Preparation and Standardisation of Potassium Permanganate Solution

Molar potassium permanganate solution is both impractical (its solubility is not high enough) and unnecessary (it would be too powerful an oxidising agent for most purposes) and this reagent is generally used at a concentration of 0.02 M. 100% pure potassium permanganate is unavailable, so that a solution of exact concentration cannot be prepared directly. A solution of approximately the required concentration is prepared and this is then standardised by titrating it against a solution which can be prepared exactly, i.e. a solution of a primary standard. For this purpose, ammonium iron(II) sulphate is used.

Iron(II) ions are oxidised to iron(III) ions, and as before, the change can be considered in terms of either (a) oxygen or (b) electrons;

(a)   In terms of oxygen

$$2Fe^+ + 2H^+ + [O] \rightarrow 2Fe^{3+} + H_2O$$
$$\underset{acid}{} \quad \underset{from \ oxidising \ agent}{[O]}$$

Since $2MnO_4^-$ provide $5[O]$,
$2MnO_4^-$ oxidise $10 \ Fe^{2+}$ ions (in acidic solution) or, **one** MnO_4^- oxidises **five** Fe^{2+} ions.

(b)   In terms of electrons.
$$Fe^{2+} - e^- \rightarrow Fe^{3+}$$

Since each MnO_4^- ion can accept 5 electrons, each is capable of oxidising (removing electrons from) five Fe^{2+} ions.
Therefore, **one** MnO_4^- ion oxidises **five** Fe^{2+} ions (in acidic solution).

The full equation for the reaction is:
$$MnO_4^- + 8H^+ + 5Fe^{2+} \rightarrow Mn^{2+} + 5Fe^{3+} + 4H_2O$$

Standard Iron(II) (Fe^{2+}) Solution

Fe^{2+} ions can be provided by dissolving iron(II) sulphate crystals in water, but it is not practical to use this substance for the standardisation of the permanganate solution since (a) it is rendered impure by efflorescence, and (b) it is very readily oxidised by atmospheric oxygen to a basic iron(III) salt:

$$12FeSO_4 + 3O_2 + 6H_2O \rightarrow 4[Fe(OH)_3Fe_2(SO_4)_3]$$

In acidic solution, a basic salt cannot exist, and so solutions containing iron(II) ions are made in acidic solution.

Ammonium iron(II) sulphate has the formula $(NH_4)_2SO_4FeSO_46H_2O$; it is obtainable pure, and atmospheric oxygen has little effect on it in acidic solution. It is therefore used as a primary standard for the standardising of potassium permanganate solution.

The reacting ratio between the MnO_4^- ions and the ammonium iron(II) sulphate is still 1:5, since each $(NH_4)_2SO_4FeSO_46H_2O$ contains **one** Fe^{2+}, and neither the ammonium ions nor the water of crystallisation react with the permanganate.

Ammonium iron(II) sulphate is generally used at a concentration of 0.1 M and since one mole of it has a mass of 392 g, a solution of concentration 39.2 grams per litre is required. 250 cm^3 of solution is adequate for standardising the permanganate solution and so 9.80 g ($\frac{39.2}{4}$) of the salt is needed.

Once this standard solution of Fe^{2+} has been prepared, the permanganate can be standardised against it. This is done by taking 25 cm^3 (measured by pipette) of the standard iron(II) solution in a conical flask, adding an excess of dilute sulphuric acid, and titrating with the permanganate solution until the pink colour of the permanganate is permanent in the flask. The concentration of the permanganate is calculated in the usual manner, i.e. by using $\dfrac{V_1M_1}{n_1} = \dfrac{V_2M_2}{n_2}$

It should be noted that potassium permanganate can also be used in neutral or alkaline solution. However, in such conditions, it is not as strong an oxidising agent, being reduced only to MnO_2, in which compound the manganese is present in the +4 oxidation state:

$$2MnO_4^- + H_2O \rightarrow 2MnO_2 + 2OH^- + 3[O]$$
$$_{+7} \qquad\qquad\quad _{+4}$$

Compare this with the reaction in acidic solution:

$$2MnO_4^- + 8H^+ \rightarrow 2Mn^{2+} + 8H_2O + 5[O]$$
$$_{+7} \qquad\qquad _{+2}$$

If insufficient acid has been added in a permanganate titration, the first reaction shown above starts to occur after the acid has been used up, resulting in a brownish precipitate of manganese dioxide. Should this occur, more acid must be added to the titration flask.

Experiment 11.1
To prepare 0.1M ammonium iron(II) sulphate solution.

Weigh out accurately 9.80 g of ammonium iron(II) sulphate crystals. Dissolve these in water in a beaker to which about 10 cm^3 of dilute sulphuric acid have been added. Pour the solution into a 250 cm^3 volumetric flask. Wash the beaker with water and add the washings to the flask. Repeat once more. Finally make the solution up to the mark on the neck of the flask with water. Stopper the flask and **mix well**.

Experiment 11.2
To standardise a solution of potassium permanganate

Fill a burette with the unknown concentration permanganate solution. Pipette 25 cm^3 of the ammonium iron(II) sulphate solution into a conical flask and add excess (about 10 cm^3) dilute sulphuric acid. Titrate with the permanganate solution until the pink colour is just permanent in the flask. (If a dark coloured precipitate (of MnO_2) should appear during the titration, add more acid). Record your results in the usual manner and carry out two further titrations to obtain consistent results.

Write out the titration conclusion, and the balanced equation for the reaction. Calculate the concentration of the permanganate solution and express this in both moles per litre and grams per litre.

Extra work: Carry out a further titration without the addition of sulphuric acid. Observe and explain the result.

Worked Example 1
In an experiment to standardise a solution of potassium permanganate, 25 cm^3 portions of 0.1 M ammonium iron(II) sulphate were titrated with the permanganate solution. The average result of several titrations was found to be 23.8 cm^3. Calculate the concentration of the permanganate (i) in terms of molarity and (ii) in grams of $KMnO_4$ per litre.

Solution
Titration Conclusion:

$23.8 \ cm^3 \ x \ KMnO_4 \equiv 25 \ cm^3 \ 0.1 \ M$ 'AmFeSO$_4$'

Balanced Equation:

$$MnO_4^- + 5 \text{ 'AmFeSO}_4\text{'} + 8H^+ \rightarrow \ldots\ldots$$

$$\frac{V_1 M_1}{n_1} = \frac{V_2 M_2}{n_2}$$

$$\therefore \quad \frac{23.8 \times x}{1} = \frac{25 \times 0.1}{5}$$

$$x = 0.021 \ mol/L = (\, 0.021 \times 158\,) \ g/L$$
$$= 3.32 \ g/L$$

("AmFeSO$_4$" = $(NH_4)_2 SO_4 FeSO_4 6H_2O$)

Use of Standard Potassium Permanganate Solution
Potassium permanganate solution, once it has been standardised, can be used to determine the concentration of any reducing agent in solution. Reducing agents which are commonly determined in this way include iron(II) ions and ethanedioic ("oxalic") acid.

Potassium permanganate and iron(II) ions react in the ratio of 1:5, and so any soluble iron(II) compound can be determined by titration with standard permanganate solution.

Ethanedioic acid is oxidised as follows:

$$H_2C_2O_4 \quad + \quad [O] \rightarrow 2CO_2 + H_2O$$
$$ \text{from the}$$
$$ \text{oxidising agent}$$

Two MnO_4^- ions provide five [O] atoms, so therefore **two** MnO_4^- ions oxidise **five** $H_2C_2O_4$ (in acidic solution), and this is the reacting ratio.

The full equation for the reaction is:

$$2MnO_4^- + 5H_2C_2O_4 + 6H^+ \rightarrow$$
$$2Mn^{2+} + 10CO_2 + 8H_2O$$

The rate of reaction is extremely low are room temperature and ethanedioic acid solutions need to be heated to about 60°C in order to be titrated with potassium permanganate.

Experiment 11.3
To determine the amount of water of crystallisation in iron(II) sulphate crystals.

Weigh out accurately about 5 g of iron(II) sulphate crystals. Dissolve these in water in a beaker. Pour the solution into a volumetric flask, wash the beaker with water (twice) and add the washings to the flask. Make the solution up to the mark with water. Stopper the flask and mix well.

Pipette 25 cm^3 of this solution into a conical flask, add excess dilute sulphuric acid, and titrate against the standard permanganate solution. Repeat to obtain consistent results.

Calculate the concentration of the iron salt, then the mass of FeSO$_4$ in grams per litre and finally the mass of it in 250 cm^3 of solution. The mass of crystalline FeSO$_4$ is known from the initial weighing, so the mass of water of crystallisation present can be calculated. This can be expressed either as a percentage or as the actual number of molecules of water in the formula FeSO$_4$ x H$_2$O (see worked example 9.3 for method of calculation).

Experiment 11.4
To find the concentration of ethanedioic ("oxalic") acid solution

Pipette 25 cm^3 of the given ethanedioic acid solution into a conical flask, [i] add excess dilute sulphuric acid and heat to about 60°C (there is no need to use a thermometer; when the bottom of the flask is just too hot to hold comfortably, it is at about the correct temperature). Titrate with standard 0.02 M permanganate solution, heating again as necessary, until the end point is reached. Repeat to obtain consistent values.

Calculate the concentration of the ethanedioic acid solution and also the number of grams of H$_2$C$_2$O$_4$ per litre:

Experiment 11.5
To determine the amount of water of crystallisation in ethanedioic acid crystals.

Weigh out accurately between 1.0 and 1.5 g of the ethanedioic acid crystals. Dissolve these in water and make the solution up to 250 cm^3 in the usual way. Pipette 25 cm^3 of this solution into a conical flask, add excess dilute sulphuric acid (about 10 cm^3), heat to about 60°C and titrate with standard 0.02 M permanganate solution. Carry out three titrations and record the results as usual.

Write out the titration conclusion and calculate the concentration of the ethanedioic acid (a) in moles per litre, (b) in grams of H$_2$C$_2$O$_4$ per litre and (c) in grams of H$_2$C$_2$O$_4$ per 250 cm^3. Hence the mass of anhydrous ethanedioic acid is found. The mass of the crystalline acid is known from the initial weighing — hence the mass of water present. This should be expressed as a percentage and also as the number of water molecules in each molecule of the crystalline acid (for method of calculation, see worked example 9.3)

Questions

Permanganate and Iron

Q.11.1   A solution of potassium permanganate was standardised against 0.1 M ammonium iron(II) sulphate solution. 25 cm^3 of the latter required 24.0 cm^3 of the permanganate solution for complete oxidation. Calculate the concentration of the potassium permanganate solution (a) in moles per litre and (b) in grams per litre.

(i)   Pipette the ethanedioic acid carefully as it is a poisonous substance. A pipette filler should be used.

Q.11.2 25 cm^3 of iron(II) sulphate solution were oxidised by 22.0 cm^3 of 0.02 M KMnO$_4$. Find the concentration of the iron(II) sulphate in terms of (a) molarity; (b) grams of iron(II) sulphate crystals (FeSO$_4$7H$_2$O) per litre.

Q.11.3 18 cm^3 of 0.022 M KMnO$_4$ oxidised 25 cm^3 of iron(II) sulphate solution which contained 22 g of iron(II) sulphate crystals per litre. Calculate the % of water of crystallisation in the crystals.

Q.11.4
(a) A standard solution of iron(II) ammonium sulphate was prepared by making 20 g of FeSO$_4$(NH$_4$)$_2$SO$_4$6H$_2$O crystals up to 500 cm^3 of solution. 25 cm^3 of this solution were found to react with 26.4 cm^3 of a solution of potassium permanganate. Calculate the concentration of the permanganate solution.

(b) The same permanganate solution was then used to find the percentage purity of a sample of impure iron(II) sulphate. 5.95 g of the iron sulphate crystals were dissolved in sulphuric acid and made up to 250 cm^3 of solution. 25 cm^3 portions of this solution were found to react with 20.7 cm^3 of permanganate solution in acidic conditions. Calculate the percentage of FeSO$_4$7H$_2$O in the crystals.

Q.11.5 Calculate the % of iron in an iron salt from the following. 25.0 g of the salt were dissolved in water and then made up to 1 litre of solution. 20 cm^3 of this solution required 20.7 cm^3 of 0.01 M KMnO$_4$ for oxidation. (It can be assumed that the iron in the iron salt is in the iron(II) state).

Q.11.6 Calculate the % of water of crystallisation in iron(II) sulphate crystals from the following experimental results: 6.25 g of the crystals were dissolved in water and made up to 250 cm^3 of solution. 25 cm^3 of this solution were found to be oxidised by 22.6 cm^3 of 0.02 M KMnO$_4$. Calculate also, "x" in the formula FeSO$_4$xH_2O.

Q.11.7 Calculate the % of iron in a sample of iron wire from the following information: 1.4 g of wire were dissolved in excess dilute sulphuric acid and the solution made up to 250 cm^3. 25 cm^3 of this solution required 22 cm^3 of 0.022 M KMnO$_4$ for oxidisation.

Q.11.8 How many cm^3 of a 0.1 M solution of Fe^{2+} ions are required to react with 0.1 g of potassium permanganate crystals dissolved in excess sulphuric acid?

Q.11.9 How many grams of potassium permanganate are needed to oxidise 25 cm^3 of a acidified 0.5 M iron(II)sulphate solution?

Q.11.10 How many grams of iron(II) sulphate crystals (FeSO$_4$7H$_2$O) would decolorise an acidified solution containing 1 g of potassium permanganate.

Q.11.11 An "iron" tablet for patients suffering from iron deficiency contains FeSO$_4$7H$_2$O. A tablet weighing 0.20 g was dissolved in an excess of dilute sulphuric acid and the resulting solution titrated with 0.018 M potassium permanganate. 7.7 cm^3 of the permanganate were needed. Calculate the percentage of the iron compound in the tablet.

Permanganate and Ethanedioic Acid

Q.11.12 Calculate the concentration of ethanedioic acid in (a) moles per litre; (b) grams of H$_2$C$_2$O$_4$ per litre, from the following information: 25 cm^3 of the ethanedioic acid, containing excess dilute sulphuric acid and heated to about 60°C, were oxidised by 21 cm^3 of 0.02 M KMnO$_4$ solution.

Q.11.13 1.20 g of ethanedioic acid crystals were dissolved in water and made up to 250 cm^3 of solution. 25 cm^3 of this solution, under the necessary conditions were oxidised by 19.0 cm^3 of 0.02 M KMnO$_4$ solution.

(i) Describe the necessary conditions.
(ii) Calculate (a) the % of water of crystallisation in the crystals; (b) "x" in the formula C$_2$H$_2$O$_4$xH_2O.

Q.11.14 A standarisation of potassium permanganate by ethanedioic acid crystals yielded the following data: 1.60 g of the crystals, H$_2$C$_2$O$_4$2H$_2$O, were made up to 250 cm^3 of aqueous solution, and 25.0 cm^3 of this solution, when acidified, required 26.2 cm^3 of the permanganate solution for oxidation. Calculate the molarity and concentration (in g/L) of the permanganate.

Q.11.15 Calculate the concentration in grams per litre of a sodium ethanedioate solution, 25 cm^3 of which were oxidised in acidic solution by 28.5 cm^3 of potassium permanganate solution containing 2.5 g of $KMnO_4$ per litre. (Sodium ethanedioate is oxidised in a similar manner to ethanedioic acid).

Q.11.16. 35 cm^3 of a potassium permanganate solution are required to oxidise a 0.215 g sample of ethanedioic acid crystals, $H_2C_2O_42H_2O$. Calculate the concentration of the permanganate in grams $KMnO_4$ per litre.

Q.11.17 1 g of potassium permanganate was dissolved in water and made up to a volume of 250 cm^3 in a volumetric flask. What volume of this solution would react with 25 cm^3 of 0.1 M ethanedioic acid (to which some sulphuric acid had been added)?

Sodium Thiosulphate

Sodium thiosulphate[i], $Na_2S_2O_3$, reacts with iodine to produce sodium iodide and a substance called sodium "tetrathionate" the equation being;

$$2Na_2S_2O_3 + I_2 \rightarrow 2NaI + Na_2S_4O_6$$

sodium   sodium
iodide   tetrathionate

This reaction is used for the estimation of free iodine, and of substances which liberate iodine from compounds during chemical reactions.

Sodium thiosulphate which is purchased as the hydrated salt, $Na_2S_2O_35H_2O$, is usually used at a concentration of 0.1 M, and this contains 24.8 grams of the crystals per litre ($M_r = 248$). As in the case of many of the compounds used for volumetric analysis, the salt is not available in a sufficient pure state to make up a 0.1 M solution directly. A solution of approximately the required concentration is therefore prepared, and then standardised against one whose concentration is exactly known. Two substances which may be used for this purpose are potassium permanganate, $KMnO_4$ and potassium iodate, KIO_3.

Indicator and End Point

A solution containing free iodine is reddish-brown in colour, whereas iodide ions (to which the iodine is converted by the thiosulphate) are colourless. However, there is no sudden colour change as the reaction proceeds — the red colour of the iodine gradually gets less and less intense until finally it disappears. An indicator is therefore necessary so that the exact end point can be found.

Starch produces a very distinct deep blue colour with free iodine, even when only tiny amounts of iodine are present and so is a very suitable indicator for this reaction. The starch is only added when most of the iodine has reacted (i.e. when the red colour has become pale yellow) and on doing this the distinctive blue colour appears. When all the iodine has reacted, the blue colour suddenly disappears.

The reason why the starch is only added near the end of the titration is as follows. Starch on being added to a solution containing iodine forms an equilibrium mixture:

I_2 + starch $\longleftrightarrow$ blue-black complex substance.

On adding thiosulphate, iodine is removed from the system and the reaction moves to the left hand side, resulting in the decomposition of the blue-black complex and hence the disappearance of the colour. However, if there is a high concentration of the complex present (as would be the case if the starch were added when the concentration of iodine was high), it will not decompose when the "right" amount of thiosulphate is added (or will not decompose at all). Thus, an incorrect titre will be obtained.

Starch solution deteriorates quite quickly and for use as an indicator it must be recently prepared. Its useful life is only about 2 — 3 weeks.

The usefulness of sodium thiosulphate lies in the fact that oxidising agents liberate iodine from acidified potassium iodide solution, the amount of iodine being proportional to the amount of oxidising agent. The liberated iodine can then be determined by titrating it with standard thiosulphate solution. Thus, thiosulphate solution is used in volumetric analysis to estimate oxidising

(i)   Pupils who develop and print their own photographs will know of sodium thiosulphate as "hypo", which is the substance that "clears" the unused emulsion in the fixing solution.

agents. Like all volumetric reagents, a standard solution of it is necessary for it to be of any value.

Solutions which are to be titrated with thiosulphate should always be made up with distilled water. Most tap water supplies contain dissolved chlorine — being present for sterilisation purposes. This element, being an oxidising agent, will liberate iodine from acidified potassium iodide solution, resulting in more liberated iodine than is due to the oxidising agent being estimated, hence too high a titre and an incorrect experimental result. Deionised water, which for most purposes is quite a satisfactory substitute for distilled water is not perfect for this purpose; deionisers only remove ions from water so that deionised water can contain some chlorine that was present in the original water.

Preparation and Standardisation of Sodium Thiosulphate Solution (using Potassium Permanganate)

An approximately 0.1 M solution of thiosulphate is prepared by dissolving about 25 g of sodium thiosulphate crystals in distilled water and making the solution up to 1 litre in the usual manner. Alternatively, since 1 litre is seldom required, 6.25 g can be made up to 250 cm^3 of solution.

In standardising the solution against permanganate, the principle is as follows. The permanganate, being an oxidising agent, liberates iodine from acidified potassium iodide — the amount of iodine being directly proportional to the amount of permanganate:

$$2KMnO_4 + 10KI + 8H_2SO_4 \rightarrow$$
$$6K_2SO_4 + 2MnSO_4 + 8H_2O + 5I_2$$

or ionically:

$$2MnO_4^- + 10I^- + 16H^+ \rightarrow 2Mn^{2+} + 8H_2O + 5I_2$$

The required information is that:
two moles of $KMnO_4$ provide **five** moles of I_2. (provided that there is an excess of both KI and acid).

Since **one** I_2 reacts with **two** $Na_2S_2O_3$, **five** I_2 react with **ten** $Na_2S_2O_3$..

So, **two** $KMnO_4$ liberate the amount of iodine which reacts with **ten** $Na_2S_2O_3$,

and this is the reacting ratio needed for

calculations. It must be stressed however, that permanganate does not **react** with thiosulphate; permanganate liberates iodine from acidified potassium iodide and it is this iodine which reacts with the thiosulphate.

$$2KMnO_4 \equiv 5I_2 \equiv 10Na_2S_2O_3$$

Potassium Iodate

Potassium iodate is suitable as a primary standard and can also be used to standardise sodium thiosulphate solution. Like potassium permanganate, it is an oxidising agent and so liberates iodine from acidified potassium iodide solution:

$$KIO_3 + 5KI + 3H_2SO_4 \rightarrow 3K_2SO_4 + 3H_2O + 3I_2$$

One mole of KIO_3 liberates **three** moles of I_2, and **three** I_2 react with **six** $Na_2S_2O_3$,

so that **one** KIO_3 is indirectly equivalent to **six** $Na_2S_2O_3$, and this is the ratio needed for calculations.

Experiment 11.6
To Prepare and Standardise a Solution of Sodium Thiosulphate.

Weigh out 6.25 g of sodium thiosulphate crystals and dissolve them in about 100 cm^3 of distilled water contained in a beaker. When the crystals have dissolved, pour the solution into a 250 cm^3 volumetric flask, rinse the beaker with distilled water and pour the wash water into the flask. Repeat this once or twice. Finally, make the solution to the 250 cm^3 mark with more distilled water. Stopper the flask, and mix well.

Fill a burette with the thiosulphate solution to be standardised. Pipette 25 cm^3 of standard 0.02 M potassium permanganate into a conical flask, add about 10 cm^3 of 10% potassium iodide solution and about 20 cm^3 of dilute sulphuric acid. Titrate with the thiosulphate solution until the solution in the flask becomes straw yellow. At this point add a few drops of starch indicator, and continue titrating until the blue colour has just disappeared. Carry out two further titrations, or more if necessary until the titres are consistent.

Record the results in the usual manner. Write out the titration conclusion and the balanced equation for the reaction. Calculate the concentration of the thiosulphate solution.

Experiment 11.7
To Prepare Standard Potassium Iodate Solution and to use it to Standardise a Solution of Sodium Thiosulphate.

Potassium iodate is normally used at a concentration of 0.02 M. Such a solution contains 4.28 g/L or 1.07 g/250 cm^3 of solution.

Weigh out accurately 1.07 g of pure potassium iodate crystals, dissolve these in distilled water in a beaker and pour the solution into a 250 cm^3 volumetric flask. Wash the beaker with distilled water several times and pour the washings into the volumetric flask. Make the volume up to exactly 250 cm^3 with more distilled water, stopper the flask and mix well.

Pipette 25 cm^3 of the solution into a conical flask, add about 10 cm^3 of 10% potassium iodide solution and 20 cm^3 of dilute sulphuric acid. Titrate the mixture with the thiosulphate to be standardised, until the solution is straw coloured. Add a few cm^3 of starch solution and continue the titration until the end point is reached. Repeat to obtain consistent titres.

Record the results in the usual manner, write out the titration conclusion and the balanced equation for the reaction. Calculate the concentration of the thiosulphate solution.

Experiment 11.8
To Determine the Amount of Sodium Hypochlorite in Bleach

The active ingredient in most commercial bleaches (e.g. Parazone) is sodium hyphchlorite, NaClO. This compound is an oxidising agent and so liberates iodine from acidified potassium iodide solution:

$$NaClO + 2I^- + 2H^+ \rightarrow I_2 + NaCl + H_2O$$

Sodium hypochlorite can therefore be determined by means of sodium thiosulphate solution.

Since $NaClO \equiv I_2$ and $I_2 \equiv 2Na_2S_2O_2$, **one** mole of NaClO requires (indirectly) **two** moles of $Na_2S_2O_2$.

Bleach as usually purchased, is too concentrated to be used directly, and so it should be diluted — quantitatively — before being used.

Procedure

Using a pipette[(i)] or burette, together with a volumetric flask, dilute a sample of bleach to exactly ten times its volume, e.g. make 10 cm^3 up to a volume of 100 cm^3.

Pipette 25 cm^3 of the diluted bleach into a conical flask, add about 10 cm^3 each of potassium iodide solution and dilute sulphuric acid. Titrate the liberated iodine with 0.1 M thiosulphate solution, adding starch indicator as the end point is approached.

Record the result in the usual manner, and carry out two further titrations, or until the results are consistent. Calculate the concentration of the sodium hypochlorite (i) in the diluted solution and (ii) in the original solution. Give the final result in both grams per litre and as a percentage (i.e. g/100 cm^3).

Worked Example 2

In an experiment to standardise sodium thiosulphate solution, 25 cm^3 of 0.02 M $KMnO_4$, to which had been added excess potassium iodide and acid, were titrated against the thiosulphate. It was found that 22.7 cm^3 of the latter were needed to react with the liberated iodine, using starch as indicator. Calculate the concentration of the thiosulphate in (a) moles per litre and (b) grams of $Na_2S_2O_35H_2O$ per litre.

Titration conclusion:

$$25 \text{ cm}^3 \text{ of } 0.02 \text{ M } KMnO_4 \equiv 22.7 \text{ cm}^3 x \, Na_2S_2O_3$$

$$2KMnO_4 \equiv 10Na_2S_2O_3$$

(from chemical equations)

$$\frac{V_1M_1}{n_1} = \frac{V_2M_2}{n_2}$$

$$\frac{25 \times 0.02}{2} = \frac{22.7x}{10}$$

(i)   A pipette filler must be used when pipetting bleach solution.

$$x = \frac{25 \times 0.02 \times 10}{2 \times 22.7}$$

$$= 0.11$$

Concentration of
$$Na_2S_2O_3 = 0.11 \text{ mol/L}$$
$$(Na_2S_2O_35H_2O = 248) = (0.11 \times 248) \text{ g/L}$$
$$= 27.3 \text{ g/L}$$

Worked Example 3

50 cm^3 of "Superbleach" were diluted to 500 cm^3 with distilled water. 25 cm^3 of this solution were mixed with an excess of potassium iodide and sulphuric acid, and the mixture was titrated with 0.11 M sodium thiosulphate solution. The average of several titrations was found to be 12.3 cm^3. Calculate the concentration of the original bleach in terms of (i) moles per litre, (ii) grams of NaClO per litre and (iii) percentage concentration.

Titration Conclusion:

25 cm^3 x NaClO $\equiv$ 12.3 cm^3 0.11 M Na$_2$S$_2$O$_3$

Reacting ratio:

NaClO $\rightarrow$ I$_2$ $\equiv$ 2Na$_2$S$_2$O$_3$
(**one** NaClO to **two** Na$_2$S$_2$O$_3$)

$$\frac{25x}{1} = \frac{12.3 \times 0.11}{2}, \quad x = 0.027 \text{ mol/L}$$

(= conc. of **diluted** solution)

$\therefore$ conc. of original solution = 0.27 mol/L
(10 times more concentrated)

(NaClO = 74.5) = (0.27 × 74.5) g/L
$$= 20 \text{ g/L}$$
$$= 2 \text{ g/} 100 \text{ cm}^3 = 2 \%$$

Questions

Q.11.18 Give short answers to each of the following questions.

(a) Name a compound containing Fe^{3+} ions and give its formula.

(b) The change from Fe^{2+} to Fe^{3+} is described as what type of reaction?

(c) What colour change indicates the end point when titrating acidified iron(II) sulphate solution with permanganate solution?

(d) What is indicated by the appearance of a dark brown precipitate during a permanganate titration?

(e) To what is ethanedioic acid converted when it is reacted with acidified permanganate solution?

(f) Why does the reaction between ethanedioic acid and permanganate solution demonstrate autocatalysts.

(g) Why are solutions of iron sulphate for titration always prepared in acidic solution?

(h) Why is permanganate titrated in acidic solution? What would happen if it were titrated under neutral or alkaline conditions?

(i) State two conditions which are necessary when titrating ethanedioic acid with permanganate solution.

Q.11.19 25 cm^3 of a solution of iodine required 27 cm^3 of 0.09 M sodium thiosulphate solution for complete reaction. Calculate (a) the molarity of the iodine solution, (b) its concentration in g/L.

Q.11.20 A standard solution of iodine was prepared by dissolving 3.3 g of pure iodine crystals in potassium iodide solution and making it up to 250 cm^3. By titration it was found that 25 cm^3 of this iodine solution reacted with 23.6 cm^3 of a solution of sodium thiosulphate. Calculate the concentration of (a) the iodine solution; (b) the sodium thiosulphate solution.

Q.11.21 2.84 g of pure iodine and 6 g of potassium iodide are dissolved in distilled water and made up to a volume of 250 cm^3 of solution. 25 cm^3 of this solution were found to react exactly with 17.7 cm^3 of sodium thiosulphate. Calculate the concentration of the thiosulphate solution.

Q.11.22 20 cm^3 of 0.02 M potassium permanganate were added to an excess of acidified potassium iodide solution. The liberated iodine was just sufficient to react with 22.6 cm^3 of a solution of sodium thiosulphate. Calculate the concentration of the latter in grams of crystals, Na$_2$S$_2$O$_3$5H$_2$O per litre.

Q.11.23 20 cm^3 of 0.02 M potassium permanganate were acidified and added to an excess of potassium iodide solution. The iodine liberated reacted with 22.3 cm^3 of a sodium thiosulphate solution. 20 cm^3 of another solution of iodine was found to react with 18.7 cm^3 of the same thiosulphate solution. Calculate the concentration of the solution of iodine.

Q.11.24　25 cm^3 of potassium permanganate solution were added to an excess of acidified potassium iodide solution. On titration, the released iodine required 27.5 cm^3 of 0.1 M sodium thiosulphate solution. Write equations for the reactions involved, and calculate the molarity of the permanganate solution.

Q.11.25　Potassium iodate reacts with acidified potassium iodide solution liberating iodine. The equation for the reaction is:

$$KIO_3 + 5KI + 6H^+ \rightarrow 3I_2 + 3H_2O + 6K^+$$

0.89 g of potassium iodate was dissolved in water and made up to 250 cm^3 of solution. To 25 cm^3 of this solution were added an excess of potassium iodide and dilute sulphuric acid. The liberated iodine reacted with 24 cm^3 of a solution of sodium thiosulphate. Calculate the concentration of the latter in grams of the hydrated salt, $Na_2S_2O_35H_2O$ per litre.

Q.11.26　1.23 g of potassium iodate, KIO_3, were dissolved in water and made up to a volume of 500 cm^3. 25 cm^3 of this solution were added to an excess of dilute acid and potassium iodide. The iodine liberated was found to react with 22.5 cm^3 of a sodium thiosulphate solution. Calculate the concentration of the latter in (i) mol/L, (ii) g of thiosulphate crystals, $Na_2S_2O_35H_2O$, per litre.

Q.11.27　Some potassium iodate crystals were dissolved in water and made up to 250 cm^3 of solution. 25 cm^3 of this were added to an excess of acidified potassium iodide and then titrated with 0.11 M sodium thiosulphate solution. The mean titre was found to be 22.2 cm^3. Calculate the mass of potassium iodate taken.

Q.11.28　Bleach contains sodium hypochlorite, NaClO, an oxidising agent which releases iodine from acidified potassium iodide. 25 cm^3 of bleach were diluted to a volume of 250 cm^3 and 25 cm^3 of this diluted solution reacted with exactly 18.5 cm^3 of 0.2 M thiosulphate solution. Calculate the percentage of chlorine in the bleach.

Q.11.29　10 cm^3 of a household bleach were made up to a volume of 250 cm^3 with water. 25 cm^3 of this were added to an excess of potassium iodide

and ethanoic acid. This was found to react with exactly 21.3 cm^3 of 0.092 M thiosulphate solution. Calculate the percentage (g/100 cm^3) of chlorine in the bleach.

Q.11.30　2.5 g of a chlorine-containing compound called bleaching powder were placed in a 250 cm^3 volumetric flask along with an excess of potassium iodide crystals. It was then acidified to liberate the iodine, and made up to the mark on the neck of the flask. 25 cm^3 of the solution reacted with exactly 20.2 cm^3 of 0.12 M thiosulphate solution. Calculate the percentage of chlorine released by the bleaching powder.

Q.11.31　A 250 cm^3 sample of chlorinated water from a swimming pool was placed in a flask along with some crystals (an excess) of potassium iodide. The liberated iodine reacted with 3.5 cm^3 of 0.01 M thiosulphate solution. Calculate the concentration of chlorine in the water, expressing the result in p.p.m.

Q.11.32　Public water supplies are sterilised by adding small amounts of chlorine. In an analysis of a water sample, 500 cm^3 of it were added to excess potassium iodide solution, and the liberated iodine was found to require 1.2 cm^3 of 0.01 M $Na_2S_2O_3$ for complete reaction. Calculate the amount of chlorine in the water in (a) moles per litre, (b) grams per litre, and (c) p.p.m.

Q.11.33　A potassium salt of ethanedioic acid has the formula $KH_x(C_2O_4)_y2H_2O$. To 25 cm^3 of a solution of this salt in water, some sulphuric acid was added and it was then heated to about 70°C. When titrated with 0.02 M potassium permanganate solution, a titre of 30 cm^3 was obtained.

(a)　Why was the sulphuric acid added?

(b)　Calculate the number of moles of $C_2O_4^{2-}$ per litre.

Another 25 cm^3 of the solution required 22.5 cm^3 of 0.1 M sodium hydroxide solution for neutralisation.

(c)　What indicator would be the correct one to use?

(d)　Calculate the number of moles of H^+ per litre of solution.

(e)　Calculate the ratio of the moles of H^+ to the moles of $C_2O_4^-$ from the results of (d) and (b).

(f)   Given that the relative molecular mass of the salt is 254, deduce the values of x and y in the formula given above.

Q.11.34   In a permanganate/ethanedioic acid titration, it was found that 24 cm^3 of 0.02 M permanganate reacted with 20 cm^3 of the ethanedioic acid solution.

(a)   What is the reducing agent in this reaction?

(b)   How is the end point of the reaction indicated?

(c)   What two conditions are necessary for the titration to work?

(d)   The first few drops of permanganate decolorise slowly while succeeding drops are rapidly decolorised. Explain why, and name this property.

(e)   Define oxidation in terms of oxidation number, and hence show that the ethanedioic acid is oxidised.

(f)   Calculate the concentration of the ethanedioic acid solution (i) in terms of molarity, and (ii) in grams of $H_2C_2O_4 2H_2O$ crystals per litre of solution.

Q.11.35   Hydrogen peroxide is an oxidising agent and therefore liberates iodine from acidified potassium iodide solution. Water is also formed in the reaction. Write a balanced equation for this reaction.

In an experiment 25 cm^3 of hydrogen peroxide solution liberated sufficient iodine to react with 15 cm^3 of 0.12 M thiosulphate solution. Calculate the molarity of the hydrogen peroxide, and its concentration in g/L

Review   When you know chapter 11, you should be able to:

(a)   Explain why potassium permanganate is an oxidising agent,

(b)   show how permanganate oxidises in acidic solution,

(c)   show how permanganate oxidises in neutral solution,

(d)   describe how to prepare ammonium iron(II) sulphate solution, and to know why it is used as a primary standard.

(e)   describe how to standardise potassium permanganate solution,

(f)   write equations for the reactions of permanganate with (a) Fe^{2+} ions, (b) ethanedioic acid,

(g)   solve problems involving permanganate with both Fe^{2+} ions and ethanedioic acid,

(h)   know how to determine the end point in such titrations,

(i)   show how sodium thiosulphate and iodine react,

(j)   explain how starch acts as an indicator

(k)   show how oxidising agents liberate iodine from acidified potassium iodide solution

(l)   describe how to standardise sodium thiosulphate solution using potassium permanganate or potassium iodate,

(m)   solve sodium thiosulphate titration problems.

The speed at which different chemical reactions occur varies considerably; some take place practically instantaneously, *e.g.* the precipitation of silver chloride on mixing solutions of silver nitrate and sodium chloride, whereas others can take days or even months to show a noticeable change, *e.g.* the rusting of iron or the fading of a newspaper. Kinetics is the study of the rates at which reactions occur, and of the various factors which influence these rates.

It is very important for chemists and chemical engineers to know all about chemical kinetics; not only do they want to turn one substance into another, they want to do it as completely as possible and, since times costs money, as **quickly** as possible.

Factors affecting Rates of Reactions

> **The rate of a chemical reaction can be defined as the change in the amount or of the concentration of either reactant or product per unit time.**

It can be expressed in a variety of units, *e.g.* moles per second (or per minute), grams (or cm^3) per second or per any other unit of time. The rate of a reaction and the time taken are inversely proportional to one another. Rate of reaction depends on a variety of conditions, as detailed below.

(i) The nature of the reactants.

In general, ionic reactions are fast because they merely involve the coming together of oppositely charged ions. When solutions of silver nitrate and sodium chloride are mixed, silver ions and chloride ions (which are already present in the solution) join together to form insoluble silver chloride which is immediately precipitated.

$$Ag^+ + Cl^- \rightarrow AgCl(\downarrow)$$

Covalent reactions are usually slower, because they involve the breaking of covalent bonds. When hydrogen and chlorine combine, the bonds in both reactants have first to be broken before atoms of hydrogen and chlorine can combine together to form hydrogen chloride.

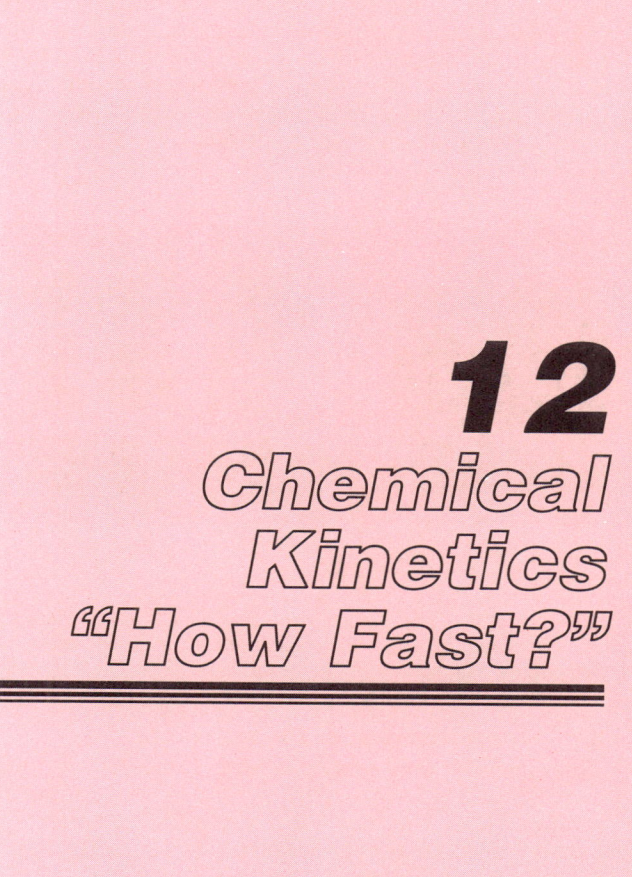

12

Chemical Kinetics "How Fast?"

$$H_2 \rightarrow 2H; \quad Cl_2 \rightarrow 2Cl;$$

$$2H + 2Cl \rightarrow 2HCl$$

(ii) State of the reactants

If one of the reactants is a solid, it generally reacts more quickly if it is finely divided. A lump of marble (calcium carbonate) takes some time to react with acid, but if the lump is first powdered, reaction is much faster. The finely divided substance has more molecules exposed to attack by acid.

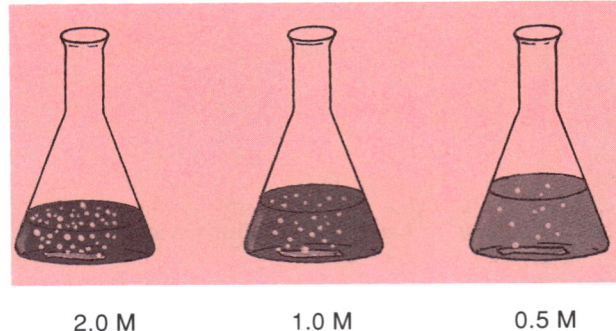

2.0 M   1.0 M   0.5 M

12.2 — In this experiment, pieces of magnesium are put into separate portions of hydrochloric acid — of different concentrations. The rate at which bubbles of hydrogen are formed clearly indicates the effect of temperature on the rate

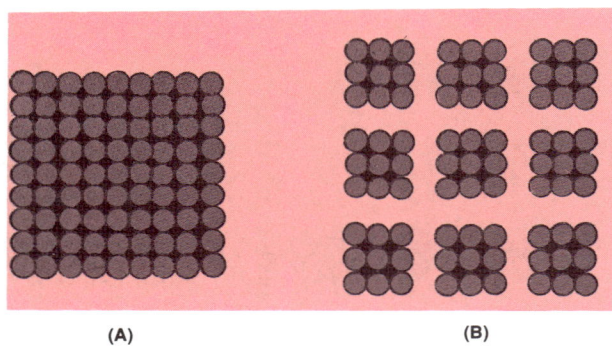

(A)   **(B)**

12.1 — (a) lump of substance; 32 molecules on surface (b) same amount of substance but divided into portions; 72 molecules on surface .

(iii) Concentration of the reactants

This greatly controls reaction rate. A law put forward in the 19th century states that at constant temperature, the rate of a chemical reaction is proportional to the concentration of each of the reacting substances.

In the reaction $A + B \rightarrow AB$, the rate is thus proportional to the concentration of A and also to the concentration of B, *i.e.* to the product of their concentrations. This can be represented as:

rate $\propto$ [A] [B], or rate = k[A][B][i]

where k is a constant.

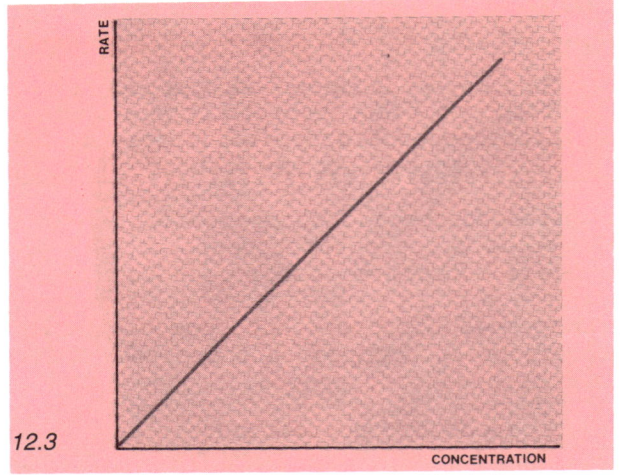

12.3

However the rate of a reaction is seldom constant for the duration of the reaction, for as the reaction proceeds, the concentrations of the reactants decrease and so the rate decreases. This effect is seen in experiments 12.5 and 12.7.

(iii) Pressure

This is only applicable to gaseous reactions and has the same effect in these as concentration has on reactions in solution.

(i)   The concentration of a substance is conventionally represented by the formula of the substance with square brackets around it. [A], for example, means "the concentration of the substance A (in moles per litre)."

(iv) Temperature

All reactions are faster at higher temperatures. An increase in temperature of 10 to 20°C generally doubles the rate of a reaction.

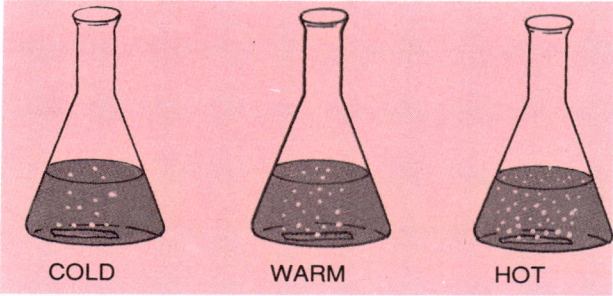

COLD   WARM   HOT

12.4 — *In this experiment, it is the temperature of the acid which differs. Again, the rate is made obvious by the rate at which hydrogen is liberated.*

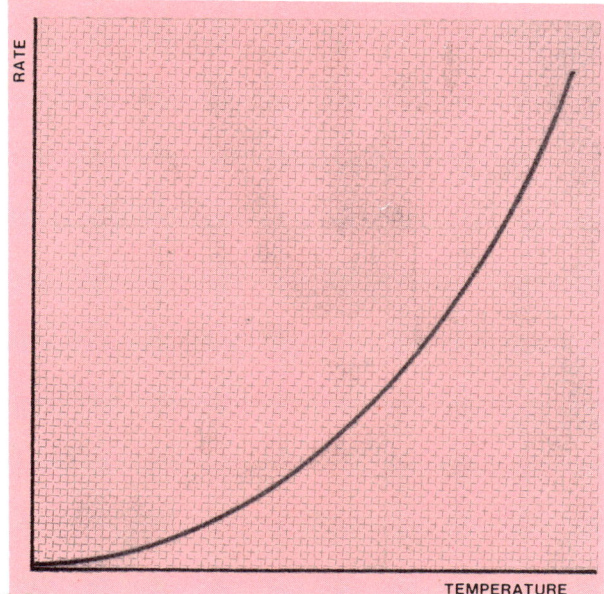

12.5 —

(v) Presence of a catalyst

Rates can be increased (and sometimes decreased) by the presence of certain substances which are not consumed in the reaction and are left chemically unchanged at the end. Such substances are called catalysts.

Experiment 12.1
To show the Difference in the Rates of Ionic and of Covalent Reactions.

Acidified potassium permanganate is decolorised by reducing agents. In this experiment, it is added to two ionic reducing agents (iron(II) ions and sulphite ions) and to two covalent reducing agents (ethanedioic acid and ethanal), and the difference in reaction rates is observed.

Into four test tubes put about 5 cm depth of :

(a) iron(II) sulphate or iron(II) ammonium sulphate solution (both contain Fe^{2+} ions)

(b) sodium sulphite solution (contains SO_3^{2-} - ions),

(c) ethanedioic acid solution,

(d) ethanal solution.

To each add about 5 drops of acidified potassium permanganate solution. If, after a minute or so, no change has occurred, gently heat the mixture until a change does occur.

Record the conclusions which can be drawn from the experiment.

Experiment 12.2
To show how Rate depends on Particle Size

Weigh out (i) a single lump of marble (calcium carbonate) of mass about 5 g, (ii) the same mass of marble "chips" and (iii) the same mass of powdered marble. Into each of the three beakers, measure 50 cm^3 of dilute hydrochloric acid. To these beakers add, simultaneously, the three weighed portions of marble, and at the same time start a stop clock or note the exact time. Let the reactions proceed, and note the time when the reaction in each of the beakers has finished.

What is the effect on the reaction rate of the size of the marble pieces? Explain why.

Experiment 12.3
To investigate how Rate of Reaction depends on Concentration.

The reaction under investigation is that in which hydrochloric acid reacts with sodium thiosulphate, giving, as one of the products, elemental sulphur (which is insoluble and therefore makes the solution cloudy as it is being formed).

$$Na_2S_2O_3 + 2HCl \rightarrow 2NaCl + S(\downarrow) + H_2O + SO_2$$

The reaction is carried out six times, with solutions of different concentrations, and in each case, the time taken for the sulphur to appear is measured (see note 1). The reciprocal of the time ($1/t$) is a measure of the reaction rate (see note 2).

A stock solution of sodium thiosulphate (0.2 M or 50 g/L) is prepared, and from this, the five other solutions of lower concentrations are made as follows:

Solution A is the undiluted stock solution, of concentration 0.2 M.

Solution B is made by taking 80 cm^3 of stock solution and diluting it to 100 cm^3. Its concentration is therefore eight-tenths of 0.2, *i.e.* 0.16 M.

Solution C contains 60 cm^3 of stock solution diluted to 100 cm^3 and has a concentration of $\frac{6}{10}$ths of 0.2 M *i.e.*, 0.12 M.

Solutions D,E and F contain 40, 20 and 10 cm^3 respectively of the thiosulphate solution, diluted to 100 cm^3 in each case; their concentrations will be 0.08 M, 0.04 M and 0.02 M

Take 100 cm^3 of the thiosulphate solution in a conical flask or beaker. Measure out 10 cm^3 of dilute hydrochloric acid in a small graduated cylinder and pour this into the thiosulphate solution, while at the same time starting a stop clock or noting the time to the nearest second. Swirl the container to mix the solution and then place it on a piece of printed paper. When the required degree of "milkiness" has been reached (see Note 1), note the time taken.

Carry out this procedure for each of the six solutions. Use the same container (or an identical one) for the solution each time. Tabulate the results, and plot a graph of rate (see note 2) against concentration. What conclusion can be drawn from this graph?

Notes

1.　Each time the experiment is carried out, the solution must have acquired the same degree of "milkiness" when the final time is taken. A satisfactory way of making sure that this is so is to put the container over printed paper, and when the print is no longer readable through the solution, the time is taken.

2.　The time taken for a reaction to occur and the average rate of reaction are inversely proportional to each other. If a reaction occurs in a short time, then the rate is high, and conversely, if a reaction takes a long time, the rate is low. The reciprocal of the time taken is therefore a measure of the rate of the reaction (the units of course are arbitrary).

Specimen Results						
Conc. of $Na_2S_2O_3$	0.2 M	0.16	0.12	0.08	0.04	0.02
Time taken / sec	16	19	26	38	77	146

Experiment 12.4
To investigate how Rate of Reaction depends on Temperature

The reaction of the previous experiment is used here, except that this time the temperature is varied rather than the concentration.

Take 25 cm^3 of the stock thiosulphate solution, dilute it to 100 cm^3 with water and pour it into the conical flask or beaker which is being used. Add 10 cm^3 of dilute hydrochloric acid, swirl the flask to mix it and observe the time. While waiting for the sulphur to appear, take the temperature of the solution. Measure the time for the usual degree of milkiness to be reached.

Take another 25 cm^3 of stock solution, dilute it to 100 cm^3 and pour it into the flask as before. This time, heat the solution to about 30°C before adding the acid. Repeat the rest of the procedure, noting the temperature while waiting for the sulphur to appear. Do this about six times, making the temperature about 10°C higher each time. Tabulate the results and plot a graph of the rate against temperature. Draw a conclusion from the graph.

Specimen Results								
Temp./°C	20	30	40	50	60	70	80	90
Time / sec.	56	29	18	12	8	6	4	between 2 and 3

Experiment 12.5
To investigate the Rate of Reaction between a Carbonate and Acid

Into a 250 cm^3 conical flask place 50 cm^3 of dilute hydrochloric acid. Weight out about 10 g of marble chips of such a size that the 10 g consists of about 30 pieces. Add the marble pieces to the flask, insert a loose plug of cotton wool into the neck of the flask and place the apparatus on the pan of a direct reading balance. Note the mass of the apparatus and at the same time start a stopclock or note the exact time.

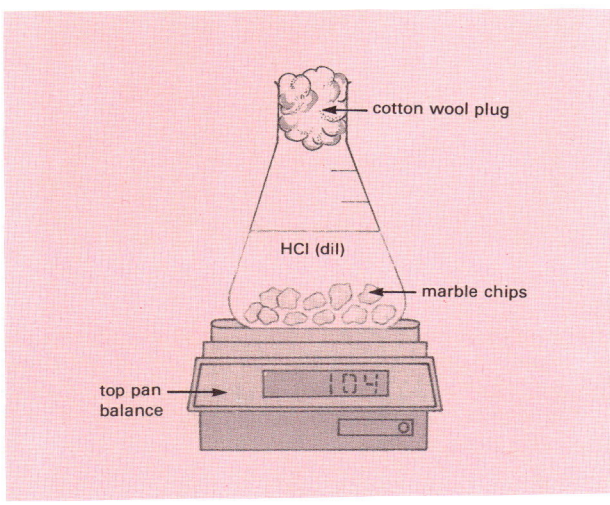

12.6 — *Calcium carbonate in hydrochloric acid.*

Leave the apparatus on the balance pan and record its mass at ½ minute intervals. Continue until the mass becomes constant; this will take about 15 minutes.

Make out a chart of the results, listing (i) time, (ii) mass of apparatus, (iii) total loss of mass. Plot a graph of total loss of mass against time.

Questions
1 Why is there a loss of mass as the reaction proceeds?
2. Why does the reaction stop?
3. What is the purpose of the cotton wool?
4. Explain the shape of the graph.
5. In what units could the rate of reaction be expressed?
6. From the graph, read off the average rate of reaction during the first minute.
7. Write the equation for the reaction.
8. Calculate the number of moles of the gas formed.
9. Calculate the number of moles of acid used.
10. Using the fact that 50 cm^3 of acid were taken initially, calculate the concentration of that acid.

11. Using exactly the same quantities of reagents, suggest how the time taken for the reaction could have been reduced.
12. In dotted lines (or in a different colour), draw a sketch of the graph that is likely to result from carrying out the experiment using 50 cm^3 of acid of half the original concentration.

Catalysis

A catalyst is a substance which alters the rate of a chemical reaction, but which is not used up, and is chemically unchanged at the end of the reaction.

The effect is known as **catalysis**. In the normal sense of the word, a catalyst speeds up a reaction *i.e.* it increases the rate of the reaction.

Hydrogen and oxygen, for example, hardly react together at all at room temperature but in the presence of platinum wire, reaction occurs rapidly and can even be explosive. Platinum is a catalyst for that reaction.

Experiment 12.6
Investigating Catalysis

Experiment A. Catalytic Decomposition of Potassium Chlorate

Potassium chlorate decomposes on being heated, yielding oxygen and potassium chloride.

$$2KClO_3 \rightarrow 2KCl + 3O_2$$

Take some potassium chlorate to a depth of about 2 cm in a test tube and support the tube diagonally in a clamp. Arrange a bunsen burner to give a medium flame (and do not readjust it), note the exact time, and commence heating the chlorate. After it has melted, hold a glowing splint at the top of the test tube to test for liberated oxygen. If the splint goes out, re-light it. Continue heating until oxygen is produced and then note the time taken.

Repeat the experiment, but this time instead of using potassium chlorate, mix it with about one quarter of its bulk of manganese dioxide. Heat as before and find out how long it takes for oxygen to be liberated. Describe the effect on the reaction of having the manganese dioxide present.

Experiment B — Catalytic Oxidation of Ethanedioic Acid

Ethanedioic acid is a reducing agent and so decolorises acidified potassium permanganate solution — which is an oxidising agent. The permanganate is converted to colourless compounds in the reaction.

$$2KMnO_4 + 6H^+ + 5H_2C_2O_4 \rightarrow$$

$$2K^+ + 2Mn^{2+} + 10CO_2 + 8H_2O$$

Take about 10 cm^3 of dilute potassium permanganate solution and acidify it by adding 1 or 2 cm^3 of dilute sulphuric acid. Add about 10 cm^3 of ethanedioic acid solution and mix well. Measure the time taken for the permanganate to lose its purple colour. While the reaction is proceeding, carry out a second experiment this time with some Mn^{2+} ions (a few drops of a solution of a manganese(II) salt) added to the ethanedioic acid. Describe your findings, and explain how this experiment illustrates autocatalysis.

Experiment C — Action of Light on Silver Chloride

Into each of two test tubes pour 5 cm^3 of dilute hydrochloric acid and the same volume of silver nitrate solution. This precipitates insoluble silver chloride. Place one tube in a dark place (*e.g.* a closed cupboard) and the other in bright light, preferably sunlight. Compare the two compounds after about 5 minutes. What effect has the light had on the silver chloride. Why do you think silver chloride is used in the manufacture of photographic paper?

Experiment D — Intermediate Compound Formation

This colourful experiment illustrates the formation of an intermediate compound during a homogeneous catalysis. The reaction is that in which Co^{2+} ions catalyse the oxidation of tartrate ions[i] by hydrogen peroxide solution, *viz.*

$$\text{tartrate ions} + H_2O_2 \xrightarrow{\text{Co}^{2+}} CO_2 + H_2O$$

Dissolve about 3 g of sodium potassium tartrate in 100 cm^3 of hot water (at about 70°C). Add 5 — 10 cm^3

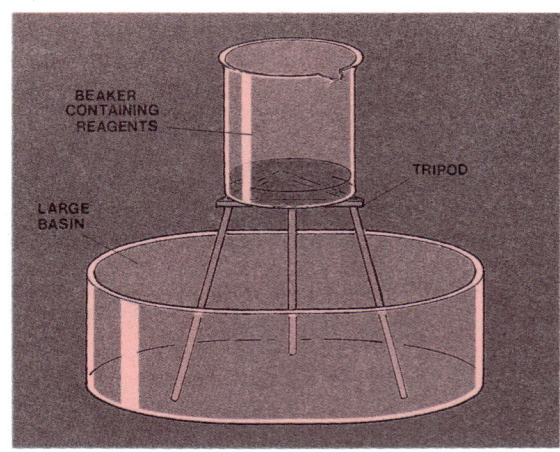

BEAKER CONTAINING REAGENTS

TRIPOD

LARGE BASIN

12.7

of cobalt chloride solution and arrange the apparatus as shown. Now add 20 cm^3 of hydrogen peroxide solution (about 20 volume) and mix. Observe and record the various changes which occur. Answer the questions which follow.

(a) What evidence is there that an intermediate compound was formed?

(b) How do you know that this compound was not one of the final products?

(c) How do you know that the catalyst was regenerated?

(d) Why did the mixture bubble?

(e) What substances were present in the final mixture?

(f) What would be the effect of carrying out the experiment (i) without the cobalt chloride? (ii) without the hydrogen peroxide? (iii) at a higher temperature?

Experiment E — The Iodine "Snake"

Place a 250 cm^3 graduated cylinder in the middle of several layers of opened-out newspaper. Into the cylinder put (i) about 5 g of solid potassium iodide, (ii) about 20 cm^3 of detergent (washing up liquid), and (iii) about 20 cm^3 of 100 volume hydrogen peroxide. The iodide ions catalyse the decomposition of the peroxide,

---

(i)   Tartaric acid is an organic form of formula $C_4H_6O_6$. The tartrate ion is $C_4H_4O_6{}^{2-}$.

releasing oxygen which, in the presence of the detergent produces foam and rises up the cylinder.

$$H_2O_2 \xrightarrow{\text{I}^-} H_2O + \tfrac{1}{2}O_2$$

Due to the fact that commercial hydrogen peroxide is usually acidic, some iodide ions (from the potassium iodide) become oxidised, forming iodine which colours the foam yellow. If the peroxide is first neutralised (by adding some sodium hydroxide solution), the foam is white.

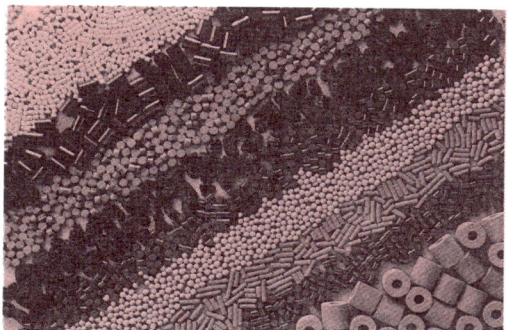

12.8 — Catalysts of various shapes and sizes, pelleted to provide large surface area.

Experiment F — Catalysis by Surface Absorption

Methanol can be oxidised by atmospheric oxygen, and this reaction is catalysed by platinum.

Set up the apparatus as shown. Heat the platinum spiral to redness and hold it in the conical flask. The reaction is exothermic and the wire remains hot. The smell of

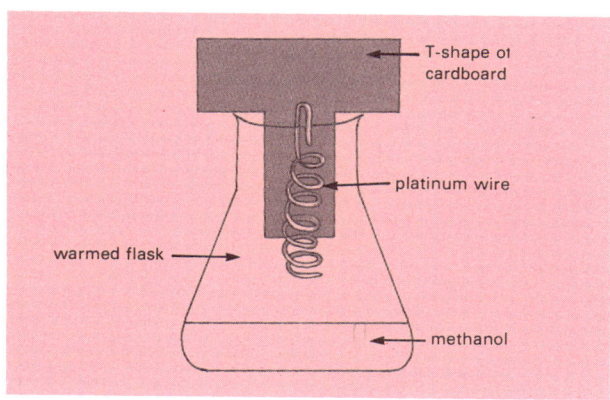

12.9 — Platinum catalysed oxidation of methanol

methanal may be noticed, but it is more likely that the mixture of methanal vapour and air will ignite, and burn with mild popping sounds. The fact that the platinum remains hot means that energy is being liberated; thus the change from methanol to methanal is an exothermic reaction.

Experiment 12.7
To investigate the Rate at which Hydrogen Peroxide is catalytically decomposed.

Set up the apparatus as shown. When everything is ready, either tilt the flask downwards so that the catalyst falls into the hydrogen peroxide (for apparatus I), or (for

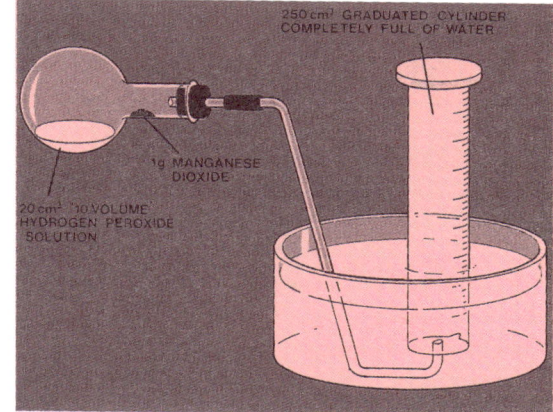

12.10 (a)

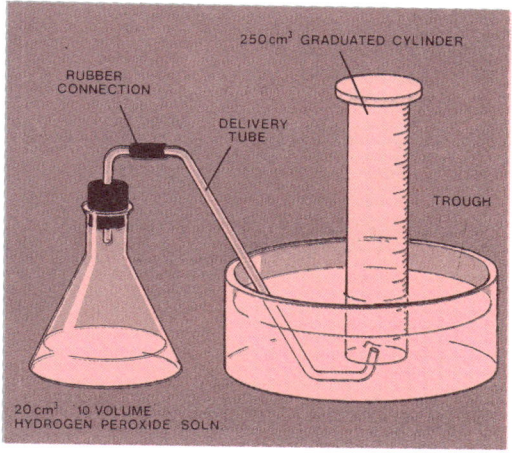

12.10 (b)

apparatus II) remove the stopper, drop in the catalyst, and quickly replace the stopper. At the same time start a stop clock or note the exact time. At half minute intervals, read the volume of the gas which has collected. Make a table of these results and then plot a graph of the volume of oxygen against time.

Repeat the experiment but this time use 50 cm^3 of peroxide of half the original concentration. Again measure, at half minute intervals, the volume of oxygen collected. On the same axes as for the previous graph, plot this second set of results.

Answer the following questions about the results of the experiment (refer to the worked example on p.147 if necessary).

(a) By referring to the graphs, state the two ways in which the results of experiment I differ from those of experiment II. Explain the reason for each of the differences.

(b) At what time was each of the reactions complete?

The following questions refer only to experiment I.

(c) What volume of oxygen had collected at 2 minutes? What was the average rate of reaction during the first two minutes?

(d) Calculate the actual rate of reaction (in cm^3 of O_2/min) at (i) 2 minutes (ii) 4 minutes.

(e) How does the rate of reaction change with time? Why?

(f) At what time had 50 cm^3 of oxygen collected?

(g) How many moles of hydrogen peroxide were used?

(h) Calculate the molarity of the original hydrogen peroxide solution.

General Features of Catalysts

There are a great number of catalysts in use today, and chemists are forever researching to find new and better catalysts to make chemical manufacture more efficient and more economic. Some catalysed reactions referred to in this book are as follows:

(a) $2H_2O_2 \xrightarrow{MnO_2} 2H_2O + O_2$

(b) $2KClO_3 \xrightarrow{MnO_2} 2KCl + 3O_2$

(c) $C_6H_{12}O_6 \xrightarrow{zymase} 2C_2H_5OH + 2CO_2$

(d) $N_2 + 3H_2 \underset{Fe}{\overrightarrow{\longleftarrow}} 2NH_3$

(e) $SO_2 + \frac{1}{2}O_2 \underset{V_2O_5}{\overset{Pt\ or}{\longleftrightarrow}} SO_3$

(f) $C_2H_4 + H_2 \xrightarrow{Ni} C_2H_6$

(g) $2MnO_4^- + 5(COOH)_2 + 6H^+ \xrightarrow{Mn^{2+}}$
$2Mn^{2+} + 8H_2O + 10CO_2$

1. A catalyst is usually specific in its action, *i.e.* it only catalyses one particular reaction or one type of reaction. In the examples, iron catalyses reaction (d), but not any of the others. Enzymes, which are biological catalysts, are even more selective in their action; reaction (c) can only be catalysed by the enzyme zymase, and this is the only reaction which zymase can catalyse.

2. The catalyst, while chemically unchanged after a reaction, can have changed physically. In reaction (a) above, if the MnO_2 is lumpy initially, it is left as a fine powder afterwards.

3. If a reaction is reversible (*e.g.* (d) and (e)) both forward and backward reactions are catalysed to the same extent, *i.e.* the position of equilibrium and the composition of the final mixture are unaffected.

4. The activity of a catalyst can be destroyed by some substances — known as **catalyst poisons**. In reaction (e) traces of arsenic destroy the activity of the platinum (and for this reason, V_2O_5 is usually preferred since it is not poisoned by arsenic).

5. The activity of a catalyst can sometimes be much improved by the presence of small quantities of other substances know as **promoters** which are not themselves catalysts. In reaction (d), a small quantity of Al_2O_3 greatly improves the effect of the iron catalyst.

6. Some substances decrease the rate of a reaction, and these are called **negative catalysts** or **inhibitors**. A small amount of glycerol is often added to commercial hydrogen peroxide because it slows down its decomposition due to the action of light. Ethanol has the same effect on the decomposition of hydrogen peroxide. Lead tetraethyl, $(Pb(C_2H_5)_4)$ is added to petrol

because it hinders the pre-ignition of the petrol vapour/air mixture when it is compressed in the engine cylinder.

7. **Autocatalysis** is the catalysis of a reaction by one of the products of that reaction. A good example is that of the oxidation of ethanedioic acid by permanganate ions, which is catalysed by Mn^{2+} ions (reaction (g)). Initially this reaction is slow, but its rate increases rapidly as the catalyst is formed.

8. **Types of Catalysis**   There are two main types of catalysis, *viz.* **homogeneous** and **heterogeneous**. In homogeneous catalysis, both catalyst and reactants are all in the same phase. *e.g* all liquids or all gaseous. Reaction (g) in which all substances are in aqueous solution, is an example of this. In heterogeneous catalysis, there is a definite boundary surface between the catalyst and the reactants. Reaction (a) (catalyst solid, reactants liquid) and (d) and (e) (catalyst solid, reactants gaseous) are examples of heterogeneous systems.

Activation Energy and Reaction Profile Diagrams

A chemical reaction between two substances is the result of their molecules colliding together. However, not all collisions between the molecules of the reacting substances result in a reaction occurring. It has been shown that two colliding molecules must possess a minimum amount of energy for a reaction to occur.

> **The minimum amount of energy which colliding molecules must posses before they can react is known as activation energy.**

Most reactions between covalent substances do not take place spontaneously — the activation energy must first be supplied to start the reaction. In other words, the system has to gain energy in some way. Normally this is provided in the form of heat, but light or electrical energy can also cause chemical reactions to take place. After the reaction has started, energy is generally released. **A reaction profile diagram** shows how the energy content of the system changes during the course of a reaction.

The changes of energy for two different reactions are shown in Fig. 12.11 For reaction I, the system

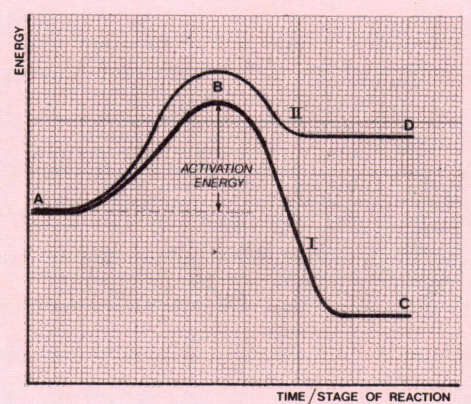

12.11

initially has energy content **A**; the activation energy is then supplied (energy content now reaches **B**) and the reaction starts. Energy is released, and when the reaction has finished, the energy content of the system has decreased to **C**. In this example, more energy was released than was supplied (**C** is lower than **A**), *i.e.* there was a net release of energy so that this reaction was an **exothermic reaction**.

Reaction II shows the energy changes for an **endothermic reaction**. More energy was supplied than was released so that the system contained more energy afterwards (point **D** on the graph) than beforehand, *i.e.* there was a net intake of energy.

A catalyst works by providing an alternative route for the reaction — a route having lower activation energy than that for the uncatalysed reaction.

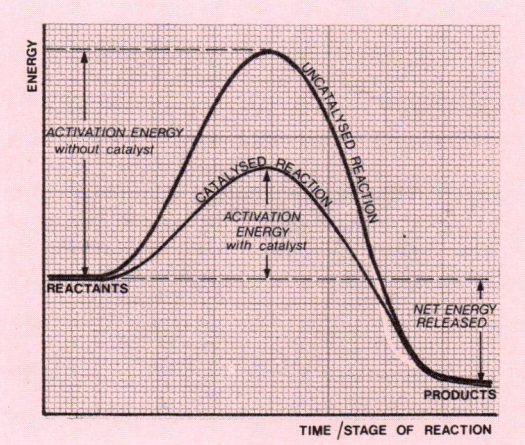

12.12

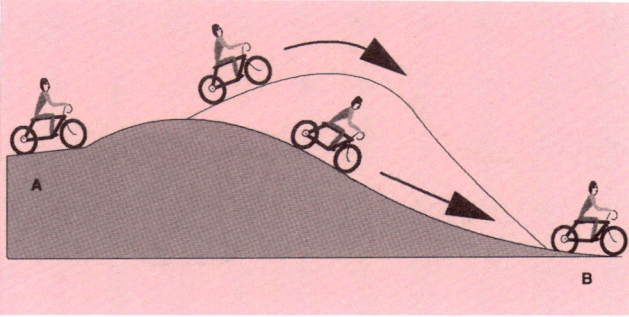

12.13 — *Two ways of getting from A to B. One requires much energy (high 'activation energy'), the other requires less energy. Note that both routes start and finish at the same*

More of the molecules will therefore have this lower amount of energy and will be able to react, and so the rate of reaction will be greater.

Catalysis Mechanisms

1. Intermediate Compound Theory

This theory suppose the formation of an unstable intermediate compound — one which is formed more readily than the product of the reaction, and also which is easily decomposed. For the reaction:

$$A + B \rightarrow AB \text{ (slow reaction)}$$

which is catalysed by the substance C, the mechanism can be represented by:

$$A + C \rightarrow AC \text{ (fast reaction)}$$

$$AC + B \rightarrow AB + C \text{ (fast reaction)}$$

AC has only a temporary existence, being decomposed as fast as it is being formed. Thus the catalyst, which has basically acted as a "carrier" is regenerated. Evidence which supports such a theory is that traces of intermediate compounds have been found in the products of catalysed reactions.

This is the mechanism by which I^- ions catalyse the decomposition of hydrogen peroxide. The intermediate substance is the IO^- ion, and the stages of the reaction are:

(i)   formation of intermediate

$$H_2O_2 + I^- \rightarrow IO^- + H_2O$$

(ii)   formation of product and regeneration of catalyst:

$$IO^- + H_2O_2 \rightarrow O_2 + I^- + H_2O$$

The net result is: $2H_2O_2 \rightarrow 2H_2O + O_2$

Catalysts which are compounds of transition metals often work in such a manner. A reaction which is catalysed by a transition metal compound and which provides evidence for the formation of an intermediate compound is the reaction in which tartrate ions are oxidised by hydrogen peroxide. This reaction is catalysed by cobalt ions and is described in Experiment 12.6 part D. The reaction is:

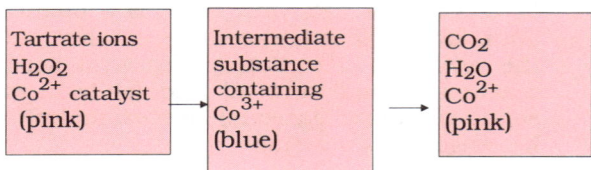

A mixture of hydrogen peroxide, cobalt chloride (*i.e.* Co^{2+}) and sodium potassium tartrate (the only common tartrate) is prepared. The mixture is pink due to the Co^{2+} ions present. Oxidation commences, the rate depending on the temperature. Much bubbling occurs as carbon dioxide is liberated, and the solution becomes blue due to the intermediate which contains cobalt ions in the blue +3 state. The bubbling ceases when oxidation has finished, and simultaneously the solution becomes pink again, as the Co^{2+} ions are regenerated.

2. Adsorption Theory

(for heterogeneous catalysis only).

Many solid substances which act as catalysts can hold appreciable quantities of gases and liquids on their surfaces; this is known as adsorption. Finely divided nickel and platinum are well known for their ability to do this.

This theory explains catalysis by suggesting that adsorption of one of the reactants on to the surface of the catalyst takes place and that the greatly increased concentration of that reactant on the surface leads to the increased rate of reaction. The fact that the more finely divided the catalyst is (*i.e.*

the greater is its surface area) the greater is its effect, supports such an idea. Examples of reactions which are catalysed in such a manner are (d), (e) and (f), p. 144

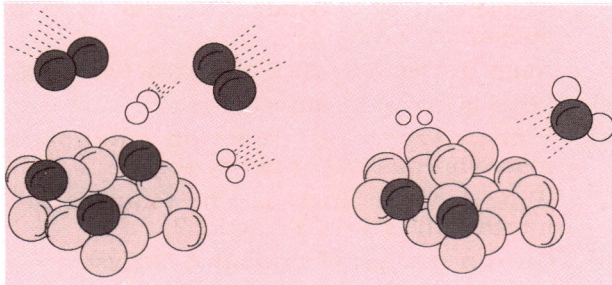

12.14 — (i) Molecules of one of the reactants are adsorbed onto the surface of the catalyst. (ii) Because of their increased concentration, molecules of the other reactant collide with them more frequently, and hence the rate of reaction is increased.

Worked Example

100 cm^3 of hydrogen peroxide solution at 32°C were mixed with 2 g of manganese dioxide, and the reaction was followed by measuring the total volume of oxygen liberated at various times. The following results were obtained.

Time / mins	1	2	3	4	5	6	8
Volume / cm^3	57	110	150	177	195	210	225

Time / mins	10	12	14	16	18	20	22
Volume /cm^3	235	242	247	248	249	250	250

(a) What is meant by the rate of a reaction?
(b) Plot a graph of the volume of the liberated oxygen against time.
(c) When was the reaction complete?
(d) When was it half complete?
(e) At what time had 170 cm^3 of oxygen been collected?

(f) What volume of oxygen was formed in 6 minutes?
(g) What percentage of the peroxide had decomposed in 6 minutes.
(h) Why was more oxygen formed in the first 6 minutes than in the next 6 minutes?
(i) What was the average rate at which oxygen was formed during the first 6 minutes?
(j) What was the actual rate of formation of oxygen at t = 6 minutes?
(k) How many moles of oxygen were formed altogether (molar volume at 32°C = 25 litres).
(l) How many moles of hydrogen peroxide were decomposed to produce that oxygen?
(m) Calculate the molarity of the hydrogen peroxide used.
(n) Name a suitable catalyst for the reaction.
(o) What mass of both catalyst and hydrogen peroxide were present at 22 minutes?
(p) On the same graph axis, sketch and label the approximate curves which would have been obtained if the 100 cm^3 of peroxide used had been half the original concentration.

Answers

(a) The rate of reaction is defined as the change in the amounts or of the concentration of the reactants (or of the products) per unit time.
(b) Fig. 12.15

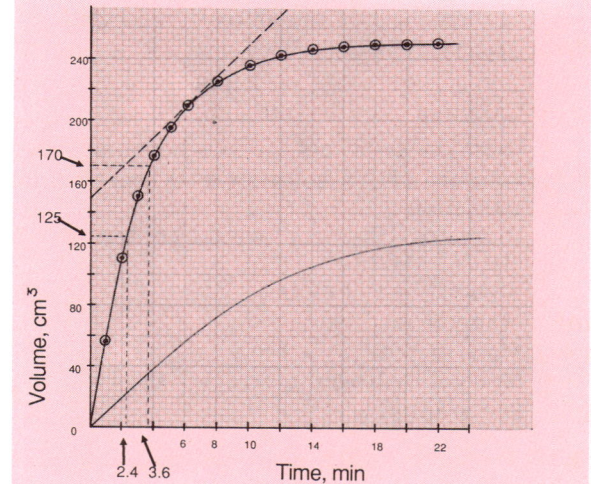

12.15 —

(c)   The reaction was complete in 20 minutes.

(d)   The reaction was half complete in 2.4 minutes. (See graph: time for 125 cm^3 of oxygen to be collected).

(e)   170 cm^3 of oxygen had been collected in 3.6 minutes (shown on graph).

(f)   210 cm^3 of oxygen were formed in 6 minutes.

(g) $$\frac{\text{volume of oxygen in 6 minutes}}{\text{total volume of oxygen}} = \frac{210 \text{ cm}^3}{250 \text{ cm}^3}$$
      = 84% of the total volume of oxygen formed, therefore 84% of the peroxide had decomposed.

(h)   More oxygen was formed in the first 6 minutes than in the second 6 because the rate of reaction was decreasing with time and so the formation of oxygen was getting slower.

(i)   Volume of oxygen in 6 minutes = 210 cm^3,
      therefore average rate = $\frac{210}{6}$ cm^3/min
      = 35 cm^3/min

(j)   The rate at $t = 6$ is 10 cm^3/minute (Method. Draw tangent to curve at $t = 6$. This tangent represents the actual rate at that instant. At that rate, the volume of oxygen would have increased from 150 cm^3 to 210 cm^3 in the 6 minutes; (60 cm^3 in 6 mins = 10 cm^3/min).

(k)   25000 cm^3 = 1 mole
      250 cm^3 = 0.01 mol of oxygen formed

(l) $2H_2O_2$ $\rightarrow$ O_2
      2 mol $\rightarrow$ 1 mol
      0.02 mol $\rightarrow$ 0.01 mol
      therefore 0.02 mol of H_2O_2 decomposed.

(m)   volume of H_2O_2 solution = 100 cm^3 (contains 0.02 mol)
      therefore 1000 cm^3 would contain 0.2 mol (10 × 0.02);
      molarity = 0.2 mol/L.

(n)   Manganese dioxide

(o)   Mass of catalyst = 2 g;
      Mass of hydrogen peroxide = 0.

(p)   See graphs.

Q.12.1   Give short answers to each of the following;

(a)   Define "rate of reaction". In what units can it be expressed?

(b)   Explain what a catalyst is.

(c)   Name a compound which catalyses the decomposition of hydrogen peroxide.

(d)   Give the equation for a reaction which is catalysed by platinum.

(e)   Acidified potassium permanganate is decolorised by substance X. What type of substance is X?

(f)   Name five factors which affect reaction rates.

(g)   What is meant by autocatalysis?

(h)   What type of reaction happens instantaneously — or nearly so?

(i)   Why does an increase in temperature increase the rate of a reaction?

(j)   Give an example of a negative catalyst.

(k)   What is meant by a catalyst poison?

(l)   Why does an increase in concentration of reactants increase the rate of a reaction?

Q.12.2   Give short answers to each of the following questions.

(a)   Define activation energy.

(b)   What effect does a catalyst have on the activation energy of a reaction?

(c)   The relationship between what two variables is shown on a reaction profile diagram?

(d)   What are the two mechanisms by which catalysts catalyse?

(e)   Give two examples where catalysts are used in industry to make processes more economical..

(f)   What reaction is shown by the "iodine snake" experiment?

(g)   By what method do cobalt ions catalyse the oxidation of tartrate ions? What evidence is there for this?

(h)   Give an example of a homogeneous catalyst and a reaction which it catalyses.

(i)   Give an example of a heterogeneous catalyst and a reaction which it catalyses.

Q.12.3   When copper(II) oxide and hydrogen peroxide are mixed, oxygen is released. In an experiment, 1 g of copper(II) oxide was added to 50 cm^3 of 2 M hydrogen peroxide. The volume of oxygen collected after various time intervals was found to be as follows:

time / sec	vol.O_2 /cm^3 (at room temperature and pressure)
5	18
10	27
15	36
20	43
30	53
40	61
50	67
60	73
75	79
90	83
105	86
120	86

(a) Draw a diagram of an apparatus suitable for this experiment.

(b) What was the purpose of (i) the hydrogen peroxide, (ii) the copper(II) oxide.

(c) Explain, with reference to the Periodic Table, why an oxide of **copper** was used.

(d) Why were readings taken more frequently in the earlier part of the experiment?

(e) Plot a graph of the results

(f) At what time was the reaction complete?

(g) At what time had half of the peroxide reacted?

(h) What four chemicals were in the apparatus at this stage?

(i) What volume of oxygen had been released at $t = 25$ sec?

(j) How many moles is this (take molar volume at room temperature and pressure to be 24 litres)

(k) How many moles of peroxide had reacted by this stage?

(l) Estimate (i) the average rate of reaction (in mol H_2O_2/sec) during the first 25 sec., (ii) the average rate during the next 25 sec, and (iii) the actual rate at $t = 25$ sec. Explain why (i) and (ii) differ.

(m) Name two ways in which the release of oxygen could have been slowed down.

(n) On the same axes, draw the graphs (in different colours) which would have been obtained if (i) 100 cm^3 of 1 M peroxide had been used, and (ii) if 25 cm^3 of 2 M peroxide had been used.

Q.12.4 The table of observations shown is taken from a laboratory investigation into the rate of decomposition of hydrogen peroxide using a manganese dioxide catalyst. For each set of initial conditions, the time taken to collect a fixed volume of gas was noted. In each experiment 50 cm^3 of aqueous hydrogen peroxide and 1 g of catalyst were used

Experiment	Concentration of aqueous hydrogen peroxide in mol/cm^3	Initial temperature in °C	Form of the catalyst	Time, in seconds to collect a fixed volume of gas
A	0.1	20	Powder	200
B	0.1	30	Powder	115
C	0.1	40	Powder	60
D	0.2	20	Powder	100
E	0.3	20	Powder	65
F	0.4	20	Pellets	130
G	0.4	20	Powder	50

(a) Draw a labelled diagram of an apparatus which could be used to perform this experiment.

(b) Write an equation for the reaction which takes place when hydrogen peroxide decomposes, and describe **one** simple test to identify the gas evolved.

(c) Which experimental results should be used to draw a graph to show the relationship between concentration of reactant and rate of reaction? Explain briefly the reasons for the choice.

(d) (i) State and explain what happens to the rate of decomposition of the hydrogen peroxide when the concentration of its solution is increased.

(ii) Explain why the use of catalyst pellets instead of powder alters the rate of reaction. (See experiments **F** and **G**).

(iii) State how **one** other factor investigated in this experiment affects the rate of reaction.

(e)   Define the term catalyst and describe briefly the essential steps of an experiment to prove that manganese dioxide acts as a catalyst in this reaction.

Q.12.5   A piece of marble (calcium carbonate) was placed in a beaker containing excess of dilute hydrochloric acid and put standing on a direct reading balance. The mass of the beaker and its contents were recorded every two minutes.

Time (mins)	Mass (g)
0	126.44
2	126.31
4	126.19
6	126.09
8	126.03
10	126.00
12	126.00

(a)   Why did the mass decrease?

(b)   Write an equation for the reaction.

(c)   Plot a graph of the results.

(d)   At which point in time was the rate of reaction highest?

(e)   Explain why.

(f)   Why was the reaction finished after 10 minutes?

(g)   State three different ways in which the reaction could have been made more rapid.

(h)   Write the name and formula of two ions which were present in the final solution.

(i)   The solution was then evaporated to dryness in the same beaker, and the mass of the beaker and remaining solid was found to be 97.63 g. Next day the mass was found to be 98.63 g. Explain what had occurred to cause this change, and name the phenomenon.

(j)   Finally, the solid was dissolved in some water and added to: (i) silver nitrate solution; (ii) sodium carbonate solution. State and explain what would be observed in each case, and write equations for the reactions which occurred.

Q.12.6   Some magnesium and an excess of dilute hydrochloric acid were reacted together. The volume of hydrogen produced was recorded every minute, giving the following results:

Time/Min	Volume of hydrogen/cm^3
0	0
1	14
2	23
3	31
4	38
5	40
6	40
7	40

(a)   What does an **excess** of acid mean?

(b)   Plot a graph of the results, labelling the axes correctly.

(c)   How much hydrogen was produced in each of the first five minutes?

(d)   When can the reaction be said to be complete?

(e)   Calculate the average rate at which the hydrogen is produced per minute.

(f)   In a similar experiment, 15 cm^3 of hydrogen were produced in the first minute. Explain whether this is a slower or a faster reaction than the one described above.

(g)   How could you make the above reaction go slower while still using the same quantities of both acid and metal?

(h)   Draw a sketch of the apparatus in which the experiment could have been carried out.

Review   When you know chapter 12 you should be able to:

(a) list five variables on which rates of reactions depend,

(b) say in what way each of these variables affects the rate,

(c) describe experiments to illustrate each of the variables,

(d) define or explain each of: rate of reaction, catalyst, catalyst poison, promoter, negative catalyst, autocatalysis, homogeneous, heterogeneous, activation energy,

(e) list the features of catalysts,

(f) describe the two mechanisms by which catalysts catalyse,

(g) plot and explain reaction rate graphs from data obtained from experiments,

(h) interpret reaction profile diagrams and show how a catalyst affects activation energy.

Reversible Reactions

Most of the reactions studied so far are ones which go to completion, or very nearly so anyway. For instance, when magnesium burns in oxygen, all of the metal is converted to magnesium oxide — there is no evidence that the reverse change occurs. There are, however, many chemical reactions which can be made to go both ways; for example, when bluestone (hydrated copper sulphate) is heated, it loses water and becomes anhydrous copper sulphate:

$$CuSO_4 5H_2O \rightarrow CuSO_4 + 5H_2O$$

Addition of water to the anhydrous copper sulphate converts it back to the hydrated salt:

$$CuSO_4 + 5H_2O \rightarrow CuSO_4 5H_2O$$

If such a reaction takes place in a closed system (no material can pass in or out), so that the reactants and products are always in contact, both reactions can (and do) occur at the same time. For example, when an acid reacts with an alcohol, an ester and water are formed, and conversely, when an ester is reacted with water, acid and alcohol are formed. Equations for such reactions are written with a reversible sign, *viz.*,

$$acid + alcohol \rightleftarrows ester + water$$

Other examples of such reactions are:

$$PCl_3 + Cl_2 \rightleftarrows PCl_5$$

$$H_2 + I_2 \rightleftarrows 2HI$$

$$N_2 + 3H_2 \rightleftarrows 2NH_3$$

$$2NO_2 \rightleftarrows N_2O_4$$

Equilibria or Equilibrium Systems

When two opposing reactions take place at the same rate, they effectively cancel each other out and the system reaches a **state of equilibrium**. Imagine that two substances A and B, react to give C and D, and that the reaction is reversible:

$$A + B \rightleftarrows C + D$$

As soon as some C and D are formed, the reverse reactions begins — at first slowly, but at an increasing rate as more C and D are formed. Meanwhile, the forward reaction slows down since

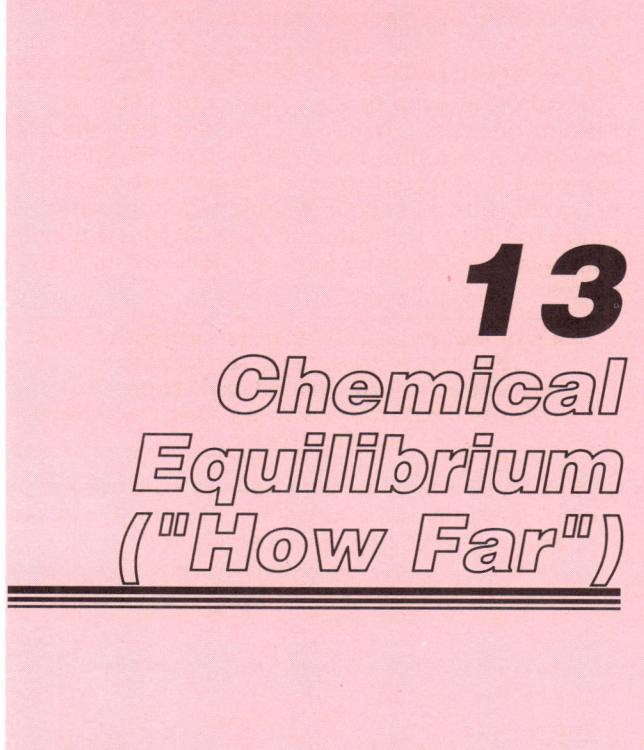

13
Chemical Equilibrium ("How Far")

A and B are being used up and their concentrations are decreasing.

A stage is therefore reached when the rates of both backward and forward reactions are equal; the system is then described as being **in equilibrium**. When equilibrium is reached there is no further change in the composition of the system; reaction however has not ceased, two opposing reactions are then proceeding at the same rate. The system is said to be in **dynamic equilibrium.**

Le Châtelier's Principle

Towards the end of the nineteenth century, a French chemist, Henri Le Châtelier, investigated changes in equilibrium systems. The result of his work is a useful guide to what happens the position of equilibrium in such a system, when a change is made to one of the external factors which affects that system. His principle, put forward in 1884, states:

> **If a system in equilibrium is subjected to a stress (*i.e.* a change in temperature, pressure, or concentration), then the system will alter so as to oppose the effect of the stress.**

To illustrate this, it is now applied to the system in which gaseous substances A, B and C are in equilibrium according to the equation:[i]

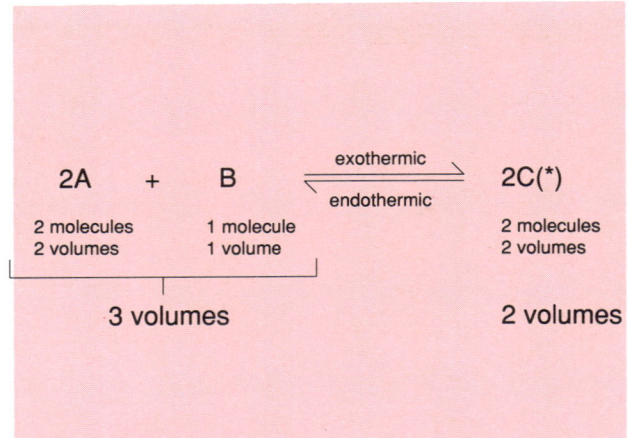

$$2A \quad + \quad B \quad \xrightleftharpoons[\text{endothermic}]{\text{exothermic}} \quad 2C(*)$$

2A	+	B		2C(*)
2 molecules		1 molecule		2 molecules
2 volumes		1 volume		2 volumes

3 volumes   2 volumes

1. **Changes in pressure:**

The pressure of a gas is directly proportional to the number of molecules per unit volume present; the greater the number of molecules, the greater is the pressure. If the pressure of the above system is increased, Le Chatelier's Principle predicts that the system will alter so as to oppose the increased pressure, *i.e.* a reaction will occur which reduces the pressure. So, in the example, the position of equilibrium moves to the right (more of C is formed) because this leads to a reduction of the total number of moles and, therefore, of the total pressure. Conversely, lowering of the pressure causes the equilibrium to move to the left.

For a reaction which occurs without change of volume (e.g. $H_2 + I_2 \rightleftharpoons 2HI$), a pressure change has no effect on the position of equilibrium. As well, it must be noted however that the only components of an equilibrium system to be affected by changes in pressure are those in the gaseous state. Thus, in an equilibrium system such as:

$$3Fe(s) + 4H_2O(g) \rightleftharpoons Fe_3O_4(s) + 4H_2(g)$$

increased pressure causes no change in the equilibrium position, because there are the same number of gaseous molecules on each side.

2. **Changes of temperature**

If the temperature is raised, the reaction which absorbs heat occurs (and thus tends to lower the temperature again). So the position of equilibrium in the example given, moves to the left, *i.e.* more of A and B are formed.

Conversely, at lower temperatures, more of C is formed.

3. **Changes in Concentration**

If more C is introduced into the system, the reaction in which C is consumed occurs *i.e.* the position of equilibrium will move to the left and more A and B will be formed.

Conversely, if C is removed from the system, the forward reaction in which C is produced will take place.

(i)   An example of such a system is $2SO_2 + O_2 \rightarrow 2SO_3$

Examples

PCl_5	$\rightleftharpoons$	$PCl_3 + Cl_2$	$\Delta H = +124 \text{ kJ}$
N_2O_4	$\rightleftharpoons$	$2NO_2$	$\Delta H = +24$
$N_2 + 3H_2$	$\rightleftharpoons$	$2NH_3$	$\Delta H = -92$
$2SO_2 + O_2$	$\rightleftharpoons$	$2SO_3$	$\Delta H = -256$
$N_2 + O_2$	$\rightleftharpoons$	$2NO$	$\Delta H = +180$
$CO + H_2O$	$\rightleftharpoons$	$CO_2 + H_2$	$\Delta H = +4$

At increased pressure, the position of equilibrium in reactions (3) and (4) moves to the right, and in reactions (1) and (2), to the left. Reactions (5) and (6) are unaffected. Decreased pressure has the opposite effects.

At increased temperature, the position of equilibrium moves to the right in reactions (1), (2), (5) and (6) and to the left in (3) and (4).

There are many reactions which can be used to illustrate Le Chatelier's Principle. The chromate/dichromate equilibrium system is very suitable, since chromate ions (CrO_4^{2-}) are yellow and dichromate ions ($Cr_2O_7^{2-}$) are orange.

$$\underset{\text{yellow}}{2CrO_4^{2-}} + 2H^+ \rightleftharpoons \underset{\text{orange}}{Cr_2O_7^{2-}} + H_2O$$

A dilute solution of potassium chromate in water is prepared. Addition of H^+ (some dilute HCl) drives the reaction to the right whereupon the orange colour due to dichromate appears. Removal of H^+ by adding OH^- (some dilute NaOH soln.) does the reverse, and the yellow colour of chromate reappears.

Experiment 13.1
Investigating Le Chatelier's Principle

Experiment A

The reaction: $N_2O_4 \underset{\text{exothermic}}{\overset{\text{endothermic}}{\rightleftharpoons}} 2NO_2$

is one which can conveniently be used to show the effect of temperature and pressure on a system in equilibrium. NO_2 gas is brown whereas N_2O_4 is practically colourless.

A glass or transparent plastic syringe is filled with nitrogen dioxide gas (which in reality is a mixture of N_2O_4 and NO_2). The pressure is then increased by pushing in the plunger and the colour becomes paler as $2NO_2$ changes to N_2O_4 [i]. On reducing the pressure again, the colour deepens as the reverse change occurs.

The effect of temperature change can be shown by filling two flasks (at room temperature) with nitrogen dioxide gas and then sealing them. One flask is then immersed in hot water and the other in iced water for about twenty seconds each. The colour of the gas in the hot flask is seen to have deepened (due to more NO_2 having been formed) and that in the cold flask to have become paler (due to less NO_2). This is in accordance with the equation: as temperature is increased the reaction proceeds in the direction: $N_2O_4 \rightarrow 2NO_2$, and as temperature is decreased, in the reverse direction.

Experiment B

The effect of changing the concentration of one of the components in an equilibrium mixture can be shown using the system:

$$Br_2 + 2OH^- \rightleftharpoons Br^- + BrO^- + H_2O$$

When bromine (which is red-brown in colour) is added to water, the above equilibrium is set up. Addition of OH^- ions (e.g. NaOH) drives the reaction to the right and the colour disappears (all the products of the reaction are colourless). Addition of acid reduces the concentration of OH^- ions (by combining with them) and the reaction is driven to the left, whereupon the colour of the bromine is again observed.

Experiment C

When an iron(III) salt (e.g $FeCl_3$) is mixed with a thiocyanate (e.g. KCNS), complex iron thiocyanate ions are formed; these are red in colour. The reaction is reversible and an equilibrium is set up:

$$FeCl_3 + CNS^- \rightleftharpoons Fe(CNS)^{2+} + 3Cl^-$$

Procedure: Mix together about 5 cm^3 of solutions of iron(III) chloride and potassium (or ammonium)

---

[i] Initially the colour deepens due the increased concentration (same amount of gas in a smaller volume) which occurs before reaction takes place, but after a few moments, the reaction occurs and the colour lightens.

thiocyanate. The red complex will be formed. Pour the solution into a beaker and dilute it with water so that the colour becomes light red. Mix well, to make the solution uniform. Half fill five test tubes with the solution. Keep one for reference.

Carry out the following tests on the others.

(a)   Add a few cm^3 of $FeCl_3$ solution.
(b)   Add a few cm^3 of thiocyanate solution.
(c)   Add a few cm^3 of dilute hydrochloric acid.

In each case, explain what is observed, and why.

(d)   Place the remaining sample in a beaker of boiling water for about 5 minutes and then compare its colour with that of the reference sample. How has the colour changed? In which direction has the reaction gone? Does this suggest that the reaction between Fe^{3+} and thiocyanate ions is exothermic or endothermic? Write the equation for the reaction, putting in the terms exothermic and endothermic above and below the reversible signs, as appropriate.

Experiment D.

When bismuth trichloride is added to water, it undergoes hydrolysis, and the following equilibrium system is set up:

$$BiCl_3 + H_2O \rightleftharpoons BiOCl + 2HCl$$

$BiCl_3$ is soluble, but the product of the reaction, bismuth oxychloride, is not, and it is formed as a white suspension in the solution.

Procedure

(a)   Take a small quantity (as much as will fit on the tip of a spatula) of bismuth trichloride and add it to some water contained in a test tube. Mix well. What is observed and why?
(b)   Predict the effect of adding hydrochloric acid to the system. Now add concentrated hydrochloric acid, drop by drop, until the change occurs. Explain why this happens.
(c)   Finally, add water to the mixture until a change occurs. What is observed? Explain why this happens.

Experiment E.

Chromate ions, CrO_4^{2-} and dichromate ions, $Cr_2O_7^{2-}$ differ in colour, and are interconvertible in solution:

$$CrO_4^{2-} \rightleftharpoons Cr_2O_7^{2-}$$

The position of equilibrium is dependent on the acidity of the solution (*i.e.* the H^+ ion concentration) and so can be changed by adding either acid or alkali to the solution.

Procedure

(a)   Take about 10 cm^3 of solutions of potassium chromate (K_2CrO_4) and potassium dichromate ($K_2Cr_2O_7$) in separate test tubes. Use these as sources of the ions. Observe and make a note of the colour of the ions of each substance.
(b)   Place about 5 cm^3 of each substance in separate test tubes. Slowly and carefully add dilute hydrochloric acid to each tube until a change of colour is observed in one of them. Note which change occurs, and to which substance.
(c)   In which direction does an excess of H^+ ions drive the reaction:

$$CrO_4^{2-} \rightleftharpoons Cr_2O_7^{2-}$$

Complete this equation by adding H^+ ions to the appropriate side, and water molecules to the other side. Then balance the equation.

(d)   To one of the tubes, now add, slowly and carefully, sodium hydroxide solution, until a colour change is observed. What substance has been formed? In which direction do OH^- ions drive the reaction:

$$CrO_4^{2-} \rightleftharpoons Cr_2O_7^{2-}$$

Complete and balance the equation by adding the proper number of both OH^- ions and water molecules to the appropriate sides of the equation.

(e)   Suggest how you might convert a sample of crystalline potassium chromate to crystalline potassium dichromate.

Experiment F.

Propanone reacts with iodine to form iodopropanone according to:

$$CH_3COCH_3 + I_2 \rightleftharpoons CH_3COCH_2I + H^+ + I^-$$

The iodine is used in solution and is reddish-brown in colour. All other substances are colourless.

Procedure

Mix about 5 cm^3 of iodine solution with about half its volume of propanone. Make the volume up to 50 cm^3 with distilled water. Half fill four test tubes with this equilibrium mixture. Keep one as a reference, and to the others add (i) a few cm^3 of propanone, (ii) a few cm^3 of concentrated hydrochloric acid (*i.e.* H$^+$) and (iii) a few crystals of potassium iodide (*i.e.* I$^-$ ions).

Record and explain what happens in each case.

Industrial Applications of Le Châtelier's Principle

In the chemical manufacturing industry, it is important to operate a process under the most suitable conditions to achieve the highest yield of product, in the shortest time, and at the lowest cost. Unfortunately it is seldom possible to achieve all of these aims at the same time, and in most cases compromises have to be made.

One important application of Le Châtelier's Principle is in the **Haber Process** for manufacturing ammonia. The reaction in this process is:

$$N_2 + 3H_2 \rightleftharpoons 2NH_3 \qquad \Delta H = -92 \text{ kJ}$$

The conditions for the maximum yield of ammonia, according to Le Chatelier, are high pressure and low temperature, and these predictions are supported by experimental evidence — as shown in the accompanying chart.

Percentage of Ammonia in Equilibrium Mixture					
Temp /°C	Pressure /atm.				
	1	10	100	200	600
200	15	50	80	90	95
300	2.2	15	50	70	85
400	0.4	4	25	40	65
500	0.13	1	10	20	40
600	0.05	0.24	5	8	

However, using a high pressure and a low temperature are not the most economical conditions for the process, as other factors are involved here. The lower the temperature, the greater is the amount of ammonia at equilibrium, but the problem is that the reaction is very much slower. It is not possible to have a high yield and a high rate at the same time. A compromise is therefore made, and most Haber processes are operated at about 500°C and in the presence of a catalyst, the usual one being finely divided iron with some Al_2O_3 which acts as a promoter.

The higher the pressure, the greater the yield of ammonia, but very high pressure plant is too costly both to construct and to maintain, so again a compromise is made, and a pressure of about 200 atmospheres is used in most ammonia plants.

Questions
Le Châtelier's Principle and Equilibrium Constant Expressions.

Q.13.1   The contact process for manufacturing sulphuric acid depends on the reaction :

$$2SO_2 + O_2 \rightleftharpoons 2SO_3 \quad \Delta H = -196 \text{ kJ/mol}$$

Explain the effect on the system if (a) the temperature is increased; (b) the pressure is decreased; (c) additional oxygen is added to the mixture; (d) some SO_3 is removed; (e) a catalyst is added.

Q.13.2   The following equilibrium exists between ICl_3 (which is a brown liquid) Cl_2 (a green gas) and ICl_5 (a yellow solid). The forward reaction is exothermic:

$$ICl_3 \quad + \quad Cl_2 \rightleftharpoons ICl_5$$

State and explain what would be **observed** if:

(a)   the temperature is raised;
(b)   the pressure is reduced;
(c)   more chlorine is added.

Q.13.3   In the case of the following equilibrium systems, predict the effect on the position of equilibrium of (i) increasing the pressure, and (ii) increasing the temperature:

(a) $2Cl_2 + 2H_2O \rightleftharpoons 4HCl + O_2$ $\qquad \Delta H = +$
(b) $CH_3COOCH_3 + H_2O \rightleftharpoons$
$\qquad\qquad CH_3COOH + CH_3OH \qquad \Delta H = -$
(c) $3O_2 \rightleftharpoons 2O_3$ $\qquad\qquad \Delta H = +$
(d) $CO + 2H_2 \rightleftharpoons CH_3OH$ $\qquad \Delta H = -$
(e) $2NO_2 \rightleftharpoons N_2O_4$ $\qquad\qquad \Delta H = -$
(f) $PCl_3 + Cl_2 \rightleftharpoons PCl_5$ $\qquad\qquad \Delta H = -$

Q.13.4 With reference to the following reaction:

$PCl_3(g) + Cl_2(g) \rightleftharpoons PCl_5(g)$ $\Delta H = -$

predict the effect on the position of equilibrium of:

(a) adding more chlorine,
(b) increasing the volume of the container,
(c) increasing the pressure,
(d) adding a catalyst,
(e) increasing the temperature,
(f) removing some PCl_5.

Q.13.5 For each of the following equilibrium systems, predict, using Le Châtelier's Principle, what happens when (a) the pressure is decreased; (b) the temperature is increased; (c) more of the first mentioned substance is added; and (d) a suitable catalyst is added.

(i) $H_2 + I_2 \rightleftharpoons 2HI$ $\Delta H = +$
(ii) $N_2O_4 \rightleftharpoons 2NO_2$ $\Delta H = +$
(iii) $CO + Cl_2 \rightleftharpoons COCl_2$ $\Delta H = -$
(iv) $CO + H_2O \rightleftharpoons CO_2 + H_2$ $\Delta H = -$

In each case, state the conditions of temperature and pressure for the maximum yield of the product.

Q.13.6 For each of the following reactions, state the optimum conditions of temperature and pressure which will give the highest yield of product(s).

(a) $PCl_5 \rightleftharpoons PCl_3 + Cl_2$ $\Delta H = +124$ kJ/mol
(b) $2NO_2 \rightleftharpoons N_2O_4$ $\Delta H = -24$
(c) $N_2 + 3H_2 \rightleftharpoons 2NH_3$ $\Delta H = -92$
(d) $2NO_2 \rightleftharpoons 2NO + O_2$ $\Delta H = +$
(e) $CO + 2H_2 \rightleftharpoons CH_3OH$ $\Delta H = -92$
(f) $2H_2 + O_2 \rightleftharpoons 2H_2O$ $\Delta H = -$

Q.13.7 For each of the above reactions (previous question) write the equilibrium constant expression, and also give the units in which each value of K is expressed.

Equilibrium Constants

For a mixture of substances in equilibrium, experiment has shown that there is a simple relationship between the concentration of the reactants and the concentration of the products — when the temperature is constant. This relationship is easily deduced from the balanced chemical equation for the reaction. If the equation for a system in equilibrium is A + B $\rightleftharpoons$ C + D, then

$$\frac{[\,C\,][\,D\,]}{[\,A\,][\,B\,]} = K$$

where K is a constant known as the equilibrium constant for the reaction. This constant, whose value depends on the temperature, is a measure of how far the reaction has proceeded when equilibrium is reached; if the forward reaction predominates, then K is greater than 1.0. The nearer to completion it goes, the greater is the value of K.

The K value (at 25 °C) for the reaction:
$SO_2 + \frac{1}{2}O \rightleftharpoons SO_3$ is about 1×10^{12} because at that temperature, that reaction goes virtually to completion. Conversely, a reaction which reaches equilibrium with very little of the product(s) present, has a very small equilibrium constant. When the system: $N_2O_4 \rightleftharpoons 2NO_2$ reaches equilibrium (at room temperature), there is very little NO_2 present and so its K value is very low, 6×10^{-3}.

Writing Equilibrium constant expressions

Not all reactions can be represented by A + B $\rightleftharpoons$ C + D, but writing the equilibrium constant expression for other reactions is easily done. The rules are simple:

1. The balanced equation for the reaction is written.

2. The concentrations of the substances on the **right hand side** of the balanced equation are put **on the top** of the expression for K, and those on the left hand side of the equation on the bottom of the expression.

3. If there is more than one mole of a substance in the balanced equation, the concentration of that substance in the expression for K is raised to a power equal to the number of moles of it in the equation, *e.g.* for the reaction:

$$2SO_2 + O_2 = 2SO_3,$$

the concentrations of both SO_2 and SO_3 will be to the power of 2, so that K will be given by:

$$K = \frac{[SO_3]^2}{[SO_2]^2[O_2]}$$

The expression for K requires the values of the **concentrations** (*i.e.* moles per litre) of the various substances present at equilibrium. However, for reactions in which the number of moles does not change, (same number of moles on left-hand side as on right-hand side of equation) the volume can be disregarded and the actual amounts (*i.e.* number of moles) of each substance used instead.

Consider the reaction: $A_2 + B_2 \rightleftharpoons 2AB$, and let the amounts of the substances at equilibrium be: $A_2 = 1$ mol, $B_2 = 2$ mol, $AB = 3$ mol, and the volume of the container be V. The concentrations will therefore be:

$$A_2 = \frac{1}{V} \text{ mol/L}$$

$$B_2 = \frac{2}{V} \text{ mol/L}$$

$$AB = \frac{3}{V} \text{ mol/L}$$

$$K = \frac{[AB]^2}{[A_2][B_2]} = \frac{\left(\dfrac{3}{V}\right)^2}{\left(\dfrac{1}{V}\right)\left(\dfrac{2}{V}\right)}$$

The Vs cancel out, leaving K equal to

$$\frac{(3)^2}{1 \times 2}$$

i.e. the actual amounts being used rather than their concentrations.

It should be noted however, that if the number of moles of reactants is different from the number of moles of products, then the Vs will not cancel, and the volume at equilibrium must be taken into account to calculate the concentrations for the K expression.

Units of K

Where there are equal numbers of moles on both sides of the balanced equation, K has no units —

it is just a number. This is because the concentration units cancel out. For example, in the reaction $A + B \rightleftharpoons C + D$, for which K is given by $\frac{[C][D]}{[A][B]}$, the units are

$$\frac{(\text{mol}/L)(\text{mol}/L)}{(\text{mol}/L)(\text{mol}/L)} \quad i.e. \text{ none}$$

For reactions where there are not equal numbers of moles, K does have units. For the reaction

$A \rightleftharpoons B + C$, K is given by $\frac{[B][C]}{[A]}$

and the units are $\frac{(\text{mol}/L)(\text{mol}/L)}{(\text{mol}/L)} = \text{mol/L}$

Information given by K

The magnitude of K gives information about the **extent** of a reversible reaction; it tells nothing about the **rate** of the reaction. **Extent and rate are completely independent of each other.** It should also be remembered that K is constant only as long as temperature is constant. At a different temperature, K for a particular reaction has a different value.

Determination of Equilibrium Constants

The value of the equilibrium constant for a particular reaction is found from experimental evidence; the reaction is allowed to reach equilibrium and the resulting mixture is then analysed to find out its composition. Knowledge of this leads to the value of K.

The following example shows how K for the reaction of ethanoic acid with ethanol (in which the ester ethyl ethanoate, and water, are formed) can be calculated.

Worked Example 1

One mole of ethanoic acid and one mole of ethanol were reacted together at 25°C until equilibrium was reached. The reaction was then stopped and the mixture made up to one litre with water. The solution was titrated with alkali to determine the amount of ethanoic acid remaining. It was found that 25 cm^3 of the solution required 16.7 cm^3 of 0.5 M sodium hydroxide for neutralisation. Calculate K for the reaction.

Solution

(i)   Calculate the amount of ethanoic acid remaining.

$$CH_3COOH + NaOH \rightleftharpoons CH_3COONa + H_2O$$

$$25 \text{ cm}^3 \ x \text{ acid} = 16.7 \text{ cm}^3 \ 0.5 \text{ M NaOH}$$

$$\frac{V_1M_1}{n_1} = \frac{V_2M_2}{n_2}$$

$$\frac{25x}{1} = \frac{16.7 \times 0.5}{1}$$

$$x = 0.33$$

i.e. the acid solution contains 0.33 moles/litre. Since the total volume is one litre, the total amount of acid remaining is 0.33 mole.

(ii)   Calculation of K

$$CH_3COOH + C_2H_2OH \rightleftharpoons CH_3COOC_2H_5 + H_2O$$

Since one mole of acid was taken and since 0.33 mole remained at equilibrium, 0.67 mole reacted. Since the acid and the alcohol react in equimolecular proportions, 0.67 mole of the alcohol also reacted and so 0.33 mole of it remained. Also 0.67 mole of the ester was produced and 0.67 mole of water. The table shows the amounts of each substance present initially, the amount by which each changed, and the amounts of each at equilibrium.

	CH₃COOH	C₂H₅OH	CH₃COOC₂H₅	H₂O
Initially	1	1	0	0
Change	-0.67	-0.67	+0.67	+0.67
At eqm.	0.33	0.33	0.67	0.67

K is given by $\dfrac{[CH_3COOOC_2H_5] \ [H_2O]}{[CH_3COOOH] \ [C_2H_5OH]}$

$$= \frac{0.67 \times 0.67}{0.33 \times 0.33} = 4$$

Once the K for a particular reaction is known, the composition of the equilibrium mixture obtained by taking the reactants in any given proportions can be calculated. The following example shows how this can be done.

Worked Example 2

Calculate the composition of the equilibrium mixture obtained from the reaction of one mole of ethanoic acid with four moles of ethanol, given that $K = 4$ at the temperature of the reaction.

Solution

Initially $[CH_3COOH] = 1$ and $[C_2H_5OH] = 4$.

If x moles of acid react, then x moles of ethanol must also react and the amounts of acid and ethanol present at equilibrium must be $(1-x)$ and $(4-x)$ respectively. Also, x moles of both ester and water must be formed.

In tabular form:

	CH₃COOH	C₂H₅OH	CH₃COOC₂H₅	H₂O
Initially	1	4	0	0
Change	-x	- x	+ x	+ x
At eqm	(1- x)	(4- x)	x	x

$$K = \frac{[CH_3COOC_2H_5] \ [H_2O]}{[CH_3COOH] \ [C_2H_5OH]}$$

$$= \frac{x \times x}{(1-x)(4-x)} = 4$$

Solving this quadratic equation gives $x = 0.93$ (or 5.73 which is impossible) Thus at equilibrium:

$CH_3COOH = (1 - 0.93) = 0.07$ moles

$C_2H_5OH = (4 - 0.93) = 3.07$ moles

$CH_3COOC_2H_5 = 0.93$ moles

$H_2O = 0.93$ moles

The answer to this problem is as shown above; it is **not** that 'x' = 0.93

Worked Example 3

Given that K for the reaction $H_2 + I_2 \rightleftharpoons 2HI$, is 64 at 400°C, calculate the mass of each of the substances present when 10 g of hydrogen react with 762 g of iodine in a closed vessel at 400°C (at which temperature the iodine is present as iodine vapour).

Solution

$$10 \text{ g } H_2 = \frac{10}{2} \text{ mol } H_2 = 5 \text{ mol of } H_2$$

$$762 \text{ g } I_2 = \frac{762}{254} \text{ mol } I_2 = 3 \text{ mol of } I_2$$

Since the equation shows **TWO** moles of hydrogen iodide being formed, the expression for the equilibrium constant is $K = \dfrac{[HI]^2}{[H_2][I_2]}$

From the information given in the equation for the reaction, if x moles of hydrogen react, then x moles of iodine must also react, and $2x$ moles of hydrogen iodide must be formed. The initial amounts, the amounts reacting and the amounts at equilibrium can be summarised in table form:

	H_2	I_2	HI
Initially	5	3	0
Change	$-x$	$-x$	$+2x$
At eqm	$(5-x)$	$(3-x)$	$2x$

$$K = \frac{(2x)^2}{(3-x)(5-x)} = 64$$

Solving this quadratic leads to $x = 2.78$ (or 5.75 which is impossible). The amount, and mass of each substance present at equilibrium is therefore:

$H_2 = (5-x) = 5-2.78 = 2.22 \text{ mol} = (2.22 \times 2) \text{ g} = 4.44 \text{ g}$

$I_2 = (3-x) = 3-2.78 = 0.22 \text{ mol} = (0.22 \times 254) \text{ g} = 55.9 \text{ g}$

$HI = 2x = 2 \times 2.78 = 5.56 \text{ mol} = 5.56 \times 128 \text{ g} = 712 \text{ g}$

Experiment 13.2
Measurement of the Equilibrium constant for the reaction

$$CH_3COOH + C_2H_5OH \rightleftharpoons CH_3COOC_2H_5 + H_2O$$

The principle of this experiment is as follows. A mixture of known amounts of ethanoic acid and ethanol is made up and allowed to come to equilibrium in the presence of sulphuric acid which catalyses the reaction. The total amount of acid in the equilibrium mixture is then found by titration with alkali.

The amount of sulphuric acid present is found by carrying out a second and similar experiment, but using water in place of the ethanoic acid and ethanol. The amount of sulphuric acid present (as found in this part of the experiment) is subtracted from the **total** amount of acid present, and so the amount of ethanoic acid in the equilibrium mixture is found. Calculation leads to the amount of the other substances present at equilibrium, and hence to the equilibrium constant, K.

Procedure

Take a clean dry bottle or flask of about 25 cm^3 to 100 cm^3 capacity and which has a good stopper (necessary to prevent the evaporation of the ethanol). By means of a burette or a 10 cm^3 pipette, measure out 10 cm^3 each of pure ethanoic acid and pure ethanol into the bottle. Add 15 drops of concentrated sulphuric acid from a burette or from a dropper having a fine tip. Stopper the bottle, shake the contents well, and set it aside for one week.

Half fill a volumetric flask with distilled water, add 15 drops of concentrated sulphuric acid from the same vessel as before, and make the solution up to the calibration mark with more distilled water. Mix well. Pipette at 25 cm^3 portion of this solution into a conical flask, add 3 drops of phenolphthalein indicator and titrate with 0.1 M sodium hydroxide solution. Carry out several more titrations until constant titres are obtained. Before putting the burette away, rinse it with some dilute acid and then with water.

After one week, pour the equilibrium mixture into a 250 cm^3 volumetric flask, rinse the bottle several times with distilled water and pour these washings into the volumetric flask also. Finally, make it up to the mark with more distilled water. Stopper it and mix well. Pipette 25 cm^3 of this solution into a conical flask, add 3 drops of phenolphthalein indicator and titrate with 0.1 M sodium hydroxide. Repeat to obtain consistent titres. After use, rinse the burette with some dilute acid, and then with water, before putting it away.

Calculations

Subtract the sodium hydroxide titres (from the two parts of the experiment) to find the volume of sodium hydroxide which would neutralise the ethanoic acid in 25 cm^3 of the equilibrium mixture. Then use the volumetric formula (V_1M_1 etc) to find the concentration (*i.e.* moles/litre) of ethanoic acid in the mixture. Knowing that the total volume of the mixture used for titration was 250 cm^3, calculate the actual number of moles of ethanoic present at equilibrium.

From the volume of ethanoic acid taken initially (10 cm^3) and its density (1.06 g/cm^3) calculate (i) the initial mass, and (ii) the initial number of moles. In the same way, calculate the amount of ethanol taken initially (density of ethanol = 0.79 g/cm^3). From the initial amount of ethanoic acid and from the amount still present at equilibrium, calculate (i) the amount which reacted, (ii) the amount of ethanol which reacted (= same number of moles), (iii) the amount of ethanol remaining (iv) the amount of ester produced and (v) the amount of water produced.

Since the total number of moles does not change during the reaction, it is unnecessary to take the volume of the solution into consideration. From the equilibrium amounts of all four substances present, calculate the value of the equilibrium constant for the reaction.

Specimen results

Volume of 0.1 M NaOH to neutralise the H$_2$SO$_4$ = 26.8 cm^3

Volume of 0.1 M NaOH to neturalise both acids (after one week) = 45.8 cm^3

Questions

Q.13.8 120 g of ethanoic acid is mixed with 138 g of ethanol and allowed to come to equilibrium according to

CH$_3$COOH + C$_2$H$_5$OH $\rightleftharpoons$ CH$_3$COOC$_2$H$_5$ + H$_2$O.
Using the given value of K (4.0), calculate (i) the number of moles, and (ii) the mass, of ethyl ethanoate which is formed.

Q.13.9 32 g of methanol and 60 g of ethanoic acid were mixed and allowed to come to equilibrium; 53.2 g of the ester were then present in the mixture. Calculate K for the reaction.

CH$_3$COOH + CH$_3$OH $\rightleftharpoons$ CH$_3$COOCH$_3$ + H$_2$O

Calculate (a) the number of moles and (b) the number of grams of each substance present when 64 g of methanol and 180 g of ethanoic acid are mixed and allowed to reach equilibrium.

Q.13.10
(a) In an experiment, 210 g of ethanoic acid and 210 g of propanol were heated together until equilibrium was reached. Titration with alkali showed that 60 g of ethanoic acid then remained. Calculate the value of K for the reaction.

(b) What mass of each substance would be present at equilibrium when 120 g of ethanoic acid were reacted with 180 g of propanol (at the same temperature)?

Q.13.11 Refer to the reaction of worked example 2 and to its value of K.

(a) What would be the composition of the equilibrium mixture resulting from the reaction of 2.5 moles of ethyl ethanoate with 1 mole of water?

(b) What mass of each substance would be present when 0.1 mole each of ethanol, ethanoic acid and water, were mixed together and allowed to come to equilibrium?

Q.13.12 Ethanol reacts with ethanal according to:

2C$_2$H$_5$OH + CH$_3$CHO $\rightleftharpoons$ CH$_3$CH(OC$_2$H$_5$)$_2$ + H$_2$O

At 25°C, 1 mole of ethanol and 0.1 mole of ethanal were mixed together and allowed to come to equilibrium. Analysis of the mixture (which had a volume of 60 cm^3) showed that it contained 0.01 mole of ethanal. Calculate the value of K for the reaction, and give its correct units.

Q.13.13 1 mole of propanoic acid and 0.5 mole of ethanol were mixed and allowed to come to equilibrium according to:

C$_2$H$_5$COOH + C$_2$H$_5$OH $\rightleftharpoons$ C$_2$H$_5$COOC$_2$H$_5$ + H$_2$O

At equilibrium, titration with alkali showed the mixture to contain 0.55 mole of unchanged acid. Calculate the value of K for the reaction. What will be the composition of the equilibrium mixture formed when 3 moles of propanoic acid and 0.5 moles of ethanol are reacted together?

Q.13.14 Calculate K for the reaction
H$_2$ + I$_2$ $\rightleftharpoons$ 2HI, at 450°C, given that when one mole each of hydrogen and iodine were mixed, the equilibrium mixture contained 1.56 moles of hydrogen iodide.

Q.13.15 Two moles of HI are introduced into a litre flask at 490°C. What will be the concentration of each of the substances present in the flask at equilibrium given that K for the reaction
H$_2$ + I$_2$ $\rightleftharpoons$ 2HI is 46 (at 490°C)

Q.13.16 Given that K for the reaction $H_2 + I_2 \rightleftharpoons 2HI$ is 64 at 400°C. Calculate the amount of each of the subsstances present at equilibrium when:

(a) 6 moles of hydrogen and 3 moles of iodine are reacted together

(b) 1 mole of H_2, 2 moles of I_2 and 3 moles of HI are reacted together.

Q.13.17 A quantity of hydrogen iodide was sealed into a container at 430°C and allowed to decompose and reach equilibrium with hydrogen and iodine. At equilibrium the concentration of hydrogen iodide was found to be 0.05 mol/L. Find the concentrations of the hydrogen and iodine. K for the reaction:

$$H_2 + I_2 \rightleftharpoons 2HI \text{ is } 60 \text{ at } 430° \text{ C.}$$

Q.13.18 K for the reaction:

$$CO + H_2O \rightleftharpoons CO_2 + H_2$$

is 5.0 at a given temperature. Analysis of an equilibrium mixture of the above system showed that it contained 0.4 mole of CO, 0.15 mole of water vapour, and 0.8 mole of hydrogen. How many moles of CO_2 were present?

Q.13.19 At a certain temperature the equilibrium constant for the system

$$CO(g) + H_2O(g) \rightleftharpoons CO_2(g) + H_2(g)$$

has the value 1.44. If equal amounts of carbon monoxide and steam are mixed and the system is allowed to reach equilibrium, what will be the composition of the equilibrium mixture? (Express the answer as percentages by volume of the total volume. Avogadro's Law may be assumed to apply).

13.20 The value for K for the reaction:

$$COCl_2 \rightleftharpoons CO + Cl_2$$

is 0.05 at 600°C. What mass of carbonyl chloride will be present in a 1 litre vessel in which 1 mole of carbon monoxide and 0.5 moles of chlorine are allowed to react to equilibrium?

Q.13.21 What do you mean by saying that a system has reached a state of equilibrium? Write the equilibrium constant expression for the reaction:

$$SO_2(g) + NO_2(g) \rightleftharpoons SO_3(g) + NO(g)$$

When 7.68 g of sulphur dioxide and 4.6 g of nitrogen dioxide were heated together in a closed vessel at a certain high temperature, it was found that at equilibrium 4.8 g of sulphur trioxide were present. Calculate the equilibrium constant for the reaction at that temperature.

Then 0.17 moles of nitrogen dioxide were added to this reaction mixture and when equilibrium was re-established it was found that an additional 0.03 moles of sulphur trioxide, had been formed. Find (i) the number of moles of each of the four gases in the final equilibrium mixture, and (ii) the value of the equilibrium constant.

How do you know that the temperature had not changed when this final equilibrium has been reached.

Q.13.22 One mole of nitrogen is mixed with 3 moles of hydrogen in a 1 litre closed container and allowed to reach equilibrium. This stage is reached when 20% of each of the reactants have reacted. Calculate K for the reaction :

$$N_2 + 3H_2 \rightleftharpoons 2NH_3$$

Q.13.23 Nitrogen and hydrogen combine together to form ammonia.

(a) One mole of N_2 and 1.5 moles of H_2 are mixed together in 1 litre vessel and allowed to react. If the reaction goes to completion, calculate the number of moles of each gas that would be present in the final mixture.

(b) The reaction however, does not go to completion, but reaches an equilibrium. At a certain temperature it is found that only 0.2 mole of nitrogen has reacted when this stage is reached. Calculate the equilibrium constant at the temperature of the reaction.

Q.13.24 Nitrogen dioxide, on being heated, dissociates according to:

$$2NO_2 \rightleftharpoons 2NO + O_2$$

When 0.5 mole of NO_2 is heated in a closed 1 litre vessel, 0.18 mole of it dissociates. Calculate (i) the number of moles of each substance then present, (ii) the value of K at the temperature of the experiment.

Q.13.25 At s.t.p. N_2O_4 is 20% dissociated into NO_2. Calculate K for the reaction $N_2O_4 \rightleftharpoons 2NO_2$.

Would the amount of dissociation increase, decrease or remain the same, if the pressure were increased? Explain your answer.

Q.13.26
(a) The value of K for the reaction $2NO_2 \rightleftharpoons N_2O_4$ is 200 L/mol at 25°C. If the concentration of N_2O_4 in a 1 litre vessel containing the gases in equilibrium is 0.02 mol/L, what is the concentration of the NO_2?
(b) Calculate the values of K for the reaction given by the equations: (i) $NO_2 \rightleftharpoons \frac{1}{2}N_2O_4$,

(ii) $N_2O_4 \rightleftharpoons 2NO_2$.

Q.13.27 Phosphorus pentachloride dissociates on being heated according to:

$$PCl_5 \rightleftharpoons PCl_3 + Cl_2$$

An equilibrium mixture in a 5 litre vessel heated to 250 °C contained 1.05 mol of PCl_5 and 1.6 mol each of PCl_3 and Cl_2. Calculate the value of K for the reaction at 250°C.

Q.13.28 When 0.5 mol of PCl_5 is heated in a 1 litre flask at a particular temperature, 20% of it dissociates. Calculate the number of moles of each gas then present, and hence find the value of K for the reaction: $PCl_5 \rightleftharpoons PCl_3 + Cl_2$.

Partial Pressures

Equilibrium constants for reactions which take place in solution are normally expressed in terms of the concentrations of the substances involved. However, for reactions involving gases, it is often more convenient to express the amount of a gas in terms of its partial pressure rather than in terms of its molar concentration. The partial pressure of a gas is really a measure of the concentration of that gas, since the partial pressure of a gas is proportional to the number of molecules of it present (and hence to its concentration).

Equilibrium constants in terms of partial pressures are denoted by K_p, whereas in terms of molar concentration, the symbol K_c is used. K_p expressions are written in the same way as those for K_c. If there are, for example, **two** moles of a substance in the equation for the reaction, the partial pressure of that substance is **squared**. For

the reaction $N_2O_4 \rightleftharpoons 2NO_2$, the equilibrium constant is given by: $K_p = \dfrac{(P_{NO_2})^2}{(P_{N_2O_4})}$ where

P_{NO_2} means the partial pressure of the gas NO_2. Like K_c, the value of K_p for a given reaction (as specified by a chemical equation) is constant at any particular temperature. Calculations involving K_p are similar to those based on K_c. The following points should be helpful when solving K_p problems:

1. For a reaction in which the number of moles beforehand is the same as the number of moles afterwards, the constant is purely a number; there are no units. (The units on the top of the fraction will cancel out with those on the bottom)

2. The **mole fraction** of a substance is the amount of that substance expressed as a fraction of the total amount present. For example, if a gaseous mixture consists of 2 moles of H_2, 2 moles of I_2 and 1 mole of HI (total = 5 moles), then the mole fraction of the hydrogen is $\frac{2}{5}$ or 0.4

3. The partial pressure of the gaseous substances present are proportional to their mole fractions. The mole fraction of hydrogen in the above example is 0.4, and so its partial pressure will be 0.4 times the total pressure.

4. The sum of the mole fractions of all the substances present in a gaseous equilibrium system must be 1. Likewise, the sum of all the partial pressures must equal the total pressure. Remembering these facts is often either necessary or is a useful check in calculations.

5. By using the general gas equation which effectively relates pressure (p) and concentration (n/V), the relationship between K_c and K_p can be deduced.

It can be shown that $K_p = K_c(RT)^{\Delta n}$, where Δn is the number of moles of products minus the number of moles of reactants. Thus, for a reaction in which there is no change in the number of moles (e.g. $H_2 + I_2 \rightleftharpoons 2HI$) the value of K_p will be the same as the value of K_c.

Worked Example 4

A mixture of oxygen and sulphur dioxide was allowed to react to equilibrium at 25 °C according to: $2SO_2 + O_2 \rightleftharpoons 2SO_3$. The total pressure of the mixture was 2 atmospheres, and the partial pressures of the oxygen and the sulphur trioxide were, respectively, 0.05 atm. and 1.85 atm.

Calculate (a) the partial pressure of the sulphur dioxide and (b) the value of K_p for the reaction.

Solution

$$\text{Pressure of } O_2 = 0.05 \text{ atm.}$$
$$\text{Pressure of } SO_3 = 1.85 \text{ atm.}$$
$$\underline{\hspace{4cm}}$$
$$= 1.90 \text{ atm}$$

$$\text{Total pressure} = 2.0 \text{ atm.}$$
$$\therefore \text{ pressure of } SO_2 = 0.10 \text{ atm.}$$

$$K_p = \frac{(P_{SO_3})^2}{(P_{SO_2})^2 (P_{O_2})} = \frac{(1.85)^2}{(0.10)^2 (0.05)} = 6.8 \times 10^3 \text{ atm}^{-1}$$

Worked Example 5

SO_2Cl_2 dissociates on being heated into sulphur dioxide and chlorine.

(a) Write an equation for the reaction.
(b) In an experiment, 6.75 g. of SO_2Cl_2 were sealed into a 1 litre vessel and the temperature raised to 375 °C. At equilibrium, the vessel contained 0.0345 moles of chlorine gas. Calculate the value of K_c for the reaction.
(c) Use the ideal gas equation to calculate the pressure (i) in Pa, (ii) in atmospheres, in the vessel at equilibrium.
(d) Calculate the partial pressure of each gas in the vessel and hence find the value of K_p for the reaction.

Solution

(a) $SO_2Cl_2 \rightleftharpoons SO_2 + Cl_2$
(b) $6.75 \text{ g } SO_2Cl_2 = \frac{6.75}{135} \text{ mol} = 0.05 \text{ mol}$ (= initial amount of SO_2Cl_2)

(c)		SO_2Cl_2	SO_2	Cl_2
	Initially	0.05	0	0
	Change	-0.0345	+ 0.0345	+ 0.0345
	At eqm	0.0155	+ 0.0345	+ 0.0345

These figures are the numbers of moles of each substance at equilibrium but since the volume of

the vessel is 1 litre, they also represent the concentrations of each (in moles/litre).

$$K_c = \frac{[SO_2][Cl_2]}{[SO_2Cl_2]}$$

$$\frac{(0.0345)(0.0345)}{0.0155} = 0.077 \text{ mol/L}$$

(c) Total moles present =
$$0.0155 + 0.0345 + 0.0345 = 0.0845$$

$375°C = 648 \text{ K}; 1 \text{ litre} = 10^{-3} \text{ m}^3; 1 \text{ atm} = 101 \times 10^3 \text{ Pa}$
$pV = nRT,$
$$p = \frac{nRT}{V} = \frac{0.0845 \times 8.31 \times 648}{10^{-3}} = 455022 \text{ Pa}$$
$$= \frac{455022}{101000} \text{ atm.} = 4.5 \text{ atm.}$$

(d)	SO_2Cl_2	SO_2	Cl_2
moles at eqm	0.0155	0.0345	0.0345
mole fractions	$\frac{0.0155}{0.0845}$ $= 0.183$	$\frac{0.0345}{0.0845}$ $= 0.408$	$\frac{0.0345}{0.0845}$ $= 0.408$
partial pressures (since total pressure = 4.5 atm)	4.5×0.183 $= 0.825$	4.5×0.408 $= 1.84$	4.5×0.408 $= 1.84$

$$K_p = \frac{(P_{Cl_2})(P_{SO_2})}{(P_{SO_2Cl_2})} = \frac{(1.84)(1.84)}{(0.825)} = 4.1 \text{ atm}$$

Questions

Q.13.29 At 1000 K, K_p for the system: $C(s) + CO_2 (g) \rightleftharpoons 2CO (g)$ is 1.9 atm. At what total pressure would an equilibrium mixture contain 0.013 mol of CO_2 and 0.024 mol of CO? (N.B. A solid does not exert a vapour pressure).

Q.13.30 The value of K_p at 25°C for the system $2NO_2 \rightleftharpoons N_2O_4$ is 0.07 atm^{-1}. In a system at equilibrium, the partial pressure of NO_2 was 14 atmospheres. Calculate the partial pressure of the N_2O_4.

Q.13.31 Phosphorus pentachloride dissociates on being heated according to:

$PCl_5 \rightleftharpoons PCl_3 + Cl_2$, for which the value of K_p is 0.17 atm. When some PCl_5 is put into a vessel and allowed to reach equilibrium, the total pressure is found to be 10 atm. Calculate the partial pressure of the chlorine then present.

Q.13.32 Nitrogen, hydrogen and ammonia form an equilibrium system according to:

$N_2 + 3H_2 \rightleftharpoons 2NH_3$. A mixture of nitrogen and hydrogen in the ratio of 1:3 was allowed to reach equilibrium at a certain temperature. It was then found that the total pressure was 400 atm. and the partial pressure of ammonia was 200 atm. Calculate the partial pressures of both the nitrogen and hydrogen, and hence find the value of K_p for the reaction.

Q.13.33 Iodine dissociates on being heated according to: $I2 \rightleftharpoons 2I$. At a certain temperature and 1 atm. pressure, iodine vapour contains 40% by volume of iodine atoms.

(a) Calculate K_p for the equilibrium.
(b) Calculate the total pressure at which the percentage of iodine atoms is reduced to 20%.

Q.13.34 At 1100 K, K_p for the system $2SO_2 + O_2 \rightleftharpoons 2SO_3$, is 0.13 atm^{-1}. 2 mol of sulphur dioxide and 1 mol of oxygen are mixed together and allowed to reach equilibrium. A 60% yield of sulphur trioxide is obtained. Calculate the total pressure of the system at equilibrium.

Q.13.35 Water vapour and carbon monoxide react according to:

$$H_2O + CO \rightleftharpoons H_2 + CO_2$$

and the forward reaction is endothermic. A mixture of water vapour, carbon monoxide and hydrogen was allowed to reach equilibrium at a certain temperature. The initial partial pressures of each of the three gases was 2 atmospheres. At equilibrium the total pressure was still the same but the partial pressure of the carbon dioxide was 1 atmosphere.

(i) Write the expression for K_p for the reaction.
(ii) Why did the total pressure not change during the reaction?
(iii) What would be the effect, if any, on K_p, of raising the temperature

(iv) Calculate K_p for the reaction.
(v) If the total pressure of the mixture is increased to 17 atm. by adding hydrogen, calculate the partial pressure of each gas when equilibrium has been re-established.

Q.13.36 At equilibrium in the reaction $N_2O_4 \rightleftharpoons 2NO_2$, it was found that the partial pressures of the two gases were, respectively, 0.6 atm. and 0.3 atm. Calculate K_p for that reaction. A container was then filled with N_2O_4 at 30 atmospheres, and set aside until equilibrium was attained. Calculate the partial pressure of each gas then present.

Q.13.37 At a certain temperature, an equilibrium mixture was found to contain 31.7 g of nitrogen, 7.0 g of hydrogen and 57.3 g of ammonia.

(a) If the mixture occupied a volume of 4 litres, calculate the value of K_c for the reaction $N_2 + 3H_2 \rightleftharpoons 2NH_3$.
(b) If the pressure in the container was 50 atmospheres, calculate the value of Kp for the reaction.
(c) Assuming the values of the pressure and volume given above, calculate the temperature of the equilibrium mixture.

Review When you know Chapter 13 you should be able to:

(a) Explain what is meant by: reversible reaction, equilibrium system, state of equilibrium, dynamic equilibrium equilibrium constant, partial pressure, K_c, K_p.
(b) State Le Châtelier's Principle and state what happens to an equilibrium system when a stated stress is applied to it.
(c) Show how Le Châtelier's Principle is relevant to industrial reactions.
(c) Describe experiments (i) to illustrate Le Châtelier's Principle and (ii) to measure the value of K for an esterification reaction.
(e) Calculate, from experimental data, the value of K for a given reaction.
(f)Solve equilibrium problems involving both Kc and Kp.

$\mathbf{P}$ure water has been shown to conduct electricity — to a very slight extent, which means that ions are present. The ionisation of water can be written as $H_2O \leftrightharpoons H^+ + OH^-$. However, this is somewhat simplified since it is known that protons (H^+ ions) cannot exist independently — they become hydrated and form oxonium ions (page 97) so that more correctly, the equation of the ionisation is $2H_2O \leftrightarrow H_3O^+ + OH^-$. The number of H_3O^+ ions is the same as the number of H^+ ions, so that it is in order to use the simplified equation.

The equilibrium constant, K, for the dissociation is given by

$$K = \frac{[H^+][OH^-]}{[H_2O]}$$

The amount of water which ionises is very very small (i.e. the equilibrium lies very much to the left hand side) so that the relative number of ions is very small and practically all of the water can be considered to be undissociated. It can be shown that only one molecule in more than 500 million is ionised. One litre of water consists of 55.55 moles of it so that $[H_2O]$ is thus constant. Thus $[H^+][OH^-]$ must also be constant. This product which is known as the **ionic product of water** (K_w), has the value 10^{-14} mol^2/L^2 at 25 °C

$$\mathbf{K_w = [H^+][OH^-] = 10^{-14} \ mol^2/L^2}$$

The value of K increases as temperature rises, but for ordinary purposes, it value at 25°C (about room temperature) is used.

The ionic product of water is a very important constant; it is the product of the H^+ and the OH^- ion concentrations in all aqueous solutions. In pure water the ions must be present in equal numbers, (since $H_2O \rightarrow H^+ + OH^-$) so that

$$[H^+] = [OH^-] = 10^{-7} \ mol^2/L^2$$

In aqueous solution, normal acidic properties are due to H^+ ions. If $[H^+]$ exceeds 10^{-7}, (e.g. 10^{-6}) the solution is acidic and if $[H^+]$ is less than 10^{-7} (e.g 10^{-8}) it means that $[OH^-]$ is greater than 10^{-7} and the solution is alkaline. It must be realised, however, that no matter how strongly acidic a solution is, there are always OH^- ions present (to maintain $[H^+][OH^-] = 10^{-14}$, the value of the ionic product). If, for example, $[H^+]$ is 10^{-1} (as in 0.1 M HCl) then $[OH^-]$ must be 10^{-13}. Since the product

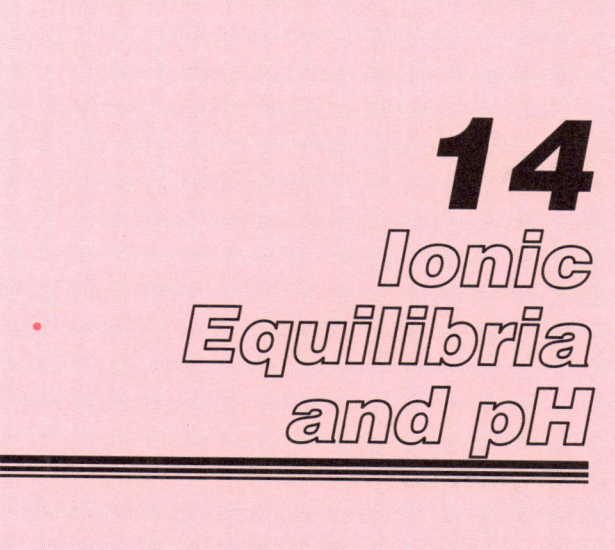

14
Ionic Equilibria and pH

of the concentrations of the ions is constant, the value of one gives information about the other.

pH

The pH of a solution is a measure of the H^+ ion concentration present and thus of its acidity or alkalinity.

Its definition is;

> **The pH is equal to minus the log (to the base 10) of the hydrogen ion concentration,**

'p' stands for '-$\log_{10}$'. In pure water, $[H^+] = 10^{-7}$ and so its pH is 7. Any other solution in which $[H^+] = [OH^-]$ has a pH of 7 and is thus neutral.

In an acidic solution $[H^+] > 10^{-7}$ (e.g. 10^{-6}) and so the pH is less than 7, and conversely in an alkaline solution the pH is greater than 7. Increasing acidity means increasing $[H^+]$ and thus decreasing pH.

It must be remembered that the pH scale is a logarithmic one, so that if $[H^+]$ changes tenfold the pH changes by only one unit.

$[H^+] = 10^0$	10^{-2}	10^{-4}	10^{-6}	10^{-7}	10^{-8}	10^{-10}	10^{-12}	10^{-14}
pH = 0	2	4	6	7	8	10	12	14
strong acids		weak acids		neu-tral	weak alkalis		strong alkalis	

pH Calculations

The pH of a solution is minus the log of the H^+ concentration, and most pH calculations involve two stages; (i) working out the value of the H^+ concentration of the given solution (although in simple problems this information may be directly given, and (ii) calculating minus the log of that value.

Calculator Calculations

Logs and exponentials are needed for pH calculations and so a scientific calculator is necessary. Details of three calculator functions might be mentioned here:

(i)   Use of the 'log' key on the calculator is straightforward; pressing it gives the log of the number already in the display.

(ii)   Pressing the exponential key (which is usually labelled either **EE** or **exp**) effectively means 'multiplied by 10 to the power of'

(iii)   It is not usually possible to directly enter a negative number into the calculator; instead, the positive value of the number is entered, followed by the +/- key, which changes its sign.

For example, to put the value 3×10^{-6} into the calculator,

press 3,   EE (or exp),   6,   and +/-   when the display should show:

$$3 - 06$$

This is read as 3 multiplied by 10 to the power of –6

Worked Examples 1 - 4

Calculate the pH of each of the following solutions:

1.   A solution whose hydrogen ion concentration is 2×10^{-2} mol/litre.

Enter this value on the calculator; press 2,   EE, 2,   +/-, then press log, followed by +/- (since **minus** the log is required):

$$[H^+] = 2 \times 10^{-2}$$

$$-\log[H^+] = 1.7 = pH$$

It is recommended that when doing pH calculations, the value of $[H^+]$ should be recorded and the laid out calculation should contain the line $[H^+] = ...$

2.   0.1 M HCl.

HCl is a strong acid and is fully dissociated in solution:

$$HCl \rightarrow H^+ + Cl^-$$

Thus 0.1 M HCl contains 0.1 mole of H^+ ions per litre:

$$[H^+] = 0.1$$

Use calculator, press 0.1,   log,   +/-

$$-\log[H^+] = 1 = pH$$

3.   0.01 M H_2SO_4.

This acid is also a strong acid, but is dibasic, so that 1 mole of the acid produces 2 moles of H^+:

$$H_2SO_4 \rightarrow 2H^+ + SO_4^{2-}$$

In 0.01 M acid therefore, the concentration of H^+ is 0.02 mol/L.

$$[H^+] = 0.02$$
$$-\log[H^+] = 1.7 = pH$$

4.   0.1 M CH_3COOH which is 1.4% ionised at this concentration.

1.4% ionised means that one mole of the acid yields only 1.4% of one mole (i.e. 0.014 moles) of H^+ ions.

$$CH_3COOH \rightarrow CH_3COO^- + H^+$$
$$1 \text{ mole} \rightarrow \qquad\qquad 0.014 \text{ moles}$$
$$0.1 \text{ mole} \rightarrow \qquad\qquad 0.0014 \text{ moles}$$

$$[H^+] = 0.0014 \text{ mol/L}$$
$$-\log[H^+] = 2.85 = pH$$

Calculating pH values of Alkaline Solutions

The simplest method of calculation is to first of all find its pOH (in other words, minus the log of its OH^- concentration). This is done in exactly the same way as calculating pH values. Since the product of $[H^+]$ and $[OH^-]$ is 10^{-14} the sum of the pH and the pOH is 14. Thus, if the pOH value is subtracted from 14, the pH value is obtained.

Worked Examples 5 - 7

5.   Calculate the pH of 0.2 M NaOH

NaOH is a strong alkali and is fully dissociated in solution.

$$NaOH \rightarrow Na^+ + OH^-$$

Thus 0.2 M NaOH contains 0.2 mole of OH^- ions per litre :

$$[OH^-] = 0.2 \text{ mol/L}$$
$$-\log[OH^-] = 0.7 = pOH$$
Therefore ,   pH = 13.3

6.   What is the pH of a solution of 2.8 g of KOH per litre?

(KOH = 56), 2.8 g KOH = $\frac{2.8}{56}$ mol = 0.05 mol.

The solution is thus 0.05 molar, and since KOH is a strong alkali (fully dissociated in solution), the concentration of OH^- is 0.05 mol/L

$$[OH^-] = 0.05$$
$$-\log[OH^-] = 1.3 = pOH$$
Therefore :   pH = 12.7

7.   What is the H^+ concentration in a solution whose pH is 2.6?

$$pH = -\log[H^+] = 2.6$$
$$\therefore \qquad \log[H^+] = -2.6$$

(use inverse log on calculator)

$$[H^+] = 2.5 \times 10^{-3} \text{ mol/L}$$

Questions

Q.14.1   Calculate the pH of solutions in which:

(a) $[H^+] = 5 \times 10^{-3}$ mol/L
(b) $[H^+] = 4 \times 10^{-12}$ mol/L
(c) $[H^+] = 10^{-7}$ mol/L
(d) $[OH^-] = 4 \times 10^{-2}$ mol/L
(e) $[OH^-] = 0.05$ mol/L
(f) $[OH^-] = 1.5 \times 10^{-9}$ mol/L

State about each solution whether it is acidic, neutral or alkaline.

Q.14.2   Calculate the pH of each of the following solutions:

(a)   0.01 M HNO_3
(b)   0.02 M H_2SO_4
(c)   a solution of hydrochloric acid containing 3.65 g of HCl per litre
(d)   A solution containing 4.9 g of H_2SO_4 per litre.
(e)   0.01 M sodium hydroxide,
(f)   0.005 M calcium hydroxide,
(g)   a solution containing 4 g of NaOH in 500 cm^3 of solution.
(h)   a solution containing 4 g of NaOH in 250 cm^3 of solution.

Q.14.3   What is the pH of each of the following solutions?

(a)   1.0 M nitric acid,
(b)   a 0.1 M solution of a monobasic (monoprotic) acid which is 3% ionised.

(c)   a solution containing 15 g of H_2SO_4 per litre,

(d)   a solution containing 15 g of NaOH per litre,

(e)   a solution containing 0.63 g of HNO_3 in 500 cm^3 of solution,

(f)   a 0.01 M solution of ethanoic acid (CH_3COOH) given that it is 4.2% ionised at this concentration.

Q.14.4   What is the hydrogen ion concentration in solutions whose pH values are: (a) 4.3, (b) 10.7, (c) 7, (d) 0?

Measurement of pH Values

1. Using pH paper

The simplest method of measuring the pH is to use pH paper or 'Universal' indicator. Unlike litmus, which can only turn red or blue and thus only show whether a substance is acidic or alkaline, these indicators have the ability to show a succession of colour changes according to the pH of the solution into which they are put. The colour which the indicator becomes is compared with a standard colour chart which relates the colour to the pH value.

14.1 —   *A pH colour chart.*

2. Using a pH meter

A pH meter is a sensitive electrical instrument fitted with a special electrode on the end of a flexible lead. When the electrode is immersed in a given solution, a potential difference directly proportional to the pH of the solution is set up, and

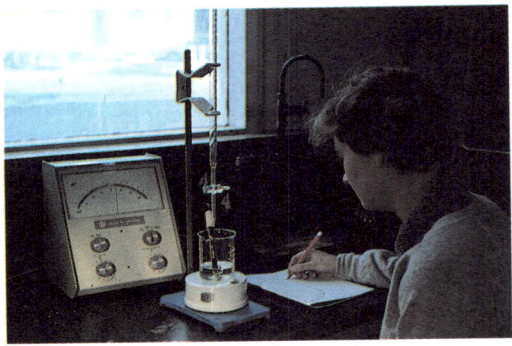

14.2 — Using a pH meter. In this experiment sodium hydroxide from the burette is being added to the hydrochloric acid contained in the beaker. The pH of the mixture is being measured at intervals and the values obtained used to plot the type of graph shown in figure 14.3. The electrode connected to the pH meter is clamped in position in the beaker and the mixture is kept stirred by the magnetic stirrer shown beneath the flask.

is recorded on the meter — which is marked in pH units rather than in volts. Before a measurement is made with a pH meter, it has first of all to be 'calibrated'; this involves putting the electrode into a solution of known pH, and then setting the meter so that that particular pH value is shown on the scale.

Experiment 14.1
Measuring pH values

Many household substances are either acidic or alkaline and in this experiment you are to measure the pH of a selection of such substances. Test as many as are conveniently available. If your teacher gives you some pH paper, the experiment can be done at home. To measure the pH of a liquid, either dip a piece of pH paper into it or add a few drops of Universal indicator.

Note the change in colour to which the indicator changes and compare this colour with the chart which relates colour and pH value. If the substance to be tested is a solid, dissolve it in water and then test it.

Suggested substances to be tested

Vinegar, ammonia solution, salt, washing soda, sour milk, lemon juice, sugar, grape juice, bread soda, soda water, caustic soda (CARE NEEDED), indigestion powder, toothpaste, rhubarb juice, acid drop sweets, milk of magnesia, coffee, detergent, bleach (CARE NEEDED), borax, raspberries, aspirin, grapefruit, vitamin C tablets, tap water.

Write in the names of the substances you have tested against its pH value on a chart such as that shown.

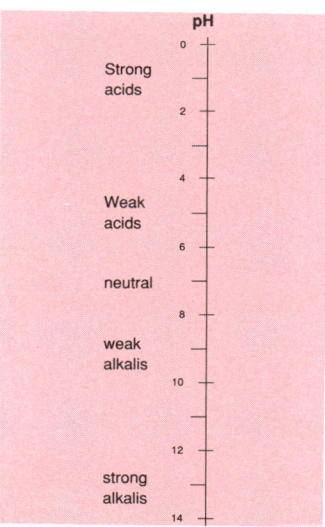

Dissociation Constants

The pH of a solution of a weak acid (or base) cannot be worked out without some information about how much the acid dissociates (ionises). This varies from acid to acid and also depends on how much the acid is diluted, *i.e.* its concentration. The dissociation constant of the acid provides the information needed to calculate the pH of a solution of known concentration (and the % dissociation if necessary).

Ethanoic acid dissociates (ionises) as follows:

$$CH_3COOH \ \rightleftharpoons \ CH_3COO^- + H^+$$

The equilibrium constant K which is given by:

$$K = \frac{[CH_3COO^-]\,[H^+]}{[CH_3COOH]}$$

is known as the dissociation constant of the acid and is denoted by K_a. In the case of ethanoic acid the value of its K_a is 1.8×10^{-5} which means that dissociation occurs to a very slight extent. Dissociation constants for other weak acids are given in the Data Section, at the end of the book.

Similarly, for weak base, *e.g.* aqueous ammonia, $NH_4OH \rightarrow NH_4^+ + OH^-$ the equilibrium constant which is given by :

$$K = \frac{[NH_4^+]\,[OH^-]}{[NH_4OH]}$$

is known as the dissociation constant for the base and is denoted by K_b.

pH values of weak acids and bases can be calculated once the dissociation constant and the concentration of the acid or base are known.

Calculation of pH Values of Weak Acid and Bases

A weak acid, HA, dissociates according to:

$HA \ \rightleftharpoons \ H^+ + A^-$ (where HA is the weak acid and A^- is its anion)

and its K_a value is given by $K_a = \dfrac{[H^+]\,[A^-]}{[HA]}$

When the acid dissociates, equal numbers of both H^+ and A^- ions are formed, so that $[H^+]$ must equal $[A^-]$. Thus,

$$K_a = \frac{[H^+]^2}{[HA]}$$

therefore, $[H^+]^2 = K_a\,[HA]$

or, $[H^+] = \sqrt{K_a\,[HA]}$

Remembering this formula is helpful in problems in which the pH of a weak acid is to be calculated.

In the same way it can be shown that for a weak base, the $[OH^-]$ value is given by;

$$[OH^-] = \sqrt{K_b\,[BOH]}$$

where K_b is the dissociation constant for the base, and [BOH] is its concentration.

Worked Example 8

Calculate the pH of 0.1 M methanoic acid (HCOOH), given that its K_a value is 1.8×10^{-4}

$$[H^+] = \sqrt{K_a\,[HCOOH]}$$

$$= \sqrt{1.8 \times 10^{-4} \times 0.1}$$

Use calculator, and enter the following:

1.8, EE (or exp), 4, +/-, × , 0.1 , =, √x (sq. root key),

when the display should read: 4.2426-03

This means 4.2426×10^{-3}, and is the value of $[H^+]$ (the 'half way' stage) i.e. $[H^+] = 4.2426 \times 10^{-3}$

Now find minus the log of that value, by pressing the log and the +/- keys, when the display should show: 2.3724 00

This is the required pH value; it should be rounded off to 2.37.

Worked Example 9

Calculate the pH value of a 0.02 M ammonia solution, given the K_b for ammonia is 1.8×10^{-5}

Solutions of ammonia are alkaline because ammonia reacts with water to produce OH^- ions according to:

$$NH_3 + H_2O \rightleftharpoons NH_4^+ + OH^-$$

Since the value of $\dfrac{[NH_4^+][OH^-]}{[NH_3][H_2O]}$

(the equilibrium constant) is constant, and the value of $[H_2O]$ is constant,

the value of $\dfrac{[NH_4^+]\,[OH^-]}{[NH_3]}$ is constant,

and the K_b value for ammonia refers to this expression.

$$[OH^-] = \sqrt{K_b\,[NH_3]}$$

$$= \sqrt{1.8 \times 10^{-5} \times 0.02}$$

Use calculator, and enter the following:

1.8, EE, 5, +/- × , 0.02, =, √x, when the value of $[OH^-]$ should show on the display;

$$[OH^-] = 6 \times 10^{-4}$$

Press log, and +/-, in order to find minus the log of that value; the calculator display should then show 3.22, which is the pOH value.

pH = 14 – pOH

  = 14 – 3.22 = 10.78 = pH of solution

Worked Example 10

Calculate the pH of the solution obtained by adding 49 cm^3 of 0.1 M NaOH to 50 cm^3 of 0.1 M HCl (for simplicity take the volume of the resulting solution to be 100 cm^3)

49 cm^3 0.1 M NaOH neutralises 49 cm^3 of 0.1 M HCl, leaving 1 cm^3 of 0.1 M HCl in excess. The amount of HCl is thus 0.0001 mole — in a volume of 100 cm^3; its concentration is therefore 0.001 mole/L or 10^{-3} M, or, put another way, there is 1 cm^3 of 0.1 M HCl in excess, but now in a volume of 100 cm^3. The 0.1 M acid has been diluted 100 times, so its concentration is now only:

$$\frac{1}{100} \times 0.1, \ i.e. \ 0.001 \text{ or } 10^{-3} \text{ M}$$

$$[H^+] = 10^{-3} \text{ mol/L}$$

$$pH = 3$$

(K_a for ethanoic acid = 1.8×10^{-5})

Questions

Q.14.5 Calculate the pH of ethanoic acid of concentration (a) 0.01 M; (b) 0.2 M (c) 3 g per litre; (d) 3 g per 250 cm^3.

Q.14.6 Given the K_a for the acid HX is 4×10^{-6} calculate the $[H^+]$ and the pH of (a) 0.1 M HX and (b) 0.01 M HX.

Q.14.7 Calculate (a) the $[H^+]$ and pH of 0.12 M ethanoic acid; (b) the pH and pOH of 0.2 M ethanoic acid.

Q.14.8 Calculate the pH of each of the following:

(a) 0.1 M nitrous acid (HNO$_2$) whose K_a value is 4.6×10^{-4}

(b) a 0.02 M solution of chloroethanoic acid ($CH_2ClCOOH$) given its K_a value is 1.3×10^{-3}

(c) a solution containing 3.4 g of hydrogen sulphide per litre

(K_a for $H_2S \longrightarrow H^+ + HS^-$ is 8.9×10^{-8})

(d) a solution containing 6.2 g of boric acid (H_3BO_3) per litre. Assume the total acidity is due to the first dissociation, for which the K_a value is 5.8×10^{-10}

(e) pure water at 100°C at which temperature its ionic product is 1×10^{-12}

(f) a solution containing 1.7 g of ammonia per 250 cm^3 of solution (K_b for ammonia = 1.8×10^{-5})

Q.14.9 What concentration of ethanoic acid is needed to give $[H^+] = 3.5 \times 10^{-4}$ mol/L?

Calculate also the pH of the solution. ($K_a = 1.8 \times 10^{-5}$)

Q.14.10 The pH of 10^{-3} M benzoic acid (C_6H_5COOH) is 3.6. Calculate its dissociation constant.

Q.14.11
Calculate $[H^+]$, $[OH^-]$, pH and pOH for each of the following solutions;

(a) 0.1 M HCl
(b) 0.0001 M $Ca(OH)_2$,
(c) 0.001 M H_2SO_4,
(d) 0.1 M NaOH,
(e) 0.01 M CH_3COOH (1.4% ionised),
(f) 1.0 M NH_3 (0.42% ionised).

Q.14.12 Calculate the pH of the solutions formed when (a) 49.5 cm^3 (b) 49.9 cm^3; (c) 50.5 cm^3; (d) 51 cm^3; of 0.1 M NaOH are added to 50 cm^3 of 0.1 M HCl (take the total volume to be 100 cm^3 in each case).

Acid/Alkali Indicators

Indicators are substances which change colour according to pH of the liquid in which they are placed. Most indicators are weak acids (but some are weak bases) and are therefore slightly dissociated in solution; the colour of the undissociated acid, HA, must be different from that of the anion A^-. In the case of methyl orange[i] for example, the acid HA is red and the anion is yellow:

$$HA \rightleftharpoons H^+ + A^-$$
$$\text{red} \qquad \text{colourless} \quad \text{yellow}$$

In acidic solution (high concentration of H^+) the equilibrium is driven to the left (in accordance with Le Châtelier) and the red colour predominates. In alkaline solution (high concentration of OH^-), H^+ ions combine with the OH^- which are thus removed, and the equilibrium moves to the right making the yellow colour of the anion predominate.

The intermediate colour (orange) is present when the red colour of the acid and the yellow of the anion are equally present, *i.e.* when $[HA] = [A^-]$. This is dependent on the K_a of the acid, which for methyl orange is 2×10^{-4}. Calculation shows that the pH is 3.7 when $[HA] = [A^-]$.

Most indicators require a range of about two pH units to show their full colour change, and in the case of methyl orange it is found that the red colour is predominant when the pH is less than 2.9 and the yellow colour when it is more than 4.6. Some indicators with this information about them are listed overleaf.

(i) The structural formula of methyl orange is :

Indicator	Colour change between the pH values
Methyl orange	Red - Yellow 2.9 - 4.6
Screened methyl orange	Violet - Green 2.9 - 4.6
Methyl red	Red - Yellow 4.2 - 6.3
Litmus	Red - Blue 5.0 - 8.0
Bromothymol - blue	Yellow - Blue 6.0 - 7.6
Phenophthalein	Colourless - Violet 8.3 -10.0

Titration Curves

Change of pH during neutralisation

When an acid is being titrated with an alkali, the pH increases during the process. The following graphs show how the pH changes during various acid-alkali titrations — of both strong and weak acids and alkalis, pH values for such graphs can be either determined experimentally — using a pH meter, such as shown on page 168 or calculated as in Worked Example 10

Choice of Indicator for Titrations

The correct indicator for a titration should show a sharp end point in a neutralisation, *i.e.* it should change colour when the exact amount (to the nearest drop) of one substance has been added to the other. The changing point must therefore appear on the vertical part of the graph showing the pH change for minimum amount of alkali (or acid) added.

When titrating a strong acid with a strong alkali (Graph 14.4 (a)), most indicators are suitable, since there is such a large change in pH value.

When titrating a strong acid with a weak alkali (Graph 14.4 (b)) an indicator which changes in the region of pH 4 to 5 is necessary; either methyl orange or methyl red is suitable here. If litmus for example were used, it would not have completely changed colour until about 52 cm^3 of the alkali had been added.

When titrating a weak acid with a strong alkali (Graph 14.4 (c)), an indicator which changes between 8 and 11 is necessary. Phenophthalein is the most suitable for this.

In titrating a weak acid with a weak base, there is no sharp change in pH value at any stage (Graph 14.4 (d)), so the exact end point cannot be shown by any indicator. Such titrations are not carried out for this reason.

Questions

Q.14.13
(a) What types of substances are usually used as indicators. Explain how they function in finding the end point of a reaction.

(b) Name suitable indicators to find the end point of the following reactions;

    (i)   NaOH and H_2SO_4;

    (ii) KOH and HCl;

    (iii) NH_3 and HCl;

    (iv) Na_2CO_3 and HCl;

    (v) KOH and CH_3COOH;

    (vi) HNO_3 and Na_2CO_3.

Q.14.14 What is meant by (i) a weak acid; (ii) the pH of a solution?

Given that the ionic product of water at room temperature is 1×10^{-14}, explain why the pH of pure water is 7.

Monochloroethanoic acid ($CH_2ClCOOH$) is a weak monobasic acid, stronger than ethanoic acid but weaker than dichloroethanoic acid ($CHCl_2COOH$).

(a) What is the pH of a 0.01 M solution of monochloroethanoic acid if its dissociation constant is 1.6×10^{-3}?

(b) By reference to the structure of monochloroethanoic acid, explain why it is a stronger acid than ethanoic acid.

(c) Explain why the following can be regarded as bases:

CH_3COO^-, CH_2ClCOO^-, $CHCl_2COO^-$

State, giving reasons, which of them is the strongest base.

Q.14.15 Methanoic acid is a weak monobasic acid which is soluble in water, ionising slightly according to the equation $HCOOH \rightarrow H^+ + HCOO^-$.

(a) Write an expression for its dissociation constant (K_a)

(b) Find the pH of a 0.1 M solution of methanoic acid given that K_a for this acid is 2.1×10^{-4}

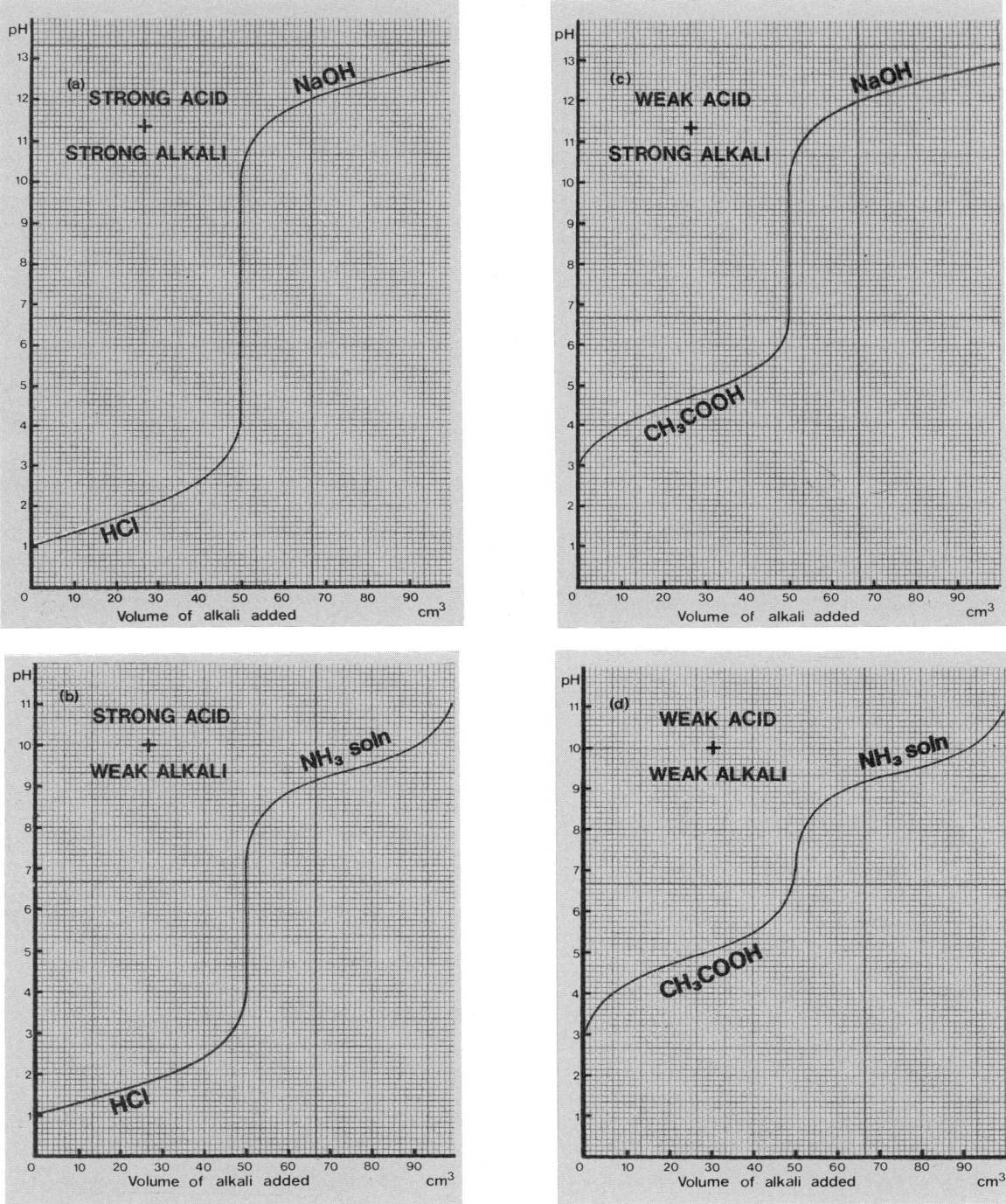

14.3 — *Titration curves, showing how the pH changes as 0. M alkali is being added to 50 cm³ of 1.0 M acid.*

(c) The dissociation constant for ethanoic acid in water is 1.8×10^{-5}. Is it a stronger or a weaker acid than methanoic acid? Explain your reasoning.

(d) What volume of 0.1 M methanoic acid would be needed to neutralise completely 25 cm^3 of 0.108 M sodium hydroxide solution?

(e) Name a suitable indicator for this titration,

(f) Assuming that the indicator you choose is a weak acid, explain briefly how it works.

Review   When you know Chapter 14 you should be able to:

(a) Explain what is meant by: ionic product of water, K_w, dissociation constant.

(b) Define pH.

(c) Calculate the pH of any strong acid or alkali, given its concentration.

(d) Calculate the pH of any weak acid or alkali given its concentration and dissociation constant.

(e) Explain how an indicator works.

(f) Say what indicator is needed for a stated acid/alkali reaction, and explain the reason for this.

Energy is involved in all chemical reactions; some reactions give out energy in one or other of its various forms — heat, light, sound, etc., while other reactions take in energy, *i.e.* require energy to make them happen. Thermochemistry is the study of the heat changes which occur during chemical reactions.

A reaction in which heat is liberated is known as an exothermic reaction.

The burning of a substance is the most common example of this type of reaction; substances which burn include all fuels and many of the elements (*e.g.* carbon, sulphur, hydrogen, magnesium), and in burning, the substance combines with oxygen and heat is liberated.

A reaction in which heat is taken in is called an endothermic reaction.

For example, in order to make nitrogen and oxygen combine together, heat must be supplied:

$$N_2 + O_2 + heat \rightarrow 2NO$$

This reaction is thus an endothermic reaction.

Heat of Reaction

This is the general name given to heat changes and its definition is:

Heat of Reaction is the heat change which occurs when a reaction takes place according to a given chemical equation.

However, it is more convenient to classify heats of reaction according to the different types of reaction — formation of compounds, combustion reactions, neutralisations, etc. The value of a heat change is conventionally given for one mole of the substance involved, and since heat is a form of energy, the units are joules. Because the joule is such a small unit, kilojoules are used in practice.

The heat of formation of a compound is the heat change which occurs when 1 mole of the compound is formed from its elements in their standard states (see note 1).

The heat of combustion of a substance is the heat change which occurs when 1 mole of the substance is burned in an excess of oxygen (see note 2.)

15

Thermo-chemistry

Notes:

1. The standard conditions to which values of heat changes apply are room temperature (which is taken as 25°C) and standard atmospheric pressure (101 kPa)

2. Burned in an excess of oxygen means that all of the elements have been converted to their normal oxides.

The reaction represented by the equation:

$$C + O_2 \rightarrow CO_2 + 393 \text{ kJ}$$

shows that 1 mole of carbon (= 12 g) combines with oxygen (also 1 mole) to produce 1 mole of carbon dioxide (= 44 g), and that 393 kJ of heat are liberated or given off.

Heat reaction is denoted by ΔH (delta H). This symbol represents the change in the heat content of the 'system' (which can be best thought of as a collection of chemicals in an isolated environment).

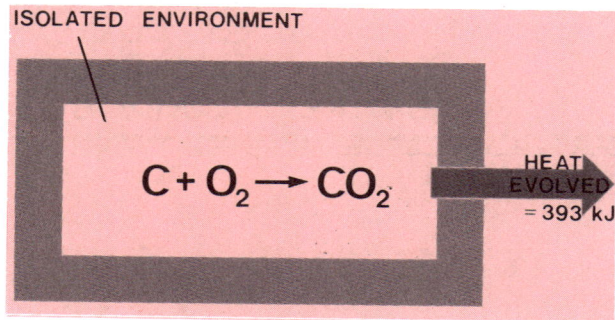

15.1

When the reaction in the above system occurs, the system is at the **loss** of heat, so therefore ΔH is minus 393 kJ. The reaction is correctly and fully represented by:

$$C(s) + O_2(g) \rightarrow CO_2(g) \qquad \Delta H = -393 \text{ kJ}$$

For an endothermic system, heat must be supplied to make the reaction occur, *i.e.* the system **gains** heat so ΔH is positive.

The full equation representing this reaction is:

$$N_2(g) + O_2(g) \rightarrow 2NO(g) \qquad \Delta H = +180 \text{ kJ}$$

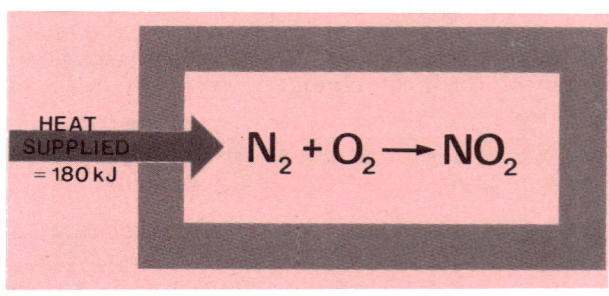

15.2

Determination of heats of combustion

The heat of combustion of a substance is an important property of it. From an industrial aspect, it provides information about the heating value (the 'calorific' value) of various fuels. From the chemical aspect, it enables many heats of formation to be calculated and hence gives information about the stability of different compounds.

Heats of combustion are measured using a bomb calorimeter. This consists of a strong cylindrical steel container with a tightly fitting screwed lid, through which an inlet tube for oxygen and a pair of electrical wires pass.

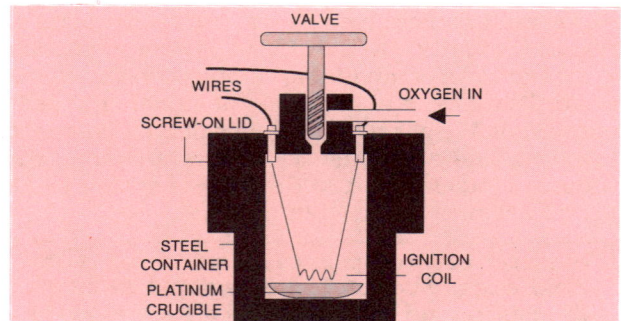

15.3

This container is the reaction vessel for the combustion reaction and when in use, it is placed in a large container of water which becomes heated due to combustion of the substance in the 'bomb'

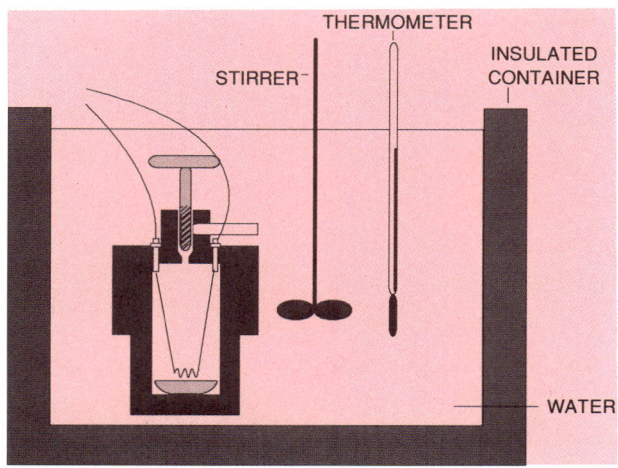

15.4

In determining the heat of combustion of a substance, a weighed quantity of it is placed in the crucible in the 'bomb', the lid screwed on tightly and oxygen pumped in to about 20 atmospheres pressure (to ensure excess), the bomb is submerged in a known mass of water in the outer container and the temperature noted. The compound is ignited electrically and it burns, liberating heat. When the reaction has finished, the final steady temperature of the water is measured.

The heat produced is calculated from the mass of water, its specific heat capacity and the rise in temperature, and hence the heat produced by the combustion of 1 mole of the substance can be found (*i.e.* its heat of combustion). Various correction factors, such as subtracting the quantity of heat provided by the heating coil to start the reaction, are applied in order to obtain a very exact value. A worked example of a typical calculation follows.

Worked Example 1

Calculate the heat of combustion of ethanol from the following experimental results, taken using a bomb calorimeter:

Mass of ethanol . . . . = 20 g

Mass of water in calorimeter . = 10 kg

Initial temperature of water . . = 18°C

Final temperature of water . = 32°C

Specific heat capacity of water = 4200 J/kg°C

Heat gained by water . . . . . . = $mc\theta$

$= 10 \times 4200 \times 14$

$= 588000$ J

$= 588$ kJ

Combustion of 20 g of ethanol liberates 588 kJ

(1 mole of C_2H_5OH = 46 g)

Therefore combustion of 46 g liberates

$\dfrac{46 \times 588}{20}$ k J $= 1352$ k J

Heat of combustion = -1352 kJ/mol.

Experiment 15.1
To estimate the heat of combustion of a substance

The heat of combustion of a substance is the heat liberated when 1 mole of the substance is burnt in excess oxygen (*i.e.* when all the elements present have been converted to their normal oxides). The principle of its measurement is that a weighed quantity of the substance is burnt and the heat produced is made to heat a measured quantity of water contained in a calorimeter. The heat gained by the water (and hence produced by the burning substance) is given by $E = mc\,\theta$, where m is the mass of water being heated, c its specific heat capacity and θ the rise in temperature. Calculation leads to the heat which would be produced by burning 1 mole of the substance.

The purpose of this experiment is to illustrate the principle of how heats of combustion are measured, rather than to give an exact value. The experiment ignores heat losses that would have to be taken into account in order to obtain accurate figures.

Procedure
Weigh an empty crucible or other small container. Place a suitable quantity of the substances in it (see notes) and reweigh. Measure 100 g of water (100 cm^3 by graduated cylinder is accurate enough) into the calorimeter and take its temperature accurately. Arrange the apparatus as shown overleaf.

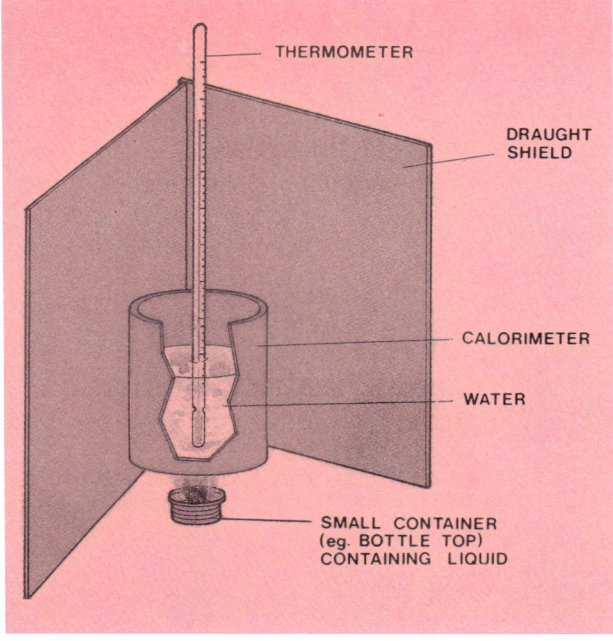

15.5

Ignite the substance and allow it to burn. When it has all burnt away, stir the water well to make its temperature uniform and then read the thermometer again. Tabulate the results as below.

Calculate the quantity of heat gained by water ($E = mc\,\theta$); this is assumed to be the same as that produced by the burning substance. Finally, by using the molecular mass of the substance, calculate the quantity of heat which would be produced by burning 1 mole of the substance.

Notes

1. If using a liquid substance, measure out 2 cm^3 of it, by means of a burette.

2. If using ethanal tetramer, use between 1.5 and 2.0 g of it.

3. If using a candle, weigh the candle before burning it, place it in position and ignite it. Heat the calorimeter until the temperature has increased by 30°C, extinguish the candle and then reweigh it to find the mass of candle wax burnt. Take the formula of candle wax to be $C_{20}H_{42}$.

Results

Record these as follows:

Mass of empty crucible . . . .

Mass of crucible with substance. . . . .

Mass of substance. . . . .

Mass of water being heated . . . .

Initial temperature. . . . .

Final temperature . . . .

Specific heat capacity of water. . . . .

Heat gained by the water. . . . .

Heat produced by combustion of the substance.

Substance used . . . .

Molecular mass of substance. . . . .

Heat of combustion of the substance. . . . .

Kilogram Calorific Values ▰▰▰

This is another heat unit, used mainly in industrial and domestic situations. It gives the heat output of a fuel per unit mass rather than per mole, and is defined as:

> **The kilogram calorific value of a fuel is the quantity of heat liberated when 1 kg of the fuel is completely burned.**

It is used by heat engineers, fuel merchants, central-heating suppliers, etc., for expressing and comparing such things as efficiencies of fuels, heat outputs of radiators and of boilers and furnaces.

It can be directly measured using a bomb calorimeter, or can be calculated from heats of combustion of fuels which have a definite molecular mass (*i.e.* ones which have a definite formula). For example, the heat of combustion of methanol (CH_3OH) is 715 kJ/mol (= 32 g).

32 g CH_3OH produce 715 kJ

$$\therefore\ 1000\text{ g}\ \text{ give }\ \frac{715 \times 1000}{32}\ \text{kJ}\ =\ 22344\text{ kJ}$$

Kilogram calorific value = 22344 kJ/kg = 22.3 MJ/kg

Kilogram Calorific Values

FUEL	FORMULA or approximate composition	CALORIFIC * VALUE	
ANTHRACITE	94% C	31.4	MJ/kg
BITUMINOUS COAL	86% C	28	MJ/kg
COKE		28	MJ/kg
PEAT	60% C 35% moisture	11.6	MJ/kg
BRIQUETTES	82% C 12% moisture	19.8	MJ/kg
LIGNITE	67% C	21	MJ/kg
WOOD	53% C 35% moisture	13	MJ/kg
PETROL	mainly C_8H_{18}	35	MJ/L
DIESEL OIL		38	MJ/kg
PARAFFIN OIL	mainly $C_{15}H_{32}$	36.7	MJ/kg
FUEL OIL		38	MJ/kg
ETHANOL	C_2H_5OH	29.8 23.5	MJ/kg MJ/L
METHANOL	CH_3OH	23.8 18.8	MJ/kg MJ/L
NATURAL GAS	CH_4	55	MJ/kg
BOTTLED GAS	$C_3H_8 + C_4H_{10}$	49.5	MJ/kg
HYDROGEN	H_2	143	MJ/kg

Note

Most figures are approximate because of variations in composition of fuels, and in the conditions of tests.

Hess's Law and Energy Cycles

Except in a few cases, heats of formation cannot be measured directly. The direct synthesis of most compounds from their elements is usually impractical. However, heats of formation can readily be calculated from heats of combustion, by making use of Hess's Law. This law states:

> **The heat change for a given reaction depends only on the initial and the final states of the system and is independent of the path followed.**

Simplified, this means that if a reaction takes place in stages, then the algebraic sum of the energy changes in the stages is the same as the energy change for the reaction if it takes place directly.

Hess's Law is illustrated in the following cycle of changes.

Carbon and hydrogen can be converted to CO_2 and H_2O either by first combining the elements to form ethyne, C_2H_2 and then burning the latter in oxygen (to give the required products), or by directly burning the elements in oxygen to give the CO_2 and H_2O. It will be seen that the total energy change is the same, irrespective of the route:

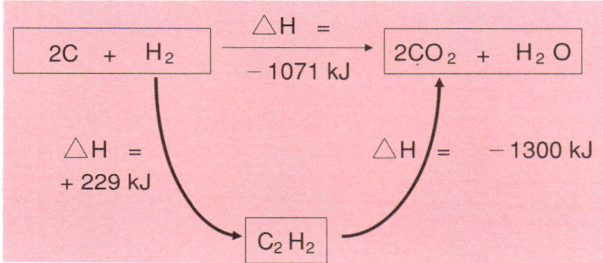

Hess's Law which can be verified experimentally and also deduced theoretically from the Law of Conservation of Energy, is the basis for thermochemical calculations; it enables heat changes of known reactions to be added, subtracted, multiplied, divided and/or reversed algebraically, in order to calculate heats which cannot be determined directly by experiment. Its use is illustrated in the following worked example of a typical calculation.

Worked Example 2[i]

Calculate the heat of formation of methane (CH_4), given the following information:

$$C + O_2 \rightarrow CO_2 \qquad \Delta H = -393 \text{ kJ} \quad (1)$$

$$H_2 + \tfrac{1}{2}O \rightarrow H_2O \qquad \Delta H = -286 \text{ kJ} \quad (2)$$

$$CH_4 + 2O_2 \rightarrow CO_2 + 2H_2O \quad \Delta H = -895 \text{ kJ} \quad (3)$$

Firstly, the equation for which the heat change is required, is written down, *viz.*

$$C + 2H_2 \rightarrow CH_4 \qquad \Delta H = ? \quad (4)$$

(i)   The Law of Conservation of Energy, or the First Law of Thermodynamics is assumed in these energy calculations. This law states " **Energy can neither be created nor destroyed, but can be changed from one form to another** " .

Secondly, the given information is rearranged as necessary, so that when all the equations are added together, that for which the heat change is required (*i.e.* equation (4)), results. To do this, equation (1) is used without change, equation (2) is doubled, and equation (3) is reversed (the sign of its ΔH must therefore be changed from - to +)

$C + O_2 \rightarrow CO_2$ $\Delta H = -393$ kJ (1)
$2H_2 + O_2 \rightarrow 2H_2O$ $\Delta H = -572$ kJ (2) × 2
$CO_2 + 2H_2O \rightarrow CH_4 + O_2$ $\Delta H = +895$ kJ (3) reversed

$\overline{C + 2H_2 \qquad \rightarrow CH_4 \qquad\qquad \Delta H = -70\ kJ}$

On adding the 3 amended equations, equation (4) which is required, is obtained — for which ΔH is calculated to be -70 kJ/mol. The whole process is really a mechanical means of calculating one heat change in a Hess cycle of reactions.

The heat of formation of a compound is usually an indication of its stability and reactivity. Most compounds are formed exothermically, which means that they contain less internal energy than the free elements from which they are formed. Such compounds are generally stable and have no tendency to revert to their component elements. Compounds which are formed endothermically contain more energy than the free elements from which they are composed. Compounds of this type are generally unstable and highly reactive — often decomposing (on being heated) to form simpler substances and releasing heat in doing so.

Use of state symbols

In doing problems, it is often very important to put in the state symbols for the various substances, because the heat change for a reaction will depend on the state of those substances. For example. hydrogen combines with oxygen to form water:

$H_2(g) + \frac{1}{2}O_2(g) \rightarrow H_2O(l)$ $\Delta H = -286$ kJ/mol

However, if the water produced is in the form of steam, the heat evolved is less because energy is required to change liquid water to vapour water:

$H_2(g) + \frac{1}{2}O_2(g) \rightarrow H_2O(g)$ $\Delta H = -242$ kJ/mol

Questions

Q.15.1   Express the following information in the form of equations:

(a)   1 mole of CO_2 on being formed from its elements liberates 393 kJ of heat.

(b)   32 g of sulphur burns in air and liberates 294 kJ of heat.

(c)   1 mole of nitrogen(II) oxide on being formed from its elements requires 90 kJ of heat.

(d)   On burning 1 mole of ethanol (C_2H_5OH) in air, 1352 kJ of heat are liberated.

(e)   When 2 g of hydrogen are burned in air, 286 kJ of heat are evolved.

(f)   The heat of formation of carbon monoxide is -110 kJ mol.

(g)   The heat of combustion of carbon monoxide is -283 kJ/mol.

(g)   When 1 g of water is formed from its elements, 15.9 kJ of heat are liberated.

Q.15.2   Given that:

$C + O_2 \rightarrow CO_2$ $\Delta H = -393$ kJ

$H_2 + \frac{1}{2}O_2 \rightarrow H_2O$ $\Delta H = -286$ kJ.

what is the quantity of liberated heat when:

(a)   1 mole of carbon is burned;
(b)   1 g of carbon is burned;
(c)   1 g of hydrogen is burned;
(d)   1 litre of hydrogen at s.t.p. is burned ?
(e)   What is the kilogram calorific value of both carbon and hydrogen?

Q.15.3   Calculate the value of ΔH for the equation $CO_2 \rightarrow C + O_2$, given that the heat of combustion of carbon is -393 kJ/mol. Find also, the heat change involved when 4 g of carbon are burned in oxygen.

Q.15.4   Given that the heat of combustion of carbon monoxide (to CO_2) is -283 kJ/mol, calculate the heat change for the following reaction:

$CO + H_2O \rightarrow CO_2 + H_2$

(Also needed:
 heat of combustion of hydrogen = -286 kJ/mol).

Q.15.5 Copper oxide is reduced to copper by reaction with carbon monoxide. Write a balanced equation for this reaction. Given the following information, calculate ΔH for that reaction.

$CO(g) + \frac{1}{2}O_2(g) \rightarrow CO_2(g)$ ΔH = -283 KJ

$Cu(s) + \frac{1}{2}O_2(g) \rightarrow CuO(s)$ ΔH = -155 kJ

Q.15.6 Ethene (C_2H_4) on reaction with hydrogen is converted to ethane (C_2H_6). Calculate ΔH for that reaction, given the following heats of combustion:

H_2 = -286 kJ, C_2H_4 = -1390 kJ, C_2H_6 = -1539 kJ.

Q.15.7 Carbon disulphide burns in oxygen according to:

$CS_2 + 3O_2 \rightarrow CO_2 + 2SO_2$ ΔH = -1072 kJ,

and the heats of combustion of carbon and sulphur are, respectively, -393 kJ and -294 kJ. Calculate the heat of formation of carbon disulphide.

Q.15.8 The table shows the heat liberated when 1 g of each of 3 different alcohols is burned in air.

Methanol (CH_3OH)	22.3 kJ evolved
Ethanol (C_2H_5OH)	29.8 kJ evolved
Propanol (C_3H_7OH)	33.5 kJ evolved

For each of these alcohols, calculate its heat of combustion in kJ/mol. From the results, estimate the heat of combustion of butanol (C_4H_9OH)

Q.15.9 On average, a person requires about 12 MJ of energy daily, to lead a normal life. If he were to obtain all his energy by eating sugar ($C_{12}H_{22}O_{11}$), what mass of it would he have to consume daily? (heat of combustion of sugar is -5670 kJ/mol).

Q.15.10 The heats of combustion of ethyne (C_2H_2) and benzene (C_6H_6) are -1299 and -3273 kJ/mol respectively. Calculate the heat change for the polymerisation of ethyne to benzene, i.e. $3C_2H_2 \rightarrow C_6H_6$, and state whether the reaction is exothermic or endothermic.

Q.15.11 Calculate the heat of formation of each of the following compounds, given its heat of combustion:

(a) Ethene, C_2H_4; heat of combustion = -1409 kJ/mol
(b) Propane, C_3H_8; heat of combustion = -2220 kJ/mol
(c) Ethane, C_2H_6; heat of combustion = -1560 kJ/mol.

Also needed: heats of combustion of carbon (-393) and hydrogen (-286 kJ/mol).

Q.15.12 The heats of formation of NO and NO_2 are +90 kJ/mol and +31 kJ/mol respectively. Calculate the heat of the reaction

$2NO + O_2 \rightarrow 2NO_2$

Is it exothermic or endothermic?

Q.15.13 Calculate the heat of formation of ammonia, given that:

$4 NH_3 + 3O_2 \rightarrow 2N_2 + 6H_2O$ ΔH = -1532 kJ

(Also needed; heat of combustion of hydrogen = -286 kJ/mol).

Q.15.14 The heat of combustion of sulphur is -297 kJ/mol and the heat of formation of sulphur trioxide is -395 kJ/mol. Calculate the quantity of heat given out when 1 kg of sulphur dioxide is converted to sulphur trioxide (This reaction is an important stage in the contact process for the manufacture of H_2SO_4).

Q.15.15 When 2 g of sulphur were completely burned in air, the heat evolved raised the temperature of 222 g of water from 18°C to 38°C. Calculate the heat of combustion of sulphur. (Specific heat capacity of water = 4200 J/kg°C)

Q.15.16 In an experiment, 560 cm^3 of ethane (at s.t.p.) were compressed with an excess of oxygen in a suitable container and ignited. It was found that the heat produced raised the temperature of 500 g of water by 18.6°C. Calculate the heat of combustion of ethane given by these figures and also its kilogram calorific value (S.H.C. of water = 4200 J/kg °C).

Q.15.17 Ammonia gas and hydrogen chloride gas can be converted to ammonium chloride solution in two ways: (i) by reacting the ammonia with hydrogen chloride gas and then dissolving the resulting compound in water, or (ii) by reacting the ammonia with water and neutralising the aqueous solution with hydrochloric acid.

Use the following information to calculate the total heat change for each route, and hence illustrate Hess's Law.

$NH_3(g) + HCl(g) \rightarrow NH_4Cl(s)$ $\Delta H = -176$ kJ

$NH_3(aq) + HCl(aq) \rightarrow NH_4Cl(aq)$ $\Delta H = -52$ kJ

$NH_3(g) + water \rightarrow NH_3(aq)$ $\Delta H = -35$ kJ

$HCl(g) + water \rightarrow HCl(aq)$ $\Delta H = -72$ kJ

$NH_4Cl(s) + water \rightarrow NH_4Cl(aq)$ $\Delta H = +17$ kJ

Q.15.18   The Thermite reaction is represented by:

$2Al + Fe_2O_3 \rightarrow 2Fe + Al_2O_3$

Calculate its heat of reaction given that the heats of formation of aluminium oxide and iron(III) oxide are, respectively, -1676 kJ/mol and -822 kJ/mol.

Q.15.19
Calculate the heats of formation of (i) methanol, and (ii) propanol, given the following heats of combustion:

    hydrogen   = -286 kJ/mol
    carbon   = -393 kJ/mol
    methanol   = -715 kJ/mol
    propanol   = -2010 kJ/mol.

Q.15.20   Diborane has the formula B_2H_6 and its heat of formation is +30 kJ/mol. Calculate its heat of combustion, given the following information:

Heat of formation of B_2O_3 = -674 kJ/mol

Heat of formation of water = -286 kJ/mol.

(diborane, on combustion, yields B_2O_3 and water).

Heat of Neutralisation

> **Heat of Neutralisation is the heat change involved when 1 mole of H^+ ions from an acid reacts with 1 mole of OH^- ions from an alkali.**

It is not necessarily the heat evolved when 1 mole of the acid is neutralised by the alkali. For HNO_3 for example, ΔH does refer to 1 mole of the acid (*i.e.* 63 g) since that amount produces 1 mole H^+ ions.

$HNO_3 \rightarrow H^+ + NO_3^-$

but for H_2SO_4, ΔH refers to one-half (or 0.5) mole of the acid (*i.e.* to 49 g) since 1 mole of the acid produces two moles of H^+:

$H_2SO_4 \rightarrow 2H^+ + SO_4^{2-}$

The heat of neutralisation of an acid by an alkali is easily measured. A thermos flask or a polystyrene beaker makes an ideal calorimeter, since there is little heat loss from either of these and their heat capacities are small. A fixed volume of standard acid (*e.g.* 100 cm^3 of 1.0 M HNO_3) is placed in the calorimeter and the volume of standard alkali required to neutralise the acid (*e.g.* 100 cm^3 of 1.0 M NaOH) placed in a beaker. The temperature of these two solutions is measured as accurately as possible, they are then mixed in the calorimeter, stirred well and the final temperature recorded when it has become steady.

The quantity of heat produced is calculated from the mass of the solution, its specific heat capacity and the rise in temperature, and thence the heat produced by neutralising 1 mole of the acid (which is the heat of neutralisation of HNO_3).

Worked Example 3

In an experiment, 200 cm^3 of 1.0 M nitric acid at 15.4°C were reacted with 200 cm^3 of 1.0 M sodium hydroxide at 16.0°C. The temperature of the resulting solution was found to be 22.6°C. Given the density of the solution (1.0 g/cm^3) and its specific heat capacity (4060 J/kg°C) calculate the heat of neutralisation of the nitric acid.

Average initial temperature

$$= \frac{15.4 + 16.0}{2} = 15.7°C$$

Final Temperature	= 22.6°C
Rise in Temperature	= 6.9°C
Mass of solution	= (400 × 1.0) g = 0.4 kg
Heat produced ($mc\theta$)	= 0.4 × 4060 × 6.9
	= 11205 J = 11.2 kJ
Amount of HNO_3	$= \frac{200 \times 1.0}{1000}$ mol
Amount of H^+	= 0.2 mol
0.2 mol H^+ produces	11.2 kJ of heat
∴ 1 mol would produce	$\frac{11.2}{0.2}$ kJ = 56 kJ
	= heat of neuturalisation.

Experiment 15.2
To measure the Heat of Neturalisation of an Acid

In this experiment, a given amount of the chosen acid is neutralised by sodium hydroxide solution, and the heat which is produced increases the temperature of the mixture. Calculation leads to the heat of neturalisation.

Measure 100 cm^3 of 1.0 M hydrochloric, nitric, or ethanoic acid (or 0.5 M sulphuric acid) into a suitable calorimeter and measure its temperature accurately. A thermometer reading to 0.1 or 0.2°C is needed. Measure into a beaker 100 cm^3 of 1.0 M sodium hydroxide solution. Rinse the thermometer and measure the temperature of the alkali. Quickly but carefully, add the alkali to the acid in the calorimeter. Mix well (if using a flask, stopper it and invert it several times). Record the highest temperature reached.

Calculate the rise in temperature (if the two starting solutions were at different temperatures, use the average as the initial temperature), and work out the amount of heat produced ($mc\theta$); the mass (which must be expressed in kg) is the total mass of the liquid being heated, and since it is a dilute solution, its density can be taken to be the same as that of water. Its specific heat capacity is almost the same as that of water (4200 J/kg°C) but the more exact values given below should be used. θ in the formula is the rise in temperature.

Calculate the amount (*i.e.* number of moles) of acid which was neutralised and finally the quantity of heat which would be produced if 1 mole of acid (but for sulphuric acid, 0.5 mole) had been used. This is the heat of neutralisation.

Specific heat capacties for various 1.0 M solutions:

sodium chloride . . . . 4060 J/kg°C,

sodium nitrate . . . . 4060 J/kg °C.

sodium sulphate . . . . 4018 J/kg° C,

sodium ethanoate . . . . 4020 J/kg°C.

Heat of Neutralisation Values ■

The heat of neutralisation of any strong acid by any strong base is almost constant — about 57.2 kJ per mole of H^+. The molecular equations for typical reactions:

$$HNO_3 + NaOH \rightarrow NaNO_3 + H_2O \qquad \Delta H = -57.3 \text{ kJ}$$

$$HCl + KOH \rightarrow KCl + H_2O \qquad \Delta H = -57.2 \text{ kJ}$$

$$\tfrac{1}{2}H_2SO_4 + NaOH \rightarrow \tfrac{1}{2}Na_2SO_4 + H_2O \quad \Delta H = -57.3 \text{ kJ}$$

make it appear as if seemingly very different reactions produce the same heat of reaction. However, remembering that all strong acids and alkalis are fully dissociated in dilute solution, writing the ionic equation for each reaction will show that the same fundamental change occurs in each, *i.e.* $H^+ + OH^- \rightarrow H_2O$. In the case of nitric acid and sodium hydroxide, for example, the breakdown of the equation is:

$$HNO_3 + NaOH \rightarrow NaNO_3 + H_2O$$

$$H^+ + NO_3^- + Na^+ + OH^- \rightarrow Na^+ + NO_3^- + H_2O$$

The real change, irrespective of what strong acid and alkali are involved is:

$$H^+ + OH^- \rightarrow H_2O, \text{ for which } \Delta H \text{ is } -57.2 \text{ kJ/mol}$$

When, however, the acid (or the base) is weak, the value of the heat of neturalisation is usually less than 57.2, e.g,

$$HCN + NaOH \rightarrow NaCN + H_2O \qquad \Delta H = -11 \text{ kJ/mol}$$

$$\tfrac{1}{2}H_2S + NaOH \rightarrow \tfrac{1}{2}Na_2S + H_2O \quad \Delta H = -16 \text{ kJ/mol.}$$

The main reason for a weak acid having a lower value is that for complete neutralisation to occur, the weak acid must first become fully dissociated, and this change is **endo**thermic. The net heat released is the 57.2 **less** the quantity required to cause complete dissociation of the weak acid (or base) into ions.

The other factor which can account for a weak acid having a different value is the heat of hydration of the anion of the acid. In the case of hydrofluoric acid (which is weak), the heat of neutralisation is **greater** than 57.2 kJ/mol. The reason for this is that the F^- ion, as soon as it is formed, becomes hydrated:

$$F^- + water \rightarrow F^-(aq)$$

and this change is exothermic, releasing more heat than is necessary to dissociate the HF into its ions, and thus **adding** to the 57.2 due to the $H^+ + OH^- \rightarrow H_2O$ reaction. The heat of neutralisation is the net result of 3 changes, viz.,

$$HF \rightarrow H^+ + F^- \text{ (endothermic)}$$

$$F^- + \text{water} \rightarrow F^-\text{(aq) (exothermic)}$$

$$H^+ + OH^- \rightarrow H_2O \text{ (exothermic)}$$

Questions

Q.15.21 Calculate the heat of neutralisation of nitric acid by sodium hydroxide from the following experimental results:

Volume of nitric acid = 100 cm^3 of 1.0 M

Volume of sodium hydroxide = 100 cm^3 of 1.0 M

Initial temperature of solutions = $17.5°C$

Final temperature of solutions = $24.4°C$

Specific heat capacity of mixture = 4080 J/kg°C

Q.15.22 Calculate the heat of neutralisation of potassium hydroxide by hydrochloric acid, given that 250 cm^3 of 0.5 M KOH at 12°C on being mixed with an equal volume of 0.5 M HCl at the same temperature attained a temperature of 15.4°C. (Assume the mixture to have the same specific heat capacity as water, i.e. 4200 J/kg°C).

Q.15.23 100 cm^3 of 0.2 M ethanoic acid were mixed with 100 cm^3 of 0.2 M sodium hydroxide solution in a polystyrene beaker of negligible heat capacity. The original temperature of the substances was 17.2°C and the final temperature was 18.5°C. Calculate the heat of neutralisation of ethanoic acid (see final note to previous question).

Q.15.24 In an experiment to measure the heat of neutralisation of sulphuric acid, the following measurements were obtained:

Initial amount of acid = 100 cm^3 of 2.0 M sulphuric acid

Initial temperature of acid = $10.2°C$

Initial amount of alkali = 200 cm^3 of 2.0 M NaOH

Initial temperature of alkali = $11.2°C$

Final temperature of mixture = $29.4°C$

Specific heat capacity of solution = 4020 J/kg°C

Calculate the result of the experiment.

Q.15.25
(a) Explain, using equations, why the heat of neutralisation of sulphuric acid by sodium hydroxide is the same as the heat of neutralisation of nitric acid by sodium hydroxide (-57 kJ/mol)
(b) Explain why the heat of neuturalisation of hydrogen sulphide (H_2S) by sodium hydroxide is different (-16 kJ/mol)

Heat of Solution

Some substances dissolve in water with the release of heat (*e.g.* NaOH) while others dissolve and absorb heat in the process (e.g NH_4NO_3) Dissolving can thus be either exothermic or endothermic.

> **The heat of solution of a substance is defined as the heat change which takes place when 1 mole of the substance is dissolved in excess solvent.**

i.e. in so much solvent that further dilution results in no more heat change.

Heat of solution is the net result of two different processes: (i) the dissociation of the ionic lattice of the solute; this process **requires** energy; (ii) the hydration of the ions so formed (*i.e.* the energy of hydration) this process **liberates** energy. If the energy of hydration is greater than the lattice energy of the solute, dissolving will be exothermic, and conversely, if the lattice energy of the solute is greater than the energy of hydration, dissolving will be an endothermic process.

Experiment 15.3
To measure heat of solution.

The heat of solution of a substance is the heat change which takes place when one mole of the substance is dissolved in excess solvent. It is easily measured — by dissolving a weighed quantity of the solute in the solvent and finding the change of temperature. The actual heat change is found from $E=mc\,\theta$, and hence the heat of solution can be calculated. Suitable substances to use are sodium hydroxide, ammonium nitrate, sodium thiosulphate.

Procedure

Measure 100 g of water (100 cm^3 by graduated cylinder is accurate enough) into a suitable calorimeter, preferably insulated (an 'aerocup' is ideal). Note its temperature as accurately as possible. Weigh out accurately about 4 g of the solute, add it to the calorimeter, stir gently until it is dissolved and read the thermometer when the temperature has become steady. Record the results below and calculate the heat change which would occur on dissolving one mole of the solute in the solvent. This is the heat of solution, assuming that further dilution causes no further heat change.

Results

Mass of water . . . . = 100 g = 0.1 kg

Initial temperature . . . .

Final temperature . . . .

Change in temperature . . . .

Specific heat capacity of solution
. . . . = 4100 J/kg $^\circ$C (average value)

Heat lost or gained by solution . . . .

Substance . . . .

Mass of substance . . . .

Molecular mass of substance . . . .

Heat of solution . . . .

Is the change exothermic or endothermic?

Questions

Q.15.26 When 10.6 g of sodium carbonate (Na_2CO_3) are dissolved in 200 g of water (an excess) the temperature of the water increased from 20°C to 22.5°C. Calculate the heat of solution of sodium carbonate.

Q.15.27 Calculate the heat of the reaction: $CuSO_4 + 5 H_2O \rightarrow CuSO_45H_2O$ given that 1 g of anhydrous copper(II) sulphate when dissolved in a large quantity of water liberates 418 J of heat, and that 5 g of hydrated copper(II) sulphate when dissolved in excess water absorbs 230 J of heat.

Q.15.28 Calculate the heat of solution of KCl, given the following:

$K(s) + \frac{1}{2}Cl_2(g) \rightarrow KCl(s)$ $\Delta H = -444$ kJ

$K(s) + \frac{1}{2}Cl_2(g) + water \rightarrow KCl(aq)$ $\Delta H = -426$ kJ

Q.15.29 The heat of formation of zinc chloride is -417 kJ/mol and its heat of solution is -66 kJ/mol. The heat of formation of hydrogen chloride is -92 kJ/mol and its heat of solution is -81 kJ/mol. Making use of this information, calculate the quantity of heat which is evolved when 1 mole of zinc completely reacts with aqueous hydrochloric acid.

Bond Energy

In chemical reactions, bonds are broken and other bonds are made. Energy is needed to break a bond and consequently energy is released when a bond is made. The energy of a bond is always calculated on the basis that the substances involved are **gaseous** atoms (or groups of atoms), *i.e.* fully separated from each other. The bond energy definition (in full, it is bond dissociation energy) is:

> **Bond energy is the energy required to break 1 mole of covalent bonds and to separate the neutral atoms formed completely from each other.**

Bond energy is also the energy **liberated** when one mole of covalent bonds is **formed**. Bond energies of diatomic molecules such as H_2 and Cl_2 can be directly determined from spectroscopic measurements, and these values along with standard heats of formation and combustion, can be used to calculate bond energies which cannot be directly determined. Bond energy values can be used to predict heat changes for many reactions and so they are important values. The following worked example illustrates how the C-H bond energy in methane is calculated from experimentally derived data.

Worked Example 4

Calculate the average C-H bond energy in methane, given the following:

(1) heat of formation of CH_4 = -75 kJ/mol

(2) heat of atomisation[(i)] of carbon
= +715 kJ/mol.

(3) H-H bond energy = +436 kJ/mol.

As with other thermochemical calculations, the best way to lay out such a problems is to (i) write the equation for which the heat change is required. (ii) write out the given information in equation form, and (iii) rearrange these equations as necessary, so that when they are all added together, the equation for the required change is obtained. It is important to use state symbols in this type of calculation since the same element may be appearing in different physical states, e.g. C(s) and C(g).

Required:

$CH_4(g) \rightarrow C(g) + 4H(g)$ $\qquad \Delta H = ?$

Given:

(1) $C(s) + 2H_2(g) \rightarrow CH_4(g)$ $\quad \Delta H = -75$ kJ
(2) $C(s) \rightarrow C(g)$ $\qquad \Delta H = +715$ kJ
(3) $H_2(g) \rightarrow 2H(g)$ $\qquad \Delta H = +436$ kJ

Rearrange the given information. Equation (1) is reversed (and the sign of the ΔH changed), equation (2) is just rewritten, and equation (3) is doubled (as well as its ΔH value).

$CH_4(g) \rightarrow C(s) + 2H_2(g)$ $\qquad \Delta H = +75$ kJ
$C(s) \rightarrow C(g)$ $\qquad \Delta H = +715$ k
$2H_2(g) \rightarrow 4H(g)$ $\qquad \Delta H = +872$ kJ

$CH_4(g) \rightarrow C(g) + 4H(g)$ $\qquad \Delta H = +1662$ kJ

The ΔH here is the energy required to break 4 moles of C-H bonds, which means that the average C-H energy is $\frac{1662}{4}$ i.e. 415 kJ/mol.

Worked Example 5

By using the required bond energies (from the given bond energy table), calculate the ΔH value for the hydrogenation of ethene.

Bond energies can be added and subtracted as necessary in order to calculate the heat of reaction for various chemical reactions. The heat change for a reaction can be found by calculating the differences between the energy required to break the bonds of the reactants molecules, and the energy liberated in the formation of the product molecule(s). This example shows the calculation of the heat change for the reaction:

Although it does not happen in practice, this reaction can be considered to take place by breaking up C_2H_4 and H_2 into free atoms (i.e. by breaking one C=C bond, four C-H bonds and one H-H bond), and the re-combining of those atoms to give C_2H_6 (i.e. by forming one C-C bond and six C-H bonds).

Breaking 1 mole of C=C requires	+ 612
Breaking 4 moles of C-H requires	
$\quad (4 \times 412)$	+ 1648
Breaking 1 mole of H—H requires	+ 436
Total energy required to break bonds	+ 2696 kJ
Forming 1 mole of C-C releases	- 348
Forming 6 moles of C-H releases	
$\quad (6 \times 412)$	-2472
Total energy released forming bonds	-2820 kJ
Net energy change (+2696 - 2820)	-124 kJ

Conclusion: $C_2H_4 + H_2 \rightarrow C_2H_6$ $\qquad \Delta H = -124$ kJ

(i) The heat of atomization of an element is the heat required to convert the element in its normal state into 1 mole of atoms in the gaseous state

TABLE OF AVERAGE BOND ENERGIES (in k J / mol)			
H-H	436	C-Br	276
H-Cl	431	C-I	238
H-Br	366	Cl-Cl	242
C-C	348	Br-Br	193
C=C	612	I-I	151
C≡C	837	N-N	163
C-O	360	N≡N	944
C=O	743	N-H	388
C-H	412	O-H	463
C-F	484	O-O	146
C-Cl	338	O=O	496

Worked Example 6

Using the bond energies of H-H (436 kJ/mol) and Cl-Cl (242 kJ/mol) and the heat of formation of hydrogen chloride (-92 kJ/mol), calculate the H-Cl bond energy.

Consider the reaction: $H_2 + Cl_2 \rightarrow 2HCl$

Energy needed to break bonds of reactants:

H_2	$\rightarrow 2H$	$\Delta H = +436$
Cl_2	$\rightarrow 2Cl$	$\underline{\Delta H = +242}$
Total energy needed		$= 678$ kJ

Energy released when HCl is formed:
(let H—Cl bond energy be x)

$2H + 2Cl \rightarrow 2HCl \qquad \Delta H = -2x$

Net change $= (678 - 2x)$
= heat of formation of **two** moles of HCl.

$\therefore 678 - 2x = 2(-92), \; x = +432$ kJ/mol

Questions

Q.15.30 Calculate the H-Br bond energy, given that its heat of formation is -52 kJ/mol. (Also needed are the H-H and Br-Br bond energy values).

Q.15.31 The heat of formation of ammonia is -46 kJ/mol. Calculate the N-H bond energy in ammonia, using this value, and the values of the H-H and N≡N bond energies. Suggest a reason why the value obtained is slightly different from that given in the table of bond energies.

Q.15.32 Making use of the heat of formation of carbon dioxide (-393 kJ/mol), the heat of atomisation of carbon (+715 kJ/mol), and the bond energy O=O, calculate (i) ΔH for the reaction $C(g) + O_2 \rightarrow CO_2(g)$, and (ii) the energy of the carbon oxygen bond in carbon dioxide.

Q.15.33 Given the following information, calculate the H-X and H-Y bond energies (all values refer to substances in the gaseous state);

2H	$\rightarrow$	H_2	$\Delta H = -436$ kJ
2X	$\rightarrow$	X_2	$\Delta H = -84$
2Y	$\rightarrow$	Y_2	$\Delta H = -168$
$H_2 + X_2$	$\rightarrow$	2HX	$\Delta H = +450$
$H_2 + Y_2$	$\rightarrow$	2HY	$\Delta H = +492$

Q.15.34 Calculate the heat of the reaction $C_2H_2 + H_2 \rightarrow C_2H_4$, using bond energy values.

Q.15.35 Calculate the heat of formation of ethane, using the bond energies of C-C, C-H and H-H, and the heat of atomization of carbon (+715 kJ/mol)

Q.15.36 Using the bond energies of H-H, I-I and H-I (299 kJ/mol) calculate the heat change for the reaction: $H_2 + I_2 \rightarrow 2HI$. Is it an exothermic or an endothermic reaction?

Q.15.37. Using the appropriate bond energy values from the table, calculate ΔH for each of the following reactions:

(a) $C_2H_4(g) + HCl(g) \rightarrow C_2H_5Cl(g)$
(b) $CH_4(g) + Cl_2(g) \rightarrow CH_3Cl(g) + HCl$
(c) $CH_4(g) + 4Cl_2(g) \rightarrow CCl_4(g) + 4 HCl(g)$
(d) $C_2H_5OH(g) \rightarrow C_2H_4 + H_2O$

Q.15.38 Use the appropriate bond energy values from the table and the heat of atomisation of carbon (+715 kJ/mol) to calculate the heat of formation of (a) propane, (b) propene, (c) propanol, (d) propanone. (N.B. The latter two compounds are liquids at room temperature and the calculations will yield their heats of formation in the gaseous state).

Q.15.39 Given these standard heats of formation, calculate ΔH for each of the reactions (a) to (c).

Com-pound	CH_3OH	CO_2	CO	H_2O	ZnO	ZnCO_3
Heat of form-ation	-239	-393	-111	-286	-348	-813 kJ/mol

(a) $2CO + O_2 \rightarrow 2CO_2$

(b) $ZnCO_3 \rightarrow ZnO + CO_2$

(c) $CH_3OH + 1\frac{1}{2}O_2 \rightarrow CO_2 + 2H_2O$

Q.15.40   A rocket propellant consists of the fuel hydrazine hydrate mixed with the oxidising agent, hydrogen peroxide; these react according to:

$N_2H_5OH + 2H_2O_2 \rightarrow N_2 + 5H_2O$

Calculate the heat of the reaction, given the following heats of formation:

N_2H_5OH = -242 kJ/mol;
H_2O_2 = -192 kJ/mol;
H_2O = -241 kJ/mol

Review   When you know chapter 15 you should be able to:

(a)   Define: heat of reaction, heat of formation, heat of combustion, heat of neutralisation, heat of solution, bond energy, kilogram calorific value.

(b)   State Hess's Law, Law of Conservation of Energy (or 1st Law of Thermodynamics).

(c)   Explain exothermic, endothermic, ΔH, 'system', $E = mc\theta$, why all strong acids have similar heats of neutralisation and why weak acids have different values.

(d)   Describe a bomb calorimeter, and describe experiments to measure heats of combustion, heats of neutralisation and heats of solution.

(e)   Solve problems involving Hess's Law and be able to calculate bond energies from thermochemical information.

The Electrochemical Series

Astudy of the properties and reactions of the various metals shows that their reactivities vary considerably. Some metals (*e.g.* sodium, potassium) are highly reactive, whereas others (*e.g.* silver, gold) hardly react at all. A metal reacts by losing electrons to form positive ions, so that the ease with which it can do this is an important property of the metal. The electrode potential of an element is a measure of the ease with which it loses electrons, and this can be investigated in an experiment using a simple electric cell.

A simple cell consists of two different metals (the electrodes) immersed in a solution of dilute acid, alkali or some other substance which can produce ions in solution. A cell produces an electric current because the different metals have different abilities to release their electrons. The metal which releases its electrons more easily becomes the negative terminal of the cell and the other metal becomes the positive terminal.

In the experiment to compare electrode potentials, one of the electrodes in the cell remains in position throughout the experiment and acts as a standard electrode. For this, a carbon rod or plate is very suitable. Different metals in turn are used as the other electrode, and for each metal used, the voltage produced by the cell is measured, using a suitable voltmeter.

16

Electrochemistry and the Electrochemical Series

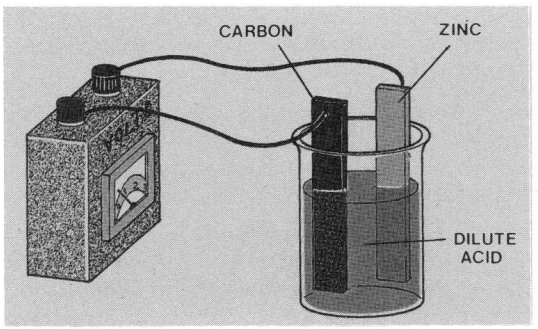

CARBON ZINC

DILUTE ACID

16.1

It will be observed that different metals give different voltages. Metals which release electrons easily give higher voltages than those which release them less easily. The voltage produced by the cell is therefore a measure of the ease with which the metal being used releases its electrons. Suitable metals which can be tried are copper, aluminium (the layer of oxide should first be sandpapered off), zinc, lead, magnesium, iron (sandpaper off any rust), tin (but not tinplate, which is mainly iron). When the measurements have been taken, the metals are arranged in decreasing order of the voltage they produce. The list of metals so arranged is their order in the electrochemical series (or 'activity' series).

Experiment 16.1
To Find the Order of Metals in the Electrochemical Series.

The electrochemical series is a list of the elements in order of their standard electrode potentials, a property which is a measure of how readily the elements lose electrons. This is correctly measured by finding the voltage produced by a cell containing one electrode of the element and one hydrogen electrode. In this experiment, whose purpose is to illustrate the principle and to find the electrochemical order of some metals, a carbon electrode is used in place of a hydrogen electrode.

Set up the apparatus as shown on page 189. Insert one of the metals to be tested into the crocodile clip (make sure that it is tightly held), and dip the metal, but not the clip, into the acid. Read and record the voltage produced. Repeat this for as many metals as are available. Sandpaper the aluminium and any of the others which look tarnished, before testing them.

Now compile another list, this time putting them in decreasing order of the voltages which they produce in the cell. This is their order in the electrochemical series.

The Electrochemical Series

For the more common metals, the order is as follows:

| potassium |
| sodium |
| calcium |
| magnesium |
| aluminium |
| zinc |
| iron |
| tin |
| lead |
| hydrogen(*) |
| copper |
| mercury |
| silver |
| gold |

* Note

Hydrogen, of course, is not a metal, but it does have the ability to release electrons (forming H^+ ions) and the relative ease with which it does this is shown by its position in the series.

It is important to remember that the order is that in which they most readily lose electrons to form positive ions; the higher up an element is, the more readily it loses electrons (which also means the stronger a reducing agent it is). The electrochemical series is a very useful means of classifying knowledge about some of the chemistry of metals.

1.   The order of the metals is the order of their reactivity in general. The metals at the top lose electrons most readily, which means that they are most reactive, and going down the series, the tendency to lose electrons decreases; thus reactivity decreases (see Table 16.1)

Conversely, compounds of the metals at the top are least reactive, since the metal ions present have least tendency to gain electrons and reform metal atoms (see Table 16.2).

2.   The series shows which elements will displace each other from solutions of their salts. Metals higher up donate electrons more easily than those lower down, so that when zinc, for example, is placed in a solution of copper sulphate, the zinc donates electrons to the Cu^{2+} ions and therefore reduces them to copper; at the same time, the zinc,

because it has lost electrons, is oxidised to Zn^{2+} ions:

$$Zn + CuSO_4 \rightarrow ZnSO_4 + Cu$$

or, ionically,

$$Zn + Cu^{2+} \rightarrow Zn^{2+} \; Cu$$

For the same reason, only metals above hydrogen can displace the latter from dilute acid:

$$Zn + H_2SO_4 \rightarrow Zn \; SO_4 + H_2$$

or ionically,

$$Zn + 2H^+ \rightarrow Zn^{2+} + H_2$$

Metals below hydrogen cannot do so:

$$Cu + H_2SO_4 \not\rightarrow CuSO_4 + H_2$$

At the very end of the electrochemical series are the non-metals *i.e.* those elements which form ions by gaining electrons. The order of the elements at the end is:

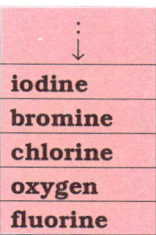

Fluorine has the greatest affinity for electrons (its electronegativity is highest), which means that it is the strongest oxidising agent. Chlorine, too, is a good oxidising agent; being nearer the end than bromine, it is a stronger oxidising agent than the latter and so will displace bromine from a solution of its ions:

$$Cl_2 + 2Br^- \rightarrow Br_2 + 2Cl^-$$

This reaction is used in the manufacture of bromine (from Br^- ions which occur in seawater).

3. The occurrence of metals in nature and their method of extraction is also related to their positions in the electrochemical series. The reactive metals at the top of the series always occur

Metal	Reaction of metal with water	Reaction of metal with dilute acid	Reaction of metal with oxygen
potassium sodium	Vigorous reaction;hydrogen displaced immediately from cold water	Dangerous reaction — should not be carried out	Burn brilliantly and quickly in air, forming oxides.
calcium	Reacts slowly liberating hydrogen	Vigorous reaction	
magnesium	Extremely slow, but reacts with steam, liberating hydrogen	Fast reaction	
aluminium zinc	React with steam; Al less reactive than Mg, and Zn and Fe less reactive still.	React, but with decreasing activity as list is descended	Slow oxidation unless heated to high temperature
iron	Slow reversible reaction with steam.		Very slow reaction with air even when heated.
copper	Do not react	Only reacts with oxidising acids	
mercury silver gold		Do not react	Do not react.

Table 16.1 — Reactivities of Metals

Metal	Effect of heat on hydroxide or carbonate	Effect of heat on nitrate	Ease of reduction of oxide by hydrogen
potassium sodium	Little or no change	Nitrite (*e.g.* KNO_2) formed	Not reduced.
calcium magnesium aluminium zinc	Metal oxide and H_2O vapour (+ CO_2 from carbonates) produced	Metal oxide, NO_2 and O_2 formed	
iron lead copper	Increasing ease of decomposition	Increasing ease of decomposition	Reduced but reversible.
			Reduction occurs easily
mercury silver gold	Metal formed	Metal formed	Oxide is reduced by heat alone (*i.e.* H_2 not needed).

Table 16.2 — Ease of Decomposition of Compounds

in the combined state while the most unreactive ones at the bottom often occur free in nature (see Table 16.3.)

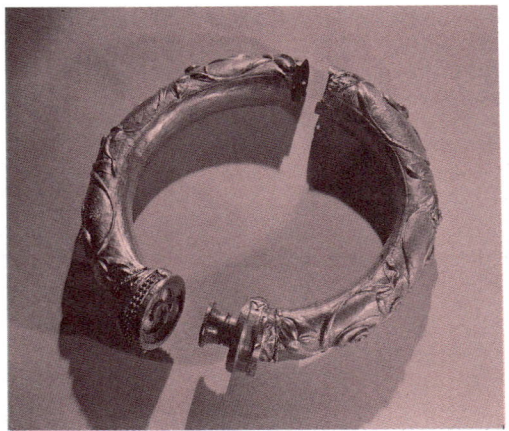

16.2 — *Gold is such an unreactive metal that articles made from it thousands of years ago are still unchanged. This torc or collar of gold, which is in the National Museum of Ireland in Dublin, dates from the early Iron Age.*

Table 16.3 — Occurences of Metals in Nature

K Na Ca Mg Al	Very reactive. Never found free in nature. All isolated after 1800. Extracted by electrolysis.
Zn Fe Pb	Moderately reactive. Found as compounds. Extracted by reduction with carbon or carbon monoxide.
Cu Hg Ag Au	Not very reactive. Can occur free in nature. Known from ancient times.

Experiment 16.2
Electrochemical displacement

The electrochemical series can be used to show which elements will displace other elements from solutions of their salts, and reactions of this type are investigated here. The higher an element is in the series, the more readily it loses electrons. Conversely, the lower it is, the more readily it gains electrons. A metal higher up will, therefore, displace one lower down, from a solution of one of its salts. By discovering that one metal displaces another, the relative positions of those two metals can be found.

1.   Take three test tubes, each containing about 5 cm^3 of zinc sulphate solution. Into these, place respectively small quantities of copper, iron (e.g. a sandpapered nail) and magnesium. After a minute or so, pour out the liquid and empty the metals onto the bench. You will see that one of the metals has become covered with zinc (from the solution); if you have difficulty in deciding which it is, compare each metal with a piece of the original metal. The zinc ions from the solution have gained electrons from the metal placed in it.

What have the atoms of this metal changed to?

What type of reaction have the zinc ions undergone?

Complete the equation for the reaction which occurred and write 'no reaction' for those which did not.

$$Zn^{2+} + Cu \rightarrow$$

$$Zn^{2+} + Fe \rightarrow$$

$$Zn^{2+} + Mg \rightarrow$$

2.   Repeat the experiment with copper sulphate solution and pieces of iron, magnesium and zinc. Complete the equations for the reactions which occurred.

$$Cu^{2+} + Fe \rightarrow$$

$$Cu^{2+} + Mg$$

$$Cu^{2+} + Zn \rightarrow$$

3.   Repeat the procedure again, using iron(II) sulphate solution and samples of copper, magnesium and zinc. Write equations for reactions which occur.

4.   Finally, try the experiment using magnesium sulphate solution and samples of copper, iron and zinc. Write equations for any reactions which occur.

5.   From the information gained in the above tests, list the metals: copper, iron, magnesium and zinc, in such an order that each metal displaces those below it from solutions of their salts, but not those above it.

6.   Test the reactivity of the same four metals with dilute acid as follows. Take approximately equal quantities of the metals (sandpaper the iron first) and simultaneously drop them into four test tubes each containing about 10 cm^3 of dilute sulphuric acid. Which is the most reactive metal? List the four metals in decreasing order of reactivity. Is the order the same as that found in the previous experiment?

Corrosion and its Prevention

It is all too common an observation that many materials, in time, corrode. Iron acquires a brown flaky surfaces known as rust, which soon crumbles away; copper surfaces exposed to the atmosphere becomes covered with a layer of a green coloured substance; a white powder forms on the surface of used dry batteries, often leading to holes in the zinc case and consequently leakage; calcium metal not stored in an airtight container changes to a white powder.

> **Corrosion can be described as the slow 'eating away' of a substance by chemical reaction — invariably oxidation — in which the metal is converted to a metal compound of some kind.**

The rate at which a metal corrodes (*i.e.* oxidises) is very much related to its position in the electrochemical series — although there are some apparent exceptions; in general though, the higher up the metal is, the faster it corrodes.

potassium sodium	tarnish immediately in air
calcium	corrodes quickly
magnesium aluminium zinc	little apparent corrosion
iron	corrodes slowly
tin lead copper	very slow corrosion
mercury silver	hardly any corrosion
gold	does not corrode

Aluminium, zinc and, to a lesser extent, magnesium, despite the fact that they do not seem to corrode, do form metal oxides on their surfaces quite quickly, but, unlike other oxides, oxides of these metals do not flake off, but stick firmly to the surface. In time, the surface of each of these metals becomes covered with a layer of oxide which prevents it from further attack. This is why these metals do not corrode to any great extent.

The rusting of iron greatly reduces its structural strength, and since iron and steel are the most widely used metals today, various methods have been devised to prevent rusting, or at least to reduce the rate at which it occurs. A number of methods involve covering the surface of the iron or steel, so that air and moisture are excluded (both air and moisture must be present for rusting to occur). The iron can be painted, covered with plastic or coated with another metal, as in 'galvanised' iron (zinc covered) or in 'tinplate' (tin covered). Electroplating with metals such as chromium, silver, copper or tin gives an attractive finish, as well as preventing corrosion. Alloying with other metals can produce non-rusting materials, such as stainless steel, which is used for draining boards and machine parts.

In a method called 'sacrificial protection' the iron is protected from rusting by connecting it to a metal higher up in the electrochemical series which oxidises instead. Bars of magnesium or zinc are often bolted to the hulls of ships (below the waterline) for the same reason.

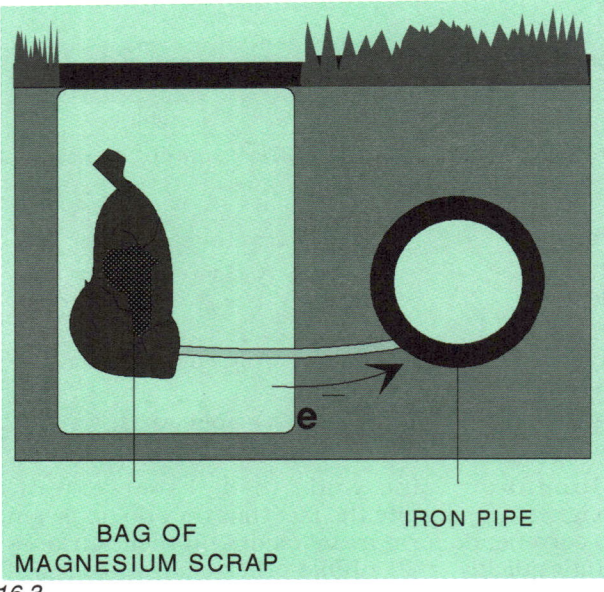

BAG OF
MAGNESIUM SCRAP

IRON PIPE

16.3

Questions

Q.16.1 Describe how you would show by experiment that (i) zinc is above copper; (ii) magnesium is above zinc; (iii) sodium is above magnesium, in the electrochemical series.

Name two elements : (a) which decompose cold water; (b) whose carbonates yield oxides on being heated; (c) which will displace iron from a solution of iron(II)sulphate, but will not decompose cold water.

Q.16.2 Heated charcoal will remove the oxygen from oxides of metals W, X and Y, but not from the oxides of Z. Metal Y will remove oxygen from the oxide of W but not from that of X.

List the four metals W, X, Y, and Z in order of decreasing reactivity.

Q.16.3 Some of the following pairs of substances can react together and some are unable to do so. For each of those pairs which can react, complete and balance the equation for the reaction, and state which substance is oxidised and which is reduced:

(a) $Fe + H^+ \rightarrow$
(b) $Ag + H^+ \rightarrow$
(c) $Ag + Fe^{2+} \rightarrow$
(d) $Ag^+ + Fe \rightarrow$
(e) $I^- + Cl_2 \rightarrow$
(f) $I_2 + Cl^- \rightarrow$
(g) $KI + Br_2 \rightarrow$
(h) $KBr + I_2 \rightarrow$
(i) $Al_2O_3 + Fe \rightarrow$
(j) $Fe_2O_3 + Al \rightarrow$

Q.16.4 Prepare an activity series for the hypothetical metals, U, V, W, X, Y and Z, from the information in the following equations:

$$H_2 + YCl_2 \rightarrow 2HCl + Y$$

$$H_2 + ZCl_2 \rightarrow \text{no reaction}$$

$$V + UCl_2 \rightarrow VCl_2 + U$$

$$W + 2XCl \rightarrow 2X + WCl_2$$

$$W + YCl_2 \rightarrow \text{no reaction}$$

$$V + XCl \rightarrow \text{no reaction}$$

Q.16.5 A new metal X is discovered and found to be divalent and between mercury and copper in the electrochemical series. State the reactions, if any, you would expect when the following reactions are carried out with compounds of X. Give equations,.

(a) the carbonate is heated;
(b) the nitrate is heated;
(c) dilute hydrochloric acid is added to the metal;
(d) hydrogen is passed over the heated metal oxide.

Q.16.6 A, B, C, D, and E are code letters for five metals. Arrange these in their correct order in the electrochemical series, from the information given below. Explain briefly your reasoning,. B is the only one of the five found free in nature. Some wire made of A when dipped into a solution of E^{2+} ions becomes coated with E. The strongest reducing agent is C. The nitrate of A decomposes at a lower temperature than that of D.

Q.16.7 In industry, copper is sometimes extracted from copper(II) sulphate solution by adding scrap iron to large tanks of the latter. The precipitated copper is then collected from the bottoms of the tanks.

(a) Explain the principle of the process.
(b) Write an equation for the reaction.
(c) How much copper would be precipitated on adding 56 kg of iron to the copper sulphate solution?

Electrochemistry

A simple experiment described in Chapter 4 showed that various compounds can conduct an electric current. Electrochemistry is the study of the chemical changes caused by electricity. Some terms and their meanings used in this topic are:

An electrolyte is a compound which in solution or in the molten state conducts an electric current and undergoes chemical change in doing so. An electrolyte must contain ions.

Good or strong electrolytes include most salts, strong acids (*e.g.* H_2SO_4, HCl) and strong alkalis (*e.g.* NaOH, KOH); such substances when dissolved in water or when molten, ionise or dissociate to a large extent and so conduct electricity well.

Weak acids and bases are poor or weak electrolytes and do not conduct electricity well — because of little dissociation and so few ions being present.

A non electrolyte is a compound which is not decomposed by an electric current. Non-electrolytes are covalent compounds and consist of molecules and not ions.

Electrolysis is the name given to the process in which an electrolyte is decomposed by electricity.

The electrodes are the conductors by which the current enters and leaves the electrolyte.

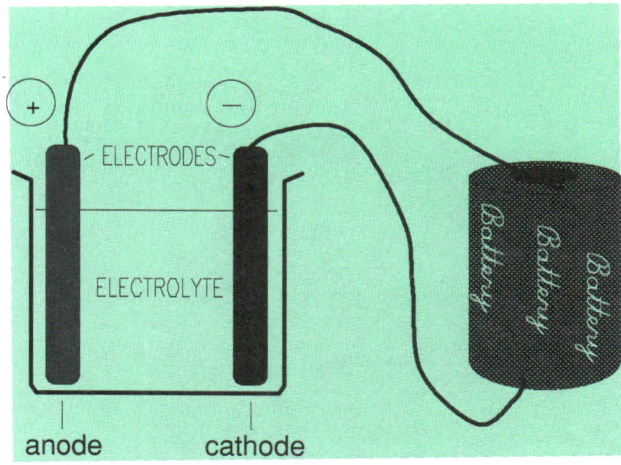

16.4

The **anode** is the positive electrode in electrolysis. Ions **lose electrons** there, so that **oxidation** occurs at the anode.

The **cathode** is the negative electrode in electrolysis. Ions **gain electrons** there so that **reduction** occurs at the cathode.

The **anion** is the ion which is attracted to the anode: it is therefore the negatively charged ion (*e.g.* Cl^-, O^{2-}).

The cation is that which goes to the cathode and hence is the positively charged ion (*e.g.* Na^+, H^+, Cu^{2+})

A **voltmeter** or **electrolytic cell** is the container fitted with electrodes and holding the electrolyte and in which electrolysis takes place.

Electrolysis of Molten Sodium Chloride

When sodium chloride is melted, the crystalline lattice breaks down and the ions are released from their fixed positions ($NaCl \rightarrow Na^+ + Cl^-$). In the molten compound, the ions have an independent existence and are free to move.

Cathode reaction: The positive sodium ions are attracted to the cathode (the negative electrode) where they gain an electron each, to become sodium atoms:

$$Na^+ + e^- \rightarrow Na$$

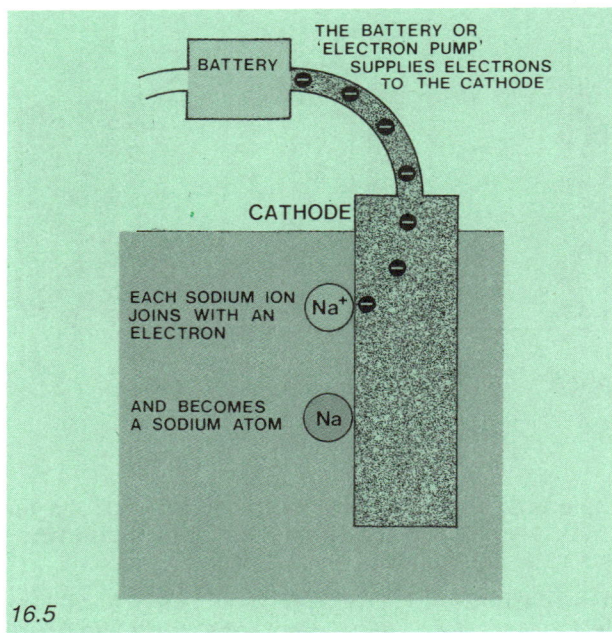

16.5

Metallic sodium is thus produced. Since the change is that of electron **gain**, it is a **reduction** reaction.

Anode reaction: The negative chloride ions are attracted to the anode where they lose an electron each to become chlorine atoms:

$$Cl^- - e^- \rightarrow Cl$$

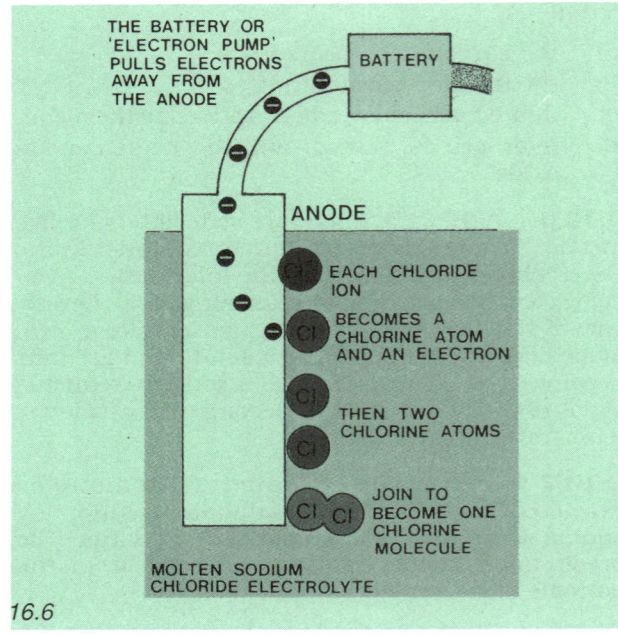

16.6

Pairs of atoms then combine together to form chlorine molecules ($2Cl^- \rightarrow Cl_2$). The chloride ions are thus oxidised and gaseous chlorine is produced. The electrons are 'pumped around' the circuit by the battery — to continue the process.

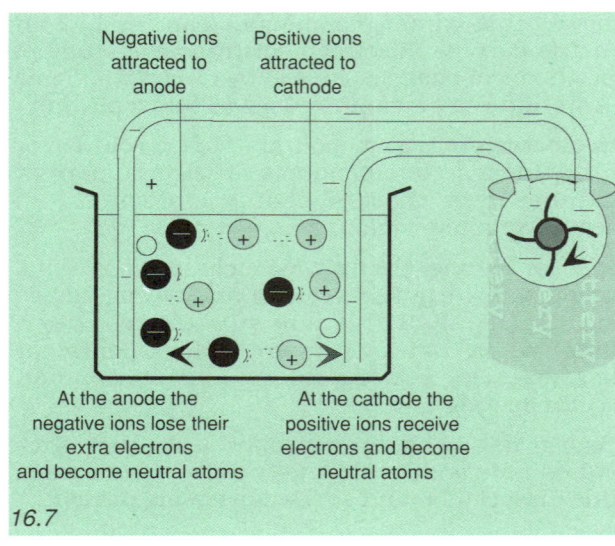

Negative ions attracted to anode

Positive ions attracted to cathode

At the anode the negative ions lose their extra electrons and become neutral atoms

At the cathode the positive ions receive electrons and become neutral atoms

16.7

The net reaction is the sum of the two electrode reactions:

$$Na^+ + e^- \rightarrow Na$$
$$\underline{Cl^- - e^- \rightarrow Cl}$$
$$NaCl \rightarrow Na + \tfrac{1}{2}Cl_2$$

It is by this process that sodium is manufactured (and chlorine is obtained as a by-product). Special electrolyte cells are built for the purpose. One of these is the Downs cell (a diagram of one of these is on page 211)

Similar reactions to those described above occur during the electrolysis of many molten salts. In general, the cathode reaction is: $M^+ + e^- \rightarrow M$ (the ion M^+ is reduced to the element M), while the reaction that occurs at the anode is $X^- - e^- \rightarrow X$ (the ion X^- is oxidised to the element X).

Electrolysis of Molten Lead Bromide

This electrolysis is very suitable as a laboratory experiment, because lead bromide has a reasonably low melting point (373°C) and so can be melted with a bunsen burner. The reactions are similar to those which occur during the electrolysis of molten sodium chloride.

On being melted, the electrolyte ionises:
$$PbBr_2 \rightarrow Pb^{2+} + 2Br^-$$

Cathode reaction: $Pb^{2+} + 2e^- \rightarrow Pb$

Metallic lead is thus produced.

Anode reaction: $2Br^- - 2e^- \rightarrow 2Br \ Br_2$

Bromine vapour is formed.

Net Result: $PbBr_2 \rightarrow Pb + Br_2$

Electrolysis of Aqueous Solutions

When an aqueous solution of an electrolyte is being electrolysed, the chemistry is somewhat more complex, because in addition to the ions produced by the electrolyte, there are some H^+ and OH^- ions too, formed from the ionisation of the water. When there are two types of ion of similar charge in a solution being electrolysed, one is usually discharged in preference to the other, rather than a mixture of the two being liberated.

For positive ions, those lower down in the electrochemical series are usually discharged first,

since they have a greater affinity for electrons than those higher up. If, for example, both Cu^{2+} and H^+ ions are present, it will be the copper ions which take electrons from the cathode, to become copper atoms (i.e. copper metal).

For negative ions, there is a similar series from which the order of discharge can be predicted. Remember that the reactions at the anode are oxidations — ions are losing electrons.

OH^-	Most easily oxidised (and therefore discharged before any of the others that are present)
I^-	
Br^-	
Cl^-	
NO_3^-	
SO_4^-	Least easily oxidised.

It might also be mentioned that the concentration of an ion is another factor which determines whether or not the ion will be released during electrolysis. An increase in the concentration of an ion helps to promote its discharge. For example, in brine (concentrated sodium chloride solution), the two cations present are Cl^- and OH^-, and although OH^- is more easily oxidised than Cl^-, it is the Cl^- which will be discharged because its concentration is so much greater than that of OH^- ion. It is by this process (electrolysis of brine) that most chlorine is manufactured industrially.

Electrolysis of Dilute Sulphuric Acid

In dilute sulphuric acid, the ions present are H^+, OH^- and SO_4^{2-}. Water provides H^+ and OH^-, and the SO_4^{2-} (and more H^+) come from the ionisation of the sulphuric acid:
$$H_2SO_4 \rightarrow 2H^+ + SO_4^{2-}$$

Cathode Reaction: As there is only one cation (H^+) the element liberated at the cathode is hydrogen:
$$2H^+ + 2e^- \rightarrow 2H \quad \text{(followed by } 2H \rightarrow H_2)$$

Anode Reaction: The two anions (OH^- and SO_4^{2-}) are attracted to the anode, but OH^- ions are oxidised more easily than SO_4^{2-} and so the reaction that occurs is:
$$2OH^- - 2e^- \rightarrow H_2O + \tfrac{1}{2}O_2$$

This reduces the OH^- ion concentration, therefore more water dissociates to maintain the ionic product for water:

$$2H_2O \rightarrow 2H^+ + 2OH^-$$

The net results of these two reactions, found by adding the equations together is that effectively water is oxidised to oxygen (N.B. one of the meanings of oxidation is removal of hydrogen).

$$H_2O - 2e^- \rightarrow \tfrac{1}{2}O_2 + 2H^+$$

The SO_4^{2-} ions remain in solution, so that the overall result of the whole process is that water is decomposed into its constituent elements, hydrogen and oxygen:

$$H_2O \rightarrow H_2 + \tfrac{1}{2}O_2$$

This reaction is often carried out in a **Hofmann Voltameter**, an apparatus in which the hydrogen and oxygen can be collected in separate graduated tubes. The gases can be shown to be present in a 2 to 1 ratio and they can be identified as hydrogen and oxygen by the usual tests.

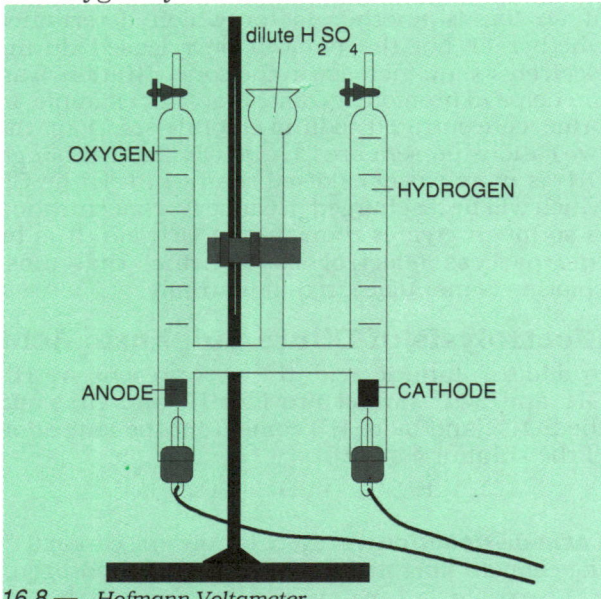

16.8 — *Hofmann Voltameter*

Electrolysis of Sodium Sulphate Solution.

The ions present in the solution are H^+ and OH^- (from the water) and Na^+ and SO_4^{2-} (from the ionisation of the electrolyte):

$$Na_2SO_4 \rightarrow 2Na^+ + SO_4^{2-}$$

Cathode reaction: The two cations are Na^+ and H^+ but since H^+ are more easily reduced than Na^+ (H is below Na in the electrochemical series) the reaction that occurs is:

$$2H^+ + 2e^- \rightarrow 2H \text{ (followed by } 2H \rightarrow H_2)$$

Anode reaction: Of the two anions present the OH^- are more easily oxidised than SO_4^{2-} and so the reaction is:

$$2OH^- - 2e^- \rightarrow H_2O + \tfrac{1}{2}O_2$$

(followed by $2H_2O \rightarrow 2H^+ + 2OH^-$)

The net result is that hydrogen and oxygen are produced.

If the reaction is carried out in a voltameter, with some universal indicator in the solution, it will be noticed that, around the cathode, the solution becomes alkaline and around that anode, acidic. This is explained as follows. At the cathode, H^+ ions are being removed from solution, thereby leaving an excess of OH^- ions, which makes the solution alkaline, and at the anode, OH^- ions are being removed, so leaving an excess of H^+, which makes the solution acidic.

Electrolysis of Copper(II) Sulphate Solution (using copper electrodes)

Copper(II) sulphate ionises in aqueous solution as follows:

$$CuSO_4 \rightarrow Cu^{2+} + SO_4^{2-}$$

so that the ions present are Cu^{2+}, SO_4^{2-}, H^+ and OH^- (the latter two from the water).

Cathode reaction: Both H^+ and Cu^{2+} ions are attracted to the cathode but the latter, being lower in the electrochemical series, are reduced more easily. The following reaction occurs:

$$Cu^{2+} + 2e^- \rightarrow Cu$$

Metallic copper is produced and is deposited on the cathode.

Anode reaction: The reaction here is different from previous ones, due to the electrode being made of copper — a more reactive element than platinum or graphite (which has been the anode in previous examples). Copper atoms are more easily oxidised than either the OH^- or the SO_4^{2-} ions in the solution and so the reaction which takes place at the anode is:

$$Cu - 2e^- \rightarrow Cu^{2+}$$

i.e. copper atoms from the electrode are oxidised to copper ions — which pass into the solution.

The net change in the process is that copper is taken from the anode and deposited on the cathode.

Uses of Electrolysis

An important industrial application of the process just described is **electroplating.** This process consists of covering one metal, often a cheap one like iron or steel, with another and usually more expensive one — to provide both protection and lustre. Car bumpers and bicycle handlebars are made of steel, but are electroplated with chromium to prevent them from rusting, and to present a good appearance. The object to be plated is the cathode of the plating bath, the anode consists of the metal which has to be deposited, and the electrolyte is a salt of the metal.

16.9 — A rack of medals being lifted out of an electroplating bath having been plated with silver.

In addition to electroplating, electrolysis has other important applications. The reactive metals (K, Na, Ca, Mg, Al) are extracted from their ores by electrolysis; some metals are purified by electrolysis (*e.g.* Cu, Ni, Pb) and anodising of aluminium makes it very resistent to corrosion and gives it a pleasant appearance. These various applications are described in Chapter 17.

Experiment 16.3
Electrolysis Experiments

It might be helpful to refer back to the results of Experiment 4.1 before doing this experiment. Set up the apparatus as shown in Fig. 4.5 (page 55) but place the electrodes in a crucible containing some solid lead bromide, rather than into a beaker of solution, Check that the circuit works by placing a piece of metal across the electrodes — when the bulb should light. Heat the crucible, gently at first and then more strongly, until the solid melts. Look for changes occurring around the electrodes. Do not continue the electrolysis for too long as one of the products is poisonous and has a very irritating smell.

Answer the following questions:

What change occurs in the structure of the lead bromide when it is melted.

Describe the appearance of the substance produced at the cathode.

What substance is it?

Give the equation for the reaction which occurs at the cathode (and in which this substance is produced).

What type of reaction is it?

What does the substance produced at the anode look like?

What substance is it?

Give the equation for the reaction in which it is produced.

What type of reaction is this?

In this next part of the experiment, a key or other metal object can be electroplated with copper — or other suitable metal.

Lightly sandpaper the surface of the object to be electroplated and connect it into a circuit as shown. It is important that the object is used as the cathode of the plating bath (i.e. connected to the negative terminal of the battery). Allow the current to flow for about 2 minutes and then remove the object and wash it with water. If the plating is patchy, the metal surface was probably not properly cleaned, or the current was too high.

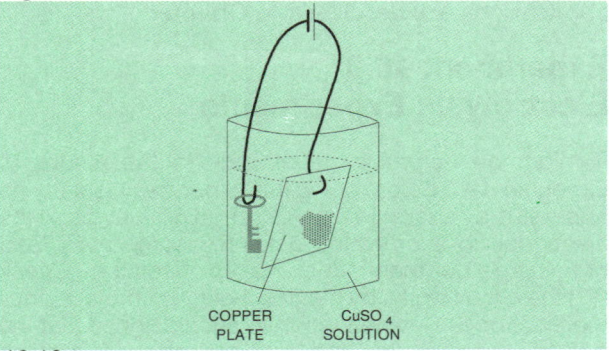

COPPER PLATE $CuSO_4$ SOLUTION

16.10

Movement of Ions during Electrolysis

There are a number of experiments which can be carried out to show that ions travel towards the electrodes during electrolysis. These make use of the fact that a number of common ions have characteristic colours (see Q.4.17 page 61). For example, copper (Cu^{2+}) ions are blue, permanganate (MnO_4^-) ions are purple and chromate (CrO_4^{2-}) ions are yellow.

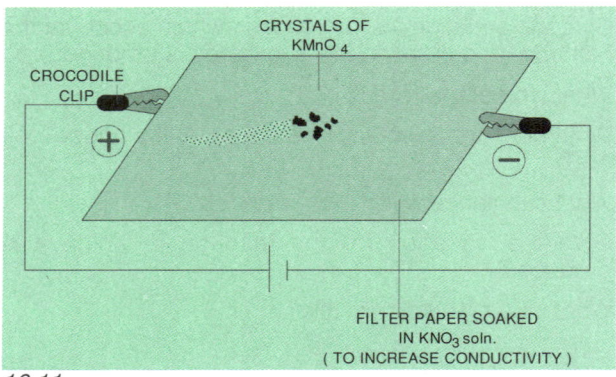

CRYSTALS OF $KMnO_4$

CROCODILE CLIP

FILTER PAPER SOAKED IN KNO_3 soln. (TO INCREASE CONDUCTIVITY)

16.11

A strip of filter paper is made to conduct by soaking it in a solution of a suitable salt (e.g. NaCl, KNO_3). A few crystals of potassium permanganate are placed on the centre of the paper which is then made part of an electric circuit as shown. On switching on the power, the purple colour of the MnO_4^- ions is observed to move towards the anode, but not in the reverse direction, (in time however, the colour spreads in all direction due to diffusion).

If the experiment is repeated using copper sulphate solution instead of potassium permanganate, the blue colour of the Cu^{2+} ion is observed to move towards the **cathode** rather than to the anode.

Fuel Cells

In the conventional type of electric cell or battery, electrical energy is produced from the reaction between chemicals which are contained **in** the cell. There is thus a limit to the quantity of electricity which can be generated in any cell. A **fuel cell** is one in which chemicals (a fuel and an oxidising agent) are fed to the cell from an external supply and in the cell they react at the electrodes to produce electricity.

In the simplest type of fuel cell, hydrogen reacts with oxygen to form water and the liberated energy is released as electrical energy. The reactions which occur and the net result are the reverse of what happens in a voltmeter in which water is being electrolysed *i.e.*,

Water + electrical energy → Hydrogen + Oxygen[i]

The apparatus for the electrolysis of water can be used to show the principle of the fuel cell. Water is electrolysed and the electrolysis continued until hydrogen and oxygen are in contact with the cathode and anode[ii] respectively. If the power supply is then disconnected and replaced by a suitable voltmeter, the latter will give a reading of about one volt.

In a commercial hydrogen/oxygen fuel cell, the electrodes are made of porous graphite which is impregnated with a catalyst to speed up the oxidation and reduction reactions which occur.

(i)   See description and diagram on page 97.
(ii)   The terms anode and cathode have the opposite meanings when used for fuel cells than when used in electrolysis. It is recommended that they not be used in the context of cells.

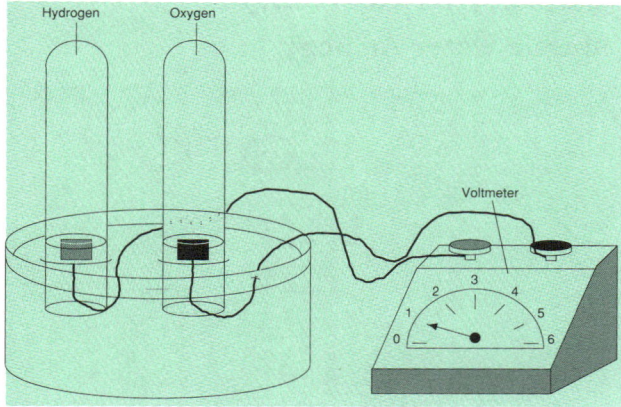

16.12

The gases diffuse through the pores and meet the electrolyte.

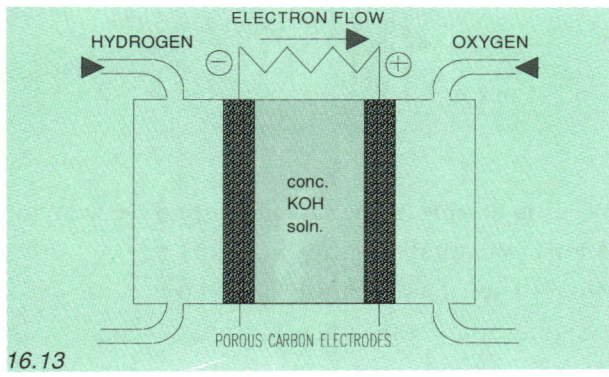

16.13

At the negative terminal of the cell where the hydrogen enters, the hydrogen is oxidised to H^+ ions; these then react with the OH^- ions from the electrolyte to form water:

$$H_2 \rightarrow 2H^+ + 2e^-$$

$$2H^+ + 2OH^- \rightarrow 2H_2O$$

The electrons which are released flow around the external circuit (driving motors, lights, etc.) to arrive back at the positive terminal. At this positive terminal, the oxygen which enters is reduced by the electrons which have travelled around the circuit, and OH^- ions are regenerated:

$$H_2O + \frac{1}{2}O_2 + 2e^- \rightarrow 2OH^-$$

The net result of all these reactions is:

$$H_2 + \frac{1}{2}O_2 \rightarrow H_2O + \text{electrical energy}$$

Advantages of such a cell as this are: (i) the substances needed are plentiful (although hydrogen is a fairly expensive fuel); (ii) the only product of the reaction is a completely harmless substance (iii) there are no moving parts to need maintenance; (iv) the process is noiseless; (v) an efficiency of about 80% is possible. Present disadvantages are that a high pressure and a temperature in excess of $200°$ C are needed for the cell to work satisfactorily, and cells are heavy and bulky. Much research however is being carried out to find effective catalysts which will make the process possible at ordinary temperatures, and as well, other possible fuels (e.g. CH_4. C_3H_8, CH_3OH) are being investigated. The oxidation of petrol in a fuel cell could be the source of power in a silent non-polluting car of the future.

Hydrogen/oxygen fuel cells have been used successfully in the U.S Gemini and Apollo space programmes of the 'seventies, to supply power for heat, light and radio communications and the by-product, water, was used for drinking by the astronauts.

Questions

Q.16.8 Each of the following compounds produces ions in solution. Write equations showing the formation of ions from each of them: sodium chloride; magnesium chloride; sulphuric acid; hydrochloric acid; copper(II) sulphate; sodium sulphate; potassium nitrate; lead(II) nitrate.

Q.16.9 Explain clearly the reactions taking place at each electrode during the electrolysis of a dilute aqueous solution of sulphuric acid and show that this is an oxidation/reduction reaction.

If 60 cm^3 of a colourless gas were formed at the cathode during this electrolysis, what gas would be formed at the anode and what would be its volume?

Q.16.10 When an aqueous solution of potassium nitrate is electrolysed, the products are hydrogen and oxygen. Also, the solution surrounding the cathode becomes alkaline and that surrounding the anode becomes acidic.

Explain these observations and write equations to illustrate your explanation. State at which electrode each of the products is formed.

Q.16.11 For the electrolysis of each of the following substances, write equations for (i) the ionisation of the electrolyte; (ii) the cathode reaction; (iii) the anode reaction; (iv) the net result which takes place. Assume that the electrodes are unreactive.

(a) concentrated hydrochloric acid;
(b) dilute hydrochloric acid;
(c) molten potassium iodide;
(d) aqueous potassium chloride;
(e) copper sulphate solution;
(f) magnesium sulphate solution;
(g) aqueous potassium hydroxide.

Q.16.12 Chlorine is manufactured by the electrolysis of brine (concentrated salt solution). There are two useful by-products, sodium hydroxide and a colourless gas. Work out the chemical reactions involved, identify the colourless gas which is formed and mention one use of each of the three products.

Faraday's Laws of Electrolysis

Michael Faraday carried out a series of experiments in which he investigated the effect of different variables on the masses of elements liberated in electrolysis. His two laws are as follows.

Law 1

> The mass of any element liberated during electrolysis is proportional to the quantity of electricity passed through the electrolyte.

Law 2

> When the same quantity of electricity is passed through different electrolytes, the masses of the different elements liberated are proportional to their relative atomic masses divided by the magnitude of the charges on their ions

i.e.

$$\frac{\text{mass}}{\text{liberated}} \propto \frac{\text{relative atomic mass of element}}{\text{magnitude of charge on ion of element}}$$

Quantity of Electricity
Simple Water Analogy

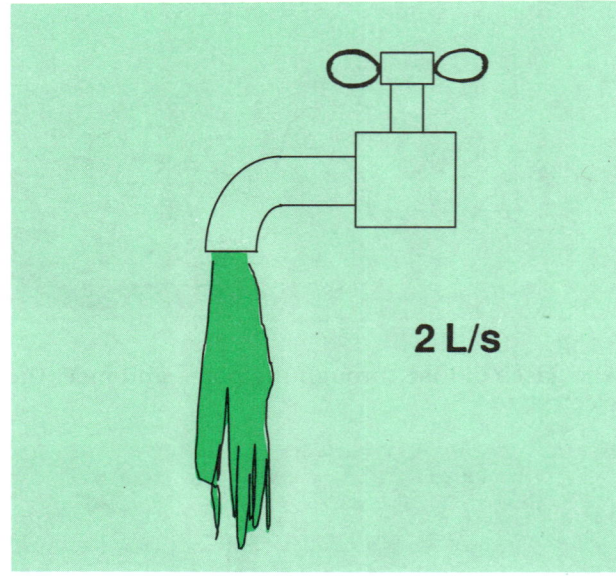

16.14

Water is flowing at the rate of 2 litres/sec from tap

After 2 sec, total quantity is 10 litres,

After 40 sec. total quantity is 80 litres,

i.e., quantity = rate of flow (current) × time

In Electricity

Current, measured in **amps**, is the rate of flow,

quantity is measured in **coulombs**.

(The symbol for current is *I*, and for quantity ,*Q*.)

After 5 sec, quantity of electricity = 10 coulombs

| **quantity of electricity** | = | **current** | × | **time** |
| (coulombs) | | (amps) | | (secs) |

$$Q = I\,t$$

1 coulomb is the quantity of electricity which flows through a wire when a current of 1 amp flows for 1 second.

The Faraday Constant

In order to liberate one hydrogen atom from a suitable electrolyte, one electron must be passed around the circuit. Therefore, to liberate one mole of hydrogen atoms (*i.e.* 1 g) one mole of electrons must be passed:

$$H^+ + e^- \xrightarrow{\text{yields}} H$$
1 electron \qquad yields \qquad 1 atom

therefore, $\begin{matrix} 1 \text{ mol of} \\ \text{electrons} \end{matrix}$ yields $\begin{matrix} 1 \text{ mol of} \\ \text{atoms} (= 1 \text{ g}) \end{matrix}$

Experiment shows that the quantity of electricity needed to liberate 1 g of hydrogen in electrolysis is 96500 coulombs; this is therefore the charge (quantity of electricity) carried by 1 mole of electrons and it is known as the Faraday Constant.

> **The Faraday Constant is the charge carried by 1 mole of electrons and is the quantity of electricity needed to liberate 1 g of hydrogen[i].**

One faraday will also liberate 1 mole of any other monovalent element (*e.g.* Na, Ag)

$$Na^+ + e^- \rightarrow Na$$
1 electron $\rightarrow$ 1 atom
$\left. \begin{matrix} 1 \text{ mole } e^- \\ 1 \text{ Faraday} \end{matrix} \right\} \rightarrow = 23 \text{ g}$

Two faradays will be necessary to liberate one mole of a divalent element such as copper, since one atom requires two electrons

$$Cu^{2+} + 2e^- \rightarrow Cu$$
$2e^- \rightarrow$ 1 Cu atom
$2F \rightarrow$ 1 mole Cu
$\qquad (= 63.5 \text{ g})$

The above shows that 193,000 coulombs (96500 × 2) are necessary to liberate 1 mole of copper. It is thus possible to calculate the mass of any element liberated in electrolysis, if the quantity of electricity passed through the electrolyte is known.

Worked Example 1

Q. A current of 10 A is passed through molten zinc bromide for 16 minutes and 5 seconds. (a) What quantity of electricity passes through the electrolyte? (b) How many moles of zinc are released? (c) What is the mass of the zinc which is formed ? (d) What other substance is formed and what is the mass of this substance ?

Solution

(a)   16 minutes + 5 seconds = 965 seconds
Quantity of electricity = current × time
= 9650 coulombs

(b) $ZnBr_2 \rightarrow Zn^{2+} + 2Br^-$

(c)   Cathode reaction:
$$Zn^{2+} + 2e^- \rightarrow Zn$$
2 electrons $\rightarrow$ 1 Zn atom
2 mol e^- $\rightarrow$ 1 mol Zn
$\left. \begin{matrix} 2 \text{ Faradays} \\ 2 \times 96500 \text{ C} \\ 193000 \text{ C} \end{matrix} \right\} \rightarrow$ 1 mol Zn

9650 C $\rightarrow \dfrac{9650}{193000}$ mol Zn

= 0.05 mol Zn
= (0.05 × 65) g
= 3.25 g Zn

(d)   Anode reaction:
$$Br^- - 2e^- \rightarrow 2Br \rightarrow Br_2$$
(hence bromine is formed)

2 electrons $\rightarrow Br_2$
$\left. \begin{matrix} 2 \text{ Faradays} \\ 2 \times 96500 C \end{matrix} \right\} \rightarrow$ 1 mol Br_2
193000 C $\rightarrow$ 160 g Br_2

9650 C $\rightarrow \dfrac{160 \times 9650}{193000}$ g Br_2

= 8 g Br_2

(i)   An alternative definition of the Faraday is the quantity of electricity required to liberate, in electrolysis one mole of a monovalent ion.
The exact value is 96,494 C/mol.

Answers

(a) = 9650 C.

(b) = 0.05 mol Zn.

(c) = 3.25 g Zn.

(d)= 8 g Br_2

Worked Example 2

Two voltameters, containing respectively molten PbI_2 and aqueous $AgNO_3$, are connected in series. In an experiment 5 g of lead were deposited from the lead iodide.

(a) What mass of silver was deposited at the same time?

(b) How many faradays were passed through the voltameters?

(c) What was the current if the electrolysis took 15 minutes?

(d) What volume of what gas (at room temperature and pressure), was liberated at the same time?

Solution

(a) Use Faraday's 2nd law

Mass of lead = 5 g

Mass of silver = x

$$\frac{\text{Atomic mass of lead}}{\text{Charge on Pb ion}} = \frac{207}{2} = 103.5$$

$$\frac{\text{Atomic mass of silver}}{\text{Charge on Ag ion}} = \frac{108}{1} = 108$$

$$\frac{5}{x} = \frac{103.5}{108}, \qquad x = 5.2 \text{ g Ag}$$

(b)
$$Pb^{2+} + 2e^- \rightarrow Pb$$
$$2e^- \rightarrow 1 \text{ atom}$$
$$2\,F \rightarrow \begin{cases} 1 \text{ mole Pb atoms} \\ 207 \text{ g Pb} \end{cases}$$
$$\frac{2 \times 5}{207}\,F \rightarrow 5 \text{ g Pb}$$
$$= 0.0483 \text{ F}$$

(c) $Q = (0.0483 \times 96500)$ C = 4662 C

t = 15 min = 900 sec
$Q = I\,t$

$4662 = I \times 900$

$$I = \frac{4662}{900} = 5.2 \text{ A}$$

(d) The anions in aqueous $AgNO_3$ are NO_3^- and OH^-

The anode reaction is:

$$2OH^- - 2e^- \rightarrow H_2O + \tfrac{1}{2}O_2$$
$$2F \rightarrow \tfrac{1}{2} \text{ mol}$$
$$= 12 \text{ L at r.t.p.}$$
$$0.0483 \text{ F} \rightarrow \frac{12 \times 0.0483}{2} \text{ L}$$
$$= 0.29 \text{ L (290 cm}^3)$$

Questions

Q.16.13   A current of 0.5 ampere flows through a solution of silver nitrate for 1 hour.

(a) Calculate the number of (i) coulombs, (ii) faradays, passed through the solution.

(b) What mass of silver is deposited during the electrolysis?

Q.16.14   Humphrey Davy discovered sodium by electrolysing molten sodium hydroxide.

(a) Calculate the mass of sodium formed when a current of 5 A flows through this electrolyte for 20 minutes?

(b) What is the other product, and what mass of it would be produced?

Q.16.15   A steady current of 0.6 A flows for 5 hours through solutions of sulphuric acid and copper sulphate in series. Calculate (a) the volume of hydrogen at s.t.p., and (b) the volume of oxygen liberated from the sulphuric acid, and (c) the mass of copper deposited in the copper sulphate cell.

Q.16.16   Calculate the mass of copper which will be deposited by a current of 1.5 A flowing for three quarters of an hour through a solution of copper sulphate.

16.15 —

Michael Faraday who was the son of a London blacksmith, was born in 1791. He received little education in his early years, being apprenticed at the age of 14 to a bookbinder. Here however, he added much to his knowledge by reading books which came to him for binding — books on science particularly impressing him. He repeated, as best he could, various experiments which were described in these.

After seven years of bookbinding, he obtained the post of laboratory assistant to Sir Humphrey Davy, Director of the Royal Institution of London. This was to prove the humble beginning of the career of one of the greatest scientists of the nineteenth century. In his spare time at the Royal Institution, he began to do experiments of his own, made discoveries and published the results of these — thus bringing himself to the notice of other scientists. In 1825, on Davy's retirement, Faraday succeeded him as Director, and here he remained until his death in 1867.

Amongst his achievements, he discovered that gases such as chlorine and carbon dioxide could be liquefied by pressure alone; he discovered **benzene** by isolating it from coal tar; he explained the catalytic action of platinum on the reaction between hydrogen and oxygen and he put forward the **laws of electrolysis** which explained how the mass of a substance liberated in electrolysis depended on the quantity of electricity. He introduced the terms **electrode, electrolyte, anode, cathode, ion** and **ionization**. However, his many discoveries in physics are even more famous and fundamental — his greatest being **electromagnetic induction**, which led to the invention of the **dynamo** and the **transformer**. He introduced the Christmas Lectures for children and gave these himself for many years. This annual series of lectures still continues and is now usually shown on television shortly after Christmas each year.

The picture shows Michael Faraday working in his laboratory at the Royal Institution.

Q.16.17
(a) Which three of the following liquids are electrolytes?
$PbI_2(l)$, $CCl_4(l)$, $HCl(aq)$, $HCl(l)$, $Na(l)$, $AgNO_3(aq)$.

(b) For each of the electrolytes give the symbols for the particles responsible for carrying the current through the liquid. List the elements released when each of these electrolytes is electrolysed (assume inert electrodes).

(c) Calculate the number of coulombs passed when 4 amps flows for 2 hours.

(d) How many faradays is that?

(e) When aluminium is discharged at an electrode, the reaction is:

$$Al^{3+} + 3e^- \rightarrow Al$$

How many faradays are needed to discharge 1 mole of aluminium?

(f) What mass of aluminium is liberated by 4 A flowing for 2 hours?

Q.16.18 A current of 5 A is passed through aqueous sodium sulphate. One litre of hydrogen, at 15°C and 100 kPa pressure is produced. Calculate (a) the time taken, (b) the volume (at the same temperature and pressure) of the other product of the reaction.

Q.16.19 What current flowing for 30 minutes through a solution of sulphuric acid liberates 56 cm³ of hydrogen at s.t.p.?

Q.16.20 0.02 faraday of electricity was passed through a solution of sodium hydroxide, the electrodes being platinum:

(a) Name the gases evolved and the electrodes at which they are liberated.

(b) Draw a labelled diagram of a suitable apparatus for this electrolysis and for the collection of the products.

(c) Write ionic equations for the reactions taking place at the two electrodes.

(d) Calculate the number of moles of each gas produced, and also the volume which each would have at s.t.p.

(e) Calculate the time needed to pass 0.02 F if the current were 2 amps.

(f) Write an equation to represent the reaction which would take place if the volumes of gas mentioned in (d) were mixed and ignited.

State the number of moles of the product which would be formed.

Q.16.21 An electric current is passed through solutions of silver nitrate, copper(II) sulphate and sulphuric acid, all in series. If 0.54 g of silver is deposited from the first solution, calculate (a) the mass of copper liberated, and (b) the volume of hydrogen, at 15°C and 98.3 kPa (98.3×10^3 N/m²) collected.

Q.16.22 Chromium chloride is electrolysed by a current of 0.5 A flowing for 579 seconds. The mass of chromium deposited is 0.052 g. Calculate:

(a) the number of coulombs of electricity,

(b) the number of moles of electrons passed through the solution.

(c) the number of moles of chromium liberated,

(d) the number of moles of electrons needed to liberate one mole of chromium,

(e) the charge of the chromium ion.

Q.16.23 Calculate the volume of hydrogen produced (at room temperature) when a current of 0.2 A is passed through dilute sulphuric acid for 9000 seconds.

Q.16.24 During the electrolysis of a solution of gold chloride, a current of 1.35 A flowing for 45 minutes deposited 2.48 g of gold. Calculate the number of faradays of electricity, and the number of moles of gold. Hence find the magnitude of the charge on the gold ion and the formula of gold chloride.

Q.16.25 In an electrolysis experiment, 5 g of copper was deposited. What mass of (a) silver, (b) zinc, (c) aluminium, would be depostied by the same quantity of electricity?

Short Answer Questions.

Q.16.26 Give short answers to each of the following questions:

(a) From the following metals, select (i) one which can, and (ii) one which cannot, displace hydrogen from dilute acid: Cu, Fe, Ag.

(b) Name a metal which is (i) more electropositive, (ii) less electropositive than hydrogen.

(c) Write an ionic equation for the reaction: $NiSO_4 + Zn \rightarrow ZnSO_4 + Ni$. Which is higher in the electrochemical series, zinc or nickel?

(d) Which statement is correct and why: (i) Sodium loses electrons more easily than magnesium because sodium is higher in the electrochemical series, OR, (ii) Sodium is higher than magnesium in the electrochemical series because sodium loses electrons more readily than magnesium does.

(e) What is the effect of passing hydrogen over heated magnesium oxide? Why?

(f) What are the three products of heating lead nitrate?

(g) What happens when magnesium is placed in a solution of Cu^{2+} ions? Why?

(h) Which ion, Cu^{2+} or Pb^{2+}, is reduced in preference to the other? What is formed when this happens ?

(i) Why could sodium not have been discovered before the 19th century?

(j) What type of chemical reaction occurs when iron rusts? Name the compound formed.

(k) What is the collective name for the ions which are attracted towards the anode in electrolysis? Give an example of such an ion.

(l) Does oxidation or reduction occur at an anode? Why?

(m) What is the overall chemical reaction which takes place in a hydrogen/alkali/oxygen fuel cell ? Which of the two reactants is the fuel for the cell?

(n) State two advantages of fuel cells over conventional electrical cells.

(o) Name the two products of electrolysing molten sodium hydride.

(p) Which product is formed at the anode in the above reaction? Write the equation for the reaction which occurs there.

(q) What reaction occurs when OH^- ions are oxidised? At which electrode does this happen.

(r) What are the products of electrolysing aqueous sodium sulphate?

(s) If the above solution contains some universal indicator, what colour would the latter become around the anode of the cell? Why?

(t) Write an equation for the reaction which occurs when an object is electroplated with silver. At which electrode does this happen?

Review When you know Chapter 16 you should be able to:

(a) Describe an experiment in which metals are arranged in order of reactivity,

(b) Describe the reactions of common metals with (i) water, (ii) dilute acid.

(c) Work out which metals can displace one another from solutions of their salts.

(d) Describe the effect of heat on metal hydroxides, carbonates and nitrates.

(e) Explain what happens when a metal corrodes, and why some reactive metals seemingly do not corrode.

(f) List ways of preventing corrosion.

(g) Define: electrolysis, electrolyte, electrode, anode, cathode, anion, cation, voltameter, coulomb, faraday.

(h) Write out the anode reaction, the cathode reaction, and the net result of electrolysing molten sodium chloride, molten lead bromide, dilute sulphuric acid, aqueous sodium sulphate, aqueous copper sulphate.

(i) Describe an experiment to show the movement of ions in electrolysis.

(j) Describe a fuel cell, and know the reactions which occur in the cell.

(k) State Faraday's Law of Electrolysis.

(l) Solve electrolysis problems involving current, time, coulombs, faradays and mass of element.

17

Metals

Metals have been known for thousands of years. From about eight that were known in Roman times, the number has increased to the eighty or so known today. Metals are amongst the most important materials of everyday life. Iron and steel are used in all modern machinery and buildings, on account of their strength and relatively low cost; copper is used for boilers because it is a good conductor of heat, and in electrical equipment because it is a good conductor of electricity; both aluminium and magnesium have low densities and are used in aircraft construction. Because lead has a high density, it is used to shield off harmful radiations such as come from X-ray machines and radioactive materials. Silver and gold are used for jewellery and for valuable ornaments because they keep their shine and do not corrode, and zinc is used for galvanising iron, to prevent it from rusting.

Apart from these familiar uses of metals, hundreds of compounds of metals are in everyday use. Such common substances as soap, salt, chalk, glass, magnetic tape, films and photographs, milk and blood, all contain metal compounds.

What is a metal, and how can one be distinguished from a non-metal? **A metal is best described as an element which ionises to give positive ions,** and the elements which do this are those which have a small number of electrons in the outer shells of their atoms. In general — though there are exceptions to nearly all of the following — metals are hard, strong and dense, have high melting and boiling points, are good conductors of heat and electricity and have a lustrous (*i.e.* shiny) appearance. Chemically, they form basic oxides, react with acids to form salts, and are good reducing agents.

Occurrence of Metals

In general, metals do not occur 'free' (*i.e.* uncombined) in nature. Apart from silver and gold, which are at the bottom of the electrochemical series, metals occur as compounds — chlorides, carbonates, oxides and sulphides being the most common. Rock and minerals containing such compounds are called **ores** of the metal.

The essential reaction in the extraction of a metal from its ore is reduction. The metal, being in the combined state, is present as metal ions and these must be reduced to atoms (*i.e.* they must gain electrons) to form the metal. The position of metal

Metal	Principal ore(s)	Formula of metal compound in ore	Method of extraction	Metal first isolated	Abundance in Earth's crust	World price sterling/ tonne (June 1989)
potassium	carnallite	$KClMgCl_2 6H_2O$	electrolysis of molten KCl	1807	1.5%	
sodium	rock salt sea water	NaCl	electrolysis of molten NaCl	1807	2.5%	
calcium	limestone	$CaCO_3$	electrolysis of molten $CaCl_2$	1808	5%	
magnesium	carnallite dolomite	$KClMgCl_2 6H_2O$ $CaCO_3MgCO_3$	electrolysis of molten $MgCl_2$	1808	3%	£2,375
aluminium	bauxite	$Al_2O_3 2H_2O$	electrolysis of molten Al_2O_3 in molten cryolite	1808	8%	£1,400
zinc	zinc blend	ZnS	reduction of ZnS by carbon	1825	< 0.1%	£950
iron	haematite magnetite	Fe_2O_3 Fe_3O_4	reduction of oxide by carbon monoxide	about 1700	6%	£188
lead	galena	PbS	reduction of lead oxide by carbon	ancient	< 0.01%	£372
copper	copper	$CuFeS_2$	roasting ore in air and then with sand	ancient	< 0.01%	£1700

in the electrochemical series is a good guide to how easily the ore can be reduced to the metal.

The metals at the top of the series, known as the electropositive or 'active' metals, are the most difficult to extract from their ores, since such metals are most stable as ions. Reduction must be carried out by the electrolysis of the molten compound. Moving down the series, reduction becomes easier. In the middle of the series the metal ores can be reduced to the metal by heating them with coke (*i.e.* carbon) which is a cheap reducing agent, and at the bottom of the series, reduction occurs when the ores are just heated. More detailed accounts of the extraction of metals from their ores are given in following sections.

Group I: The Alkali Metals

Most of the metals of everyday life (iron and steel, copper, aluminum, etc) are strong and hard, and have high melting points, but the metals of Group I, and to a lesser extent those of Group II, differ considerably in such properties. The Group I metals are so soft that they can be cut with a knife and most are so light that they float on water. Their most striking feature, however, is their extreme activity.

This group of elements, called the alkali metals because they form alkalis when they react with water, consist of lithium, sodium, potassium, rubidium and caesium. Having only one electron in the outer shells of their atoms means that their ionisation energies are low and that they easily attain a noble gas structure. Because of this, they are very reactive elements; the react with both air and water and must be stored under oil. Tongs should be used in handling them — not bare hands. The latter two members of the group are relatively uncommon and the following properties and reactions refer mainly to lithium, sodium and potassium.

Physical Properties

They are all soft silvery metals. When cut with a knife they show a shiny surface — but this rapidly tarnishes when exposed to air. They are less dense than water, have very low melting points and low boiling points. They are very good conductors of heat and electricity.

Chemical Reactions

They readily lose an electron from the outer shells of their atoms (*i.e.* they are very electropositive) and so are good reducing agents — being themselves oxidised in such reactions. They burn in air with brightly coloured flames (lithium - red; sodium - yellow; potassium - lilac) forming the metal oxide or peroxide (Na and K only):

$$4Li + O_2 \rightarrow 2Li_2O$$

$$2Na + O_2 \rightarrow Na_2O_2$$

$$2K + O_2 \rightarrow K_2O_2$$

The oxide in each case is soluble in water to give an alkaline solution of the metal hydroxide. They react vigorously with water. When a piece of the metal about the size of a pea is dropped on the surface of water, it melts into a ball (except Li) and rushes about on the surface, causing hydrogen gas to be liberated. The water is converted to a solution of the metal hydroxide (strongly alkaline):

$$e.g. \ 2Na + 2H_2O \rightarrow 2NaOH + H_2$$

They combine readily with halogens and other non-metals:

$$2Na + Cl_2 \rightarrow 2NaCl$$

$$2K + Br_2 \rightarrow 2KBr$$

$$2Li + H_2 \rightarrow 2LiH$$

Many metal oxides and halides, on being heated with an alkali metal, are reduced to the metal:

$$AlCl_3 + 3Na \rightarrow Al + 3NaCl$$

In all the chemical reactions, potassium reacts most vigorously, then sodium, and lithium reacts least vigorously.

They all have a valency of one, and are good reducing agents. Their salts are stable to heat, and are soluble in water.

Property	Lithium	Sodium	Potassium
Atomic Number	3	11	19
Electron structure	2,1	2,8,1	2,8,8,1
Atomic radius (nm)	0.133	0.157	0.203
Ionic radius (nm)	0.078	0.098	0.133
Ionisation energy (kJ/ mol)	520	495	420
Electrode potential(V)	-3.03	-2.72	-2.92
Electro-negativity	1.0	0.9	0.8
m.p.(°C)	186	98	63
b.p.(°C)	1336	877	757
Density (g/cm³)	0.53	0.97	0.86
Hardness	hard	soft	very soft
Reaction with air	slow	fast	very fast
Colour of flame when burning	red	yellow	violet
Reactivity	Reactive	very reactive	extremely reactive

Sodium Hydroxide

Commonly called **caustic soda** (caustic means burning) because it attacks most animal and vegetable material, sodium hydroxide is one of the important chemical compounds of industry. It is white deliquescent solid, extremely soluble in water, and dissolves exothermically, to give a strong alkaline solution.

Sodium hydroxide solution reacts with many substances; it neutralises all acids and converts acidic oxides and amphoteric oxides to their sodium salts:

$$NaOH + H_2SO_4 \rightarrow NaHSO_4 \rightarrow H_2O$$

$$2NaOH + H_2SO_4 \rightarrow Na_2SO_4 + 2H_2O$$

$$2NaOH + SO_2 \rightarrow Na_2SO_3 + H_2O$$

$$2NaOH + ZnO \rightarrow Na_2ZnO_2 + H_2O$$

Silica, SiO_2, one of the main components of glass, is attacked by concentrated sodium hydroxide solution:

$$2NaOH + SiO_2 \rightarrow Na_2SiO_3 + H_2O$$

This explains why glass stoppers become sealed into reagent bottles (plastic stoppers are preferable for alkali bottles) and why burette taps stick in their sockets after alkalis have been used in them — unless they are rinsed with acid and then with water before being put away.

Manufacture of Sodium

Sodium and the other alkali metals are much too reactive to occur free in nature; they are all found as compounds. Sodium occurs as sodium chloride, in the form of rock salt and in the sea. Potassium and sodium were first isolated by Sir Humphrey Davy in 1807. Using a large battery of the recently invented Volta's cells, he electrolysed molten potash (KOH) and soda (NaOH) respectively, to produce the metals. Within a year, Davy also isolated magnesium, strontium, barium and calcium by similar methods.

Sodium is obtained by the electrolysis of molten sodium chloride, in cells specially designed for the purpose. The reactions involved in the process are as follows.

When molten, sodium chloride is dissociated into its ions:

$$NaCl \rightarrow Na^+ + Cl^-$$

The positive ions (Na^+) are attracted to the cathode (negative electrode) where they each gain an electron to become sodium atoms; the negative chloride ions go to the anode (positive electrode) where they lose an electron each, to become chlorine atoms:

At cathode: $Na^+ + e^- \rightarrow Na$

At anode: $Cl^- - e^- \rightarrow Cl$
(followed by $2Cl \rightarrow Cl_2$)

Chlorine gas is thus a by-product of the reaction.

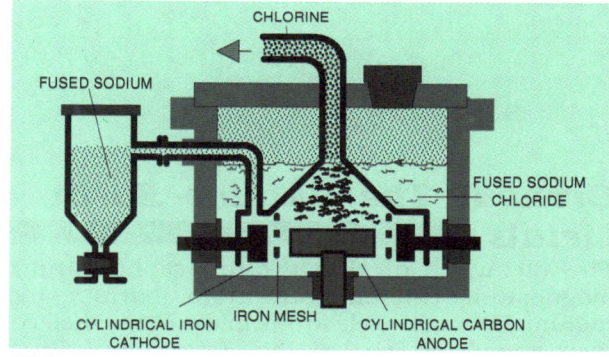

17.1 — *The Downs cell for making sodium and chlorine, by the electrolysis of fused sodium chloride. In this cell, the electrodes are close together, so making the resistance of the cell low, but the products of electrolysis (i.e. the sodium and chlorine) are separated from each other so that recombination cannot occur. A typical cell of this type is 2.5 metres high and 1.5 meters in diameter, and the current used is 30,000 amps at 6.7 volts.*

Use of Sodium

Apart from sodium, which has a great number of industrial applications, the alkali metals have few uses. The most important use of sodium is in the manufacture of tetra-ethyl lead, a petrol additive. Sodium is also used in the manufacture and purification of gold and silver, in the extraction of titanium from its ore (TiO_2 is a fundamental constituent of modern white paints), as a coolant in certain types of nuclear reactor and in the familiar amber-coloured street lights.

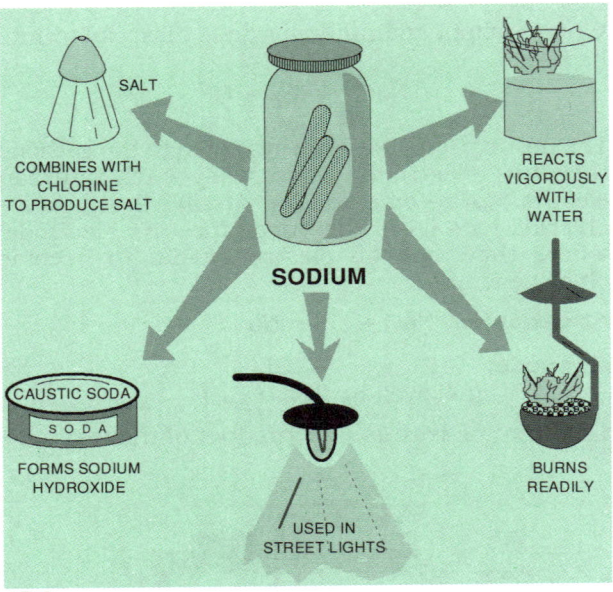

SALT

COMBINES WITH
CHLORINE
TO PRODUCE SALT

REACTS
VIGOROUSLY
WITH
WATER

SODIUM

CAUSTIC SODA
S O D A

FORMS SODIUM
HYDROXIDE

BURNS
READILY

USED IN
STREET LIGHTS

17.2

Group II: The Alkaline- Earth Metals

The elements of this group are beryllium, magnesium, calcium, strontium, barium and radium. Having two electrons in the outer shells of their atoms means that they form ions (with a charge of +2) relatively easily and are therefore reactive metals — though not as reactive as those of Group I. Magnesium and calcium are the common elements of Group II

Physical Properties of Magnesium and Calcium.

Both are silvery coloured metals of low density and fairly low melting and boiling points. Because they are both reactive, their surfaces are normally covered with a thin film of oxide so that the true colour of the metal cannot be seen. They are good conductors of heat and electricity and are much harder than the Group I metals. Magnesium is normally encountered in the laboratory as thin ribbon, and calcium as small chips which are very brittle.

Chemical Reactions

They are both very electropositive, and readily combine with oxygen and other electronegative elements. They burn in air, or more vigorously in oxygen, forming their oxides:

$$2Mg + O_2 \rightarrow 2MgO$$

They also combine directly with nitrogen, sulphur and halogens. Calcium combines directly with hydrogen:

$$3Mg + N_2 \rightarrow Mg_3N_2$$
$$Ca + S \rightarrow CaS$$
$$Mg + Cl_2 \rightarrow MgCl_2$$
$$Ca + H_2 \rightarrow CaH_2$$

Both are good reducing agents. Magnesium, once ignited, will continue to burn in steam, sulphur dioxide, carbon dioxide and the oxides of nitrogen, reducing them to the element in every case:

$$Mg + H_2O \rightarrow MgO + H_2$$

$$2Mg + CO_2 \rightarrow 2MgO + C$$

Calcium will decompose cold water:

$$Ca + 2H_2O \rightarrow Ca(OH)_2 + H_2$$

Both metals react with acids, liberating hydrogen and forming their salts:

$$Mg + H_2SO_4 \rightarrow MgSO_4 + H_2$$

Magnesium will displace less electropositive metals from solutions of their salts:

$$Mg + CuSO_4 \rightarrow Cu + MgSO_4$$

or, $$Mg + Cu^{2+} \rightarrow Cu + Mg^{2+}$$

Manufacture of Magnesium and Calcium

The principal sources of magnesium are magnetite ($MgCO_3$), dolomite ($MgCO_3CaCO_3$) and the sea, which contains Mg^{2+} ions. Calcium occurs naturally as limestone, chalk, calcite and marble, all of which are essentially $CaCO_3$, and as gypsum, which is hydrated calcium sulphate, $CaSO_42H_2O$.

Both metals are manufactured by similar methods, *viz.*, by the electrolysis of their molten chlorides. The chemical changes which occur in the process are similar to those which take place when molten sodium chloride is electrolysed.

In the molten state, the ions dissociate:

$$MgCl_2 \rightarrow Mg^{2+} + 2Cl^-$$

At the cathode, magnesium ions are reduced to magnesium metal:

$$Mg + 2e^- \rightarrow Mg^{2+}$$

while at the anode, chloride ions are oxidised to chlorine gas:

$$2Cl^- - 2e^- \rightarrow 2Cl \rightarrow Cl_2$$

Magnesium alloys have low densities and high strength and are used for aircraft construction. Magnesium powder is used in fireworks, and photographic flash bulbs contain magnesium wire in an atmosphere of oxygen. Because of magnesium's reactivity, it is used as sacrificial protection (see p.194) for iron.

While calcium compounds are important and useful, calcium metal itself has very few uses. It is used in laboratories as a reducing agent.

Questions

Q.17.1   What is produced when sodium is (i) burned, (ii) reacted with water, (iii) reacted with chlorine. Write an equation for each reaction, say which of the reactants is oxidised and which is reduced. Give the reasons for your answers.

Q.17.2   What are the alkali metals? Why are the so called? In which Group of the Periodic Table do they occur? List three properties which are common to all metals, and three which show trends (*i.e.* a gradual change in properties).

Q.17.3   Sodium is extracted from its ore by electrolysis

(a)   From what compound is sodium extracted?

(b)   Before electrolysis, the sodium compound must be heated to about 800°C. Why?

(c)   What change occurs to its structure when this is done?

(d)   At which electrode of the electrolysis cell is the sodium produced?

(e)   Write an equation for the reaction which occurs there.

(f)   Is this reaction an oxidation, a reduction, or neither ? Why?

(g)   What substance is formed at the other electrode?

(h)   Write an equation showing how this substance is formed.

(i)   Draw a diagram showing the structure of a molecule of this substance.

(j)   Write the equation for the net result of the whole process.

Q.17.4   Sodium reacts with aluminium chloride. Show that this is a redox reaction and use (a) oxidation numbers and (b) electron transfer, to indicate what is oxidised and what is reduced.

Q.17.5   Magnesium combines with chlorine to form magnesium chloride. What type of bond is present in this compound? Draw a diagram showing its structure and write down its formula.

Q.17.6
Sodium and chlorine are both manufactured by the electrolysis of molten sodium chloride. Calculate (a) the mass of sodium and (b) the volume of chlorine (at s.t.p.) produced when 10 amps are passed through molten sodium chloride for 30 minutes. (Value of the Faraday = 96500 C).

Aluminium
Aluminium is the most abundant metal and the third most abundant element in the Earth's crust. Its compounds are not only plentiful, but they are widely distributed, usually combined with silicon and/or oxygen. They include clays of various kinds *e.g.* china clay ($Al_2Si_2O_72H_2O$), mica ($K_2Al_2Si_6O_{16}$), corundum (Al_2O_3), cryolite (Na_2AlF_6), and bauxite ($Al_2O_32H_2O$).

Manufacture

Stage 1: Production of Alumina
The main ore of aluminium is bauxite, which is mainly hydrated Al_2O_3 but along with some oxides of iron, titanium and silicon. Bauxite contains from 50 to 70% Al_2O_3. The first stage of manufacture involves extracting pure Al_2O_3 from the bauxite ore. The ore is crushed and dissolves in hot concentrated sodium hydroxide solution. The Al_2O_3, being amphoteric, reacts with the alkali and forms sodium aluminate.

$$2NaOH + Al_2O_3 \rightarrow 2NaAlO_2 + H_2O$$

The impurities — mainly oxides of iron and titanium, and silicates — do not dissolve and are filtered off as a sludge. The filtrate is then diluted and 'seeded' with pure $Al(OH)_3$ crystals. This encourages crystallisation, and solid $Al(OH)_3$ is precipitated.

$$NaAlO_2 + 2H_2O \rightarrow Al(OH)_3 + NaOH$$

The aluminium hydroxide is then heated to over 1000°C, when the combined water is driven off, leaving pure alumina (Al_2O_3)

$$2Al(OH)_3 \rightarrow Al_2O_3 + 3H_2O$$

Stage 2: Extraction of the Metal.

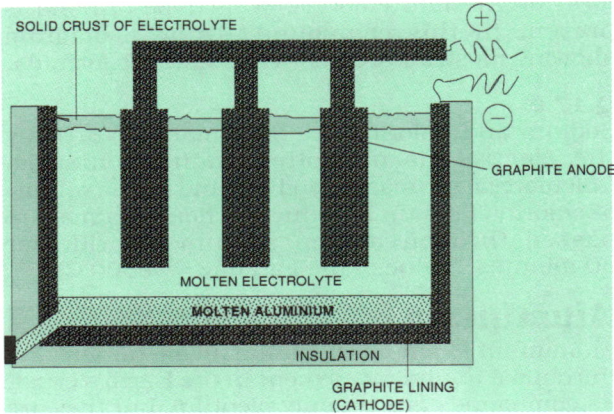

17.3

The extraction of the metal from the metal oxide is done electrolytically, *i.e.* by electrolysis. However, the melting point of the oxide is above 2000°C and this makes its direct electrolysis impracticable. The problem is overcome by dissolving the alumina in molten cryolite, Na_3AlF_6 ,which melts at about 900°C. The cathode is the graphite lining of the cell, and a number of graphite blocks act as anodes. Electrolysis yields aluminium and oxygen, at cathode and anode respectively, and the reactions are as follows:

$$Al_2O_3 \rightarrow 2Al + 3O^{2-}$$

At cathode: $2Al_3 + 6e^- \rightarrow 2Al$

At anode: $3O^{2-} - 6e^- \rightarrow 1\frac{1}{2}O_2$

The pure aluminium which forms at the cathode is molten at the temperature of the cell, and it runs to the bottom where it is tapped off from time to time. The oxygen which is liberated at the anodes reacts to a certain extent with the graphite and oxidises it to carbon dioxide. The anodes are therefore slowly burnt away and have to be replaced at intervals. The cryolite remains unchanged and can be used indefinitely. The electrolyte is kept molten by the passage of the electric current.

An enormous current is required to produce appreciable amounts of the metal and sufficient power must be supplied to keep the electrolyte molten. A typical cell uses 100,000 amps at 6 volts (this is 600 kilowatts) and will take almost 30 hours to produce one tonne of the metal. An aluminium producing works (an aluminium 'smelter') will have a great number of cells in use at any one time and so much electricity is therefore needed that aluminium production is only carried out where cheap electricity is available. In the U.K. the largest works are in Scotland, alongside hydroelectric power stations.

Properties of Aluminium

Aluminium is a silvery coloured metal, m.p. 660°C and b.p. 2400°C. It is a light metal, having a density of only 2.7 g/cm^3 which is about one third that of steel. It is very malleable and a very good conductor of both heat and electricity. Pure aluminium is rather soft, but by alloying it with small amounts (of the order of 5%) of other metals (*e.g.* copper), very strong, light, materials are formed. Dozens of different aluminium alloys are available.

Its position in the electrochemical series suggests that it should be a fairly reactive element, but its reactions show otherwise. It is very resistant to corrosion, and is unaffected by air, water or steam. This stability is due to a thin invisible layer of the oxide which is formed on the surface of the metal once it is exposed to air. Whereas the oxide of other elements (iron in particular) usually flakes off to expose fresh metal, so that corrosion (oxidation) continues, aluminium oxide forms an impervious layer which stays on the metal surface and prevents further oxidation.

Aluminium is amphoteric, reacting with both acids and alkalis to form salts:

$$Al + 6HCl \rightarrow AlCl_3 + 3H_2$$
aluminium
chloride

$$2Al + 2NaOH + 2H_2O \rightarrow 2NaAlO_2 + 3H_2$$
sodium
aluminate

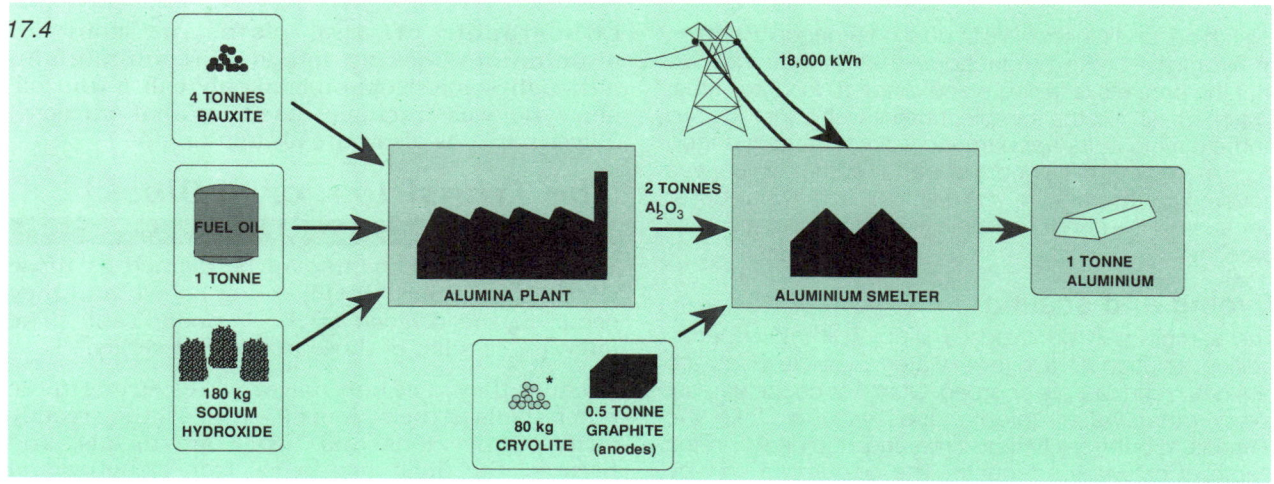

17.4

4 TONNES BAUXITE

FUEL OIL
1 TONNE

180 kg SODIUM HYDROXIDE

ALUMINA PLANT

2 TONNES Al₂O₃

18,000 kWh

ALUMINIUM SMELTER

1 TONNE ALUMINIUM

*
80 kg CRYOLITE

0.5 TONNE GRAPHITE (anodes)

* not consumed

Because of this latter reaction, aluminium saucepans should not be cleaned with alkaline cleaning agents such as washing soda.

Anodising

Aluminium is resistant to corrosion because of the protective layer of oxide which forms on its surface. The thickness of this layer can be artificially increased by a process called **anodising.** In this process, the aluminium to be anodised is made the anode of an electrolytic cell containing dilute sulphuric acid — which on electrolysis yields hydrogen at the cathode and oxygen at the anode (see page 197). The oxygen produced at the aluminium anode reacts with it to thicken the layer of Al_2O_3 on its surface. A freshly formed surface layer of Al_2O_3 is initially rather porous and can be dyed very satisfactorily by immersing the aluminium in a solution of the dye. All this results in an attractive appearance and extra protection from corrosion. Anodised aluminium is used for items such as saucepan lids and metal panels for decorative purposes in buildings.

Experiment 17.1
Anodising aluminium

Preparation of sample

Aluminium to be anodised must be quite clean and free from grease. Take the piece of metal to be anodised and thoroughly wash it with hot detergent solution. Hold it only by the edges. Rinse it in clean water. If it appears greasy, it will have to be dried and degreased with a solvent such as trichloroethane, and then dried once again.

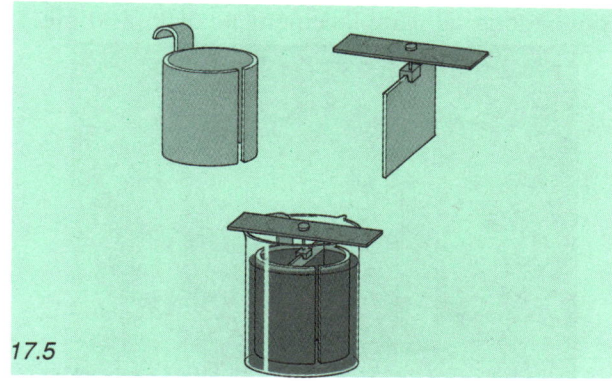

17.5

Anodising

Bend a piece of thin aluminium sheet (not the sample to an anodised) into a cylindrical shape so as to fit inside a beaker. This cylinder is the cathode. It is useful if this piece has a projecting lug. Attach a wire, via a crocodile clip, to the sample, and suspend the sample inside the cylindrical cathode. A suitable way of doing this is to have the crocodile clip attached to a wooden bar — such as shown. Make sure the cathode and the sample (which is the anode) are not touching each other. Carefully pour enough dilute sulphuric acid into the beaker until almost all of the sample is immersed. Connect the cell to a power supply of about 12 volts, making sure that the sample is the anode.

Switch on, and electrolysis should commence. Bubbles of hydrogen being produced at the cathode indicate that the process is taking place. After 10 to 15 minutes, switch off, lift out the sample, rinse it well under the tap and examine it. Its appearance will not have changed very much, but the anodised part (*i.e.* that which was covered by the electrolyte) will look somewhat duller because of the almost invisible film of transparent oxide present.

Dyeing and sealing

The sample can be dyed by dipping it into a nearly boiling solution of a dye in water. Suitable dyes are eosin, alizarin, purple or green 'Quink' or cochineal, but many other water soluble dyes will do. Take the aluminium out from time to time and decide when the depth of colour is adequate. The colour can now be sealed in and made permanent by immersing the dyed sample in boiling water for about two minutes.

Uses of Aluminium

Aluminium has become the second most widely used metal today, and is finding more and more applications as a replacement for iron and steel.

17.6 — An aluminium printing plate on a lithographic printing press at Folens Publishers, Tallaght, Co. Dublin.

Because of its strength (as an alloy), low density, and resistance to corrosion, it is used in aircraft bodywork, superstructure of ships, buildings and machinery, and door and window frames. Because of its good heat conductivity, it is used for car engines and radiators and cooking utensils, and owing to its good electrical conductivity and lightness, it is used for overhead electric cables. It is very malleable and so is easily rolled into sheets.

Lithographic printing plates are made of aluminium. Cooking foil is pure aluminium, although some people mistakenly call it 'tin foil' since tin was originally used for that purpose. 'Silver paper' is also pure aluminium foil !

The Transition, or 'd-Block' Elements

The transition elements can be defined as those which have a partially filled d subshell, and they occur in the d-block of the Periodic Table. The following is a list of those in the first series.

Because they have only one or two electrons in the outer shells of their atoms (*i.e.* the 4s) they readily form positive ions and hence are metals, and because the difference in electron structures of successive members occurs in the penultimate shells (*i.e.* the 3d) these metals have many properties in common. They have reasonably small atomic radii and have loose packed structures, so they are dense metals with high melting and boiling points. They have good mechanical strength, and readily form alloys with both themselves and with other elements. They are thus typical metals in all respects, and are widely used in industry and in everyday life.

Atomic number	Element	Electron configuration
21	scandium	$1s^2,2s^2,2p^6,3s^2,3p^6,4s^2,3d^1$
22	titanium	$1s^2,2s^2,2p^6,3s^2,3p^6,4s^2,3d^2$
23	vanadium	$1s^2,2s^2,2p^6,3s^2,3p^6,4s^2,3d^3$
24	chromium	$1s^2,2s^2,2p^6,3s^2,3p^6,4s^1,3d^5$
25	manganese	$1s^2,2s^2,2p^6,3s^2,3p^6,4s^2,3d^5$
26	iron	$1s^2,2s^2,2p^6,3s^2,3p^6,4s^2,3d^6$
27	cobalt	$1s^2,2s^2,2p^6,3s^2,3p^6,4s^2,3d^7$
28	nickel	$1s^2,2s^2,2p^6,3s^2,3p^6,4s^2,3d^8$
29	copper	$1s^2,2s^2,2p^6,3s^2,3p^6,4s^1,3d^{10}$
30	zinc	$1s^2,2s^2,2p^6,3s^2,3p^6,4s^2,3d^{10}$

There are a number of properties however, which are characteristic only of themselves and not of other metals. They show variable valency or oxidation state, they form coloured ions (and hence coloured compounds) and they act as catalysts in many chemical reactions. These properties are due to the ease with which electrons can move from one subshell to another. The colours of the more common ions of these metals are as follows:

Ion	Colour
Sc^{3+}	Colourless
Ti^{3+}	Purple
V^{3+}	Violet
Cr^{3+}	Green
Mn^{3+}	Red
Mn^{2+}	Pink
Fe^{3+}	Yellow / Brown
Fe^{2+}	Green
Co^{2+}	Pink
Ni^{2+}	Green
Cu^{2+}	Blue
Zn^{2+}	Colourless

Iron, copper and zinc are the most important and widely used of the transition metals and are described in greater detail in the following sections.

Iron

Iron, the second most abundant metal in the Earth's crust, has been known to man as a useful element for thousands of years. It is found in all parts of the world, the main ores being **haematite** (Fe_2O_3), magnetite (Fe_3O_4) and limonite or brown iron ore ($Fe_2O_3H_2O$). Another common mineral containing iron is iron pyrites or 'fools gold' (FeS_2), This is a gold coloured solid with a metallic appearance, and it often occurs in coal seams. Its colour fooled many of the miners and prospectors of the last century who mistook it for gold, hence its name.

Although the scale of iron production has increased enormously over the past hundred years or so, the principles involved in extracting the metal from its ore have remained much the same since Roman times. Most of the ore used today contains other substances such as calcium, silicon, oxygen, phosphorus and sulphur, along with the iron, and the process in which these other substances are removed or reduced to a minimum to leave nearly pure iron is called **smelting**. Huge furnaces known as **blast furnaces** are used for the smelting of iron.

The Blast Furnace

Described simply, a modern blast furnace is a tall steel cylindrical vessel, which can be as big as 70 metres high and 11 metres in diameter. It is lined on the inside with firebricks, and on the outside at the top is an arrangement for the addition of the raw materials without allowing the escape of gas from inside, as well as the outlet pipes to take away this gas. At the base of the furnace, just above the hearth, are a series of nozzles, called tuyeres, through which a blast of very hot air is blown — hence the name of this type of furnace.

The furnace is charged from the top with a mixture of iron ore, coke and limestone, while the superheated air (sometimes enriched with oxygen) at about 600°C is blown in through the tuyeres at the bottom. The coke plays a triple role in the furnace process. Firstly, it is the fuel to provide the heat, secondly it provides the reducing agent to reduce the iron oxide to iron, and lastly it acts as a physical support for the materials in the furnace, being very suitable for this because it is porous enough to allow the hot gases to flow upwards and the molten products to trickle downwards.

17.7 — Transition metal compounds are usually coloured. This picture shows samples (left to right) of nickel sulphate, potassium chromate, potassium dichromate, potassium permanganate, iron(III)oxide, iron(II)sulphate, manganese dioxide, copper sulphate and cobalt nitrate.

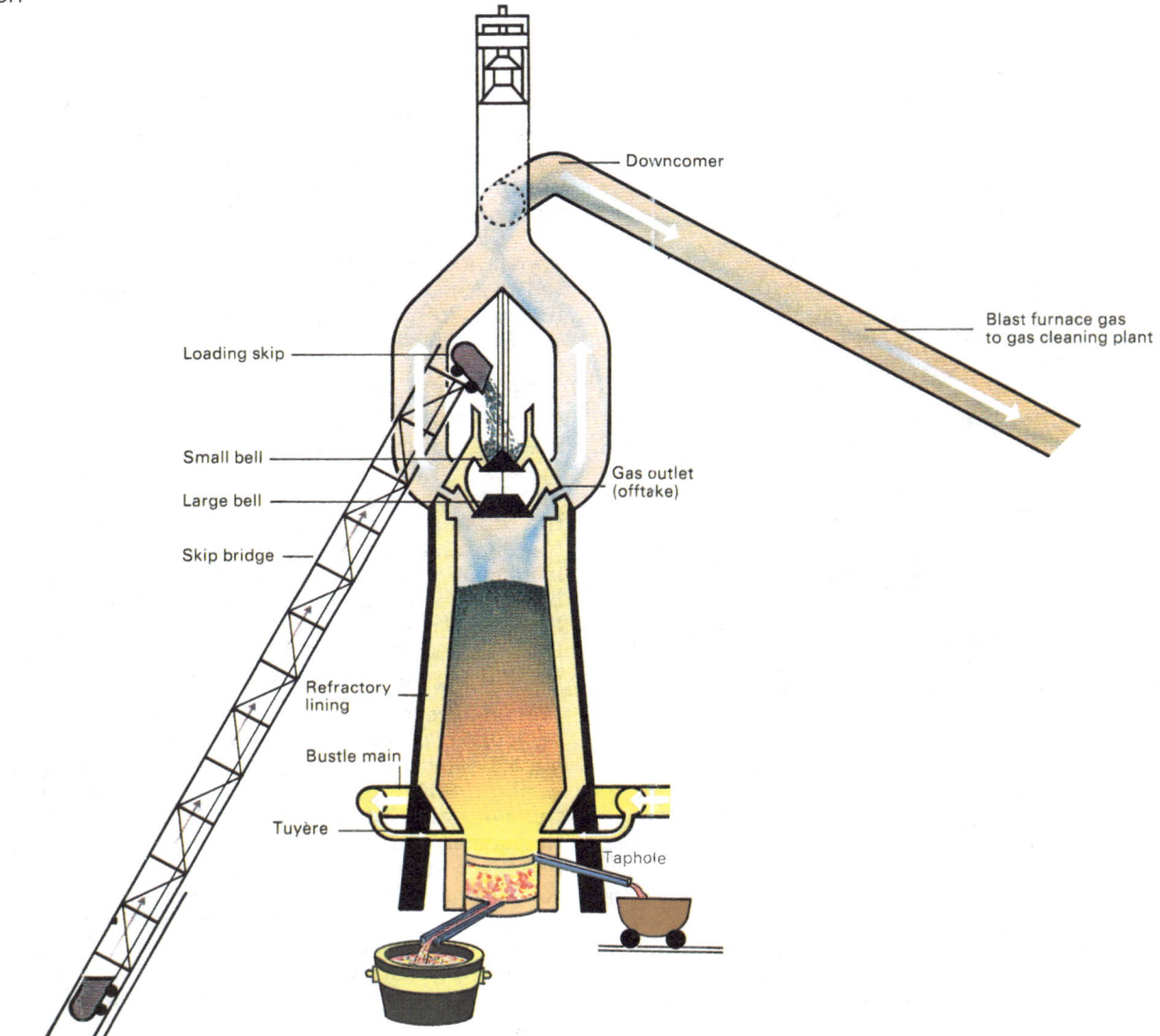

Downcomer

Blast furnace gas
to gas cleaning plant

Loading skip

Small bell

Large bell

Gas outlet
(offtake)

Skip bridge

Refractory
lining

Bustle main

Tuyère

Taphole

17.8 — The Blast Furnace

Several different reactions occur during the smelting process:

(i)   The oxygen in the hot air causes the coke to burn fiercely, forming carbon dioxide:

$$C + O_2 \rightarrow CO_2 + heat$$

This reaction is exothermic and the temperature at the bottom of the furnace can be as high as 1900°C. The high temperature is necessary for two reasons:

(a)   the next three reactions, described below, are endothermic, and take in heat as they occur; this causes the furnace temperature to decrease in the upwards direction, (b) when the iron is produced, it melts and can flow down to the bottom of the furnace.

(ii)   The carbon dioxide moves upwards through hot coke, which reduces it to carbon monoxide:

$$CO_2 + C \rightarrow 2CO$$

The carbon monoxide is necessary for the next stage.

(iii)   The carbon monoxide then reduces the iron oxide in the ore to iron:

$$Fe_2O_3 + 3CO \rightarrow 2Fe + 3CO_2$$

The molten iron drips down through the furnace and forms a layer on the hearth.

(iv)   Higher up the furnace, the limestone decomposes, forming calcium oxide (lime) and carbon dioxide:

$$CaCO_3 \rightarrow CaO + CO_2$$

(v)   The calcium oxide reacts with impurities in the ore (mainly SiO_2 in the sand and clay) and forms what is called a 'slag' of molten calcium silicate:

$$CaO + SiO_2 \rightarrow CaSiO_3$$

This slag runs to the bottom of the furnace and being less dense than the molten iron, floats on top of the iron. The slag and the iron are tapped off separately at regular intervals (every four to six hours or so) throughout each day. The slag solidifies on cooling and is broken up to provide material for road construction and making lightweight building blocks.

The hot gas which leaves the top of the furnace contains a high proportion (25 - 30%) of unused carbon monoxide and consequently is a good fuel. It is cleaned and then piped to special stoves ('Cowper' stoves) where it is burned to heat the incoming air which goes to the furnace. This preheating avoids the cooling effect that cold air would produce, and so saves fuel.

The whole process is continuous, raw materials being constantly added at the top, and molten iron and slag being tapped off at the bottom, and a blast furnace will continue doing this until the firebrick lining starts to disintegrate — after two or three years, by which time as much as a million tonnes of iron may have been produced. The furnace is then emptied, allowed to cool (this can take up to five weeks!) and relined, to start up production once more.

From an energy point of view, a blast furnace can be extremely efficient, When full use is made of the gas generated, heat loss can amount to as little as 5%. The manufacture of iron which has been described is a good example of a continuous process, but it gives little idea of the actual magnitude of the plant or the amounts of materials involved. A modern blast furnace is capable of producing more than 1000 tonnes of molten iron every 24 hours.

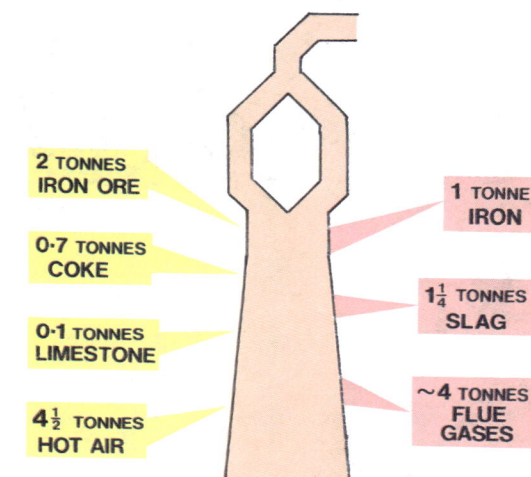

17.9 —   Blast Furnace input and output

17.10 —   A Blast Furnace in South Wales

Iron straight from the blast furnace, is called **pig iron**. Because of the impurities present, its melting point is much lower ($1200^{\circ}C$) than that of pure iron ($1540^{\circ}C$), and so it is easily melted and cast into moulds to make objects like lamp posts. As such, it is known as **cast iron.**

Wrought iron is the purest form of iron, and is obtained by heating cast iron with iron oxide. The oxygen from the iron oxide oxidises the various impurities (C,S,O,Si) to either gaseous oxides or to

CHARGING HOT METAL

SAMPLING

SLAGGING

CHARGING SCRAP

'BLOW'

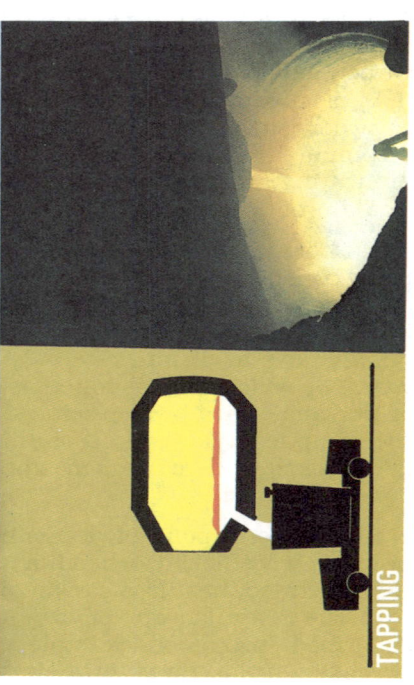

TAPPING

17.11

a slag. Unlike cast iron, wrought iron can be worked ('wrought') by blacksmiths into horseshoes, ornamental gates etc. Wrought iron has to a large extent been replaced by mild steel which is cheaper to produce.

Steel

There is no single substance called steel; there are dozens of different types of steel — of different compositions and with different properties. 'Ordinary' steel can be described as an alloy of iron containing a small but fixed amount (up to 1.5%) of carbon. The many special steels which are available have several other metals mixed in as well.

The properties of a steel depend not only on its composition but also on any heat treatment given to it subsequent to manufacture.

Pig iron, with its high proportion of impurities, is too brittle for most purposes, and the bulk of what is produced in blast furnaces is converted into steel. The basic principle of the steelmaking process involves removing most of the carbon and practically all of the other impurities (Si, S, P) by oxidising them, and then adding the right amount of each of the required elements. Of the main steelmaking processes in use today, the one by which most steel is manufactured is the **basic oxygen process**. This modern method is fast and over 300 tonnes of steel can be produced in as little as 40 minutes.

A modern converter for the basic oxygen process is a huge, steel, pear-shaped vessel of up to 300 tonnes capacity, mounted so that it can be tilted either way for charging and tapping. A water-cooled tube, called a lance, can be lowered vertically into the vessel to deliver a high powered jet of pure oxygen at great speed. A hood is arranged so that it can come down over the mouth of the vessel to carry away the gases and fumes which are produced, and this eliminates atmospheric pollution.

The converter is charged with molten pig iron from the blast furnace, along with up to about half of its mass of scrap iron or steel. The lance is lowered into position and the oxygen is blow onto, and into, the metal for 15-20 minutes. This oxidises the impurities rapidly, (carbon to CO_2 and sulphur to SO_2) and these escape as gases. Lime is added to combine with the less volatile oxides (P_2O_5 and SiO_2) which are converted to a slag, composed mainly of $Ca_3(PO_4)_2$ and $CaSiO_3$. The slag floats on the molten steel. After a sample of the steel has been taken, analysed and confirmed to be of the

PROPERTIES AND USES OF DIFFERENT TYPES OF IRON AND STEEL			
Material	Properties		Uses
Cast iron (contains up to 4 % C)	Brittle, high compression strength but little tensile strength, cannot be welded		Car engine blocks, fire grates, bunsen burner bases, pipes, machinery, man hole covers , railings, radiators
Wrought iron (99 % iron)	Purest form of iron, soft, bends easily, can be worked (hammered, bent, welded) without breaking.		Nails, bolts, gates, chains, horse shoes.
Soft steel (up to 0.15 % C)	Soft, strong , ductile.	strength decreases ductility decreases / hardness increases	Wire, rivets , cans, car bodies.
Mild steel (0.15 - 0.25 % C)	Strong , ductile.		Machines, girders, ships.
medium steel (0.25 - 0.5 % C)	Hard, not so strong, low ductility.		Springs, rails.
Hard steel (0.5 - 1.7 % C)	Hard, brittle, low ductility.		Tools, scissors, knives, razors.

correct composition, the lance is withdrawn, the vessel tilted and the molten steel poured into a waiting ladle. Once the pouring is complete, the vessel is tilted in the opposite direction and the residual slag tipped into a slag ladle for removal to a slag pool. This slag can be used as a fertiliser, since it contains phosphates.

17.13 One of the copper cathodes being placed in the electrolysis bath. During the process it will increase in size as pure copper is plated on to it.

Copper

Like its close chemical relations silver and gold, copper has been known to man from early times. All three metals can be found free in nature and it is likely that the early civilisations used copper to make utensils and ornaments. Bronze, made by melting copper and tin together, was discovered about 3000 B.C. and this was the start of the bronze age.

Occurence and Extraction

The main ore of copper is **copper pyrites**, which is mainly $CuFeS_2$. Since both iron and sulphur have to be removed in the extraction, there are several stages in the process. The ore is first heated in air; this converts the iron and sulphur to their oxides, leaving the copper as copper(I) sulphide (equation (i)). The sulphur dioxide, being a gas, escapes and is collected, usually for sulphuric acid manufacture. Sand is then added, and the heating continued, but in the absence of air; this converts the iron oxide to a molten slag, which is poured away (equation (ii)). Finally, the copper sulphide is heated with the right amount of air for the sulphur to be oxidised, but not the copper (equation (iii))

(i) $2CuFeS_2 + 4O_2 \rightarrow Cu_2S + 3SO_2 + 2FeO$

(ii) $SiO_2 + FeO \rightarrow FeSiO_3$

(iii) $Cu_2S + O_2 \rightarrow 2Cu + SO_2$

17.12 — Molten pig iron being poured into a basic oxygen furnace for conversion to steel.

Chemical Properties of Iron

Iron is a silvery grey metal, m.p. 1530°C and b.p. 3000°C. It is reasonably dense (7.8 g/cm^3). It is easily magnetised.

It combines on heating with many non metals, *viz* oxygen, halogens, nitrogen, sulphur, and carbon. Iron filings burn in oxygen with a shower of bright sparks. On exposure to moist air, iron forms a surface layer of the hydrated oxide, $Fe_2O_3 3H_2O$, commonly called rust. Unlike aluminium oxide the layer of iron oxide is porous and easily flakes off and so oxidation or rusting can continue. At red heat, iron reacts reversibly with steam:

$$3Fe + 4H_2O \rightleftharpoons Fe_3O_4 + 4H_2$$

The copper which is produced contains 2-3% impurities, mainly iron and sulphur, but small amounts of arsenic, bismuth, zinc, lead, silver and gold may also be present. As such, the copper is unsuitable for most purposes, particularly for electrical work, which requires very pure metal. Even very small amounts of impurities in copper can considerably reduce its electrical conductivity.

Purification is done by electrolysis. Blocks of the impure metal are used as anodes and thin sheets of pure copper as cathodes. The electrolyte is copper sulphate solution. The chemical reactions which occur are described elsewhere (Chapter 16) but the net result is that copper is dissolved off the anodes, and deposited as pure metal on the cathodes, which therefore increase in size. Impurities which are insoluble fall to the bottom of the cell and form what is called anode 'sludge' — a rather unglamorous name for a material which often contains silver and gold! Impurities such as these are very valuable by-products and are naturally recovered.

Properties and Uses

Copper is an attractive golden-brown shiny metal, of density 8.92 g/cm^3, m.p. 1080°C and b.p. 2600°C. It is very malleable (sheets can be made as thin as 0.004 mm) and ductile (1 g can be drawn into wire 200 m in length). Its conductivity of both heat and electricity are second only to silver. It mixes well with other metals, and many copper alloys are in everyday use.

Being near the bottom of the electrochemical series, it is not a highly reactive metal. When heated to about 300°C in air or oxygen, it slowly forms copper oxide on its surface, and when left exposed to the atmosphere for a long period of time it forms a basic sulphate $CuSO_43Cu(OH)_2$, which protects it from further reaction. The familiar green seen on roofs and domes of buildings is due to this substance. Copper is not attacked by water or steam, or by dilute non-oxidising acids such as hydrochloric. Oxidising acids (HNO_3 and conc. H_2SO_4) react with it, being themselves reduced in the reaction to NO_2 (or NO) and SO_2 respectively:

$$Cu + 4HNO_3 \rightarrow Cu(NO_3)_2 + 2NO_2 + 2H_2O$$

$$Cu + 2H_2SO_4 \rightarrow CuSO_4 + SO_2 + 2H_2O$$

Each of the many and varied uses of copper is due to one or more of its properties just described. The most important single use is in the manufacture of wires, cables and other electrical conductors, and about half of the copper which is manufactured is for this purpose. Copper is also used for boilers, piping and radiators, and for soldering iron 'bits' . It is used for roofing and decorative work. Its alloys (see table overleaf) are widely used and a large amount of copper goes to the manufacture of these.

Zinc

Zinc is not strictly a transition metal, as its d orbital in the penultimate shell is full (Zn = $1s^2, 2s^2, 2p^6, 3s^2, 3p^6, 4s^2, 3d^{10}$). It lacks the characteristic properties of transition elements, having only the one valency (of 2) and forming white compounds.

The main ore of zinc is **zinc blende**, which is the sulphide of the metal, ZnS. The metal is extracted by first roasting the ore in air, where oxidation takes place, zinc oxide and sulphur dioxide being formed. The metal oxide is then reduced by heating it with powdered coke, when the metal is formed. The liquid zinc is run into moulds in which it solidifies:

$$2ZnS + 3O_2 \rightarrow 2ZnO + 2SO_2$$

$$ZnO + C \rightarrow Zn + CO$$

17.14 Farmyard gates being lifted out of a bath of molten zinc, having been galvinised. The bath shown contains 200 tonnes of zinc and must constantly be kept at a temperature of 450˙C.

Properties and Uses

Zinc is a brittle silvery grey metal, with reasonably low melting and boiling points (419°C and 910°C respectively). It is a fairly reactive metal, as is indicated by its position in the electrochemical series. It combines directly with oxygen, halogens, phosphorus and sulphur when heated with them, and it displaces hydrogen from dilute acids, *e.g.*

$$Zn + H_2SO_4 \rightarrow ZnSO_4 + H_2$$

Like aluminium, zinc is amphoteric, so it reacts also with alkalis:

$$Zn + 2NaOH \rightarrow Na_2ZnO_2 + H_2$$
$$\text{sodium zincate}$$

The main use of zinc is in galvanising iron to inhibit corrosion, and this is usually done by dipping the article to be covered into a bath of molten zinc. The zinc protects the iron in two ways; firstly by excluding air and moisture from the surface of the iron so that it cannot oxidise. Secondly (and this is relevant when the iron becomes old and scratched), since zinc is more electropositive (higher up the electrochemical series) than iron, it oxidises and forms ions in preference to the iron, which is thus still protected. Everyday galvanised articles include dustbins and buckets, water tanks and electricity pylons.

Composition and Uses of some Alloys		
Alloy	Percentage composition (*)	Uses
Brass	70 Cu, 30 Zn	ornaments, bearings, screws, bulb caps
Bronze	85 Cu, 15 Sn	bearings
Cupro-nickel	75 Cu, 25 Ni	'silver' coins
Coinage bronze	97 Cu, 2.5 Zn, 0.5 Sn	copper coins
Constantan	60 Cu, 40 Ni	electric fire elements
18 carat gold	75 Au, 25 Cu	jewellery
Solder	60 Sn, 40 Pb	joining wires and pipes
Duralium	96 Al, 4 Cu	kitchen utensils, aircraft
Alnico	Fe, Al, Ni, Co	permanent magnets

(*) These are approximate as variations are common

Questions

Q.17.7   In the extraction of aluminium from its ore, the ore is crushed and dissolved in hot sodium hydroxide. The solution which is formed is filtered and the filtrate 'seeded' with aluminium hydroxide. The precipitate which forms is collected and roasted to about 1000°C, producing alumina. This compound is dissolved in fused cryolite and electrolysed, whereupon aluminium is formed.

(a)   What is the name of the ore of aluminium?

(b)   What aluminium compound does it contain?

(c)   Why is the ore crushed?

(d)   What aluminium compound is formed on reaction with the sodium hydroxide?

(e)   What substances are filtered off?

(f)   What is the purpose of seeding?

(g)   What substance is precipitated on seeding?

(h)   What is driven off when this substance is roasted?

(i)   Why is such a high temperature needed?

(j)   What is the formula for alumina?

(k)   Why is the alumina dissolved in fused cryolite?

(l)   What does 'fused' mean?

(m)   Of what material is the cell (i) anode, (ii) cathode made ?

(n)   At which electrode is aluminium formed?

(o)   Give the equation for the reaction at this electrode.

(p)   Is this reaction an oxidation, a reduction, or neither ? Why?

(q)   What substance is formed at the other electrode ?

(r)   Give the equation to show how this substance is formed.

(s)   How is the electrolyte kept molten?

(t)   Why is aluminium extracted by electrolysis rather than using coke (as is the case for iron and zinc)?

(u)   One of the electrodes has to be replaced at intervals. Which electrode is this, and why?

(v)   Name a by-product of the process.

(w)   Although aluminium is high in the electrochemical series, it is quite resistant to corrosion. Why?

(x)   How can its resistance to corrosion be further increased?

(y)   How is this process carried out?

(z)   Calculate the length of time needed to produce 1 kg of aluminium, when the current through the cell is 30,000 amperes.

Q.17.8   In the blast furnace, iron is produced from iron ore. In the process a mixture of three substances, the ore, the fuel, and a third substance, is fed into the top of the furnace.

(a)   Name and give the formula for a common ore of iron.

(b)   What substance is used to heat the furnace?

(c)   Write an equation to show how this substance produces the heat.

(d)   What gas converts the iron ore to iron?

(e)   Show how this gas is formed.

(f)   Write an equation for the iron ore to iron reaction.

(g)   Is this reaction an oxidation, a reduction or neither?

(h)   Why is air blown into the furnace?

(i)   Where is it blown in?

(j)   Why is hot air used?

(k)   Name the third material added at the top of the furnace.

(l)   Write an equation to show what happens to this substance when it is heated.

(m)   What is the purpose of this substance?

(n)   What would be the effect on the process of not adding this third substance?

(o)   In what part of the furnace does the iron collect?

(p)   In addition to the iron, another substance collects here. What is this substance and how is it formed?

(q)   For what is it used?

(r)   What two gases are expelled from the furnace, and from what part of it?

(s)   One of these gases is used in the process. Which gas is this and for what is it used.

(t)   What is the name given to the crude iron produced by the blast furnace?

(u)   What are the main impurities in this iron?

(v)   What effect do these impurities have on the iron?

(w)   How are these impurities removed when iron is made into steel?

(x)   In steel manufacture, huge quantities of a common non-metallic element are required. What element is this, and what is its source.

(y)   What other element, in addition to iron, is contained in steel.

(z)   Why is most of the iron from the blast furnace immediately made into steel?

Q.17.9   Pure copper is manufactured in two main stages : (i) the extraction of the metal from its ore (smelting), and (ii) purification of the crude copper by electrolysis.

(a)   Name the main ore of copper.

(b)   In addition to the copper, what other elements are normally present?

(c)   What is the chemical formula of the ore?

(d)   In the first stage of smelting, the ore is heated in air. To what is it converted in this process.

(e)   What gas is a by-product of this stage?

(f)   For what is this gas normally used?

(g)   What solid is then added in order to remove the other metal which is present.

(h)   What useful by-product is formed and for what is it used?

(i)   What reaction takes place in the last stage of the extraction process?

(j)   What impurities are still present in the crude copper?

(k)   What electrolyte is used in the purification process?

(l)   What material forms the cathode of the electrolysis cell?

(m)   Write an equation for the cathode reaction.

(n)   Of what substance is the anode made?

(o)   Write an equation for the anode reaction.

(p)   At which electrode is the pure copper formed?

(q)   At which electrode does oxidation occur? Why?

(r)   How does the concentration of the electrolyte change during the process?

(s)   What change (if any) can be seen during the electrolysis?

(t)   What impurities are recovered from the electrolysis process?

Q.17.10

(a) Copper is purified by electrolysis. Calculate the mass of pure copper formed in this process by a current of 3000 A flowing for 1 hour.

(b) Mention three uses of copper in everyday life, and say which property of the metal makes it suitable for each of these used.

(c) Describe what you would see if copper(II) nitrate crystals [$Cu(NO_3)_2 3H_2O$] were heated until no further change occurred. Name the products formed, and write equations for the two reactions which take place.

Q.17.11 Give the name and formula for a common ore of zinc and describe the chemistry involved in extracting zinc from it. Mention two industrial uses of zinc. How would you prepare a sample of zinc oxide from zinc? What is meant by the statement 'zinc oxide is amphoteric'? Illustrate your answer with chemical equations.

Q.17.12 Describe the changes which take place when: (a) zinc carbonate is strongly heated in air; (b) excess zinc is placed in copper(II) sulphate solution; (c) zinc is added to dilute sulphuric acid; (d) zinc oxide is reacted with hydrochloric acid; (e) zinc oxide is heated with sodium hydroxide solution. What important property of zinc oxide is illustrated by the answers to (d) and (e)?

Q.17.14 Describe the characteristic properties of the transition elements and their compounds, illustrating your answer with examples. Would you classify zinc as a transition element? Explain your answer, mentioning relevant properties of this element and its compounds.

Q.17.14 Select five metals from: sodium, magnesium, aluminium, calcium, copper, iron, zinc — and for each metal (i) write its electronic configuration; (ii) give the name and formula for

the ore of the metal; (iii) write an equation showing how the metal is extracted from its ore; (iv) list two common uses of the metal.

Q.17.15 Which of the following properties makes aluminium suitable for each of the uses listed below; silvery colour; good heat conductor; good electrical conductor; resistant to corrosion; low density; malleable; ductile; non-poisonous; reducing agent;- (a) aircraft; (b) overhead electrical cables; (c) car cylinder head; (d) milk bottle tops; (e) 'silver' paint; (f) cooking utensils.

Give equations for the reactions of aluminium with (i) oxygen; (ii) chlorine; (iii) iron(III) oxide, stating what is oxidised and what is reduced in each case.

Review When you know chapter 17 you should be able to:

(a) Explain each of: metal, ore, electropositive, alkali metal, transition element, d-block element, anodising, alloy.

(b) Describe the properties of the alkali metals, the alkaline earth metals, sodium hydroxide, aluminium, iron, copper, zinc.

(c) State the ores of each of: sodium, magnesium calcium, aluminium, iron copper, zinc, and describe how each of these metals is extracted from its ore.

(d) Answer questions 17.7, 17.8 and 17.9.

(e) Describe how iron is converted to steel and why this is done.

(f) Know the characteristic properties of transition elements.

(g) State how and why aluminium is anodised.

(h) List the common uses of sodium, magnesium, calcium, aluminium, iron, copper, zinc.

Carbon is an element on which all life depends. All animal and vegetable matter, both alive and dead, is mainly composed of carbon compounds. Although the amount of carbon in the Earth's crust is less than 1%, it is one of the most widely distributed elements in nature — present virtually everywhere except in water.

Carbon occurs in the atmosphere as carbon dioxide, in the earth as fossil fuels — coal, petroleum and natural gas all of which are made up of carbon compounds; as diamonds and graphite which are pure carbon, and as metal carbonates in rocks, which are very widespread. The most abundant of the naturally occurring carbonates is calcium carbonate, $CaCO_3$, which occurs as limestone, chalk and marble. Most of the central plains of Ireland is limestone, with much in other parts as well. Dolomite, $CaCO_3MgCO_3$ is a double carbonate; it occurs widely and is named after the Dolomites in the Italian Alps; magnesite is $MgCO_3$ and along with dolomite is used as an ore for magnesium; siterite or 'spathic iron ore' is $FeCO_3$. Other carbonates which occurs naturally, but only in small quantities in rock veins and so are uneconomic to mine, are malachite $CuCO_3Cu(OH)_2$, calamine $ZnCO_3$ and witherite $BaCO_3$.

The Element Carbon

Carbon exists in several different forms — called **allotropes**. Graphite and diamond are pure forms of carbon, and the impure forms include charcoal, coke and lampblack.

Allotropes can be described as the different physical forms of the same element, due to different arrangements of the atoms of the element.

Graphite

Graphite which is the usual form of carbon, occurs in quantity in Sri Lanka, Germany and the U.S.A. Natural sources, however, cannot provide all that is needed, and most of today's graphite is manufactured. This is done by heating coke and sand to 2500 $^{\circ}$C when the following reactions occur:

$$SiO_2 + 3C \rightarrow SiC + 2CO$$

$$SiC \rightarrow Si + C$$

Graphite is a shiny black crystalline substance and is soft, slippery and a reasonably good conductor

18
Carbon in Nature

of electricity. It does not melt but sublimes at 3500°C. It is very unreactive and cannot be dissolved in any common solvent. Its structure has been determined by X-ray analysis, and has been shown to consist of layers of carbon atoms arranged in 6-membered rings. The layers can slide over one another, resulting in the slippery nature of graphite and its use as a lubricant (see figure 5.3, page 66).

Graphite is used for the brushes of electric motors and dynamos, for badminton racket frames, as electrodes for electrolysis and in dry batteries, as a lubricant (particularly for high temperature work where an oil would vaporise), in the core of certain types of nuclear reactor, and to make pencil 'lead'. For this latter purpose, it is mixed with clay and extruded through a small hole (rather like toothpaste being squeezed out of a tube) and then baked. The more graphite in the mixture the softer the lead; the lead for a 'B' pencil has, thus, more graphite in it than the lead for an 'H' pencil.

Diamond

Diamonds are found in igneous rocks, and most of the world's supply of them comes from South Africa. When they come out of the ground, they look like small shiny pebbles and it requires skilled craftsmen to split, cut and polish them before they have the shape and sparkle that one associates with diamonds.

Diamond's structure is a lattice of carbon atoms, in which each atom is joined by covalent bonds to four other atoms, to form a 3-dimensional structure which is very rigid and hard. A diamond crystal is really a single giant molecule. Diamond is the hardest natural substance known. It is chemically very unreactive, (see figure 5.2 page 66).

It has an unusually high refractive index (2.4); this gives diamond its characteristic sparkle and is why it is used as a gemstone — although only about one fifth of the world's diamonds are used in this way. The main use of diamonds results from their extreme hardness, and is for cutting and drilling purposes. Saws used for cutting glass and concrete have teeth which are tipped with diamond, and rock drills such as those used for boring oil wells are diamond tipped also. Most glass cutters contain a small diamond and record players often have a diamond as a stylus.

18.1 — *An oil well drill bit*

Charcoal

Charcoal is a black powdery solid which can be made by heating wood out of contact with air. It is often stated as being non-crystalline, but modern X-ray analysis has shown that it in fact consists of tiny fragments of graphite, but in a disordered arrangement. In bulk therefore, charcoal can be regarded as non-crystalline. Charcoal readily combines with oxygen and so is a good reducing agent. On heating a mixture of lead oxide and charcoal for example, metallic lead is formed, and carbon dioxide liberated:

$$2PbO + C \rightarrow 2Pb + CO_2$$

Industrially, carbon (in the form of coke) is used for reducing the oxides of iron, zinc and lead to their metals. Charcoal has the ability of adsorbing coloured substances on its surface, and hence is a good decolorising agent, particularly for vegetable dyes. If a solution of litmus is boiled with some charcoal and then filtered, the filtrate will be a clear colourless liquid. Brown sugar is refined to white sugar in this way.

Properties of the Carbon Allotropes

In physical properties the allotropes differ considerably, but chemically they are all similar. Carbon is not a highly reactive element, but when heated it combines directly with some metals, and with oxygen, sulphur and fluorine. There are two common oxides, carbon monoxide and carbon dioxide. In a plentiful supply of air or oxygen, carbon burns to form carbon dioxide but in a limited air supply, the main product is the monoxide.

Physical Properties

Property	Diamond	Graphite	Charcoal
Form	Octahedral crystals	Hexagonal plates, metallic lustre	Amorphous (*i.e.* non crystalline)
Colour	Transparent when pure	Dark grey or black	Black
Hardness	Hardest natural substance	Soft and slippery	Variable, often brittle
Density (g/cm^3)	3.52	2.26	1.5 - 1.8
Electrical conductivity	Non-conductor	Conductor	Non-conductor

Carbon Dioxide

Carbon dioxide is formed whenever carbon or any of its compounds burns in a plentiful supply of air or oxygen:

$$C + O_2 \rightarrow CO_2$$
$$CH_4 + 2O_2 \rightarrow CO_2 + 2H_2O$$

It is also produced when any carbonate or hydrogencarbonate reacts with dilute acid, or is decomposed by being heated *e.g.*,

$$K_2CO_3 + H_2SO_4 \rightarrow CO_2 + K_2SO_4 + H_2O$$

$$Mg(HCO_3) + 2HCl \rightarrow 2CO_2 + MgCl_2 + 2H_2O$$

$$ZnCO_3 \xrightarrow{heat} CO_2 + ZnO$$

$$2NaHCO_3 \xrightarrow{heat} CO_2 + Na_2CO_3 + H_2O$$

In the laboratory, carbon dioxide is normally prepared by reacting either marble 'chips' (calcium carbonate) or sodium carbonate with dilute hydrochloric acid.

$$CaCO_3 + 2HCl \rightarrow CaCl_2 + CO_2 + H_2O$$

It is moderately soluble in water, but since it is slow to dissolve, it can be collected over water. However, if dry CO_2 is required, it should be collected by upwards displacement of air. Industrially, CO_2 is obtained by a by-product of fermentation processes, such as brewing, and also from lime kilns — in which limestone ($CaCO_3$) is roasted to produce quicklime (CaO)

Properties of Carbon Dioxide

CO_2 consists of linear covalent molecules, the oxygen atoms being joined by double bonds to the carbon atom in the centre, *i.e.*

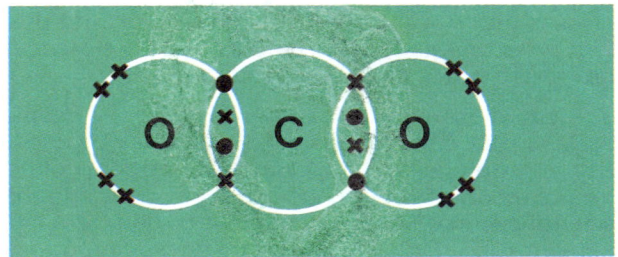

18.2

It is a colourless, odourless gas with a density of about $1\frac{1}{2}$ times that of air. It can be liquefied by just compressing it; at $15^{\circ}C$ a pressure of about 50 atmospheres causes it to condense and it can then be stored in cylinders. On being cooled to $-78^{\circ}C$, it freezes to a white solid which is known as 'dry ice'. This substance sublimes on being allowed to warm.

It neither burns nor supports normal combustion. Some vigorously burning substances (*e.g.* magnesium) will continue to burn in it, and when this happens, the CO_2 is reduced to either carbon or carbon monoxide:

$$2Mg + CO_2 \rightarrow 2MgO + C$$

It is moderately soluble in water with which it reacts to produce a solution of carbonic acid:

$$CO_2 + H_2O \rightarrow H_2CO_3$$

It is thus an acidic oxide (for a fuller description of the acidic properties of carbon dioxide, see the following section).

Uses of Carbon Dioxide

1.   Carbon dioxide is moderately soluble in water, but, under pressure, a much larger volume can be made to dissolve, producing 'soda water'. The sharp taste of this is due to the acidity of the gas. All fizzy drinks likewise contain dissolved carbon dioxide.

2.   Some types of fire extinguisher consist of a steel cylinder containing carbon dioxide under pressure. When directed at a fire and turned on, a blast of very cold gas strikes the fire, cools it and excludes the air, so the fire is unable to burn. No mess is made because there is no residue and this type of extinguisher can be used on an electrical fire where water would be dangerous.

3.   Another important use is as a cooling agent, and, for this, solid carbon dioxide ('dry ice') is used. Dry ice sublimes at -78 °C and is used for cooling ice cream and frozen foods during transit, and for scientific experiments which must be done at a low temperature. Dry ice leaves no mess, produces much lower temperatures then ordinary ice, and lasts much longer. It is also used to produce artificial 'smoke' on stage and in films.

4.   It is used in the manufacture of other chemicals like sodium hydrogencarbonate, urea and indigestion powders.

5.   It is used as a coolant in some types of nuclear reactor.

Carbon Monoxide ▬▬▬▬

Carbon monoxide is formed whenever carbon or carbon-containing compounds are burned in a limited supply of air. It can be prepared in the laboratory by reducing carbon dioxide with either charcoal or zinc powder (neither of these reducing agents is strong enough to reduce the CO_2 to carbon), or by dehydrating methanoic acid (using concentrated H_2SO_4)

$$CO_2 + C \rightarrow 2CO$$

$$CO_2 + Zn \rightarrow CO + ZnO$$

$$HCOOH \xrightarrow[-H_2O]{c.H_2SO_4} CO$$

It is insoluble in water and can be conveniently collected over water.

Properties of Carbon Monoxide

Its molecular structure is not simple, but the bonding is mainly covalent, and the molecules, having only two atoms, are linear.

It is a colourless odourless gas with a density almost the same as that of air, and it is insoluble in water.

It burns in air with a blue flame, forming carbon dioxide. A blue flame on top of the fuel in a charcoal burner, coke fire or closed anthracite stove is often visible. This is due to carbon monoxide burning. Carbon monoxide does not normally react with either acids or alkalis and is thus a neutral oxide [i]. It is a good reducing agent and is used industrially to reduce several metal ores to the metal, *e.g.* the blast furnace reaction:

$$Fe_2O_3 + 3CO \rightarrow 2Fe + 3CO_2$$

It is very poisonous as it combines with the haemoglobin in blood, making the blood unable to transport oxygen around the body. The fact that it is odourless makes it particularly dangerous, as one can be breathing it without being aware of it. The exhaust fumes of a car engine contain carbon monoxide and this is why a car engine should never be run in a closed garage.

Carbonic Acid/Carbonates / Hydrogencarbonates ▬▬▬▬

Carbon dioxide reacts reversibly with water, to form carbonic acid, which is a weak acid as it is only dissociated slightly in solution:

$$CO_2 + H_2O \rightleftharpoons H_2CO_3 \rightleftharpoons 2H^+ + CO_3^{2-}$$

(i)   Under pressure, carbon monoxide reacts with sodium hydroxide, to give sodium methanoate, so in this reaction, it is acting as an acidic oxide: $CO + NaOH \rightarrow HCOONa$

It is also an unstable acid and exists only in solution. Attempts to isolate it by evaporating the solution only causes it to decompose and form CO_2 again. Salts of carbonic acid, on the other hand, are both stable and important. There are two series of salts: normal carbonates, in which both of the hydrogen atoms of the acid have been replaced, and hydrogencarbonates, in which only one of the hydrogen atoms has been replaced.

The reaction of carbon dioxide with limewater [Ca(OH₂) solution] which is used as a test for the gas, is an acid-base reaction. The limewater becomes 'milky' owing to the formation of the insoluble salt calcium carbonate, which is formed as follows:

$$CO_2 + Ca(OH)_2 \rightarrow CaCO_3 + H_2O$$

With excess carbonic acid, *i.e.*, if carbon dioxide continues to be bubbled through the limewater, the calcium carbonate redissolves and becomes clear. This is due to the formation of calcium hydrogencarbonate, which is soluble (like all hydrogencarbonates):

$$CaCO_3 + CO_2 + H_2O \rightarrow Ca(HCO_3)_2$$

Calcium hydrogencarbonate is one of the compounds which causes temporary hardness in water (the chemistry of hard water is discussed in Chapter 21), and it is also responsible for the formation of stalactites and stalagmites. This latter process happens in two stages:

(i)   Rain containing dissolved carbon dioxide (therefore essentially carbonic acid) reacts with surface limestone and converts it to calcium hydrogencarbonate, as indicated by above equation. The latter compound is soluble and goes into solution in the rainwater. This rainwater permeates into the ground, and at times finds itself dripping from the roof of a cave.

(ii)   Where the solution evaporates, the calcium hydrogencarbonate decomposes, the above reaction is reversed, and calcium carbonate is deposited, a little at a time, on the roof and the floor of the cave, causing stalactites to grow downwards, and stalagmites to grow up. In time, these two can meet and form the type of pillar that can be seen in limestone caves.

18.3

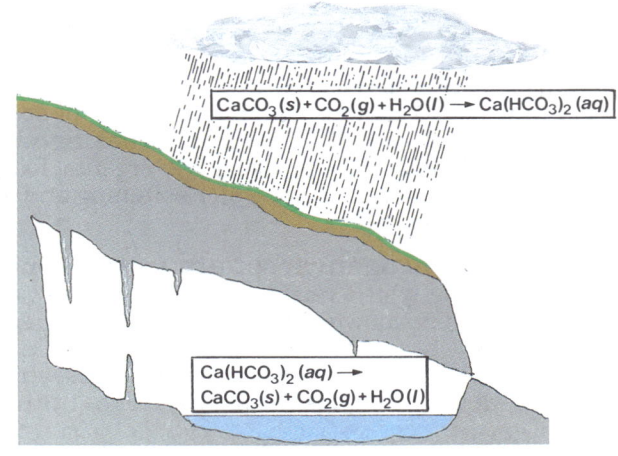

18.4

Carbon dioxide, on account of its being acidic, reacts readily with all alkalis; it is quickly absorbed by sodium hydroxide solution, forming sodium carbonate in solution:

$$2NaOH + CO_2 \rightarrow Na_2CO_3 + H_2O$$

or with excess of CO_2, forming sodium hydrogencarbonate:

$$NaOH + CO_2 \rightarrow NaHCO_3$$

All hydrogencarbonates, and most carbonates, decompose on being heated, and both evolve carbon dioxide on treatment with acid.

They can be distinguished from each other by adding magnesium sulphate solution. On doing this, a carbonate gives a white precipitate of magnesium carbonate, this salt being insoluble:

$$XCO_3 + MgSO_4 \rightarrow MgCO_3(\downarrow) + XSO_4$$

A hydrogencarbonate, on the other hand, yields no precipitate (all hydrogencarbonates being soluble), but when the solution is boiled, a precipitate is formed (because all hydrogencarbonates decompose on being heated, to give the corresponding carbonate:)

$$X(HCO_3)_2 + MgCO_3 \rightarrow Mg(HCO_3)_2 + XSO_4$$

$$Mg(HCO_3)_2 \xrightarrow{heat} MgCO_3(\downarrow) + H_2O + CO_2$$

Sodium Carbonate (or 'soda ash' as it is called) is an important substance in the chemical industry. Its main use is in the manufacture of glass, which is done by fusing a mixture of soda, limestone and sand. It is also used in making other chemicals drugs and dyes, soap, detergents, foods and drinks, waterglass, for water softening and for refining oil and gas.

Sodium hydrogencarbonate (or 'bicarbonate of soda' to many) is a raising agent used in baking. On its own it is known as breadsoda, and, on being heated in a bread mix which is being cooked, it decomposes and liberates carbon dioxide, which lifts the dough and gives the bread its light texture:

$$2NaHCO_3 \rightarrow Na_2CO_3 + CO_2 + H_2O$$

A mixture of sodium hydrogencarbonate and tartaric acid (a weak edible acid) is called 'baking powder' and this acts in two ways: the hydrogencarbonate decomposes as already described, and then the acid reacts with the resulting carbonate and liberates more carbon dioxide.

It is also used as a remedy for indigestion, neutralising excess of acidity in the stomach, and is present in many commercial preparation such as *Alka Seltzer*.

Limestone, which is nearly pure calcium carbonate, is a sedimentary rock, precipitated over long periods of time from the sea, and also formed from layers of shells and coral being compressed and hardened. For the chemical industry, it is a cheap, readily available and very important raw material. It is used directly in the extraction of iron from its ore in the blast furnace (see page 219) and in the manufacture of cement and concrete and of glass materials which are of great importance in the modern age.

When limestone is roasted in a limekiln, carbon dioxide is liberated, and 'quicklime' (CaO) is formed. Most of this is then 'slaked' (*i.e.* reacted with the right amount of water) to form calcium hydroxide or 'slaked lime' $Ca(OH)_2$

$$CaCO_3 \rightarrow CaO + CO_2$$

$$CaO + H_2O \rightarrow Ca(OH)_2$$

Slaked lime is used for making mortar for building, for neutralising acidic soils (so that crops can be grown properly) and for neutralising acidic wastes from various industrial processes, before they can be discharged.

The Carbon Cycle

The atmosphere contains a reasonably constant 0.03% of carbon dioxide, despite the fact that enormous amounts of carbon and carbon compounds (*i.e.* fossil fuels) are continuously being burnt and so producing CO_2, and that the 10^9 human inhabitants of the Earth, along with all the other animals present, are continually breathing out and producing more CO_2. Counteracting this addition of carbon dioxide to the atmosphere is photosynthesis — the reaction in which green plants using the Sun's energy, absorb CO_2 and moisture to produce carbohydrates and liberate oxygen. This interchange of carbon in the form of various compounds between the earth and the atmosphere is called the Carbon Cycle.

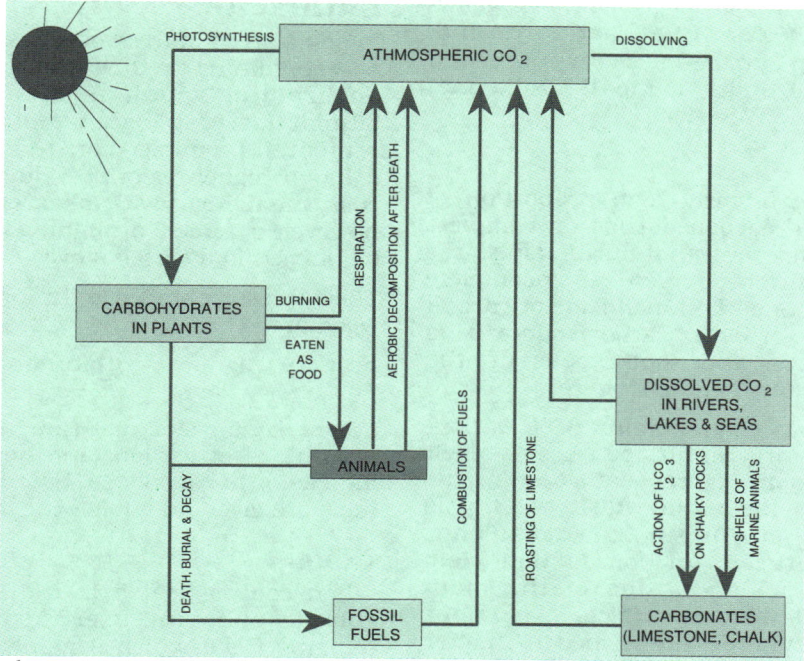

18.5 — *The carbon cycle*

Fossil Fuels

The stored chemical energy in most of today's fuels originally came from the Sun. Through the ages, plant and animal remains have been buried underground and compressed to become our supply of coal, oil, natural gas and peat. These fuels are known as fossil fuels, and there is little or no doubt as to how they were formed.

About 300 million years ago, huge forests covered coastal areas. In what is now Europe, the climate was much warmer and there were large areas of dense forests of trees, ferns and mosses. These died and were replaced by others, and in time thick layers of plant matter, called peat, covered the forest floor. Following geographical changes, the sea gradually swept through these forests, covering everything with mud and sand. Thousands of years later, the seas retreated and new forests grew. All this happened many times over millions of years and so the layers of decayed vegetation were buried deeper and deeper under layers of mud and sand. The compressed peat slowly turned into coal, first of all to a soft brown coal called lignite, and then, under further extremes of temperature and pressure, into bituminous coal, the ordinary black coal in common use today.

Man has used coal since ancient times. Originally it was dug from seams near the surface — this method is called open-cast mining. It is only in the last 250 years or so that deep underground mines have been sunk to extract the coal from far beneath the Earth's surface.

As vegetation decays (and so as the peat turns into coal) methane is formed. This gas, known to many miners as 'fire damp', often occurs with coal (and oil) deposits, having been trapped under layers of impervious rocks. In the 19th century, before the use of electric light in coal mines, it was dreaded by miners on account of the explosive mixture which it forms with air and many accidents in mines were due to it. It was because of this that Sir Humphrey Davy invented the miners' safety lamp in 1815.

Over the ages, huge quantities of methane have collected in porous sandstone, trapped beneath impervious rocks. These reservoirs have been found in many places — the Sahara, the North Sea, Holland, many areas in the U.S.A. and, more recently, off the south coast of Ireland. In much of the U.K at present, the supply of domestic gas is natural gas from the North Sea, and in Ireland, Kinsale gas is being supplied to many towns and cities, *e.g.* Cork, Dublin, Dundalk, Kilkenny, Limerick, Mallow and Waterford.

Coal

Most fuels contain a fairly high proportion of carbon and so yield carbon dioxide on complete combustion. It is important that burning fuels are supplied with sufficient oxygen, as incomplete combustion produces carbon monoxide or carbon in the form of soot, or both. Carbon monoxide is extremely poisonous and soot blocks up the chimneys and pollutes the atmosphere.

Ordinary bituminous coal contains 86% carbon, and burns satisfactorily in an open fire — albeit very inefficiently, since more heat goes up the chimney than into the room which the fire is heating. Coal too, contains sulphur and sulphur compounds, and these, on combustion yield sulphur dioxide, which is one of the main atmospheric pollutants. The effects of sulphur dioxide in the atmosphere are described in Chapter 22.

Anthracite

In some areas of the world, a very hard and shiny coal containing up to 96% carbon is found. This is anthracite, which is older in origin than bituminous coal. Because of the higher carbon content, it produces more heat per unit mass (*i.e.* it has a higher 'calorific value') than bituminous coal, and it burns with a smokeless flame. It needs however, a 'forced' draught, which means it must be burned in a closed stove.

The successive stages in the formation of coal from wood are:

peat $\rightarrow$ lignite $\rightarrow$ bituminous coal $\rightarrow$ anthracite,

the percentage of moisture decreasing and the percentage of carbon (and hence calorific value) increasing at each stage. Calorific values of several fuels are given on a following table.

Coke

When coal is heated in the absence of air, the volatile substances are driven off and coke remains. Coke, which is mainly carbon, is light and porous and burns cleanly, and it is an important

18.6 — *Powered rotary cutters in a coal mine.*

industrial fuel as well as an important reducing agent. Also produced from coal in the coking process is coal gas; this was widely used in the 19th century for lighting, and well into the 20th century for domestic heating and cooking, but with the advent of electricity and the wider use of oil products, its use for these purposes has virtually died out. Town gas of today is either natural gas or is made from naptha, a petroleum product.

Kilogram Calorific Values

The kilogram calorific value of a fuel is a measure of the heat output of the fuel when it is burned. This topic is described in the chapter on Thermochemistry (see. p. 179) and a list of kilogram calorific values for many of the common fuels is given.

Questions

Q.18.1 Give short answers to each of the following questions:

(a) Define allotropes.
(b) State two important uses of graphite.
(c) Name a non-crystalline allotrope of carbon.
(d) What two compounds are usually reacted together to prepare carbon dioxide?
(e) What is the shape of a carbon dioxide molecule?
(f) Write an equation for the reaction between magnesium carbonate and sulphuric acid.
(g) What is the main component of Kinsale gas?
(h) Name and give the chemical formula for the solute in limewater.
(i) What is the milky substance formed when carbon dioxide is bubbled through limewater?
(j) Why does breadsoda make bread rise?
(k) Describe a test by which carbon monoxide could be distinguished from hydrogen.
(l) Name a solid fossil fuel and state its approximate composition.
(m) Write an equation to show the use of carbon monoxide as a reducing agent.
(n) The fuel coke consists mainly of what substance?
(o) What happens to a solution of calcium hydrogencarbonate when it is heated?
(p) What compound is formed when methanoic acid is dehydrated?
(q) Name a suitable dehydrating agent for (p).
(r) What substance can be used to distinguish between solutions of a carbonate and of a hydrogencarbonate.
(s) Name two ways in which atmospheric carbon dioxide is returned to the ground.
(t) What is the formula for limestone? What is formed when it is heated?

Q.18.2
(a) List three contrasting properties of diamond and graphite;
(b) Explain what is meant by a 'crystal lattice'. Draw diagrams of the crystal lattice of both diamond and graphite, and explain how these lattices account for the differences in properties of the two allotropes.

Q.18.3 Diamond and graphite are allotropes of carbon. Explain why:

(a) diamond has a greater density than graphite;
(b) diamond is much harder than graphite;
(c) diamond is a non-conductor of electricity, but graphite is a conductor;
(d) great pressure is necessary in making diamond from graphite.

Q.18.4 Describe what is observed when carbon dioxide is bubbled into limewater until no further change occurs. Explain using equations, the changes which occur.

Q.18.5 Write equations for each of the following reactions:

(a) the burning of carbon in air;
(b) the burning of propane (C_3H_8) in air;
(c) the reduction of lead oxide by carbon monoxide;
(d) the action of carbon dioxide on limewater;
(e) the reaction of nitric acid with barium carbonate;
(f) the effect of heat on sodium hydrogencarbonate;
(g) the reaction of sodium carbonate with magnesium sulphate solution;
(h) the reaction between carbon dioxide and potassium hydroxide solution.

Q.18.6 A substance is thought to be either sodium carbonate or sodium hydrogencarbonate. Describe chemical tests which could be carried out in order to decide which substance it is. Give equations for any reactions mentioned.

Q.18.7 State two ways in which carbon dioxide is constantly being added to the atmosphere. Why does the amount of this gas in the atmosphere remain at about 0.03%? Mention three important uses of carbon dioxide.

Q.18.8

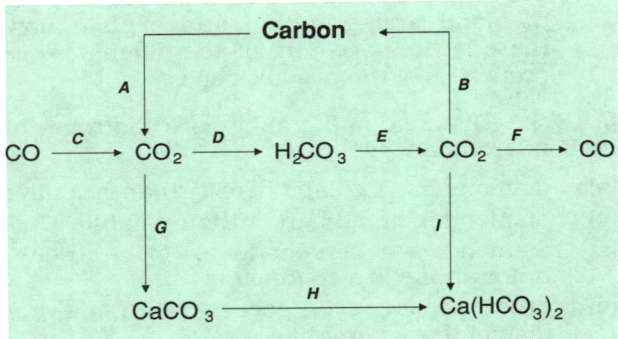

For each of the conversions **A** to **I** in the above scheme (i) state briefly how the conversion can be carried out, naming any other reagent used; (ii) write an equation for the reaction. (Diagrams and description of apparatus are not required).

Q.18.9 Name three elements present in coal, and describe how coal was formed in the earth. Describe what happens when coal is strongly heated in the absence of air. What are the various substances which are formed?

Review When you know Chapter 18, you should be able to:

(a) State the different ways in which carbon and its compounds occur in Nature,

(b) Define allotropes; list the allotropes of carbon, and say how they differ.

(c) Describe how carbon dioxide and carbon monoxide can be prepared.

(d) Describe the properties and reactions of carbon dioxide and carbon monoxide

(e) Explain how carbon dioxide reacts with water and with limewater.

(f) Explain the difference between metal carbonates and hydrogencarbonates, describe the effect of heat on them, and tell how to distinguish between them.

(g) Write the formula for limewater, limestone, carbonic acid, and any metal carbonate or hydrogencarbonate.

(h) Describe the carbon cycle.

(i) Describe the differences between coal, anthracite, and coke.

(j) Define the kilogram calorific value.

After oxygen, nitrogen is probably the next most essential element for life, for it is one of the constituent elements in proteins, and proteins are vital to all living things. They are the material from which much of animal bodies consist; skin, muscle and hair are all made of protein, and without it, animals could not grow or maintain healthy bodies. Nitrogen occurs free (*i.e.* uncombined) in nature, making up about 78% of the atmosphere. It consists of diatomic molecules which are extremely stable, and in which the two atoms are held together by a triple covalent bond:

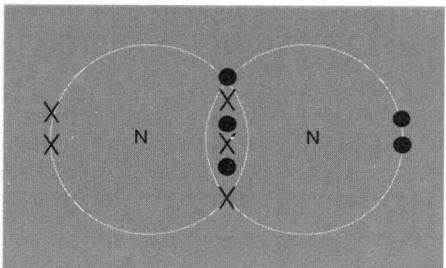

19.1 — *(N₂ molecule)*

Chemically, nitrogen gas is rather inert (unreactive) and combines directly with few other elements, but its compounds are of immense importance in today's world.

Fixation of Nitrogen

This is the name given to any process in which atmospheric nitrogen is made to combine with other elements to make useful compounds. Fixation of nitrogen occurs to a small extent in nature, but artificial fixation is done on a massive scale during the manufacture of ammonia.

At very high temperatures, nitrogen and oxygen combine together to form nitrogen monoxide, NO. This happens during thunderstorms when the flash of lightning provides the high temperature:

$$N_2 + O_2 \rightarrow 2NO \qquad \Delta H = +180 \text{ kJ}$$

Nitrogen monoxide combines with oxygen from the air to form nitrogen dioxide (NO_2), which then dissolves in rainwater to give a mixture of nitrous and nitric acids (HNO_2 and HNO_3). In this way, a considerable amount of atmospheric nitrogen is brought to earth and deposited in the soil. The presence of nitrogen compounds in the soil is an essential requirement for healthy plant growth and so fixation of nitrogen is of considerable importance to agriculture and food production.

19
Nitrogen and its Compounds

Some plants are able to fix nitrogen naturally, but the amount of nitrogen fixed by both plants and lightning is not nearly adequate for today's needs.

In the late 19th century, a search started for an artificial means of nitrogen fixation, and the first successful process, conceived by two Norwegians, Birkeland and Eyde, was basically just a copy of natural fixation. Instead of lightning (as in nature), an electric arc was used to produce the high temperature necessary to make the nitrogen and oxygen combine together. The yield was small but electric power in Norway was cheap. Birkeland and Eyde's process is now obsolete, having being superseded by better and less costly methods, particularly the **Haber process** in which atmospheric nitrogen is combined with hydrogen to make ammonia. Named after Fritz Haber, the German chemist who discovered how to make the two elements combine together directly, this process was developed commercially in Germany during World War 1, largely to provide nitric acid for the manufacture of explosives, and fertilisers which were needed for food production.

The Haber Process - Manufacture of Ammonia

At ordinary temperatures and pressures there is little reaction between nitrogen and hydrogen, but under pressure they combine (reversibly), forming an equilibrium mixture of nitrogen, hydrogen and ammonia:

$$N_2 + 3H_2 \rightleftharpoons 2NH_3 \qquad \Delta H = -92 \text{ kJ}$$

The amount of ammonia in the equilibrium mixture depends on both temperature and pressure, and in accordance with Le Chatelier's Principle (Chapter 13), the higher the pressure, the greater is the percentage of ammonia present. It would therefore appear best to carry out the reaction at the highest possible pressure. However, with increasing pressure, the cost of industrial plants becomes much greater — reaction vessels and pipes have to be thicker, and compressors have to be more powerful. So the chemical engineers have to decide on a compromise between high yield at high cost, and lower yield at lower cost. In practice, most Haber processes are operated at about 200 atmospheres pressure.

The reaction is exothermic and so the lower the temperature the more ammonia will be present in the equilibrium mixture. Contrary to this though is the fact that the lower the temperature, the longer is the time taken for the reaction to reach equilibrium; it would therefore be uneconomical to carry it out at too low a temperature. A compromise has again to be made, this time between a high yield after a long time, and a lower yield in a shorter time. About 550°C is the usual operating

19.2

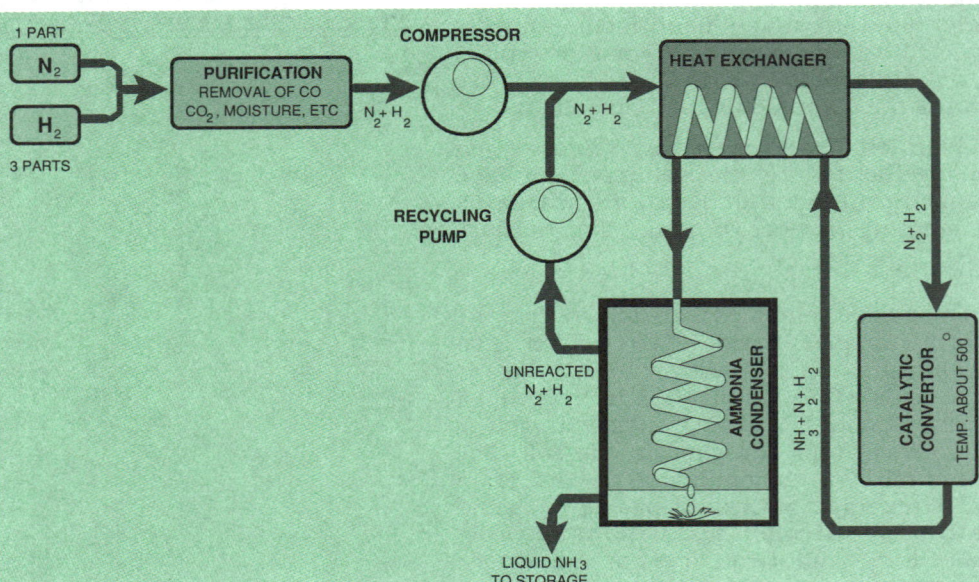

temperature for the process. Suitable catalysts however, increase the rate to make it worthwhile, even at 550°C. The catalyst used is finely divided iron, mixed with some aluminium and potassium oxides, which act as promoters.

The schematic diagram shows the stages in the whole process. Hydrogen is obtained from the steam reforming of either natural gas or naptha (see page 251), and the nitrogen comes from the atmosphere. The gases are purified and compressed, and then passed through a heat exchanger where they are heated up to the required 550°C or thereabouts. In the converter, the hot gases pass over the catalyst, where reaction takes place and some ammonia is formed. Since the reaction is exothermic, the gases leaving the converter are at a higher temperature than those entering. They are cooled by being passed through the heat exchanger, in which they give up their surplus heat to heat the gases coming into the converter. Finally, the mixture of gases is cooled, causing the ammonia (which is still under pressure) to liquefy, whence it is run off to storage. The unreacted nitrogen and hydrogen are continuously recycled, so that eventually all of the incoming gases are converted to ammonia. A photograph of the N.E.T. ammonia plant at Marino Point, Cork is shown on page 14.

Laboratory Preparation and Properties

Ammonia is conveniently prepared by reacting any ammonium salt with an alkali, *e.g.*

$$NH_4Cl + NaOH \rightarrow NH_3 + NaCl + H_2O$$

The alkali removes the H^+ from the NH_4^+ ion in the salt, which therefore becomes NH_3, so, effectively, the reaction can be represented by :

$$NH_4^+ + OH^- \rightarrow NH_3 + H_2O$$

Ammonia cannot be dried by any of the usually drying agents, because it reacts with them. It is normally dried by passing it through a container of calcium oxide, which absorbs moisture. It cannot be collected over water because it is highly soluble in it, but being less dense than air, it can be collected by downwards displacement of air.

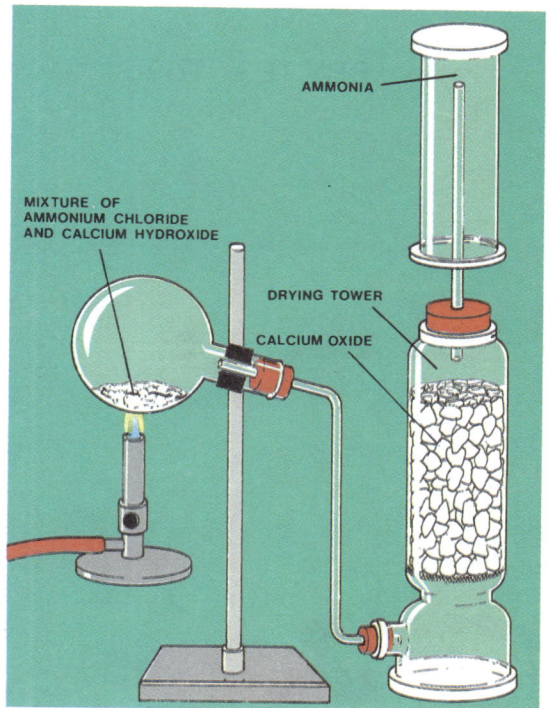

19.3

Experiment 19.1
Investigating properties of Ammonia

Prepare some ammonia as follows. Mix 5-10 grams of ammonium sulphate (or chloride) with about the same amount of calcium hydroxide. Arrange the apparatus as shown. Gently heat the mixture until a piece of damp red litmus paper at the mouth of the collecting test tube turns blue. Then remove the test tube and put a cork in it. Collect three more tubes of the gas in a similar manner. These test tubes must be quite dry.

(1) Complete the equation for the reaction:
     $Ca(OH)_2 \quad + \quad \rightarrow \quad + \quad \rightarrow$
(2) What colour is the gas?
(3) Smell it carefully and describe its smell.

Find out how soluble it is in water by placing a test tube of the gas, mouth downwards, in water and then removing the cork.
(4) What happens?
(5) Why?
(6) Is the solution in water acidic or alkaline?

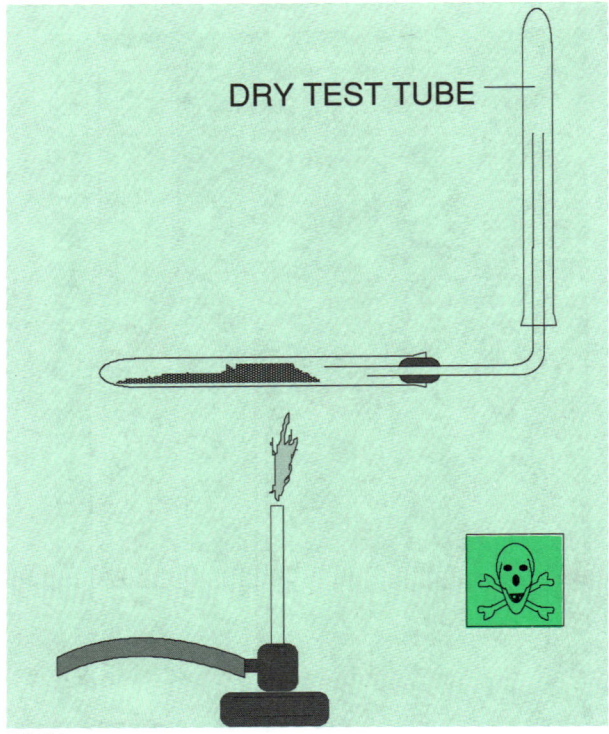

DRY TEST TUBE

19.4

Devise a method of showing that the gas is less dense than air.

(7) Describe how you do this, and say what the conclusion is.

(8) Does the gas burn?

(9) Does it support combustion?

Dip a glass rod into concentrated hydrochloric acid and then place it in a test tube of ammonia.

(10) Describe the appearance of the substance formed. This substance is formed by the direct combination of ammonia and hydrogen chloride.

(11) Write the equation for the reaction and name the product.

Some ammonium salts undergo 'thermal dissociation' (dissociation on being heated). Heat a small quantity of ammonium chloride in a test tube, held in a sloping position, and observe carefully what happens. The space above the solid contains the two gases which are combined together to form the salt. The reaction here is thus the reverse of what happened in the last test.

(12) Write an equation for the change which occurs on heating.

Properties of Ammonia

Ammonia is a colourless gas with a characteristic, pungent smell, it is less dense than air (approximately one-half air) and is extremely soluble in water. It does not normally burn and does not support combustion. The molecule, which is covalent and pyramidal in shape (see Figs. 4.4 and 5.9) contains a lone pair of electrons, which means that it can accept a proton and form the NH_4^+ ion:

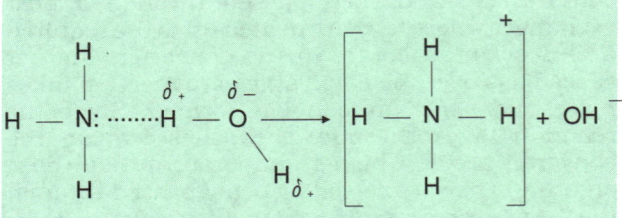

Ammonia, therefore, is a base. When dissolved in water, the following reactions occurs, but the position of equilibrium lies very much to the left:

$$NH_3 + H_2O \rightleftharpoons NH_4^+ + OH^-$$

weak base   strong conjugate acid

It neutralises acids and forms salts:

$$2NH_3 + H_2SO_4 \rightarrow (NH_4)_2SO_4$$

$$NH_3 + HCl \rightarrow NH_4Cl$$

This latter reaction is utilised in testing for both ammonia and hydrogen chloride; when these two gases are brought into contact with each other, dense white fumes of ammonium chloride are formed. Thus to test whether an unknown gas is ammonia or not, hydrogen chloride is mixed with it and if dense white fumes are formed, then the unknown is ammonia.

Ammonia is an important industrial chemical. Its main use is in the manufacture of fertilisers e.g. ammonium sulphate, ammonium nitrate. It is used in industrial refrigeration plants and as a starting material for the manufacture of nitric acid (this is done by oxidising ammonia in the presence of a catalyst), certain plastics and glues.

Domestically, ammonia solution is used as a grease solvent.

Nitric Acid

Nitric acid is manufactured on a large scale by the catalytic oxidation of ammonia. There are three main stages in the process:

Stage 1

A mixture of ammonia and an excess of air is passed through a platinum-rhodium gauze (the catalyst) at a temperature of about 900°C. This oxidises the ammonia to nitrogen monoxide:

$$4NH_3 + 5O_2 \rightarrow 4NO + 6H_2O \quad \Delta H = -903 \text{ kJ}$$

The reaction is exothermic and the heat evolved keeps the catalyst at the high temperature required, and as well is used to generate steam for use in other parts of the factory. A 96-98% conversion is achieved.

Stage 2

In this stage the nitrogen monoxide is cooled, and it then spontaneously combines with more oxygen (from the air) to form nitrogen dioxide:

$$2NO + O_2 \rightarrow 2NO_2$$

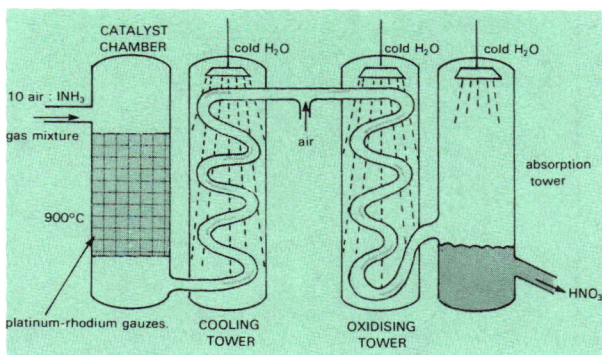

19.5 — *The industrial manufacture of nitric acid.*

Stage 3

Here, the nitrogen dioxide is reacted with water and more oxygen (again from the air) to form nitric acid:

$$4NO_2 + O_2 + 2H_2O \rightarrow 4HNO_3$$

This is done in large adsorption towers in which the gases are forced upwards through the solution which in turn descends, and so thorough mixing occurs. Acid containing 68% HNO_3 can be produced and this is the usual concentration of 'concentrated nitric acid'

Properties of Nitric Acid

Nitric acid is a clear, colourless liquid, although it is often coloured pale yellow because of some dissolved nitrogen dioxide. The normal concentrated acid contains about 68% HNO_3, has a density of 1.4 g/cm^3 and boils at 86°C. It has an irritating pungent smell and is highly corrosive, Chemically, it acts both as an acid and as an oxidising agent.

1. As an acid:

It is a strong acid and shows the usual acidic properties. It ionises in solution, yielding H^+ ions and nitrate ions:

$$HNO_3 \rightarrow H^+ + NO_3^-$$

The solution thus conducts electricity. The dilute acid reacts with metal oxides, hydroxides and carbonates, forming the metal nitrate and water in each case, along with CO_2 in the case of carbonates.

2. As an oxidising agent:

It is a strong oxidising agent, and is normally reduced to either nitrogen monoxide (NO) or nitrogen dioxide (NO_2) as it oxidises. Which oxide is formed depends mainly on the concentration of the acid; concentrated acid tends to produce NO_2 and dilute acid normally yields NO.

$$2HNO_3 \rightarrow H_2O + 2NO_2 + [O] \searrow \text{ taken by the substance}$$
$$2HNO_3 \rightarrow H_2O + 2NO + 3[O] \nearrow \text{ being oxidised}$$

It reacts with metals, including those below hydrogen in the electrochemical series forming the metal oxide, one of the oxides of nitrogen and water. The metal oxide initially formed (being a base) then reacts with more acid, to form the metal nitrate and water.

The main use of nitric acid is in the manufacture of fertilisers (this takes about 75% of the acid). Another 15% is used in making explosives (most of which are nitrates, or organic compounds containing the nitro (NO_2) group, and the rest is used in making dyes, *Nylon*, *Terylene*, photographic chemicals and for refining certain metals.

Nitrates

Nitrates, which are the salts of nitric acid, are all crystalline solids and are soluble in water, in which they ionise to give NO_3^- ions, in addition to the metal ion. The stability of metal nitrates to heat depends on the position of the metal in the electrochemical series. Nitrates of metals high in the series (*e.g.* Na, K) are quite stable and are decomposed only to a small extent, being mainly converted to the corresponding nitrite, *e.g.*

$$KNO_3 \rightarrow KNO_2 + \frac{1}{2} O_2$$

Nitrates of metals lower down (from Ca to Cu) are decomposed, forming the metal oxide, nitrogen dioxide and oxygen, *e.g.*

$$Mg(NO_3)_2 \rightarrow MgO + 2NO_2 + \frac{1}{2} O_2$$

Nitrates of metals at the very bottom of the series are converted to the metal itself, *e.g.*

$$AgNO_3 \rightarrow Ag + NO_2 + \frac{1}{2} O_2$$

The decomposition of ammonium nitrate is a special case. On being heated, it decomposes into nitrous oxide, N_2O, and water (vapour):

$$NH_4NO_3 \rightarrow N_2O + 2H_2O$$

Nitrous oxide, commonly called 'laughing gas' is an anaesthetic and is manufactured in this way.

The 'Brown Ring' Test for Nitrates

Since all nitrates are soluble in water, they cannot be detected by the formation of a precipitate, as can chlorides and sulphates. The 'brown ring' test is done as follows.

A cold saturated solution of iron(II) sulphate is added to a solution of the substance and mixed. Concentrated sulphuric acid is then poured down the inside of the test tube to form a layer at the bottom. The formation of a brown ring at the junction of the two liquids confirms that the substance is a nitrate.

The reactions here are not simple, but basically are as follows:

The concentrated sulphuric acid on reaction with the nitrate yields nitric acid, which is reduced by the iron(II) ions to form nitrogen(II) oxide, NO. This then combines with iron(II) sulphate and forms the compound $FeSO_4NO$, which is the brown substance in the brown ring of the test.

Fertilisers

The Need for More Food

The world's population in 1980 was somewhere in the region of four billion (4×10^9) and it is growing at an enormous rate. At present, the rate of increase is about 80 million per year — more than the entire population of Ireland, England, Scotland and Wales. There is not enough food available for such an overpopulated world; while those that live in Europe are generally well fed, at least 400 million people in other parts of the world do not have enough to eat, and many more do not have the right kind of food. The pictures of starving people that one sees in the newspapers and on television from time to time are a grim reminder of this fact. So it is one of today's greatest problems, and therefore a challenge to man, that so many millions of people live on, or near the verge of starvation.

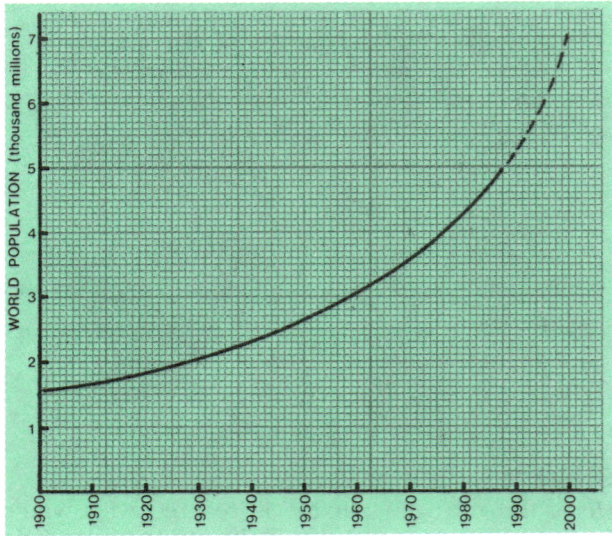

19.6

There is an urgent need to increase food production enormously. Most food comes from the ground, either directly (cereals, fruit, vegetables) or indirectly (meat, milk, eggs). However, the amount of land available for food production in the world is limited — many areas are unsuitable because of terrain, lack of water, too much heat, not enough heat, etc. and so it is imperative that the land which is available is used to its maximum capacity. Of the several ways of achieving this, the most important is by the use of suitable plant foods or fertilisers. When it is realised that fertilisers can treble crop yields, their importance becomes obvious.

19.7 — The grass in the centre of the picture has received no fertiliser.

Foods that grow consist mainly of carbohydrates and proteins. Carbohydrates, which are compounds composed of carbon, hydrogen and oxygen, are manufactured by photosynthesis, from the CO_2 in the air and the moisture in the soil (using sunlight as the energy source).

Proteins

Proteins are nitrogen-containing organic compounds build up from amino acids, and they form much of the body tissue of both plants and animals. Animals (including humans) acquire proteins from the food they eat. Meat, eggs, fish, milk, peas and beans are all high protein foods. Plants are the original source of all proteins because the cows, hens, fish, and other animals get their protein from the plants which they in turn eat. Plants, in order to manufacture protein, therefore need nitrogen.

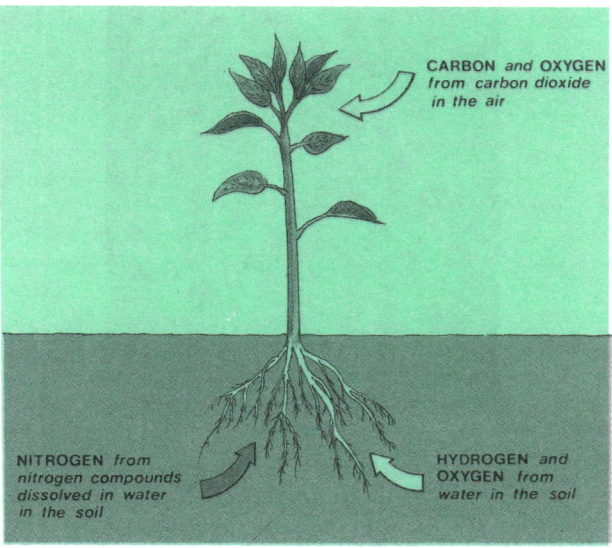

19.8 How a plant obtains the carbon, hydrogen, oxygen and nitrogen it needs.

Legumes

Some plants, notably those of the legume family (peas, beans, clover) have swellings called nodules on their roots. These nodules contain nitrogen-fixing bacteria that convert atmospheric nitrogen to nitrates, which can then be used by the plant as its nitrogen source.

Most plants however, cannot use the nitrogen from the air, it must be in the soil in the form of soluble nitrogen compounds (*e.g.* nitrates and ammonium salts) which the plant takes in through its roots. As crops are grown and harvested, nitrogen is removed from the soil, so unless it is replaced from time to time, the soil will run out of it and be of little use for agriculture.

Two of the several other elements which are needed by plants for healthy growth are phosphorus and potassium and these are also taken in through plant roots. Like nitrogen, compounds of these elements must also be added to the soil to keep it fertile. Phosphorus (in the form of phosphate) stimulates root development and early growth and

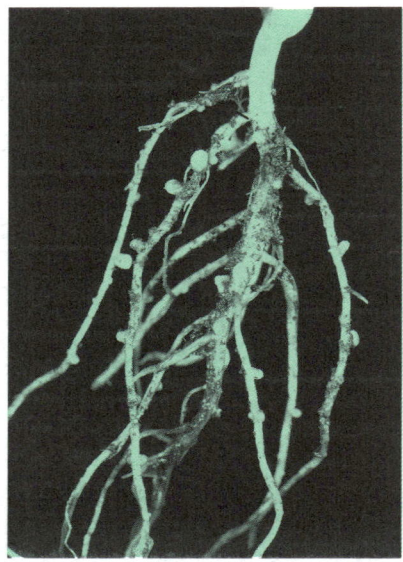

19.9

Chemical name	Commercial name	Formula	Percentage of nitrogen
Ammonium sulphate	Sulphate of ammonia	$(NH_4)_2SO_4$	21.2
Ammonium nitrate	'Nitram'	NH_4NO_3	34.5
Calcium ammonium nitrate	'Nitrochalk' 'C.A.N.'	NH_4NO_3 and $CaCO_3$	26
Urea		$CO(NH_2)_2$	46.6

Ammonium sulphate is made by neutralising ammonia with sulphuric acid, and ammonium nitrate is formed when ammonia is neutralised with nitric acid. Calcium ammonium nitrate contains ground limestone, which is present to reduce the acidity of an over-acidic soil (most plants grow best in soil whose pH is about 6.5). Urea is made by reacting carbon dioxide with ammonia, under pressure:

$$CO_2 + 2NH_3 \rightarrow CO(NH_2)_2 + H_2O$$

Apart from its use as a fertiliser, urea is also used in making textiles and adhesives and is an ingredient of urea-formaldehyde plastics.

helps crops to ripen earlier. Potassium is necessary for plants to make full use of all the nitrogen available in the soil and it also helps in the manufacture of carbohydrate and in maintaining resistance to drought and disease.

Element	Importance	Fertiliser containing it
Nitrogen	Growth of stems	KNO_3; $(NH_4)_2SO_4$; NH_4NO_3; urea; calcium ammonium nitrate
Phosphorus	Root growth	Ammonium phosphate; superphosphate
Potassium	Flowers	KCl, KNO_3

Nitrogen Fertilisers

There are a number of 'straight nitrogen' (nitrogen only) fertilisers, of which the more important are shown in the table.

Phosphate, Potash and 'Compound' Fertilisers

The main phosphorus fertilisers are ammonium phosphate (this is also a nitrogen source) and 'superphosphate' which is mainly $Ca(H_2PO_4)_2$. Phosphorus occurs naturally as phosphate rock, $Ca_3(PO_4)_2$, and comes mainly from Tunisia and Senegal. As such it is insoluble in water and therefore of little value as a fertiliser. Sulphuric acid converts phosphate rock to suitable soluble compounds which can be used as fertilisers:

$$H_2SO_4 + Ca_3(PO_4)_2 \rightarrow H_3PO_4 + CaSO_4$$
phosphoric acid

$$\downarrow NH_3$$

$(NH_4)_3PO_4$
ammonium phosphate

$$H_2SO_4 + Ca_3(PO_4)_2 \rightarrow Ca(H_2PO_4)_2 + CaSO_4$$
'superphosphate'

Potassium fertilisers are generally referred to as 'potash' fertilisers ; the most common is KCl, known to many farmers by its old chemical name of 'muriate of potash' (200 years ago, hydrochloric acid was called muriatic acid) Potassium chloride comes mainly from Germany and France, where it occurs naturally.

19.10 — A selection of fertilisers. The NPK value refers to the % of each of the three elements (i.e. N, P and K) present in the fertiliser.

Quite often a soil or a crop requires more than one plant food at a time and so it is an obvious economy of a farmer's time, labour and machinery to mix the fertilisers and spread them all at once. For this purpose, many 'compound' fertilisers are available. These contain all of the three main plant nutrients (N, P, K) but is must be pointed out that the name 'compound' fertiliser is a misnomer, since they are only mixtures of the various compounds which contain the required element.

Experiment 19.2
To determine the percentage of ammonia in an ammonium salt or fertiliser.

The most reliable method for the determination of ammonia in an ammonium salt (or an ammonium fertiliser) is as follows. A weighed amount of the salt is boiled with an excess of alkali. The liberated ammonia is passed into an excess but known amount of acid. The ammonia reacts with the acid and neutralises an equivalent amount of it. The excess of acid is then determined by titration with alkali, and hence the

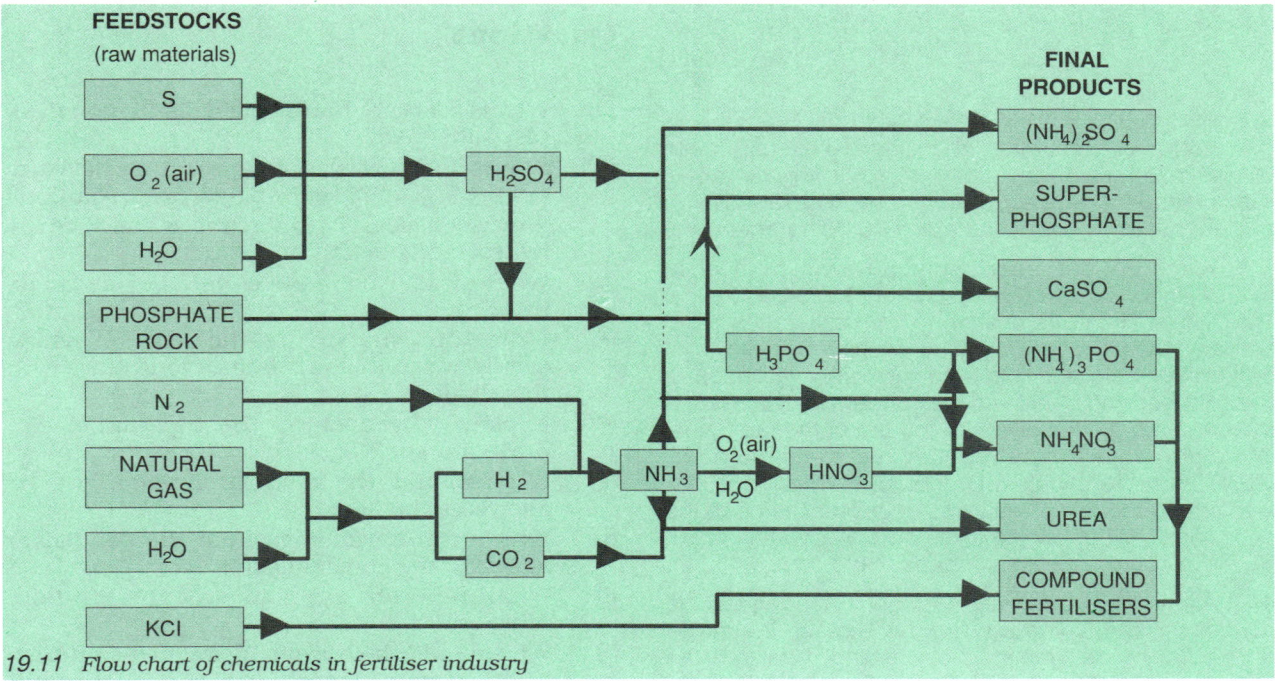

19.11 Flow chart of chemicals in fertiliser industry

amount used to neutralise the ammonia is found. From this, the amount of ammonia in the sample of the ammonium salt is calculated.

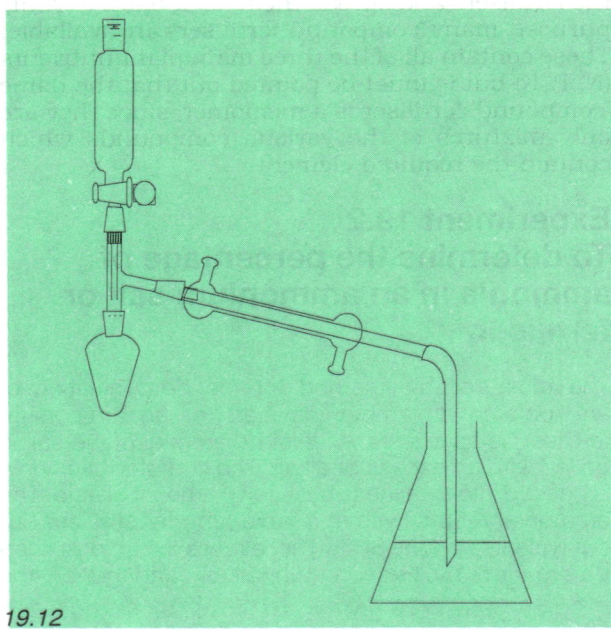

19.12

1.   Set up the apparatus as shown.

2.   Weigh out accurately about 2 g of the fertiliser into a distillation flask (a 100 cm³ flask, or larger, is recommended). Add about 25 cm³ of dilute (about 3 M) sodium hydroxide, and some anti-bumping agent.

3.   Measure out accurately 50 cm³ of 1.0 M hydrochloric acid (or 0.5 M sulphuric) into the conical flask. Slowly heat the mixture in the flask until it boils. Since ammonia is very soluble in water and even more so in dilute acid, there is a considerably likelihood of the acid 'sucking back' into the condenser. If this tends to happen, momentarily open the tap of the tap funnel in order to equalise the pressure. Let the mixture boil **GENTLY** for 10 minutes. Do not let the flask boil dry. Add small amounts of water, as necessary, through the tap funnel. When doing this, add the water **VERY SLOWLY**, otherwise a suck back may occur.

4.   Allow the apparatus to cool, disconnect the condenser and, using a wash bottle, wash the inside of the condenser, letting the washings run into the conical flask. Do the same with the delivery tube.

Transfer the solution from the conical flask to a 250 cm³ volumetric flask, taking whatever precautions are necessary to ensure that it is completely transferred. Make it up to exactly 250 cm³ with water.

5.   Titrate 25 cm³ samples of this solution with 0.1 M sodium hydroxide. Repeat until three consistent titres have been obtained.

6.   Empty the burette and wash it, first with some dilute acid and then with water.

Calculation of Results

Do this by working out each of:

(i)   the concentration of the excess acid solution,

(ii)   the actual amount (i.e. moles) of acid in the 250 cm³ of excess acid solution,

(iii)   the amount of acid taken initially (i.e. the amount in the 50 cm³ of 1.0 M HCl),

(iv)   the amount of acid used (to neutralise the ammonia),

(v)   the amount of ammonia liberated.

Hence find the mass of ammonia in the given salt. Express this as a percentage of the mass of the salt.

Questions

Q.19.1

(a)   Why is a larger-than-needed distillation flask recommended?

(b)   Why is it not necessary to accurately measure out the 25 cm³ of sodium hydroxide solution?

(c)   Why is it necessary to accurately measure the hydrochloric acid?

(d)   What measuring vessel should be used to do this?

(e)   Write the equation for the reaction which occurs when the ammonium ions react with the alkali.

(f)   Explain why opening the tap funnel can prevent a suck-back.

(g)   Why should the distillation flask not be allowed to boil dry?

(h)   Why are the washings from the condenser added to the conical flask?

(i)   What indicator is suitable for the titration; Why?

(j)   Why should the burette be washed with both acid and water at the end of the experiment?

Worked Example

3.0 g of a crushed fertiliser were placed in a distillation apparatus along with about 50 cm^3 of 2.0 M sodium hydroxide. The solution was boiled and the distillate absorbed into 50 cm^3 of 1.0 M hydrochloric acid contained in a conical flask. When the reaction had finished, the contents of the flask were transferred to a 250 cm^3 volumetric flask. The conical flask was washed and the washings were added to the volumetric flask also. The solution was then made up to exactly 250 cm^3, and mixed well. 25 cm^3 portions of this solution were titrated with 0.1 M sodium hydroxide and the mean titre was found to be 20.0 cm^3.

(a) Calculate the concentration of the excess hydrochloric acid solutions and the amount of acid present in the 250 cm^3 of solution.
(b) Calculate the amount of hydrochloric acid taken initially, and hence find the amount of used to neutralise the ammonia.
(c) Calculate the amount of ammonia formed
(d) Work out the percentage of (i) ammonia, and (ii) nitrogen, in the fertiliser.

25 cm^3 x HCl neutralised 20.0 cm^3 of 0.1 M NaOH

$$HCl + NaOH \rightarrow NaCl + H_2O$$

$$\frac{V_1 M_1}{n_1} = \frac{V_2 M_2}{n_2}$$

therefore,

$$\frac{25\ x}{1} = \frac{20.0 \times 0.1}{1}$$

Cross multiply and solve for x,

x = 0.08 mole per litre.

0.08 mol/L = 0.02 mol/250cm^3 = excess HCl

Amount of HCl in 50 cm^3 of 1.0 M solution =

$$\frac{50 \times 1.0}{1000}\ mole = 0.05\ mole$$

HCl taken initially = 0.05 mole
HCl left over   = 0.02 mole

therefore, HCl used = 0.03 mole

$$HCl + NH_3 \rightarrow NH_4Cl$$

SInce the amount of HCl used was 0.03 mol, therefore the amount of NH$_3$ formed was 0.03 mol.

Amount of NH$_3$ = 0.03 mol = (0.03 $\times$ 17) g = 0.51 g

Amount of nitrogen

= 0.03 mol = (0.03 $\times$ 14) g = 0.42 g

Percentage of NH$_3$ = $\dfrac{0.51 \times 100}{3.0}$ = 17%

Percentage of nitrogen = $\dfrac{0.42 \times 100}{3.0}$ = 14%

Questions

Q.19.2
(a) What type of bond is present in the nitrogen molecule?
(b) How many electrons are involved in it?
(c) What is the percentage of nitrogen in the air?
(d) What is meant by the fixation of nitrogen?
(e) Name two ways in which it is fixed naturally.
(f) What scientist devised the modern method of fixing it artificially?
(g) What substances are reacted together in this process?
(h) Why is nitrogen essential to life?

Q.19.3 The following passage about ammonia taken from the notebook of a not-too-knowledgeable pupil contains many mistakes. Rewrite it, correcting the mistakes which are present.

'Ammonia gas is usually prepared in the laboratory by heating ammonium chloride with calcium chloride, and then passing the gas through concentrated sulphuric acid in order to dry it. Since it is more dense than air, it is collected by unpwards displacement of air. It is colourless odourless gas, is very soluble in water, and the solution turns blue litmus red. It forms dense white fumes of chlorine when reacted with sodium chloride'.

Q.19.4
(a) Name two compounds which when reacted together product ammonia.
(b) Describe with the aid of a diagram, an experiment in which ammonia was prepared and collected. Give the equation for the reaction which occurred.

(c) Name one drying agent which (i) could be used, and (ii) one which could not be used, to dry the ammonia in the experiment.

(d) What happens when a gas jar of ammonia is opened, mouth downwards, in a basin of water? Why?

(e) List the properties of ammonia.

(f) Give the equations for the reactions of ammonia with (i) water, (ii) hydrogen chloride.

(g) How could ammonia be converted to ammonium nitrate?

(h) What is formed when ammonium nitrate is heated?

(i) What do you think is formed when ammonia reacts with (i) chlorine, (ii) copper(II) oxide? (both of these substances are oxidising agents).

Q.19.5 Ammonia is manufactured by reacting nitrogen and hydrogen according to:

$$N_2 + 3H_2 \rightleftharpoons 2NH_3$$

(a) What does the symbol $\rightleftharpoons$ mean?

(b) What is the source of the nitrogen?

(c) What is the source of the hydrogen?

(d) According to Le Chatelier's Principle, what combination of temperature and pressure will give the highest yield of ammonia?

(e) What temperature and pressure are actually used?

(f) Why are these conditions chosen?

(g) What catalyst is used?

(h) A promoter is also used. What is its purpose?

(i) What happens to the nitrogen and hydrogen which have not reacted when they leave the converter?

(j) What volume of ammonia is obtained when 1 litre of nitrogen and 3 litres of hydrogen (all at the same temperature and pressure) combine together?

Q.19.6 Nitric acid is manufactured from ammonia via two intermediate compounds

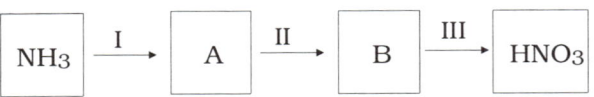

(a) Name the two compounds A and B.

(b) What substance is reacted with the ammonia in reaction I?

(c) What type of reaction is this?

(d) What catalyst is used?

(e) At what temperature is the reaction carried out?

(f) Give the equation for reaction II

(g) What type of reaction is this?

(h) What is the appearance of substance B.

(i) What substances are reacted with compound B at III?

(j) What mass of nitric acid could be obtained from 17 g of ammonia?

Q.19.7 This paragraph is about nitrogen. Rewrite it, choosing the correct word from each of the pair in brackets.

Air is a (mixture/compound) which contains (one-fifth/four-fifths) nitrogen. The symbol for nitrogen is (N/N$_2$) and the gas is made up of (molecules/atoms) of formula (N/N$_2$). It is therefore a (monatomic/diatomic) gas. Nitrogen is needed by plants to make (proteins / sugars). Most plants are unable to take nitrogen directly from the (water/air), so the gas must be 'fixed'. Some is fixed by (rain/lightning) and some is fixed by (leaves/bacteria), but most is fixed artificially by the (Haber/contact) process in which (ammonia/sulphuric acid) is manufactured. In this process, the nitrogen is first reacted with (hydrogen/oxygen) to give the (gas/solid) NH$_3$. This is then made into (nitric/phosphoric) acid which is used to make fertilisers such as ammonium (sulphate/nitrate).

Q.19.8

(a) Name the type of compound containing nitrogen which is present in all plants and animals.

(b) What are the three main plant nutrients? Why is each important?

(c) During what atmospheric conditions can nitrogen from the air be converted directly to a nitrogen compound?

(d) What family of plants can directly utilise atmospheric nitrogen? Name such a plant.

(e) Name a natural fertiliser.

(f) What is a nitrogenous fertiliser?

(g) Name and give the formulae for three manufactured nitrogenous fertilisers.

(h) What is a compound fertiliser?

(i) Why is a compound fertiliser inappropriately named?

(j) State a typical NPK value of a compound fertiliser.

(k) Calculate the percentage of nitrogen in ammonium sulphate

(l) Of what value is this fertiliser to plants?

(m) What two compounds are used to manufacture it?

(n) Write an equation for its preparation.

(o) Some fertilisers are acidic. What substance is added to land to reduce the acidity caused by such fertilisers?

(p) Land which is intensely farmed needs regular applications of fertiliser. Why.

Q.19.9 Ammonia is synthesised in the Haber process according to

$$N_2 + 3H_2 \rightleftharpoons 2NH_3; \qquad \Delta H = -92 \text{ kJ/mol.}$$

(a) What does the word 'synthesised' mean?

(b) What is the effect of raising the pressure on
(i) the percentage of ammonia formed at equilibrium?
(ii) the rate of formation of ammonia?

(c) What is the effect of raising the temperature on
(i) the percentage of ammonia formed at equilibrium?
(ii) the rate of formation of ammonia?

(d) What is the effect of using a catalyst on
(i) the percentage of ammonia formed at equilibrium?

(ii) the rate of formation of ammonia?

(iii) the rate of decomposition of ammonia?

(e) A typical plant producing ammonia operates at a temperature of 800 K and a pressure of $2 \times 10^7 \text{ N/m}^2$. If the volume of the vessel is 100 m^3, calculate the number of moles of gas present ($R = 8.31$).

(f) If the gaseous mixture in the vessel consisted of 10% nitrogen, 30% hydrogen, and 60% ammonia, calculate the values of Kc and Kp for the equilibrium present.

Q.19.10 Lead nitrate, sodium nitrate and silver nitrate are all decomposed on being heated. These reactions are illustrated by the equations:

$$2Pb(NO_3)_2 \rightarrow 2PbO + 4NO_2 + O_2$$

$$2NaNO_3 \rightarrow 2NaNO_2 + O_2$$

$$2AgNO_3 \rightarrow 2Ag + 2NO_2 + O_2$$

(a) From the results of these reactions, place the metals lead, sodium and silver in order of reactivity (most reactive first), and explain why you have selected this order.

(b) Describe how you would use the first two reactions to distinguish between samples of lead nitrate and sodium nitrate.

(c) How could you separate the nitrogen dioxide (b.p. $21°C$) and the oxygen (b.p. $-183°C$) which are formed in the first reaction?

(d) What would you expect to happen on heating potassium nitrate?

Problems

Q.19.11 8.0 g of an ammonium fertiliser were boiled with an excess of solution of sodium hydroxide. The ammonia which was evolved was passed into and absorbed by 50 cm^3 of 1.5 M sulphuric acid. The solution was then made up to 100 cm^3 and the excess of acid was determined by titration. It was found that 25 cm^3 of the solution needed 10.4 cm^3 of 1.2 M sodium hydroxide for neutralisation. Calculate the percentage of ammonia in the fertiliser.

Q.19.12   1.0 g of an ammonium fertiliser was boiled with an excess of a sodium hydroxide solution, and the ammonia evolved was absorbed in 100 cm^3 of 0.5 M hydrochloric acid. The solution was then made up to 250 cm^3 with water. 25 cm^3 of this solution required 15 cm^3 of 0.1 M sodium hydroxide for complete neutralisation. Calculate the percentage of ammonia in the fertiliser.

Q.19.13   A 10 cm^3 portion of an ammonium sulphate solution was boiled with an excess of sodium hydroxide. The ammonia gas was absorbed in 50 cm^3 of 0.1 M hydrochloric acid. To neutralise the excess of acid, 21.5 cm^3 of 0.098 M NaOH were needed. Calculate the molarity of the ammonium sulphate solution, and its concentration in g/L.

Q.19.14   A household cleaner contains ammonia. A 25.4 g sample of the cleaner is dissolved in water and made up to 250 cm^3. A 25 cm^3 portion of this solution requires 37.3 cm^3 of 0.36 M sulphuric acid for neutralisation. What is the percentage by mass of ammonia in the cleaner?

Q.19.15   A fertiliser contains ammonium sulphate and potassium sulphate. A 0.225 g sample of the fertiliser was warmed with sodium hydroxide solution. The ammonia evolved required 15.7 cm^3 of 0.1 M hydrochloric acid for neutralisation. Calculate the percentage of ammonium sulphate in the sample.

Q.19.16   Calculate the percentage of ammonia in an ammonium fertiliser from the following data: 1.65 g of the fertiliser were boiled with 50 cm^3 of 1.0 M sodium hydroxide solution. The excess of alkali required 25.4 cm^3 of 0.1 M hydrochloric acid for neutralisation.

Q.19.17   0.5 g of impure ammonium chloride is warmed with an excess of sodium hydroxide solution. The ammonia liberated is absorbed in 25 cm^3 of 0.2 M sulphuric acid. The excess of sulphuric acid requires 5.6 cm^3 of 0.2 M sodium hydroxide solution for neutralisation. Calculate the percentage of ammonium chloride in the sample.

Review   When you know Chapter 19 you should be able to:

(a)   Explain what is meant by fixation of nitrogen, and how this process occurs both naturally and artificially.

(b)   Give a detailed account of the Haber Process.

(c)   Describe: laboratory preparation of ammonia, the properties of ammonia, how ammonia is converted to nitric acid, the effect of heat on nitrates, the brown ring test, an experiment to find the percentage of ammonia in an ammonium fertiliser.

(d)   Explain what each of the following is: carbohydrate, protein, legume, fertiliser, nitrogenous fertiliser, 'compound' fertiliser.

(e)   List the three main plant nutrients and state which compounds used in fertilisers contain each of these substances.

(f)   Solve numerical problems involving ammonia and fertilisers.

Hydrogen

Hydrogen was discovered in 1766 by Henry Cavendish, a rather eccentric and very wealthy Englishman, who devoted his life to scientific investigations. Cavendish was also the first to show that water is a compound of hydrogen and oxygen only — until then it was thought that water was an element.

Hydrogen is not found in the uncombined state on earth, except in trace amounts in volcanic gases, but as a compound it occurs widely. All animal and vegetable matter contains hydrogen; petroleum and natural gas contain hydrogen and two-thirds of the atoms in every water molecule are atoms of hydrogen. There are more compounds of hydrogen than of any other element. In the atmosphere of the sun and of the stars, hydrogen is present to a large extent. There, nuclear fusion of hydrogen atoms into other elements provides the vast quantities of energy liberated by these bodies.

Manufacture

At present, the main source of hydrogen in Britain and Ireland is natural gas. In Ireland the gas comes from the Kinsale field off the south coast, and in the UK, North Sea gas is used. The hydrogen is produced from it by a process called **steam reforming**. This involves reacting the natural gas with steam at a temperature of about $900^{\circ}C$, when the following change occurs:

$$CH_4 + H_2O \rightarrow CO + 3H_2$$

The mixture of gases which is produced is then mixed with more steam and passed over a heated Fe_2O_3 catalyst. This reaction, known as the **shift reaction**, results in the carbon monoxide being converted to carbon dioxide, and more hydrogen being formed (the previously made hydrogen is unaffected);

$$H_2O + CO \rightarrow CO_2 + H_2$$

The carbon dioxide is removed by dissolving it in water under pressure.

Hydrogen can also be produced from naphtha (a mixture of hydrocarbons in the C_6 and C_7 region) by steam reforming followed by the shift reaction. Electrolysis of a dilute solution of either acid or alkali is another method by which hydrogen is produced. This gives very pure hydrogen, but cheap electricity is necessary to make it a worthwhile process.

20
Hydrogen and Oxygen

20.1 — The Hon.Henry Cavendish (1731 - 1810) was one of the most remarkable and oddest men of science of the 18th century. He was a millionaire but lived the life of a recluse, devoting all his time to the study of science. He made numerous and important discoveries in heat, electricity, gravitation and chemistry, but the records of much of his work remained in his note-books, unread, until many years after his death. Nevertheless, he published enough to earn himself a European reputation for his painstaking experiments and accurate observations. He is best known for his discovery of hydrogen and for being the first person to 'weigh' the Earth.

He lived alone in a large house in London (one of three which he owned), and in it the drawing room was a laboratory, with a forge next door, and an observatory upstairs. Many stories are told about Cavendish and his strange ways: he disliked meeting people and went out only at night; he possessed only one suit at a time and was quite often shabbily dressed and out of date; he disliked women and communicated with his housekeeper by leaving notes for her; it is said that he gave her a standing order to serve roast mutton for dinner every day so that he would not have to be bothered with questions about food; he refused to sit for his portrait and this picture of him was done without his knowledge — it is the only one of him which exists.

The **Cavendish Laboratory** in Cambridge University is his national memorial and contains much of the scientific apparatus he used.

The particular method by which hydrogen is manufactured depends on the raw materials (including electricity) most economically available, at the time and place. In the laboratory, hydrogen is usually obtained by reacting zinc with either dilute sulphuric or hydrochloric acid.

Properties of Hydrogen

Hydrogen is a colourless, odourless, neutral gas and is practically insoluble in water. It is the lightest of all substances, its density being only 0.09 grams per litre at s.t.p. Its boiling point is very low (-253°C), and this makes it very difficult to liquefy. It is a reasonably reactive element, combining directly with both metals and non-metals.

It combines with electropositive metals such as sodium, potassium and calcium to produce ionic hydrides, in which the hydrogen is present as the H^- ion (note: a normal hydrogen ion or proton is H^+). It combines with non-metals to produce covalent hydrides, *e.g.* ammonia, water, hydrogen sulphide, hydrogen chloride. It is flammable, and burns in air or oxygen to produce water (vapour). Mixtures of hydrogen and oxygen are explosive. It removes the oxygen from many metal oxides, reducing them to the corresponding metal.

Uses of Hydrogen

About 75% of manufactured hydrogen is converted into ammonia by the Haber process (see Chapter 19), most of which is then made into nitric acid and fertilisers. It is used to 'harden' oils to make them into fats suitable for margarine production (Chapter 25). It is used to manufacture methanol (Chapter 26) and hydrochloric acid (Chapter 23). Liquid hydrogen is used as a fuel in many rockets; the Saturn V rockets which were used for the Apollo missions to the moon in the 'seventies used liquid hydrogen (along with liquid oxygen) to provide power. It is used for filling balloons to carry weather instruments up into the atmosphere, but, because of its high flammability, its use for this purpose is limited. For many years in the early 1900s airships filled with hydrogen travelled widely (including making hundreds of Atlantic crossings) carrying passengers and cargo, but a number of disasters, due to the hydrogen exploding, put an end to this method of travel.

Hydrogen is a potentially important fuel but, at present, its high cost of production has limited its use as such. It is capable of driving internal combustion engines without producing the harmful by-products associated with petrol, or alternatively it can be used to produce electricity in fuel cells (see page 200). It is possible that, with increasing amounts of relatively cheap electricity available from nuclear power stations, hydrogen could be produced much more cheaply by electrolysis. It burns cleanly and can be stored in liquid form.

Oxygen

Oxygen is the most abundant of all elements, occurring in nearly all rocks and clays, in the atmosphere (21% free oxygen), in water (89% combined oxygen along with some dissolved oxygen) and in all living things, both vegetable and animal (about 70% of the human body is oxygen, much of it in the form of water).

Manufacture of Oxygen

Pure oxygen is a substance which is in constant demand in large quantities, particularly for use in industry and in medicine. It is extracted from its obvious source, the atmosphere, by first liquefying the air and then fractionally distilling it; this separates the various components since they have different boiling points.

The principle involved in the liquefaction of air is fairly simple. When a gas is compressed, heat is produced. Most pupils will be familiar with this

20.2 — The **Rev. Joseph Priestley**, who lived 200 years ago, is regarded as the discoverer of oxygen. Priestley was born in 1733, but although trained for the church, he had a great interest in science from an early age, and gave many lectures in it. There was a brewery next door to his home in Leeds, and there he had access to chemical apparatus and supplies of carbon dioxide with which he did many experiments. He made soda water for the first time. He was first to prepare many common gases including ammonia, nitric oxide, nitrous oxide, carbon monoxide and sulphur dioxide. He invented the 'trough and jar' method of collecting gases over water.

His most famous experiment took place on Sunday 1st August, 1774. He heated 'red calx of mercury' (mercury oxide) using a burning lens, and discovered that a gas was given off which made a candle burn with a "remarkable vigorous flame", and which made a mouse very lively when placed in it. He breathed the gas (oxygen) himself and wrote in his notes "In time, pure air may become a fashionable article of Luxury". Priestley travelled around Europe and was friendly with other scientists such as Antoine Lavoisier, James Watt and Benjamin Franklin.

Towards the end of his life, Priestley went to live with his sons in the United States, where he died in 1804.

fact; it is very noticeable when a bicycle tyre is being pumped up, the air in the pump gets quite hot. Conversely, when a compressed gas is allow to expand, the gas cools. If air is released from a tyre, particularly from a car tyre in which it is under higher pressure, it is noticeably cold. Liquefaction of air makes use of this effect. Air, which has first of all been freed from dust, carbon dioxide and moisture is compressed; this causes it to heat up. It is then passed through a heat exchanger where it is strongly cooled by very cold nitrogen leaving the fractionating column. The cold compressed gas is allowed to expand, and this cools it so much more than it liquefies. The liquid air so formed is a mixture of liquid oxygen and nitrogen, with varying quantities of the noble gases. This mixture is then fractionated, yielding first of all nitrogen at -196 °C, and then oxygen, at -183°C.

Some industries, particularly steelmaking, need so much oxygen that they have their own oxygen making plants, which pump the gas directly to where it is to be used. Countries with an abundance of hydroelectric power produce oxygen by the electrolysis of dilute acid or alkali. In the laboratory oxygen is readily prepared by decomposing hydrogen peroxide solution. This is done by just adding some manganese dioxide, which acts as a catalyst for the decomposition.

20.4 — A liquid oxygen tanker being filled. The clouds are caused by some of the very cold liquid vaporising as it enters the tanker — which initially is at a much higher temperature than the boiling point of the liquid.

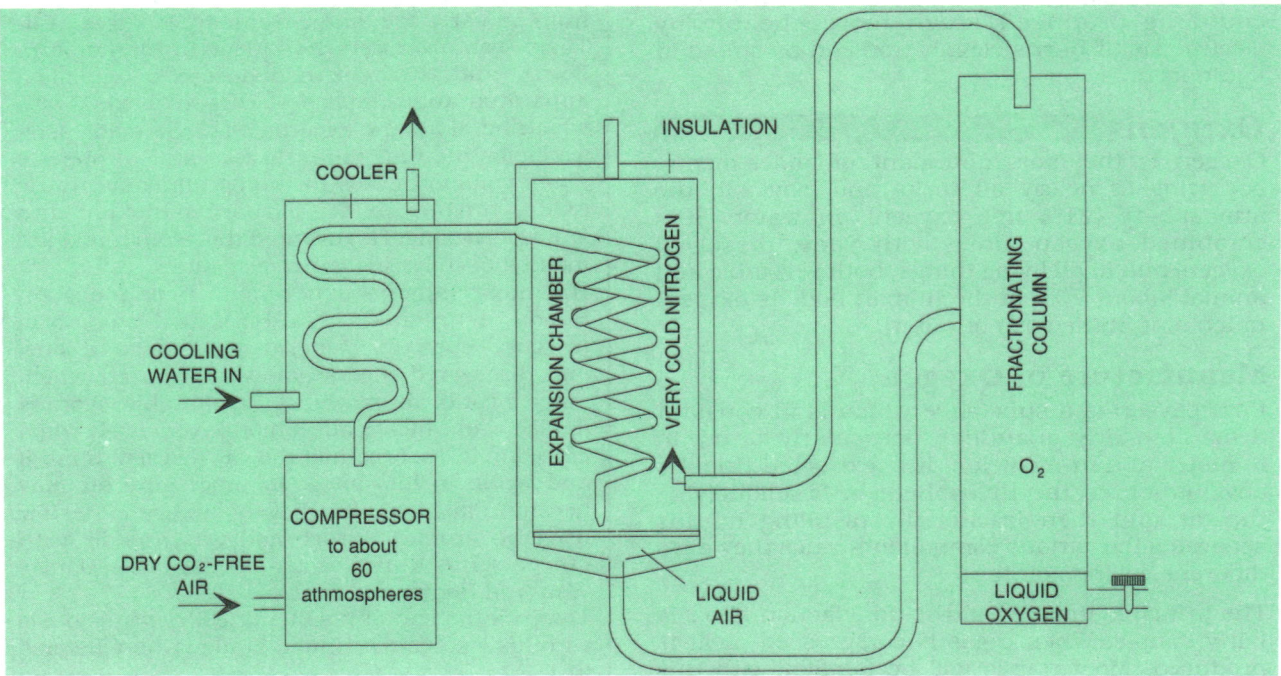

20.3

Properties of Oxygen

Oxygen is a colourless, odourless gas, with a density slightly greater than that of air. Its solubility in water is small; about 40 cm^3 of the gas dissolve in a litre of water at room temperature. This small solubility, however, is of vital importance to fish and other aquatic life, which could not survive without it.

It is a vigorous supporter of combustion; anything which burns in air burns faster, and with a hotter flame, in oxygen. It is very reactive in other ways, and combines directly with nearly every other element, forming the oxide of the element; elements which do not combine directly include the halogens and unreactive metals like gold, but oxides of these elements can be made indirectly. The usual test for oxygen gas is that it relights a glowing splint. As a general rule, oxides of metals are basic and oxides of non-metals are acidic. The nature and properties of various oxides are described in greater detail in following sections.

Use of Oxygen

1. The main consumer of oxygen is the iron and steel industry, which uses about 75% of the supply. The oxygen is an essential requirement for the conversion of pig iron to steel and it is also used to enrich the air supply to the blast furnace in which iron is extracted from iron ore.

2. A great number of uses are connected with breathing. Oxygen is used to help many patients with breathing difficulties, for rescue work in mines, fire and drowning accidents, for flying and climbing at high altitudes, for space exploration, in submarines and sub-aqua diving work.

3. Oxygen is used to make flames hotter. Acetylene (ethyne) burning in oxygen produces the hottest flame obtainable from any known combination of gases, reaching as high as 3000°C — about twice the m.p. of steel. This flame is used for cutting and welding steel, see Fig.25.7. Mixtures of hydrogen and oxygen, and of propane and oxygen, are used for similar purposes. Rockets must carry a supply of oxygen for the fuel to burn in space. The Saturn V rockets at 'lift-off' carried over 2000 tonnes of liquid oxygen, using it initially at a rate of about 12 tonnes per second!

Oxides of Elements

Oxides are compounds of two elements, one of which is oxygen. Oxides vary considerably in their structure and properties, but as a general rule metal oxides are ionic and basic (because the electronegativity difference between oxygen and a metal is large), and non-metal oxides are covalent (because the electronegativity difference between the elements is small) and are either acidic or neutral. The table shows how the acidic/basic nature of the oxides change, in moving from left to right across a period of elements.

Classification of Oxides

1. **Basic oxides** are metal oxides which **react with acids** to produce salts and water only, *e.g.*

$$MgO + H_2SO_4 \rightarrow MgSO_4 + H_2O$$

Those which are soluble in water form alkaline solutions:

$$Na_2O + H_2O \rightarrow 2NaOH$$

2. **Acidic oxides** are oxides which **react with alkalis** to produce salts and water. Those which are soluble in water produce acids:

$$CO_2 + 2NaOH \rightarrow Na_2CO_3 + H_2O$$

Element	Na	Mg	Al	Si	P	S	Cl
Formula of oxide	Na_2O	MgO	Al_2O_3	SiO_2	P_2O_5 P_2O_3	SO_3 SO_2	Cl_2O_7 Cl_2O
Valency of element	1	2	3	4	5 3	6 2	7 1
Nature of oxide	strongly basic	basic	ampho-teric	Weakly acidic	acidic	acidic	strongly acidic
Type of structure	GIANT IONIC			GIANT MOLEC.	SIMPLE MOLECULAR		
Table 20.1 : Classification Of Oxides							

$$SO_3 + H_2O \rightarrow H_2SO_4$$

Most non-metal oxides are of this type.

3.   Amphoteric oxides are metal oxides which show both basic and acidic properties, *i.e.* they form salts with both acids and alkalis. Most of the oxides of this type are of metals near the middle of the periodic table:

$$ZnO + H_2SO_4 \rightarrow ZnSO_4 + H_2O$$

$$ZnO + 2NaOH \rightarrow Na_2ZnO_2 + H_2O$$
sodium zincate

4.   Neutral oxides are oxides which show neither basic nor acidic properties. There are only few such oxides, *viz.* N_2O, NO, CO.

5.   Peroxides are oxides which contain 2 oxygen atoms joined together. Hydrogen peroxide has the structure H—O—O—H, and the few metal peroxides (*e.g.* Na_2O_2) contain the ion $(O—O)^{2-}$.

Oxides of Hydrogen

Water
The most common oxide, H_2O, is amphoteric. Its structure, molecular shape and reactions are described in other chapters (pages 54, 59, 68 and 97)

Hydrogen Peroxide
H_2O_2 can be prepared by reacting barium peroxide with dilute sulphuric acid;

$$BaO_2 + H_2SO_4 \rightarrow BaSO_4 + H_2O_2$$

Properties: Pure hydrogen peroxide is a pale blue viscous liquid of b.p. $150^{\circ}C$, but it is very unstable and readily decomposes, and is rarely encountered in the laboratory because of this. It is usually stored and used in aqueous solution.

It decomposes on being heated, forming oxygen and water:

$$2H_2O_2 \rightarrow O_2 + 2H_2O$$

Many finely divided solids (*e.g.* MnO_2) catalyse this reaction and are added to hydrogen peroxide in order to prepare oxygen. Other substances, particularly some organic compounds[i] (*e.g.*

glycerol), retard the reaction or act as negative catalysts, and are often added to hydrogen peroxide solutions in storage, to prevent their decomposition.

Hydrogen peroxide is thus an oxidising agent. It oxidises, for example, iron(II) to iron(III) ions, sulphite to sulphate ions, and iodide ions to free iodine.

$$2FeSO_4 + H_2O_2 + H_2SO_4 \rightarrow Fe_2(SO_4)_3 + 2H_2O$$
$$Na_2SO_3 + H_2O_2 \rightarrow NaSO_4 + H_2O$$
$$2KI + H_2O_2 + 2H^+ \rightarrow I_2 + 2K^+ + 2H_2O$$

or, ionically

$$2Fe^{2+} + H_2O_2 + 2H^+ \rightarrow 2Fe^{3+} + 2H_2O$$
$$SO_3^{2-} + H_2O_2 \rightarrow SO_4^{2-} + H_2O$$
$$2I^- + H_2O_2 + 2H^+ \rightarrow I_2 + 2H_2O$$

The molecule has the structure shown below, the atoms being joined by covalent bonds:

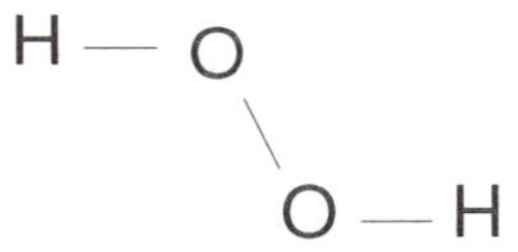

H — O
        \\
         O — H

Group I Metal Oxides
The oxides of lithium, sodium and potassium are obtained when the metals are oxidised. Lithium forms only a monoxide (Li_2O) but the others form higher oxides as well (Na_2O_2, KO_2). They are all white cyrstalline solids and they are basic in that they form salts with acids, and strong alkalis with water.

$$Li_2O + H_2SO_4 \rightarrow Li_2SO_4 + H_2O$$

$$Na_2O + H_2O \rightarrow 2NaOH$$

Metal peroxides liberate oxygen when added to water:

$$Na_2O_2 + H_2O \rightarrow 2NaOH + \tfrac{1}{2}O_2$$

(i)   Organic compounds are compounds of carbon. Chapters 24 - 29 deal with organic chemistry.

Group II Metal Oxides

The oxides of magnesium and calcium (MgO, CaO) can be obtained by heating the metals in oxygen. They are both white crystalline solids (MgO has a cubic ionic lattice like NaCl) and they are basic in their reactions, forming salts with acids, and alkalis with water:

$$CaO + 2HCl \rightarrow CaCl_2 + H_2O$$

$$MgO + H_2O \rightarrow Mg(OH)_2$$

Group III, Aluminium Oxide (Alumina)

Al_2O_3 is a white, very hard, crystalline solid, of very high melting-point. It occurs naturally in 'bauxite' which is the main ore from which aluminium is manufactured.

It is a covalent compound and is amphoteric, reacting with acids to form aluminium salts, and with alkalis to yield salt-like compounds called aluminates:

$$Al_2O_3 + 6HCl \rightarrow 2AlCl_3 + 3H_2O$$

$$Al_2O_3 + 2NaOH \rightarrow 2NaAlO_2 + H_2O$$
sodium aluminate

Oxides of Group IV elements

The two common oxides of carbon, carbon dioxide and carbon monoxide, are described on pages 229 and 230

Group V, Oxides of Nitrogen

There are several different oxides of nitrogen. Two of the common ones are nitrogen monoxide or 'nitric oxide' (NO) and nitrogen dioxide (NO_2)

Nitrogen monoxide

This can be prepared by reacting 50% nitric acid with copper. It can be collected over water since it is insoluble in it:

$$8HNO_3 + 3Cu \rightarrow 3Cu(NO_3)_2 + 2NO + 4H_2O$$

It is a colourless gas, of unknown smell as it is spontaneously and immediately oxidised to nitrogen dioxide on contact with oxygen. It is a neutral oxide. Its structure is not simple, but the bonding is mainly polar covalent.

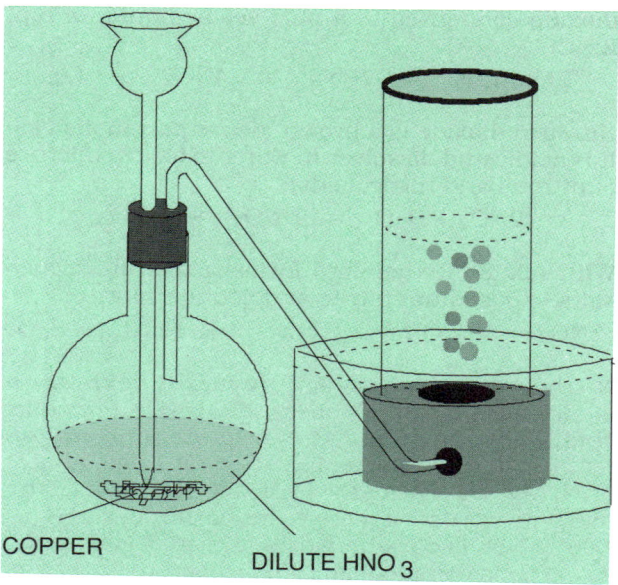

COPPER DILUTE HNO$_3$

20.5 — *Preparation of nitrogen monoxide*

Nitrogen dioxide

This can be prepared by heating most metal nitrates, but lead nitrate is particularly suitable since it does not contain any water of crystallisation. Oxygen is liberated as well but the two gases can be separated by passing them through a freezing mixture, in which the nitrogen

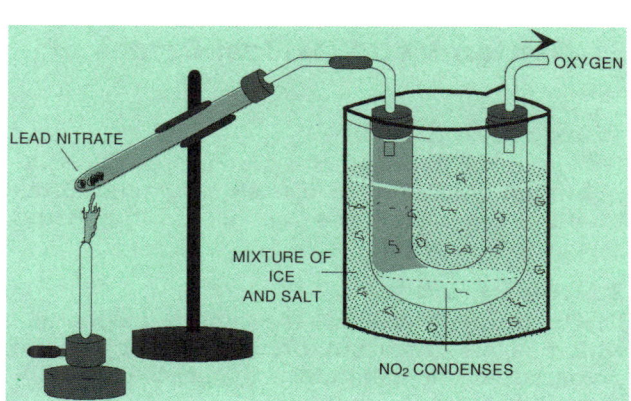

OXYGEN

LEAD NITRATE

MIXTURE OF ICE AND SALT

NO$_2$ CONDENSES

20.6 — *Preparation of nitrogen dioxide.*

dioxide condenses to a pale yellow liquid, of b.p. 22°C:

$$2Pb(NO_3)_2 \rightarrow 2PbO + 4NO_2 + O_2$$

Nitrogen dioxide is a brown, dense poisonous gas. It is acidic and dissolves in water to form a mixture of nitrous and nitric acids:

$$2NO_2 + H_2O \rightarrow HNO_2 + HNO_3$$

With alkalis it therefore forms a mixture of two salts, *e.g.* sodium nitrite and sodium nitrate:

$$2NO_2 + 2NaOH \rightarrow NaNO_2 + NaNO_3 + H_2O$$

Nitrogen dioxide, NO_2, normally exists in equilibrium with the dimer[i] dinitrogen tetroxide, N_2O_4, the ratio of the two depending on temperature. At low temperatures it exists almost entirely as the pale yellow N_2O_4; as the temperature is increased the colour darkens as NO_2 (which is dark brown) is formed. Dissociation into NO_2 is complete at 150°C, when the colour is dark brown. (On further heating it is decomposed into nitrogen monoxide and oxygen).

$$N_2O_4 \underset{cool}{\overset{heat}{\rightleftarrows}} \underset{\substack{dark \\ brown}}{2NO_2} \underset{cool}{\overset{heat}{\rightleftarrows}} \underset{colourless}{2NO + O_2}$$

Group VI, Oxides of Sulphur

There are five known oxides of sulphur but only two, sulphur dioxide, SO_2 and sulphur trioxide, SO_3, are important. These are described in detail in Chapter 22.

Transition Metal Oxides; Oxides of Iron.

1. Iron(II) oxide

FeO is a black powder with an ionic lattice like that of sodium chloride. It is a basic oxide and forms iron(II) salts with acids, *i.e.* it has the usual properties of a metal oxide.

2. Iron(III) oxide

Fe_2O_3 occurs naturally as the mineral 'haematite', which is an important ore of iron. It can be prepared in the laboratory by heating iron(III) hydroxide or iron(II) sulphate.

$$2Fe(OH)_3 \rightarrow Fe_2O_3 + 3H_2O$$
$$2FeSO_4 \rightarrow Fe_2O_3 + SO_2 + SO_3$$

It is a rust-coloured solid and has an ionic structure. It is amphoteric, reacting with acids to give iron(III) salts and with alkalis to give ferrates:

$$Fe_2O_3 + 2NaOH \rightarrow \underset{sodium\ ferrate(III)}{2NaFeO_2} + H_2O$$

Oxides of Copper

Copper(I) oxide

Cu_2O is formed when basic solutions of copper(II) salts are heated with reducing agents. A convenient way to do this is to react Fehling's solution (a complex Cu^{2+} salt) with glucose (a reducing agent):

$$2Cu^{2+} + 4OH^- \longrightarrow Cu_2O + 2H_2O + \underset{\substack{taken\ by \\ reducing \\ agent}}{[O]}$$

or, in terms of electrons,

$$2Cu^{2+} + 2OH^- + \underset{\substack{supplied\ by \\ reducing \\ agent}}{2e^-} \longrightarrow Cu_2O + H_2O$$

Copper(I) oxide is a red insoluble powder. It is basically covalent in structure, each oxygen atom being surrounded by four copper atoms and each copper lying midway between two oxygen atoms:

$$
\begin{array}{ccc}
Cu & & Cu \\
\downarrow & & \downarrow \\
Cu\!-\!\!-O\!-\!\!-Cu\!-\!\!-O\!-\!\!-Cu \\
\uparrow & & \uparrow \\
Cu & & Cu
\end{array}
$$

It is a basic oxide and forms salts when reacted with acids, but, as many copper(I) salts are unstable, they are immediately decomposed yielding the copper(II) salts and metallic copper:

$$Cu_2O + H_2SO_4 \rightarrow CuSO_4 + Cu + H_2O$$

Copper(II) oxide

CuO is formed when copper(II) nitrate, carbonate or hydroxide is heated. It is a black insoluble powder and the bonding is predominantly ionic. It

---

(i)   A dimer is a molecule made up of two simpler molecules joined together.

Element	Formula	Name	Appearance	Bonding	Structure	Reaction with water
H	H_2O	Water	Colourless liquid	Pola r covalent	V - shaped molecule	———
Li	Li_2O CaO	Lithium, oxide etc	White crystalline solid	Ionic	Ionic lattice of Li^+ and O^{2-}	Soluble, forming alkaline solution
Mg	MgO	Magnesium oxide	White crystalline solid	Ionic	Ionic lattice of Mg^{2+} and O^{2-}	Soluble, forming alkaline solution
Al	Al_2O_3	Aluminium oxide (alumina)	White crystalline solid	Polar covalent	Molecules of Al_4O_6	None
C	CO_2	Carbon dioxide	Colourless gas	Pola r covalent	Linear molecules	Slightly soluble forming weakly acidic solution
N	NO_2	Nitrogen dioxide	Brown gas	Polar covalent	V - shaped molecule	Soluble, forming acidic solution
S	SO_2	Sulphur dioxide	Colourless gas	Polar covalent	V - shaped molecule	Very soluble, forming acidic solution
Fe	Fe_2O_3	Iron (III) oxide	Red powder	Ionic	Ionic lattice	None
Cu	CuO	Copper (II) oxide	Black powder	Mainly ionic	Ionic lattice	None
Zn	ZnO	Zinc oxide	White powder	Mainly covalent	Linear molecules	None

Table 20.2: Summary of the Properties of the Normal Oxides of Elements

is a basic oxide and yields copper(II) salts on reaction with acids:

$$CuO + 2HNO_3 \rightarrow Cu(NO_3)_2 + H_2O$$

Zinc Oxide

There is only one oxide of zinc, ZnO. It is a white insoluble powder and the bonding is mainly covalent.

It is an amphoteric oxide, reacting with acids to give the corresponding zinc salts, and with alkalis to yield metal zincates:

$$ZnO + 2HCl \rightarrow ZnCl_2 + H_2O$$

$$ZnO + 2NaOH \rightarrow Na_2ZnO_2 + H_2O$$
$$\text{sodium zincate}$$

Questions

Q.20.1

(a) Outline a method by which oxygen is manufactured from air.

(b) State two methods by which this gas can be conveyed to the consumer.

(c) Describe two large scale uses for the gas.

(d) Give equations for two reactions in which oxygen is produced.

(e) Name two gases which are compounds and which burn in air or oxygen. Write equations for the reactions which take place.

Q.20.2 What is meant by steam reforming? Describe how hydrogen can be produced by this process from (a) natural gas; (b) propane. Mention one other way in which hydrogen can be produced. Describe three important uses of hydrogen.

Q.20.3 Name the products formed when each of the following elements reacts with excess of oxygen: (a) carbon; (b) magnesium; (c) hydrogen; (d) copper. Write equations for the reactions, if any, of these products with (i) dilute hydrochloric acid; (ii) sodium hydroxide solution. If no reaction occurs, write 'no reaction'. State the type of oxide formed by each of the four elements.

Q.20.4 Select a typical ionic oxide and a typical covalent oxide. Give the name and formula of each, and in tabular form, compare and contrast their appearance, structure, behaviour in water and acid/base character.

Q.20.5 The observations below relate to four oxides, **A**, **B**, **C** and **D**. Classify the oxides in each case, name one oxide which has the properties indicated.

A is a white crystalline solid which reacts vigorously with water, forming a solution which turns blue litmus paper red.

B is a white powder which is insoluble in water. It forms colourless solutions when separate portions are warmed with (i) dilute hydrochloric acid (ii) concentrated sodium hydroxide solution.

C is a white solid reacts vigorously with water forming a white suspension. When this is filtered, the filtrate turns red litmus paper blue.

D is a colourless gas which is insoluble in water.

Q.20.6 Carbon dioxide is an **acidic oxide** and copper oxide is a **basic oxide**. Describe what is meant by each of these terms. What type of elements, in general, form each of these types of oxide? Name two other examples of each type. Describe how you would test an oxide in order to classify it. State three ways in which metal oxides differ from non-metal oxides.

Q.20.7 Give short answers to each of the following questions:

(a) By what process is oxygen produced industrially?

(b) Name two by-products of the above process.

(c) What is the most important industrial use of oxygen?

(d) What is a peroxide?

(e) Name a peroxide which is (i) a solid and (ii) a liquid.

(f) In what form does most of the Earth's hydrogen occur?

(g) How can it be extracted from that form?

(h) How is hydrogen produced industrially?

(i) For what is most of the manufactured hydrogen used?

(j) Name two advantages of hydrogen as a motor fuel.

(k) What is an amphoteric oxide?

(l) Where, in general, do the elements which form amphoteric oxides, occur in the Periodic Table?

(m) Show why water is regarded as being amphoteric.

(n) What are the trends in the ionic character of oxides in moving (i) from L to R across a period of elements, (ii) down a group of elements?

(o) Name and give the formula for the two neutral oxides.

Q.20.8 Hydrogen has similarities to both the alkali metals and the halogens in its chemical behaviour. Describe two ways in which it resembles the alkali metals (chemically) and two ways in which it resembles the halogens. Explain, with examples, how the type of bond in hydrides depends on the element to which the hydrogen is attached.

Q.20.9 From the following list: CO_2; P_2O_5; Li_2O; NO_2; NO; SiO_2; CuO; Al_2O_3; Fe_2O_3; MgO; select:

(i) a basic oxide which is soluble in water,

(ii) a highly coloured acidic oxide;

(iii) a neutral oxide;

(iv) an amphoteric oxide;

(v) a coloured solid oxide;

(vi) a covalent oxide;

(vii) an ionic oxide

(viii) an oxide whose molecules are linear;

(ix) an oxide which has a giant structure;

(x) an oxide which reacts with sulphuric acid to form a coloured solution.

Review When you know chapter 20 you should be able to:

(a) State how both hydrogen and oxygen occur in nature.

(b) Describe how each is produced industrially.

(c) List three uses of each element.

(d) Describe the properties of each.

(e) List the five classes into which oxides can be divided, and give examples of each.

(f) State about each example, its (i) appearance, (ii) type of bonding, (iii) reaction (if any) with water, (iv) acid/base nature.

(g) State how both nitrogen monoxide and nitrogen dioxide can be prepared.

(h) Explain what is meant by each of: steam reforming, shift reaction, amphoteric, peroxide.

20.7 — After the release of the first hot air balloon (by the Montgolfier brothers) from Paris in 1783, **Professor Charles**, of Gas Law fame, became interested in this invention and decided to build a different type of balloon — one filled with hydrogen. This he did and, observed by practically the whole population of Paris, he released the first hydrogen balloon. It travelled 9.5 km in three quarters of an hour, before coming down. Some months later, he built a larger, man-carrying balloon and, with a friend, ascended to a height of 250 metres in it. Later on the same day, he alone ascended to 3 km, but at that height his ears began to ache, and he rapidly descended. In spite of his successful trip, he never made another ascent.

His interest in balloons led him to his experiments on expanding gases, and in 1787, he established the law relating the volume and temperature of a gas — Charles' Law.

Pictured right is an artist's impression of the historic first ascent of a manned hydrogen balloon, on Dec. 1st 1783.

21
Water

Water is such a common substance that probably not many people ever think much about it. For most, it is a substance that comes out of the tap as it is needed, for drinking, cleaning, washing, cooking, or, in quantity, is something to enjoy looking at, swimming or fishing in or sailing on. Few people know where it has come from, how it gets to the tap or what has been done to it before it does so. Most people just take water for granted.

Water is a vital necessity of everyday life. Apart from its obvious uses in the home, it is required in enormous quantities in farming and food processing factories, in raising steam to drive turbines and other machinery, for producing hydroelectricity, for cooling in industry, in carrying away wastes, in bleaching and dyeing, as a solvent, and as a raw material for the manufacture of many important chemicals. Water is contained in virtually everything that people eat and drink and about 80% of the human body is water. Without water, life on earth could not survive.

21.1 — *Ice crystals seen under a microscope*

Chemically, water is a very simple substance, but its properties and reactions are not what might be expected from a substance made up of such small molecules. Its boiling and melting points are abnormally high, as are its specific latent heats; it expands as its temperature approaches its freezing point; it forms extremely well defined crystals (of ice) when it freezes; it dissolves, to some extent at least, a vast number of substances — so much so that completely pure water is rare; it causes acids to ionise and it causes hydrolysis[i] to varying extents, of many substances — both simple inorganic salts, such as sodium carbonate and complex organic compounds, like starch.

Many of the reactions of water are due to the fact that the bonds in its molecules are very polar, and most of the abnormal properties result from its shape and the hydrogen bonding which occurs between its molecules. Bonding in water and its effects are described in Chapter 4.

Hardness in Water

Because water is such a good solvent, practically all water supplies contain dissolved substances; many of these substances are beneficial but some of them create problems by being present. People whose water supplies come from limestone regions will know that it is quite difficult to obtain a lather with soap, and before the lather is produced, a dirty looking scum forms in the water. Water which does this is said to be **hard**. Hardness in water is caused by dissolved calcium salts, particularly calcium sulphate ($CaSO_4$), and calcium hydrogencarbonate, $Ca(HCO_3)_2$, (and to a lesser extent the corresponding salts of magnesium).

There are several different soaps — all chemically similar — but one of the most common is sodium stearate, $C_{17}H_{35}COONa$; this is the sodium salt of the 'long chain' stearic acid, $C_{17}H_{35}COOH$. When soap is dissolved in hard water, it reacts with the Ca^{2+} ions present, to form calcium stearate, which is insoluble and is precipitated as a scum in the water:

$$2C_{17}H_{35}COONa + Ca^{2+} \rightarrow (C_{17}H_{35}COO)_2Ca(\downarrow) + 2Na^+$$

soap   ions in   scum
the hard water

The soap will only form a lather after all of the Ca^{2+} ions have been precipitated and so the soap used in doing this is wasted. As well, the undesirable scum forms.

Types of Hardness

There are two types of hardness, temporary and permanent:

1. **Temporary hardness** is due mainly to dissolved calcium hydrogencarbonates; this type of hardness can be removed by boiling the water which contains it, since hydrogencarbonates are decomposed on being heated — giving a precipitate of the corresponding carbonate:

$$Ca(HCO_3)_2 \rightarrow CaCO_3(\downarrow) + H_2O + CO_2$$

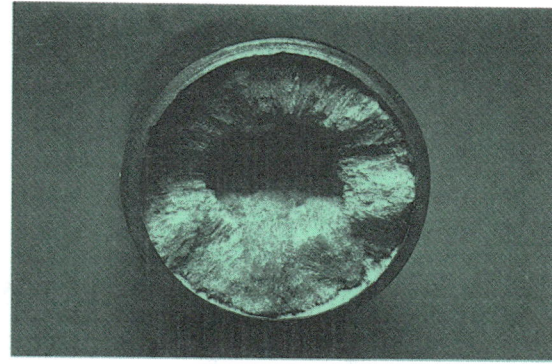

21.2 — An example of a badly 'furred' water pipe.

The 'fur' or 'scale' which accumulates inside kettles in hardwater regions is calcium carbonate formed by the above reaction. In a kettle, an accumulation of 'fur' may be a bit of a nuisance, but on a large scale, such as inside boilers and central heating pipes, fur can be a serious problem. Boilers become less efficient because the deposit is a bad

---

(i)   Hydrolysis is a reaction in which substances are decomposed by water, the water becoming decomposed in the process also. Hydrolysis reactions are described elsewhere (Chapters 14 and 28)

conductor of heat (and so fuel is wasted) and pipes in time can become blocked. In industry, where vast quantities of water are used, any hardness in the water must be removed (i.e. the water must be 'softened') before the water enters a heating system.

2.   **Permanent hardness** in water is hardness which is not removed by boiling the water and is mainly caused by dissolved calcium sulphate. Sulphates are not decomposed on being heated.

Methods of Softening Water

Temporary hardness is removed by boiling, as has been described, but there are a number of general methods for removing both types of hardness at the same time.

1.   **Distillation** removes all dissolved matter, but on a large scale it would be too costly because of the amount of energy needed to boil the water.

2.   **Using 'Washing 'Soda'** ($Na_2CO_3 10H_2O$). The addition of this substance is a simple method of removing hardness from water. It reacts with the Ca^{2+} ions in the water and precipitates them as $CaCO_3$:

$$Na_2CO_3 + Ca^{2+} \rightarrow CaCO_3 (\downarrow) + 2Na^+$$

The Na^+ ions which are formed remain in the water but they do not cause hardness. Bath salts consist of coloured and perfumed washing soda crystals and their main effect is to soften the water so that soap lathers in it more easily.

3.   **Ion Exchange using 'Zeolites':** Compounds called zeolites (sold under the trade name 'Permutit') consists of complex sodium aluminium-silicates and these have the ability to exchange their sodium ions for the calcium (or magnesium) ions in the water. The water to be softened is passed through a cylinder containing the zeolite, when the following reaction occurs[i]:

$$Ca^{2+} + Na_2Z \rightarrow CaZ + 2Na^+$$

The Ca^{2+} ions are thus removed from the water and become part of the zeolite. In time, all the sodium ions of the zeolite have been replaced by calcium ions, so that the zeolite is no longer able to soften water. However, the zeolite can be converted to its original state quite easily, by just allowing it to soak in concentrated salt solution for a few hours, when the reverse reaction occurs:

$$CaZ + 2Na^+ \rightarrow Ca^{2+} + Na_2Z$$

The excess salt solution, containing the Ca^{2+} ions from the zeolite, is run off to waste, and the zeolite is then ready to soften more water. This type of softener is often found in factories and homes.

4.   **Modern Ion-Exchange Resins:** A more modern method uses a mixture of two types of ion-exchange resin. One type is capable of replacing Ca^{2+} ions by H^+, while the other can substitute OH^- for both HCO_3^- and SO_4^{2-}:

$$Ca^{2+} + resin\ 1 \rightarrow 2H^+ + spent\ resin$$

$$HCO_3^- + resin\ 2 \rightarrow OH^- + spent\ resin$$

The H^+ and OH^- ions which are formed then combine together to produce water. Thus the water leaving the ion exchanger is ion free. It may however contain dissolved non-ionic solids and dissolved chlorine present in the original water supply. Water softened in this way is called **deionised water**, and small deionisers which produce this are widely available for laboratory use.

Advantages of Hard Water

Although hard water at times creates various problems (already referred to), it has advantages over soft water for several purposes. It generally has a better taste and so is more satisfying to drink; the calcium present is essential for healthy bones and teeth in the human body, and hard water is particularly suitable for brewing, i.e. making beer and ale.

Q.21.1
(a)   Explain what is meant by each of: hard water, temporary hardness, permanent hardness.

(b)   How could you test a sample of hard water to find out if the hardness was temporary or permanent?

(c)   Name two compounds which cause each type of hardness.

(i)   Z represents the zeolite anion

(d) How does hard water react with soap? State two disadvantages of this reaction.

(e) Mention and explain one other disadvantage of hard water.

(f) Mention two advantages of hard water.

(g) Explain with the appropriate chemical equations why the addition of washing soda removes hardness in water.

Q.21.2 Atmospheric carbon dioxide dissolved in rainwater causes the water to be hard in limestone districts.

(a) What compound is formed when carbon dioxide reacts with rain?

(b) Show by an equation how this compound reacts with limestone.

(c) What type of hardness is formed?

(d) Why is the hardness described in this way?

(e) How does this type of hardness cause 'fur' in kettles?

(f) Why must water for use in industrial boilers be softened?

(g) Explain how this is done.

Q.21.3 Soap solution from a burette was added to samples of different types of water, until a permanent lather was formed. Fresh samples of each of the type of water were then boiled, cooled, and the experiment repeated. The following results were obtained:

Sample	Vol. of soap solution needed	
	Initially	After boiling
W	6.5	3.5
X	11.5	11.5
Y	11.5	0.5
Z	0.5	0.5

Which of the samples could have been:

(i)   Distilled water,

(ii) $Ca(HCO_3)_2$ soln.,

(iii) tap water,

(iv) $MgSO_4$ soln.,

(v) Na_2CO_3 soln.,

(vi) $CaCl_2$ soln.

Explain each of your answers.

Water Supplies

The availability of adequate supplies of clean safe drinking water is one of the necessities of life, and providing it is one of the tasks of the various county councils and corporations throughout the country.

Each person, on average, uses about 140 litres of water per day, made up as follows:

Purpose	Litres
Toilet flushing	50
Personal washing	40
Washing clothes	17
Dish washing	14
Gardening	6
Cooking	10
Drinking	3

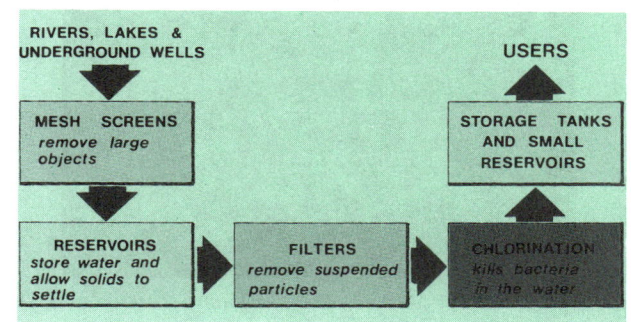

21.3

Industry uses huge quantities of water, much of it for cooling purposes. The E.S.B. power station at Poolbeg, Dublin, needs about 1200 million litres of water daily. The N.E.T. factory which manufactures ammonia at Marino Point in Cork Harbour requires about one million litres of water daily. It has been estimated that it requires 10 litres of water to make one newspaper, and half a million litres to make one new car.

Most Irish water supplies come from rivers and lakes, often being stored in reservoirs before going to the water works for purification. There are a number of stages in this process and these are usually as follows:

1.   The water first of all passes through a series of graded screens, which remove large suspended matter, such as pebbles and loose vegetation.

2.   Substances called 'flocculating agents' (*e.g.* aluminium sulphate) are then added. These cause any suspended solids and organic matter to coagulate (stick together) so that they can be filtered off more easily.

3.   Filtration is usually done by sand filters; these consist of beds of sand, about 1 m thick, with fine sand on top and coarse sand below — all being supported on a layer of gravel. As the water percolates down through this, algae and bacteria, which soon develop on the upper layers, remove any nitrates and phosphates present and cause any organic matter to be oxidised to simple compounds such as CO_2. The surface layers of sand have to be replaced at intervals.

21.4 —   *The sand filters at Dublin County Council's water treatment works, at Leixlip.*

4.   The clean water from the filters is then sterilised by adding chlorine; this destroys any pathogenic[i] bacteria such as those causing typhoid and cholera — water borne diseased that were so rampant in the nineteenth century. The amount of chlorine added to the water is carefully controlled: too little (< 0.1 mg/L) will not fulfil its purpose, and too much (> 1.0 mg/L) gives the water an unpleasant taste and smell.

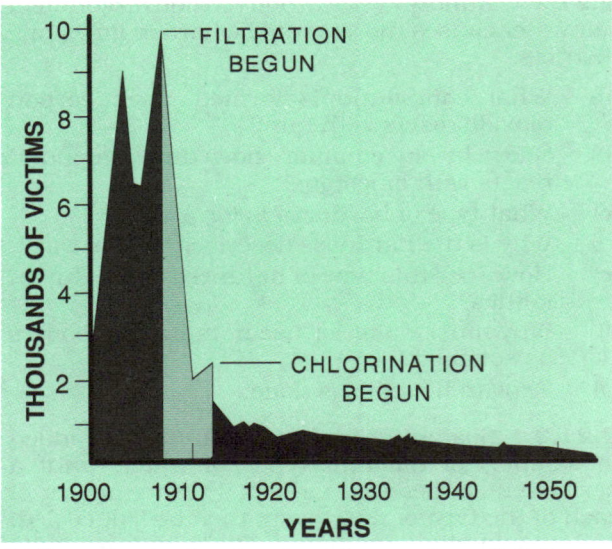

21.5 —   *Graph showing how the number of victims of typhoid changed when water treatment was introduced.*

5.   In Ireland and several other countries, water authorities are obliged to add fluorine (in the form of one of its compounds) at a concentration of about 1 p.p.m. The presence of fluoride in drinking water has been shown to reduce dental decay, which is one of the most prevalent diseases in the Western World.

6.   If necessary, lime is added to bring the pH value to about 7.5

Finally, at the end of the whole process, various chemical and biological tests are carried out, to ensure that the water is clean, pure, disease-free and has no colour, taste or smell.

(i)   *i.e.* disease causing

Water Pollution

Pollution kills 4,000 fish in rivers of Munster

Heavy river pollution from silage

21.6 — 2 newspaper headings

Newspaper headings such as the above are unfortunately all too common nowadays; the two shown appeared during the same month in the *Irish Times*. One referred to rivers in Munster, and the other to rivers in counties Kildare, Dublin and Meath. Pollution can be described as the release of substances into the environment in quantities which damage man's health and/or his environment.

At the beginning of the nineteenth century, pollution of rivers and lakes was virtually unknown, and in Ireland it is only in comparatively recent times that pollution of fresh water has become a problem. Polluted water can be recognised by several symptoms, though not all of these are necessarily present at the one time: it is opaque and the colour is often dirty green or brown; bubbles of methane or hydrogen sulphide (rotten egg gas) come from the bottom; the soil or sand on the bank is coloured dark grey or black; the usual plant and animal life is absent, with perhaps dead fish floating about; there is often an excessive amount of algae. In a recent survey, it was shown that nearly one fifth of Ireland's inland waters are polluted, and in several areas there are regular fish kills every year.

21.7 — A fish kill

Water pollution is caused by an excess of substances which are toxic, or which make a demand on the dissolved oxygen in the water. The more common pollutants found in water in this country are the following:

(i) **Untreated sewage** from towns and cities;

(ii) **Pig and poultry slurry,** responsible for many of the country's polluted lakes, particularly those in counties Cavan, Monaghan, Longford and Westmeath,

(iii) **Silage effluent**[i] from farms,

(iv) **Fertilisers** washed out of farming lands by rain, into rivers and lakes;

(v) **Factory effluent** from a variety of manufacturing industries, creameries, beet factories, meat processing factories;

(vi) **Detergents** from homes and factories.

Normal aquatic life is dependent on dissolved oxygen in water, the oxygen normally being acquired by absorption from the atmosphere; this process occurs continuously but rather slowly. Pollutants use up the dissolved oxygen in several ways. Organic matter (*e.g.* sewage, slurry, silage effluent) is slowly decomposed by aerobic bacteria (basically this is oxidation) to simple compounds, such as CO_2, and water. Fertilisers (and also phosphates from washing powders) reaching the water, remove the dissolved oxygen indirectly;

(i) Wash water, or water carrying waste materials from farms, industries etc. is known as effluent.

when the water becomes enriched with nitrates and phosphates, there is excessive growth of water plants, particularly algae. The latter grows very rapidly forming **'algal bloom'**.

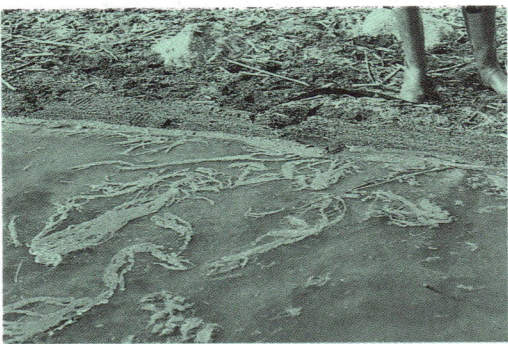

21.8 — Algal Bloom

The abnormal growth of water plants causes them to use up considerably more dissolved oxygen than they would normally require. As well, the decaying vegetation, which results when the plants die, takes more oxygen.

> **The enrichment of water by nutrients, which results in deoxygenation, is known as eutrophication.**

It should be realised that it is only in quantity that the substances mentioned cause pollution in rivers and lakes; in sufficiently small amounts, any or all of the above can be present with no ill effects whatever. It will also be seen that although many of the common pollutants are waste materials, this is not necessarily the case. Included in the list are fertilisers, substances which are absolutely essential to enable sufficient food for today's over-populated world to be produced, but which, when they get into rivers or lakes, can become pollutants.

Biochemical Oxygen Demand (B.O.D.)

The effect of a pollutant in a river or lake can be estimated in a general way by measuring the rate at which oxygen is needed for its decomposition, and for this purpose the **B.O.D. test** is used.

> **The Biochemical Oxygen Demand is the amount of dissolved oxygen consumed by biochemical action, when a sample of water is kept in the dark at 20°C for five days.**

The test is carried out by adding well-oxygenated water to a sample of the water under test, and then measuring the initial oxygen concentration. The sample is stored at 20°C in the dark (to prevent possible photosynthesis replacing the oxygen) for five days after which the oxygen concentration is again measured. The difference between the two dissolved oxygen values represents the demand which the pollutants have for the oxygen in the water and the value is a rough indication of the amount of organic matter in the sample. Five days is chosen because most organic matter has decomposed in that time.

B.O.D. values are normally expressed in p.p.m. and range from zero (for clean unpolluted water) to about 30,000 for silage effluent.

Sewage Disposal

At the beginning of the 19th century, sewage disposal in towns was simple — it was usually just thrown into the streets.

From there it was washed away when it rained or else it was removed and buried in the soil on the outskirts of the town. The increase in both population and the size of towns in the 19th century resulted in deplorable sanitary conditions, and epidemics of the waterborne diseases, typhoid and cholera, were common when sewage found its way into drinking water supplies.

Things have improved since then. As well as a piped system for the removal of sewage, many authorities now treat, and make harmless, the sewage before returning the water from it to rivers, lakes or to the sea. Sewage treatment is essentially a process of water recycling and consists basically of removal of solid organic matter as a 'sludge' (primary treatment) and oxidation and microbiological decomposition of the organic matter left in solution and in suspension (secondary treatment), leaving clean, solid-free and disease-free water.

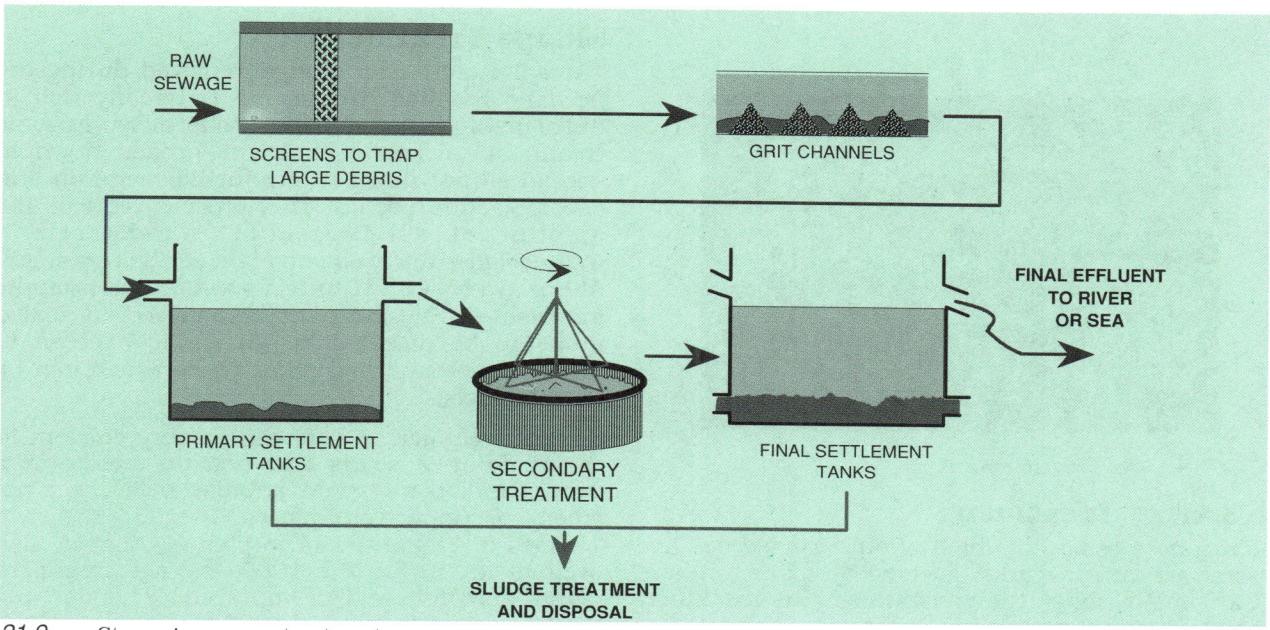

21.9 — Stages in sewage treatment process.

There are variations of the sewage treatment process, but they all follow the same general pattern.

Primary Treatment

Sewage arriving at a sewage treatment plant is made up of the effluent, or wastewater, from homes (water from sinks, baths, washing machines, toilets), factories (water used for chemical processes, washwater, etc.) and, in some cases, rainwater from streets and roads. It is mainly liquid, solid matter making up only about 2% of the total volume.

Primary treatment is essentially **physical**. The incoming sewage first passes through a screening arrangement which removes large solid matter and other debris. Next, it goes through grit traps in which grit and small stones settle so that they can be removed at intervals. The sewage now passes to large deep tanks, called settlement or sedimentation tanks. In these, much of the suspended solid matter settles out as a sludge, over a period of about 3 hours. About 60% of the solids and 25% of the B.O.D. are removed from the wastewater at this stage. Mechanical scrapers remove the sludge from the bottoms of the tanks while the liquid flows over the tops, to go to the next stage of the process.

Secondary Treatment

The processes here basically **biological**. The liquid from the first stage is passed to large aeration tanks in which the dissolved organic matter and the organic matter still in suspension are both chemically oxidised and decomposed by micro-organisms such as protozoa, fungi and aerobic[i] bacteria. These organisms feed on organic matter in the water and convert it to simple inorganic compounds such as carbon dioxide, nitrates, etc. The liquid can remain up to 16 hours in these tanks. A mechanical agitator continuously churns up the liquid so that it absorbs oxygen from the air.

The effluent from these tanks is comparatively clean and inoffensive, but it still contains dissolved phosphates (and nitrates), and some suspended solids which require removal. Phosphates come from washing powders, in which they are present because they give a 'whiter' wash, but being plant nutrients, they can cause pollution by eutrophication.

(i)   Aerobic = requiring oxygen
        Anaerobic = not requiring oxygen.

21.10 — Secondary treatment.

Tertiary Treatment

Phosphate removal, which is only carried out by some treatment works, is done by adding either Ca^{2+} or Al^{3+} ions; this precipitates it as insoluble calcium (or aluminium) phosphate.

From here, the liquid flows to final settlement tanks. Here, the process and the mechanical arrangements are similar to those in the primary settlement tanks. The last of the solid matter settles out and the output from these tanks is clean transparent water with a very low B.O.D. (about 10 p.p.m.) and it is then discharged into a convenient river or lake or into the sea.

21.11 — The purified water leaving the final settlement tank is so clear that it is almost unnoticable as it flows over the tiled bottom around the outside of the tank.

Sludge Treatment

The solid matter or 'sludge' removed during the primary and final treatments is usually rich in nutrients and can be made into fertiliser. In some treatment works, the sludge is broken down in special sludge tanks where further aeration and decomposition occurs. This process reduces the amount of solid residue, which from a well-designed and well-run plant can be very small. Alternatively — and this is a practice that is on the increase — the sludge is transferred to sealed tanks to be digested by anaerobic bacteria to produce methane and other gases which can be used as fuels.

Sewage treatment plants can be very efficient in the removal of solids and organic matter from water, and, contrary to popular belief, are not smelly or unpleasant places. In 1957 the river Thames in England was so polluted that no fish lived in it. During the 1960s sewage treatment plants were built and/or improved for London and towns on the Thames. In 1968, 41 species of fish were found in the river, and by 1978, the number known there had reached 200. As the Thames flows through one of the most densely populated areas of the world and receives about 2300 million litres of treated sewage daily, it shows how satisfactory the treatment can be.

Pollution by Sewage

Given sufficient time, all sewage naturally decomposes; bacteria and oxygen cause it to break down into harmless products. Small amounts of pollutants can be run into rivers with no adverse effects, but if the river becomes overloaded with them, the biochemical self-purification system is unable to cope, the river becomes devoid of dissolved oxygen and everything living in it dies. It has become polluted and a possible health hazard. Not long ago, rivers and lakes could adsorb all the waste which was dumped into them; today the quantity is too great.

The disposal of untreated sewage into the sea is less dangerous than when it is put into rivers or lakes. The sea dilutes it to a much greater extent; salt water kills most fresh water micro-organisms and marine organisms break down organic matter. In time, the sewage will break down, and if it is discharged well out into the sea, causes little or no pollution.

Q.21.4 Give short answers to each of the following questions.

(a) What is the difference between distilled water and deionised water?

(b) What is the source of the water supply to your own home?

(c) A flocculating agent is added to water at the water works. What is its purpose. Name such a substance.

(d) Following this, what is done to the water?

(e) What should the pH of water for domestic use be?

(f) Why is lime sometimes added to water supplies?

(g) What is meant by fluoridation of water? Why is water fluoridated in this country?

(h) Why do cholera and typhoid seldom occur in Ireland nowadays?

(i) How can fertilisers cause water to be polluted?

(j) Name two other sources of pollution in Irish rivers and lakes.

(k) What are the symptoms of polluted water?

(l) What is meant by eutrophication?

(m) Name a substance which causes eutrophication.

(n) Define B.O.D.

(o) Why, in the B.O.D. test, is the water stored in the dark?

(p) What does the B.O.D. value of a water sample indicate?

(q) Should the B.O.D. of domestic water supplies be high or low? Why?

(r) Incoming sewage to the treatment works is first screened. What does this mean?

(s) What does the primary treatment of sewage involve?

(t) What is meant by sedimentation in the sewage treatment process?

(u) Microorganisms take part in which stage of sewage treatment? What do they do in the water?

(v) What chemical change occurs at the same time?

(w) Explain (i) effluent, (ii) aerobic.

(x) What is the source of phosphates in sewage? Why should they be removed?

(y) How are phosphates removed?

(z) Name two uses to which the sludge from sewage treatment works can be put.

Water Analysis

Total Suspended and Dissolved Solids

Suspended solids are insoluble substances which are too finely divided to settle, either on the top or the bottom of the water, and so remain distributed throughout the water, but without being dissolved in it. Substances such as particles of plant and animal matter, silt, etc, make up the suspended solids. The amount of these in a sample of water can be determined by weighing a sheet of filter paper having as fine a pore size as possible, filtering through it a measured quantity of the water being analysed (a reasonably large volume *e.g.* 1 litre, should be taken), drying the filter paper, and then reweighing. The increase in mass is the amount of solids in the sample. Suspended solids are usually expressed in parts per million (p.p.m) which is the same as milligrams (mg) per litre [i]

The dissolved solids are estimated by filtering a sample of the water being analysed (to remove the suspended solids), then measuring a known volume of it into a weighed beaker, evaporating the solution to dryness and reweighing. The mass of dissolved matter in the known volume of water is thus found, and hence the amount in p.p.m can be calculated.

---

[i] One litre of water has a mass of one million milligrams (*i.e.* 1000 g) so giving the concentration in mg/L is the same as expressing it in p.p.m.

Experiment 21.1
Estimation of Suspended and Dissolved Solids in Water

1. Suspended Solids

Weigh as accurately as possible, a sheet of fine filter paper. Take a known volume[i] of the water being investigated and filter it through the weighed paper. Remove the filter paper from the funnel and completely dry it over gentle heat or in a warm oven. Reweigh the paper.

Calculate the mass of the solid matter, *i.e.* the increase in mass of the paper, Express the amount of solid matter (i) in grams per litre of the sample, and (ii) in parts per million.

2. Dissolved Solids

Weigh a clean dry beaker. Add 100 cm^3 of the filtered water from the previous experiment, and then evaporate it to dryness. A convenient way of doing this is to place the beaker in an oven at 105°C for half an hour or so. The dissolved solids will remain in the beaker. Allow the beaker to cool and then reweigh it.

Calculate the mass of the solid matter (i) in the sample, (ii) per litre of the sample, and (iii) in parts per million.

pH

The pH of a water sample is best measured with a pH meter, but it can also be found (though with slightly less accuracy) using either pH paper or Universal indicator solution (details of this are described in Chapter 14)

Total Hardness

The total hardness in a water sample is best determined by using **e**thylene**d**iamine**t**etra**a**cetic acid or as it is invariably called, **edta**. This substance is a tetrabasic (= 4 replaceable hydrogen atoms) organic acid of formula:

formula to follow organic acid of the formula

and it has the ability to react with metal ions (usually in a 1:1 ratio, irrespective of the magnitude of the charge on the metal ion) and form stable soluble complexes.

The acid is not very soluble in water, and the disodium salt is usually used. If, for simplicity, the formula for **edta** is abbreviated to H_4Y, the disodium salt is Na_2H_2Y, and the reaction with calcium ions is:

$$Na_2H_2Y \ + \ Ca^{2+} \ \rightarrow \ CaH_2Y \ + \ 2Na^+$$

| edta | | | complex | | |
| edta disodium salt | | | of edta with Ca | | |

In determining hardness in water, the water is titrated with standard edta solution containing a suitable indicator. In order to obtain a sharp and accurate end point, it is necessary to carry out the titration at a particular pH value — dependent on the metal ion being determined, and this is achieved by adding a small quantity of a buffer solution to the solution being titrated. For the determination of Ca^{2+} and Mg^{2+} a buffer solution maintaining a pH of about 10 is required. The indicator eriochrome black T[ii] is normally used.

The disodium salt of edta is obtainable in a sufficiently pure state to prepare a standard solution directly. A solution of molarity 0.02 is suitable and this is prepared by dissolving 7.44 g of the salt ($Na_2H_2Y2H_2O$) in distilled water and making the solution up to 1 litre in the usual manner. Standard edta solution should be stored in plastic bottles as it has the power to extract metal ions out of glass.

(i)   If the water is very clean, a large volume (*e.g.* 1 litre) will be necessary to obtain a weighable amount of solid matter, but if the water is obviously dirty, a smaller volume (*e.g.* 500 or 200 cm^3) will suffice.

(ii)   Also called solochrome black

A sample of the water (50 or 100 cm^3) is measured into a conical flask and a few cm^3 of the buffer solution with a 'pinch' of the indicator (which is dry powder) are added. In the presence of metal ions, the indicator is red. Standard edta solution from a burette is run into the flask until the end point is reached. This is the point at which all the metal ions have become complexed by the edta and when this has happened, the colour of the free indicator (blue) appears. The volume of edta solution added is a measure of the total amount of Ca^{2+} and Mg^{2+} present in the sample.

Total hardness of water is normally expressed as parts per million of CaCO$_3$, *i.e.* even though some is present as magnesium compounds, and even though it is actually present as the hydrogencarbonate and the sulphate the amount is expressed as if it were all there as CaCO$_3$.

Experiment 21.2
To Determine the Total Hardness in Water

Fill a burette with 0.02 M edta solution. Measure out 100 cm^3 of the water sample into a conical flask. Add about 2 cm^3 of the buffer solution and a 'pinch' of solochrome black indicator (it is a dry powder). In the presence of the metal ions in the water, the indicator is red. Titrate with the edta solution until the indicator turns blue. As the end point is approached, the edta must be added very slowly and the flask swirled continuously — because the reaction between the edta and the metal ions is fairly slow.

Carry out several titrations and record the results in the usual manner. Calculate the concentration of hardness in the water, expressing the results in (i) grams of CaCO$_3$ per/litre and (ii) parts per million CaCO$_3$. (A worked example is given on page 274)

Dissolved Oxygen

The standard method for the determination of this is the **Winkler Method**, and the principle of it is as follows. A suitable stoppered bottle (of about 200 cm^3 capacity) is filled with the water being analysed, and to it is added some concentrated manganese sulphate solution and alkaline potassium iodide solution. It is important that the bottle should be completely full so that atmospheric oxygen is excluded. The manganese salt and the alkali react together to produce a white precipitate of manganese(II) hydroxide:

$$Mn^{2+} + 2OH^- \rightarrow Mn(OH)_2$$

The oxygen dissolved in the water oxidises this to brown manganese(III) hydroxide[i].

$$4Mn(OH)_2 + O_2 + 2H_2O \rightarrow 4Mn(OH)_3$$

Concentrated acid is now added and in the presence of this, the Mn(OH)$_3$ oxidises the iodide ions (from the KI) to free iodine and at the same time the manganese(III) is reduced back to manganese(II):

$$6H^+ + 2I^- + 2Mn(OH)_3 \rightarrow I_2 + 6H_2O + 2Mn^{2+}$$

Finally, the amount of liberated iodine is determined in the usual way, *i.e.* by titration with standard thiosulphate solution.

Since:

$$1 \text{ mole } O_2 \rightarrow 4 \text{ moles } Mn(OH)_3 \rightarrow 2 \text{ moles } I_2$$

the amount of liberated iodine is a measure of the amount of dissolved oxygen in the water sample.

Experiment 21.3
Estimation of Dissolved Oxygen in Water

Pour a small quantity of water into a stoppered bottle of about 250 cm^3 capacity, shake it about vigorously to thoroughly wet the sides of the bottle, and then empty out the water. Completely fill the bottle with the water to be analysed, making sure that there are no trapped air bubbles. If taking the water from a pond, river or other natural source, take the sample from well below the water's surface.

Using a dropper placed well below the surface of the water, add 1 cm^3 each of manganese(II) sulphate

---

(i) There are different opinions as to the formula of the brown precipitate which is formed, among which are MnO$_2$H$_2$O; MnO(OH)$_2$; Mn$_2$O$_3$; Mn(OH)$_3$. It seems probable that its composition, especially in contact with water, is variable. In the long run it makes no difference, since the brown precipitate is reduced back to its original state *i.e.* Mn^{2+}.

solution and alkaline potassium iodide solution. Stopper the bottle carefully, making sure that no air is trapped (a few cm^3 of water will overflow at this stage). Shake the bottle well for about half a minute and then allow the precipitate to settle. Carefully add 1 cm^3 of concentrated sulphuric acid and re-stopper the bottle — avoiding trapping any air. Shake gently to redissolve the precipitate. Iodine should now be released, making the solution turn reddish brown. If all of the solid does not dissolve, add a few more drops of acid.

The liberated iodine is now determined using sodium thiosulphate solution. Measure out two 100 cm^3 samples into clean conical flasks and titrate each of these with 0.02 M thiosulphate solution in the usual way. Add starch indicator as the end point is approached, and titrate until the blue colour has just disappeared.

Record the results in the usual way, and then calculate the concentration of the dissolved oxygen in the water, expressing the result in (i) grams of O_2 per litre, and (ii) parts per million.

Worked Example 1

In an experiment to determine the total amount of hardness in water, 100 cm^3 of the water were measured into a conical flask. 2 cm^3 of a pH = 10 buffer solution and some solochrome indicator were added and the mixture was titrated with 0.02 M edta solution The average titre was found to be 12.5 cm^3. Calculate the total amount of hardness in the water. Explain also why a buffer solution was added and why edta solution should be stored in plastic bottles.

Answers

Volume of water analysed = 100 cm^3

Volume of 0.02 M edta = 12.5 cm^3

1 mole Ca^{2+} ≡ 1 mole edta

$$\frac{V_1 M_1}{n_1} = \frac{V_2 M_2}{n_2}$$

$$\frac{100 \times x}{1} = \frac{12.5 \times 0.02}{1} \quad \begin{array}{l} (\ x = \text{molarity} \\ \text{of } Ca^{2+} \text{ in} \\ \text{water }) \end{array}$$

$$x = \frac{12.5 \times 0.02}{100} = 0.0025 \text{ mol/L}$$

$$= (0.0025 \times 100) \text{ g/L of } CaCO_3 \quad (CaCO_3 = 100)$$

$$= 0.25 \text{ g/L} = 250 \text{ mg/L} = 250 \text{ p.p.m.}$$

A buffer solution is needed to maintain the pH at a value of 10. In the absence of the buffer, or at an incorrect pH, the indicator will either not change at the correct end point or will not change at all. Edta is stored in plastic bottles because it is capable of extracting metal ions out of glass.

Worked Example 2

In a Winkler experiment to determine the amount of dissolved oxygen in water, the usual procedure was carried out. At the end of the experiment, it was found that the iodine released by 210 cm^3 of the treated water required 7.5 cm^3 of 0.02 M sodium thiosulphate solution. The water temperature was 15°C.

(a) What were the first two reagents added to the water sample?

(b) Why were they added well below the water surface?

(c) What visible change did this cause?

(d) What deduction could be made if a white precipitate were formed?

(e) Why would Winkler's method be unsuitable for water which had been chlorinated?

(f) Calculate the amount of dissolved oxygen in the water sample. Express this (i) moles per litre, (ii) grams per litre (iii) p.p.m. (iv) percentage saturation.

Answers

(a) Alkaline potassium iodide solution and manganese(II) sulphate solution.

(b) There are two reasons for adding them well below the surface: (i) so that atmospheric oxygen will not react with them, and (ii) so they will not be displaced by the stopper when it is put back in the bottle.

(c) A brown coloured precipitate is formed.

(d) There was no dissolved oxygen in the water.

(e) Chlorine in an oxidising agent and will liberate iodine from acidified potassium iodide solution. The titre would therefore be equivalent to the amount both oxygen **and** chlorine dissolved in the water.

(f)

$$\frac{V_1 M_1}{n_1} = \frac{V_2 M_2}{n_2}$$

$$\frac{210 \times x}{1} = \frac{7.5 \times 0.02}{4}$$

$$x = \frac{7.5 \times 0.02}{4 \times 210}$$

$= 0.00018 \text{ mol/L} \qquad = 0.0057 \text{ g } (O_2 = 32)$

Concentration of oxygen in water

$= 0.0057 \text{ g/L} = 5.7 \text{ mg/L} = 5.7 \text{ p.p.m.}$

Concentration of oxygen in water saturated with oxygen at 15 $^\circ$ C = 10.2 p.p.m.[(i)]

Percentage saturation

$$= \frac{5.7 \times 100}{10.2} = 56\%$$

Alternatively:

Since: $O_2 \rightarrow 4Mn(OH)_3 \rightarrow 2I_2 \rightarrow 4Na_2S_2O_3$

1 mole $O_2 \equiv 4$ moles thiosulphate

moles of thiosulphate $= \dfrac{7.5 \times 100}{1000}$

Therfore, moles of oxygen in 210 cm^3 of water

$$= \frac{7.5 \times 0.02}{4 \times 1000}$$

Therefore moles of oxygen per litre

$$= \frac{7.5 \times 0.02 \times 1000}{4 \times 1000 \times 210}$$

$$= 0.00018 \text{ mole}$$

and thereafter as in previous method.

Questions

Q.21.5 In order to measure the amount of suspended solids in water, a 1200 cm^3 sample of the water was filtered through a weighed filter paper. After drying the filter paper, its mass had increased by 0.060 g. Calculate the amount of solids present, giving the result in p.p.m.

Q.21.6 600 cm^3 of water were filtered through a fine pore filter paper of mass 0.84 g. After being dried, the mass of the paper was 0.96 g.

200 cm^3 of the filtered water were evaporated to dryness in a beaker of mass 120.11 g. After doing this, the mass of the beaker and residue was found to be 120.47 g.

From the above measurements, calculate the amounts of both suspended solids and dissolved in the water.

Q.21.7 A 50 cm^3 sample of water was analysed in order to find the amount of hardness present. On titration with 0.025 M edta, the sample required 15 cm^3 of the solution for reaction. Calculate the amount of hardness, giving the results as p.p.m. of CaCO$_3$.

Q.21.8 In an experiment a 25 cm^3 sample of water containing a few cm^3 of a suitable buffer solution was titrated with 0.01 M edta solution. 15 cm^3 of the latter were needed.

(a) What do the letters edta stand for?
(b) Calculate the amount of hardness in the water, giving the result in p.p.m. of CaCO$_3$.
(c) Name a suitable indicator for the titration.
(d) What is a buffer solution?
(e) What would be the effect of carrying out the titration without a buffer solution?

Q.21.9 A 100 cm^3 sample of tap water was placed in a conical flask along with 2 cm^3 of a suitable buffer solution and some solochrome black indicator. On being titrated with 0.01 M edta solution, an average titre of 17.5 cm^3 was found. Calculate the amount of hardness in the water, giving the result in (i) g of Ca^{2+} ions per litre, and (ii) p.p.m. CaCO$_3$.

Q.21.10 100 cm^3 of tap water were placed in a conical flask along with 2 cm^3 of a suitable buffer solution and some solochrome black indicator. On titration with 0.01 M edta solution, an average titre of 21.0 cm^3 was found. A second 100 cm^3 sample of the same water which had been boiled for

[(i)] See chart on page 379.

10 minutes and cooled, was titrated and this time the average titre was found to be 12 .0 cm^3. Calculate the amounts of both permanent hardness and temporary hardness in the water, giving the results in p.p.m.

Q.21.11   25 cm^3 of a solution of magnesium sulphate were titrated with 0.10 M edta solution and the average titre was found to be 15.0 cm^3. Calculate the concentration of MgSO$_4$ in the solution.

If the solution had been prepared by dissolving 7.38 g of magnesium sulphate crystals in a total volume of 500 cm^3 of solution, calculate the percentage of water of crystallisation in the crystals. Calculate also, the value of **x** in the formula MgSO$_4$**x**H$_2$O

Q.21.12   4.00 g of a sample of impure zinc sulphate were dissolved in water and made up to a volume of 250 cm^3. 25 cm^3 of this solution were found to react with 24 cm^3 of 0.1 M edta solution. Calculate the percentage purity of the zinc sulphate.

Q.21.13   3.00 g of crushed sea shells were weighed out and dissolved in dilute nitric acid. The solution was neutralised and made up to a volume of 250 cm^3. 25 cm^3 portions of this were titrated with 0.1 M edta solution, and the mean titre was found to be 30.0 cm^3. Calculate the percentage of calcium in the shells.

Q.21.14   An experiment was carried out to measure the B.O.D. of some canal water. A 250 cm^3 sample was collected and to it were added small volumes of (i) concentrated manganese sulphate and alkaline potassium iodide solutions and (ii), concentrated sulphuric acid. This mixture on being titrated with 0.02 M sodium thiosulphate solution gave a titre of 40.0 cm^3. A second 250 cm^3 sample was stored in an airtight, completed filled bottle for 5 days in the dark and a similar test was carried out on it. This time the titre was 5 cm^3.

(a)   What precautions were necessary in collecting the sample?

(b)   Why were the solutions which were added concentrated?

(c)   What visible changes occurred on adding the reagents at (i) and at (ii)?

(d)   Give the equation for the titration reaction.

(e)   What indicator was needed?

(f)   Calculate the oxygen content of the water (i) initially, and (ii) after five day period.

(g)   Why was the sample stored (i) in a completely filled bottle, (ii) in an airtight bottle, (iii) in the dark?

(h)   Calculate the B.O.D. of the water.

Q.21.15   The following is an account of an experiment in which a pupil was determining the amount of hardness in water.

'A burette was rinsed with water and filled to the 0 cm^3 mark with 0.02 M edta solution. 100 cm^3 of hard water were measured, using a washed pipette, into a washed conical flask. A few drops of starch indicator were added and the characteristic red colour appeared. Edta solution was added, 1 cm^3 at a time, from the burette, and the indicator changed to blue after 11 cm^3 of it had been run into the flask. The flask and pipette were washed and three more titrations carried out, the resulting titres being 10 cm^3, 10 cm^3 and 9 cm^3. The average titre was calculated to be 9.7 cm^3.'

In the above account of the experiment, there are 8 errors, and 2 essential requirements have not been mentioned. List the 8 errors, and say what should have been done in each case. Mention the two missing requirements, and for each, state what would have happened if the experiment had been carried out without these requirements.

Assuming that the average titre, as calculated, was correct, work out the amount of hardness in the water, giving the results in (i) g of Ca^{2+} per litre, (ii) p.p.m. of CaCO$_3$.

Q.21.16   The following results were obtained from a Winkler determination of dissolved oxygen in water; volume of water taken 150 cm^3; volume of thiosulphate solution required 12.0 cm^3; concentration of thiosulphate solution 0.02 molar. Calculate the amount of dissolved oxygen in the water.

Q.21.17   In a Winkler determination of dissolved oxygen in tap water, 121 g of water were taken. The liberated iodine in the experiment required 20 cm^3 of 0.01 M thiosulphate solution. Calculate the quantity of dissolved oxygen in the water, giving the result in p.p.m.

Q.21.18 A sample of river water was analysed as follows. A 250 cm^3 of water had 2 cm^3 each of concentrated manganese(II) sulphate and concentrated alkaline potassium iodide solutions added to it. A brown precipitate of manganese(III) hydroxide was formed. The mixture was acidified and the iodine which was released was found to react with 10 cm^3 of 0.02 M sodium thiosulphate solution. Calculate the number of moles of:

(i)   sodium thiosulphate in the titre.
(ii)   iodine released,
(iii) manganese(III) hydroxide formed,
(iv)   dissolved oxygen in the water sample.

Hence find the concentration of dissolved oxygen in the water. Express the answer in (i) moles per litre, and (ii) p.p.m.

Q.21.19 In a Winkler determination, 200 cm^3 of pond water were analysed by the usual method. The liberated iodine was found to react with 12 cm^3 of 0.02 M sodium thiosulphate solution. Calculate the amount of dissolved oxygen in the water and give the results in both mol/L and p.p.m.
If the amount of dissolved oxygen in saturated water (at the temperature of the experiment) is 12.0 p.p.m., calculate the percentage saturation in the pond water.

Q.21.20 A Winkler determination was carried out on a sample of water from a river. It was found that 150 cm^3 of water released sufficient iodine to react with 8.0 cm^3 of 0.022 M thiosulphate solution.

A second 150 cm^3 sample of the water was stored in the dark for five days and then analysed as before. This time the thiosulphate titre was 3.8 cm^3.

Calculate the amount of dissolved oxygen in the water (i) initially and (ii) after the five day period. Hence, find the B.O.D. value of the water.

Q.21.21 A sample of polluted water was analysed by the Winkler method. 200 cm^3 of the water released sufficient iodine to react with 12.0 cm^3 of 0.01 M sodium thiosulphate solution. Calculate the p.p.m. of dissolved oxygen in the water.
A second 200 cm^3 sample was taken and analysed five days later. This time the titre was 0.1 cm^3. Explain why such a low titre could be obtained and why it would not be possible to calculate a B.O.D. value from these figures.
A third 200 cm^3 sample was taken and made up to 2 litres with well oxygenated water. 200 cm^3 of this were analysed and the liberated iodine needed 23 cm^3 of 0.01M thiosulphte.

Another 200 cm^3 of the diluted polluted water were suitably stored for five days and then analysed. This time the thiosulphate titre was 5.5 cm^3.

Calculate the initial, and the five day, dissolved oxygen values. Hence, find the B.O.D. of the diluted water sample and of the original sample.

Q.21.22 A sample of badly polluted water was analysed as follows.
A Winkler determination on 300 cm^3 of the water gave a thiosulphate (of concentration 0.02 M) titre of 9.0 cm^3.
A sample of the water was then diluted by taking 50 cm^3 of it and making it to 1 litre with fresh well-oxygenated water. 300 cm^3 of this gave a thiosulphate titre of 15.0 cm^3.

A 300 cm^3 sample of the above solution was suitable stored for five days and the titre this time was 4.0 cm^3.

Calculate (i) the amount of dissolved oxygen in the original water sample, and (ii) its B.O.D. value. Express each value in p.p.m.

Review When you know Chapter 21, you should be able to:

(a)   Explain what each of the following is: hard water, soft water, temporary hardness and permanent hardness (and state the cause of each), distilled and deionised water, ion exchange, flocculation, eutrophication, algal bloom, micro-organism.

(b)   State the reactions which occur when: hard water reacts with soap, temporarily hard water is heated, carbon dioxide reacts with limestone.

(c)   Describe: how water is softened, how water is purified for domestic use, the three stages of sewage treatment.

(d)   List the substances which cause pollution in water and state the effects of each.

(e)   Define B.O.D.

(f)   Give the meaning of aerobic, anaerobic, hydrolysis.

(g)   Describe experiments to measure the amount of suspended solids, dissolved solids, hardness, dissolved oxygen, in water.

(h)   Answer questions 21.1, 21.2, 21.4

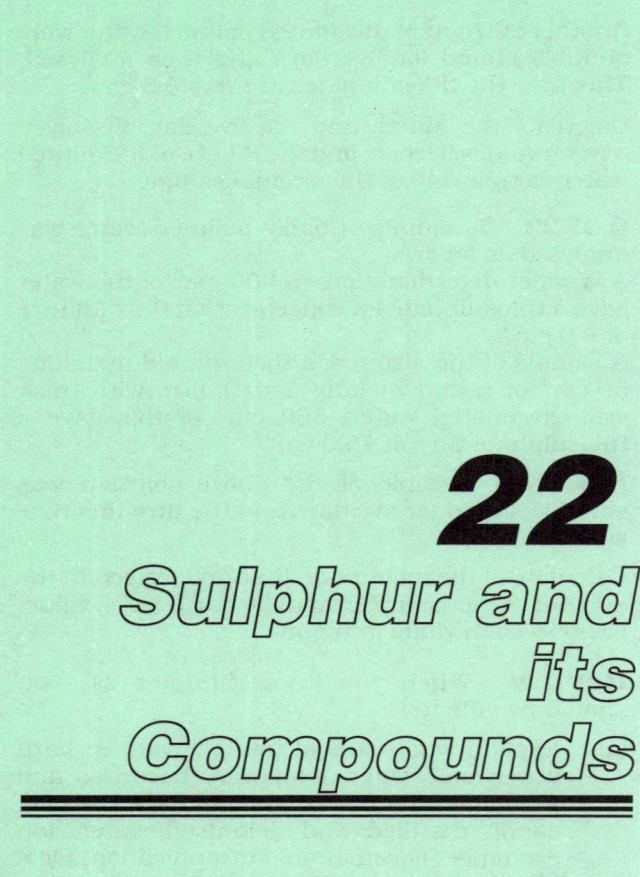

22

Sulphur and its Compounds

Sulphur is a yellow, solid, non-metallic, element, which occurs free in large deposits in Texas and Louisiana (U.S.A.), Poland and Mexico, and also in smaller amounts in various volcanic regions of the world, such as Sicily. It also occurs in the form of metal sulphides, *e.g.* iron pyrites (FeS_2); copper pyrites ($CuFeS_2$); zinc blende (ZnS).

There are several allotropes of sulphur, but the normal form — rhombic sulphur — is a crystalline solid, composed of 8-membered rings of sulphur atoms. It is soluble in several covalent solvents (*e.g.* carbon disulphide, methylbezene) and its m.p. is 113°C. It is very reactive and combines directly with most other elements. It burns in air or oxygen with a blue flame, forming sulphur dioxide, which is its normal oxide. It combines with hydrogen to give hydrogen sulphide (rotten egg gas) which is a very poisonous substance and is weakly acidic. Metals combine with sulphur to form metal sulphides:

$$S + O_2 \rightarrow SO_2$$
$$H_2 + S \rightarrow H_2S$$
$$Fe + S \rightarrow FeS$$

Sulphur Dioxide

Sulphur dioxide is produced whenever sulphur, or any compound containing it burns in air or oxygen. In the laboratory, it is most conveniently prepared by reacting sodium sulphite, Na_2SO_3, with sulphuric acid. It is soluble in water and so cannot be collected over water; its usual means of collection is by upward displacement of air;

$$Na_2SO_3 + H_2SO_4 \rightarrow Na_2SO_4 + SO_2 + H_2O$$

Properties and Uses

Sulphur dioxide is a colourless gas with a pungent choking smell and has a density of about twice that of air. It is very poisonous, particularly to lower forms of life, such as micro-organisms; for this reason it is often used in preserving canned fruit. Its boiling point is -10°C and so it is easily liquefied. Small cylinders of liquefied SO_2 are common in laboratories. Its molecules are V-shaped and the bonding is polar covalent.

It is very soluble in water with which it reacts to form a solution of sulphur**ous** acid, H_2SO_3:

$$H_2O + SO_2 \rightarrow H_2SO_3$$

It is thus an acidic oxide and consequently reacts with alkalis forming salts:

$$SO_2 + NaOH \rightarrow NaHSO_3$$
sodium
hydrogensulphite

$$SO_2 + 2NaOH \rightarrow Na_2SO_3 + H_2O$$
sodium
sulphite

Moist SO_2 is very readily oxidised to form sulphuric acid and so it is a powerful reducing agent:

$$H_2O + SO_2 + [O] \rightarrow H_2SO_4$$

It reduces for example, Fe^{3+} ions to Fe^{2+}; halogens to halide ions; permanganate ions (MnO_4^-) to manganese ions (in acidic solution). This last reaction can be used as a test for the gas, since permanganate ions are purple and Mn^{2+} are practically colourless. Potassium permanganate solution is thus decolorised when added to sulphur dioxide:

$$5SO_2 + 2H_2O + 2MnO_4^- + 6H^+ \rightarrow$$
$$5H_2SO_4 + 2Mn^{2+}$$

Many coloured substances lose their colour on being reduced, and are thus bleached by moist SO_2. In the manufacture of paper, wood pulp is bleached in this way, also wool, and straw used for making straw hats.

The main importance of sulphur dioxide is that it is an intermediate compound in the manufacture of sulphuric acid from sulphur.

Sulphurous Acid and Sulphites

Sulphur dioxide reacts reversibly with water, forming a solution of sulphurous acid, which is a weak dibasic acid:

$$SO_2 + H_2O \rightleftharpoons H_2SO_3$$

When the solution is boiled, the sulphur dioxide is driven off, so that the pure acid cannot be isolated. Salts of sulphurous acid, however, are quite stable. Being a dibasic acid, it forms two series of salts — sulphites and hydrogensulphites:

$$H_2SO_3 \xrightarrow{NaOH} NaHSO_3 \xrightarrow{NaOH} Na_2SO_3$$
sodium   sodium
hydrogensulphite   sulphite
+ H_2O   + H_2O

Both sulphites and hydrogensulphites are decomposed by dilute strong acids, yielding SO_2 *e.g.*

$$Na_2SO_3 + 2HCl \rightarrow 2NaCl + SO_2 + H_2O$$

Sulphur Trioxide

Sulphur trioxide as such is of little importance, but as a stage in the manufacture of sulphuric acid from sulphur it is extremely important. It is formed by the catalytic oxidation of SO_2 and this occurs when a mixture of hot SO_2 and air (or oxygen) is passed over heated platinum or vanadium pentoxide (V_2O_5), both of which catalyse the reaction:

$$SO_2 + \frac{1}{2}O_2 \xrightarrow{\text{Pt or} \atop V_2O_5} SO_3$$

Sulphur trioxide is a white crystalline solid which melts at $17^\circ C$. It is very hygroscopic and reacts with water with considerable violence, releasing much energy and forming sulphuric acid:

$$SO_3 + H_2O \rightarrow H_2SO_4$$

It is thus an acidic oxide. Its molecules are planar covalent, and have the structure:

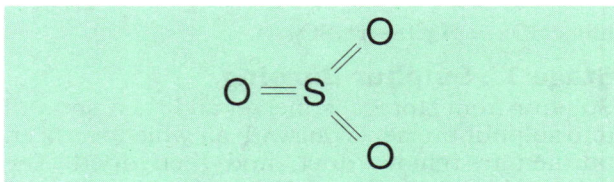

Sulphuric Acid

The only place the average person sees sulphuric acid is in his car battery, but in industry it is one of the most widely used of all manufactured chemicals. About 3.5 million tonnes are used in Britain and Ireland each year and world production is over 100 million tonnes per year. It is used in practically all chemical industries and there are few materials or goods in which it is not used at some stage of their manufacture.

Manufacture of Sulphuric Acid

The main method by which sulphuric acid is manufactured is known as the **Contact Process**. For this the starting materials are sulphur, air and water, and the essential reactions are (i) sulphur is burned in air to produce sulphur dioxide; (ii) the

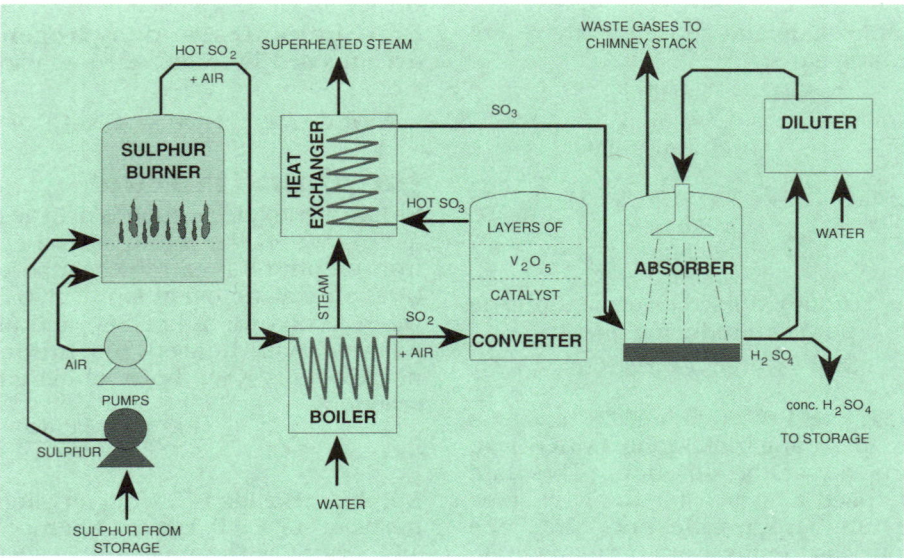

22.1 — Simplified flow diagram of sulphuric acid manufacture.

sulphur dioxide is oxidised catalytically to sulphur trioxide ; (iii) the sulphur trioxide is reacted with water to produce sulphuric acid:

(i) $S + O_2 \rightarrow SO_2$

(ii) $SO_2 + \frac{1}{2}O_2 \rightarrow SO_3$

(iii) $SO_3 + H_2O \rightarrow H_2SO_4$

Stage 1 : Sulphur Burning

Sulphur from storage is melted and then sprayed into sulphur burner, along with air which has been purified to remove dust, and then dried. The sulphur burns, producing sulphur dioxide and the heat of combustion (-291 kJ/mol) causes the temperature to reach about 1000°C. This very hot gas thus contains valuable energy and also is too hot for the next stage of the process. It is therefore passed into a waste heat boiler in which it gives up its heat to convert water into steam. In doing so, its temperature is reduced to about 450°C.

Stage 2 : Catalytic Conversion of SO$_2$ to SO$_3$

Sulphur dioxide, along with unused oxygen (and nitrogen) from the air, enters the converter which contains beds of V_2O_5 catalyst. The reaction of SO_2 with oxygen is reversible and exothermic:

$$SO_2 + \frac{1}{2}O_2 \rightleftharpoons SO_3 \qquad \Delta H = -98 \text{ kJ/mol}$$

So, according to Le Chatelier's Principle, the lower the temperature, the greater the yield of SO_3 at equilibrium. However, at low temperatures, the reaction is slow, and the time taken to reach equilibrium is long. A compromise between high yield and low rate, and high rate and low yield, has therefore to be chosen and 450°C is the usual operating temperature. The catalyst is spread out so that the maximum surface area is in contact with the reacting gases. A conversion rate of about 99.5% can be achieved in a modern plant.

Since the reaction is exothermic, heat is produced in the converter, and the gases leaving it are at a higher temperature than those entering. The exit gases are therefore cooled by passing them through a heat exchanger in which they convert the steam made in the waste heat boiler, into superheated steam, at about 500°C and 40 atmospheres pressure.

Platinum can also be used to catalyse this conversion and it is a more efficient catalyst. However, it is much more easily 'poisoned' (made ineffective) by impurities in the reactants and because of this it has been found to be less economic to use.

Stage 3: Absorption of SO$_3$

Sulphur trioxide cannot be directly absorbed in water because the gas first comes into contact with the water vapour over the liquid and reacts with it. This produces a stable mist of tiny droplets which will not condense but would pass right through the absorber and be emitted into the atmosphere. The gas is therefore dissolved in concentrated sulphuric acid (which it does readily) and this is then diluted with the right amount of water to react with the dissolved SO_3. The net result is that the SO_3 is reacted with water, producing H_2SO_4.

Plant Emission

The nitrogen which enters the sulphur burner in the original air is carried right through the plant and sent up the chimney stack to be emitted to the atmosphere. Inevitably some unreacted SO_2 is emitted too, but in a modern plant, the amount is minimal (about 0.2%) compared with SO_2 emissions from other sources, such as power stations.

22.2 —   A sulphuric acid plant.

Use of the 'waste' heat

The superheated steam generated in the heat exchangers is utilised in various ways; it supplies the heat necessary to melt the sulphur initially and to keep it molten until it reaches the sulphur burner; it heats the incoming air to the burner and so avoids a cooling effect; it works various pumps needed in the plant. Many sulphuric acid plants incorporate their own electricity generating stations, using the high pressure steam to drive generators in the conventional manner. The electricity generated is used in the plant and this either reduces or eliminates the cost of electricity.

Properties of Sulphuric Acid

Pure sulphuric acid is a thick colourless oily liquid. The normal laboratory concentrated acid contains 98% H_2SO_4, and has a density of 1.85 g/cm^3 and boils at 338°C. It is corrosive and dangerous and should always be treated with care. Chemically, it behaves in 3 different ways, *viz*, (1) as an acid, (2) as an oxidising agent and (3) as a drying and dehydrating agent.

1.   **As an Acid**: It is a strong dibasic acid with the usual acidic properties.

It ionises in solution :

$$H_2SO_4 \rightarrow 2H^+ + SO_4^{2-}$$

and so the solution conducts electricity. The dilute acid reacts with most metals, liberating hydrogen and producing metal sulphates. It reacts with bases, forming salts and water, and with metal carbonates, giving off carbon dioxide, and forming salts and water. Being a dibasic acid, it forms two series of salts, *viz*. sulphates and hydrogensulphates. Most metal sulphates are soluble in water, the common exceptions being those of barium, lead and calcium.

2.   **As an Oxidising Agent:** The concentrated acid is a strong oxidising agent, normally being reduced to SO_2 as it oxidises:

$$H_2SO_4 \rightarrow H_2O + SO_2 + [O]$$
$$\text{taken by}$$
$$\text{reducing agent}$$

It reacts with metals, including those below hydrogen in the electrochemical series, forming the metal oxide, sulphur dioxide, and water. The metal oxide being a base, then reacts with more acid to form a salt and water. With copper for example, the reactions are:

$$Cu + H_2SO_4 \rightarrow CuO + H_2O + SO_2$$

$$CuO + H_2SO_4 \rightarrow CuSO_4 + H_2O$$

The overall result is:

$$Cu + 2H_2SO_4 \rightarrow CuSO_4 + 2H_2O + SO_2$$

Likewise, it can oxidise carbon to CO_2, sulphur to SO_2, hydrogen bromide to bromine and iron(II) salts to iron(III) salts.

3.   **As a Drying and Dehydrating Agent**: Concentrated sulphuric acid has a tremendous affinity for water and considerable energy is released when cold concentrated acid is added to cold water; the mixture can instantly reach a

temperature of well over 100°C. Because of this, diluting the acid **must** be done by adding the acid to a large volume of water, and never the other way round. Adding water to acid would result in so much heat being produced that the initial water would instantly turn to steam and cause the acid to splutter and splash dangerously.

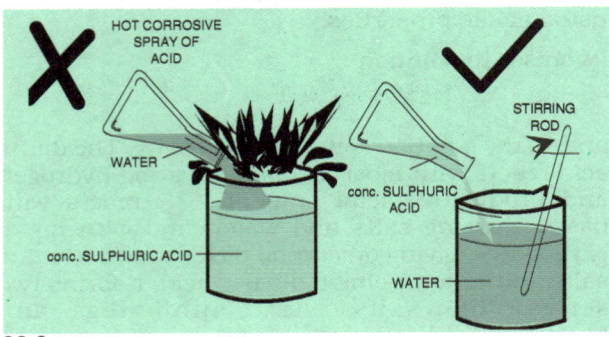

22.3

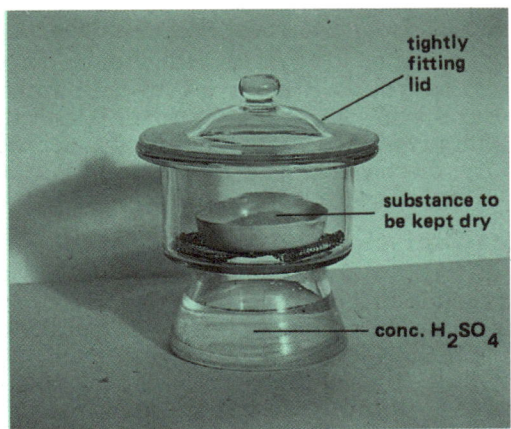

22.4 — *Desiccator*

The concentrated acid can extract the elements of water from compounds. Bluestone ($CuSO_4 5H_2O$) becomes dehydrated and changes to white anhydrous copper sulphate. Sugar becomes carbon:

$$C_{12}H_{22}O_{11} \rightarrow 11H_2O + 12C$$

Ethanol is dehydrated to ethene, and methanoic acid is converted to carbon monoxide:

$$C_2H_5OH - H_2O \rightarrow C_2H_4$$
$$HCOOH - H_2O \rightarrow CO$$

The concentrated acid often is used to dry gases (with the exception of ammonia), by bubbling them through it, and it is also used in a desiccator, a vessel for keeping materials absolutely dry.

Uses of Sulphuric Acid

As mentioned earlier sulphuric acid is one of industry's most used chemicals. A recent breakdown of its uses is shown — see figure 22.5.

Tests for Sulphates and Sulphites

Sulphates and sulphites[i] in solution can be detected by adding barium chloride solution.

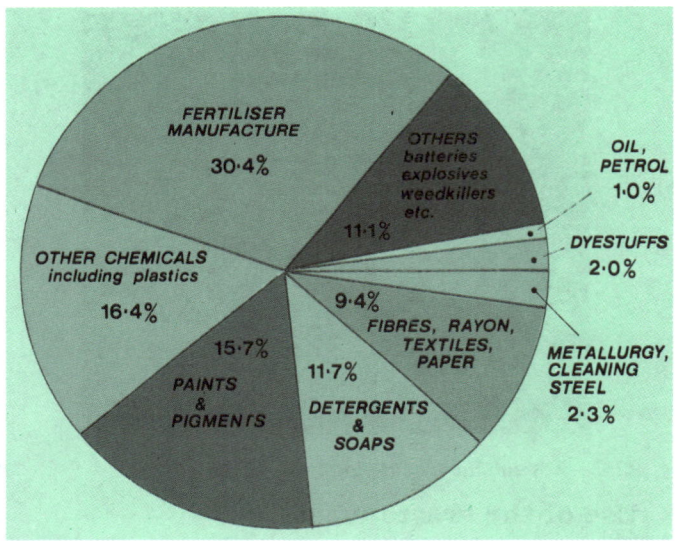

22.5

Both sulphates and sulphites in solution yield white precipitates on adding barium chloride solution:

$$XSO_4 + BaCl_2 \rightarrow BaSO_4(\downarrow) + XCl_2$$

$$XSO_3 + BaCl_2 \rightarrow BaSO_3(\downarrow) + XCl_2$$

(i)   Experimental details for these tests are given on Page 103

Sulphites however, are decomposed by acid, so if dilute acid is then added and the precipitate dissolves, the substance is a sulphite, whereas, if it remains, the substance is a sulphate

$$BaSO_3 + 2HCl \rightarrow BaCl_2 + SO_2 + H_2O$$

$$BaSO_4 + 2HCl \rightarrow \text{no reaction.}$$

Thiosulphates

The only common thiosulphate is sodium thiosulphate, $Na_2S_2O_3$,. Photographers know this substance as 'hypo' and use it when developing films to dissolve away (as a complex substance) unused silver halides from the emulsion on the film, so making the film no longer sensitive to light; this process is called fixing.

In the laboratory, sodium thiosulphate is used in volumetric analysis for estimating iodine in solution. This technique is described elsewhere (Chapter 11.)

Thiosulphate in solution is detected by adding dilute acid; SO_2 is evolved and a fine whitish precipitate of sulphur is formed:

$$Na_2S_2O_3 + 2HCl \rightarrow 2NaCl + SO_2(\uparrow) + S(\downarrow)$$

Air Pollution

Clean air is a substance which is becoming less and less common; in towns and cities at present, it is virtually unknown. Man is constantly adding to the air a variety of substances which damage both himself and his environment. Air pollution is caused by waste products from factories, power stations, homes, cars and other forms of transport, and the amount of such substances has increased enormously during the last fifty years or so, particularly in those parts of the world which have become industrial and affluent, e.g. Western Europe, U.S.A, Japan. The disposal of man's unwanted and unusable materials is a major problem today.

The burning of fossil fuels, necessary to provide heat, electricity and transport, produces most of the common air pollutants. Most fuels contain small amounts of sulphur, which, on combustion, yields sulphur dioxide, to be released into the atmosphere. Coal and fuel oil can contain up to 3% sulphur, so that domestic fires, central heating boilers, industrial furnaces and power stations all contribute to atmospheric sulphur dioxide. It has

Table 22.1 — Major Air Pollutants

Air Pollutant	Source	Effects	Methods of reduction
Sulphur dioxide (SO_2)	Burning fossil fuels	Causes acid rain, attacks limestone buildings.	Remove sulphur from fuels before burning. Remove SO_2 from chimney gases of power stations.
Nitrogen oxides (NO, NO_2)	Vehicle exhausts, burning of fuels	Contributes to acid rain and 'smog'	Fit catalytic converters to vehicle exhausts. Modify engines to run on a weaker mixture of fuel and air.
Carbon dioxide (CO_2)	Burning fuels	Causes "greenhouse effect"	Can only be reduced by burning less fossil fuels.
Carbon monoxide (CO)	Burning fuels, vehicle exhausts, cigarette smoke.	Poisonous to animals including humans	Ensure vehicle engines are well maintained. Prevent cigarette smoking.
Hydrocarbons	Vehicles exhaust, burning fuels	Contributes to acid rain and 'smog'	Fit catalytic converters to vehicle exhausts. Modify engines to run on a weaker mixture of fuel and air
Smoke	Burning fuels, untuned vehicle engines	Damages lungs, reduced photosynthesis in plants, dirties buildings	Use smokeless fuel. Make sure engines and burners have plenty of air to burn fully.

been estimated that the UK releases about five million tonnes of SO_2, into the air each year.

Smoke, produced by burning coal, consists of particles of carbon and other solids, and these, in time, are deposited somewhere — on buildings, on people, on traffic and on the ground. The dirty stonework, so common on buildings of towns and cities, is largely caused by deposited smoke.

The engines of cars, lorries and motor cycles emit a number of poisonous substances — carbon monoxide, oxides of nitrogen, unburnt hydrocarbons, volatile lead compounds, and, all to often, dirty smoke from poorly maintained engines. The oxides of nitrogen result from the combining of atmospheric oxygen and nitrogen at the high temperature of the spark produced by the sparking plug inside the engine. The lead compounds come from the tetraethyl lead which is contained in petrol (in order to improve engine performance). Lead is a cumulative poison which means that once it is taken into the human body, it remains there. Too much lead in the body can cause brain damage and even death.

Sulphur dioxide is possibly the worst of the common air pollutants. It is toxic to both plants and animals; it can damage or kill crops and other vegetation; it can impair breathing and damage lung tissue. For old people with weak hearts and people suffering from bronchitis, it can be a killer, particularly if smoke is also present in the air. In the atmosphere, sulphur dioxide can become oxidised to sulphur trioxide, so that when it rains, sulphurous and sulphuric acids are formed and fall to earth. Over towns and industrial areas in particular, rain is usually quite acidic. 'Acid rain' accelerates metal corrosion and attacks the stonework of buildings, causing it to wear and crumble,

In Ireland, the highest concentrations of atmospheric sulphur dioxide and smoke occur in central Dublin, and Cork city. It has been found that about half of all air pollutants in the country come from the Dublin and Cork areas; this is due to the high concentration of people, traffic and industry in those places.

There is a growing awareness at the present time regarding the dangers of air pollution, and various measures are being taken to reduce it. Power stations are built with very high chimneys to disperse their waste gases over a wide area, in order to reduce the local concentration of these

22.6 — *These photographs of one of the statues on top of the Bank of Ireland, Dublin, show the damage caused by years of air pollution. The picture on the left was taken before restoration, while that on the right shows the statue at present, looking as it did originally.*

gases; new chemical plants are required to have very high standards of air pollution control; unleaded petrol is becoming available in many parts of the world — including Ireland — and reduction of the lead content is being made obligatory elsewhere; 'smokeless zones' have been created in parts of the UK (e.g. London) which means that open coal fires are illegal; most factories have 'electrostatic precipitators' in their chimney stacks, and these remove most of the smoke from the waste gases which are being discharged.

Questions

Q.22.1 Describe the reaction which takes place when copper is heated with concentrated sulphuric acid. The resulting gas is passed into (a) litmus solution; (b) chlorine water; (c) a solution of potassium permanganate. What would be observed in each case and what are the explanations for the various observations?

Q.22.2 Sulphur dioxide can be prepared by the reaction between hydrochloric acid and sodium sulphite.

(a)   State the conditions necessary to give a steady reaction.
(b)   Explain, using a diagram, how you would collect the gas.
(c)   Give the equation for the reaction.
(d)   State one distinctive test for the gas. When sulphur dioxide is passed into chlorine water, the following reaction takes place:

$$2H_2O + SO_2 + Cl_2 \rightarrow 4H^+ + SO_4^{2-} + 2Cl^-$$

(i) Interpret this equation in terms of oxidation and reduction.

(ii) Describe and explain chemical tests by which you could confirm that the products of the reaction are those indicated by the equation.

Q.22.3 When bromine water is added to a gas jar containing sulphur dioxide, the bromine is reduced and the SO_2 is oxidised.

(a)   To what is the SO_2 oxidised?
(b)   Write an equation for the reaction.
(c)   What visible change occurs in the jar?
(d)   How would you carry out a chemical test to confirm that the reaction had taken place?

Q.22.4 Describe how you would test for the following ions in solution; (a) sulphate; (b) sulphite; (c) thiosulphate.

Q.22.5 Over 90% of the sulphur dioxide which is released into the atmosphere is in the northern hemisphere of the world. What is the possible explanation for this? Should this give man cause for concern? Why ? Describe two harmful effects of the pollution of the atmosphere by sulphur dioxide.

Q.22.6 In a coal fired power station, 1000 tonnes of coal are burned each day. The average sulphur content of coal is 1.6% by mass. Calculate the mass of sulphur dioxide produced by the power station each day. What happens to this gas? Name three effects caused by its presence. Name three other substances released by the burning of coal.

Q.22.7 The modern method for sulphuric acid manufacture involves a 3 stage process.

(a)   Name the process.
(b)   Name the three raw materials used.
(c)   Which two of these are reacted together in stage 1?
(d)   What substance is formed in this stage?
(e)   Is the reaction in this stage exothermic or endothermic?
(f)   What chemical reaction occurs in stage 2?
(g)   At what temperature does this reaction take place?
(h)   What would be the effect of increasing the temperature used?
(i)   What is done to the product of this stage to make sulphuric acid?
(j)   What precautions are necessary in the last stage?
(k)   Explain why.
(l)   Which stage of the process is catalysed?
(m)   What catalyst is used?
(n)   What would be the effect of not using a catalyst?
(o)   At which stage is the third raw material added?
(p)   What is the maximum amount of sulphuric acid which could be produced from 1 tonne (1000 kg) of sulphur?
(q)   Why is this amount never achieved in practice?

Q.22.8 Write balanced equations for each of the following reactions:

(a) the production of hydrogen from sulphuric acid,

(b) the reaction of sulphuric acid with sodium carbonate,

(c) the reaction of concentrated sulphuric acid with ethanol,

(d) the oxidation of hydrogen iodide by sulphuric acid,

(e) the reaction of ammonia with sulphuric acid.

(f) the effect of sulphuric acid on barium chloride solution,

(g) the effect of sulphuric acid with sodium sulphite,

(h) the dissolving of sulphur dioxide in water,

(i) the decolorisation of acidified potassium permanganate solution by sulphur dioxide,

(j) the addition of sodium thiosulphate crystals to dilute hydrochloric acid,

(k) the reaction of sodium thiosulphate solution with iodine.

Review When you know Chapter 22 you should be able to:

(a) List some reactions in which sulphur dioxide is formed.

(b) List the properties of sulphur dioxide, and say how it is converted to sulphur trioxide.

(c) Describe in detail the Contact Process.

(d) Describe the three ways in which sulphuric acid reacts.

(e) Describe the tests for sulphite, sulphate, and thiosulphate ions.

(f) List the causes and effects of the various pollutants in the atmospheres.

Fluorine, chlorine bromine and iodine are the elements of Group 7 of the periodic table and are known as the **halogens**. They are a good example of a 'family of elements', as they have many properties and reactions in common. Of the four elements, **chlorine** is the most common and the most important, and its chemistry is described in detail.

23.1 — Chlorine is a greenish gas, bromine a red volatile liquid and iodine a dark grey crystalline solid.

Chlorine

Chlorine was discovered in 1774 by the Swedish chemist Scheele, who prepared it by the action of hydrochloric acid on 'black oxide of manganese'. The gas was shown to be an element and given its name (on account of its green colour) by Davy in 1810.

Occurence

Chlorine is much too reactive an element to occur free (*i.e.* uncombined), it is found only in the combined state — mainly as sodium chloride — in the form of rock salt and in sea water. Sodium chloride is the source of almost all chlorine (and of most sodium compounds).

Manufacture of Chlorine

Chlorine is a vital necessity for the manufacture of many everyday substances and it is manufactured in large quantities — by the electrolysis of brine (saturated sodium chloride solution). Details of this are given in Chapter 16.

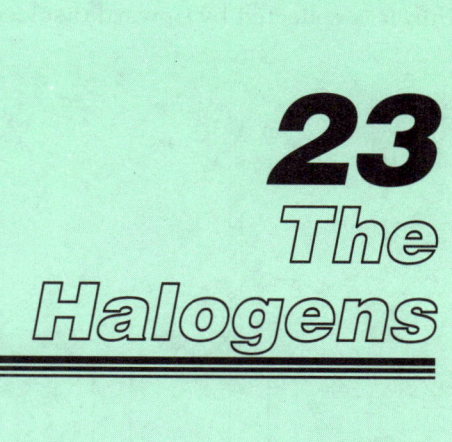

23
The
Halogens

Preparation of Chlorine

The simplest way to prepare chlorine is to react concentrated hydrochloric acid with potassium permanganate

$$16HCl + 2KMnO_4 \rightarrow 2KCl + 2MnCl_2 + 8H_2O + 5Cl_2$$

or, ionically,

$$16H^+ + 10Cl^- + 2MnO_4^- \rightarrow 2Mn^{2+} + 8H_2O + 5Cl_2$$

Chlorine prepared in this manner contains some hydrogen chloride gas, but this can be removed by bubbling the gas through water. The chlorine can be dried by passing it through concentrated sulphuric acid and, since it is much denser than air, it is collected by upward displacement of air.

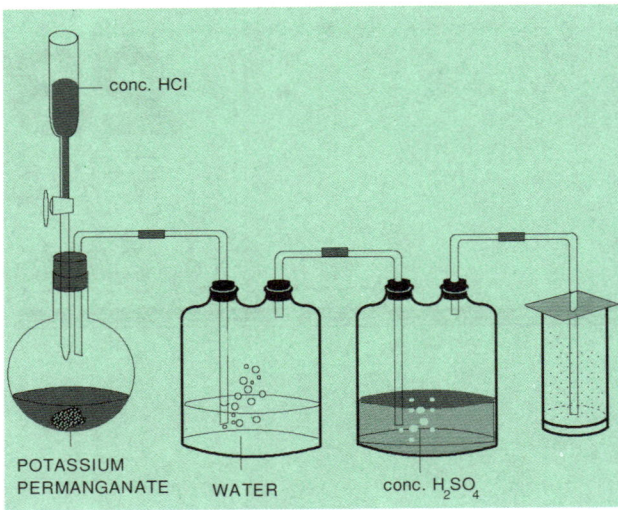

23.2 — Preparation of Chlorine.

Physical Properties of Chlorine

Greenish gas with pungent choking smell. Very poisonous; it causes inflammation of the lungs and mucous membranes. Density = 3.17 g/L (air $\times 2\frac{1}{2}$). Moderately soluble in water (about 2 volumes of gas in 1 volume of water). Easily liquefied (b.p. -34°C) under pressure alone (7 atmospheres at room temperature).

Chemical Reactions

1. With metals:

Chlorine is an extremely reactive element; it combines directly with all metals forming metal chlorides:

$$Mg + Cl_2 \rightarrow MgCl_2$$
$$2Na + Cl_2 \rightarrow 2NaCl$$

Where a metal has more than one valency; the chloride of the metal in its higher valency state is formed; iron is converted to iron(III) chloride:

$$2Fe + 3Cl_2 \rightarrow 2FeCl_3$$

2. With non-metals:

It combines directly with most non-metals:

$$2P + 5Cl_2 \rightarrow 2PCl_5$$

A mixture of hydrogen and chlorine combines slowly in daylight, but on exposure to ultra-violet light or on ignition, it combines explosively.

$$H_2 + Cl_2 \rightarrow 2HCl$$

In the dark, there is no reaction.

3. Oxidising Reactions:

Chlorine is a strong oxidising agent:

(a) It can remove hydrogen from the hydrides of non-metals, forming hydrogen chloride and leaving the non-metal element.

$$Cl_2 + H_2S \rightarrow 2HCl + S$$

Burning hydrocarbons (*e.g.* turpentine $C_{10}H_{16}$ or candle wax) continue to burn in chlorine; black clouds of soot are produced and hydrogen chloride gas is liberated:

$$C_{10}H_{16} + 8Cl_2 \rightarrow 16HCl + 10C$$

(b) It can displace the less electronegative bromine (and iodine) from solutions of bromides (and iodides):

$$Cl_2 + 2KBr \rightarrow 2KCl + Br_2$$

or, ionically,

$$Cl_2 + 2Br^- \rightarrow 2Cl^- + Br_2$$

This process is used in the extraction of bromine from the bromides in sea water. Its reaction with iodides is similar.

(c) It can oxidise iron(II) chloride to iron(III) chloride; and sulphite ions to sulphate ions:

23.3 — Chlorine is so reactive that it spontaneously combines with powdered antimony — forming antimony(III) chloride. This photograph was taken in a dark room when antimony powder was dropped into a jar of chlorine gas. The light comes solely from the chemical reaction.

$$2FeCl_2 + Cl_2 \rightarrow 2FeCl_3$$

$$K_2SO_3 + Cl_2 + H_2O \rightarrow K_2SO_4 + 2HCl$$

or ionically,

$$SO_3^{2-} + Cl_2 + H_2O \rightarrow SO_4^{2-} + 2HCl$$

4. Reaction with water:

A solution of chlorine in water ('chlorine water') is acidic, due to the presence of some hydrochloric and hypochlorous acids:

$$Cl_2 + H_2O \rightarrow \underset{\substack{\text{hydro–}\\\text{chloric acid}}}{HCl} + \underset{\substack{\text{hypochlorous}\\\text{acid}}}{HClO}$$

Hypochlorous acid is not very stable and the solution readily decomposes, especially when exposed to sunlight, yielding oxygen:

$$2HClO \rightarrow 2HCl + O_2$$

Moist chlorine is a bleaching agent, due to the presence of the hypochlorous acid; this reacts with many organic dyes, and converts them, by oxidation, to colourless compounds. Common substances bleached by chlorine are litmus, grass and ink.

5. Reaction with alkalis:

Chlorine reacts readily with cold alkalis forming a mixture of a chloride and a hypochlorite:

$$2NaOH + Cl_2 \rightarrow \underset{\substack{\text{sodium}\\\text{chloride}}}{NaCl} + \underset{\substack{\text{sodium}\\\text{hypochlorite}}}{NaClO} + H_2O$$

The solution so formed is a very good bleaching agent and is available commercially as *Parazone, Milton, Domestos*.

Uses of Chlorine

Well over half of the commercially produced chlorine is used in the manufacture of chlorine-containing organic compounds. Examples of these are tetrachloromethane and trichloroethene (both are solvents and dry-cleaning agents), chloroethane (a local anaesthetic), and also used in manufacturing dichloro-methane (a solvent used as a paint remover), 1,2-dichloroethane (for manufacturing the plastic PVC), antiseptics (*Dettol* and *TCP*) and insecticides.

Other important uses are for the manufacture of hydrochloric acid, for sterilising water supplies and swimming baths and for bleaching cotton, linen and paper.

Chlorine is easily liquefied under pressure and is stored and transported in steel cylinders.

Bromine

Bromine, like chlorine, is too reactive to occur free. It occurs mainly as sodium, potassium and magnesium bromides which are present in sea water.

Physical Properties of Bromine

Dark red liquid with pungent very irritating smell. Heavy; density = 3.12 g/cm^3. Very volatile (b.p. = 50°C). It gives off a red/brown vapour at room temperature. This liquid causes painful burn-like wounds and the vapour is poisonous.

Slightly soluble in water (4.3 $g/100\ cm^3$); the solution is known as 'bromine water'. Very soluble in non-polar solvents such as trichloroethane or tetrachloromethane.

Summary of Properties of Group 7 Elements

Property	Fluorine	Chlorine	Bromine	Iodine
Atomic number	9	17	35	53
Relative Atomic Mass	19	35.5	80	127
Electron structure	2,7	2,8,7	2,8,18,7	2,8,18,18,7
Atomic Radius (nm)	0.072	0.099	0.114	0.133
Ionisation Energy (kJ/mol)	1682	1255	1142	1008
Electronegativity	4.9	3.0	2.8	2.4
Density (g/cm^3)	1.11 (l)	1.56 (l)	3.12 (l)	4.93 (s)
m.p. (^{o}C)	-220	-101	-7	+114
b.p. (^{o}C)	-188	-35	+59	+184
Colour	pale yellow	light green	dark red	dark grey
Reactivity		————————> decreases ——————————>		

Chemical reactions

It is similar to chlorine, but is less reactive. Thus it combines directly with most elements although heat or a catalyst is often necessary to start the reaction, *e.g.*

$$2Na + Br_2 \rightarrow 2NaBr$$

$$H_2 + Br_2 \rightarrow 2HBr$$

$$2P + 3Br_2 \rightarrow 2PBr_3$$

When dissolved in water, it reacts forming a mixture of hydrobromic and hypobromous acids — this liberates oxygen when heated or when exposed to sunlight:

$$Br_2 + H_2O \rightarrow HBr + HBrO$$

$$2HBrO \rightarrow 2HBr + O_2$$

Bromine reacts with alkalis in a similar way to chlorine. It also displaces iodine from solution of iodides:

$$Br_2 + 2I^- \rightarrow I_2 + 2Br^-$$

Use of Bromine

Its main use is for the manufacture of 1,2-dibromoethane which is added to petrol to prevent lead (from the anti-knock agent, lead tetra-ethyl) being deposited in the cylinders. It is also used to make bromides for use in medicine and photography, and in the laboratory it is used in testing for unsaturation in organic compounds (Chapter 25).

Iodine

Iodine occurs to a very small extent in sea water in the form of iodides, but the main source of the element is the compound sodium iodate ($NaIO_3$) which occurs in the Chile saltpetre ($NaNO_3$) deposits.

Physical Properties of Iodine

Dark grey crystalline solid with metallic lustre. Density 4.9 g/cm^3. It sublimes on heating, producing a violet vapour, which dissociates on further heating above 77°C: $I_2 \rightleftharpoons 2I$

$$\text{m.p.} = 114^oC, \text{b.p.} = 184^oC$$

The vapour is irritating and poisonous. Almost insoluble in water but soluble in organic solvents *e.g.* ethanol, tetrachloromethane.

Chemical Reactions

It is not so reactive as the other halogens but combines directly with many elements, although it is usually necessary to provide heat and/or a catalyst.

Iodine dissolves readily in potassium iodide solution, in which it forms the tri-iodide, KI_3:

$$KI + I_2 \rightarrow KI_3 \quad (i.e. \text{ K}^+ \text{ and I}_3^-)$$

It reacts quantitatively with sodium thiosulphate:

$$I_2 + 2Na_2S_2O_3 \rightarrow 2NaI + Na_2S_4O_6$$

This reaction is of importance in volumetric analysis for the estimation of oxidising agents (which liberate free iodine from acidified potassium iodide solution). Iodine also produces a deep blue colour with starch solution.

Uses of iodine

Iodine kills germs and a 2% solution of it in alcohol is an antiseptic which is known as 'tincture of iodine'. Iodine is an essential element for healthy growth and it is used in a number of medical preparations.

Fluorine

Fluorine is a pale yellow, extremely poisonous gas with an irritating smell. It is the most reactive of all elements, combining directly with every element except oxygen and some of the noble gases. It is also the most electronegative element and this is why some fluorine compounds do not show a continuation of the trends shown by HI, HBr and HCl, e.g. boiling points.

Experiment 23.1
Some reactions of the halogens and the halides

A. Note the smell of chlorine water — this is the same as that of chlorine gas.

B. Place two pieces of litmus paper, red and blue, into some chlorine water.

(1) What happens the litmus paper?

(2) Is chlorine water acidic or alkaline, or can you tell?

(3) How would you describe the effect which chlorine water has on litmus?

Chlorine water, in addition to dissolved chlorine, contains two acids — formed by the reaction of chlorine molecules with water.

(4) Complete the equation for this reaction:
$$H_2O + Cl_2 \rightarrow ... + ...$$

C. Repeat the previous experiment, but use bromine water instead of chlorine water.

(5) Describe your conclusions.

D. Add a small crystal of iodine to a few cm^3 of water and shake.

(6) Does it dissolve?

(7) Why/why not?

Now add about 5 cm^3 of potassium iodide solution and shake.

(8) What happens?

Iodine combines with potassium iodide to form a soluble compound of formula KI_3.

(9) Write the balanced equation for this reaction.

'Iodine solution' usually contains this compound, and since it is easily decomposed, iodine solution behaves as if it were a solution of iodine in water.

E. Take a few cm^3 of iodine solution from the previous experiment, and fill the test tube almost to the top with water. Add a few drops of starch solution.

(10) What is the result?

This reaction is used as a test for iodine. Show that it is a very sensitive test by adding just a few drops of iodine solution to a test tube full of water, mixing and then adding some starch solution.

(11) Is the characteristic colour formed?

F. Add a few cm^3 of chlorine water to some potassium bromide solution in a test tube and mix.

(12) What is observed?

(13) What is the coloured product?

(14) Complete and balance the equation:
$$Cl_2 + KBr \rightarrow ... + ...$$

(15) Write the ionic equation for the same reaction.

(16) What is oxidised in this reaction?

(17) What is reduced?

(18) What is the oxidising agent?

(19) What is the reducing agent?

G. Add a few cm^3 of chlorine water to some potassium iodide solution in a test tube.

(20) What substance is liberated?

(21) Complete the equation: $Cl_2 + I^- \rightarrow .. + ...$

(22) What type of reaction is the above?

(23)   Copy out the following and fill in the gaps: chlorine has ... the iodide ions to ... and in doing so, chlorine is ... to ....

H.   Sometimes it is difficult to distinguish between bromine and iodine by their colours in aqueous solution, but in trichloroethane solution, they show very different colours. Add about $1cm^3$ of trichloroethane (preferably from a dropper) to a few cm^3 of (a) bromine water and (b) iodine solution. Cork each tube and shake.

(24)   What colour is bromine in trichloroethane?

(25)   What colour is iodine in trichloroethane?

I.   Chlorine can oxidise bromide ions to bromine, and iodine ions to iodine.

(26)   Is it more likely that bromine will oxidise iodide ions to iodine or that iodine will oxidise bromide ions to bromine?

(27)   Describe how you do this.

(28)   Complete and balance each of the following equations or write 'no reaction' as appropriate:
   (i) $Br_2 + I^- \rightarrow$
   (ii) $I_2 + Br^- \rightarrow$

(29)   List the elements bromine, chlorine and iodine in decreasing order of oxidising ability.

(30)   Which most readily gains electrons?

(31)   Which least readily gains them?

J.   Take a few cm^3 of freshly prepared iron(II) sulphate solution and acidify it with about $1 cm^3$ of dilute sulphuric acid. Add some chlorine water and mix. Now add sodium hydroxide solution.

(32)   What colour is the precipitate?

(33)   What substance is it ?

(34)   What happened the iron(II) ions on adding the chlorine water?

(35)   Complete and balance the equation:
   $Fe^{2+} + H^+ + Cl_2 \rightarrow ... + ...$

K.   Take a few cm^3 of sodium sulphite solution, and add a few cm^3 of chlorine water. Now identify the acid radical or anion in the resulting solution (tests for acid radicals, experiment 8.3).

(36)   What radical or anion is present?

(37)   What change did the sulphite undergo?

(38)   Why?

(39)   Complete and balance the equation:
   $SO_3^{2-} + H_2O + Cl_2 \rightarrow ... + ,,,$

L   Compare the chloride, bromide and iodide of silver with each other as follows. Into three test tubes put $5 cm^3$ each of solutions of a chloride (e.g. NaCl), a bromide (e.g. K Br) and an iodide (e.g. KI) [i] Add a few cm^3 of silver nitrate solution to each.

(40)   What colour is silver chloride? silver bromide? and silver iodide?

(41)   Write the equation for the formation of one of these substance. Now to each test tube add about $5 cm^3$ of aqueous ammonia. Cover the top of each tube and mix well by inverting several times.

(42)   What happens to the silver chloride?

((43)   and to the silver bromide?

(44)   and to the silver iodide?

These reactions are used in analysis to identify and distinguish between the halide ions.

M.   Lead iodide has a very bright and characteristic colour. It is insoluble in water and so can be prepared by an ion exchange reaction. Prepare some.

(45)   What colour is lead iodide?

(46)   Write down the equation for the reaction in which you prepared it

---

(i)   If only the solid is available, dissolve a quantity about the size of a pea in a test tube half full with water.

The Hydrogen Halides.

Compound	Formula	b.p.°C	m.p.°C
Hydrogen fluoride	HF	19.5	-89
Hydrogen chloride	HCl	-84	-115
Hydrogen bromide	HBr	-67	-87
Hydrogen iodide	Hl	-35	-51

The hydrogen halides are the compounds of the halogens with hydrogen, They are all colourless, pungent smelling and poisonous gases which dissolve in water to give acidic solutions. They are made by the direct synthesis (*i.e.* combining together) of the two elements. Hydrogen chloride is the most common and most important.

Hydrogen Chloride

Preparation of Hydrogen Chloride

Hydrogen chloride is manufactured by simply burning hydrogen in chlorine. Much of the manufactured hydrogen chloride is immediately reacted with water to produce hydrochloric acid.

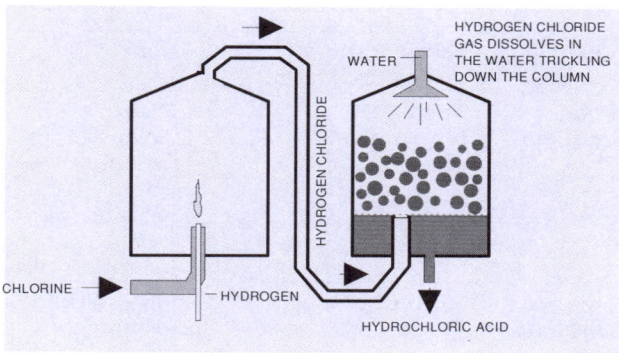

23.4

In the laboratory, hydrogen chloride is best prepared by heating concentrated sulphuric acid with sodium chloride, when the following reaction occurs:

$$NaCl + H_2SO_4 \rightarrow HCl + NaHSO_4$$

The gas is soluble in water and is collected by the upward displacement of air.

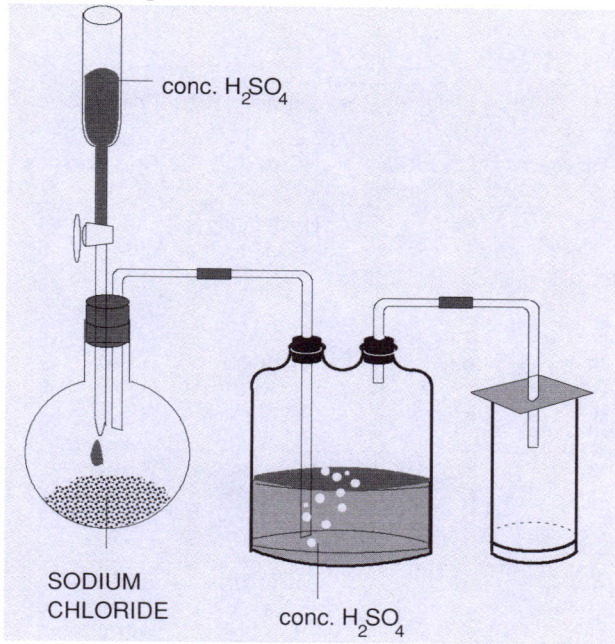

23.5 — *Preparation of Hydrogen Chloride*

Properties of Hydrogen Chloride

It is a colourless, pungent smelling gas which fumes in moist air and its density is about 1.5 times that of air. It neither burns nor supports combustion. It is highly soluble in water (500 : 1) with which it reacts to form a solution of hydrochloric acid:

$$HCl + H_2O \rightarrow H_3O^+ + Cl^-$$

It forms dense white fumes with ammonia and this reaction is used as a test for the gas:

$$HCl + NH_3 \rightarrow NH_4Cl$$

Its molecules, being diatomic, are linear, and the bonding is polar covalent due to the electronegativity difference between the two elements.

Hydrochloric acid is a strong acid and shows the usual acidic properties, as described on page 98.

Uses

Its various uses include cleaning metal surfaces before galvanising, manufacturing glucose from starch and making PVC from ethene. It is used in the manufacture of various drugs, dyes and photographic chemicals.

Summary of the Properties of the Normal Chlorides of Elements						
Element	Formula of chloride	Name	Appearance	Bonding	Structure	Reaction with water
H	HCl	Hydrogen chloride	Colourless gas	Polar covalent	Linear molecules	Very soluble forming strongly acidic solution
Li Na K	LiCl NaCl KCl	Lithium, chloride, etc.	White crystalline solid	Ionic	Ionic lattice of Li^+ and Cl^-	Very soluble forming neutral solution
Mg Ca	$MgCl_2$ $CaCl_2$	Magnesium chloride etc.	White crystalline solid	Ionic	Ionic lattice of Mg^{2+} and Cl^-	Very soluble forming slightly acidic solution
Al	$AlCl_3$	Aluminium chloride	White crystalline solid	Polar covalent	Molecules of Al_2Cl_6	Hydrolysed by water, forming $Al(OH)_3$ and HCl
C	CCl_4	Tetrachloro-methane	Colourless liquid	Polar covalent	Tetrahedral molecules	None
P	PCl_5	Phosphorus (v) chloride	Pale yellow crystalline solid	Polar covalent	Trigonal bipyramidal molecules	Reacts violently forming acidic solution of H_3PO_4 and liberating HCl
Fe	$FeCl_3$	Iron(III) chloride	Yellow-brown crystalline solid	Polar covalent	Molecules of Fe_2Cl_6	Very soluble, forming weakly acidic solution
Cu	$CuCl_2$	Copper chloride	Brown solid (green when hydrated)	Polar covalent	Covalent lattice	Soluble, forming weakly acidic solution

Detection of Halide Ions

Most metal halides are soluble in water, and on addition of silver nitrate solution, the insoluble silver halide is precipitated, *e.g.*

$$Cl^- + AgNO_3 \rightarrow AgCl + NO_3^-$$

Silver chloride is white and is soluble in dilute ammonia solution; silver bromide is very pale yellow and is only slightly soluble in ammonia solution; silver iodide is yellow and insoluble in ammonia solution. Hence, by noting the appearance of the precipitated silver halide and its behaviour with aqueous ammonia, the original halide ion can be identified.

Conclusion

The halogens are a group of elements which show many similarities to each other, making them one of the best defined families in the periodic table. They are all diatomic, non-metallic elements with poisonous irritating vapours. They are all electronegative and combine with (a) non-metals, forming molecular substances and (b) metals, forming ionic lattices. They all combine with hydrogen forming very soluble gases which give acidic solutions. Where properties differ, there is generally a gradual change or a trend in values between those of successive elements (although those of fluorine often do not conform) *e.g.* values of melting and boiling points and of density increase with atomic number, the colour darkens and reactivity decreases significantly.

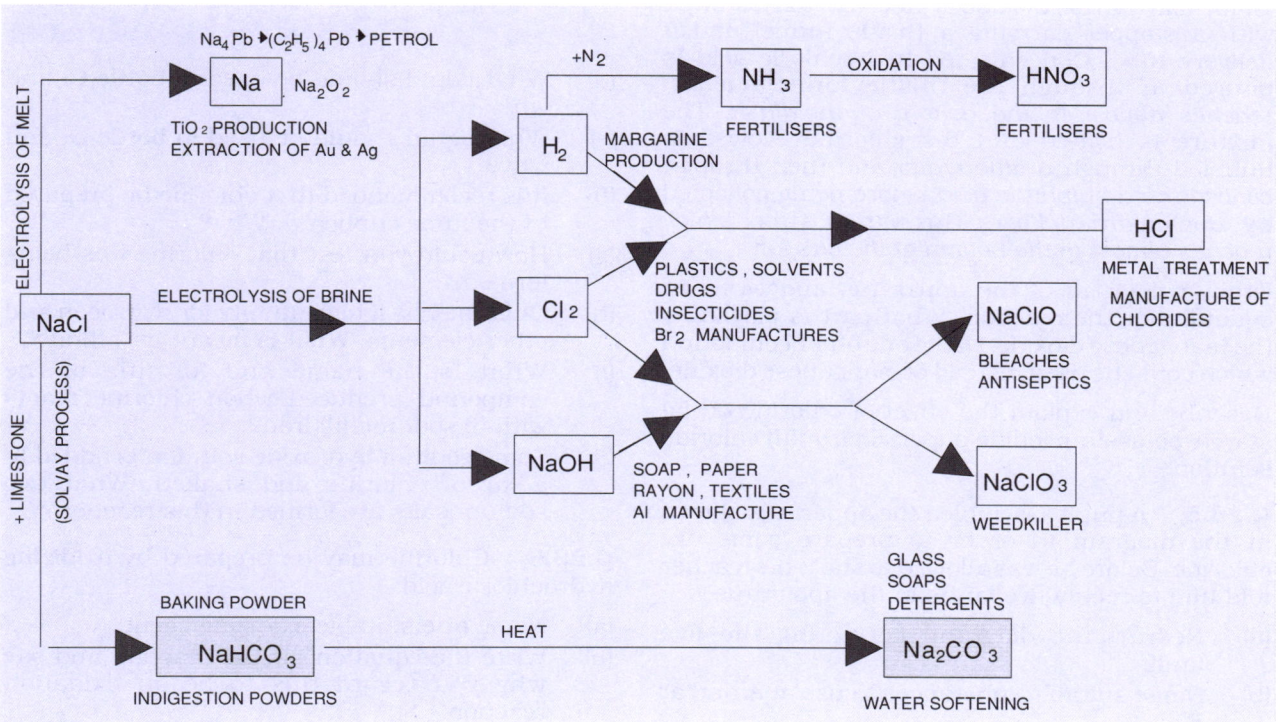

23.6 — Chemicals from salt.

Questions

Q.23.1 List eight properties of the halogens which are common to all members and eight properties which show trends in values. Indicate what the trends are.

Q.23.2 Which halogen has (a) the lowest m.p.; (b) the lowest b.p.; (c) the highest b.p.; (d) the greatest density; (e) the smallest atom, (f) the greatest ionisation energy; (g) the largest ion; (h) the greatest reactivity; (j) the greatest oxidising ability.

Q.22.3 Describe with the aid of a diagram, an experiment in which dry chlorine is prepared and collected.

Q.23.4 Give reasons for the items which are *in italics* in the following directions for the laboratory preparation of chlorine:

'Some manganese dioxide is placed in a flask fitted with a stopper carrying a thistle funnel and a delivery tube. Concentrated hydrochloric acid is poured in through the thistle funnel *which reaches almost to the bottom of the flask*. The mixture is heated and the chlorine evolved is bubbled through *a little water* and then through *concentrated sulphuric acid* before being collected by *downward delivery* through a tube *which reaches almost to the bottom of the gas-jar.*

Draw a diagram of the apparatus and write an equation for the reaction. What part is played by the manganese dioxide. Name one other compound which could be used instead of manganese dioxide.

Describe and explain the effect of chlorine on (a) starch-potassium iodide paper; (b) iron(II) chloride solution.

Q.23.5 A pupil assembled the apparatus shown in the diagram in order to prepare some dry chlorine. Before he was allowed to start, his teacher told him to rectify five faults in the apparatus.

(a) Redraw the diagram, correcting the five faults.

(b) Name suitable substances to use at **A** and at **B**.

(c) Write an equation for the reaction between these substances.

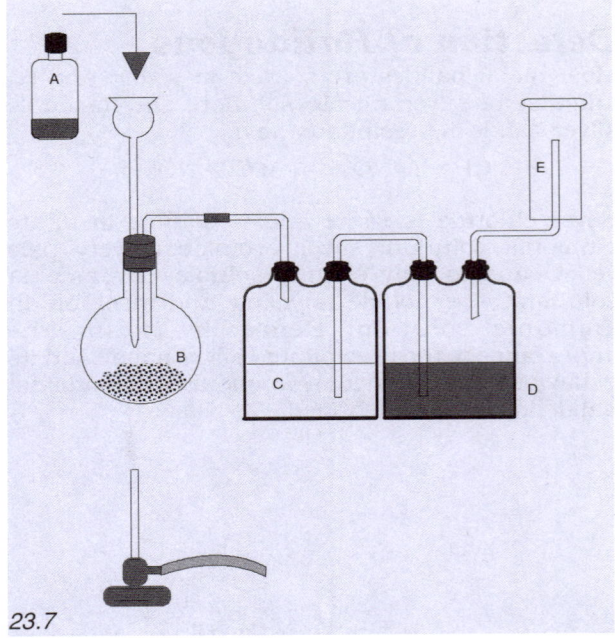

23.7

(d) What liquid should be used in bottle C, and why?

(e) What liquid should be used in bottle D, and why?

(f) It is recommended that chlorine be prepared in the fume cupboard. Why?

(g) How could you test that chlorine was being formed?

(h) Chlorine has a high affinity for hydrogen and other elements. What is meant by 'affinity'?

(i) What is the name and formula of the compound produced when chlorine reacts with (i) sodium; (ii) iron?

(j) Some sodium hydroxide solution is added to a jar of chlorine and shaken. What two sodium salts are formed in this reaction?

Q.23.6 Chlorine may be prepared by oxidizing hydrochloric acid:

(a) Name **one** suitable oxidizing agent.

(b) Write the equation for the reaction and say why you regard this to be an oxidation reaction.

(c) State how you would react the oxidising agent with hydrochloric acid so as to produce a reasonable quantity of chlorine for use in the laboratory (a diagram is not required).

(d) Why is it desirable to wash the chlorine with a little water before collecting it? Why would it be incorrect to use sodium hydroxide solution to wash the gas?

(e) State how you would collect the chlorine. Why is the method of collection suitable?

(f) Give **one** chemical test for chlorine.

(g) Describe **one** experiment you have seen in which chlorine reacts with a named metallic element.

(h) Warming a gaseous oxide of chlorine, Cl_xO_y causes it to decompose:

$$2Cl_xO_y \rightarrow xCl_2 + yO_2$$

In an experiment, 20 cm^3 of the oxide gave 20 cm^3 of chlorine and 10 cm^3 of oxygen (all gas volumes being measured at the same temperature and pressure). Calculate the formula of this oxide showing your reasoning clearly.

Q.23.7 Give the reason for each of the following statements:

(a) The b.p. of sodium chloride is much higher than that of hydrogen chloride.

(b) A chloride ion is much larger than a chlorine atom.

(c) The ionisation energy of chlorine is much greater than that of iodine.

(d) Bromine can displace iodine from potassium iodide solution, but cannot displace chlorine from potassium chloride solution.

(e) The electronegativity of bromine is less than that of fluorine.

(f) Hydrogen iodide has a boiling point much higher than that of hydrogen chloride.

(g) Hydrogen fluoride has a boiling point much higher than that of hydrogen chloride.

(h) Iodine dissolves in potassium iodide solution but not in water.

Q.23.8 Give the equations for the reactions of:

(a) chlorine with; water: sodium hydroxide solution; phosphorus

(b) bromine with: hydrogen; magnesium; potassium iodide solution;

(c) iodine with: hydrogen, sodium, potassium iodide solution.

Q.23.9 On a graph, plot (a) the boiling points; (b) the densities, of the hydrogen halides against their relative molecular masses. Explain the unusual features shown on the graphs.

Q.23.10 Select a typical ionic chloride and a typical covalent chloride. Give the name and formula of each, and, in the form of a table, compare and contrast their appearance, structure, behaviour in water, and acid/base character.

Review When you know Chapter 23 you should be able to:

(a) Describe the lab. preparation and industrial manufacture of chlorine.

(b) Describe the properties, reactions and uses of chlorine.

(c) Describe the properties and reactions of bromine, iodine and hydrogen chloride.

(d) Describe the tests for the chloride, bromide and iodide ions.

(e) Give the formula, and describe the appearance, type of bonding and structure, and the reaction with water of the chlorides of each of: hydrogen, the alkali metals, magnesium and calcium, aluminium, phosphorus, iron and copper.

24
Introduction to Organic Chemistry

Carbon Compounds

Carbon is a unique element; it forms well over two million compounds — about four times more than the compounds of all other elements put together. Because of this, the chemistry of carbon compounds is a separate branch of chemistry, and is known as **organic chemistry**.

Originally, organic chemistry was the branch of chemistry concerned with substances derived from living organisms (*i.e.* plants and animals) as it was thought that such substances were essentially different from those extracted from minerals and other non-living sources. Organic substances were thought to have some 'Vital Force' present and so were impossible to prepare by the usual chemical methods. This fallacy was overcome in the 19th century when several typical organic substances (*e.g.* urea, NH_2CONH_2) were prepared from purely inorganic materials, and so the idea of the 'Vital Force' slowly disappeared. Nevertheless, organic chemistry is still essentially concerned with substances of plant and animal origin because all such substances consist of compounds of carbon.

Carbon forms such a large number of compounds because of the ability of its atoms to string together in 'chains' (both 'straight' and 'branched') and in 'rings' and in mixtures of the two. The formulae of some typical organic compounds showing the arrangements of the atoms illustrate this.

In general, molecules of organic compounds are much larger than those of inorganic compounds; compare those molecules shown above with typical inorganic molecules, *e.g.* H_2O, H_2SO_4, $Ca(OH)_2$, NH_4Cl. Simple organic compounds do exist too, whose molecules contain as few as 5 atoms.

Although organic molecules are generally large, they are made up of relatively few elements; carbon and hydrogen occur in all compounds; oxygen in a great many, and nitrogen, halogens and sulphur are often present too. The vast majority of organic compounds do not contain any of the other 98 elements.

The huge number of organic compounds can be divided into two main classes — aliphatic and aromatic compounds. **Aliphatic** compounds are those whose molecules contain **'chains'** of carbon atoms; 'iso-octane' and sodium palmitate (illustrated in Fig.24.1) are examples of aliphatic compounds.

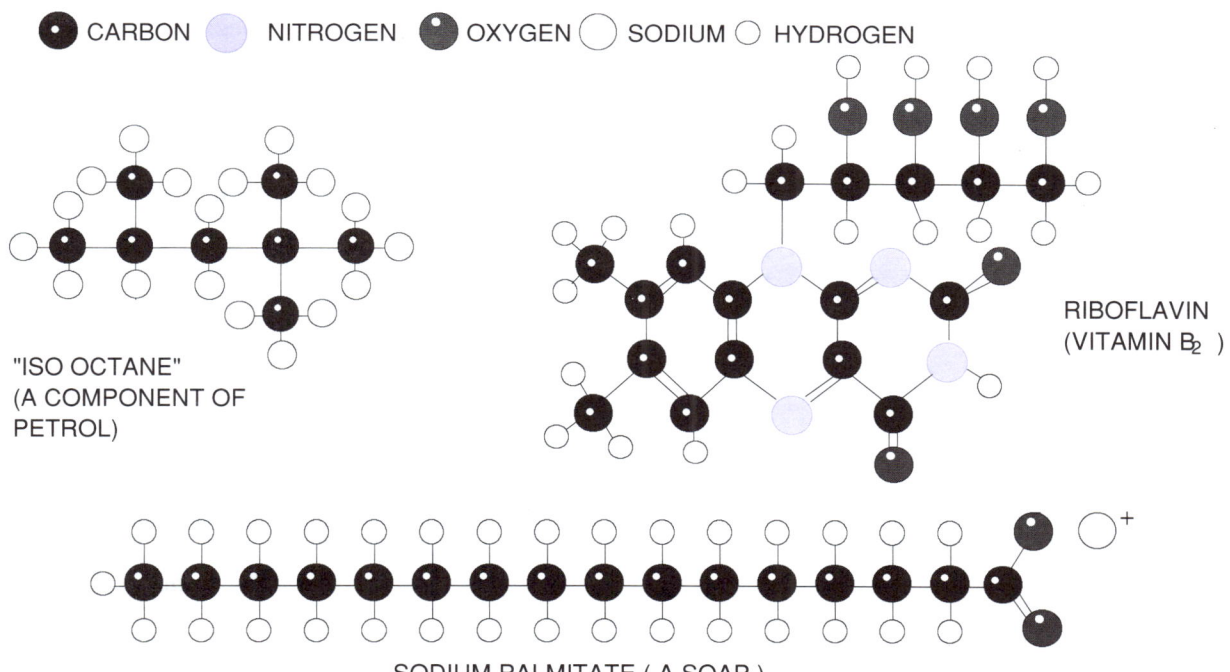

● CARBON ◯ NITROGEN ● OXYGEN ◯ SODIUM ◯ HYDROGEN

"ISO OCTANE"
(A COMPONENT OF
PETROL)

RIBOFLAVIN
(VITAMIN B_2)

SODIUM PALMITATE (A SOAP)

24.1 Structures of some everyday organic molecules.

Aromatic compounds contain a special type of 6-membered ring of carbon atoms, known as a benzene ring; Vitamin B contains such a ring and is therefore an aromatic compound.

Both aliphatic and aromatic compounds can be divided into a number of different 'families' or homologous series of compounds.

> **A homologous series is a group of compounds, all members of which contain the same 'functional group' of atoms, and successive members of a homologous series differ in size by CH₂.**

The alcohols are an example of a homologous series. The first few members of this series (in which the functional group is OH) are:

Methanol	CH_3OH
Ethanol	C_2H_5OH
Propanol	C_3H_7OH
Butanol	C_4H_9OH

All members of any given homologous series can be prepared by similar methods, have similar chemical properties, show a graduation in physical properties and can be represented by a general formula. All members of the alcohols, for example, can be represented by the formula $C_nH_{2n+1}OH$

> **A functional group is a group of atoms on which the characteristic properties of a particular homologous series depend.**

The properties of the group largely determine the properties of the compounds in which the group occurs. This is why all members of a homologous series have similar chemical properties. The number of functional groups is relatively small, and so by knowing the properties and reactions of these groups, the chemistry of a very large number of compounds is known [i].

The most common functional groups are listed in figure 24.2

NAME OF SERIES	STRUCTURE	CONDENSED STRUCTURAL FORMULA
ALKANE		$-C\!-\!C-$
ALKENE		$>\!C\!=\!C\!<$
ALKYNE		$-C\!\equiv\!C-$
ALCOHOL	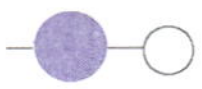	$-$ OH
ALDEHYDE		$-$CHO
KETONE		$-$CO$-$
CARBOXYLIC ACID	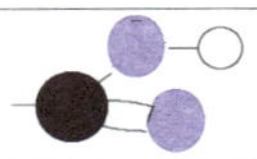	$-$COOH
ESTER		$-$COO$-$

24.2 — *Characteristic structures and functional groups.*

Isomerism and Structural Formula.

In inorganic chemistry, a molecular formula is usually sufficient to distinguish one compound from another; H_2SO_4 for example, represents only one compound, namely sulphuric acid. In organic chemistry, however, a molecular formula can represent (and usually does) several different compounds; C_2H_6O can be either of 2 compounds, namely methoxymethane, in which the atoms are arranged like

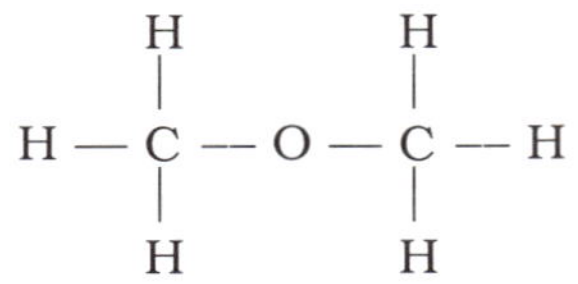

$$
\begin{array}{ccccccc}
 & H & & & & H & \\
 & | & & & & | & \\
H - & C & - O - & C & - H \\
 & | & & & & | & \\
 & H & & & & H &
\end{array}
$$

or ethanol, whose arrangements of atoms is

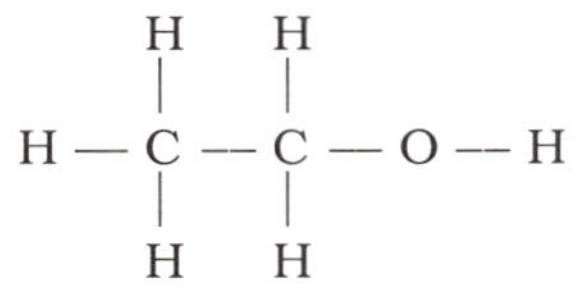

$$
\begin{array}{ccccccc}
 & H & & H & & & \\
 & | & & | & & & \\
H - & C & - & C & - O - H \\
 & | & & | & & & \\
 & H & & H & & &
\end{array}
$$

> **Isomers are compounds which have the same molecular formula but differ in the way in which their atoms are arranged (*i.e.* in structural formulae).**

The existence of such compounds is called **isomerism**.

Because of isomerism, molecular formulae are usually insufficient to distinguish one compound from another, and structural formulae showing the arrangements of the atoms in the molecules are necessary. The structural formulae shown above are the full structural formulae (known as graphic formulae) of the compounds methoxymethane and ethanol. When writing graphic formulae, it is necessary to remember that 4 bonds must be joined to each carbon atom (*i.e.* its valency is 4), 2 to each oxygen and one to each hydrogen or halogen atom.

Graphic formulae are slow and cumbersome to write and to save space and time, the same information can be given in a condensed form. This is done, by writing in a row, the longest chain of carbon atoms in the molecule, and putting immediately after each of these carbon atoms the atoms or groups which are joined to it. The 2 formulae above can be condensed to CH_3OCH_3 and CH_3CH_2OH (or C_2H_5OH). This method also

---

(i)   A completely accurate knowledge of properties is not always possible, for the reactions of a group depend to some extend on what the group is joined to and what other groups are present.

emphasises the grouping(s) of atoms and shows which functional groups are present. Two further examples follow:

$$H - \underset{\underset{H}{|}}{\overset{\overset{H}{|}}{C}} - \overset{\nearrow OH}{\underset{\searrow O}{C}} = CH_3COOH$$

$$H - \underset{\underset{H}{|}}{\overset{\overset{H}{|}}{C}} - \underset{\underset{H}{|}}{\overset{\overset{OH}{|}}{C}} - \underset{\underset{H}{|}}{\overset{\overset{H}{|}}{C}} - H = CH_3CHOHCH_3$$

Atomic Models

There are several types of model available for showing the structure of molecules. Two are illustrated; the model in each case is that of ethanol (C_2H_5OH)

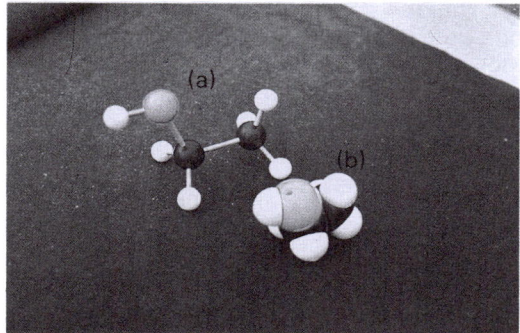

24.3

Model (a) clearly shows what atoms are joined together but this type of model gives a false impression of relative sizes and distances; atoms in reality are not isolated from each other by the distance suggested in the model. Model (b) is a truer representation of the structure, but it is not so easy, particularly in the case of a large molecule, to see which atoms are joined to which.

Bonding in Organic Compounds

Being composed of non-metals, bonding in organic compounds is predominantly covalent. This means in general, that compounds have low melting points and boiling points, are insoluble in water but soluble in non-polar solvents, are non-electrolytes, and that their reactions are slow and do not necessarily go to completion. Many organic compounds decompose on being heated and few of them are stable above a temperature of about 500°C.

Analysis of Organic Compounds

Analysis of a compound involves breaking it down into simpler substances in order to find out, firstly what elements are present in it (this is called **qualitative analysis**), and secondly to find out the amounts of each of those elements present (this is **quantitative analysis**). Quantitative analysis may be done by weighing (**gravimetric analysis**) or, in the case of gaseous compounds, by measuring volumes (this technique is called **eudiometry**).

Gravimetric Analysis

As an example of how a gravimetric analysis is done, the method for determining both carbon and hydrogen is described. In order to find out the amount of each of these elements present in a compound, a known mass of the dry compound is heated in a combustion tube through which pure dry oxygen is passing. The carbon in the compound is oxidised to carbon dioxide and the hydrogen to steam or water.

The mass of carbon dioxide is measured by absorbing it in a weighed tube of soda lime or potassium hydroxide (and reweighing it

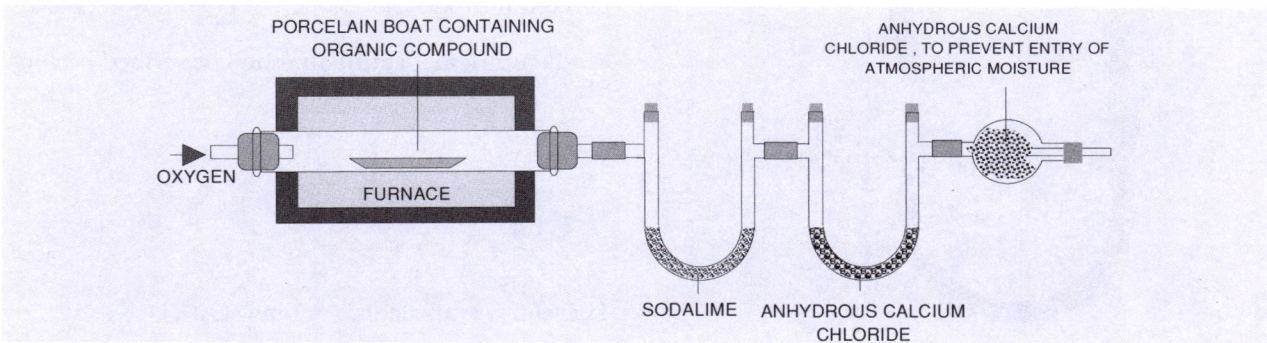

24.4 — *Apparatus for estimation of carbon and hydrogen.*

afterwards) and the water is found by absorbing it in a weighed tube of anhydrous calcium chloride.

As $\frac{12}{44}$ths of the mass of CO_2 is carbon ($CO_2 = 44$; $C = 12$), and $\frac{2}{18}$ths of the water is hydrogen ($H_2O = 18$; $H_2 = 2$), the masses of each of these two elements can be found (see Worked Example 1).

Eudiometry

The empirical formulae of gaseous organic compounds is more conveniently determined by means of an eudiometer. This is a graduated glass vessel with a spark gap by means of which a gas inside the vessel can be ignited. There is an arrangement for making the pressure inside the apparatus equal to that outside, so that the volume of the gas within can be measured at atmospheric pressure.

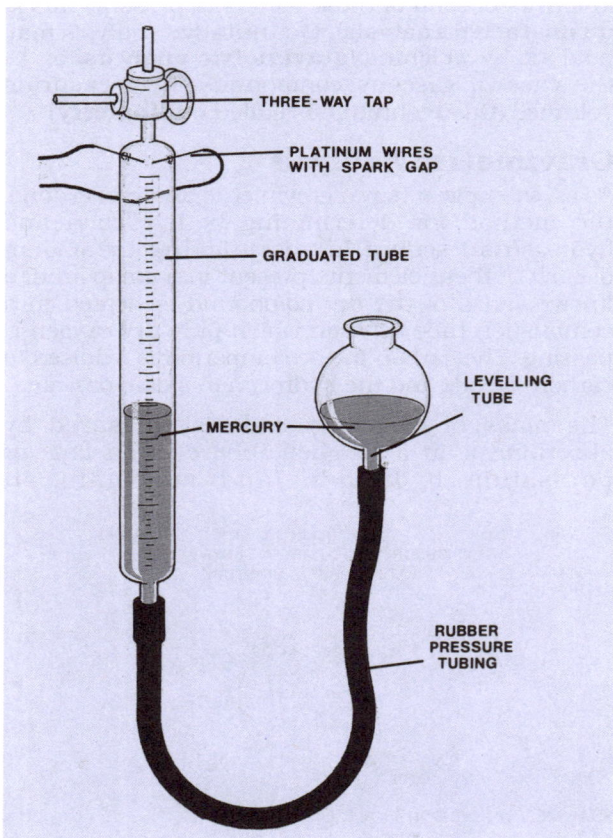

THREE-WAY TAP

PLATINUM WIRES WITH SPARK GAP

GRADUATED TUBE

LEVELLING TUBE

MERCURY

RUBBER PRESSURE TUBING

24.5

A measured volume of the gas is mixed with a measured volume of oxygen (which must be in excess) and this mixture is then ignited by means of a spark. The carbon in the compound burns to produce carbon dioxide and the hydrogen present forms water (vapour). The apparatus is cooled to room temperature, the water vapour condenses, and the volume (of the CO_2 and excess oxygen) is noted. Alkali solution is added to absorb the CO_2, and the decrease in volume (= volume of CO_2) is measured. The remaining gas is the excess oxygen. calculation (as in worked example 2) leads to the empirical formula of the compound.

Worked Example 1

An organic compound contains carbon, oxygen and hydrogen. On combustion in an excess of oxygen, 0.64 g of the compound gave 1.45 g of carbon dioxide and 0.59 g of water. Calculate the percentage of each of the elements in the compound and hence find its empirical formula.

Solution

Mass of carbon $= \dfrac{12 \times 1.45}{44} = 0.40$ g

mass of hydrogen $= \dfrac{2 \times 0.59}{18} = 0.066$ g

mass of (C + H) $= (0.40 + 0.066) = 0.466$ g

mass of oxygen $= (0.64 - 0.466) = 0.174$ g

percentage carbon $= \dfrac{0.40 \times 100}{0.64} = 62.5\%$

percentage hydrogen $= \dfrac{0.066 \times 100}{0.64} = 10.3\%$

percentage oxygen $= \dfrac{0.174 \times 100}{0.64} = 27.2\%$

Find empirical formula (method described on Page 88)

		ratio
$C = \dfrac{62.5}{12} = 5.1$		3
$H = \dfrac{10.3}{1} = 10.3$		6
$O = \dfrac{27.2}{16} = 1.7$		1

Therefore, empirical formula $= C_3H_6O$

Note: If it is only the empirical formula that is needed (and not the percentage composition as specifically asked in this particular problem), there is no need to calculate the latter. The ratio can be found by just dividing the mass of each element by the relative atomic mass of that element.

e.g.,				ratio
C	$= \dfrac{0.40}{12}$	$=$	0.033	3
H	$= \dfrac{0.066}{1}$	$=$	0.066	6
O	$= \dfrac{0.174}{16}$	$=$	0.011	1

Worked Example 2

To 20 cm^3 of a gaseous hydrocarbon contained in a eudiometer, 80 cm^3 of oxygen were added, and the mixture was ignited. After the reaction, the apparatus was allowed to cool to room temperature, and the remaining gases occupied 70 cm^3. After shaking with potassium hydroxide solution, the volume was reduced to 30 cm^3. Calculate the formula of the hydrocarbon.

Solution

$$C_xH_y + O_2 \rightarrow CO_2 + O_2 + H_2O$$

20 cm^3 80 cm^3

$\underbrace{\qquad\qquad}$

70 cm^3

Absorb CO_2

V becomes 30 cm^3 (= excess O_2)

$\therefore CO_2 = 40$ cm^3

$\therefore O_2$ used $= (80 - 30) = 50$ cm^3

$$C_xH_y + O_2 \rightarrow CO_2 + H_2O$$

20 cm^3 50 cm^3 40 cm^3

(moles and volumes are proportional (Avogadro))

$\therefore 20C_xH_y + 50O_2 \rightarrow 40CO_2 + ?H_2O$

$\therefore 2C_xH_y + 5O_2 \rightarrow 4CO_2 + ?H_2O$

No. of C atoms $= 4 = 2x$, $\therefore x = 2$, *i.e.* C_2H_y

No. of [O] atoms on L.H.S. $= 10$ (*i.e.* $5O_2$),

$\therefore$ no. on R.H.S. $= 10$

$4CO_2$ contain 8 [O] atoms,

$\therefore 2$ [O] atoms in the H_2O, $\therefore 2H_2O$, $\therefore 4$ H atoms

$2y = 4$, $y = 2$, $\therefore C_2H_2$ = formula

Problems

Gravimetric Analysis

Q.24.1 A gaseous organic compound has the following gravimetric composition: carbon 80%, hydrogen 20%. The mass of 1 litre of the compound is 1.35 g. What is the compound?

Q.24.2 3.9 g of a hydrocarbon, on combustion, gave 13.2 g of carbon dioxide and 2.7 g of water. Calculate the empirical formula for the compound.

Q.24.3 3.0 g of a hydrocarbon gave 8.8 g of carbon dioxide and 5.4 g of water. What is the empirical formula of the compound?

Q.24.4 1.00 g of a organic compound containing carbon, hydrogen and oxygen, on combustion, yielded 1.45 g of CO_2 and 0.59 g of water. Calculate the empirical formula of the compound.

Q.24.5 0.5 g of an oxygen-containing organic compound gave, on combustion, 0.69 g of carbon dioxide and 0.56 g of water. Calculate the empirical formula of the compound.

Q.24.6 0.69 g of a compound containing C, H and O gave, on combustion, 1.32 g of CO_2, and 0.81 g of water. Calculate its empirical formula.

Q.24.7 0.785 g of an organic compound containing carbon, hydrogen and chlorine gave, on combustion, 1.32 g of carbon dioxide and 0.63 g of water. Calculate the empirical formula of the compound.

Q.24.8 A compound containing carbon, hydrogen and nitrogen, on combustion, gave 3.696 g of CO_2 and 0.882 g of water. The same mass of the compound in an experiment in which the nitrogen was removed from it, gave 157 cm^3 of nitrogen at s.t.p. Calculate the empirical formula of the compound.

Q.24.9 0.493 g of a compound containing C, H and O, gave on combustion, 0.881 g of CO_2 and 0.359 g of water. Calculate its empirical formula.

Q.24.10 1.48 g of a compound containing C, H and O, gave 2.64 g of CO_2 and 1.08 g of H_2O on combustion. 0.082 g of the compound displaced 27 cm^3 of air, measured at 17°C and 98.3 kPa pressure. Calculate the molecular formula of the compound.

Eudiometry

Q.24.11 18 cm^3 of a hydrocarbon gas were mixed with 75 cm^3 of oxygen. The mixture was ignited and allowed to cool, after which the volume was found to be 48 cm^3. This was reduced to 12 cm^3 when potassium hydroxide was added. What was the formula of the hydrocarbon?

Q.24.12 After 40 cm^3 of a hydrocarbon had been sparked with 200 cm^3 of oxygen, the gaseous mixture occupied a volume of 160 cm^3, and this was reduced to 80 cm^3 by the addition of strong alkali. Assuming that all volumes were measured at the same temperature and pressure, calculate the formula for the hydrocarbon.

Q.24.13 A mixture of 25 cm^2 of a gaseous hydrocarbon and 96 cm^3 of oxygen is ignited. After being cooled to room temperature, the volume is found to have contracted by 50 cm^3. On addition of KOH solution, there is a further contraction of 25 cm^3. Calculate the formula for the hydrocarbon.

Q.24.14 25 cm^3 of a gaseous hydrocarbon were mixed with 200 cm^3 of oxygen and exploded. After cooling, the residual gases occupied 137.5 cm^3. The volume was reduced by 100 cm^3 when potassium hydroxide solution was added. The remaining gas was found to be oxygen. What was the formula for the hydrocarbon?

Q.24.15 When 15 cm^3 of a gaseous hydrocarbon were exploded with 60 cm^3 of oxygen (an excess), the final volume was 45 cm^3. This decreased to 15 cm^3 on treatment with sodium hydroxide solution. What was the formula of the hydrocarbon?

Q.24.16 10 cm^3 of a gaseous hydrocarbon at room temperature and pressure were mixed with 100 cm^3 of oxygen. After sparking the mixture and allowing it to return to its original conditions, the total volume was found to be 95 cm^3. This contracted to 75 cm^3 when in contact with a concentrated solution of sodium hydroxide. What was the formula of the hydrocarbon?

Q.24.17 The complete combustion of 448 cm^3 (at s.t.p.) of a volatile organic compound in an excess of oxygen produced 0.08 mole of carbon dioxide. Calculate the number of carbon atoms in each molecule of the compound.

Q.24.18 At 110°C, a gaseous hydrocarbon gave nine times its own volume of oxidation products when sparked with just sufficient oxygen for complete combustion. Two thirds of the residual gas proved to be soluble in sodium hydroxide and the rest condensed on cooling. Calculate the formula of the hydrocarbon.

Q.24.19 Ethene burns in oxygen to give carbon dioxide and water. What is the volume of the resulting gas when 10 cm^3 is sparked with 60 cm^3 of oxygen (all volumes at room temperature and pressure) ?

Q.24.20 20 cm^3 of a gaseous hydrocarbon were mixed with 150 cm^3 of oxygen and exploded. After cooling to the original room temperature, the remaining gases occupied 100 cm^3. Introducing KOH solution reduced this volume by 80 cm^3. The remaining gas was oxygen. Find the molecular formula of the gas, and write the structural formulae and names for the two possible isomers.

'Quickfit' Organic Preparation Apparatus

Sets of 'Quickfit' apparatus consist of a number of pieces of interchangeable glass components. These can quickly and readily be assembled in many ways to make any of the standard apparatus required for organic preparations. The components have ground glass cones and sockets which connect together and these are made to accurate standards and are airtight when connected. This eliminates the need for rubber stoppers and glass tubing, it reduces time, and corrosive and inflammable liquids and gases are contained more easily. Such glassware is naturally expensive and it must be treated with care.

Setting up.

The ground glass surface should be absolutely free from grit or dirt. A very thin smear of petroleum jelly (e.g. 'Vaseline') should be rubbed on the top portion of the cone before connecting it into a socket; this reduces the risk of seizure. When putting rubber tubing onto the condenser nozzle, lubricate the nozzle by wetting it and slide the tubing on gently, holding the condenser as near to the nozzle as possible. When removing the rubber tubing, again be gentle and if the tubing appears to have stuck, ask your teacher for help.

An apparatus is rigid when assembled and therefore undue stress can lead to breakage.

Supporting, rather than tightly clamping, should always be the principle when setting up. The neck of the flask should be held in a cork or rubber-padded clamp, or, if the padding has worn away (as it soon does), the clamp should have a thick wad (32 thicknesses) of scrap paper. The clamp must be tight enough to hold the flask securely, but not so tight that the flask has no 'play'. Other pieces of glassware connected to the flask should be adequately supported by a slightly-loose clamp. Be sure that the rubber tubing to the condenser is kept well away from the bunsen flame.

Heating

Direct heating of the pear-shaped flask with a small flame is quite satisfactory. Using an ordinary bunsen burner, turn down the gas to make the flame about 3 cm high. Allow sufficient air in to make the flame blue; do **not** use a yellow flame; this will cover the flask with soot. To promote smooth boiling, add a few pieces of anti-bumping agent, *e.g.* broken porcelain.

Cleaning

Assemblies should be dismantled and cleaned immediately after use. Water and brush will remove most substances used in simple preparations. An occasional wash-up in hot water with detergent is recommended. The ground glass

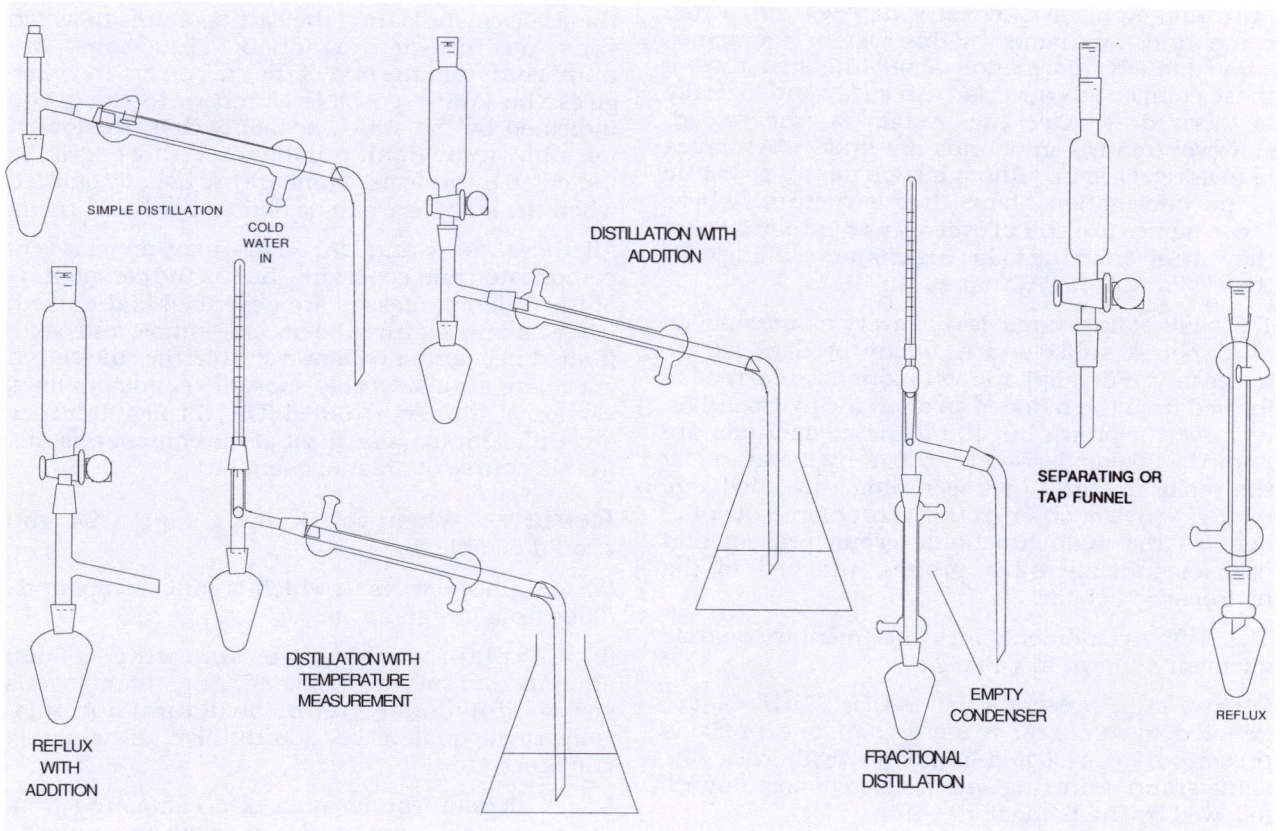

SIMPLE DISTILLATION

COLD WATER IN

DISTILLATION WITH ADDITION

REFLUX WITH ADDITION

DISTILLATION WITH TEMPERATURE MEASUREMENT

SEPARATING OR TAP FUNNEL

EMPTY CONDENSER

FRACTIONAL DISTILLATION

REFLUX

24.6

joints should be particularly well cleaned. Glassware washed with detergent should be rinsed in plain water before being left to dry.

The accompanying diagrams show the various arrangements which are required for the experiments to be described.

IUPAC Nomenclature for Organic Compounds

There are so many organic compounds, particularly when isomers are taken into account, that it was a real problem at one time to give them all different names. As more and more compounds were discovered and synthesised over the years, it was found necessary to devise a systematic method of giving each one a unique name. A system which is in use today is due to the International Union of Pure and Applied Chemistry (IUPAC) and when compounds are named by this system, the names convey much information about the structure of these compounds and also can easily and logically be derived — once the system is understood. However, many compounds are known by names of historical origin, although such names give little or no information about their structure. Where these names are still in everyday or industrial use, they are given in the following chapters, along with the systematic IUPAC name.

The basis of the system is that every name consists of a root, a suffix and as many prefixes as are necessary. For aliphatic compounds, the root is formed from the name of an aliphatic hydrocarbon (*e.g.* meth-, prop-, but-) and the compounds are named as being derived from that hydrocarbon by the replacement of hydrogen atoms by alkyl (*e.g.* methyl, ethyl) or other groups (*e.g.* chloro-). A suffix denotes the main functional group present and prefixes indicate other groups attached to the hydrocarbon chain.

The suffixes commonly met in elementary organic chemistry shown in Table 24.1.

Other groups present such as CH_3, C_2H_5, Cl, are denoted by prefixes; if more than one prefix is present, they are listed in alphabetical order. The same group occurring say twice, is denoted by 'di' followed by the name of the group.

Table 24.1		
Functional Group		Name
—COOH	(*)	-oic acid
—COOR	(*)	alkyl.......oate
—CHO	(*)	-al
—CO—	(*)	-one
—C≡N	(*)	-onitrile
—OH		-ol

(*) The carbon atom in these groups is counted in the carbon chain which forms the root.

In order to show the positions at which substituent atoms or groups are attached, the carbon atoms of the parent hydrocarbon (*i.e.* the root) are numbered from one end to the other. The appropriate numbers then precede the names of the prefixes, indicating the carbon atoms to which those groups are attached. The atoms are numbered from the end of the carbon chain which gives the lowest possible numbers to the group indicated by the suffix, or failing that, the lowest possible individual numbers to those groups indicated by prefixes. Numbers are usually omitted when the structure can be deduced without them.

All these rules and directions may appear very complicated and confusing, but as the compounds of the different classes are described and named, IUPAC nomenclature will become simple and clear. It must be mentioned however, that the rules given above are a considerably shortened and simplified version of the very detailed IUPAC rules, but they are sufficient to name most of the compounds met in this course of organic chemistry.

Review When you know Chapter 24 you should be able to:

(a)   State the ways in which organic compounds differ from inorganic ones.

(b)   Explain each of the following terms: aliphatic, aromatic, benzene ring, homologous series, functional group, structural formula, isomerism, qualitative, quantitative, gravimetric, eudiometry.

(c)   Calculate the formula of a compound from the results of a quantitative analysis experiment.

(d)   Describe the care needed when using 'Quickfit' glassware.

Hydrocarbons are compounds containing carbon and hydrogen only and both aliphatic and aromatic hydrocarbons exist. Aliphatic hydrocarbons can be divided into three groups or homologous series, namely, alkanes, alkenes and alkynes.

The **alkanes** are compounds in which the carbon and hydrogen atoms in each molecule are joined to each other by single bonds (*i.e.* by single pairs of electrons shared between the two joined atoms). Such compounds are said to be **saturated**. An example of an alkane is ethane, whose structure is shown below.

Molecules of the **alkenes** contain a double bond (*i.e.* two shared pairs of electrons) between two of the carbon atoms present. These compounds are said to be **unsaturated**. Ethene (shown below) is an example of this series.

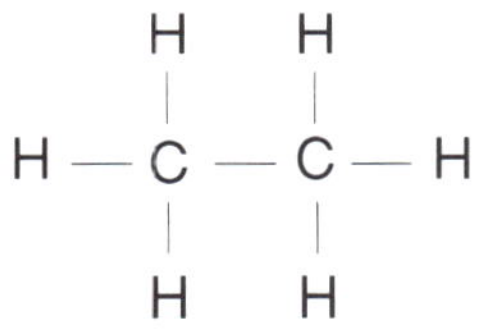

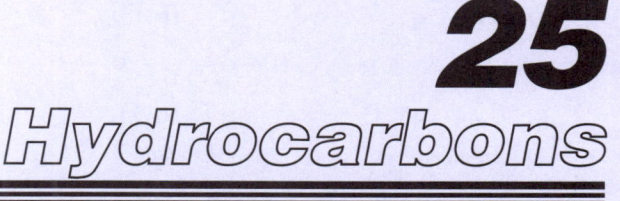

Ethane
(an alkane)

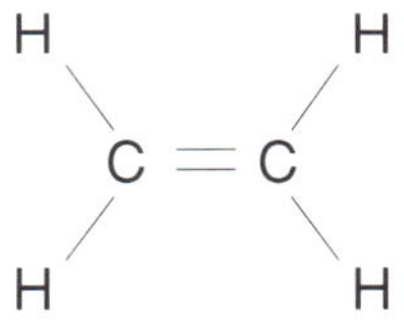

Ethene
(an alkene)

Ethene
(an alkyne)

The **alkynes** contain a triple bond between two of the carbon atoms in each of the molecules and are also termed **unsaturated**. Ethyne is a member of this series.

The Alkanes

These compounds are of great importance because they are the main constituents of crude oil or petroleum. The simplest member of the series is **methane;** its formula is CH_4 and it consists of a carbon atom joined to four hydrogen atoms, arranged tetrahedrally, see figure 25.1

25
Hydrocarbons

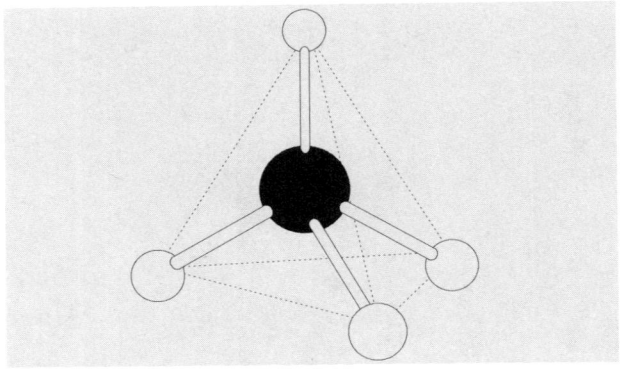

25.1

The next few members of the series are ethane (C_2H_6), propane (C_3H_8) and butane (C_4H_{10}). Their graphic formulae are as follows:

Ethane

Propane

Butane

The bonds around each carbon atom are arranged tetrahedrally. The shape of the propane molecule, for example, is shown below.

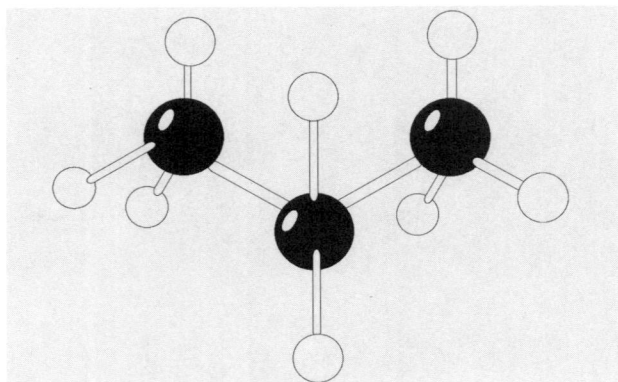

25.2 — *Shape of a propane molecule.*

There are two possible structures for butane, *i.e.* there are two isomers of C_4H_{10}. In addition to the structure shown above, the atoms can be arranged as follows:

The next member is pentane, C_5H_{12} and three isomers of this compound are possible:

(a)

(b)

(c)

Nomenclature (see pp. 306)

The basic idea of the IUPAC system in naming these compounds is that they are named as being derivatives of the alkane with the longest continuous chain of carbon atoms. The compound with the structure of isomer (b) above, is named as being a derivative of butane (even though it is an isomer of pentane), since the longest charbon chain has four atoms (but .... = 4); the atoms in this chain are then numbered from whichever end gives the lowest numbers to the atoms which have groups attached. In this example, the chain is therefore numbered from the right hand end, *i.e.*

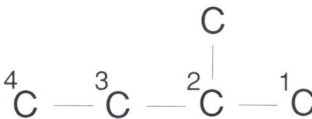

The name of the isomer is 2-methyl-butane, since there is a methyl (-CH$_3$) group attached to the second carbon atom.

The name of isomer (c) of the pentane structure shown above is 2,2-dimethylpropane. (The longest carbon chain has three atoms (prop... = 3) and there are two methyl groups, both attached to carbon atom number 2).

Alkyl Radicals

When a hydrogen atom is missing from an alkane molecule, the group of atoms which remains is called an alkyl radical. Alkyl radicals are named by replacing the ending *-ane* of the alkane by *-yl*. Methane, for example is CH$_4$; the group of atoms CH$_3$ is the methyl radical. The first 4 alkyl radicals are thus:

CH$_3$	methyl
C$_2$H$_5$	ethyl
C$_3$H$_7$	propyl
C$_4$H$_9$	butyl

Questions

Q.25.1 Give the IUPAC name of 'iso-octane', whose structure is shown on page 299.

Q.25.2 Draw the full structural formulae, and name each of the following compounds:

(a) CH$_3$CH(CH$_3$)CH$_2$CH$_3$

(b) CH$_3$CH(CH$_3$)CH(CH$_3$)CH$_3$

(c) CH$_3$CH$_2$CH$_2$CH(CH$_3$)CH$_3$

(d) CH$_3$CH$_2$CH(C$_2$H$_5$)CH$_2$CH$_3$

(e) CH$_3$CH(CH$_3$)C(CH$_3$)$_2$CH$_3$

(f) CH$_3$CHClCH$_2$CH$_3$

(g) CH$_3$CCl$_2$CH$_2$CH$_3$

(h) CH$_3$CHClCHClCH$_3$

(i) CH$_3$CH(CH$_3$)CHCl$_2$

(j) CH$_3$C(CH$_3$)$_2$CCl$_2$CH$_2$CH$_3$

Q.25.3 There are four isomers of the compound of formula C$_4$H$_9$Cl. Draw the graphic formula and give the name of each of them.

Q.25.4 Draw the graphic formulae and give the names of (a) the five isomers of hexane, and (b) the nine isomers of heptane.

Q.25.5 Draw the graphic formulae and name the isomers of C$_3$H$_6$Cl$_2$.

Q.25.6 For each of the following compounds (i) draw its structural formula; (ii) write down its molecular formula:

(a) 2-chloro-pentane;

(b) 1-chloro-2-methyl-butane;

(c) 1-chloro-2, 2-dimethyl-propane;

(d) 3-chloro-pentane;

(e) 2-chloro-2-methyl-butane.

How are all the compounds related?

Methane, CH$_4$

Methane is often called 'marsh gas' due to the fact that it is produced in marshes and stagnant water by the bacterial decomposition of vegetable matter; bubbles breaking the surface of stagnant ponds consist of methane. It also occurs with oil and coal deposits, and in the last century, before the use of electric light in coal mines, it was known to the miners as 'fire damp' and dreaded by them on account of the explosive mixture which it forms with air.

Methane is also produced in the digestive systems of animals, by bacteria in the intestines; it has been estimated that a cow produces about 500 litres of methane per day. In recent years since the price of oil has increased so much, some farmers have been experimenting with the production of methane by decaying cow manure.

25.3 — *Manure being loaded into 'digesters' for methane production. Digesters are strong sealed tanks in which the organic material decays — anaerobically — and generates methane.*

Physical Properties of Methane

Colourless odourless gas. Boiling point -162°C. Density 0.81 g/L (air × 0.5). Practically insoluble in water.

Chemical Reactions.

Chemically, methane (like the other alkanes) is rather inert and undergoes few reactions.

1. It burns readily (with a blue non-luminous flame) to produce CO_2 and water vapour:

$$CH_4 + 2O_2 \rightarrow CO_2 + 2H_2O$$

2. Because it is a saturated compound (*i.e.* it contains only single bonds), **it can react only by 'substitution'** (*i.e.* by replacement of its hydrogen atoms by other atoms). It reacts with chlorine in the presence of ultraviolet light to yield, chloromethane, along with hydrogen chloride

$$CH_4 + Cl_2 \rightarrow CH_3Cl + HCl$$

Further reaction leads successively to:

chloromethane, dichloromethane, trichloromethane (commonly called chloroform) and tetrachloromethane:

trichloromethane   tetrachloromethane

Hydrogen chloride is liberated at each stage.

Reaction Mechanism

This is similar to that of the reaction of hydrogen with chlorine *i.e.* $H_2 + Cl_2 \rightarrow 2HCl$. The first stage is the **homolytic fission** of a chlorine molecule, by ultra-violet light:

$$Cl{:}Cl + \text{u.v. photon} \rightarrow Cl^\bullet + Cl^\bullet$$
(initiation stage)

The free chlorine atoms attack CH_4 molecules, forming HCl and free CH_3 radicals. These radicals have an unpaired electron and are therefore highly reactive; they attack chlorine molecules, forming chloromethane and free Cl atoms. A chain reaction is thus initiated:

$$Cl^\bullet + CH_4 \rightarrow HCl + {}^\bullet CH_3$$
$${}^\bullet CH_3 + Cl_2 \rightarrow CH_3Cl + Cl^\bullet$$

The chain can be terminated by any of the following reations:

$$^{\bullet}CH_3 + Cl^{\bullet} \rightarrow CH_3Cl$$

$$^{\bullet}CH_3 + {^{\bullet}CH_3} \rightarrow C_2H_6$$

$$Cl^{\bullet} + Cl^{\bullet} \rightarrow Cl_2$$

Various other propagation stages result in the formation of further substituted produces e.g.

$$^{\bullet}Cl + CH_3Cl \rightarrow {^{\bullet}CH_2Cl} + HCl$$

$$^{\bullet}CH_2Cl + Cl_2 \rightarrow CH_2Cl_2 + Cl^{\bullet}$$

Manufacture and Use

The main source of methane is natural gas but small amounts are also obtained by the bacterial decomposition of sewage. It is used as a fuel and in the manufacture of hydrogen and other chemicals. Methane can be pumped through pipelines, or liquefied and transported by tanker.

Ethane, C_2H_6

Ethane is very similar to methane. Its only difference is that, due to its greater molecular mass, it has a higher boiling point ($-89°C$) and greater density (1.34 g/L). It burns to produce CO_2 and water and undergoes substitution when reacted with chlorine.

$$C_2H_6 + 3\tfrac{1}{2}O_2 \rightarrow 2CO_2 + 3H_2O$$

$$C_2H_6 + Cl_2 \rightarrow C_2H_5Cl + HCl$$
$$\text{chloroethane}$$

General Properties of the Alkanes

They are colourless gases (CH_4 to C_4H_{10}), liquids (C_5H_{12} to $C_{15}H_{32}$) and solids ($C_{16}H_{34}$ and higher), are insoluble in water and have no taste or smell. They all burn readily in air (forming CO_2 and water) and their main use is as fuels. Natural gas, which is nearly pure methane, is in widespread use for domestic and industrial heating, bottled gas (e.g. Calor-Kosangas, Ergas) is mainly butane, petrol is a mixture of isomers of hexane (C_6H_{14}), heptane (C_7H_{16}) and octane (C_8H_{18}) and paraffin oil consists of alkanes in the range C_9H_{20} to $C_{16}H_{34}$. Candle wax is approximately $C_{20}H_{42}$. Apart from combustion, alkanes are rather unreactive and only react by substitution. They can all be represented by the general formula C_nH_{2n+2} (where n is the number of carbon atoms per molecule.)

The accompanying table shows how their physical properties depend on the number of carbon atoms in their molecule (i.e. on their molecular mass):

Compound	Formula	b.p. ($°C$)	m.p. ($°C$)	density (g/cm^3)
Methane	CH_4	-162	-183	0.42*
Ethane	C_2H_6	-89	-183	0.55*
Propane	C_3H_8	-42	-188	0.58*
Butane	C_4H_{10}	-1	-138	0.58*
Pentane	C_5H_{12}	36	-130	0.63
Hexane	C_6H_{14}	69	-95	0.66
Heptane	C_7H_{16}	98	-91	0.68
Octane	C_8H_{18}	126	-57	0.70
Nonane	C_9H_{20}	151	-54	0.72
Decane	$C_{10}H_{22}$	174	-30	0.73
Dodecane	$C_{12}H_{26}$	216	-10	0.75
Tetra-decane	$C_{14}H_{30}$	254	+6	0.76
Eicosane	$C_{20}H_{42}$	343	37	0.79

(* = as liquids)

Experiment 25.1
Reactions of methane (and of other alkanes)

(1)   What colour is methane?
(2)   Has it a smell?

Ignite a tube of the gas.
(3)   What colour is the flame?
(4)   Is soot formed?

As soon as the flame goes out, add some limewater, cork the tube and shake.
(5)   What is observed?
(6)   Why?
(7)   Write an equation for the combustion of methane.

Investigate the density of the gas by finding out if it can be poured upwards or downwards.
(8)   Is the gas more dense or less dense than air?

Find out if the gas is soluble in any of: water, ethanol, hexane, as follows. Pour about 3 cm^3 of the liquid into a test tube of the gas, cork the tube, shake it and then remove the cork while the mouth of the tube is under water.

(9)   In which liquid (if any) is the gas soluble?

Obtain a test tube of chlorine and selotape it, mouth to mouth, to a test tube of methane. Place the tubes in sunlight or artifically produced u.v. light for a few hours. Open the tubes and insert a glass rod which has been dipped in concentrated ammonia solution.

(10)   What is observed?

(11)   What does this test confirm the presence of?

(12)   Write an equation for the reaction between methane and chlorine.

The Alkenes

The alkenes are characterised by a double bond between two of the carbon atoms in the molecule. The first two members of the series are ethene, C_2H_4 and propene, C_3H_8, whose structures are:

The next member, butene, C_4H_8, has 3 isomers, whose structures and names are as follows:

But - 1 - ene

But - 2 - ene

2 - methyl - prop - 1 - ene

Nomenclature

As may be seen in these examples, the position of the double bond in the alkenes is indicated by writing the number of the carbon atom after which the double bond occurs, in the middle of its name. Following are two further examples of double bonded compounds illustrating their nomenclature:

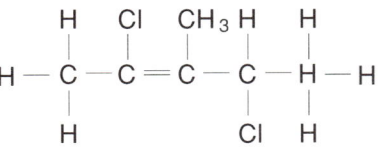

2 - methyl - but - 2 - ene

2,4 - dichloro - 3 - methyl - pent - 2 - ene

Questions

Q.25.7   Draw the structural formulae of each of the following compounds:

(a)   2-methyl-but-2-ene

(b)   3-ethyl-pent-1-ene

(c)   2,3-dichloro-but-2-ene

(d)   2,3-dibromo-pent-1, 3-diene.

(e)   1,3-dichloro-2,4-dimethyl-pent-2-ene

Q.25.8   Draw the structures and name the isomers of

(a)   butene; (b)   pentene.

Q.25.9   Draw the graphic formula and give the name of each of the following:

(a) $(CH_3)_2C=CH_2$

(b) $(C_2H_5)_2C=CH_2$

(c) $CH_3CH=C(CH_3)_2$

(d) $(CH_3)_2CHC(CH_3)=CH_2$

Q.25.10   Name each of the following compounds:

(a) $CH_3CH_2CHCH_2$

(b) $CH_3CHCClCH_2Cl$

(c) $CH_3CBrC(CH_3)CH_2CH_3$

(d) $CH_3CH_2CH_2C(CH_3)CHCl$

(e) $CH_3CClCHCClCHCl$

Ethene, C_2H_4 ('Ethylene')

This is the simplest member of the alkenes; it is most easily prepared in the laboratory by the dehydration of ethanol:

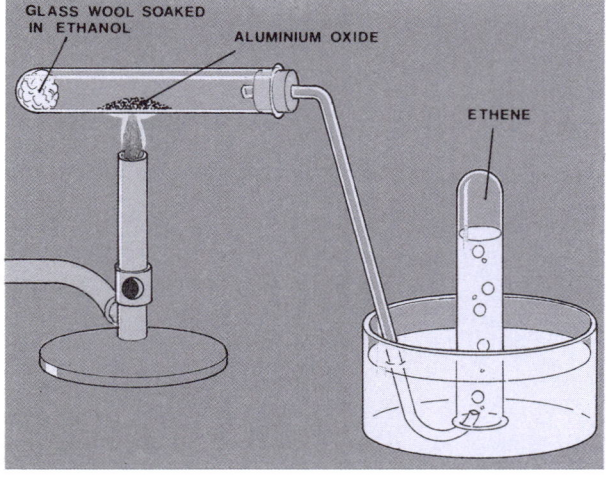

The dehydration is most easily done by passing ethanol vapour over heated aluminium oxide, Al_2O_3, which causes it to be dehydrated. Ethene is insoluble in water and so can be collected in the usual way over water.

Alternatively, the ethanol can be dehydrated by heating it with concentrated sulphuric acid. However, if ethene is prepared by this method, it should be passed through sodium hydroxide solution to remove the small quantities of CO_2 and SO_2 which are produced by side reactions.

Experiment 25.2
Preparation of Ethene.

Fill a test tube to a depth of about 5 cm with ethanol, and then push in a loose wad of glass wool or cotton wool to soak up the liquid. While holding the test tube horizontally, place about 2 g of aluminium oxide half way along it. Assemble the apparatus as shown in the diagram. Have ready some test tubes filled with water, but do not put the first of them in position until the air from inside the apparatus has been displaced.

Heat the aluminium oxide, gently at first and then more strongly with a bunsen. Sufficient heat should reach the ethanol at the end of the test tube to vaporise it but it may be necessary to **momentarily** apply some heat directly to the ethanol to achieve this. As the ethanol vapour passes over the heated aluminium oxide, it becomes dehydrated, yielding ethene, which then passes down the delivery tube to be collected.

Collect five tubes of the gas and place corks in each when full. On ceasing heating and to prevent a 'suck back', either lift the end of the delivery tube out of the water, or loosen the stopper in the test tube.

Experiment 25.3
Reactions of ethene

(1) Has the gas a smell?

Ignite a tube of the gas.
(2) What colour is the flame, and is soot formed?

As soon as the flame goes out, add some limewater, cork the tube and shake.
(3) What is observed?
(4) and why?
(5) Write an equation for the combustion of ethene.

25.4

Add about 1 cm^3 of bromine solution[i] to a tube of ethene, cork the tube, and shake.
(6) What change occurs?

There is only one substance formed in this reaction.
(7) Write an equation for the change.
This reaction is a standard test for a carbon-carbon double bond.

Add about 1 cm^3 of bromine water to a tube of ethene, cork the tube, and shake.
(8) Record your observation, write an equation for the reaction and name the product.

Physical Properties of Ethene

Colourless gas with sweetish smell. Boiling point -104°C. Density 1.25 g/L (slightly less dense than air). Practically insoluble in water; soluble in non-polar (*i.e.* organic) solvents.

Chemical Reactions

1. It burns readily with a luminous flame to form CO_2 and water:

$$C_2H_4 + 3O_2 \rightarrow 2CO_2 + 2H_2O$$

2. Chemically, ethene and the other alkenes are much more reactive than the alkanes; their **characteristic reactions are 'addition' reactions,** in which the double bond 'opens up' making it possible for various substances to add on directly and produce saturated compounds:

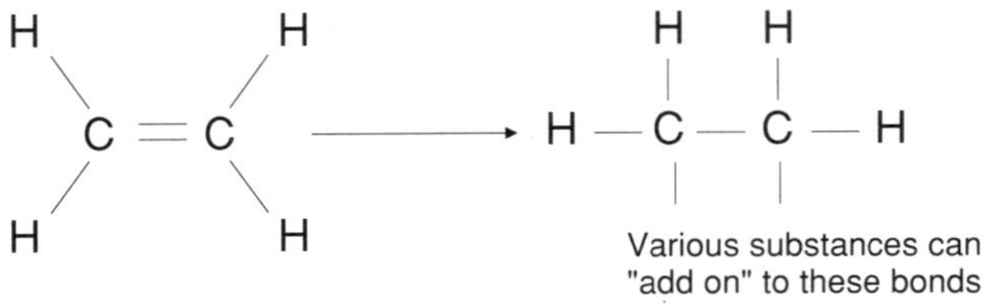

Various substances can "add on" to these bonds

Examples of the addition reactions of ethene are:

(a) Hydrogen at 200°C and in the presence of a nickel catalyst adds on to form ethane. Addition of hydrogen in this manner is called **hydrogenation**:

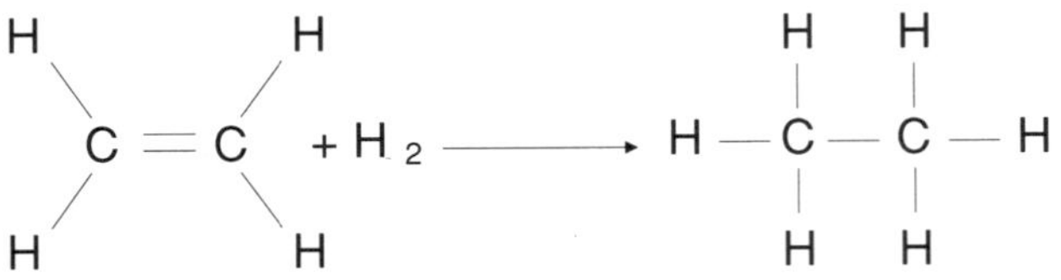

(b) Chlorine and bromine (in $CHCl_3$ or CH_3CCl_3 solution) add on readily giving 1,2-dichloroethane (or dibromo):

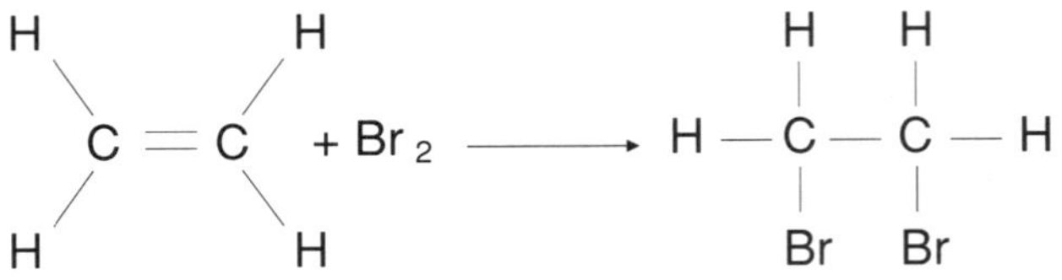

If a few drops of bromine solution are added to an unsaturated compound, the bromine solution will be decolorised. This is a simple and useful test for unsaturation in a compound.

(c) Hydrogen halides add on to form, for example, bromethane:

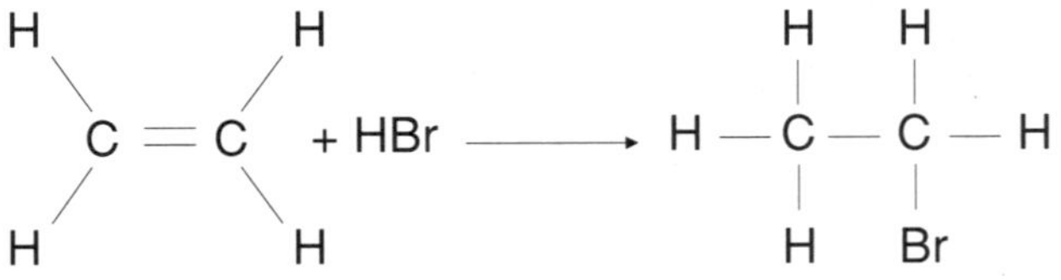

(i) Bromine dissolved in CH_3CCl_3

(d) With steam, under high pressure and in the presence of a catalyst, ethene becomes hydrated, forming ethanol:

$$\begin{array}{c} H \\ C \end{array} = \begin{array}{c} H \\ C \end{array} + HOH \longrightarrow H - C - C - H$$

(e) With dilute potassium permanganate solution, ethene is both oxidised and hydrated, forming ethane-1,2-diol:

$$\begin{array}{c} H \\ C \end{array} = \begin{array}{c} H \\ C \end{array} + H_2O + [O] \longrightarrow H - C - C - H$$

This compound is commonly called 'ethylene glycol' and is the main constituent of 'anti-freeze' used in car engines in winter time.

Mechanism of Addition to a Double Bond or Ionic Addition

Ethene and bromine react together to produce 1,2-dibromoethane. This reaction **can** occur in the dark, which suggests that the mechanism is **not** a free radical mechanism, such as that involved in the chlorination of methane (already described).

Addition to a double bond involves **heterolytic fission** and the formation of ions, and the following is accepted as being the mechanism for the reaction:

$$C_2H_4 + Br_2 \rightarrow C_2H_4Br_2$$

1. The reaction is initiated by the 'end on' approach of a bromine molecule towards the double bond of the ethene molecule:

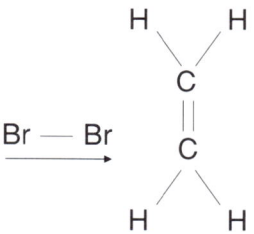

2. Since the double bond is a region of negative charge (it consists of 2 pairs of electrons), it causes the bromine molecule to be polarised, by repelling the shared pair of electrons in it to the far end:

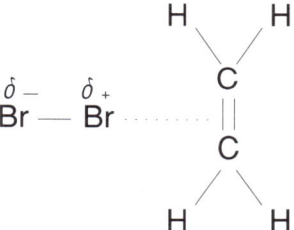

3. The positively charged bromine atom attracts electrons from the double bond and forms a covalent bond with one of the carbon atoms, leaving the other carbon atom positively charged (such a carbon atom is called a **carbonium ion**). The other bromine atom has now been converted to a negative bromide ion.

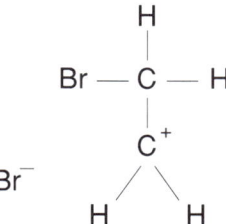

4. The presence of the carbonium ion makes the substance very unstable, and it quickly combines with the bromide ion to form 1,2-dibromoethane:

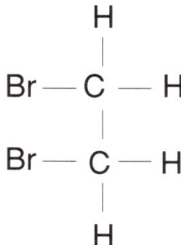

Evidence for this mechanism comes from the fact that when the reaction is carried out in the presence of Cl^- ions some

$$H-\underset{\underset{Br}{|}}{\overset{\overset{H}{|}}{C}}-\underset{\underset{Cl}{|}}{\overset{\overset{H}{|}}{C}}-H$$

is formed, as well as the main product. This suggests that the intermediate carbonium ion has been formed, and has reacted with Cl^- as well as with the Br^- ions.

Polymerisation of Ethene

Polymerisation is a process in which many small and simple molecules join together to form a much larger molecule, known as a polymer. When ethene is subjected to high temperature and pressures, or to certain catalysts, it polymerises and forms polyethene, which is the well known plastic called 'polythene'.

'n' varies between about 100 and 700; polythene thus consists of many hundreds of ethene molecules joined together. Polymerisation is described in greater detail in Chapter 29.

Manufacture and Use of Ethene

Great quantities of ethene are produced during the cracking of petroleum (see page 324). It is used in the manufacture of polythene and various other organic chemicals — ethanol and the plastic polystyrene being two of the most important.

Propene and the Other Alkenes

Propene resembles ethene in its physical and chemical properties. Because of its greater molecular mass, its boiling point and density are higher then those of ethene. Its main chemical reactions are additions across the double bond and these are similar to those of ethene. As with the alkanes, the lower members of the alkenes (C_2 to C_4) are gases, then come the liquid members and finally solids when the number of carbon atoms reaches 15. They are all practically insoluble in water but soluble in organic solvents and they can all be represented by the general formula CnH_2n. They are more reactive than the alkanes and add directly to hydrogen, halogens, etc. in the same manner as does ethene.

The Alkynes

This series is characterised by a carbon-carbon triple bond in the molecules of the compounds. **Ethyne**, C_2H_2, the simplest member, is the only one of any importance. Industrially it is known as 'acetylene' and is used to produce the flame for cutting and welding steel. Its structure is:

$$H-C \equiv C-H$$

Experiment 25.4
Preparation of Ethyne

Ethyne is most conveniently prepared by the action of water on calcium(II) dicarbide, CaC_2:

$$CaC_2 + 2H_2O \rightarrow Ca(OH)_2 + C_2H_2$$

The gas is usually contaminated with traces of phosphine (PH_3) and hydrogen sulphide (H_2S), caused by the presence of impurities (Ca_3P_2 and CaS) in the calcium(II) dicarbide; these gases can be removed by bubbling the gas through acidified $CuSO_4$ solution before being collected.

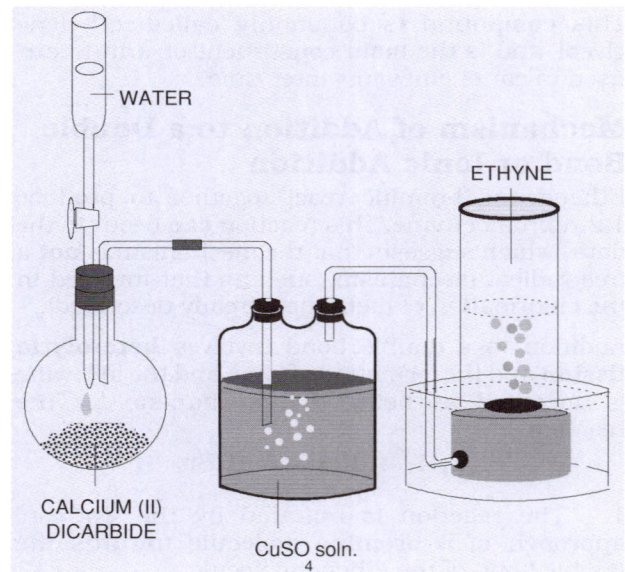

25.5

Set up the apparatus as shown. Allow the water to drop on to the calcium dicarbide, at such a rate as to give a slow steady stream of ethyne. Collect six test tubes of the gas, and place a cork in each when full.

Experiment 25.5
Reactions of Ethyne

It will be noticed that the gas has a smell, but this is mainly due to impurities; pure ethyne is practically odourless.

Ignite a tube of the gas.

(1) Note the colour of the flame, and whether or not soot is produced.

(2) Explain your observation.

Add about 1 cm^3 of bromine water and shake.

(3) Record your observation, write an equation for the reaction and name the product.

Add about 1 cm^3 of bromine solution and shake.

(4) What change occurs?

(5) Write an equation for the reaction and name the product.

Add a few cm^3 of silver nitrate solution to a tube of the gas. The precipitate formed is silver dicarbide, Ag_2C_2, and this substance is unstable and explosive when dry. Filter off the solid, spread out the filter paper on a gauze and heat gently over a low bunsen. As the silver dicarbide dries out, it decomposes into its elements with an explosive sound. Do not stand too close while this is happening.

Physical Properties of Ethyne

Colourless gas with slightly sweetish smell. Boiling point -84°C. Density 1.16 g/L (slightly less dense than air). Sparingly soluble in water but soluble in organic solvents. Liquid ethyne is very unstable and cannot be stored as such under pressure alone; under about 12 atmospheres pressure, a considerable quantity of it dissolves in propanone and it is in this form that it is stored and transported in steel cylinders.

Chemical Reactions

1. It burns in air with a luminous and very smoky flame, due to unburnt carbon. Mixed with the correct proportion of oxygen, it burns with a non-luminous flame which can reach a temperature as high as 3000°C (the 'oxy-acetylene' flame):

$$2C_2H_2 + 5O_2 \rightarrow 4CO_2 + 2H_2O$$

25.6 — A ' profile cutting" machine in use. The principle of oxygen cutting is that when pure oxygen impinges on steel at yellow heat (about 500˚C), the hot metal is eroded away as metal oxide and the steel is thus cut. Machines of this type can cut steel up to 15 cm thick. Here, two cutters are mounted and operated simultaneously. The cutters follow a path which is determined by the shape of a template, on the table beside the operator. The three tubes going to each of the cutters carry the fuel (acetylene or propane), oxygen for combustion and oxygen for cutting.

2. Like ethene, it is unsaturated and its characteristic chemical reactions are **addition reactions**. With ethyne, however, addition reactions take place in 2 stages, the C≡C bond being converted to C=C and then to C-C.

(a) With hydrogen in the presence of a nickel catalyst at 200°C, it is converted to ethene and then to ethane:

$$H-C \equiv C-H \xrightarrow[\text{Ni catalyst}]{H_2}$$

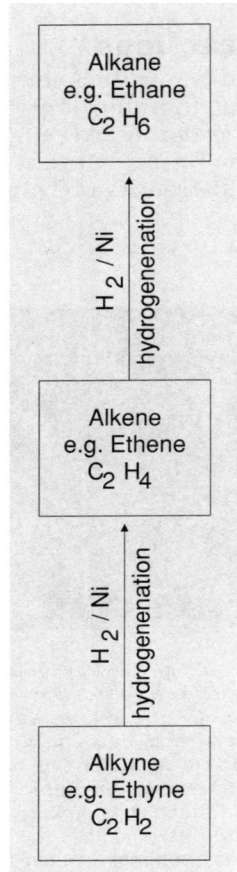

25.7

(c)   Like ethene, it adds on hydrogen halides:

$$H-C\equiv C-H \xrightarrow{HCl}$$

Chloroethene
("vinyl chloride)

$$\downarrow HCl$$

1,1 - dichloroethane

(d)   Under pressure, and in the presence of a catalyst, hydrogen cyanide adds on to ethyne, forming propenonitrile (nitrile = CN group), or as it is commonly called, acrylonitrile:

$$H-C\equiv C-H + HCN \longrightarrow$$

Acrylonitrile is the monomer for the manufacture of acrylic fibres.

(e)   When bubbled into dilute H_2SO_4 at 60°C in the presence of $HgSO_4$ which acts as a catalyst, water adds on, forming ethanal, an important industrial compound:

$$H-C\equiv C-H + H_2O \longrightarrow$$

(b)   In a similar manner, chlorine and bromine add on as follows:

$$H-C\equiv C-H \xrightarrow{Br_2}$$

1,2 - dibromoethene

$$\downarrow Br_2$$

1,1,2,2 - tetrabromoethane

3   **Substitution** : When ethyne is bubbled into, or shaken with, a solution of silver nitrate, a whitish precipitate, which rapidly turns grey is produced. This precipitate, which can be considered a substitution product of ethyne, is silver dicarbide:

$$C_2H_2 + 2AgNO_3 \rightarrow C_2Ag_2 (\downarrow) + 2HNO_3$$

This reaction is not given by the alkenes and so can be used to distinguish between alkenes and alkynes. Silver dicarbide is unstable and decomposes explosively into its elements when dried.

Manufacture and Use of Ethyne

Industrially, ethyne is prepared by the same reaction as in the laboratory preparation described earlier. Apart from its use in 'oxy-acetylene' torches for cutting and welding steel, it is used in manufacturing ethanal (CH_3CHO), chloroethene (C_2H_3Cl), and propenonitrile (C_2H_3CN). On polymerisation, chloroethane forms the plastic PVC, and propenonitrile becomes the synthetic fibre sold as *Acrilan* and *Courtelle*.

Aromatic Compounds

Benzene

Aromatic chemistry is based on a compound called **benzene** — a compound which differs in many ways from the various aliphatic compounds already described.

Structure of Benzene

When benzene was first isolated (in 1825) and its molecular formula (C_6H_6) determined, its structure was quite a puzzle to chemists for some time. The ratio of carbon atoms to hydrogen atoms suggested that it was highly unsaturated (the corresponding alkane, hexane, has fourteen hydrogen atoms to each six carbons) but yet it showed none of the characteristic reactions of double or triple bonds; instead it showed some reactions of fully saturated compounds *e.g.* replacement of hydrogen by chlorine in u.v. light. It was a German chemist, Friedrich Kekule who, in 1865, proposed a possible solution; Kekule suggested a structure of six carbon atoms arranged in a ring, linked by alternate double and single bonds, *i.e.*

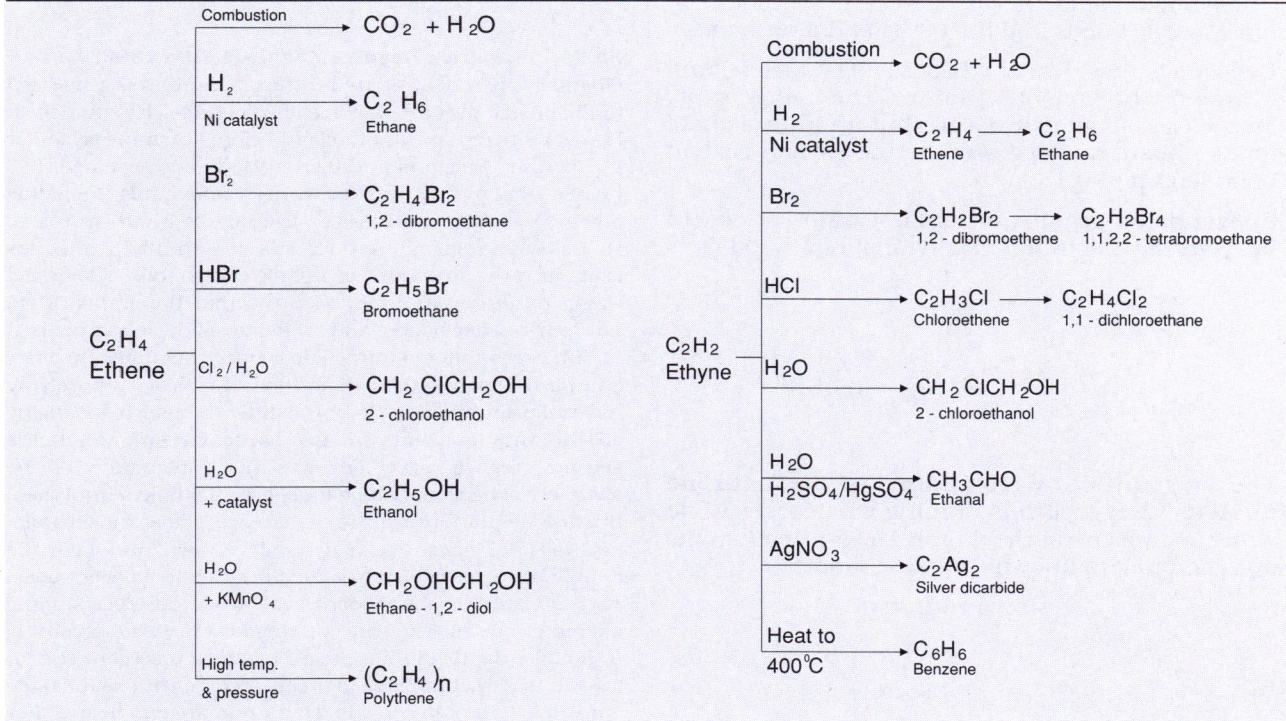

Summaries of the reactions of ethene and ethyne.

However, this structure was not fully satisfactory because it did not explain the absence of the characteristic double bond reactions, and also it would have meant that there were two isomers of the compound formed by replacing two adjacent hydrogen atoms by, for example, chlorine atoms, *viz.*

In practice only one such compound was, and still is, known. Further evidence against Kekule's structure is that his arrangement indicated two different carbon/carbon bond lengths: the C-C distance (now known to be 0.154 nm) and that of C=C (which is 0.134 nm). Modern methods of measurement (using X-rays and electron diffraction) have shown all the bonds to be the same length, *viz.* 0.139 nm, a value intermediate between the 0.154 nm of single bonds and the 0.134 of double bonds.

Benzene is now described as having a special and characteristic type of structure. The bonds, thus, are neither single nor double but an intermediate type of bond, as suggested by the carbon-carbon bond length of 0.139 nm.

Conventional graphic formulae cannot represent benzene satisfactorily. The symbol now used is

The ring structure is known as the **benzene nucleus** (though it has nothing whatsoever to do with the nucleus of the atom); any group of atoms attached to it is known as a **side chain**:

(structure of methylbenzene)

25.8 — Friedrich Augusta Kekule (1829 - 1896)

Originally a student of architecture, Kekule was converted to chemistry by Professor Liebig's lectures. He studied in France, Switzerland and England before becoming professor in Ghent (in Belgium) and then in Bonn (in Germany).

Kekule's main work was on carbon compounds, including ethyne, which he synthesised from carbon and hydrogen. He is best remembered for his two brilliant theories explaining the structures of organic compounds. The first of these, published in 1858, assumes that the carbon atom has four valency bonds, and that some of these can be used to link carbon atoms into chains; until this time, chemists had been denoting the composition of molecules purely by molecular formulae — there was little thought of arranging all the various atoms in any particular order. Kekule's second great achievement was his explanation of the structure of benzene, which had posed a problem until then. In 1865 he put forward the well known plane ring formula, and in 1872 suggested a dynamic version, in which the double bonds oscillated from one position to adjacent ones. This is similar to the modern view, which involves shifting shared electrons. The benzene ring formula was, according to Kekule, the result of a dream in which a serpent caught its own tail. "Let us learn to dream, gentlemen", said Kekule " but let us beware of publishing our dreams before they have been put to the proof of our waking understanding".

Manufacture and Use of Benzene

Benzene was first isolated about 1825 by Michael Faraday, who is mainly remembered for his great achievements in electromagnetism, but who also carried out many chemical investigations. Benzene was discovered in an oil which was deposited when a certain type of illuminating gas used in the nineteenth century was being compressed into cylinders. Faraday purified this oil by distillation and isolated the new compound, benzene. Some years afterwards, the German chemist Hofmann, showed that this same compound could be obtained from coal tar — from which same source benzene was obtained for many years.

Coal tar is produced, along with coke, coal gas and other substances, when coal is heated in the absence of air. When the tar, which is a black, viscous liquid, is fractionated, in the same manner as is petroleum, about two hundred different compounds can be isolated. These compounds, which include many aromatic hydrocarbons — benzene (C_6H_6); methylbenzene ($C_6H_5CH_3$); dimethylbenzenes ($C_6H_4(CH_3)_2$); naphthalene ($C_{10}H_8$) are the starting points for the manufacture of hundreds of everyday chemicals.

Large quantities of benzene are converted to ethylbenzene, which is then made into 'styrene' and this, on polymerisation, becomes the everyday substance polystyrene — used for packaging, insulation, electrical components, etc. Polystyrene is described in detail in Chapter 29. Benzene is also used in the manufacture of dyes, insecticides, detergents and other common materials.

Petroleum

Crude oil or petroleum is a substance on which modern life depends. In one way or another it is used by everybody every day. Over a third of the world's power comes from petroleum, and well over half the total production of organic chemicals is derived from it. As a fuel, it is used to drive cars, ships and aircraft, and to provide heat and light for homes, schools, offices and factories. As a lubricant, it keeps machinery running smoothly, and as bitumen, it is used to surface roads and other similar areas. As a source of hundreds of important chemicals, it is used to make many everyday substances, such as plastics, fibres, drugs, detergents, paints, polishes, ointments, solvents, insecticides and weedkillers. To keep

25.9 — Some everyday aromatic compounds.

pace with the huge demand for petroleum products, there has grown up one of the largest, most advanced and mechanised industries in the world.

The origin of petroleum is not absolutely certain, but it is probable that it was formed over millions of years by the decay of marine plants and animals which had become covered with layers of rock, silt and mud. Under the great pressure caused by these layers, and the heat from the Earth's interior, decomposition of the organic matter resulted in petroleum. Some evidence for this theory is provided by the fact that petroleum is often found with natural gas (which is mainly methane) and methane is formed by decaying animal and vegetable matter.

Relatively few people ever see the raw material petroleum — a black, evil smelling, viscous liquid, which is made up of many hundreds of different hydrocarbons mixed together. As it comes out of the ground, it is of little use to anyone; it must be 'refined' or converted into useful products. The first stage in the refining process involves separating the hydrocarbon mixture into 'fractions' of different boiling points.

Fractional Distillation or 'Fractionation'

Fractional distillation is the process in which a mixture of liquids is separated into components of different boiling points (or different ranges of boiling points)

On an industrial scale, this is achieved in a fractionating column — a tall steel tower, which may be up to 60 metres high. The inside of the column is divided at intervals by a number of horizontal trays with holes in them. The column is kept very hot at the bottom but the temperature

25.10 — *An oil platform in the North Sea.*

25.11 — *Fractionating columns at one of Shell's refineries.*

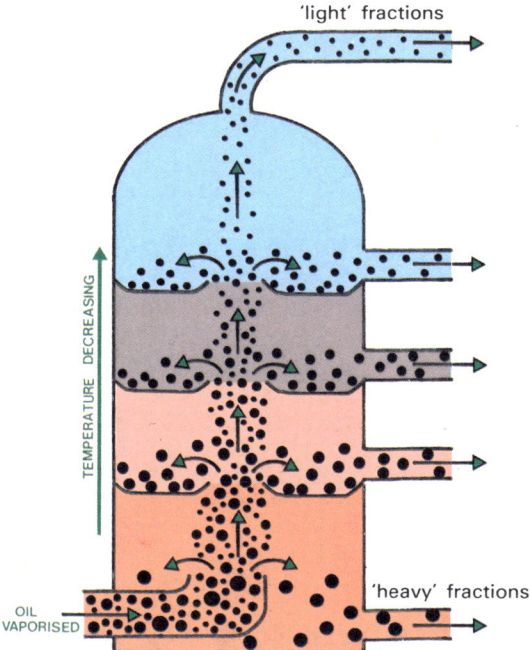

'light' fractions

TEMPERATURE DECREASING

OIL VAPORISED

'heavy' fractions

25.12 — *The principle of fractionation.*

gradually falls towards the top, so that each tray is a little cooler than the one below it. The crude oil is first heated in a furnace and then passed into the lower part of the column. Most of the fractions in the oil are already boiling, so they vaporise and rise up the column through the holes in the trays, losing heat as they rise. When each fraction reaches the tray where the temperature is just below its own boiling point, it condenses and changes back to a liquid on the tray. The different fractions which are thus separated from each other are drawn off by pipes from the various trays. More hot crude oil flows in near the base of the column, so that the process goes on continuously.

The most volatile fraction comes out of the top of the column and consists of gases (*i.e.* the compounds of lowest molecular mass), most of which are used in the refinery process. The least volatile fraction (compounds of highest molecular mass) go to the bottom of the column.

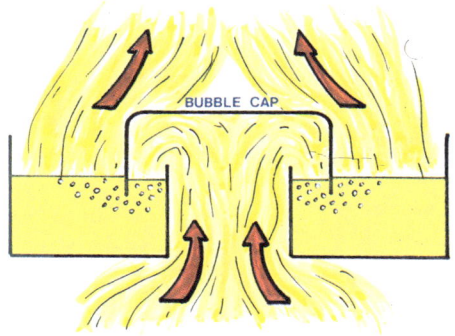

BUBBLE CAP

25.13 — *The vapours passing through a bubble cap.*

Fraction	Approximate percentage present	Boiling point range/$^{\circ}$C	Carbon atoms per molecule
Petroleum gas	1	-10 — +10	1 - 4
Gasoline	5	10 — 70	5 - 6
Naphtha	16	70 — 150	6 - 8
Kerosine	15	150 — 250	8 - 12
Gas Oil	20	250 — 350	20 - 35
Fuel Oil		350 — 500	above 35
Residue		above 500	

Composition of a typical Middle East oil

Experiment 25.6
Fractional Distillation of Crude Oil

Set up the apparatus as shown. Have three receiving flasks ready. Heat the distillation flask, gently at first and then more strongly, until distillation starts. Continue heating and collecting the distillate until the temperature reaches 70°C.

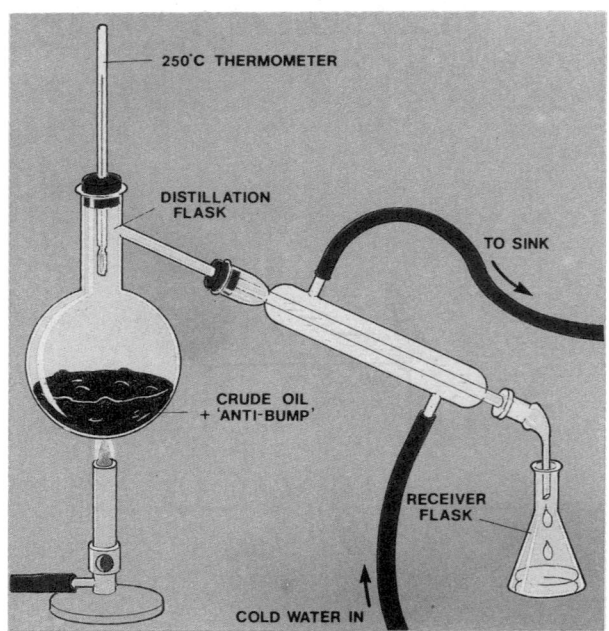

Replace the receiving flask with a fresh one and start collecting the next fraction. When the temperature reaches 100°C, turn off the cold water supply to the condenser, disconnect the inlet tube at the tap and allow the condenser to empty. Hot vapour at more than 100°C entering a cold condenser could cause it to crack. A condenser used without water is known as an **air condenser**. Continue heating until the temperature reaches 150°C and then again replace the receiving flask.

Collect another fraction between 150°C and 250°C (**Warning**: High Temperature) or as high a temperature as can be obtained.

For each of the three fractions, record (i) its appearance, (ii) its viscosity (resistance to flow or 'thickness') and (iii) its flammability. To test the latter, ignite a few cm^3 of the fraction placed on an inverted crucible lid. Compare the ease with which each fraction ignites and burns.

Q.25.11   Answer the following questions about the fractions:

(a)   Which fraction is darkest in colour?
(b)   Which is the most viscous?
(c)   Which is the most flammable?
(d)   Which has the most carbon atoms per molecule?
(e)   Which burns with the smokiest flame?
(f)   Why?
(g)   Which condensed least efficiently?
(h)   What remains in the distillation flame?
(i)   State two uses for this material.
(j)   From which fraction is petrol made?
(k)   Give the name of this fraction.
(l)   Give the formula for one of the hydrocarbons in this fraction.
(m)   From which fraction is aircraft fuel produced?

Cracking (or 'Cat' Cracking)

The gasoline and naphtha fractions are the fractions from which petrol is made and these are needed in the greatest quantities to satisfy the enormous demands of modern motoring. Distillation alone cannot provide sufficient petrol to meet that demand.

The problem is solved by converting those fractions for which there is the least demand, into fractions

25.14

for which there is the most demand. These changes are carried out in oil refineries and the main processes are **cracking**, **polymerisation,** and **reforming**. Cracking involves making small molecules from large ones, polymerisation is the opposite — building large molecules from small ones, and reforming basically involves turning straight chain hydrocarbons into branched chain isomers (which burn better in car engines). This 'playing about' with molecules — converting them from one type to another — is typical of the chemistry which has evolved with the growing petroleum industry of this century.

25.15 — A catalytic 'cracker'.

> **Cracking is the breaking down of long chain hydrocarbon molecules into smaller molecules,**

and is done by heating them to high temperatures in the presence of suitable catalysts. On doing this, the large less-volatile molecules split into two or more smaller molecules, which have therefore lower boiling points. A molecule of $C_{12}H_{26}$ for example, could yield but-l-ene, pentane, and propene. Note that for each bond which is split, a double bond must be formed in one of the resulting molecules. Cracking therefore, as well as producing the more useful alkanes, also provides a supply of alkenes, which are important 'building-block' chemicals for the plastics industry.

(Bonds about to be broken)

The Petrochemicals Industry

The large scale manufacture of chemicals from petroleum and natural gas is one of the largest and most important of all chemical industries. Chemicals from petroleum are the starting point for making thousands of everyday materials and goods. Alkenes are produced in enormous quantities during the crackling of petroleum, and because of their ability to readily undergo addition reactions, they are particularly suitable as starting compounds for the manufacture of many petrochemicals. Ethene, in particular, is one of the most important, and is the raw material for making PVC, polythene, polystyrene, polyesters (e.g. Terylene), ethanol, ethanoic acid, ethylene glycol (anti-freeze), petrol additives, synthetic rubbers, and many more.

Experiment 25.7
Cracking a hydrocarbon

In this experiment, paraffin is cracked by passing its vapour over heated porcelain pieces or steel wool, both of which catalyse the reaction.

Put about 5 cm³ of liquid paraffin into a test tube and then add some glass wool to soak it up. Hold the tube horizontally, place a pile of porcelain pieces in the middle of the tube and then arrange the apparatus in the same way as for the preparation of ethene (shown in figure 25.4). Heat the middle of the tube fairly strongly and at intervals heat the end of the tube to vaporise the paraffin. Collect four test tubes of the gas but discard the first of these which will be mainly expanded air, and put a cork in each tube when it is full. Loosen the stopper in the apparatus immediately heating is stopped, to prevent a 'suck'back'

Tests on the gas

Ignite a tube of the gas.
(1) What colour is the flame?
(2) Is soot formed?
(3) Is the flame characteristic of the alkanes or of the alkenes?

To another tube of the gas add about 1 cm^3 of bromine solution and shake.
(4) What change occurs?
(5) What does this reaction confirm the presence of?

Repeat the procedure of the previous test, but use bromine water instead.
(6) What does the test show?
(7) What evidence is there that the original hydrocarbon has been   cracked?
(8) Write an equation for a cracking reaction of decane, assuming that two of the products are ethene and propene.

Questions

Q.25.12   On the same axes, plot graphs of (i) the boiling points, (ii) the melting points, of the alkanes against their relative molecular masses (data on page 379). Explain the trends shown by the graphs.

Q.25.13   Explain, with the aid of examples, the following terms: aliphatic, aromatic, hydrocarbon, straight chain hydrocarbon, branched chain hydrocarbon, homologous series, functional group, alkane, alkene, alkyne, empirical formula, molecular formula, structural formula, isomer, saturated compound, unsaturated compound, alkyl radical, dehydration reaction, substitution reaction, addition reaction.

Q.25.14   Give short answers to each of the following questions:

(a) What is the general formula for (i) the alkanes, (ii) the alkenes?
(b) Give the name and formula for the third member of (i) the alkanes, (ii) the alkenes.

(c) Give the meanings of the terms **saturated** and **unsaturated** as used in organic chemistry.
(d) Complete and balance the equations
(i) $C_3H_8 + O_2 \rightarrow$
(ii) $C_3H_8 + Cl_2 \rightarrow$
(iii) $C_3H_6 + Cl_2 \rightarrow$
What names describe the types of reaction at (ii) and (iii) above?
(f) How would you distinguish experimentally between (i) C_2H_4 and C_2H_6 and (ii) between C_2H_4 and C_2H_2?
(g) What is observed when ethene reacts with bromine solution?
(h) What does the above observation prove about ethene?
(i) Name the compounds: $CH_3CHClCH_3$, C_2H_5OH
(j) What compound on dehydration produces ethene? Name a suitable dehydrating agent.
(k) Give the name and formula for the compound which is formed when ethene is hydrated.
(l) Complete: Water reacts with .... to produce eth....
(m) What is the characteristic feature of the alkynes? What characteristic type of reaction do these compounds undergo?
(n) From what source is ethene obtained industrially? For what is it used?
(o) Explain what is meant by (i) fractionation, (ii) cracking.
(p) What must be done to a hydrocarbon to 'crack' it? Why is this process carried out?
(q) Name the compounds:

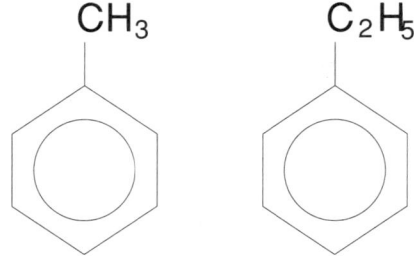

(r) The heat of combustion of propane is -2220 kJ/mol. Calculate the heat liberated on burning 11 g of propane.

(s) What volume of oxygen (at room temperature and pressure) would be required for the above?

(t) What is the formula of the alkane whose molecular mass is 114?

(u) By what type of reaction does chlorine react with methane? What is formed when chlorine undergoes homolytic fission?

(v) 7 g of an alkene reacts with exactly 16 g of bromine. Calculate the formula of the alkene, and name it.

Review   When you know Chapter 25, you should be able to:

(a) Explain what is meant by each of: hydrocarbon, alkane, alkene, alkyne, alkyl radical, isomerism, saturated, unsaturated, addition, substitution, hydrogenation, polymerisation, fractionation, cracking, homolytic fission, heterolytic fission.

(b) State the general formula for the alkanes, alkenes and alkynes, and give the name and formula for any member of any of these series.

(c) Use the IUPAC rules to name any given isomer, and draw the structure of any named isomer.

(d) Describe experiment to (i) prepare ethene, (ii) prepare ethyne, (iii) fractionate a sample of petroleum (iv) crack a long chain alkane.

(e) Describe the properties of the alkanes, alkenes, and alkynes.

(f) Describe the structure of benzene and name some simple aromatic compounds.

(g) Describe the mechanisms of the reaction between (i) methane and chlorine, and (ii) ethene and bromine.

(h) Explain the processes involved in refining petroleum.

Oil Products and their Uses
$\longrightarrow$

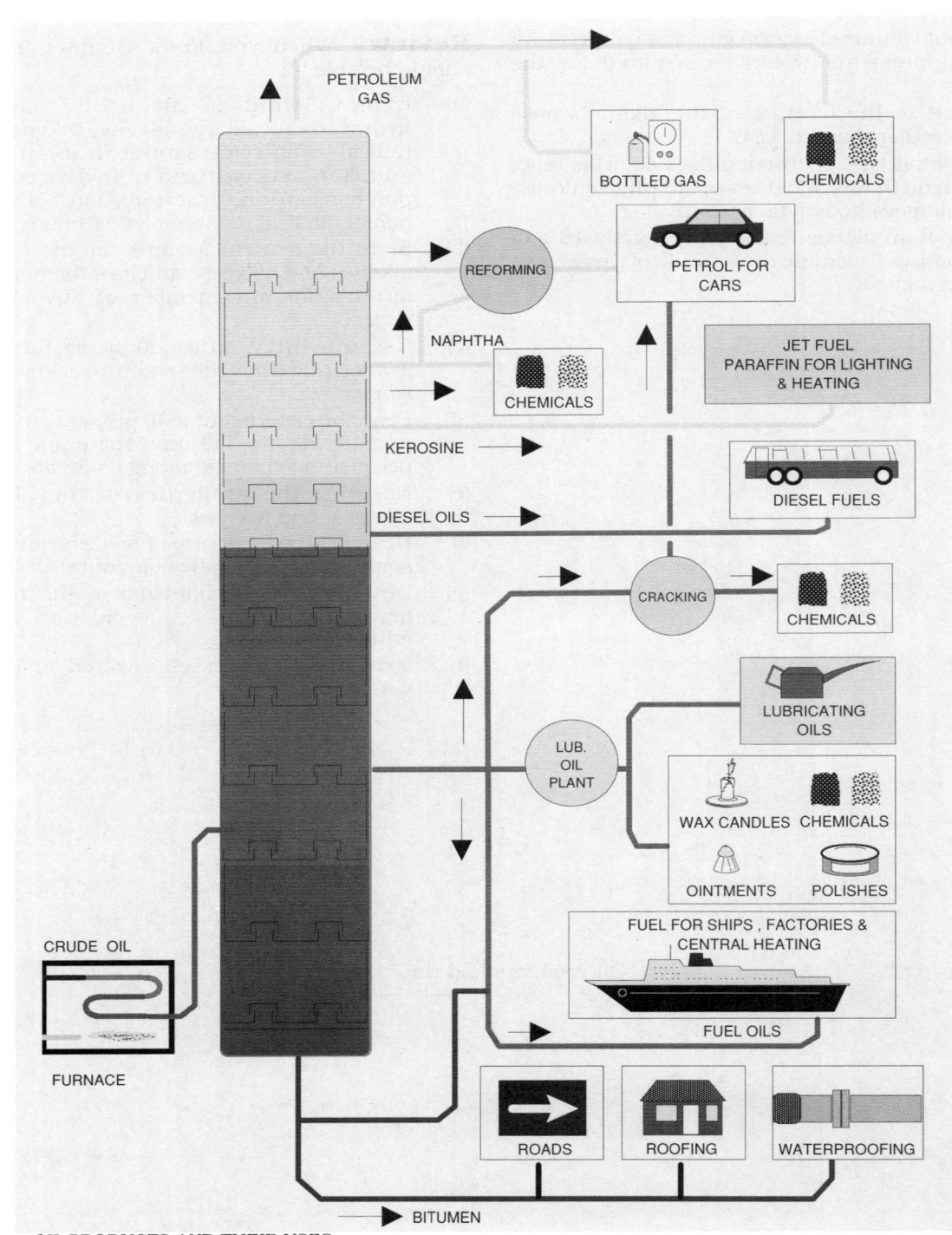

PETROLEUM GAS

BOTTLED GAS

CHEMICALS

REFORMING

PETROL FOR CARS

NAPHTHA

CHEMICALS

JET FUEL
PARAFFIN FOR LIGHTING & HEATING

KEROSINE

DIESEL OILS

DIESEL FUELS

CRACKING

CHEMICALS

LUBRICATING OILS

LUB. OIL PLANT

WAX CANDLES   CHEMICALS

OINTMENTS   POLISHES

FUEL FOR SHIPS, FACTORIES & CENTRAL HEATING

FUEL OILS

CRUDE OIL

FURNACE

ROADS

ROOFING

WATERPROOFING

BITUMEN

25.16 — *OIL PRODUCTS AND THEIR USES.*

Aliphatic alcohols are compounds in which a hydroxyl group (-OH) is attached directly to an alkyl radical. They can be regarded as being derived from the alkanes by the replacement of a hydrogen atom by a hydroxyl group — although they cannot be prepared in such manner.

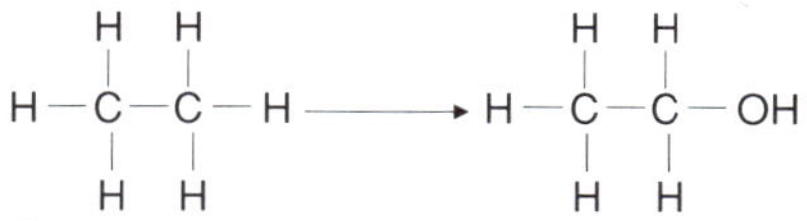

The first few members of the series are:

Methanol	CH_3OH
Ethanol	C_2H_5OH
Propanol	C_3H_7OH
Butanol	C_4H_9OH

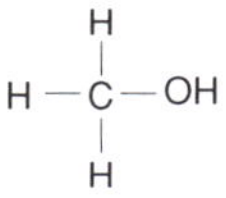

Methanol

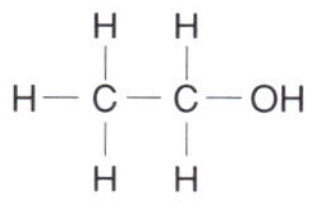

Ethanol

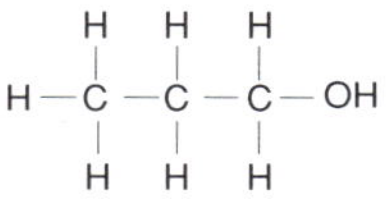

Propan-1-ol   and   Propan-2-ol

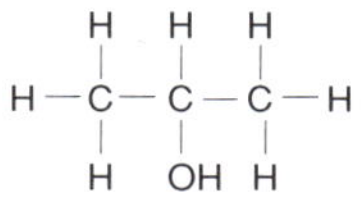

There are 4 isomers of butanol.

The alcohols are named by substituting the ending **-ol** for **-e** in the name of the corresponding alkane.

(*e.g.*, methane → methanol).

Alcohols can be classified into primary, secondary, and tertiary.

A primary alcohol is one in which there is one (and only one) carbon atom joined to the carbon atom to which the OH group is attached. Examples of primary alcohols are methanol, ethanol and proan-1-ol, as illustrated. Primary alcohols can be represented in general by **RCH₂OH**, where R is an alkyl radical (or a hydrogen atom in the case of methanol).

A secondary alcohol has two carbon atoms joined to the carbon atom attached to the OH group; an example is propan-2-ol. The general formula for a secondary alcohol is **RCHOHR** (the alkyl radicals can be the same of different).

A tertiary alcohol has three carbon atoms joined to the carbon atom attached to the OH group. The simplest tertiary alcohol is 2-methyl-propan-2-ol, whose graphic formula is:

26
Alcohols

$$\begin{array}{c}
H \\
| \\
H-C-H \\
| \\
H \quad\quad H \\
| \quad\quad | \\
H-C-C-C-H \\
| \quad | \quad | \\
H \quad OH \quad H
\end{array}$$

Ethanol

Ethanol, the second member of the series, is by far the most common and the most important of the primary alcohols and is often referred to as just 'alcohol'. It is the alcohol which occurs in all beers, wines and spirits and which is also a very important and widely used industrial chemical.

Manufacture of Ethanol

1. By Fermentation

Fermentation is the process in which organic matter is slowly broken down into simple substances by the action of enzymes — complex chemical substances which occur in yeast and are highly effective catalysts for certain reactions. The action of enzymes is very specific — one enzyme usually causing only one particular reaction. A common example of fermentation is the conversion of glucose into ethanol and CO_2, by the action of the enzyme zymase. The overall change can be represented by:

$$C_6H_{12}O_6 \rightarrow 2C_2H_5OH + 2CO_2$$

In manufacturing ethanol, the starting material is often sucrose — in the form of molasses, which is the syrupy liquid remaining after the crystallisation of cane sugar (it contains about 50% sucrose). Yeast is added to the sucrose solution and the enzyme 'invertase', present in the yeast, causes the sucrose to be converted to two simpler isomeric sugars, glucose and fructose.

$$\underset{\text{sucrose}}{C_{12}H_{22}O_{11}} + H_2O \xrightarrow{\text{invertase}} \underset{\text{glucose}}{C_6H_{12}O_6} + \underset{\text{fructose}}{C_6H_{12}O_6}$$

Then the zymase, also present in the yeast, breaks down these sugars and converts them to ethanol and CO_2:

$$C_6H_{12}O_6 \xrightarrow{\text{zymase}} 2C_2H_5OH + 2CO_2$$

2. By Hydration of Ethene

Large quantities of ethene are produced as a by-product during the cracking of petroleum. Ethene is used mainly for the manufacture of plastics, and for making ethanol and other chemicals.

Direct **hydration** of ethene gives ethanol:

$$C_2H_4 + H_2O \rightarrow C_2H_5OH$$

The reaction is carried out by passing a mixture of ethene and steam, under pressure and at about 300° C, over a catalyst of phosphoric acid adsorbed on to silica.

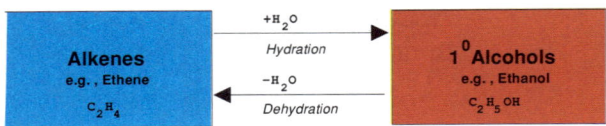

26.1

Physical Properties of Ethanol

Colourless liquid with pleasant smell. Volatile, b.p. 78° C. Density 0.79 g/cm^3. Miscible with water and with organic (*i.e.* non-polar) solvents in all proportions. Poisonous.

Chemical reactions

1. **Combustion:** It burns with a pale blue flame forming CO_2 and water:

$$C_2H_5OH + 3O_2 \rightarrow 2CO_2 + 3H_2O$$

2. **Oxidation:** It can readily be oxidised to ethanal, which, with excess oxidising agent, can be further oxidised to ethanoic (acetic) acid

$$CH_3CH_2OH \xrightarrow{[O]} CH_3CHO \xrightarrow{[O]} CH_3COOH$$

The oxidising agent usually used for this reaction is a mixture of sodium (or potassium) dichromate and sulphuric acid, which react together to provide oxygen atoms as follows:

$$Na_2Cr_2O_7 + 4H_2SO_4 \rightarrow$$
$$Na_2SO_4 + Cr_2(SO_4)_3 + 4H_2O + 3[O]$$

or, ionically,

$$Cr_2O_7{}^{2-} + 8H^+ \rightarrow 2Cr^{3+} + 4H_2O + 3[O]$$

The **breathalyser test**, which is given to suspected drunken drivers, makes use of this reaction.

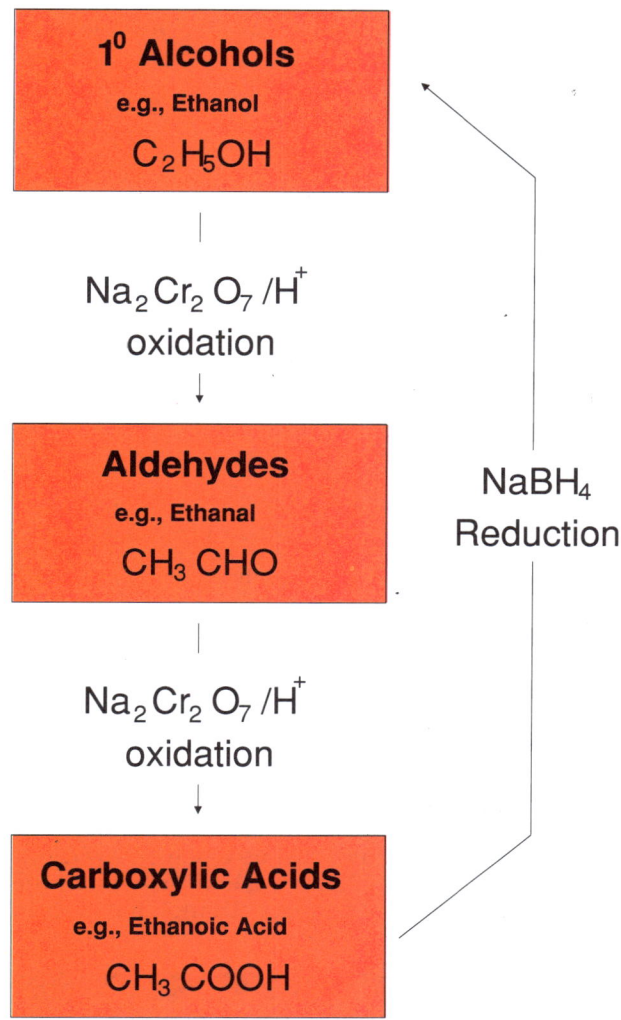

26.3 — A breathalyser. The dichromate crystals are contained in the glass tube attached to the bag.

ester is the equivalent of the salt. Esters and salts, however, have very dissimilar properties; esters are covalent compounds whereas salts are ionic.

A neutralisation reaction:

$$CH_3COOH + NaOH \rightarrow CH_3COONa + H_2O$$

ethanoic acid — Sodium ethanoate (a salt)

An esterification:

$$CH_3COOH + C_2H_5OH \rightleftharpoons CH_3COOC_2H_5 + H_2O$$

ethanoic acid — Ethyl ethanoate (an ester)

Another difference between the reactions is that a neutralisation (being an ionic reaction) is practically instantaneous and goes to completion, whereas an esterification is a reversible reaction and how far the reaction goes depends on the equilibrium constant for the reaction.

Ethanol reacts with acids forming ethyl esters; with ethanoic acid, as in the above equation, the ester ethyl ethanoate is formed. Esterifications are usually carried out in the presence of concentrated sulphuric acid, which both acts as a catalyst for the reaction, and also absorbs the water formed in the process — thereby preventing the backward reaction and moving the position of equilibrium to the right so that a higher yield of ester is formed.

4.   Halogenation:

The phosphorous pentachloride (PCl5), a reagent which replaces an OH group by a chlorine atom, reacts with ethanol, converting it to chloroethane:

$$C_2H_5OH + PCl_5 \rightarrow C_2H_5Cl + POCl_3 + HC$$

26.2
Potassium dichromate is orange in colour, and on reaction with alcohol it is reduced to Cr^{3+} ions, which are green. If a person on breathing into the breathalyser changes the colour of the orange dichromate to green, it is a strong indication that he has been consuming alcohol.

3.   Esterfication: This is a reaction in which an acid and an alcohol react together to form an ester and water. It resembles, to some extent, the inorganic reaction between an acid and an alkali in which a salt and water are formed (*i.e.* a neutralisation). The

Phosphorus pentachloride is converted to phosphorus trichloride oxide ($POCl_3$) and HCl gas is liberated. This reaction is used as a standard test for an OH group in a compound.

5. Reaction with Metals:

When ethanol reacts with sodium (or potassium), the hydrogen atom of the OH group is replaced by a sodium (or potassium) atom, forming sodium ethoxide (or potassium ethoxide), a salt-like compound, and hydrogen liberated:

$$C_2H_5OH + Na \rightarrow C_2H_5ONa + \tfrac{1}{2}H_2$$

Apart from this reaction, ethanol and other alcohols show no acidic properties.

6. Dehydration:

There are two ways in which ethanol can be dehydrated, but the more important of them results in ethene being formed. This occurs when ethanol is heated with excess concentrated sulphuric acid at a temperature of about 170°C. Each molecule of ethanol loses one molecule of water:

Uses of Ethanol

Apart from its presence in beers, wines and spirits, ethanol is an important solvent — for paints, varnishes, polishes, perfumes, toilet preparations, dyes and drugs. It is used in the manufacture of many other organic compounds, and it is used as a fuel and as a preservative for biological specimens.

Methanol (CH_3OH)

Methanol, the first member of the series, is very similar to ethanol in most respects. It is a colourless volatile liquid but its boiling point (64°C) is lower than that of ethanol because of its smaller molecular mass. It is miscible with water and with organic solvents in all proportions. It is more poisonous than ethanol and can cause blindness, insanity and death.

Its chemical reactions, which are summarised below, resemble those of ethanol — with the exception of dehydration to form an alkene (since there is no alkene with only one carbon atom).

1. Combustion:

$$CH_3OH + 1\tfrac{1}{2}O_2 \rightarrow CO_2 + 2H_2O$$

2. Oxidation:

$$CH_3OH \rightarrow \underset{\text{Methanal}}{HCHO} \rightarrow \underset{\text{Methanoic acid}}{HCOOH}$$

3. Esterfication:

$$CH_3OH + CH_3COOH \rightarrow \underset{\text{Methyl ethanoate}}{CH_3COOCH_3} + H_2O$$

4. Halogenation:

$$CH_3OH + PCl_5 \rightarrow CH_3Cl + POCl_3 + HCl$$

5. Reaction with Metals:

$$CH_3OH + Na \rightarrow \underset{\substack{\text{Sodium} \\ \text{methoxide}}}{CH_3ONa} + \tfrac{1}{2}H_2$$

Uses of Methanol

Large quantities of methanol are converted to methanal ('formaldehyde') (which is used as a preservative and to make various plastics), and other methyl compounds. Methylated spirits is a mixture of approximately 10% methanol and 90% ethanol, with small quantities of an unpleasant tasting substances and a dye. This mixture can be bought for use as a fuel and as a solvent, without having to pay the high excise duty which the Government levies on pure ethanol for use in drinks.

Alcohols as Fuels

There is much research being done at the present time into finding alternative fuels to petrol. Alcohols, and in particular methanol, are likely to become of major importance for this purpose in the future.

World production of methanol at present is about 11 million tonnes per year, largely for the manufacture of plastics and glues, but small amounts (in the region of 10%) are blended into petrol in several countries, *e.g.* France, Germany, Holland. There is a major methanol fuel programme presently under way in New Zealand. Methanol can be manufactured from virtually any carbon-containing substance such as coal, gas, peat, wood and even refuse. Natural gas is the preferred raw material at the moment, since manufacture of methanol from it is efficient and reactively cheap. Methanol can be made from renewable sources, such as wood, and in some European countries there are already pilot plants producing it from wood and straw.

Ethanol is another possible fuel of the future since it can readily be produced by fermentation of substances containing starch and/or sugar. In Brazil at present, vast quantities of sugar cane are grown, fermented to produce alcohol, and mixed with petrol. Ordinary petrol is not available in that country: instead, the pumps deliver 'gasohol' which is a mixture of 80% petrol and 20% ethanol. No alternation to car engines is needed for them to run on this mixture. In both the USA and Sweden at present, crops are being grown for the purpose of producing ethanol for use as fuel.

General Properties of Alcohols

The OH group is considerably polar so that in alcohols there is consequent association between molecules, particularly those of low molecular mass:

$$R - \overset{\delta-}{O} - \overset{\delta+}{H}$$
$$\overset{}{H} - \underset{\delta+}{O} - \underset{\delta-}{R}$$

This results in alcohols having higher boiling points than alkanes of similar molecular mass (the first few members of the alkanes are gases, whereas the first members of the alcohols are liquids; there are no gaseous alcohols). The effect is greatest in the first few members of the series, in which the alkane portion of the molecule is relatively small, and so the OH group has a predominant influence on the properties of the compound.

The polarity of the OH group also explains why the lower alcohols are completely miscible with water. Higher alcohols, in which the alkyl group is larger and has more influence, become progressively more like the alkanes; $C_{16}H_{33}OH$ for example, is a waxy solid which is insoluble in water.

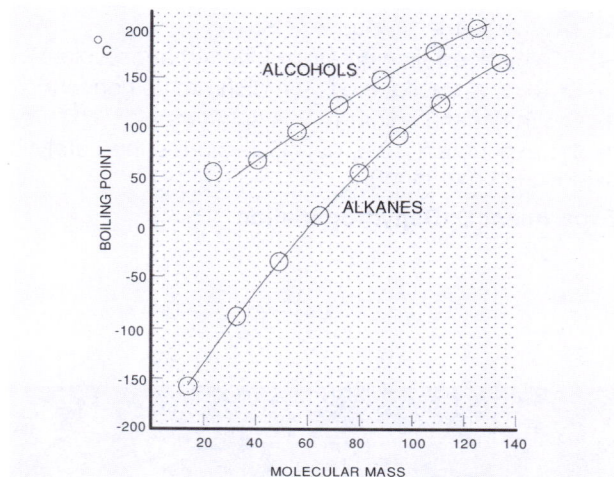

26.4 — *Graph of b.p. of (a) alcohols and (b) alkanes, against molecular mass.*

Chemically, the alcohols are very similar and undergo the following reactions:

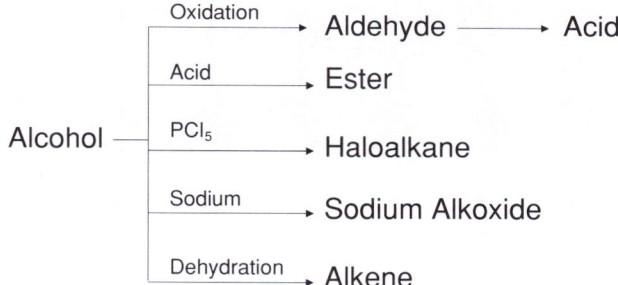

Experiment 26.1
Reactions of Ethanol

The reactions of ethanol are typical of the reactions of any primary alcohol.

Experiment A : Combustion
Ignite about 2 cm^3 of ethanol in an evaporating basin or other suitable container.

(1)   What colour is the flame?

(2)   Write an equation for the reaction which occurs.

Experiment B: Oxidation
Take about 5 cm^3 of potassium dichromate solution and add 5 drops each of ethanol and concentrated sulphuric acid. Warm gently, but do not boil. Note the irritating smell of the product.

(3) What is the product?

(4) Why does dichromate solution change colour?

(5) To what substance is the dichromate converted?

(6) What is the colour of this substance?

(Note: experiment 12.6, part F, illustrates the catalytic oxidation of methanol).

Experiment C: Dehydrogenation

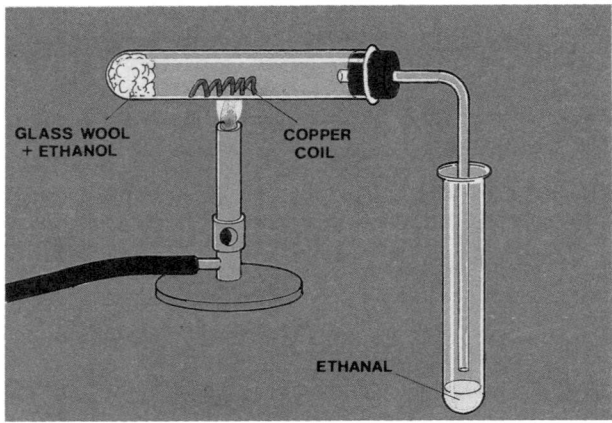

26.5

Dehydrogenation is removal of hydrogen, and thus is an oxidation reaction. Copper catalyses the dehydrogenation of ethanol. Set up the apparatus as shown. Heat the copper, gently at first, and then more strongly. At intervals, apply some heat to the ethanol in order to vaporise it. As the vapour passes over the hot copper, it becomes dehydrogenated. The product is driven down the delivery tube and collects in the cooled test tube.

(7) To what is the ethanol converted in the reaction?

(8) Why is the collecting tube kept cold?

This reaction can also be shown in the following way. Boil a small quantity of ethanol with an electric heater (there must be no naked flames nearby which could ignite the vapour). At a safe distance, heat a copper coin to near redness. Hold the hot coin in the ethanol vapour. The copper catalyses the oxidation of the ethanol, and at the same time, any copper oxide on the coin becomes reduced, thus cleaning the coin. When the coin is removed from the vapour, it quickly re-oxidises.

Experiment D: Esterfication

Take about 2 cm^3 each of ethanol and ethanoic acid in a test tube, and add 10 drops of concentrated sulphuric acid. Shake carefully to mix the contents, and then gently warm (**DO NOT BOIL**) the mixture for a few minutes. Note the pleasant smell. Pour the mixture into cold water when the product, being insoluble, should be observed floating on top.

(9) What is the product of the reaction?

(10) Write an equation for the reaction.

(11) Why does it float on the water?

(12) What is the purpose of the sulphuric acid?

Experiment E: Halogenation

This experiment should be done in the fume cupboard. To about 1 cm^3 of ethanol add a very small quantity (about the size of a match head) of phosphorus pentachloride, PCl_5. Test the fumes evolved with moist blue litmus paper.

(13) What is the result, and why?

Now test the fumes with a glass rod which has been dipped into concentrated ammonia solution.

(14) What happens, and why?

(15) Write an equation for the reaction and name all the products.

Experiment F: Acidic Nature

Add some sodium hydrogencarbonate solution to the few cm^3 of ethanol.

(16) Is carbon dioxide liberated?

(17) Is ethanol acidic?

Experiment G: Reaction with Metals

Strongly electropositive metals react with alcohols. To 2 or 3 cm^3 of ethanol, add a piece (about the size of a small pea) of dry sodium. Test the gas liberated with a lighted splint.

(18) What gas is evolved?

When the metal has fully reacted, pour the resulting solution on to a watch-glass, and evaporate it to dryness over a beaker of boiling water.

(19) What is the white compound which crystallises?

(20) Write an equation for the reaction.

Now add some water to this substance and test the solution that is formed with litmus. Work out what is produced.

(21)   Write an equation for this last reaction.

Haloalkanes

These are the compounds in which a halogen atom has replaced a hydrogen atom of an alkane molecule, *e.g.* chloromethane, bromoethane. They are produced by several different reactions:

1.   By the reaction of the alcohol with phosphorus pentachloride, *e.g.*

$C_2H_5OH + PCl_5 \rightarrow C_2H_5Cl + POCl_3 + HCl$

2.   By the reaction of the alkane with the halogen, *e.g.*

$C_2H_6 + Cl_2 \rightarrow C_2H_5Cl + HCl$

3.   By the reaction of the alkene with the hydrogen halide, *e.g.*

$C_2H_4 + HCl \rightarrow C_2H_5Cl$

Apart from the simplest members, which are gases, most of the haloalkanes are sweet-smelling volatile liquids which are insoluble in water. One of the important reactions of a haloalkane is its hydrolysis, particularly in the presence of alkali —

in which reaction it is converted to its corresponding alcohol (along with the sodium or potassium halide):

$$RX + NaOH \rightarrow ROH + NaX \quad (X = halogen)$$

e.g. $C_2H_5Cl + NaOH \rightarrow C_2H_5OH + NaCl$

Experiment 26.2
Hydrolysis of a Haloalkane

Hydrolysis of a haloalkane produces an alcohol. Tertiary haloalkanes are more easily hydrolysed than either primary or secondary, and on hydrolysis, they form tertiary alcohols.

$$R-\underset{\underset{R}{|}}{\overset{\overset{R}{|}}{C}}-Cl \xrightarrow{NaOH} R-\underset{\underset{R}{|}}{\overset{\overset{R}{|}}{C}}-OH + NaCl$$

In this experiment, 2-chloro-2-methyl propane is hydrolysed, by reacting it with sodium hydroxide solution.

Into each of two test tubes, put about 3 cm^3 of 2-chloro-2-methylpropane and about the same volume of very dilute sodium hydroxide solution. Set one tube aside for about 15 minutes.

To the other tube, add a few drops each of dilute nitric acid and silver nitrate solution.

(1)   What is meant by hydrolysis?

(2)   Draw the structural formula for 2-chloro-2-methylpropane.

(3)   What type of bond joins the chlorine and carbon atoms?

(4)   For what is the addition of nitric acid and silver nitrate a test?

(5)   What happens when these reagents were added to the chloroalkane?

(6)   Explain why?

To the second tube, after the 15 minutes, add a few drops of dilute nitric acid and silver nitrate solution. Observe what happens, Then add a few cm^3 of aqueous ammonia and mix well.

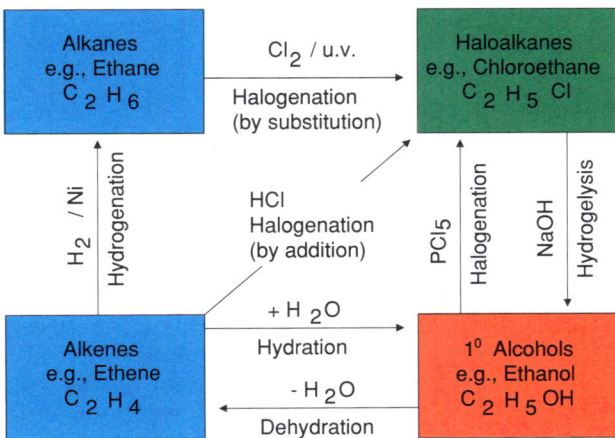

26.6

(7) What was formed when the silver nitrate was added? Why?

(8) What happened when the ammonia was added?

(9) What ion did this test prove to be present?

(10) To what alcohol was the 2-chloro-2-methylpropane converted in the experiment? Draw its structure, and write an equation for the hydrolysis reaction which occurred.

(11) How would the result have differed if water were used for the hydrolysis rather than alkali solution.

(12) What reagent could be used to convert the alcohol back to the starting compound?

Summary of the reactions of ethanol.

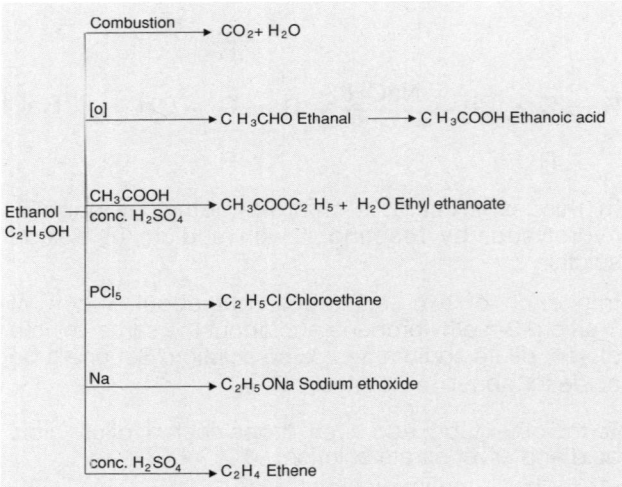

Ethanol C_2H_5OH

- Combustion → $CO_2 + H_2O$
- [o] → CH_3CHO Ethanal → CH_3COOH Ethanoic acid
- CH_3COOH conc. H_2SO_4 → $CH_3COOC_2H_5 + H_2O$ Ethyl ethanoate
- PCl_5 → C_2H_5Cl Chloroethane
- Na → C_2H_5ONa Sodium ethoxide
- conc. H_2SO_4 → C_2H_4 Ethene

Inter-relationships of Homologous Series

It may have been observed so far, that many reactions of a particular compound frequently involve its conversion to the corresponding (*i.e.* with the same number of carbon atoms) member of a different homologous series, *e.g.* hydrogenation of an alkene yields an alkane and oxidation of an alcohol produces an aldehyde. The chart facing, summarises the ways in which members of various homologous series can be converted to members of other series.

Questions

Q.26.1 Draw the structure and name each of the compounds of formulae:

(a) $CH_3CH_2CHOHCH_3$
(b) $CH_3CHClCHOHCH_3$
(c) $CH_3CCl_2CHOHCH_3$
(d) $CH_3CH(CH_3)CHClCH_2OH$.
(e) $CH_3C(CH_3)_2CHOHCH_2Cl$
(f) $CH_3C(CH_3)(OH)CH_2Cl$

Q.26.2
(a) Draw the structures and give the names of four isomers of butanol, C_4H_9OH.

(b) List each of the isomers as being a primary, secondary or tertiary alcohol, as appropriate.

Q.26.3
(i) How is each of the following conversions carried out?

(ii) Classify each as one of : oxidation, hydration, dehydration, hydrolysis, halogenation, substitution.

(a) ethene → ethanol
(b) ethanol → ethanoic acid,
(c) ethanol → chloroethane,
(d) ethane → chlorethane,
(e) ethanol → ethanal,
(f) ethanol → sodium ethoxide,
(g) ethanol → ethene
(h) ethene → chloroethane,
(i) chloroethane → ethanol
(j) sodium ethoxide → ethanol

(iii) Write an equation for each reaction.

Q.26.4
(a) Give two reasons why methanol has a much higher boiling point than methane.

(b) Explain how you could distinguish between samples of methanol and ethanol.

(c) What is formed when methanol reacts with each of: sodium, PCl_5, acidified potassium dichromate solution, methanoic acid?

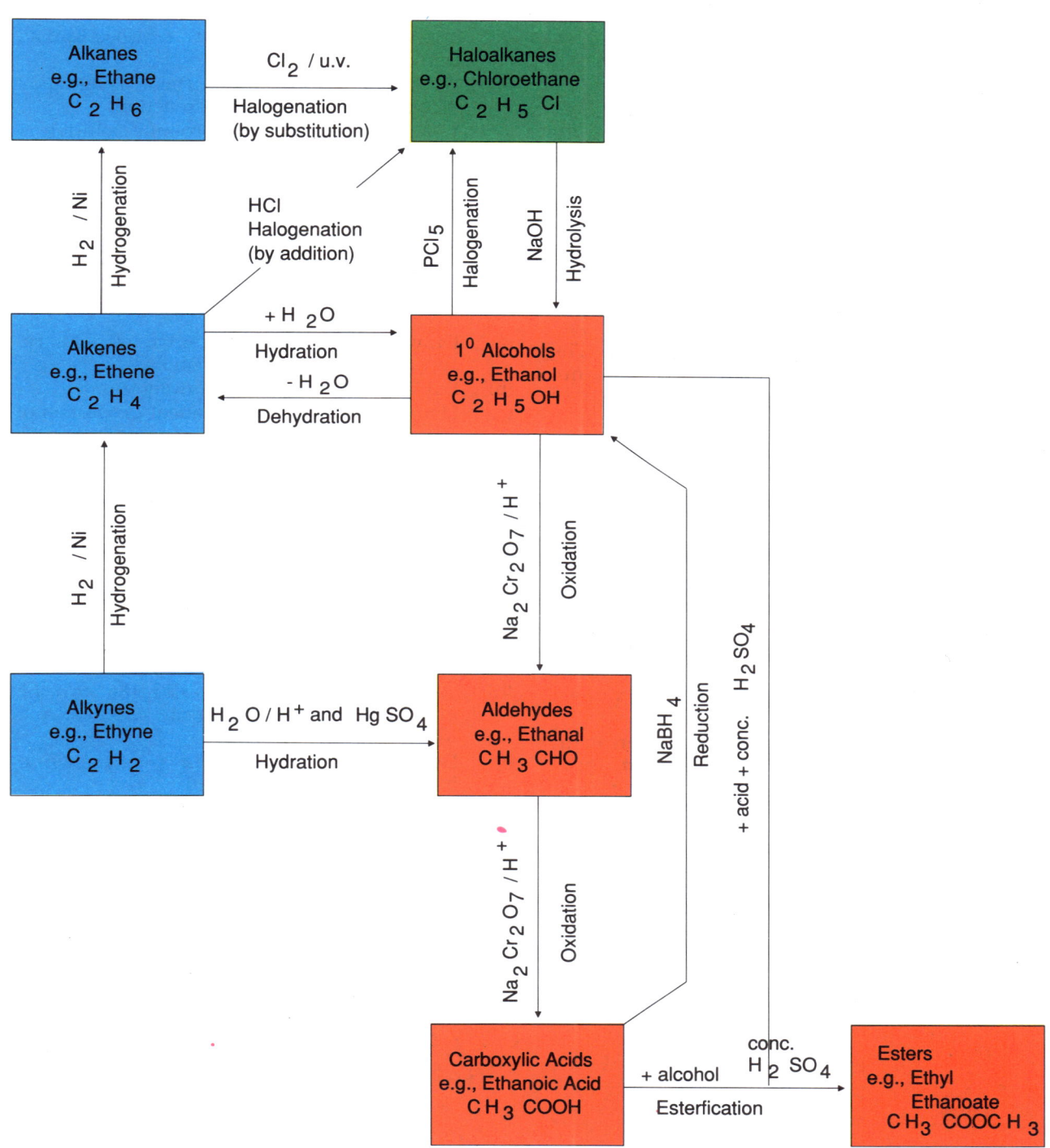

26.7

Q.26.5 By means of equations, show how 1-bromopropane could be prepared from each of (a) propane, (b) propene, (c) propan-1-ol.

Classify each reaction as a substitution or an addition reaction.

Draw the structure of 2-bromopropane, and suggest how it could be prepared.

Q.26.6 The following is an account of an experiment in which ethene is prepared by dehydrating ethanol, using manganese dioxide as catalyst.

The apparatus is set up as shown below. The mixture in the flask is heated, the ethanol vaporises, and is dehydrated by the manganese dioxide, forming ethene:

$$2CH_3OH \xrightarrow{MnO_2} C_2H_4 + H_2O$$

The ethene is bubbled through concentrated sulphuric acid to dry it, after which it is collected by displacing air from gas jars. After sufficient gas is collected, the apparatus is left to cool before being dismantled'.

The experiment as described, will not work — for a number of reasons.

(a) Redraw the diagram, correcting the various faults shown.
(b) Rewrite the account of the experiment, stating how the experiment **should** have been carried out.
(c) One of the statements in the account would lead to an accident. Which statement is this,

and what would happen if the procedure as described, is carried out?

(d) What is observed when ethene is ignited? Write an equation for that reaction.
(e) What is observed when bromine solution is added to a jar of ethene? Write an equation for the reaction, name the product, and state what that reaction proves.
(f) How is ethene produced commercially, and for what is it used?

Review When you known Chapter 26 you should be able to:

(a) Draw the structural formulae of primary, secondary and tertiary alcohols.
(b) Explain how ethanol is manufactured.
(c) List the physical and chemical properties of ethanol and methanol.
(d) Give the names and structures of the two oxidation products of both ethanol and methanol, and state the oxidising agent commonly used.
(e) Explain the chemistry of the breathalyser test.
(f) Write about the potential of alcohols as fuels.
(g) Explain each of: fermentation, hydration, dehydration, dehydrogenation, esterification, halogenation.
(h) Describe how the haloalkanes can be produced from alkanes, from alkenes, and from alcohols.
(i) Describe what reaction occurs when haloalkanes are hydrolysed.
(j) Rewrite Fig. 26.7 from memory.

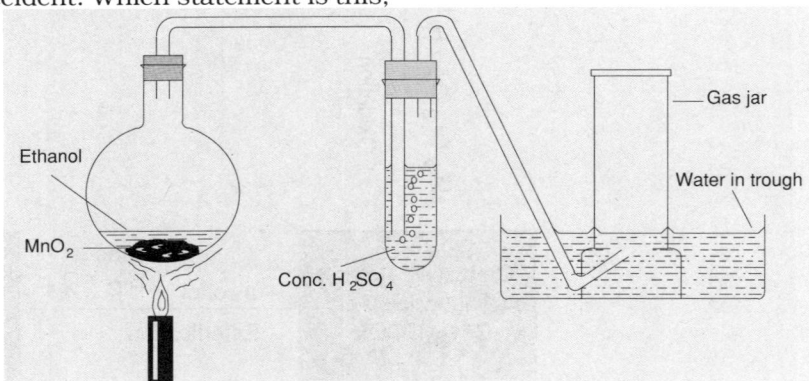

26.8

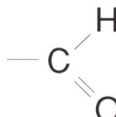The aldehyde functional group is

$$-C \overset{H}{\underset{O}{\|}}$$

so that aldehydes in general can be represented by

$$R-C \overset{H}{\underset{O}{\|}}$$

where R in an alkyl radical. Ketones have a second alkyl radical in place of the hydrogen atom in the aldehyde group, so their general structure is:

$$R-\overset{R}{\underset{|}{C}}=O$$

Because the carbonyl group, *i.e.* —

$$\diagdown_{C}=O$$

is common to both series of compounds they have many similar properties and reactions. The

$$\overset{\delta^+}{C} \overset{\delta^-}{=} O$$

group is considerably polar, so that association occurs, and therefore both aldehydes and ketones have higher boiling points than alkanes of similar molecular mass. As well, it means that the lower members of each series are soluble in water. The chemical reactions of the C=O group (to be described) are shown by both series of compounds. Another similarity is that both are obtained on oxidation of alcohols, aldehydes from primary alcohols and ketones from secondary alcohols.

27
Aldehydes and Ketones

$$R-\underset{\underset{H}{|}}{\overset{\overset{H}{|}}{C}}-OH \xrightarrow{[o]} R-C\overset{\overset{H}{\diagup}}{\underset{\diagdown}{O}} + H_2O$$

Primary alcohol   Aldehyde

$$R-\underset{\underset{H}{|}}{\overset{\overset{R}{|}}{C}}-OH \xrightarrow{[o]} R-\overset{\overset{R}{|}}{C}=O + H_2O$$

Secondary alcohol   Ketone

Aldehydes

The first members of the series are:

Methanal[*] HCHO $H-C\overset{\diagup H}{\diagdown O}$

Ethanal[*] CH_3CHO $H-\underset{\underset{H}{|}}{\overset{\overset{H}{|}}{C}}-C\overset{\diagup H}{\diagdown O}$

Propanal[*] C_2H_5CHO (CH_3CH_2CHO) $H-\underset{\underset{H}{|}}{\overset{\overset{H}{|}}{C}}-\underset{\underset{H}{|}}{\overset{\overset{H}{|}}{C}}-C\overset{\diagup H}{\diagdown O}$

Aldehydes are named by replacing the final -e of the corresponding alkane with the ending -al (methane → methanal). The most important member of the series is **ethanal** (CH_3CHO).

Ethanal (CH_3CHO), or 'Acetaldehyde'

Preparation of Ethanal

The normal laboratory preparation is by the oxidation of ethan**ol**, using a mixture of sodium dichromate and sulphuric acid. (How these substances react is described on page 330/331).

$$C_2H_5OH \xrightarrow{[O]} CH_3CHO + H_2O$$

Sodium dichromate is used in preference to the potassium salt as it is more soluble in the presence of ethanol. The oxidation is carried out by heating together the alcohol and the oxidising agent in a distillation apparatus. The reaction is exothermic, and little heat is necessary once the reaction has started. During the reaction, the colour of the

mixture changes from orange (the colour of the dichromate ions) to green (the colour of the Cr^{3+} ions). In order to prevent further oxidation of the aldehyde (to the acid), the alcohol is kept in excess, and the volatile aldehyde is distilled off as it is formed. However, even with these precautions, some ethanoic acid may be formed. Other impurities likely to be produced are ethene and ethoxyethane ($C_2H_5OC_2H_5$) formed by dehydration of ethanol, and ethyl hydrogensulphate formed by the reaction of ethanol and sulphuric acid. As well, the distillate may contain water and unreacted ethanol.

Experiment 27.1
Preparation of Ethanal

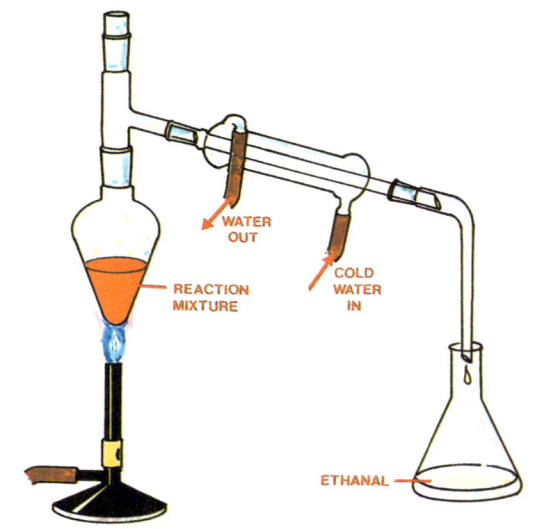

27.1 —

Prepare a solution of 10 g of sodium dichromate in 20 cm^3 of water, and pour this into the distillation flask. Add a few pieces of anti-bumping agent, and then arrange the apparatus for distillation with addition, as shown. **Slowly and carefully**, and with cooling as required, mix 5 cm^3 of concentrated sulphuric with 10 cm^3 of ethanol in a small conical flask or beaker. Pour this mixture into the tap funnel.

Heat the flask, gently, until the dichromate solution is **almost** boiling, and then remove the bunsen. Slowly (*i.e.* **drop by drop**) add the mixture from the tap funnel.

The reaction may start immediately, but if not, heat it gently until it does. Then distil slowly, adding the mixture form the tap funnel at about the same rate as the ethanal distills over. Continue heating until about 10 cm^3 of distillate have been collected; by then, practically all of the ethanal will have distilled over. Do not allow the distillation flask to become less than half full, as charring may then occur, and this makes the flask very difficult to clean.

Questions

Q.27.1   In order to prepare ethanal, a distillation apparatus was set up. The flask contained 60 cm^3 of 40% sulphuric acid along with some silica granules and in the tap funnel was a mixture of 30 g of sodium dichromate, 50 cm^3 of water and 30 cm^3 of ethanol The acid was heated to almost boiling and the heat then removed. The mixture from the tap funnel was added, dropwise, to the hot acid. The ethanal vapour which was formed was condensed and collected in a flask cooled with a mixture of ice and water. The ethanal was purified by fractional distillation and this resulted in 11.5 g of the product.

(a)   What precautions should have been taken when mixing the acid and alcohol? Why?

(b)   What was the purpose of the silica granules?

(c)   Why was the heating stopped before the addition of the ethanol?

(d)   State and explain the colour change that was observed during the experiment.

(e)   Why was the receiving flask cooled with iced water?

(f)   Mention two points in the procedure which ensure that the main product was ethanal.

(g)   What impurities were likely to have been present?

(h)   Use oxidation numbers to show that the ethanol was oxidised and the dichromate ions were reduced during the experiment.

(i)   Write and balance the equation of the reaction of ethanol and acidified dichromate.

(j)   Given that the density of ethanol is 0.8 g/cm^3, calculate (i) the mass of ethanol taken, (ii) the mass of sodium dichromate needed, and (iii) the theoretical mass of ethanal which should be formed.

(k)   Why was much less formed?

(l)   Calculate the percentage yield of ethanal in the experiment.

(m)   Give the name and formula of the product which would be formed if oxidation had been allowed to proceed further.

(n)   What would have been the product if, instead of ethanol, (i) propan-1-ol, or (ii) propan-2-ol had been used.

Industrial Manufacture of Ethanal

1.   When ethyne (obtained from the action of water on calcium dicarbide) is bubbled into dilute H$_2$SO$_4$ in the presence of HgSO$_4$ (which acts as a catalyst) it becomes hydrated and forms ethanal:

$$C_2H_2 \; + \; H_2O \; \rightarrow \; CH_3CHO$$

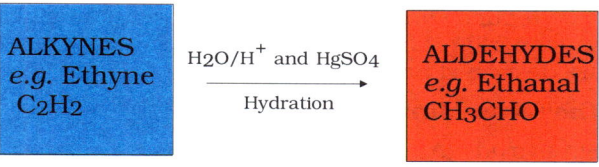

27.2

2.   Ethanol is oxidised by passing its vapour, mixed with air, over a heated silver or copper catalyst:

$$C_2H_5OH \; + \; \tfrac{1}{2}O_2 \; \rightarrow \; CH_3CHO \; + \; H_2O$$

This reaction can be easily demonstrated. See Experiment 26.1 (c)

Physical Properties of Ethanal
Colourless liquid with pungent smell. Volatile, boiling point is 21°C. Miscible with water and with organic solvents in all proportions.

Chemical Reactions:
1.   Combustion
It burns in air to form CO$_2$ and water vapour:

$$CH_3CHO \; + \; 1\tfrac{1}{2}O_2 \; \rightarrow \; 2CO_2 \; + \; 2H_2O$$

2. Oxidation

One of the most important properties of the aldehyde group is the ease with which it is oxidised to the carboxylic acid group (-COOH):

Ethanal, on oxidation, is converted to ethanoic acid:

$$CH_3CHO \xrightarrow{[O]} CH_3COOH$$

Acidified potassium dichromate or potassium permanganate can be used as the oxidising agent.

Because of the ease with which aldehydes are oxidised they are good reducing agents. They give a silver mirror with ammoniacal silver oxide and they reduce Fehling's solution to a red precipitate of copper(I) oxide. These tests for reducing agents are described below.

The Silver Mirror Test.

Silver oxide (Ag_2O) dissolves in aqueous ammonia forming the complex ion $Ag(NH_3)_2^+$. This solution is called ammoniacal silver oxide or **'Tollens' Reagent'**. It is prepared by adding aqueous ammonia drop by drop to silver nitrate solution until the precipitate of Ag_2O formed has almost redissolved. Chemically, it can be regarded as Ag_2O.

When a solution of ammoniacal silver oxide is heated with some ethanal in a test tube, it is reduced to metallic silver by the aldehyde — which at the same time, is oxidised to the acid:

$$CH_3CHO + Ag_2O \rightarrow 2Ag + CH_3COOH$$

The silver is deposited on the sides of the test tube, producing a silver mirror — hence the name of the test. Glass is silvered industrially by a similar reaction.

Fehling's Solution

When copper(II) sulphate solution ($CuSO_4$) is added to sodium hydroxide, a blue precipitate of copper(II) hydroxide ($Cu(OH)_2$) is formed:

$$CuSO_4 + 2NaOH \rightarrow Cu(OH)_2 + Na_2SO_4$$

However, in the presence of sodium potassium tartrate, a complex copper(II) tartrate is formed, which is soluble and so remains in solution. This solution, which is royal blue, is known as Fehling's solution. Chemically, it can be regarded as $Cu(OH)_2$.

On treatment with a reducing agent such as ethanal, the copper(II) is reduced to copper(I) which is produced as the oxide (Cu_2O):

$$CH_3CHO + 2Cu(OH)_2 \rightarrow Cu_2O + CH_3COOH + 2H_2O$$

The formation of a red precipitate (of Cu_2O which is insoluble) is evidence that the Fehling's solution has been reduced and that the aldehyde is therefore a reducing agent.

3. Reduction:

On being reduced with, for example, hydrogen, in the presence of a nickel catalyst, aldehydes are converted back to the corresponding alcohol; ethanal is therefore converted to ethanol:

$$CH_3CHO + H_2 \rightarrow C_2H_5OH$$

4. Condensation Reactions:

A condensation is a reaction between two different molecules which combine together to form a more complex molecule, with the elimination of water or other simple substance such as NH_3 or HCl.

Ethanal condenses with several compounds; these reactions can be represented in general by:

where H_2X is the compound with which it condenses.

An example of a compound which condenses with ethanal is hydrazine, H_2NNH_2, and when it does so, it forms ethanal hydrazone:

In practice though, hydrazine itself is seldom used for this reaction, but a substituted hydrazine called 2,4-dinitrophenylhydrazine. In this compound, a large group of atoms, the 2,4-dinitrophenyl group, replaces one of the hydrogen atoms of the hydrazine. The reaction, however, is identical to that shown above, and the condensation product is called a 2,4-dinitrophenylhydrazone:

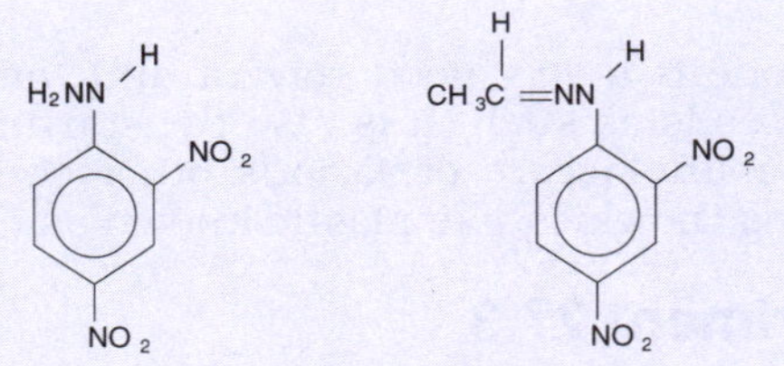

2,4 - dintro phenylhydrazine

Ethanal 2,4 - dinitro phenylhydrazone

The main purpose of carrying out this reaction is that it is a means of identifying a C=O group in a compound; the advantage of using the substituted hydrazine is that the condensation product is an insoluble solid and hence is formed much more readily and can be isolated more easily. A solution of 2,4-dinitrophenylhydrazine is known as **Brady's reagent**. Most 2,4-dinitrophenylhydrazones are red or yellow in colour

5. Chlorination:

When chlorine is bubbled into ethanal, the three hydrogen atoms of the CH_3 group are successively replaced by chlorine atoms, forming trichloroethanal (commonly called 'chloral'):

$$CH_3CHO + 3Cl_2 \rightarrow CCl_3CHO + 3HCl$$

This reaction, a typical alkane-type substitution, is not a reaction of the CHO group, but of the alkane end of the molecule. The product on hydration ('chloral hydrate') is used medically as a sleep inducing agent.

Methanal (HCHO) or 'Formaldehyde'

The first member of the aldehydes, methanal, differs to some extend from other aldehydes. Due to its very low molecular mass, it is the only member which is a gas under normal conditions and, because there are 2 oxidizable hydrogen atoms present (the extra one in place of what is normally an alkyl radical) it is more powerful reducing agent than other aldehydes. It can be prepared by the oxidation of methanol:

$$CH_3OH \xrightarrow{[O]} HCHO + H_2O$$

This is generally done by passing a mixture of methanol vapour and air (or oxygen) over a heated platinum catalyst. Industrially, it is manufactured in a similar manner.

Chemical Reactions

In most ways, its reactions resemble those of ethanal. It burns to produce CO_2 and water. It is powerful reducing agent being oxidised to methanoic acid (HCOOH) as it reduces:

$$HCHO \xrightarrow{[O]} HCOOH$$

It reduces Fehling's solution and gives a silver mirror with ammoniacal silver oxide. It condenses with Brady's reagent to give methanal-2,4-dinitrophenylhydrazone. One of the ways in which methanal differs from ethanal is that, since there is no alkyl group present, it cannot be chlorinated.

Uses

The chief use of methanal is in the manufacture of certain plastics and resins (see page 363) *e.g. Bakelite* and urea-formaldehyde resins. A 40% solution of methanal in water is called 'formalin' and is used for preserving biological specimens.

Ketones

Ketones have the general structure

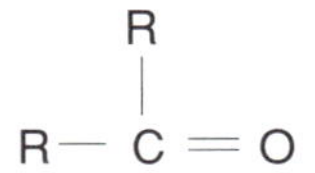

$$R - \overset{\displaystyle R}{\underset{\displaystyle |}{C}} = O$$

where the Rs are alkyl radicals (which may be the same or different). The only ketone of any importance is the first member of the series, in which the Rs are CH_3 groups. Having a chain of 3 carbon atoms per molecule and being a ketone, its name is **propanone**.

Experiment 27.2
Preparation of Propanone

Propanone is prepared by the oxidation of the secondary alcohol, propan-2-ol:

$$CH_3CHOHCH_3 \xrightarrow{[O]} CH_3COCH_3 + H_2O$$

In the laboratory, the oxidation is carried out in an identical manner as the oxidation of ethanol to ethanal, *i.e.* by distilling the alcohol with a mixture of sodium dichromate and sulphuric acid. (See Experiment 27.1. The same quantities and experimental instructions apply).

Industrially, the oxidation is done by passing the alcohol over a heated copper catalyst — which causes dehydrogenation (= oxidation) of the alcohol:

$$CH_3CHOHCH_3 \xrightarrow{[-H_2]} CH_3COCH_3 + H_2O$$

Physical Properties of Propanone

Colourless liquid with pleasant smell. Volatile, b.p. 56°C. Miscible with water and with organic solvents in all proportions.

Chemical Reactions.

1. Combustion

It burns with a non-luminous flame to produce CO_2 and water:

$$CH_3COCH_3 + 4O_2 \rightarrow 3CO_2 + 3H_2O$$

2. Oxidation

Ketones are not easily oxidised and, therefore unlike aldehydes, are not reducing agents. Propanone does not reduce Fehling's solution or ammoniacal silver oxide. When propanone is **very strongly** oxidised, a C-C bond is broken and it yields ethanoic acid and CO_2.

3. Reduction:

When reacted with hydrogen in the presence of a nickel catalyst, propanone is reduced to propan-2-ol:

$$CH_3COCH_3 + H_2 \rightarrow CH_3CHOHCH_3$$

4. Condensation

Propanone condenses with Brady's reagent (2,4-dinitrophenylhydrazine) to form propanone 2,4-dinitrophenylhydrazone.

[R= 2,4 dinitrophenyl group]

5. Chlorination:

When chlorine is bubbled into propanone, the hydrogen atoms are successively replaced by chlorine atoms:

$$CH_3COCH_3 + Cl_2 \rightarrow CH_3COCH_2Cl + HCl$$
Chloropropanone

Uses

Propanone is a very good solvent and one of its main uses is as such. It is also the starting point for the manufacture of various other chemicals, including the glass-like plastic known as *Perspex*.

Experiment 27.3
Properties and reactions of aldehydes and ketones

Aldehydes and ketones are similar in that they both contain the carbonyl group (C=O), but they differ in that aldehydes are reducing agents (because the -CHO group can be oxidised to -COOH) whereas ketones are not. Thus, some reactions (*i.e.* those of the C=O group) are common to both classes of compound, but others (those of the -CHO) are not. The compounds investigated in these experiments are the aldehyde ethanal and the ketone propanone.

(a) **Solubility** : Test the solubility of each of the given compounds in water. Do this by adding 1 or 2 cm^3 of the compound to the same volume of water and shaking.

(1) What is your conclusion?
(2) Explain why this is so.

(b) **Oxidation** : (i) To about half a test tube of water add 1 cm^3 each of potassium permanganate solution and dilute sulphuric acid. Now add 1 cm^3 of ethanal. Mix and warm gently.

(3) What colour change occurs?
(4) When this colour change occurs to potassium permanganate solution, it confirms the presence of what type of reagent?
(5) Thus, ... is a .... agent?
(6) In the reaction, the ethanal is .... and is converted to ....

(ii) Repeat the above test using propanone instead of ethanal.

(7) What happens and why?

(c) **Fehling's Test**: Prepare working Fehling's solution by mixing together about 3 cm^3 each of

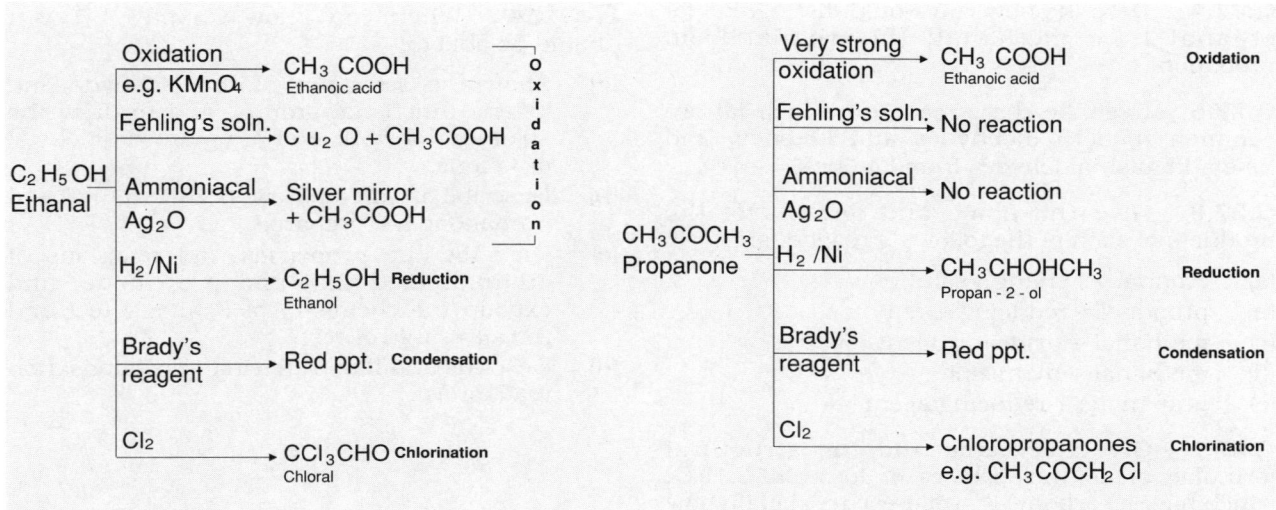

Fehling's solutions A and B. The resulting solution should be clear and royal blue in colour. Add to it about 1 cm^3 of ethanal. Invert to mix, boil gently and allow to cool.

(8) What visible change occurs?
(9) What substance is precipitated?
(10) What type of reaction has happened to the Fehling's solution?
(11) What type of reagent is ethanal?

Repeat the test using propanone instead of ethanal.
(12) What happens and why?

(d) **Silver mirror test** (reaction with ammoniacal silver oxide): To about 5 cm^3 of silver nitrate solution in a thoroughly clean test tube, add a few drops of sodium hydroxide solution; this precipitates silver oxide (Ag$_2$O). Now add aqueous ammonia, a few drops at a time and shaking after each addition, until the precipitate is almost redissolved. Add a few drops of ethanal and warm gently — preferably in a water bath.

(13) Has a silver mirror formed on any part of the glass?
(14) What change has occurred to the silver oxide?
(15) What type of reagent is ethanal ?

Repeat the test using propanone instead of ethanal.
(16) What happens and why?

(e) **Condensation reaction** :The hydrazones of the lower aldehydes and ketones are difficult to isolate, but the 2,4-dinitrophenylhydrazones are readily obtained. To about 5 cm^3 of 2,4-dinitro- phenylhydrazine reagent (Brady's reagent), add a few drops of ethanal. Shake to mix, and heat gently if necessary..

(17) Describe the product and name it.

Repeat the test using propanone instead of ethanal.
(18) Describe the product and name it.
(19) The formation of a condensation product confirms the presence of what group in a molecule?

Questions

Q.27.2 What characteristic property of aldehydes distinguishes them from ketones? What two reactions could be used to distinguish between the two classes of compound?

Q.27.3 Give equations to illustrate each of the following changes and name all the compounds present: (a) the conversion of an alcohol to an aldehyde; (b) the oxidation of a secondary alcohol; (c) the reduction of a ketone; (d) a condensation reaction of an aldehyde; (e) the oxidation of an aldehyde; (f) a substitution reaction of an aldehyde.

Q.27.4 Describe how you would distinguish (a) ethanal from methanal; (b) ethanal from propanone.

Q.27.5 Describe three reactions which (a) are common to both aldehydes and ketones, and (b) distinguish aldehydes from ketones.

Q.27.6 Give the name and formula of the products of each of the following reactions:

(a)   ethanal + Fehling's solution →
(b)   propanal + reducing agent →
(c)   methanal + oxidising agent →
(d)   methanal + hydrazine →
(e)   propanone + reducing agent →

Q.27.7 Give the name and the structural formulae of all the isomers of formula C_4H_8O, which have a carbonyl group present. Explain how you would distinguish between the different compounds.

Q.27.8 A compound of molecular mass 72 was found to have the following gravimetric composition: carbon 66.7%; hydrogen 11.1%; oxygen 22.2%. The compound condensed with Brady's reagent but did not reduce Fehling's solution. Deduce the structural formula of the compound and give its name.

Review   When you know Chapter 27, you should be able to:

(a)   Show the structure of the aldehyde and ketone functional groups, and to draw the structural formulae of any named aldehyde or ketone.

(b)   Describe in detail how both ethanal and propanone are prepared.

(c)   Describe the properties and reactions of ethanal, methanal and propanone, and explain the chemistry of Fehling's test and the silver mirror test.

(d)   Describe and illustrate what a condensation reaction is.

Carboxylic Acids

The functional group in all organic acids is the carboxyl group, -COOH, or structurally,

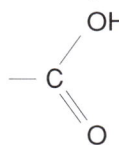

When this group is joined to an alkyl radical, the series of acids which results is known as the alkanoic acids. In the first member of the series, the 'alkyl radical' is simply a hydrogen atom and the acid is called methanoic acid, HCOOH.

The first four acids are:

Methanoic acid	**HCOOH**
Ethanoic acid	**CH₃COOH**
	(also called Acetic acid)
Propanoic acid	**C₂H₅COOH**
	(or **CH₃CH₂COOH**)
Butanoic acid	**C₃H₇COOH**
	(or **CH₃CH₂CH₂COOH**)

The name of the acid is obtained by replacing the final 'e' of the name of the corresponding alkane by 'oic'.

The acids can be prepared by oxidising either the corresponding primary alcohol or the aldehyde:

$$RCH_2OH \xrightarrow{[O]} RCHO \xrightarrow{[O]} RCOOH$$

The acidity of molecules containing a COOH group (*i.e.* its tendency to form $RCOO^-$ and H^+) is due to the considerable polarity of the O-H bond. This is caused, not primarily by the difference between the electronegativities of the oxygen and hydrogen atoms (if it were, alcohols, R—O—H, would be acidic), but by the presence of the second oxygen atom, which causes 'electron shift' through the molecule:

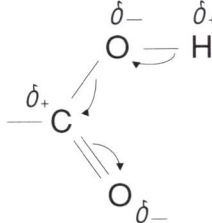

Oxygen, being highly electronegative, attracts electrons from the double bond towards itself and

28
Carboxylic Acids and Esters

so leaves the carbon atom slightly positive. The latter therefore attracts electrons from the C—O bond and also from the O—H bond, making this O—H bond more polar than it would normally be — so polar that it ionises to a small extent.

This electron shift along a chain of atoms is called the **inductive effect.** The longer the chain of atoms, the smaller is the effect. It is not normally noticeable beyond 4 atoms.

Organic acids differ from inorganic acids in several ways:

(i)   Although there may be many hydrogen atoms present in the molecule, it is only the hydrogen atom of the COOH group that is acidic, *i.e.* that ionises and can be replaced by a metal. Ethanoic acid, CH₃COOH, has 4 hydrogen atoms in its molecule but only the last one is acidic — the other three are part of the alkane chain and undergo alkane type reactions *i.e.* substitutions.

(ii)   The replaceable hydrogen atom is written last in the formula, whereas in inorganic acids it is usually written first, *e.g.* H_2SO_4.

(iii)   Organic acids are usually much weaker than inorganic acids, *i.e.* they ionise to a much lesser extent.

Because of the polar nature of the COOH group, it causes association between molecules, making the acids have higher boiling points than alkanes of similar molecular mass and also making the lower members soluble in water. As the length of the carbon chain increases, the acids become waxy solids which are insoluble in water — very much resembling the higher alkanes.

Ethanoic or Acetic Acid (CH₃COOH)

Ethanoic acid is the most important and the best known of the alkanoic acids; domestically it is used in dilute solution as 'vinegar', for preserving and flavouring food.

Experiment 28.1
Preparation of Ethanoic Acid

In the laboratory, ethanoic acid is normally prepared by the strong oxidation of ethanol:

$$CH_3CH_2OH \xrightarrow{[O]} CH_3CHO \xrightarrow{[O]} CH_3COOH$$

The oxidising agent is the usual acidified sodium dichromate solution.

To ensure that the alcohol is oxidised to the full extent, and that the acid is formed rather than the aldehyde,
(i) an excess of oxidising agent is used, and
(ii) the mixture is refluxed.

Refluxing is a technique in which volatile substances are heated together but with an arrangement to prevent loss of any of the substances by evaporation.

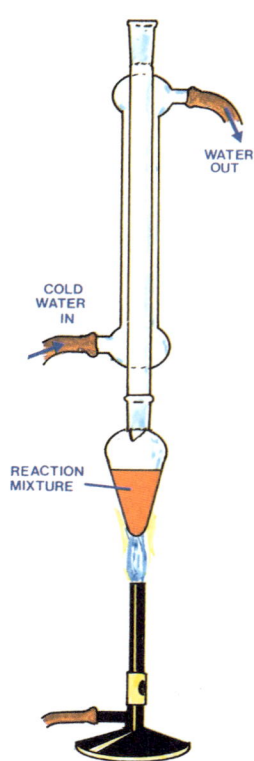

WATER OUT

COLD WATER IN

REACTION MIXTURE

28.1 —   *Reflux apparatus*

When the mixture in the flask is boiled, the vapour which is formed enters the condenser, where it is cooled, causing it to condense and run back down into the flask. In the experiment, any aldehyde which evaporates from the mixture is thus returned to the flask to be further oxidised to the acid.

When the reaction is complete, the apparatus is rearranged for distillation and the acid distilled off.

Take 10 cm^3 of water in a 50 or 100 cm^3 boiling flask, and add, **slowly and carefully**, 6 cm^3 of concentrated sulphuric acid, putting in about 1 cm^3 at a time. Swirl the flask after each addition to mix the contents, and when necessary, cool the flask by holding it under a stream of running water from the tap. Then add 10 g of sodium dichromate and some anti-bumping agent (use a paper funnel when doing this to prevent the solid sticking to the inside of the neck of the flask). Arrange the apparatus for reflux with addition.

Mix, in the tap funnel, 5 cm^3 of ethanol and 10 cm^3 of water. Add this, a little at a time **through the condenser**, to the oxidising mixture in the flask. After each addition, mix the contents **VERY THOROUGHLY**, by vigorously shaking the flask. Cool the flask if necessary by immersing it in cold water in a beaker. When all the ethanol has been added, heat the flask on a water bath, and reflux the mixture for about 30 minutes.

Remove the water bath, allow the apparatus to cool for a few minutes, and then rearrange it for distillation. Heat the flask either directly with a small flame, or over a gauze, and collect the first 20 cm^3 of distillate. This is mainly an aqueous solution of ethanoic acid.

Physical Properties of Ethanoic Acid

Colourless liquid with characteristic smell of vinegar.

The anhydrous acid (which is known as glacial ethanoic acid) has a melting point of 17 $^{\circ}C$, so that on cold days it solidifies — forming ice-like crystals. Its boiling point (118$^{\circ}C$) is abnormally high because of molecular association due to hydrogen bonding.

It mixes with water and with organic solvents in all proportions.

Chemical Reactions

1. Salt formation: Although it is a weak acid, it is one of the strongest of the organic acids ($K_a = 1.8 \times 10^{-5}$). It ionises as follows:

$$CH_3COOH \rightarrow CH_3COO^- + H^+$$
$$\text{Ethanoate ion}$$

It turns blue litmus red; reacts with the strongly electropositive metals forming salts (ethanoates) and liberating hydrogen; liberates CO_2 from metal carbonates and hydrogencarbonates; neutralises bases forming salts and water:

$$CH_3COOH + Na \rightarrow CH_3COONa + \tfrac{1}{2}H_2$$

$$2CH_3COOH + Na_2CO_3 \rightarrow 2CH_3COONa + CO_2 + H_2O$$

$$CH_3COOH + NaHCO_3 \rightarrow CH_3COONa + CO_2 + H_2O$$

$$CH_3COOH + NaOH \rightarrow CH_3COONa + H_2O$$

The liberating of CO_2 from sodium hydrogencarbonate solution is often used as a test for an organic acid.

2. Esterfication: It reacts (reversibly) with alcohol, forming esters and water:

$$CH_3COOH + C_2H_5OH \rightleftharpoons CH_3COOC_2H_5 + H_2O$$
$$\text{Ethyl ethanoate}$$

3. Reaction with Cl_2: In the presence of u.v. light, chlorine replaces the 3 hydrogen atoms of the CH_3 group, forming successively, monochlorethanoic acid, dichlorethanoic acid and trichloroethanoic acid. Due to the inductive effect, these acids are stronger than ethanoic acid; trichloroethanoic acid is comparable in strength to the mineral acids. Their K_a values are:

monochlorethanoic acid	$K_a = 1.6 \times 10^{-3}$
dichlorethanoic acid	$K_a = 5.1 \times 10^{-2}$
trichloroethanoic acid	$K_a = 8.3 \times 10^{-1}$

4. Reduction: Organic acids are difficult to reduce and ordinary reducing agents have little effect on them. On treatment with very strong reducing agents (e.g. sodium borohydride) they are reduced directly to the corresponding alcohol. Ethanoic acid is therefore reduced to ethanol:

$$CH_3COOH \xrightarrow{NaBH_4} C_2H_5OH$$

5. Oxidation: Ethanoic acid is very stable to all oxidising agents. It burns, when vaporised, forming CO_2, and water vapour.

Manufacture and Use of Ethanoic Acid

Industrially ethanoic acid is manufactured by using air to oxidise ethanol in the presence of a catalyst which aids this reaction. The acid can also be manufactured from butane (or naphtha) by catalytic oxidation (also using air) at about 200°C. This process involves breaking down the 4-carbon chain of butane molecule, and results in various by-products (e.g methanoic acid, alcohols) in addition to the ethanoic acid:

$$C_4H_{10} + O_2 \quad \xrightarrow[200°C \ 200 \ atm]{Co(CH_3COO)_2} \quad CH_3COOH$$
$$+$$
$$by–products$$

The U.S.A. manufactures most of its ethanoic acid by this method, because butane is relatively plentiful there; a type of natural gas that occurs in certain areas of the U.S. is rich in butane.

Its main use is in the manufacture of 'cellulose acetate' which is used for packaging and in producing rayon. It is also used as a solvent and in the manufacture of other chemicals.

Vinegar is made from beers and wines and contains about 5% ethanoic acid. Beers and wines go sour on exposure to air, due to bacterial oxidation of ethanol and consequent formation of ethanoic acid. This process is slow under normal conditions, but in manufacturing vinegar, the reaction is speeded up using suitable bacteria.

Methanoic Acid (HCOOH)

Methanoic acid occurs in the stings of ants, bees and other insects and in the stinging nettle. It can be prepared by oxidising methanol with sodium dichromate and sulphuric acid.

Physical Properties of Methanoic Acid

Colourless liquid with pungent smell. Like ethanoic acid it is associated by hydrogen bonding and this accounts for its abnormally high boiling point (101°C) for such a small molecule mass. Due to it being considerably polar, it is miscible with water in all proportions.

Chemical Reactions

Chemically, methanoic acid shows considerable differences from other acids.

1.   **Stability**: It is very unstable and decomposes on being heated, forming CO_2 and hydrogen:

$$HCOOH \quad \rightarrow CO_2 + H_2$$

2.   **Oxidation**: Unlike all other acids, it has a CHO group in its structure and so resembles aldehydes. It is therefore a strong reducing agent since it can be oxidised to CO_2 and water:

$$HCOOH \quad \xrightarrow{[O]} \quad CO_2 \quad + \quad H_2O$$

It reduces Fehling's solution, gives a silver mirror with ammoniacal silver oxide and decolorises potassium permanganate solution.

3.   **Dehydration**: When heated with concentrated sulphuric acid, it is dehydrated and converted to carbon monoxide:

$$HCOOH \quad \xrightarrow{c. \ H_2SO_4} \quad CO \ + \ H_2O$$

This reaction provides a convenient method of preparing carbon monoxide in the laboratory.

4.   **As an Acid**: It behaves normally, reacting with bases to form salts, and with alcohols to form esters:

$$HCOOH \ + \ NaOH \ \rightarrow \ HCOONa \ + \ H_2O$$

$$HCOOH + C_2H_5OH \ \rightarrow \ HCOOC_2H_5 \ + \ H_2O$$

It is a stronger acid than acetic acid, having a K_a of 1.8×10^{-4}.

Experiment 28.2
Properties and reactions of carboxylic acids

The acids investigated in this experiment are methanoic (HCOOH), and ethanoic or acetic (CH₃COOH). Anhydrous ethanoic acid is often referred to as 'glacial' ethanoic acid.

Ethanoic acid

(a) Solubility

(1) Test the solubility of ethanoic acid (anhydrous) in water and in various organic solvents (*e.g.* ethanol, propanone, ethyl ethanoate, trichloromethane, methylbenzene). Take about 1 or 2 cm^3 of each liquid for the test. List those liquids in which the acid is soluble.

(b) Acidic Nature

(2) What is the effect of ethanoic acid on litmus?

Add a short length (about 5 cm) of magnesium ribbon to some ethanoic acid solution.

(3) What are the two products of this reaction?

(4) Write out the equation for the reaction?

(5) What gas is liberated?

(6) How can it be identified?

(c) Esterification

Take about 3 cm^3 each of ethanol and anhydrous ethanoic acid and $\frac{1}{2}$ cm^3 (10 drops) of concentrated sulphuric acid (**CARE**) in a test tube. Shake carefully and warm (do not boil) the mixture for a few minutes. Note the pleasant smell of ester. Pour the mixture into cold water (in which the ester is insoluble) and observe it floating on top.

(7) Write out the equation for the reaction and name the products.

(d) Halogenation

This experiment must be done in the fume cupboard. To 1 cm^3 of anhydrous ethanoic acid, add a small quantity (as much as will fit on the tip of a spatula) of PCl_5. Test the fumes evolved with:

   (i) pieces of moist red and blue litmus paper.

(8) What is the result and why?

   (ii) a glass rod dipped in concentrated ammonia solution

(9) What happens and why ?

(10) Write out the equation for the reaction of the acid with PCl_5 and name all the products.

Methanoic acid

If desired, tests (a), (b) and (c) can be applied to this acid, but the results are similar to those obtained with ethanoic acid in each case.

(e) Stability

Saturate a loose plug of glass wool in the bottom of a test tube with methanoic acid (about 5 cm^3) and heat it strongly. Test the gases evolved with a lighted splint and with lime water.

(11) What reaction has occurred?

(f) Oxidation

   (i)   Prepare some ammoniacal silver oxide solution (described in Expt. 27.2) and add a few drops of methanoic acid. Warm gently.

   (ii)   To some methanoic acid in a test tube add a few cm^3 of acidified (dilute H_2SO_4) potassium permanganate solution. Heat if necessary. What is observed and why?

(g) Dehydration

To 1 cm^3 of methanoic acid add about 1 cm^3 of concentrated sulphuric acid (with care). Warm gently. Test the gas evolved with a lighted splint.

(16) What reaction has occurred?

Esters

An ester is the compound obtained when the hydrogen of the carboxyl group of an acid is replaced by an alkyl radical. An introduction to esters is given on page 331.

$$CH_3COOH \quad \rightarrow \quad CH_3COOC_2H_5$$
Ethanoic acid   Ethyl   ethanoate

$$C_2H_5COOH \quad \rightarrow \quad C_2H_5COOCH_3 \text{ [i]}$$
Propanoic acid   Methyl propanoate

The name of the ester, as can be seen above, is derived from the acid radical and the alkyl group which makes up its structure. The term ester is

---

(i)   Note that the 2 esters shown are isomers of each other; they are also isomeric with butanoic acid (C_3H_7COOH). Every ester has an isomeric acid.

usually restricted to the products of organic acids only.

Esters are prepared by heating together the appropriate acid and alcohol (which provides the alkyl radical) in the presence of concentrated sulphuric acid — which both acts as a catalyst for the reaction and also absorbs the water produced in the process, giving a higher yield of ester.

$$R - C \overset{OH}{\underset{O}{\Big|}} + R'OH \rightleftharpoons R - C \overset{OR'}{\underset{O}{\Big|}} + H_2O$$

Acid + Alcohol $\rightleftharpoons$ Ester + Water

R and R^1 can be either the same or different. All esters are very similar chemically, and the properties and reactions of one example is representative of all.

Experiment 28.3
Preparation of ethyl ethanoate

Ethyl ethanoate is prepared by refluxing together glacial (*i.e.* 100%) ethanoic acid and ethanol with concentrated sulphuric acid:

$$CH_3COOH + C_2H_5OH \rightarrow CH_3COOC_2H_5 + H_2O$$

The sulphuric acid serves two purposes : (i) it catalyses the reaction, and (ii) it absorbs the water which is formed, so preventing the reverse reaction. The ester is generally impure, containing small quantities of unreacted ethanoic acid and ethanol, with probably some ethene, ethoxyethane, and water which is formed in the reaction.

Into a 50 cm^3 or a 100 cm^3 boiling flask, place 15 cm^3 of ethanol and 12 cm^3 of anhydrous ethanoic acid. Add some small pieces of anti-bumping agent and then set up the apparatus for reflux with the flask placed in a beaker of water, the flask being about half immersed in the water. **Slowly and carefully** add 8 cm^3 of concentrated sulphuric acid through the condenser from a small graduated cylinder or tap funnel. Heat the water bath and allow the mixture to reflux for 20 to 30 minutes.

Remove the water bath, let the apparatus cool for several minutes and then rearrange it for distillation. Heat the flask over a gauze or directly with a **small flame** and collect the distillate until the boiling point reaches 80°C. The distillate consists mainly of the required ester, but mixed with some water, ethanoic and sulphuric acids, and probably excess ethanol.

Transfer the distillate to a tap funnel and add 10 cm^3 of sodium carbonate solution (to neutralise acid impurities). Insert the stopper and shake the mixture, releasing the pressure at intervals. Allow the layers to separate and discard the aqueous (lower) layer. Wash the ester again, in a similar manner but with 10 cm^3 of water this time. Finally run the ester into a small dry conical flask and add some anhydrous sodium sulphate or fused calcium chloride to dry it. The ester can be further purified by redistilling it, and collecting the fraction of boiling between 75°C and 79°C.

Physical Properties of Ethyl Ethanoate

Colourless liquid with pleasant 'fruity' smell. Volatile; b.p. 77°C. Density = 0.9 g/cm^3. Practically insoluble in water but soluble in organic solvents.

Chemical reactions

Esters are comparatively unreactive and undergo few reactions.

1. Combustion

It burns to produce carbon dioxide and water.

2. Hydrolysis[i]

It is hydrolysed to form ethanoic acid and ethanol. The hydrolysis is catalysed by both H^+ ions (*i.e.* by acids) and OH^- ions (*i.e.* by alkalis.) The acid catalysed hydrolysis is a reversible reaction.

$$CH_3COOC_2H_5 + H_2O \rightleftharpoons CH_3COOH + C_2H_5OH$$

An alkaline hydrolysis is called a **saponification** because this type of reaction is involved in the manufacture of soap from fats and oils.

$$CH_3COOC_2H_5 + NaOH \rightarrow CH_3COONa + C_2H_5OH$$

(i)   A hydrolysis can be defined as the chemical decomposition of a compound by water, the water itself also reacting. In general, a hydrolysis can be represented as: XY + H_2O -> XOH + HY

Experiment 28.4
Hydrolysis of ethyl benzoate

Hydrolysis of an ester (the reverse of esterification) yields the acid and alcohol from which the ester was formed:

$$RCOOR^1 + H_2O \rightarrow RCOOH + R^1OH$$
ester　　water　　　acid　　alcohol

This reaction is catalysed by both H^+ ions (*i.e.*, dilute acid) and OH^- ions (dilute alkali). However, using the latter as the catalyst has the advantage that the reverse reaction is prevented, since the acid is neutralised and converted to a salt as it is formed. Such a reaction is called a saponification.

Into a 50 or 100 cm^3 boiling flask, place 7 cm^3 of ethyl benzoate and 30 cm^3 of sodium hydroxide solution. Add some pieces of anti-bumping agent and then arrange the apparatus for reflux. Heat the flask over a wire gauze or directly with a small flame, and boil the mixture gently for 30 minutes.

Complete the equation for the reaction occurring during this time.

$$C_6H_5COOC_2H_5 + NaOH \rightarrow ....+ ....$$
ethyl　benzoate

Allow the apparatus to cool and then rearrange it for distillation. Boil the mixture and collect the first 15 cm^3 of distillate — which will be mainly an aqueous solution of ethanol. Verify this, by carrying out some of the tests for that compound, *e.g.* test B of Experiment 26.1.

The liquid remaining in the flask is a solution of sodium benzoate. Pour this into a beaker, rinse out the flask with a small quantity of water and add this to the beaker. To liberate the benzoic acid, add dilute hydrochloric acid, a few cm^3 at a time and with stirring, until the solution is acidic to litmus. Write the equation for the reaction occurring here.

Filter off the solid, on a Buchner funnel if possible, wash it with several portions of water, and then allow to dry. This is the benzoic acid.

Further Work
1. Weigh the benzoic acid when dry, and calculate the percentage yield of it. To do this, first calculate the mass of benzoic acid that could have been produced, knowing the equation for the reaction and that the starting quantity of ethyl benzoate was 7 cm^3 which is 7.4 g. Then divide the actual quantity produced by the quantity which could have been produced, and multiply the result by 100 to convert to a percentage.

2. Find the melting point of the benzoic acid, as described in Experiment 1.1.

3. Recrystallise the benzoic acid from hot water. Do this by dissolving it in the minimum quantity of hot (80° - 90°C) water, filtering the solution while hot (heat the filter funnel) and allowing to cool. When cold, filter off the crystals and allow to dry. Find their melting point as described in Experiment 1.1.

Occurence and uses of Esters
Esters are distributed widely in nature. The lower members have pleasant 'fruity' smells and are responsible for the scents of flowers and the flavours of fruits. Many perfumes and artificial flavouring essences contain manufactured esters, *e.g.* ethyl butanoate (pineapple); octyl ethanoate (orange); methyl-butyl ethanoate (pear). Natural fats, vegetable oils and waxes all consist of esters. The lower esters are all good solvents, and are used as such in, for example, quick-drying paints and varnishes.

Fats and Oils
All fats and vegetable oils are esters of the trihydric alcohol, propane-1,2,3-triol (commonly called glycerol, or 'glycerine') with various long chain carboxylic acids such as palmitic, stearic or oleic:

$C_{15}H_{31}COOH$ = palmitic acid

$C_{17}H_{35}COOH$ = stearic acid

$C_{17}H_{33}COOH$ = oleic acid (contains double bond)

$$\begin{array}{l} CH_2\text{---}OH \\ | \\ CH\text{---}OH \ = \ Propane\text{--}1,2,3\text{--}triol \\ | \qquad\qquad\qquad [glycerol] \\ CH_2\text{---}OH \end{array}$$

For example the substance 'tripalmitin' which occurs in palm oil, is the ester glycerol tripalmitate, and has the structure:

$$\begin{array}{l} C_{15}H_{31}COO\text{-----}CH_2 \\ | \\ C_{15}H_{31}COO\text{-----}CH \\ | \\ C_{15}H_{31}COO\text{-----}CH_2 \end{array}$$

If the substance is a solid at room temperature it is called a fat and if it is a liquid, it is known as an oil. Naturally occurring oils, such as those which come from olives, coconuts, and peanuts, usually contain esters of unsaturated acids, whereas the fats (*e.g.* beef fat, mutton fat) contain esters of saturated acids.

Hydrogenation of Vegetable Oils

Fats and oils are primarily important as foodstuffs, providing (along with carbohydrates) the energy required by the body. Fats, being solid, are more useful for cooking and eating than oils, and oils can be changed into fats by hydrogenation. This process, technically known as **'hardening'** of oils, is carried out on a large scale industrially and is done by bubbling hydrogen through the heated oil in the presence of a nickel catalyst. This results in hydrogen molecules adding across the double bonds present in the oil molecules, thereby producing saturated compounds which have higher m.p. and will be solid at room temperature. Margarine is made by mixing hardened oils with various fats, colouring matter, vitamins and skim milk to produce butter substitutes. 'Soft' margarines such as *'Flora'* are soft (and therefore easily spreadable) because they have a relatively low m.p. This is due to their containing a high proportion of esters of unsaturated acids such as linoleic ($C_{17}H_{31}COOH$), which has two double bonds in its molecule.

Soaps

Soaps are the sodium and potassium salts of long chain carboxylic acids like stearic, palmitic and oleic — the same acids which occur as glycerol esters in natural oils and fats, and it is by the hydrolysis of these esters that soaps are produced. In manufacturing soap, fats and oils are boiled in large vats with alkali, (either sodium hydroxide or potassium hydroxide solution) until they are converted to glycerol and the salts of the acids present *e.g.*

$$C_{15}H_{31}COO{-}CH_2$$
$$C_{15}H_{31}COO{-}CH \; + \; 3NaOH \rightarrow C_{15}H_{31}COONa \; + \; CHOH$$
$$C_{15}H_{31}COO{-}CH_2 \quad\quad\quad\quad C_{15}H_{31}COONa \quad CH_2OH$$

Glyceryltripalmitate (tripalmitin) + 3NaOH Alkali → $C_{15}H_{31}COONa$ Sodium palmitate (a soap) + CH_2OH CHOH CH_2OH Glycerol

This type of reaction is called saponification (literally 'soap making'). The glycerol, which is a by-product, is used for making medical and pharmaceutical products, in baking, and for manufacturing nitroglycerin explosives.

Experiment 28.5
Preparation of Soap

Soap is made by the saponification of any animal or vegetable oil or fat. Such compounds consist of the glycerol esters of long chain acids, such as palmitic acid ($C_{15}H_{31}COOH$). Saponification is an alkaline hydrolysis of these esters, and results in glycerol and the sodium (or potassium) salt of the long chain acid. These salts are soaps.

Procedure

Place about 5 g of lard, 3 g of sodium or potassium hydroxide pellets and 40 cm^3 of ethanol (which acts as solvent) in a 100 cm^3 (or larger) round bottomed flask. Attach a reflux condenser and boil the mixture gently for about 30 minutes. By this time, most of the fat will have been saponified.

Allow the apparatus to cool and then rearrange it for distillation. Boil the mixture to distil off the alcohol solvent. Continue doing so until either 30 cm^3 of alcohol have been collected or the temperature of the vapour which is distilling goes above 80°C. The liquid then remaining in the flask is a mixture of soap and excess of alkali.

Quickly pour the hot mixture into about 100 cm^3 of brine contained in a beaker. The alkali is soluble in brine[i] but the soap is not, and hence is precipitated. Filter off the soap and wash it (while still in the filter) with more brine in order to remove alkali still clinging to it. A Buchner funnel is particularly suitable for this part of the

---

(i)   Saturated salt (NaCl) solution

procedure. Finally spread the soap on to paper and leave it to dry.

Tests:

(i) Test a portion of the soap for its lathering properties by rubbing it with water between the hands. (However, as the soap is still likely to contain free alkali, the hands should be well rinsed with plain water after carrying out this test).

(ii) Add another portion of the soap to some hot water, shake well and observe the result. This test works better if distilled water is used.

Summary of the Reactions of Ethanoic Acid

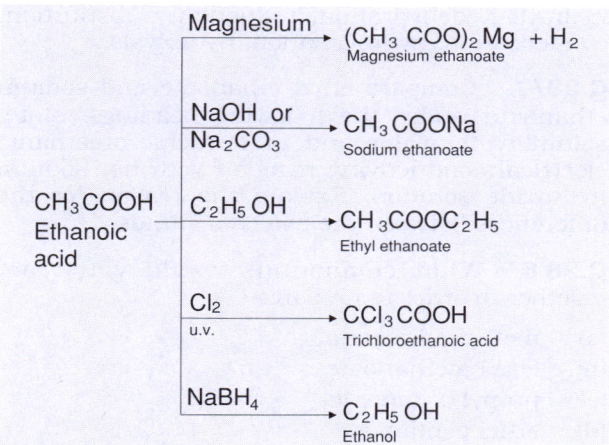

Questions

Q.28.1 Give short answers to each of the following questions.

(a) What is the structure of the carboxyl group?

(b) Give the name and formulae for the first three carboxylic acids.

(c) State three differences between organic and inorganic acids.

(d) By what process is ethanoic normally prepared?

(e) What is observed when ethanoic acid is added to $NaHCO_3$ solution? Why?

(f) What compound, on strong oxidation, is converted to methanoic acid?

(g) Why is methanoic acid a reducing agent?

(h) What visible change occurs on heating methanoic acid with Fehling's solution.

(i) What gas is formed when methanoic acid reacts with concentrated H_2SO_4?

(j) What type of reaction is:
$$CH_3COOH \rightarrow C_2H_5OH ?$$

(k) Name a reagent which can cause the above reaction.

(l) Why have organic acids higher boiling points than alkanes of similar molecular mass?

(m) How is ethanoic acid produced industrially?

(n) Under what conditions is ethanoic acid converted to monochloroethanoic acid?

(o) What is the general formula for an ester?

(p) Give two reasons why sulphuric acid is used when preparing an ester?

(q) What is a hydrolysis reaction?

(r) What compounds are formed when methyl propanoate is boiled with some dilute acid?

(s) Give the name and formula of a long chain carboxylic acid.

(t) What type of compound is a fat or vegetable oil?

Q.28.2

(a) Write equations for the reactions of ethanoic acid with (i) magnesium (ii) potassium hydroxide, (iii) ammonia, (iv) ethanol, (v) methanol, (vi) sodium borohydride. Name the product(s) in each case.

(b) What reagent could be used to distinguish between ethanoic acid and methanoic acid. What would happen with each acid, and why?

Q.28.3 In an experiment to prepare ethanoic acid by the usual method, a mixture of 10 cm^3 of sulphuric acid, 16 cm^3 of water and 14 g of sodium dichromate was placed in a boiling flask, along with a few pieces of broken porcelain. The flask was then fitted with a reflux condenser. A mixture of 4 cm^3 of ethanol and 10 cm^3 of water was slowly poured down the condenser. The mixture was refluxed for 30 minutes and then distilled. The equation for the reaction is:

$$2Na_2Cr_2O_7 + 3C_2H_5OH + 8H_2SO_4 \rightarrow$$
$$2Cr_2(SO_4)_3 + 2Na_2SO_4 + 3CH_3COOH + 8H_2O$$

(a) What precaution was necessary (i) when preparing the solution of sulphuric acid, and (ii) when adding the dichromate solution to the flask ? Explain why.

(b) Some of the water was put directly into the flask and the rest was added through the condenser, rather than it all being put in together. Why is the recommended procedure preferred?

(c) Why was the mixture poured down the condenser rather than put directly into the flask.

(d) What colour change was observed during the experiment? Why?

(e) Why was the mixture refluxed? How does a reflux condenser operate.

(f) Draw a diagram to show a reflux apparatus and how the condenser is connected to the water supply.

(g) What was the purpose of the porcelain pieces?

(h) What was the purpose of distilling the mixture ?

(i) Why is sulphuric acid used in preference to (i) hydrochloric acid, (ii) nitric acid.

(j) Why is it possible that some ethanal could have been formed in the experiment?

(k) Why is it unlikely that much of it was present after the experiment?

(l) Given that the density of ethanol is 0.8 g/cm^3 and that 1.6 g of ethanoic was formed, calculate the percentage yield in the experiment.

(m) Show by calculation that 14 g of sodium dichromate was sufficient.

(n) How could you tell, at the end of the experiment, that the acid present was ethanoic acid, and not just sulphuric acid which had distilled over?

Q.28.4 Name the acids whose formulae are:

(a) $CH_2ClCOOH$,
(b) CCl_3COOH,
(c) CH_3CCl_2COOH,
(d) $CH_2ClCHClCOOH$,
(e) $CH_3CH(CH_3)COOH$
(f) $CH_3CH_2C(CH_3)_2COOH$
(g) $CH_3(CH_2)_4COOH$,
(h) $(COOH)_2$

Q.28.5 Explain each of the following terms; (a) dehydration, (b) neutralisation, (c) esterification, (d) halogenation, (e) hydrolysis.

Illustrate each explanation with an example taken from the following list:

(i) $2CH_3COOH + CuO \rightarrow (CH_3COO)_2Cu + H_2O$
(ii) $CH_3COOH + Cl_2 \rightarrow CH_2ClCOOH + HCl$
(iii) $CH_3COOH + CH_3OH \rightarrow CH_3COOCH_3 + H_2O$
(iv) $CH_3COOCH_3 + H_2O \rightarrow CH_3COOH + CH_3OH$
(v) $CH_3CH_2OH \rightarrow C_2H_4 + H_2O$

Q.28.6 With what should propan-1-ol be reacted in order to convert it to (i) propanoic acid, (ii) propyl ethanoate, (iii) propene, (iv) propanal, (v) chloropropane? Write an equation for each reaction and select, from the following list, the appropriate term to describe each of those reactions: neutralisation, oxidation, esterification, hydration, dehydration, reduction, substitution, condensation, hydrogenation, hydrolysis.

Q.28/7 Compare ethyl ethanoate and sodium ethanoate under the following headings: state; solubility in water and in tetrachloromethane; electrical conductivity; reaction with hot sodium hydroxide solution, Explain the reason for the differences between the two compounds.

Q.28.8 What compounds would you react together in order to prepare:

(a) methyl ethanoate,
(b) ethyl methanoate,
(c) propyl butanoate,
(d) ethyl pentanoate,
(e) butyl propanoate,
(f) pentyl hexanoate.

Write an equation for each reaction and describe how the reaction could be carried out in practice.

Q.28.9 Explain what is meant by each of the following terms: (a) natural oil; (b) animal fat; (c) soap; (d) saponification; (e) hardening of oils. Illustrate each explanation with a formula, equation or other example.

Q.28.10 0.367 g of an organic acid on complete combustion gave 0.73 g of carbon dioxide and 0.30 g of water. The relative molecular mass of the acid was found to be 88. Find the acid's percentage composition, molecular formula and write any possible structural formulae.

Q.28.11 1 g of an organic acid was neutralised by 13.5 cm^3 of 1.0 M NaOH. Calculate the molecular mass of the acid and identify it.

Q.28.12 1.2 g of an organic acid were dissolved in 250 cm^3 of 0.1 M NaOH solution. The excess alkali was neutralised by 40 cm^3 of 0.125 M HCl. Identify the organic acid.

Q.28.13 2.2 g of an ester were refluxed with 100 cm^3 of 1.0 M sodium hydroxide solution for one hour. After cooling, the volume was made up to 250 cm^3 with pure water. 25 cm^3 of this diluted solution reacted with 15 cm^3 of dilute hydrochloric acid of concentration 0.5 mol/L, using phenolphthalein as indicator.

(a)   Assuming that hydrolysis was complete, determine the molecular formula of the ester,

(b)   Write the names and structural formulae of **all** of the esters having that molecular formula,

(c)   Write the names and structural formulae of the alcohols obtained by hydrolysing each of the esters given in (b).

Review When you know Chapter 28 you should be able to:

(a)   Show the structure of the carboxylic acid group, and draw the structural formula for any named acid or ester.

(b)   Explain why the COOH group is acidic.

(c)   Describe in detail the following experiments: (i) preparation or ethanoic acid, (ii) preparation of an ester, (iii) hydrolysis of an ester, (iv) preparation of a soap.

(d)   Describe the properties of ethanoic and methanoic acids.

(e)   Describe the structure of natural oils and fats, and show what happens when they are saponified.

(f)   Explain each of: inductive effect, esterification, refluxing, hydrolysis, saponification, hydrogenation, hardening of oils.

29
Plastics and Polymers

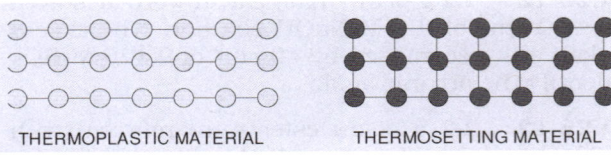

THERMOPLASTIC MATERIAL   THERMOSETTING MATERIAL

29.1

Plastics

There is no single material called 'plastic'. Plastics are a large family of materials which have several features in common, the most important being that they soften and can be moulded by heat and pressure, and that they all consist of polymers — giant molecules built up from thousands of smaller molecules, combined together to form a repeating structure. Many polymers have 50,000 atoms or more in their molecules. Many natural polymers exist (e.g. proteins, starch, cellulose, rubber) but all plastics consist of synthetic (i.e. man-made) polymers, most of which are made from chemicals derived from coal or oil.

Plastics can be divided into two main classes, thermoplastics and thermosetting plastics.

Thermoplastics are ones which can be repeatedly softened by heating and thus can be moulded and remoulded many times. Their structure is a network of polymer chains but the chains are not joined to each other. On being heated, the intermolecular forces holding the chains together are weakened, so that the chains can slide over each other; the plastic is thus softened. Thermoplastics, therefore, are not used to make objects which have to withstand high temperatures. Examples of this type of plastic are polythene, P.V.C., polystyrene and nylon.

Thermosetting plastics consist of a network of cross-linked polymer chains and are moulded during their manufacture when the cross-links are formed. Thermosetting plastics cannot be resoftened on heating and thus have greater heat resistance then thermoplastic. Examples of thermosetting plastics are 'Bakelite', 'Formica' polyurethane, and epoxy resins such as 'Araldite'.

29.2

Polymerisation

Polymerisation occurs in two different ways—by addition and by condensation.

1.   Addition Polymerisation

This is the direct joining together of many small molecules of a single compound (called the monomer) to form the very large molecule of the polymer. This process can only happen when the monomer is unsaturated, and addition polymerisation is thus characteristic of ethene and substituted ethenes. All polymers formed in this way are thermoplastic.

2.   Condensation Polymerisation

This is the joining together of many molecules of two different compounds to form the large polymer molecule, water (or other simple compound like HCl) being eliminated in the process. *Terylene* (page 363) is one of the best known condensation polymers. Both thermoplastics and thermosetting plastics can result from the process.

Addition Polymers

Polythene (Polyethene)

Polythene, now one of the most widely used polymers ('plastic bags') was discovered quite by accident in the 1930s during research experiments (carried out by I.C.I.) in which the effect of very high pressure on chemical reactions was being studied. In one of these experiments, involving ethene, a small quantity of a white solid was produced, which proved to have interested properties. It was resistent to chemicals, could be moulded by heat and pressure and was a very good electrical insulator. That small beginning led to an industry which now produces millions of tonnes of polythene each year. Polythene is manufactured by the same process in which it was discovered, *i.e.* by subjecting ethene to high temperatures ($100°$ - $300°$ C) and pressures (1000 - 2000 atmospheres). These conditions result in the double bonds of the ethene opening up and adjacent molecules joining together, to produce chains of up to 50,000 ethene molecules in length:

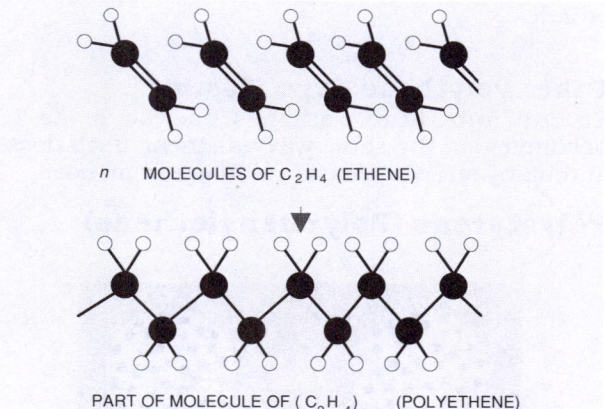

n MOLECULES OF C_2H_4 (ETHENE)

PART OF MOLECULE OF $(C_2H_4)_n$ (POLYETHENE)

29.3   Structure of polythene

The product, known commercially as 'polythene' (or, more precisely as 'low density polythene') is a strong translucent plastic, is chemically inert, quite flexible and is an excellent electrical insulator. From it, buckets, lunch boxes, bags and wrapping film, fertiliser sacks and 'squeezy' bottles are manufactured. Its disadvantage is that it softens at the temperature of boiling water.

In the mid 1950s a German chemist called Ziegler discovered a method of polymerising ethene without using the high temperatures and pressures previously needed. His method was based on the use of special catalysts (now called Ziegler catalysts), and much lower temperatures (100° - 150°C) and pressure (5 - 30 atmospheres) were sufficient. The product obtained by this method has longer polymer chains than the polythene made by the earlier method and they are also more closely packed together, so that the polymer has a higher density. It is used to manufacture milk crates, dustbins, washing-up bowls and unbreakable bottles. Recently, it has been produced in very thin sheets for packaging. Bags made of this type of polythene make a 'crackling' sound when crumpled.

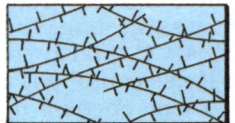 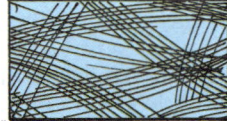

29.4 —

Other Polythene Type Plastics

Several substituted ethenes can be made to polymerise in the same way as ethene itself does, and many such polymers are in everyday use.

Polystyrene (Polyphenylethene)

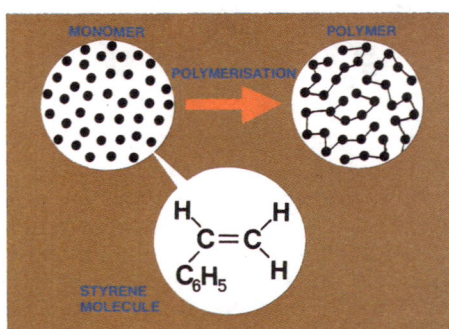

29.5 —

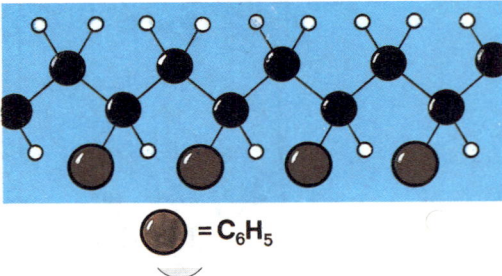

$\bigcirc$ $= C_6H_5$

29.6 — *Structure of polystyrene*

Every year, polystyrene replaces more and more paper and cardboard, glass and ceramics, metals and other materials — especially for the storage of food. The method by which phenylethene ('styrene') is polymerised is typical of several other addition polymerisations.

A compound, called an initiator, decomposes on being heated, producing free radicals. Organic peroxides (*e.g.* dibenzoyl peroxide) act in this way:

$$C_6H_5CO\text{-}O\text{-}O\text{-}COC_6H_5 \quad \rightarrow \quad 2C_6H_5CO\text{-}O^\bullet$$

One of the resulting radicals adds on to the phenylethene:

The product in turn, adds on to another molecule of phenylethene:

A chain reaction thus ensues and further additions produce the long chains of the polymer. However, the chain reaction can be terminated by the chance collision of any two free radicals *e.g.*

Polystyrene is a strong but brittle glass-like plastic. It is an excellent electrical insulator and is easily coloured. It is used to make yogurt and cream containers, vending cups, egg boxes, ball point pens, cotton reels, refrigerator linings and electrical components.

Expanded Polystyrene:

By adding a substance which generates gas on being heated, styrene on polymerisation forms the polymer as a solid foam, having a volume of about fifty times that of the unexpanded polymer; this material thus has a very low density. It is used for ceiling tiles and for packing delicate goods, such

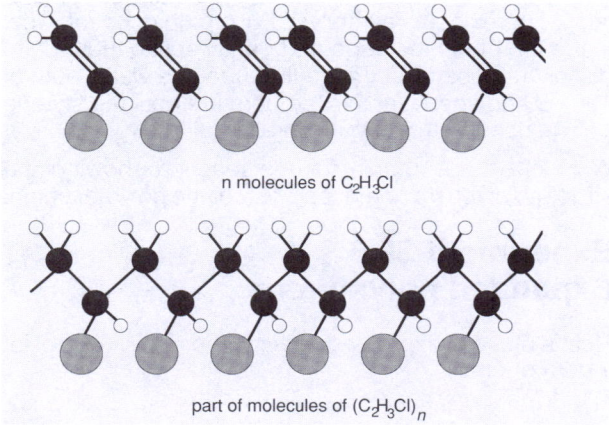

n molecules of C_2H_3Cl

part of molecules of $(C_2H_3Cl)_n$

29.7

as cameras and scientific instruments, and for making theatrical props.

The disadvantages of polystyrene, which limit its use, are that it softens at fairly low temperature (about 90°C) and that sunlight, in time, causes discoloration and makes it very brittle.

Polyvinyl Chloride, P.V.C.

Polyvinyl chloride (frequently referred to as just 'vinyl') is another important plastic. It is more rigid than polythene but by adding a substance called a 'plasticiser', which acts as a lubricant between the long polymer chains and enables them to slide over each other more readily, it can be made very flexible, without losing its strength. In one or other of its forms, it is used to manufacture a wide variety of goods — electric cable covering, floor tiles, gramophone records, gutters and drainpipes

$$\left(\begin{array}{cc} H & H \\ | & | \\ -C & -C- \\ | & | \\ H & CN \end{array} \right)_n$$

('*Wavin*'), hosepipes, car upholstery, shower curtains, baby pants, raincoats, and 'vinyl' wallpaper.

Polyacrylonitrile

Propenonitrile ($CH_2{=}CHCN$), commonly called acrylonitrile, polymerises to form polyacrylonitrile:

This polymer, when made into fibres, has a wool-like appearance and texture, and is used as a wool substitute for making such things as carpets, pullovers, skirts, scarfs and wigs. It is sold

$$\left(\begin{array}{cc} F & F \\ | & | \\ -C & -C- \\ | & | \\ F & F \end{array} \right)_n$$

under the trade name *Orlon*.

Acrilan and *Courtelle* are co-polymers (2 polymers joined together) which contain polyacrylonitrile. Fibres such as *Orlon* and *Acrilan* are often loosely referred to as 'acrylics'.

Polytetrafluoroethene (P.T.F.E.)

This polymer, which is more commonly known by its trade name *Teflon*, is very inert, resisting reaction with practically all substances. It is also very hard and is comparatively stable to heat, not softening below 320°C. It is used for coating cooking utensils to give them a non-stick surface, for seals and gaskets, and for electrical insulation at high voltages.

Experiment 29.1
To distinguish between thermoplastics and thermosetting plastics.

Take two pieces of plastic, one of each type. Find out which is which by heating each well above a bunsen

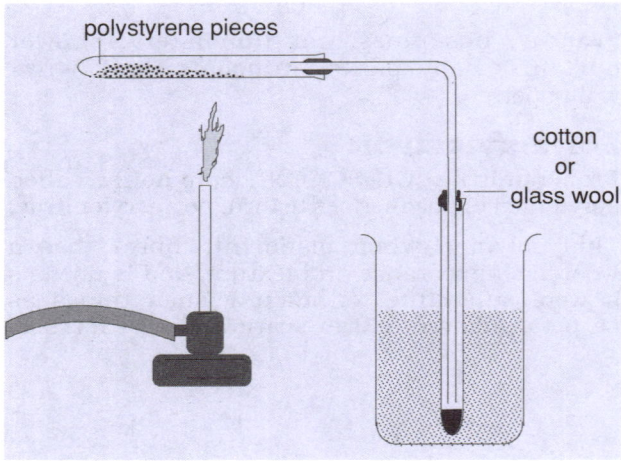

polystyrene pieces

cotton or glass wool

29.8

burner flame. Hold the piece of plastic in a pair of tongs when doing this, and do not let it catch fire; if this happens extinguish the flame by plunging the sample into cold water.

(1) What happens to the thermoplastic when it is heated?

(2) What happens to the thermosetting plastic when it is heated?

Experiment 29.2
Styrene and polystyrene

Before starting these experiments, read the footnote[i] about the nature of styrene.

(a) Depolymerisation of polystyrene.

Fill a test tube to a depth of about 3 cm with pieces of polystyrene (these can be cut from an empty yogurt pot) and then arrange the apparatus as shown. Heat the test tube gently, to convert the polymer to the monomer — which distills over and collects in the cooled test tube.

What evidence shows this to be chemical change and not just the melting of the polymer?

(b) Polymerisation of styrene.

Take about 5 cm^3 of styrene and add about 0.3 g of lauroyl peroxide as a catalyst. Put a plug of cotton wool in the top of the test tube and gently shake the tube to dissolve the catalyst. Place the tube in a water bath at 100 °C and keep it at this temperature until the styrene polymerises — this should take 20 minutes.

Write out the equation for the reaction showing the structure of the monomer and part of the polymer chain.

Experiment 29.3
Expanded polystyrene.

Heat a piece of expanded polystyrene gently (do not let it burn or char).
(1)   What happens?

Place a few drops of each of several solvents (*e.g.* ethanol, propanone, ethyl ethanoate, trichloroethane, hexane or petrol) at different positions on a piece of the polystyrene.
(2)   List those substances in which the polymer is soluble.

Heat a piece of solid (not expanded) polystyrene gently, until it softens, note that it becomes quite pliable. Bend it and allow it to cool.
(3)   What happens?
(4)   What type of plastic, therefore, is polystyrene?

Burn a very small piece.
(5)   Describe the type of flame and say whether soot is formed.
(6)   What does this indicate about the composition of polystyrene?

(i)   Styrene is very flammable and has a harmful vapour which is irritating to the skin, eyes and lungs. If small quantities are used and the laboratory is well ventilated, there is little danger.

Condensation Polymers

Polyesters

As the name suggests, polyesters are polymers containing the ester structure:

The best known and most important of the polyesters is that formed by the condensation of benzene-1,4-dicarboxylic acid (commonly called terephthalic acid) and the dihydric (= 2 OH groups) alcohol ethane-1,2-diol or 'ethylene glycol'. Both of these monomers are obtained from petroleum.

The polyester shown above is best known by the I.C.I trade name of *Terylene*, derived from the common names of the two monomers, *Ter*ephthaleic acid and eth*ylene* glycol. *Terylene*, which is produced as a fibre, is very strong when wet or dry, is resistant to shrinkage, creasing, abrasion, mildew and sunlight. It is used to make blouses, dresses, shirts, ties, trousers, curtains, tablecloths, sewing threads, pillow and quilt filling, yacht sails, protective clothing and car safety belts.

Experiment 29.4
'Bakelite' (Phenol-methanal polymer)

This is a condensation polymer, formed as follows:

(continued on page 366)

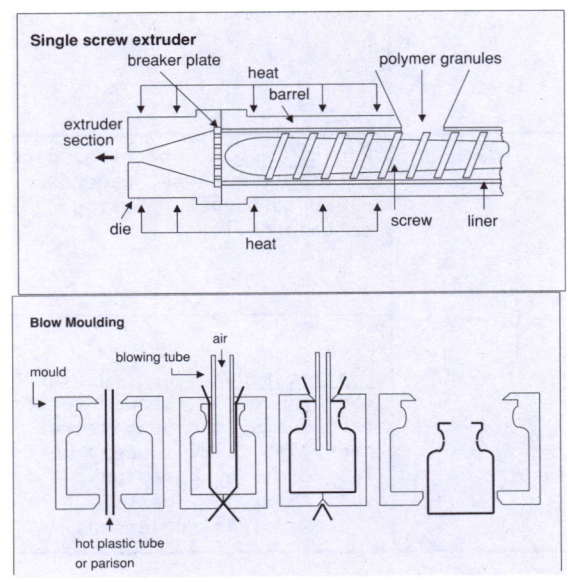

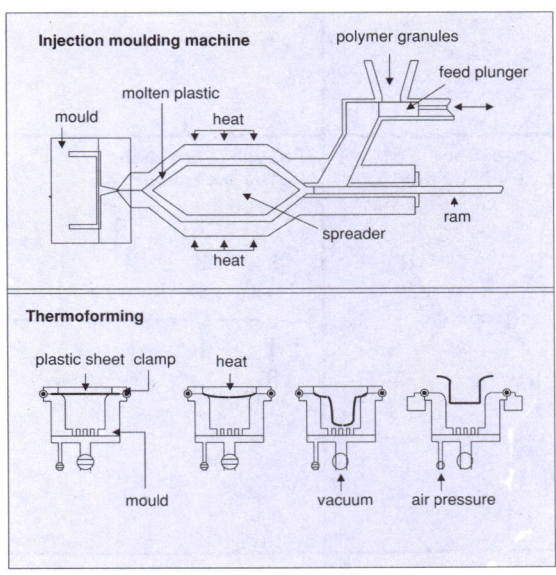

29.9 — *Techniques for shaping thermoplastics: extrusion; injection moulding; blow moulding; thermoforming.*

MONOMER	POLYMER NAME POLYMER STRUCTURE	MAIN USES
Ethene	Polyethene Polythene	Low density polyethene Fertiliser and rubbish bags, squeezy detergent and washing-up liquid bottles, milk bottles, packaging film. High density polyethene Bleach bottles, milk bottle crates.
Propene	Polypropene or Polypropylene	Crates, chairshells, pipes, packaging film for biscuits etc., laboratory sinks.
Phenylethene Styrene	Polyphenylethene Polystyrene	Rigid polystyrene Food containers, yogurt pots, vending machine cups, ballpoint pen cases, flower pots, cotton reels. Expanded polystyrene Insulation, ceiling tiles, food trays, egg boxes, packing for cameras etc.
Chloroethene Vinyl chloride	Polychloroethene Polyvinylchloride P.V.C.	Rigid P.V.C. Guttering, pipes and fittings, bottles, records, clear corrugated roofing, curtain rails. Plasticised P.V.C. Insulation for wire and cable, shower curtains, rain coats, car upholstery, packaging film, squeezy bottles, leathercloth, hosepipes, soft toys, baby pants, floor and wall coverings.

Monomer	Polymer	Uses
Methyl 2-methyl-propenoate Methyl methacrylate,	Poly(methyl 2-methylpropenoate) Polymethyl methacrylate, 'Perspex',	Glass substitute for lighting displays and signs, lighting fittings, simple lenses, furniture, baths, dentures, record player lids.
Propenonitrile, Acrylonitrile	Polypropenonitrile, Polyacrylonitrile, 'Courtelle', 'Orlon', Acrilan',	Cases for food mixers, car rear-light covers, refrigerator linings, sweaters and scarfs, carpets.
Tetrafluoroethene	Polytetrafluoroethene 'Teflon', 'Fluon'	Non-stick coatings for cooking utensils, low friction dry bearings sealing material (e.g., plumbers' tape).
Hexane-1,6-dioic acid Hexane-1,6-diamine $HO-\overset{O}{C}-(CH_2)_4-\overset{O}{C}-OH$ $H_2N-(CH_2)_6-NH_2$	'Nylon', Polyamide $-\overset{O}{C}-(CH_2)_4-\overset{O}{C}-\overset{H}{N}-(CH_2)_6-\overset{H}{N}-$	Tights, underwear, socks, ropes, parachutes, carpets, power tool housings, gear wheels curtain rail fittings, bearings, packaging film, brush hairs.
Benzene-1,4-dicarboxylic acid (Terephthalic acid) Ethane-1,2-diol (Ethylene glycol) $HOOC\bigcirc COOH$ $HO-(CH_2)_2-OH$	'Terylene', Polyester	Clothes, recording tape, photographic film, food and liquid packaging
isocyanates + alcohols e.g., $O=C=N-R-N=C=O$ $HO-R-OH$	Polyurethanes	Upholstery, cushions, in furniture etc. thermal insulation.
1,2-epoxy-3-chloropropane 2,2-diphenylpropane	an epoxy resin	Corrosion resistant paints, electrical insulation, adhesives.
Phenol, Methanal	Phenol methanal Phenol formaldehyde,	Handles for pots and irons, plug tops, switch covers, table tops, buttons, lavatory seats, lampholders, picnic crockery.

Place 4 cm^3 of 'formalin' (40% aqueous methanal) in a test tube, add about 2 g of phenol $^{(i)}$ and 10 drops of sodium hydroxide solution (to catalyse the polymerisation). Stir well and then clamp the tube in a stand, preferably in the fume cupboard, and warm it over a small bunsen flame until a viscous red resin is formed; this takes about 30 minutes. Decant off any water present. If the resin is now baked in a over at about 50 $^{\circ}$C for several hours, a hard plastic is obtained, this is *'Bakelite'*.

Questions

Q.29.1 Explain, with an example of each, the following terms; thermoplastic; thermosetting plastic; addition polymer; condensation polymer.

Draw a section of each of the following polymer molecules, showing two repeating units; polyvinyl chloride; *Terylene*; polystyrene, polyacrylonitrile, polytetrafluorethene.

Q.29.2 Draw a section of a polythene molecule, showing the units present and the bonding between them. Name another polymer of the same type.

Terylene is formed by a condensation polymerisation. Explain this term and show the structure of the recurring group in the polymer chain.

Q.29.3 Explain the meaning of (i) addition polymerisation; (ii) condensation polymerisation. Draw the structure of part of the polymer chain of a polymer formed by each of these methods. List two uses of each polymer.

Q.29.4 Ethene is made on a industrial scale by crackling naphtha in the presence of steam at 900°C at just above atmospheric pressure.

(a) Explain what is meant by 'cracking'.
(b) Why is the process operated at a comparatively low pressure?
(c) Show by means of an equation how ethene could be obtained by the cracking of octane.
(d) Ethene has been referred to as a building block chemical. What is meant by this?

(e) Show by means of equations how ethene could be converted into (i) chloroethene; (ii) phenylethene (styrene).
(f) Name a material in everyday use made from each of these substances.
(g) Give the structural formula for each of these materials.

Q.29.5 Propenonitrile (acrylonitrile) is made on a large scale by passing a mixture of propene, ammonia and air over a catalyst at 450°C. The principal overall reaction may be represented as:

$$2CH_2=CHCH_3 + 3O_2 + 2NH_3 \rightarrow$$
$$2CH_2=CHCN + 6H_2O$$

(a) Name a possible source or method of manufacture of each of the reactants.
(b) Write out the structural formulae for the propene and the propenonitrile.
(c) What common everyday product is manufactured from propenonitrile?
(d) Draw the structure of part of the molecule of the product.
(e) Propenonitrile has been described as a dangerous chemical. Give some possible reasons why this might be so.

Review When you know Chapter 29 you should be able to:

(a) Explain what each of the following is: polymer, plastic, thermoplastic, thermosetting plastic, addition polymerisation, condensation polymerisation.
(b) Draw the structure of part of the polymer chain of each of polyethene, polystyrene, P.V.C., polyacrylonitrile, polytetrafluoroethene, a polyester, and list some uses of each of these.
(c) Describe experiments (i) in which styrene is polymerised, and (ii) polystyrene is depolymerised.
(d) Describe the mechanism by which styrene polymerises.

(i) **Care:** phenol is a skin poison, If any touches your hands, wash it off immediately with soap and water.

Percentage Yields

There are many chemical reactions which do not go to completion. In particular, organic reactions never give a yield of 100% and the figure is often considerably lower. The percentage yield is the actual yield expressed as a percentage of the theoretical yield — as calculated from the stoichiometry of the reaction.

$$\text{Percentage yield} = \frac{\text{Actual yield} \times 100}{\text{Theoretical yield}}$$

Example

In an experiment, 23 g of ethanol are reacted with an excess of ethanoic acid and concentrated sulphuric acid, 33 g of ethyl ethanoate are obtained. Calculate the percentage yield.

Method

The equation is:

$$C_2H_5OH + CH_3COOH \rightarrow CH_3COOC_2H_5 + H_2O$$

46 g ethanol   forms   88 g ethyl ethanoate

23 g should give $\dfrac{23 \times 88}{46}$ g = 44 g of ethyl ethanoate

Actual mass obtained = 33 g

Percentage yield = $\dfrac{33 \times 100}{44}$ = 75%.

Problems on Percentage Yield

Q.30.1 In the preparation of oxygen from potassium chlorate, the reaction is:

$$2KClO_3 \rightarrow 2KCl + 3O_2$$

60 g of potassium chlorate yielded 16 g of oxygen. Calculate the percentage yield.

Q.30.2 In the extraction of aluminium from alumina (Al_2O_3), each 100 kg of alumina provides 45 kg of the metal. Calculate the percentage yield for this process.

Q.30.3 7 g of ethene are made by the action of concentrated sulphuric acid on 23 g of ethanol. Calculate the percentage yield for this reaction.

30
Miscellaneous Topics and Revision Questions

Q.30.4   Nitrogen monoxide is prepared by the reaction:

$$3Cu + 8HNO_3 \rightarrow 3Cu(NO_3)_2 + 2NO + 4H_2O$$

If 12.7 g of copper are used, and the volume of nitrogen monoxide is 1.12 L at s.t.p., what is the percentage yield?

Q.30.5   Phenol, C_6H_5OH, is converted to trichlorophenol, $C_6H_2Cl_3OH$. If 488 g of product are obtained from 250 g of phenol, what is the percentage yield?

Q.30.6   59 g of ethanoic acid, CH_3COOH, are obtained from the oxidation of 50 g of ethanol. C_2H_5OH. What percentage yield does this represent?

Q.30.7   1.7 g of hexanone, $C_6H_{12}O$, is converted to its 2,4-dinitrophenylhydrazone. After isolation and purification, 4.236 g of the product, $C_{12}H_{18}N_4O_4$ are obtained. What percentage yield does this represent?

Q.30.8   Sulphur dioxide can be prepared by roasting iron disulphide FeS_2 in air. The equation for the reaction is: $4FeS_2 + 11O_2 \rightarrow 2Fe_2O_3 + 8SO_2$.

If 200 g of FeS_2 produce 107 g of SO_2, what is the percentage yield?

Q.30.9   Nitrous oxide, N_2O, is made by heating ammonium nitrate until it decomposes. The only other product of the reaction is steam.

In an experiment, 10 g of ammonium nitrate yielded 2.85 L of nitrous oxide at room temperature. Assuming that the molar volume at room temperature is 24 L, calculate the percentage yield for the reaction.

Q.30.10   5 g of methylbenzene are oxidised by potassium permanganate according to the equation:

$$2KMnO_4 + C_6H_5CH_3 \rightarrow$$
$$2MnO_2 + C_6H_5COOH + 2KOH,$$

and 1.22 g of benzoic acid are produced.

(a)   How many moles of methylbenzene are used?
(b)   How many moles of benzoic acid are produced?
(c)   What is the percentage yield for the reaction?

Ionic Equations

A conventional chemical equation summarises what changes take place in a chemical reaction. An **ionic equation** shows exactly just what change or changes occur. In most reactions involving ions, there are ions present which do not do anything, they are there before the reaction and there afterwards. Such ions are called **spectator ions**.

For example, when sulphuric acid is added to sodium hydroxide solution, sodium sulphate and water are formed. The reaction is conventionally represented by:

$$H_2SO_4 + 2NaOH \rightarrow Na_2SO_4 + 2H_2O$$

Three of these substances are ionic, and in solution the ions are independent particles and are free to move about. H_2SO_4 in solution consists of two H^+ ions and an SO_4^{2-} ion; NaOH is composed of Na^+ and two OH^- ions and Na_2SO_4 is made up of two Na^+ ions and an SO_4^{2-} ion. So, when the above equation is rewritten, listing the ions that are present, it becomes:

$$2H^+ + SO_4^{2-} + 2Na^+ + 2OH^- \rightarrow 2Na^+ + SO_4^{2-} + 2H_2O$$
$$\underbrace{[\quad\quad]}_{H_2SO_4} \quad \underbrace{[\quad\quad]}_{2NaOH} \quad \underbrace{[\quad\quad]}_{Na_2SO_4}$$

It can be seen that SO_4^{2-} and $2Na^+$ are present both before and after the reaction, i.e. they have not done anything — they are spectator ions.

Deleting these from the equation, the equation then becomes:

$$2H^+ + 2OH^- \rightarrow 2H_2O,$$

and this is the change which really occurs when sulphuric acid is neutralised by sodium hydroxide.

In a similar way, the change that really occurs when magnesium reacts with sulphuric acid is:

$$Mg + 2H^+ \rightarrow Mg^{2+} + H_2$$

Why? $Mg + H_2SO_4 \rightarrow MgSO_4 + H_2$

$$Mg + 2H^+ + SO_4^{2-} \rightarrow Mg^{2+} + SO_4^{2-} + H_2$$

The sulphate ion, SO_4^{2-}, is only a spectator ion.

Q.30.11 Write each of the following equations in its ionic form.

(a) $Cl_2 + MgBr_2 \rightarrow MgCl_2 + Br_2$

(b) $2HCl + Mg \rightarrow MgCl_2 + H_2$

(c) $Mg + CuSO_4 \rightarrow MgSO_4 + Cu$

(d) $HCl + NaOH \rightarrow NaCl + H_2O$

(e) $2HNO_3 + Ca(OH)_2 \rightarrow Ca(NO_3)_2 + 2H_2O$

(f) $SnCl_4 + 2FeCl_2 \rightarrow SnCl_2 + 2FeCl_3$

Q.30.12 Write each of the following equations in its ionic form.

(a) $Na_2SO_3 + 2HCl \rightarrow 2NaCl + SO_2 + H_2O$

(b) $Na_2CO_3 + H_2SO_4 \rightarrow Na_2SO_4 + CO_2 + H_2O$

(c) $Na_2S_2O_3 + 2HCl \rightarrow 2NaCl + SO_2 + H_2O + S$

(d) $NH_4Cl + NaOH \rightarrow NaCl + NH_3 + H_2O$

(e) $MnO_2 + 4HCl \rightarrow MnCl_2 + Cl_2 + 2H_2O$

(f) $2FeCl_2 + Cl_2 \rightarrow 2FeCl_3$

Q.30.13 Balance each of the following difficult equations and then rewrite it in its ionic form.

(a) $H_2O_2 + KBr + H_2SO_4 \rightarrow Br_2 + H_2O + K_2SO_4$

(b) $Fe + HNO_3 \rightarrow Fe(NO_3)_3 + NO_2 + H_2O$

(c) $KIO_3 + KI + H_2SO_4 \rightarrow I_2 + K_2SO_4 + H_2O$

(d) $KMnO_4 + H_2SO_4 + FeSO_4 \rightarrow$
$K_2SO_4 + MnSO_4 + Fe_2(SO_4)_3 + H_2O$

(e) $Na_2Cr_2O_7 + H_2SO_4 + HI \rightarrow$
$Na_2SO_4 + Cr_2(SO_4)_3 + H_2O + I_2$

(f) $KMnO_4 + H_2SO_4 + H_2C_2O_4 \rightarrow$
$K_2SO_4 + MnSO_4 + CO_2 + H_2O$

Solving Quadratic Equations

A quadratic equation is one whose form is:
$$ax^2 + bx + c = 0$$

The solution to such an equation is given by the formula

$$x = \frac{-b \pm \sqrt{b^2 - 4ac}}{2a}$$

In the equation: $4x^2 + 5x - 6$

$a = 4$, $b = 5$, $c = -6$, and it is solved as follows:

(i) The coefficients are substituted into the formula, which then becomes

$$x = \frac{-5 \pm \sqrt{5^2 - 4(4)(-6)}}{2(4)}$$

(ii) The value under the square root sign is calculated. Calculators with bracket facilities can solve this in one operation by pressing the following sequence of keys:
5, x^2, -, (, 4, $\times$, 4, $\times$, 6, +/- (to enter the 6 as minus),), =, and this evaluates to 121. Pressing the square root key gives 11.

(iib) For calculators without the bracket facility, the [4(4)(-6)] is first calculated by pressing :
4, $\times$, 4 , $\times$ 6, +/- (to enter the 6 as minus), =, and this gives -96. Then clear the display. This is followed by : 5, x^2, -, 96, +/- (to change the 96 to minus), +, which gives 121. Pressing the square root key then gives 11.

(iii) The calculation is continued as at both (a) and (b) shown below:

(a) for the + option in the formula, press the keys as follows (having first cleared the display):
5, +/-, +, 11, =, $\div$, 2, $\div$, 4, =, and this gives the answer 0.75.

(b) For the - option in the formula, press:
5, +/-, -, 11, =, $\div$, 2, $\div$, 4, =, and this gives the result -2.

Thus the two solutions to the given equation are x = 0.75 and -2.

Q.30.14 Name one example of each of the following:

(i) a dibasic acid;

(ii) a triatomic gas present in air;

(iii) an insoluble metal sulphate;

(iv) an oxidising agent;

(v) a normal salt;

(vi) the element which is in both Group 3, and Period 3 of the Periodic Table;

(vii) a substance which liberates carbon dioxide on treatment with acid;

(viii) a substance which forms a white precipitate when added to sodium chloride solution.

Q.30.15 Give the exact symbols for the atoms or ions which contain the following particles:

(a) 6 protons, 6 neutrons, 6 electrons;

(b) 6 protons, 8 neutrons, 6 electrons;

(c) 17 protons, 18 neutrons, 17 electrons

(d) 17 protons, 18 neutrons, 18 electrons;

(e) 17 protons, 20 neutrons, 18 electrons,

(f) 26 protons, 30 neutrons, 26 electrons;

(g) 26 protons, 30 neutrons, 23 electrons.

Q.30.16 The following is a list of substances: butane; diamond; ethane; ethanol; ethene; graphite; iodine; 2-methylpropane; propane; sodium chloride.

Explain the meaning of each of the following terms, choosing suitable examples from the above list to illustrate your answers. Each substance may be used once, more than once, or not at all: (a) allotropes; (b) structural isomers; (c) empirical formula and molecular formula; (d) molecular crystals.

Q.30.17 What is meant by (i) atomic number; (ii) mass number; (iii) isotopes? Using the two isotopes of chlorine $^{35}_{17}Cl$ and $^{37}_{17}Cl$, as your example, explain why (a) the two isotopes have identical chemical properties; (b) the relative atomic mass of chlorine is not a whole number.

Q.30.18 How many protons, neutrons and electrons are in each of the following:
$^{12}CO_2$; $^{14}CO_2$; NH_3 ; NH_4^+ ?

Q.30.19 Describe (i) the general appearance (at room temperature); (ii) the type of bonding in, and (iii) the effect of water on, each of the following: CaO; SO_2; $LiCl$; HBr; NH_3; NH_4Cl; ZnO.

Q.30.20 Give the name and formula of:

(a) one hydride which reacts with water to give an alkaline solution, and one which reacts to give an acidic solution.

(b) one oxide which reacts with water to give an alkaline solution and one which reacts to give an acidic solution:

(c) one chloride where chlorine is combined with a metal and one where it is combined with a non-metal.

Describe the appearance and the type of bonding present in the case of each of the six compounds you have named above.

Q.30.21 Distinguish clearly between the members of the following pairs. Illustrate your answers with examples:

(a) a peroxide and a dioxide;

(b) ionisation and dissociation;

(c) a hydride and a hydrate;

(d) mass number and relative atomic mass;

(e) a base and an alkali;

(f) isomers and isotopes.

Q.30.22 The letters A to F refer to the following substances:

A = dry hydrogen chloride;

B = a solution of HCl in water;

C = a solution of HCl in dry methylbenzene;

D = glacial (pure) ethanoic acid;

E = a solution of ethanoic acid in water;

F = a solution of NaOH in water
(the solutions are all of the same concentration).

(a) Which three substances would not affect dry blue litmus paper?

(b) Which two would be good conductors of electricity?

(continued)

(c) Which would have the lowest pH value?

(d) What would you expect to happen if C were shaken with water? Write an equation for the change.

(e) Write an equation for the reaction of B and F. What would be the pH of the product?

Q.30.23 A solution of sodium hydroxide containing 1.5 g in 250 cm^3 of solution was titrated with a solution of 0.1 M hydrochloric acid;

(a) Write down the molarity of the sodium hydroxide solution.

(b) What volume of acid would be needed to react with 20 cm^3 of the alkali solution?

(c) Calculate the pH of each solution.

(d) Name a suitable indicator for the titration.

(e) Outline briefly, how you would carry out the titration.

Q.30.24

(a) What are the products of the reaction of an acid with a base?

(b) Give three other characteristics of an acid and three other characteristics of a base.

(c) What kind of a heat change occurs when an acid reacts with a base?

(d) Describe how you could prepare solid sodium chloride by the action of an acid with a base.

(e) If acid containing 3.65 g of HCl were used, what mass of sodium chloride would be obtained?

Q.30.25 A solution of $Ba(OH)_2$ (a strong electrolyte) reacts with sulphuric acid (another strong electrolyte) to form a white precipitate and a solution that is a non-conductor of electricity:

(a) what is a strong electrolyte?

(b) what is the white precipitate formed?

(c) write an equation for the reaction.

(c) why does the solution not conduct electricity?

Q.30.26 'Borax', $Na_2B_4O_7 10H_2O$, is a base in aqueous solution because the borate ion reacts with water according to:

$$B_4O_7{}^{2-} + 7H_2O \rightarrow 4H_3BO_3 + 2OH^-$$

(a) what can you deduce about the nature of boric acid (H_3BO_3)?

(b) What name is given to the type of reaction in which borax reacts with water?

(c) Calculate the oxidation number of boron in (i) borax; (ii) boric acid.

(d) How many (i) moles; (ii) grams; of borax will react with 1 mole of H^+ ions from acid?

Q.30.27 Explain what is wrong with each of the following statements, all of which are untrue:

(a) The mass number of an element is the same as its relative atomic mass.

(b) Covalent substances are all gases, liquids or low m.p. solids.

(c) The heat of vaporisation of CH_4 (8.3 kJ/mol) is much lower than that of NaCl (171 kJ/mol); this proves that covalent bonds are much weaker than ionic bonds.

(d) The atomic radius of hydrogen is the radius of the 1s orbital.

(e) All atoms of any given element are identical.

(f) Copper reacts with nitric acid according to:

$$Cu + 2HNO_3 \rightarrow Cu(NO_3)_2 + H_2$$

(g) The pH of 10^{-7} M HCl is 7.

(h) Hydrogen and oxygen combine together to form hydrogen peroxide according to:

$$H_2 + O_2 \rightarrow H_2O_2$$

(ix) Fluorine, on reaction with oxygen, is oxidised to F_2O.

(x) Sodium, on reaction with hydrogen, is reduced to NaH.

Q.30.28 An element Z reacts with hydrochloric acid releasing hydrogen:

$$2Z + 6HCl \rightarrow 2ZCl_3 + 3H_2$$

It was found that 3 g of Z reacted with exactly 17 cm^3 of 10 M hydrochloric acid. Calculate the mass of Z which reacts with 6 moles of HCl. Then use the equation to deduce the atomic mass of Z.

Q.30.29 A gas jar contains 12.6 g of C_3H_6.

(a) How many moles of C_3H_6 are present?

(b) How many moles of hydrogen atoms are contained therein?

(c) How many moles of carbon atoms are present?

(continued)

(d) How many molecules are present?

(e) What volume does it occupy at s.t.p.?

(f) Write an equation for its combustion.

(g) How many moles of oxygen molecules are required for combustion of C_3H_6 in the gas jar?

(h) How many grams of oxygen are required?

(i) How many moles of CO_2 are produced?

(j) What is the mass of CO_2 produced?

(k) What volume, at s.t.p., does the CO_2 occupy?

Q.30.30   Describe how you would distinguish chemically between the following pairs of substances. Illustrate your answers with equations where possible:

(a) sodium chloride and sodium sulphate:

(b) sodium chloride and sodium iodide:

(c) sodium carbonate and sodium hydrogencarbonate;

(d) carbon monoxide and hydrogen;

(e) zinc and iron.

(f) 0.1 M hydrochloric acid and 0.1 M ethanoic acid:

(g) common salt and castor sugar:

(h) nitric acid and hydrochloric acid.

Q.30.31   What is meant by (i) an acid, (ii) a molar solution of an acid?

Ethanoic acid, CH_3COOH, is a monobasic acid.

(a) What ions are present in an aqueous solution of ethanoic acid?

(b) How many grams of ethanoic acid are present in 500 cm^3 of a molar solution?

(c) A molar solution of ethanoic acid conducts electricity, but not so well as a molar solution of hydrochloric acid. What explanation can you offer for this fact?

Calculate (i) the minimum volume of molar hydrochloric acid required to react with 1 gram of calcium carbonate; (ii) the volume of gas which would be evolved at s.t.p.

Q.30.32   Practical Observations

What would you **observe** in each of the following reactions, and what is the cause of each of those observations?

(a) CO_2 is passed into limewater.

(b) Ammonia is mixed with hydrogen chloride.

(c) Sodium is added to water.

(d) Some MnO_2 is added to hydrogen peroxide solution.

(e) Ethyne gas is ignited.

(f) Iodine crystals are heated.

(g) Some $BaCl_2$ solution is added to sulphuric acid.

(h) Bromine solution is added to ethene.

(i) A splint moistened with sodium chloride solution is held in a bunsen flame.

(j) Dilute HCl is added to limestone.

(k) A solution of calcium hydrogencarbonate is heated.

(l) Some ethanal is added to Fehlings' solution and heated.

(m) Some acidified permanganate solution is added to a solution of Fe^{2+} ions.

(n) Solid sodium hydroxide is left exposed to the air for a day.

(o) Solutions of potassium iodide and silver nitrate are mixed.

(p) Acidified potassium dichromate solution is added to ethanol and heated.

(q) Concentrated nitric acid is added to copper.

(r) A gas jar containing nitrogen monoxide is opened.

(s) A hot platinum wire is held over methanol.

(t) Hydrogen peroxide is added to acidified KI solution.

(u) Soap is added to calcium chloride solution.

(v) Lead nitrate crystals are heated.

(w) Universal indicator is added to ethanoic acid.

(x) Dilute HCl and sodium thiosulphate solution are mixed.

(y) Copper carbonate is heated.

(z) Some KI crystals are added to chlorine water.

Q.30.33   An organic compound contains 24.7% carbon, 2.1% hydrogen and the rest is chlorine. Calculate its empirical formula. If its molecular mass is 97, what is its molecular formula? Draw two possible structures and name them.

Q.30.34   A compound containing carbon, hydrogen and oxygen, contains 64.9% carbon and 13.5% hydrogen. Calculate its empirical formula. Given that its relative molecular mass is 74, write out the structural formulae for three isomers.

Q.30.35 Two organic compounds (A) and (B) have the same percentage composition: carbon 52.2% , hydrogen 13.1% and oxygen 34.7%. Each has a molecular mass of 46. (A) yielded hydrogen when reacted with sodium, and gave fumes of hydrogen chloride with PCl_5. (B) gave no visible effect with either reagent. Deduce the structural formula of both (A) and (B).

Q.30.36 By means of equations using the compounds containing three carbon atoms, illustrate each of the following conversions. Name all compounds involved.

(a) chlorination of an alkane,
(b) bromination of an alkene,
(c) dehydration of an alcohol,
(d) oxidation of an aldehyde,
(e) condensation of a ketone,
(f) neutralisation of an acid,
(g) hydrolysis of a chloroalkane,
(h) oxidation of a secondary alcohol,
(i) hydrogenation of an alkene,
(j) combustion of an alkyne,
(k) formation of an ester,
(l) saponification of the ester formed in (k).

Q.30.37 What reagent could be used to distinguish between each of the following pairs of compounds? Explain how you would tell which is which:

(a) hexane and hexanol;
(b) ethanoic and methanoic acids;
(c) ethanol and ethanal;
(d) propane and propene;
(e) propanal and propanone;
(f) ethanoic and ethanedioic (oxalic) acids;
(g) ethanol and ethyl ethanoate.

Q.30.38 List six reactions you would expect to be shown by the following substance. Illustrate each reaction by an equation:

$$HO-CH = CH-COOH$$

Q.30.39 Study the following reaction and then answer the questions which follow:

$$\begin{array}{cccc} \mathbf{A} & \mathbf{B} & \mathbf{C} & \mathbf{D} \\ C_2H_6 & \xrightarrow{Br_2} C_2H_5Br & \xrightarrow{NaOH} C_2H_5OH & \rightarrow CH_3CHO \\ & & \downarrow & \downarrow \text{oxidation} \\ & & \mathbf{F}\ C_2H_4 & \mathbf{E} \end{array}$$

(a) Name the compounds, A, B, D, E, F
(b) Write down the structural formulae of B, D, E, F.
(c) Give the necessary conditions to change C into F.
(d) Show, by means of an equation, how D is converted into E.
(e) Show, by means of an equation, how C reacts with E. Name the products formed.
(f) To what homologous series do each of A and F belong?
(g) What chemical test could be used to distinguish between A and F?

Q.30.40 1 mole of a hydrocarbon X burned, producing 8 moles of CO_2 and 4 moles of steam, with no other products. When 1 mole of X was shaken with an excess of bromine, only 1 mole of bromine was used.

(a) Calculate the molecular formula for X.
(b) Suggest a structural formula for it.

Q.30.41 Measurements on an alkene showed that 100 cm^3 of the gas weighed 0.229 g at 25°C and 1 atm. pressure. 25 cm^3 of the alkene reacted with 25 cm^3 of hydrogen. Find the molecular mass and the molecular formula of the alkene. Name and give the structural formulae of two alkenes which have this molecular formula.

Q.30.42 An organic liquid contains C, H and O. On oxidation, 0.25 g of the liquid gave 0.595 g of carbon dioxide and 0.304 g of water. When vaporised, 0.25 g of the liquid occupied 131 cm^3 at 200°C and 1 atm. pressure. Find (a) the empirical formula, (b) the molecular formula of the liquid. (c) Write the structural formulae of compounds with this molecular formula.

Q.30.43 A compound **A**, of relative molecular mass 114 was found to have the following gravimetric composition; carbon 63.2%, hydrogen 8.8%, oxygen 28.0%.

When it was boiled with sodium hydroxide, two compounds were formed. These were **B**, a white crystalline solid which contained sodium, and **C**, a colourless liquid of molecular mass 60.

When hydrochloric acid was added to **B**, compound **D** was formed along with sodium chloride. **D** reacted with hydrogen in the presence of nickel to give **F** which was an acid.

Compound **C** on oxidation formed compound **E** which gave a positive silver mirror test, and **E** on further oxidation produced **F**.

Deduce the identities of compounds **A** to **F** and write equations for the reactions mentioned.

Q.30.44 A gaseous hydrocarbon **A** was found to contain 85.7% carbon and 14.3% hydrogen. When 80 cm^3 of it were injected into a evacuated gas syringe at 20 ° C and 101 kPa pressure, the mass of the syringe increased by 0.14 g.

Calculate the empirical formula and the molecular formula of the hydrocarbon. Name it and draw its structural formula.

On reaction with steam in the presence of a suitable catalyst, a mixture of two isomers **B** and **C** was formed. On oxidation, isomer **B** formed a ketone **D**, while **C** formed an acid **E**.

Another compound **F**, which was composed of 23.8% carbon, 5.9% hydrogen and 70.3% chlorine, reacted with sodium hydroxide to produce **G** and sodium chloride.

When **E** and **G** were reacted together, compound **H**, which contained four carbon atoms per molecule, was formed. Deduce the identities of **A** to **H**, and write equations for the reactions mentioned.

Q.30.45 A gaseous hydrocarbon **A** of density 2.5 g/L at s.t.p., was found to decolorise bromine solution. When this hydrocarbon was hydrogenated, compound **B** was formed.

B on reaction with chlorine gave **C**, along with a gas **D**. **C** on reaction with alkali produced **E** and an inorganic compound **F**.

When **E** was vaporised and its vapour passed over heated porcelain pieces, the original compound, **A**, was formed. Give names and formulae of the compounds **A** to **F** and write equations for the reactions mentioned.

Q.30.46 An organic compound, on analysis, was found to contain carbon, hydrogen and oxygen only. On combustion, 1 g of the compound produced 1.5 g of carbon dioxide and 0.41 g of water.

The molecular mass was determined by spectrometry, and was found to be about 177.

The compound was found to be insoluble in water but it dissolved in sodium hydroxide solution. Also, on treatment with sodium hydrogencarbonate solution, it evolved carbon dioxide.

1 g of the compound was dissolved in 200 cm^3 of 0.1 M NaOH. The resulting solution was then titrated against 0.1 M hydrochloric acid. 25 cm^3 portions of the solution required 10.8 cm^3 of the acid for neutralisation.

The compound was found to react with 2,4-dinitrophenylhydrazine but did not reduce Fehling's solution. It did not decolorise bromine water but when treated with PCl$_5$, HCl was liberated.

Deduce a structure which satisfies the above facts.

Answers to Problems

6.1 78.3 cm^3
6.2 1.9 L
6.3 566 cm^3 , 746 cm^3
6.4 546 cm^3
6.5 199 cm^3
6.6 539 cm^3
6.7 213 cm^3, 280 cm^3
6.8 362 cm^3
6.9 20 kPa, 80 kPa
6.10 1.0, 0.2, 1.2
6.11 0.3, 0.5, 0.1
6.12 4 g, 2 g, 24 g, 28 g, 71 g, 18 g
6.13 0.25 mol, 0.5, 0.1, 0.25, 0.1, 0.5
6.14 (a) 4 g, 40 g, 12 g, 32 g,
(b) 2.5, 0.25, 4, 3
(c) 1.5×10^{24}, 1.5×10^{23}, 2.4×10^{24}, 1.8×10^{24}
6.15 (a) 28 g, 44 g, 17 g, 16 g
(b) 0.36, 0.23, 0.59, 0.63
(c) 2.14×10^{23}, 1.36×10^{23}, 3.53×10^{23}, 3.76×10^{23}
(d) 4.28×10^{23}, 4.1×10^{23}, 1.42×10^{23}, 1.89×10^{23}
6.16 (i) 5, 0.25, 0.25
(ii) 3×10^{24}, 1.5×10^{23}, 1.5×10^{23}
(iii) 6×10^{24}, 3×10^{23}, 3×10^{23}
6.17 (i) 6×10^{22}, 6×10^{24}, 3×10^{22}, 1.2×10^{24}, 6×10^{21}
(ii) 1.8×10^{23}, 1.8×10^{25}, 2.1×10^{23}, 4.8×10^{24}, 3.0×10^{22}
6.18 (a) 6×10^{22}, (b) 6.7×10^{24}
6.19 44, CO_2 or N_2O
6.20 3.17 g/L, 35.7 L, 112 L, 1.25 g/L, 5.6 L, 2.86 g/L
6.21 1.25 g/L, 1.96 g/L, 1.43 g/L, 1.51 g/L, 0.71 g/L, 1.25 g/L
6.22 11.2 L, 2.24 L, 5.6 L, 4.48 L, 1.4 L, 0.8 L
6.23 1.25 g, 3.92 g, 4.3 g, 6.07 g, 3.57 g, 7.5 g
6.24 (a) 16, CH_4, (b) 100   (c) 64, SO_2
6.25 190
6.26 160, Br_2
6.27 58
6.28 99
6.29 0.0134, 224
6.30 28
6.31 28
6.32 58
6.33 32

6.34 72
6.35 64
6.36 64
6.37 45.3 s
6.38 25 cm^3
6.39 35.5
6.40 10.81
6.41 200.8
6.42 87.712
6.43 207.27
6.44 77%, 23%
6.45 95.25, 4.8%

7.3 30.4%, 22.2%, 14.9%, 82.4%, 28.0%
7.4 82.4%, 21.2%, 87.5%, 35.0%
7.5 46.7%, 70.0%, 72.4%, 62.9%
7.6 36%
7.7 26.2%, 7.5%, 66.3%
7.8 40.0%, 56.3%, 65.3%, 51.0%, 47.0%
7.9 (a) and (b) 85.7%, 14.3%
7.11 ZnO, $SnCl_2$, Fe_2O_3, SF_6
7.12 SO_2Cl_2, Na_2ZnO_2, $MgCl_26H_2O$, $MgSO_47H_2O$
7.13 $Na_2S_2O_3$, $BaCl_22H_2O$
7.14 $K_2Cr_2O_7$
7.15 $C_2H_4O_2$, $C_3H_6O_3$
7.16 H_2O_2
7.17 0.02 mol, 2.13 g, 0.06 mol, 1:3, $FeCl_3$
7.18 Cu_2O
7.19 0.0075 mol, 0.015 mol, PbI_2
7.20 Cu_2S
7.21 67%, CuI
7.22 35.2%, $ZnCO_3$
7.23 18
7.24 8
7.25 24.5
7.26 52
7.27 55
7.28 7.1 g, 2.4 L
7.29 40.6 g
7.30 3.2 g, 2.4 L
7.32 48 g, 4 g, 12 g, 156 g
7.33 2 L, 22.4 L
7.34 0.8 g, 600 cm^3
7.35 22 g, 11.2 L
7.36 10.6 g
7.37 4.4 g, 2.24 L
7.38 22.4 L, 44.8 L, 22.4 L, 36 g
7.39 10.6 g, 2.24 L

7.40	0.05 mol, 0.2 mol, 6.3 g, 1.12 L, 3×10^{22}
7.41	1.6 mol, 100.8 g, 67 cm^3, 75 g, 0.8, 17.9 L, 4.8×10^{23}
9.7	1, 2, 0.1, 5, 0.1, 0.2
9.8	1000, 2000, 100, 10, 20, 100, 1000
9.9	1.25, 50
9.10	0.575 M, 56.4 g/L
9.11	0.16 M, 8.96 g/L
9.12	9.6 g
9.13	1.04 M, 38 g/L
9.14	0.5 M, 31.5 g/L
9.15	9.26 M, 338 g/L
9.16	85.3 g/L
9.17	0.2 M, 0.12 M, 12.72 g/L
9.18	23.6
9.19	63%, 10
9.20	60.6%, 9
9.21	0.1 M, 2
9.22	13.4%, 1
9.23	2
9.24	0.05 M, 2
9.25	0.225 M, 130
9.26	0.154 M, 104
9.27	0.238 M, 210
9.28	56
9.29	10.8%
9.30	72, 56
9.31	100, 40
9.32	79.5
9.33	68.8%
9.34	96.4
9.35	1.776 g/L
9.36	5%
11.1	0.021 M, 3.3 g/L
11.2	0.088 M, 24.5 g/L
11.3	45.3%
11.4	(a) 0.0193; (b) 93.4%
11.5	11.6%
11.6	45%, 7
11.7	96.8%
11.8	31.6 cm^3
11.9	0.395 g
11.10	8.8 g
11.11	96.3%
11.12	0.042 M, 3.78 g/L
11.13	28.75%, 2
11.14	0.0194 M, 3.06 g/L
11.15	6.04 g/L
11.16	0.0195 M, 3.08 g/L
11.17	39.5 cm^3
11.19	0.0486 M, 12.34 g/L
11.20	0.052 mol I_2/L, 0.11 mol $Na_2S_2O_3$/L
11.21	0.127 M
11.22	0.0885 M, 21.9 g/L
11.23	$Na_2S_2O_3$ = 0.0897 M, I_2 = 0.042 M
11.24	0.022 M
11.25	25.7 g/L
11.26	0.0766 M, 19 g/L
11.27	0.87 g
11.28	0.74 mol/L
11.29	6.96%
11.30	34.37%
11.31	4.96 p.p.m.
11.32	0.000012 M, 0.00085 g/L, 0.85 p.p.m.
11.33	(b) 0.06 M; (d) 0.09 M; (e) 3:2; (f) 3,2
11.34	(i) 0.06 M, (ii) 7.56 g/L
11.35	0.036 M, 1.224 g/L
13.8	1.57 mol, 138.2 g
13.9	6.6, (a) 1.3, 0.3, 1.7, 1.7 mol, (b) 78 g, 9.6 g, 125.8 g, 30.6 g
13.10	(a) 6.25, (b) 80 g, 20 g, 170 g, 30 g
13.11	(a) 0.5 mol acid, 0.5 alcohol, 2.0 ester, 0.5 water (b) 2.76 g, 2.12 g, 4.75 g, 2.77 g
13.12	0.072 $(mol/L)^{-1}$
13.13	7.36; 2.51, 0.01, 0.49, 0.49
13.14	50.3
13.15	H_2 = I_2 = 0.23 mol/L, HI = 1.54 mol/L
13.16	(a) 3.2, 0.2, 5.6, (b) 0.25, 1.25, 4.5
13.17	0.0065 mol/L
13.18	0.375
13.19	CO = H_2O = 22.7%, CO_2 = H_2 = 27.3%
13.20	0.46 mol = 45.5 g
13.21	1.5; 0.03, 0.18, 0.09, 0.09; 1.5
13.22	0.0145
13.23	(a) 1 mol NH_3, 0.5 mol N_2; (b) 0.274
13.24	(i) 0.32, 0.18, 0.09; (ii) 0.028
13.25	0.2
13.26	(a) 0.01 mol/L; (b) 14.14, 0.005
13.27	0.488
13.28	0.4, 0.1, 0.1; 0.025
13.29	1.57 atm.
13.30	13.72 atm.
13.31	1.14 atm.
13.32	50 and 150 atm., 2.37×10^{-4}
13.33	0.267, 5.34 atm.
13.34	0.13, 104 atm.
13.35	(iv) 3; (v) 1.5, 1.5, 13.5, 0.5
13.36	0.15 atm., 28.96 and 2.08 atm.
13.37	(a) 3.75, (b) 0.006, (c) 31°C.

14.1 2.3, 11.4, 7, 12.6, 12.7, 5.2

14.2 2, 1.4, 1, 1, 12, 12, 13.3, 13.6

14.3 0, 2.5, 0.51, 13.6, 1.7, 3.4

14.4 5×10^{-5}, 2×10^{-11}, 1×10^{-7}, 1

14.5 3.37, 2.72, 3.02, 2.72

14.6 3.7

14.7 (a) 1.47×10^{-3}, 2.83, (b) 2.72, 11.28

14.8 2.2, 2.3, 4.0, 5.1, 6, 11.4

14.9 6.8×10^{-3}, 3.46

14.10 6.25×10^{-5}

14.11 pH = 1, 10.3, 2.7, 13, 3.85, 11.62

14.12 3.3, 4, 10.7, 11

14.14 (i) 2.4

14.15 (ii) 2.34, (iv) 27 cm^3

15.2 393, 32.75, 143, 12.8 kJ; 32.7, 143 MJ /kg

15.3 +393 kJ, -131 kJ/mol

15.4 +3 kJ

15.5 -128 kJ/mol

15.6 -137 kJ/mol

15.7 +91 kJ/mol

15.8 -714, -1371, -2010, -2658 kJ/mol

15.9 723 g

15.10 -624 kJ

15.11 +51, -103, -84 kJ/mol

15.12 -118 kJ

15.13 -46 kJ/mol

15.14 1532 kJ

15.15 298.4 kJ/mol

15.16 1562 kJ/mol, 52.1 MJ/kg

15.17 (i) -159 kJ, (ii) -159 kJ

15.18 -854 kJ

15.19 -250, -313 kJ/mol

15.20 -1562 kJ/mol

15.21 -56.3 kJ/mol

15.22 -57.1 kJ/mol

15.23 -54.6 kJ/mol

15.24 56.4 kJ/mol

15.26 21 kJ/mol

15.27 -78.4 kJ

15.28 +18 kJ/mol

15.29 -137 kJ/mol

15.30 366.5 kJ/mol

15.31 391 kJ/mol

15.32 (i) -1108, (ii) +802 kJ/mol

15.33 35 and 56 kJ/mol

15.34 -187 kJ/mol

15.35 -86 kJ/mol

15.36 -11 kJ/mol

15.37 -55, -115, -460, +45 kJ

15.38 -103, +21, -266, -210 kJ/mol

15.39 -564, +72, -726 kJ

15.40 -579 kJ

16.13 1800 C, 0.0186 F, 2 g

16.14 1.43 g, 0.5 g O_2

16.15 1.25 L, 625 cm^3, 3.55 g

16.16 1.33 g

16.17 28800 C, 0.298 F, 2.68 g

16.18 1613 s, 500 cm^3 O_2

16.19 0.27 A

16.20 H_2: 0.01 mol = 224 cm^3, O_2: 0.005 mol = 112 cm^3, 16.1 min, 0.01 mol

16.21 0.159 g, 61 cm^3

16.22 289.5 C, 0.003, 0.001, 3, +3

16.23 224 cm^3

16.24 0.0378 F, 0.0126 mol, +3

16.25 17 g, 5.11 g, 1.42 g

19.9 (e) 3×10^5 mol, (f) 14.8, 3.33×10^{-13}

19.11 21.25%

19.12 59.5%

19.13 0.145 M, 19.1 g/L

19.14 18%

19.15 46%

19.16 25.3%

19.17 95%

21.5 50 p.p.m.

21.6 200 p.p.m., 1800 p.p.m.

21.7 750 p.p.m.

21.8 600 p.p.m.

21.9 (i) 0.07 g/L, (ii) 175 p.p.m.

21.10 120 p.p.m., 90 p.p.m.

21.11 0.06 M, 51.2%, 7

21.12 96.6%

21.13 40%

21.14 (f) 25.6, 3.2, (h) 22.4 p.p.m.

21.15 0.0776 g/L, 194 p.p.m.

21.16 12.8 p.p.m.

21.17 13.2 p.p.m.

21.18 (i) 0.0002 mol/L, 6.4 p.p.m.

21.19 0.0003 mol/L, 9.6 p.p.m., 80%

21.20 (i) 9.39 p.p.m., (ii) 4.46 p.p.m.; 4.93 p.p.m.

21.21 4.8 p.p.m.; 9.2 and 2.2 p.p.m.; 7 and 70 p.p.m.

21.22 (i) 4.8 p.p.m. in original; 8.0 and 2.13 p.p.m. in diluted sample; BOD of original sample = 117 p.p.m.

24.1 C_2H_6
24.2 CH
24.3 CH_3
24.4 CH_2O
24.5 CH_4O
24.6 C_2H_6O
24.7 C_3H_7Cl
24.8 C_6H_7N
24.9 $C_3H_6O_2$
24.10 $C_3H_6O_2$
24.11 C_2H_6
24.12 C_2H_4
24.13 CH_4
24.14 C_4H_{10}
24.15 C_2H_4
24.16 C_2H_2
24.17 4
24.18 C_6H_6
24.19 50 cm^3
24.20 C_4H_{10}

27.8 C_4H_8O

28.3 (l) 38%
28.10 54.5% C, 9.1% H, 36.4% O, $C_4H_8O_2$
28.11 74
28.12 CH_3COOH
28.13 88, $C_4H_8O_2$

30.1 68%
30.2 85%
30.3 50%
30.4 37.5%
30.5 93%
30.6 90.4%
30.7 88.4%
30.8 50.1%
30.9 95%
30.10 0.0543, 0.01, 18.4%
30.23 0.15 M, 30 cm^3, 13.2, 1
30.24 5.35 g
30.28 105.9 g, 52.9
30.29 0.3, 1.8, 0.9, 1.8×10^{23}, 6.72 L, 1.35 mol, 43.2 g, 0.9 mol, 39.6 g, 20.16 L
30.31 30 g, 20 cm^3
30.33 $C_2H_2Cl_2$
30.34 $C_4H_{10}O$
30.35 C_2H_6O
30.40 C_8H_8
30.41 56, C_4H_8
30.42 $C_4H_{10}O$, 74
30.43 A = $C_6H_{10}O_2$
30.44 A = C_4H_8, F = CH_3Cl
30.45 A = C_4H_8
30.46 E.F. = $C_3H_4O_3$, M.F. = $C_6H_8O_6$, 2 COOH groups, C=O and OH groups.

ELECTRONEGATIVITIES OF THE ELEMENTS

LEICTRIDHIÚLTACHTAÍ NA nDÚL
(Pauling)

1	2											3	4	5	6	7	0
H 2·1																	He —
Li 1·0	Be 1·5											B 2·0	C 2·5	N 3·0	O 3·5	F 4·0	Ne —
Na 0·9	Mg 1·2											Al 1·5	Si 1·8	P 2·1	S 2·5	Cl 3·0	Ar —
K 0·8	Ca 1·0	Sc 1·3	Ti 1·5	V 1·6	Cr 1·6	Mn 1·5	Fe 1·8	Co 1·8	Ni 1·8	Cu 1·9	Zn 1·6	Ga 1·6	Ge 1·8	As 2·0	Se 2·4	Br 2·8	Kr —
Rb 0·8	Sr 1·0	Y 1·2	Zr 1·4	Nb 1·6	Mo 1·8	Tc 1·9	Ru 2·2	Rh 2·2	Pd 2·2	Ag 1·9	Cd 1·7	In 1·7	Sn 1·8	Sb 1·9	Te 2·1	I 2·5	Xe —
Cs 0·7	Ba 0·9	La-Lu 1·1-1·2	Hf 1·3	Ta 1·5	W 1·7	Re 1·9	Os 2·2	Ir 2·2	Pt 2·2	Au 2·4	Hg 1·9	Tl 1·8	Pb 1·8	Bi 1·9	Po 2·0	At 2·2	Rn —
Fr 0·7	Ra 0·9	Ac 1·1	Th 1·3	Pa 1·5	U 1·7	Np-Lw 1·3											

FIRST IONIZATION ENERGIES OF THE ELEMENTS
(in kiloJoules per mole)

CÉAD-FHUINNIMH IANÚCHÁIN NA nDÚL
(ina kJ an mól)

1	2											3	4	5	6	7	0
H 1310																	He 2370
Li 519	Be 900											B 799	C 1090	N 1400	O 1310	F 1680	Ne 2080
Na 494	Mg 736											Al 577	Si 787	P 1060	S 1000	Cl 1260	Ar 1520
K 418	Ca 590	Sc 632	Ti 661	V 649	Cr 653	Mn 715	Fe 761	Co 757	Ni 736	Cu 745	Zn 908	Ga 577	Ge 761	As 967	Se 941	Br 1140	Kr 1350
Rb 402	Sr 548	Y 636	Zr 669	Nb 653	Mo 695	Tc 699·	Ru 724	Rh 745	Pd 803	Ag 732	Cd 866	In 556	Sn 707	Sb 833	Te 870	I 1010	Xe 1170
Cs 377	Ba 502	La 540	Hf 531	Ta 577	W 770	Re 761	Os 841	Ir 887	Pt 866	Au 891	Hg 1010	Tl 590	Pb 715	Bi 774	Po 812	At —	Rn 1040
Fr —	Ra 510	Ac 669															

Tá na Dúile Tearc-Chré agus na hActinídí fágtha ar lár.   The Rare Earth Elements and the Actinides have been omitted.

THE CHEMICAL ELEMENTS

Atomic number	Element	Symbol	Relative atomic mass	Melting point $^{\circ}$C	Boiling point $^{\circ}$C	Density g/cm^3	Date of discovery
1	Hydrogen	H	1.00797	−259	−253	0.00008	1766
2	Helium	He	4.0026	−270	−269	0.00017	1868
3	Lithium	Li	6.939	180	1330	0.53	1817
4	Beryllium	Be	9.0122	1280	2700	1.9	1827
5	Boron	B	10.811	2000	3000	2.3	1808
6	Carbon (graphite)	C	12.0115		4200	2.2	*
7	Nitrogen	N	14.0067	−210	−196	0.00117	1772
8	Oxygen	O	15.9994	−219	−183	0.00132	1774
9	Fluorine	F	18.9984	−220	−188	0.0016	1886
10	Neon	Ne	20.183	−249	−246	0.0008	1898
11	Sodium	Na	22.9898	98	890	0.97	1807
12	Magnesium	Mg	24.312	650	1110	1.7	1808
13	Aluminium	Al	26.9815	660	2060	2.7	1825
14	Silicon	Si	28.086	1410	2700	2.4	1823
15	Phosphorus	P	30.9738	44	280	1.8	1669
16	Sulphur	S	32.064	119	445	2.1	*
17	Chlorine	Cl	35.453	−101	−35	0.003	1774
18	Argon	Ar	39.948	−189	−186	0.0017	1894
19	Potassium	K	39.102	64	760	0.86	1807
20	Calcium	Ca	40.08	850	1440	1.6	1808
21	Scandium	Sc	44.956	1400	2500	3.1	1879
22	Titanium	Ti	47.90	1670	3300	4.5	1789
23	Vanadium	V	50.942	1900	3400	6.0	1801
24	Chromium	Cr	51.996	1900	2500	7.2	1797
25	Manganese	Mn	54.9380	1250	2000	7.4	1774
26	Iron	Fe	55.847	1540	3000	7.9	*
27	Cobalt	Co	58.9332	1490	2900	8.9	1735
28	Nickel	Ni	58.71	1450	2800	8.9	1751
29	Copper	Cu	63.54	1080	2500	9.0	*
30	Zinc	Zn	65.37	419	910	7.1	17th century
31	Gallium	Ga	69.72	30	2200	5.9	1875
32	Germanium	Ge	72.59	950	2800	5.4	1886
33	Arsenic	As	74.9216		615	5.7	13th century
34	Selenium	Se	78.96	217	690	4.8	1817
35	Bromine	Br	79.909	−7	58	3.1	1826
36	Krypton	Kr	83.80	−157	−153	0.0035	1898
37	Rubidium	Rb	85.47	39	700	1.5	1861
38	Strontium	Sr	87.62	770	1380	2.6	1808
39	Yttrium	Y	88.905	1500	3000	4.5	1794
40	Zirconium	Zr	91.22	1900	4000	6.5	1789
41	Niobium	Nb	92.906	2500	4800	8.5	1801
42	Molybdenum	Mo	95.94	2620	5000	10.2	1782
43	Technetium	Tc	(99)	2200	4600	11.5	1937
44	Ruthenium	Ru	101.07	2500	4000	12.2	1845
45	Rhodium	Rh	102.905	1960	3700	12.4	1803
46	Palladium	Pd	106.4	1550	3000	12.0	1803
47	Silver	Ag	107.870	961	2200	10.5	*
48	Cadmium	Cd	112.40	320	765	8.7	1817
49	Indium	In	114.82	156	2000	7.3	1861
50	Tin	Sn	118.69	232	2600	7.3	*
51	Antimony	Sb	121.75	630	1400	6.6	*
52	Tellerium	Te	127.60	450	990	6.2	1782

Atomic number	Element	Symbol	Relative atomic mass	Melting point °C	Boiling point °C	Density g/cm³	Date of discovery
53	Iodine	I	126.9044	114	183	4.9	1811
54	Xenon	Xe	131.30	−112	−108	0.005	1898
55	Caesium	Cs	132.905	29	680	1.9	1861
56	Barium	Ba	137.34	710	1600	3.5	1805
57	Lanthanum	La	138.91	920	3500	6.2	1839
58	Cerium	Ce	140.12	800	3000	6.7	1803
59	Praseodymium	Pr	140.907	935	3100	6.8	1885
60	Neodymium	Nd	144.24	1020	3100	7.0	1885
61	Promethium	Pm	(147)**	1030	2700		1945
62	Samarium	Sm	150.35	1080	1600	7.6	1879
63	Europium	Eu	151.96	830	1430	5.3	1901
64	Gadolinium	Gd	157.25	1320	3000	7.9	1886
65	Terbium	Tb	158.924	1400	2600	8.3	1843
66	Dysprosium	Dy	162.50	1500	2400	8.5	1886
67	Holmium	Ho	164.930	1500	2500	8.8	1879
68	Erbium	Er	167.26	1500	2700	9.0	1843
69	Ehulium	Tm	168.934	1550	2000	9.3	1879
70	Ytterbium	Yb	173.04	824	1500	7.0	1878
71	Lutetium	Lu	174.97	1700	3330	9.9	1907
72	Hafnium	Hf	178.49	2000	5000	13.1	1923
73	Tantalum	Ta	180.948	3000	5400	16.6	1802
74	Tungsten	W	183.85	3400	6000	19.3	1789
75	Rhenium	Re	186.2	3200	5630	21.0	1925
76	Osmium	Os	190.2	2700	5000	22.6	1804
77	Iridium	Ir	192.2	2440	5300	22.5	1804
78	Platinum	Pt	195.09	1770	4000	21.4	1735
79	Gold	Au	196.967	1060	2700	19.3	*
80	Mercury	Hg	200.59	−39	357	13.6	*
81	Thallium	Tl	204.37	300	1460	11.8	1861
82	Lead	Pb	207.19	327	1744	11.3	*
83	Bismuth	Bi	208.980	270	1560	9.8	16th century
84	Polonium	Po	(210)	254	1000	9.3	1898
85	Astatine	At	(210)	302			1940
86	Radon	Rn	(222)	−71	−62	0.009	1900
87	Francium	Fr	(223)	30	650		1936
88	Radium	Ra	(226)	700	1500	5.0	1898
89	Actinium	Ac	(227)	1050	3000		1899
90	Thorium	Th	232.038	1700	4000	11.6	1829
91	Protactinium	Pa	231	1200	4000	15.4	1917
92	Uranium	U	238.03	1130	3800	19.0	1789
93	Neptunium	Np	(237)	640		19.5	1940
94	Plutonium	Pu	(242)	640	3200	19.6	1940
95	Americium	Am	(243)	1200	2600	11.7	1944
96	Curium	Cm	(247)				1944
97	Berkelium	Bk	(249)				1949
98	Californium	Cf	(251)				1950
99	Einsteinium	Es	(254)				1952
100	Fermium	Fm	(253)				1953
101	Mendelevium	Md	(256)				1955
102	Nobelium	No	(259)				1958
103	Lawrencium	Lw	(257)				1961
104	Unnilquadium†	Unq	(261)				1969
105	Unnilpentium†	Unp	(262)				1970
106	Unnilhexium†	Unh	(263)				

*Known in Roman times.   †IUPAC recommended names.

**Atomic masses shown in brackets are the mass numbers of the most stable known isotopes.

p.p.m. of oxygen in water saturated with oxygen
(for fresh water at sea level)

Temp (^{o}C)	p.p.m.
0	14.6
1	14.2
2	13.9
3	13.5
4	13.2
5	12.8
6	12.5
7	12.2
8	11.9
9	11.6
10	11.3
11	11.1
12	10.8
13	10.6
14	10.4
15	10.2
16	10.0
17	9.7
18	9.5
19	9.4
20	9.2
21	9.0
22	8.8
23	8.7
24	8.5
25	8.4

Relative Atomic Masses
(for calculations)

Aluminium	27
Barium	137
Bismuth	209
Bromine	80
Calcium	40
Carbon	12
Chlorine	35.5
Chromium	52
Cobalt	59
Copper	64
Fluorine	19
Hydrogen	1
Iodine	127
Iron	56
Lead	207
Lithium	7
Magnesium	24
Manganese	55
Mercury	201
Nickel	59
Nitrogen	14
Oxygen	16
Phosphorus	31
Potassium	39
Silicon	28
Silver	108
Sodium	23
Sulphur	32
Tin	119
Titanium	48
Zinc	65

EXAMINATION TECHNIQUE

BEFORE THE EXAM make sure you have all the equipment you are likely to need, viz., several pens or biros including a colour or two, pencils, pencil sharpener and rubber, calculator and spare batteries, ruler, compass and science stencil.

GENERAL ADVICE

When you receive your exam paper, read the instructions at the beginning of it. Quickly read through the questions and decide on which ones you are going to answer. If there are six questions to be done in three hours, allow about 25 minutes for each question; this will give spare time at the end, and also allow you to over-run the allotted time if there are some particularly long questions.

For each of the questions you decide to do, spend a few minutes planning how you are going to answer it. Jot down, on rough paper, the main points required. Arrange them in some sort of logical order. When you are reasonably satisfied with your list, start writing.

Answer first those questions to which you best know the answers, but do not spend more than the calculated time on each. Always attempt the full number of questions, paying due heed to those which are compulsory.

Time is valuable in Leaving Certificate exams. Do not waste it. Ignore your surroundings; valuable time can be wasted if you allow yourself to be distracted.

PRESENTATION OF ANSWERS

Read each question carefully and answer **exactly** what is asked. For example, if the question asks you to **name** the substances formed when zinc reacts with dilute sulphuric acid, writing down H_2 and $ZnSO_4$ will not gain full marks; the required answer is

'hydrogen and zinc sulphate'.

And again, if a question asks 'How would you measure the percentage of water in copper sulphate crystals ($CuSO_4 5H_2O$), working out the answer by calculation i.e. $\left(\dfrac{90 \times 100}{250}\right)$ is not answering what is asked; the question asks how would you **measure** i.e. it requires the description of an experiment.

Write concisely but fully on each of the points to be discussed or described. Do not digress; refer to the question frequently to check that you are still keeping to the point(s) asked. As a general rule, you should spend more time on, and write more about those parts of the question for which there are more marks.

Write clearly and legibly. It is often easier and quicker to give answers as a series of short sentences rather than writing in a very literary way – as is required for example in an English essay.

Attempt all parts of each of the chosen questions. A missing answer gains no marks; an attempted answer, however poor, may gain some marks. Leave space for any information which you cannot remember, it may occur to you later.

Diagrams Where possible, illustrate all descriptions with suitable diagrams. Diagrams look best if they are drawn in pencil and labelled in ink. A science stencil is **most** useful for drawing quick neat diagrams. Do not waste time in colouring a diagram unless (a) it adds to the information being given (e.g. in showing the visible spectrum) or (b) you have time to spare at the end **after** all the written work has been checked.

A diagram must work. The one shown here would gain few marks because one mistake and one omission in it would make it unworkable.

Definitions These need to be learned and known by heart. A definition is a short sentence stating **exactly** what is meant by a scientific term. A vague statement will gain few marks. Where possible, illustrate all definitions with an example, e.g., 'the atomic number of an element is the number of protons in an atom of that element, e.g., the atomic number of carbon is 6'.

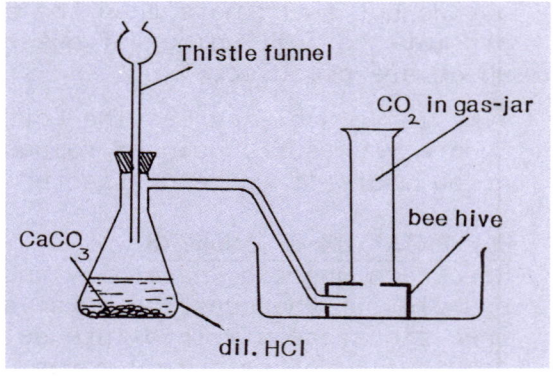

Laws Unless otherwise asked, a law should be stated in words. For example, do not give Boyle's Law as pV is constant. (However, if you do not know the law, giving pV is constant is certainly better than nothing at all!)

All questions and parts of questions should be clearly labelled in the margin of every page of your answer sheets.

At the end of each answer, leave ten or so lines of space for additional information which may occur to you later, and also to improve appearance (a crowded page is not pleasing to look at, and is also more difficult to follow)

DESCRIPTIVE QUESTIONS
If you are asked to describe an experiment, do so under the following headings:
(a) Diagram (see note about diagrams)

(b) Method; mention the **essential** points in the procedure (e.g., the alkali was put into a **conical** flask), but leave out irrelevant information (e.g., the burette was set up using a burette clip attached to a stand). State the readings or observations taken, mentioning any precautions taken in order to obtain an accurate result.

(c) Calculations (if any); take imaginary but reasonable values, **or** use symbols. Show how the result is calculated.

(d) Conclusion: state clearly what the experiment proved or measured. If it was numerical, be sure and give the units of the result, e.g., 'concentration of the acid was 1.2 **moles/ litre'**

'Describe the properties of' type of question.

Physical properties of a substance include:
colour, state smell,
density (this can always be calculated for gases),
solubility in water and in non-polar solvents,
melting point and boiling point.

Chemical properties include:
does it burn?
'does it support combustion' (if it is a gas)
action of water, acids, alkalis, heat,
special properties, e.g., carbon dioxide turns limewater milky.

Reactions mentioned should be accompanied by the appropriate chemical equations.

CALCULATION QUESTONS
Start all calculation questions with the appropriate equation, e.g.
$pV = nRT$,   or $Zn + H_2SO_4 \longrightarrow ZnSO_4 + H_2$
Write down the given information, and work out how you can use the equation to work out the required information.

Show your reasoning clearly in working through a problem. Then if you do make a mathematical slip, you can still gain high marks by showing that you knew and understood the principle(s) involved.

Highlight your final answer clearly, for example, by putting a box around it. Be sure and give the units in which numerical quantities are expressed, e.g., 15 kg, 0.3 mole, 1.2 moles/litre. This is particularly important in giving your final answer.

Attempt all the calculation parts in any question you do - even if you know you cannot complete them. Do use **all** the given information in some way or other.

AT THE END
It is very important to have some time available at the end, in which to read over all you have written and particularly to check calculations. Any errors which you detect should be neatly corrected.

Do not leave the exam hall until the full time is up. Use every available minute to try and improve or add something useful to your answers.

N.B. The exam paper itself provides certain necessary information, such as chemical constants, relative atomic masses, etc., and can also contain other useful information such as chemical terms, formulae and spellings.

Index

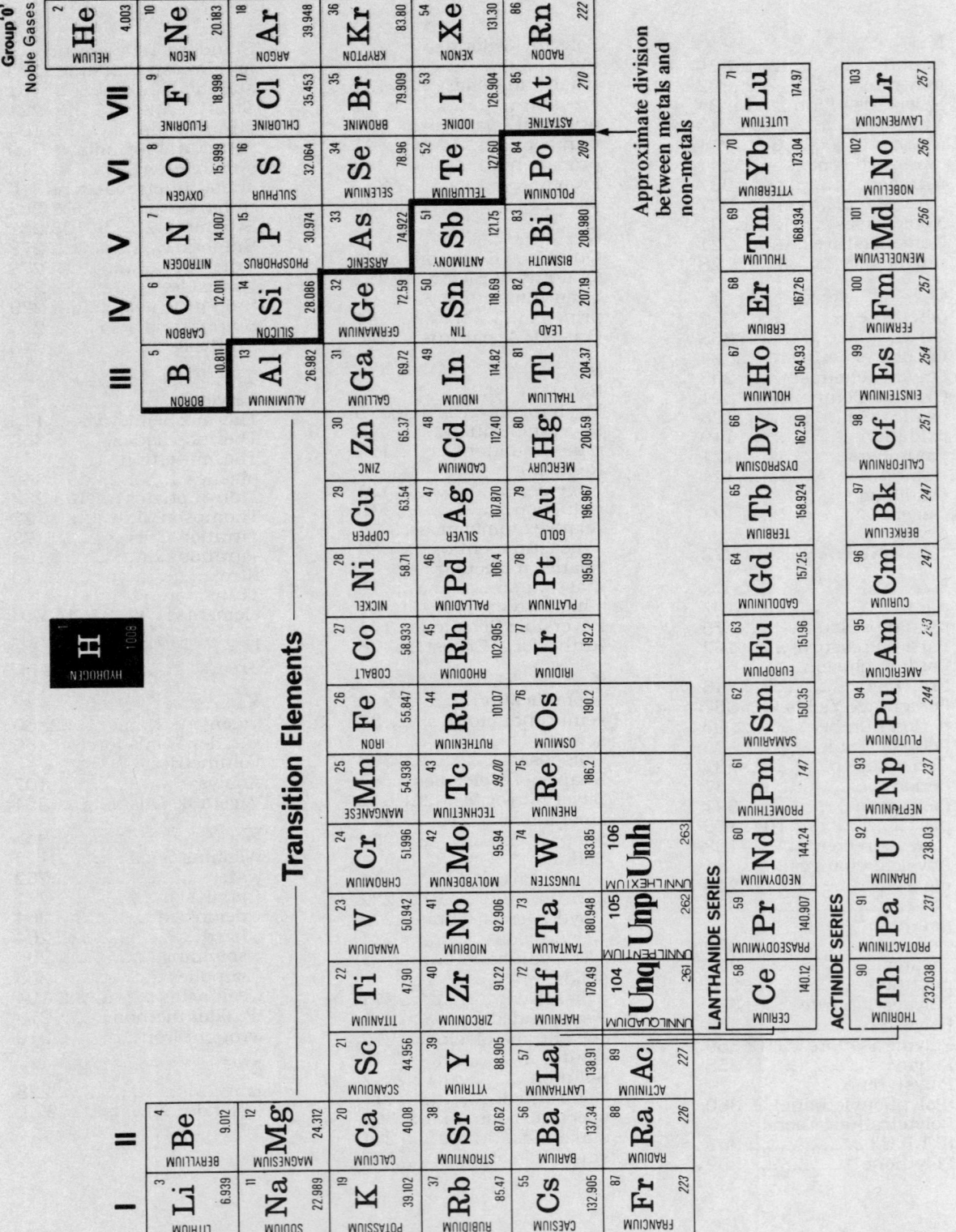

The Periodic Table of the Elements